REF 917.8 JOU   873361

The Journals of the Lewis &
Clark expedition, August 25

D1294914

For Reference

Not to be taken

from this library

Bellevue Public Library

The Journals of the Lewis and Clark Expedition, Volume 3

August 25, 1804–April 6, 1805

Sponsored by the Center for
Great Plains Studies,
University of Nebraska-Lincoln
and the American
Philosophical Society, Philadelphia

A Project of the Center for
Great Plains Studies,
University of Nebraska-Lincoln
Gary E. Moulton, Editor
Thomas W. Dunlay, Assistant Editor

The Journals of the Lewis & Clark Expedition

August 25, 1804–April 6, 1805

University of Nebraska Press
Lincoln and London

The preparation and publication of this volume
were assisted by grants from
the National Endowment for the Humanities.

Copyright 1987 by the University of Nebraska Press
All rights reserved
Manufactured in the United States of America

The Paper in this book meets the minimum
requirements of American National Standard for
Information Sciences—Permanence of Paper for
Printed Library Materials, ANSI z39.48-1984.

Library of Congress Cataloging-in-Publication Data

(Revised for volume 3)
The Journals of the Lewis and Clark expedition.

Vol. : Gary E. Moulton, editor; Thomas W. Dunlay,
assistant editor.
Includes bibliographical references and indexes.
Contents: v. 1. Atlas of the Lewis & Clark
expedition—v. 2. August 30, 1803-August 24, 1804—
v. 3. August 25, 1804-April 6, 1805.
1. Lewis and Clark Expedition—(1804-1806)—Collected
works.   2. West (U.S.)—Description and travel—
To 1848—Collected works.   3. United States—Exploring
expeditions—Collected works.   I. Lewis,
Meriwether, 1774-1809. II. Clark, William, 1770-1838.
III. Moulton, Gary E.   IV. Dunlay, Thomas W., 1944—

F592.4   1983   917.8'042   82-8510
ISBN 0-8032-2861-9 (V. 1)   ISBN 0-8032-2875-9 (V. 3)

Contents

Preface

It is a pleasure to acknowledge again all those persons who have helped with this new edition of the journals. The individuals named in volume 2 have continued with their encouragement and assistance, while the Lewis and Clark Trail Heritage Foundation has given financial support, as has Lyle S. Woodcook of St. Louis. Other persons have been aiding the project more recently: Jeffery R. Hanson, University of Wisconsin–La Crosse, John Ludwickson, Nebraska State Historical Society, and Thomas O. Holtzer, University of Nebraska–Lincoln, answered some difficult ethnological, archaeological, and entomological questions, while Vernon Volpe, University of Nebraska, and Jennifer Frost of the project, assisted in the research tasks.

Linguistic data in the notes were provided by the following individuals. Dakota language: Raymond J. DeMallie, Indiana University. Dakota words are written in the orthography of Eugene Buechel, *A Dictionary of the Teton Dakota Sioux Language*, edited by Paul Manhart (Pine Ridge: Red Cloud Indian School, 1970). All words are accented on the second syllable unless otherwise indicated. Arikara language: Douglas R. Parks, Indiana University. Hidatsa language: A. Wesley Jones, Mary College, Bismarck, North Dakota. Mandan language: Robert C. Hollow, State Historical Society of North Dakota. Arikara, Hidatsa, and Mandan words are written in the orthographies given in Douglas R. Parks, A. Wesley Jones, and Robert C. Hollow, eds., *Earth Lodge Tales From the Upper Missouri: Traditional Stories of the Arikara, Hidatsa, and Mandan* (Bismarck: Mary College, 1978), pp. 122–24. Two changes have been made in the Mandan orthography: extra-short vowels are written here raised above the line instead of using smaller type size, and nasal vowels are marked by *ŋ* instead of by a smaller type size *n*.

EDITORIAL SYMBOLS AND ABBREVIATIONS

[roman]   Word or phrase supplied or corrected.

[roman?]   Conjectural reading of the original.

[*italics*]   Editor's remarks within a document.

[*Ed: italics*]   Editor's remarks that might be confused with
                     EC, ML, NB, WC, or *X.*

[*EC: italics*]   Elliott Coues's emendations or interlineations.

[*ML: italics*]   Meriwether Lewis's emendations or interlineations.

[*NB: italics*]   Nicholas Biddle's emendations or interlineations.

[*WC: italics*]   William Clark's emendations or interlineations.

[*X: italics*]   Emendations or interlineations of the unknown or an
                     unidentified person.

⟨roman⟩   Word or phrase deleted by the writer and restored
                     by the editor.

SPECIAL SYMBOLS OF LEWIS AND CLARK

α   Alpha

∠   Angle

☽   Moon symbol

☞   Pointing hand

★   Star

☉   Sun symbol

♍   Virgo

COMMON ABBREVIATIONS OF LEWIS AND CLARK

Altd., alds	altitude, allitudes
Apt. T.	apparent time
d.	degree
do.	ditto
h.	hour
id., isd.	island
L. L.	lower limb
L., Larb., Lard., Lbd., or Ld. S.	larboard (or left) side
Lad., Latd.	latitude
Longtd.	longitude
m., mts.	minute
M. T.	mean time
mes., mls., ms.	miles
obstn.	observation
opsd.	opposite
pd., psd.	passed
pt.	point
qde., quadt., qudt.	quadrant
qtr., qutr.	quarter
s.	second
S., St., Star., Starbd. Stb., Stbd., or S.	starboard (or right) side
sext., sextn., sextt.	sextant
U. L.	upper limb

Note: abbreviations in weather entries are explained with the first weather data, following the entry of January 31, 1804.

Vermillion River, South Dakota, through Winter at Fort Mandan, North Dakota

August 25, 1804–April 6, 1805

On August 25, 1804, while their three boats proceeded upriver, the two captains and several men went ashore near the mouth of the Vermillion River in present southeast South Dakota to visit a hill which the Indians of the vicinity insisted was haunted by evil spirits. Moving on upstream past the mouth of the James River, they paused from August 28 to 31 at the Calumet Bluff on the present Nebraska side of the Missouri to council with the Yankton Sioux, the first of this numerous tribe and the first of the truly nomadic Plains Indians they had met.

The captains were pleased with the council, but as they moved on they were increasingly anxious about George Shannon, the youngest member of the Corps of Discovery, who had been missing since August 28, when he was sent out to locate two stray horses. Mistakenly believing that the boats had gone ahead of him, Shannon hurried up the river trying to overtake them, although they were actually behind him. Not until September 11 did they overtake the young man, now weak from hunger.

The party was now entering the semi-arid High Plains, previously unknown to Anglo-Americans, and they were encountering some of the region's characteristic plant and animal species. In present northeast Nebraska they first saw a prairie dog "town" and obtained a specimen of that animal. In modern South Dakota, as September wore on, they also discovered the coyote, the pronghorn, the mule deer, the jackrabbit, and the magpie.

Some miles north of the White River, on September 16 and 17, they paused for two days to rest, dry out their baggage, and perhaps to make some decisions. From the first, the captains had intended to send back, before winter, a small party of men carrying dispatches, journals, and specimens to be shipped to President Jefferson. They had never found an opportune time, and it was here that they decided not to send out the return party until the following spring. Lewis wrote several pages of journals during the two days halt, the first such daily journal-keeping he appears to have done since May.

Leaving the rest camp, they traveled around the remarkable "Grand Detour" of the Missouri River and arrived on September 24 at the mouth of the present Bad River, which they called the Teton, for it was there that they met a large number of the Teton Sioux. Here they had their first really hazardous and potentially violent encounter with Indians on the journey, arising from the arrogance of some of the chiefs, disagreements among the Sioux leaders, and very likely confusion resulting from the lack of a Sioux interpreter. The Sioux attempted to bully the Corps of Discovery as they did trading parties, but the captains were not prepared to submit. As they saw it, they represented the dignity of the United States, and their pride and a military conception of security required that they show a readiness to fight. Rightly or wrongly they believed that the Tetons planned a surprise attack on their boats and they remained uneasy until they left those bands behind.

A few days later, on October 8, they reached the villages of the Arikaras in what is now northern South Dakota. Their reception by these sedentary farmers was far more encouraging than that of the Tetons, and the party remained until the eleventh. The captains hoped to serve as peacemakers between the Arikaras and the Mandans and Hidatsas farther upriver and as they departed they took an Arikara chief with them to act as ambassador to the two tribes. On October 13 Private John Newman was arrested and tried for "having uttered repeated expressions of a highly criminal and mutinous nature"; the verdict was guilty and he received seventy-five lashes and was dishonorably discharged, although he remained with the party until spring doing hard labor. Newman was repentant, but the captains refused to reinstate him.

The party arrived on October 25 at the Mandan and Hidatsa villages, 164 days and about 1,510 miles out from Camp Dubois. Here they were met with a mixed reception and informed the Indian leaders of the change in official sovereignty. Winter was near and the Indians and various white traders told the captains that the Missouri would soon freeze; they decided, therefore, to discharge some of their French boatmen and make their winter quarters in the vicinity of these friendly tribes, from whom they could obtain corn to supplement the results of their hunting. On November 3 the party began the construction of Fort Mandan, on the eastern side of the Missouri a few miles below the mouth of the

Knife River in west-central North Dakota and nearly opposite the lower Mandan village.

The stockaded log fort would be their home for five months, during a bitter Northern Plains winter in which temperatures sometimes dropped to over forty degrees below zero Fahrenheit and venturing outside was likely to result in frostbite. Nevertheless, Clark describes the party as being in good spirits. It was by no means a period of idleness, although Lewis notes playing backgammon at least once. Hunting, in spite of the fierce cold, was frequently necessary to provide meat. Indians visited the fort constantly and the chiefs, at least, expected to be entertained by the captains. The smiths were kept busy making tomahawks for the visiting warriors, in exchange for corn. The men visited the villages regularly and some of them contracted venereal disease as a result.

For the captains the period was occupied not only with diplomacy but with attempts to counter Sioux attacks on the village tribes, with preparations for continuing their journey in the spring, and with evaluating what they had already learned. Traders and Indians provided information that went into the large map of the West that Clark prepared, still largely conjectural beyond Fort Mandan but now incorporating Indian information about rivers and mountains west to the continental divide. The Mandan and Hidatsa villages were a center of intertribal trade, and the captains met members of the Cheyenne, Assiniboine, and Cree tribes.

Soon after the Corps of Discovery settled in for the winter, more traders arrived from Canada representing the competing Hudson's Bay and North West companies. The captains had no objections to the British engaging in legitimate trade with the Indians on what was now American soil, but they suspected that the traders were trying to win the political allegiance of the village tribes away from the United States. The traders consistently denied such intrigues, but the Americans were not convinced and even believed that the British were trying to sabotage the expedition itself.

At Fort Mandan other persons were added to the party. Toussaint Charbonneau, an independent Canadian trader living at one of the Hidatsa villages (now called Sakakawea), had two Shoshone wives, natives of the Rocky Mountains along the continental divide and later captives of the Hidatsas. Charbonneau hired out his services and those of his consorts as interpreters for the trip across the mountains; in fact, only one of his wives, Sacagawea, who gave birth to a son during the winter, actually made the trip. In time she became the most famous member of the party after the two leaders themselves. Baptiste Lepage, another Frenchman living with the Mandans, also joined up as an enlisted soldier to replace Newman.

In March the ice began breaking up in the Missouri, and the Corps of Discovery started preparations for a departure in early April. Having decided to send the keelboat back to St. Louis with the returning soldiers and discharged *engagés,* they built several new canoes from cottonwood logs and prepared specimens, journals, and maps to send back to Jefferson, including a live prairie dog and several live birds. The permanent party now consisted of the two captains, three sergeants, twenty-three privates, Drouillard, Charbonneau, Sacagawea and her infant, and York. Up to Fort Mandan the route had been known to whites and even mapped to some degree, but now the party faced a long journey through country known only in part from sketchy Indian information. Just five weeks short of a year after leaving Camp Dubois, they set out on April 7, with still half a continent to cross before they reached the Pacific.

The Journals of the Lewis and Clark Expedition, Volume 3

August 25, 1804–April 6, 1805

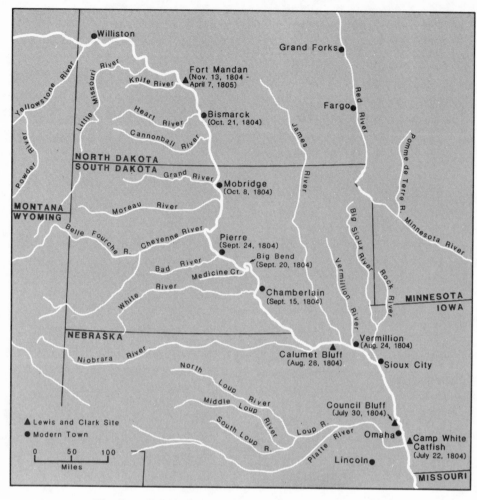

The Expedition's Route, August 25, 1804–April 6, 1805

Chapter Six

From the Vermillion to the Teton River

August 25–September 24, 1804

[Clark]

Augt. 25th Satturday 1804   This morning Capt Lewis & my Self G D. Sjt. Ouderway Shields J. Fields colter Bratten Cane Labeeche corp Wovington Frasure & York Set out to Visit this mountain of evel Spirits,[1] we Set out from the mouth of the White Stone Creek,[2] at 8 oClock, at 4 miles Cross the Creek in an open plain, at 7 ms. the dog gave out & we Sent him back to the Creek   at 12 oClock we rose the hill   Some time before we got to the hill we obsevd. great numbers of Birds hovering about the top of this Mound   when I got on the top those Birds flw off. I discovered that they wer Cetechig [catching] a kind of flying ant[3] which were in great numbers abought the top of this hill, those insects lit on our hats & necks, Several of them bit me verry Shart [sharp?] on the neck, near the top of this nole I observed three holes which I Supposed to be Prarie Wolves or Braroes,[4] which are numerous in those Plains.   this hill is about 70 foot high in an emince Prarie or leavel plain   from the top I could not observe any woods except in the Missourie Points and a few Scattering trees on the three Rivers in view. i' e' the Soues River below, the River Jacque above & the one we have[5] crossed   from the top of this Mound we observed Several large gangus of Buffalow & Elk feeding   upwards of 800 in number   Capt Lewis being much fatigued and verry thursty obliged us to go to the neares water which we Could See, which was the W Stone Creek at

right angles from the Course we came out, and we got water in three
miles in the Creek above whre the beaver had damed it up   after a Delay
of about one hour & a half we Set out for our boat, Cross the Creek three
times wast deep, passing down an ellgent bottom of about a mile in width
bordered by a ridge of about 50 feet from the top of which it was leavel to
the river, we proceeded on by a Circular Derection to the place we Crossed
this Creek going out where we delayed for the men to rest themselves
about 40 minits in a small grove   here we got Great quantities of the best
largest grapes I ever tasted, Some Blue Currents still on the bushes, and
two kind of Plumbs, one the Common wild Plumb the other a large Yellow
Plumb growing on a Small bush, this blumb is[6] about double the Size of
the Common and Deliscously flavoured—[7]   Those plains are leavel without much water and no timber   all the timber on the Stone River would
not thickly timber 100 acres of land—   we returned to the boat at Sunset,
my Servent nearly exosted with heat thurst and fatigue, he being fat and
un accustomed to walk as fast as I went was the Cause—   we Set fire to
the Praries in two Places to let the Sous know we were on the river and as
a Signal for them to Come to the river above, our Party in the Boat & one
Perogue undr. the Comd of Sergt. Pryor answered us by firing a prarie
near them.   we proceeded on to the place we Camped last night, and as it
began to rain and verry dark, we Concluded to Stay all night, our boys
prepared us a Supper of jurked mee[t] and two Prarie Larks (which are
about the Size of a Pigeon and Peculier to this country)[8] and on a Buffalow roabe we Slept verry well   in the morning we proceeded on and
joined the boat at 6 miles, they had camped[9] & were Jurking an Elk & 5
Deer which R. Fields & Shannon had brough in.   from the Mound to the
Hill S. S. mo: of R. Soues S 70° E. to the opsd. Hills S. 45° E. and to the
woods near River au Jacque is West—

[Clark][10]

Augt. 25th Satturday   wind S E   The Boat under Serjt Pryor after
drying some goods which got wet in the french Perogue & jurking the
meet killed yesterday Set out at 12 oClock and proceeded on Six miles
and Camped on the L. S.   passed a Bluff of blue earth[11] at 3 miles and a

large Sand Island in a bend to the S. S. at 5 miles, R Fields brought in 5 Deer, G Shannon an Elk this eveng: rain   *at 3 oClock Murcky. 86 abo O,*[12]

Course, Destance & Reffurence august 25th 1804

S. 72° W.	1	me. the S. S. opposit a ⟨Bluff⟩ of Blue earth on the L. S.
West	½	me. on the S. S. opposite the Bluff, the River verry narrow
N. 22 E	3	ms. to a pt. of high willows of the L. S. opposit a Sand Isd. in a bend
N. 40 W.	1	me on the L. S. opsd. an Island afore Said
S. 86 W	½	on the L. S. to a point of willows, where the Boat lay Sinc
Miles	6	last night Sunset.

[Clark]   *25th August Satturday 1804*[13]

a Cloudy morning   Capt Lewis & my Self Concluded to go and See the Mound which was viewed with Such turrow by all the different Nation in this quarter, we Selected Shields J. Fields, W Bratten, Sergt. Ordway, J Colter, Can, ⟨& york⟩ and Corp Worbington & Frasure, also G. Drewyer and droped down to the mouth of White Stone River where we left the Perogue with two men and at 200 yards we assended a riseing ground of about Sixty feet, from the top of this High land the Countrey is leavel & open as far as Can be Seen, except Some few rises at a Great Distance, and the *Mound* which the Indians Call Mountain of *little people* or Spirits   this mound appears of a Conic form & is N. 20° W. from the mouth of the Creek, we left the river at 8 oClock, at 4 miles we Crossed the Creek 23 yards wide in an extensive Valley and continued on   at two miles further our Dog was So Heeted & fatigued we was obliged Send him back to the Creek, at 12 oClock we arrived at the hill   Capt Lewis much fatigued from heat the day it being verry hot & he being in a debilitated State from the Precautions he was obliged to take to provent the affects of the Cobalt, & Minl. Substance which had like to have poisoned him two days ago, his want of water, and Several of the men complaining of Great thirst, detur-mined us to make for the first water which was the Creek in a bend N. E. from the mound about 3 miles—   aftr a Delay of about 1 hour & a half to

9

recrut our party w[e] Set out on our return down the Creek thro: the bottom of about 1 mile in width, Crossed the Creek 3 times to the place we first Struck it, where we geathered Some delisious froot Such as Grapes Plumbs, & Blue Currents   after a Delay of an hour we Set out on our back trail & arrived at the Perogue at Sun Set   we proceedd on to the place w[e] Campd. last night and Stayed all night.

☞ This Mound is Situated on an elivated plain in a leavel and extensive prarie, bearing N. 20° W. from the mouth of White Stone Creek *Nine* Miles, the base of the Mound is a regular parallelagram the long Side of which is about 300 yards in length the Shorter 60 or 70 yards— from the longer Side of the Base it rises from the North & South with a Steep assent to the hight of 65 or 70 feet, leaveing a leavel Plain on the top of 12 feet in width & 90 in length.   the North & South part of this mound is joins by two regular rises, each in Oval forms of half its hight forming three regular rises from the Plain   the assent of each elivated part is as Suden as the principal mound at the narrower Sides of its Bass—

The reagular form of this hill would in Some measure justify a belief that it owed its Orrigin to the hand of man; but as the earth and loos pebbles and other Substances of which it was Composed, bare an exact resemblance to the Steep Ground which border on the Creek in its neigh-bourhood we Concluded it was most probably the production of nature—.

The only remarkable Charactoristic of this hill admiting it to be a natu-rial production is that it is insulated or Seperated a considerable distance from any other, which is verry unusial in the naturul order or disposition of the hills.

The Surrounding Plains is open void of Timber and leavel to a great extent: hence the wind from whatever quarter it may blow, drives with unusial force over the naked Plains and against this hill; the insects of various kinds are thus involuntaryly driven to the mound by the force of the wind, or fly to its Leward Side for Shelter; the Small Birds whoes food they are, Consequently ⟨they are⟩ resort in great numbers to this place in Surch of them; Perticularly the Small brown [14] Martin of which we saw a vast number hovering on the Leward Side of the hill, when we approached it in the act of Catching those insects; they were So gentle that they did not quit the place untill we had arrivd. within a fiew feet of them—

One evidence which the Inds Give for believeing this place to be the residence of Some unusial Spirits is that they frequently discover a large assemblage of Birds about this mound— is in my opinion a Suffient proof to produce in the Savage mind a Confident belief of all the properties which they ascribe it.

from the top of this Mound we beheld a most butifull landscape; Numerous herds of buffalow were Seen feeding in various directions, the Plain to North N. W & N E extends without interuption as far as Can be Seen—

From the Mound

to the mouth of Stone River is S. 20° E 9 miles.
to the woods near the mouth of River Jacque is West—
to the High land near the mouth of Souis River is S. 70° E.
to the high land opposit Side or near the Maha Town is S. 45 E.

Some high lands to be Seen from the mound at a Great distance to the N. E Some Nearer to the N W. no woods except on the Missouris Points

if all the timber which is on the Stone Creek was on 100 a[c]res it would not be thickly timbered, the Soil of those Plains are delightfull—

Great numbers of Birds are Seen in those Plains, Such as black bird, Ren [*X: wren*] or Prarie burd a kind of larke about the Sise of a Partridge with a Short tail &c. &.[15]

25th Augt the Boat under the Comd. of Sergt. Pryor proceeded on in our absence (after jurking the Elk I Killed yesterday) Six Miles and Camped on the Larboard Side R Fields brought in five Deer. George Shannon Killed an Elk Buck Some rain this evening.

we Set the Praries on fire as a Signal for the Soues to Come to the river.

Course Dist & refers. Augt. 25th

S. 72° W	1	me. on the pt. on S. S. opsd. a Bluff of Blue Clay which is on the L. S.
West	½	me. on the pt. S. S. opsd. the Bluff
N. 22° E	3	mes. to a pt. of high willows on the L. S. opsd. a Sand Island passed a Sand bar on the L. S.
N. 40° W.	1	Me. on the L. S. opsd. Sand Isd.

S. 86° W.   ½   Me. on the L. S. to a pt. of willows the Camp.

           6
           =

[Lewis]   August the 25th[16]

on our return from the mound of sperits saw the first *bats* that we had observed since we began to ascend the Missouri—

also saw on our return on the Creek that passes this mound about 2 M. distant S. a bird of heron kind as large as the Cormorant short tale long leggs of a colour on the back and wings deep copper brown with a shade of red.   we could not kill it therefore I can not describe it more particularly.

1. "G D." is Drouillard. "Cane" may be here written "Carre"; in Codex B it is "Can" or "Carr." He may be the "E. Cann" listed as an *engagé* in the Field Notes for July 4. Clarke (MLCE), 68–69; Osgood (FN), 118 and n. 2. The mound is Spirit Mound, Clay County, South Dakota. See August 24, 1804.

2. Vermillion River, which they reached on August 24.

3. Probably the harvester ant, *Pogonomyrmex* sp.

4. The prairie wolf is the coyote, *Canis latrans,* and the braro is the badger, *Taxidea taxus.* See September 18, 1804, and July 30, 1804, respectively for the two species.

5. The entry shifts here from document 44 to document 46 of the Field Notes. Clark used a circled number "3" on both sheets to connect the two parts.

6. Here on the reverse of document 46 are the barely legible deleted words: I walked on Shore. Documents 45 and 46 of the Field Notes were once apparently part of a single sheet that was divided. In the process these words were cut in two that appear partly on each sheet. Whatever sentence was intended was not continued. The text of the two documents are mixed between August 24 and 25.

7. The "Blue Currants" are either *Ribes odoratum* Wendl. f., buffalo currant, or *R. americanum* Mill., wild black currant. The common wild plum is *Prunus americana* Marsh. and the "Yellow Plumb" is *P. mexicana* Wats., big-tree plum. Barkley, 134–35, 146, 147.

8. This is probably the same bird Clark calls "the Sise of a Partridge" in Codex B this day (see n. 15). Coues labels it the western meadowlark, *Sturnella neglecta* [AOU, 501.1], then unknown to science. Another source suggests the yellow rail, *Coturnicops noveboracensis* [AOU, 215]. Coues (HLC), 1:87; Holmgren, 31.

9. The boats, under Pryor's command, had camped on the larboard side, near the Cedar-Dixon county line, Nebraska. *Atlas* map 17; MRC map 29; MRR maps 80, 81.

10. This second entry for August 25 is on document 47 of the Field Notes. Biddle's notation at the top of the sheet reads "Aug. 25 to Aug. 30th." Immediately above the entry date is written "92½" and a circled 10 comes right after the date and day. See August 24, 1804, n. 2. This entry for August 25 is written over some figures, many of which are illegible due to an ink blot:

12

24 ¾

1?

1? ¼

10 ½

7

9
___

½

11. Perhaps Carlile Shale, a gray marine shale that sometimes has a bluish hue, or outcrops of Graneros Shale, most of which is dark gray.

12. This appears to be the only temperature reading taken between May 14 and September 19, 1804. Whatever the reason for the hiatus, it was not for lack of a thermometer, as this recorded temperature proves. See below, September 19, 1804.

13. Biddle has apparently made red marks through some of the scientific material in this entry.

14. This word could be read as "Crows" or "Grows." Biddle and Thwaites both have "brown," which seems correct. Possibly the bank swallow, *Riparia riparia,* [AOU, 616] or the northern rough-winged swallow, *Stelgidopteryx serripennis* [AOU, 617]. Holmgren, 32, and personal communication, August 9, 1984.

15. This bird "the Sise of a Partridge" may be the same as the one in the Field Notes of this day, "about the Size of a Pigeon" (see n. 8 for this day). The sentence itself is unclear as to whether the wren or the lark is the "Praire bird." Biddle punctuates it so as to make it the wren. Coues (HLC), 1:87. For the wren, see Holmgren, 34.

16. Lewis's natural history notes from Codex Q. The bats could be any of a number of species that are widely dispersed on the plains. The "bird of heron kind" may be either the American bittern, *Botaurus lentiginosus* [AOU, 190], or the immature black-crowned night-heron, *Nycticorax nycticorax* [AOU, 202]. Jones et al., 64–96; Holmgren, 23, 31.

[Clark]

26th August Sunday 1804   arrived at the boat at 9 oClock A. M.   Set out at 10 oClock after Jurking the meet & Cutting the Elk Skins for a Toe Roap and proceeded, leaving G. Drew[yer] & Shannon to hunt the horses, ⟨at 9 miles⟩ the river verry full of Sand bars and Wide   Course S. 66° W. 2 mes. to a Sand bar Makeing out from the S. S.   N. 82° W. 7 mes. to a pt. of willows S S   passd. a Island & large Sand bars on both sides   river wide and a Clift of White earth on the L. S of 2 ms. in length to a point of Willows on the S. S opposit *Arch* Creek[1]   above the mouth of this Creek a Chief of the Maha nataton displeased with the Conduct of Black bird the main Chief came to this place and built a Town[2] which was called by his name *Petite Arch* (or Little Bow)   this Town was at the foot of a Hill in a handsom Plain fronting the river and Contained about 100 huts & 200 men, the remains of this tribe Since the Death of Petite arch has joined the remaining part of the nation   This Creek is Small— we apt. Pat Gass Sergeant Vice Floyd Dicesed, Geathered great quantites of Grapes & three Kinds of Plumbs, one yellow round, & one ovel, & the Common wild Plumb.[3]   Misquetors bad to night—[4]   I have apt. you[5]

[Clark]   26th *August Sunday* 1804

(Joined the Boat at 9 oClock A M)   after Jurking the meat Killed yesterday and prepareing the Elk Skins for a Toe Roape we Set out ⟨and⟩ Leaveing Drewyer & Shannon to hunt the horses which was lost with directions to follow us Keeping on the high lands.

proceeded on   passed a Clift of White & Blue or Dark earth[6] of 2 miles in extent on the L. S. and Camped on a Sand bar opposed the old village Called *Pitite Arc*   a Small Creek falls into the river 15 yds wide below the Village on the Same Side L. S   this village was built by a Indian Chief of the Maha nation by the name of Pitite arc (or little Bow) displeasd. with the Great Chief of that nation (Black Bird) Seperated with *200* men and built a village at this place.   after his death the two villages joined, apt. Pat Gass a Sergt. Vice Floyd Deceased

Great qts. of Grape, Plumbs of three Kinds 2 yellow and large of on[e] of which is long and a 3rd kind round & red all well flavored.   perticularly the yellow Sort.[7]

Course Distance & refrs. Augt. 26th

S. 66° W.   2   mes. to a Sand bar makeing out from the S. S.
N. 82 W.   7   ms. to a pt. of Willows on the S. S.   passed an Island on S S and
             9   large Sand bar on both Sides of the river and Camped[8] opposit the mouth of *Aec* [NB: arc] Creek   the river below wide

[Lewis]   *Orders August 26th 1804.*[9]

The commanding officers have thought it proper to appoint Patric Gass, a Sergeant in *the corps of volunteers for North Western Discovery*, he is therefore to be obeyed and respected accordingly.

Sergt. Gass is directed to take charge of the late Sergt. Floyd's mess, and immediately to enter on the discharge of such other duties, as by their previous orders been prescribed for the government of the Sergeants of this corps.

The Commanding officers have every reason to hope from the previous faithfull services of Sergt. Gass, that this expression of their approbation will be still further confirmed, by his vigilent attention in future to his duties as a Sergeant.   the Commanding officers are still further confirmed in the high opinion they had previously formed of the capacity, deligence and integrety of Sergt. Gass, from the wish expresssed by a large majority of his comrades for his appointment as Sergeant.

Meriwether Lewis
Capt. 1st U' S. Regt Infty.
Wm Clark Cpt &.

1. Present Bow Creek, Cedar County, Nebraska. "Pettite Arch" and "Village" appear on Evans's map 1 (*Atlas* map 7). *Atlas* map 18; MRC map 29; MRR map 81.

2. An Omaha Indian village called "Bad Village" was built near the mouth of Bow Creek in the early eighteenth century. The same general location was the site of a later Omaha village, "Little Bow" (from the French *Petite Arch* of Clark). The location Clark gives for the village is questionable. Nicollet shows an "Old Mahaw Village" near the August 25 camp. Nicollet (MMR), 399; Lewis, 290 and n.; Wood (TL); Fletcher & La Flesche, 1 : 85–86; *Atlas* map 18. Ludwickson, Blakeslee, & O'Shea, 79–85, discuss the historical (and confusing) record of the locations of the villages.

3. For these plums see previous day's entry. The identification of a third species of wild plum for this area may be in error. The "ovel" plum may be a variant of the common wild plum.

4. Probably *Aedes vexans*.

5. An incomplete sentence, apparently a draft for a document appointing Gass as sergeant. The number 9 follows this—the day's mileage accumulation.

6. The white material probably is Niobrara Chalk which overlies the Carlile Shale (the dark material) in this region. Both are Late Cretaceous in age. The white color might refer to a calcareous zone within the Carlile.

7. This passage is crossed out in red, apparently by Biddle.

8. In Clay County, South Dakota, opposite the mouth of Bow Creek and at the lower end of later Audubon Bend. *Atlas* map 18; MRC map 29; MRR map 81.

9. From the Orderly Book in Lewis's hand, except for Clark's own signature.

[Clark]

27th *August* Monday, this morning the Morning Star was observed to be very large, G Drewyer Came up and informed that he Could neither find Shannon or the horses, he had walked all night— we Sent Shields & J. Fields back to look for Shannon & the horses and to Come up with us on the river above at the grand Callemet or River KaCure[1] & we Set out under a Gentle Breeze from the S. E. proceeded on passed a Bluff at 7 mes. Several mile in extent of white Clay Marl or Chalk, under this bank we discovered Large Stone resembling lime incrusted with a Substanc like Glass which I take to be Cabolt, also ore,[2] three mes above this Bluff we Set the Prarie on fire, to let the Soues Know we wished to see them at two oClock an Indian Swam to the Perogue, we landed & two other Came they were boys, they informed us that the *Souex* were Camped near, on the R Jacke one Maha boy informed us his nation was gorn to make a peace with the Pania's [Pawnee] we Send Sjt. Pryor & a frenchman with the Interptr. Mr. Durion to the Camp to See & invite their Great Chiefs to Come and Counsel with us at the Callemet Bluffs [*blank*] Mile abov on L. S.— we proceed on 1½ miles farther & Camped S S.[3]

N. 73 W.	7	mes. to the upper pt of Calx or Chalk Bluffs on L. S. passd. a large Sand bar on L. S. & 2 on S S.
North	3	mes to a tree in the bend to S. S.
W.	2 ½	m to the mouth of rive Jacque[4] S. S. the Sisze of R [Soes?]
S. 80 W.	1 ½	on the Side of a large mud bar on the S. S. and Camped.
	14	

[Clark]   27th *August Monday* 1804

This morning the Star Calld. the morning Star much larger than Common G. Drewyer Came up and informed that he Could neither find Shannon nor horses, we Sent Shields & J Fields, back to hunt ⟨Sha⟩ Shannon & the horses, with derections to Keep on the Hills to the Grand Calumet above on River *Ka cure* [*NB: quecure*].

We Set Sail under a gentle Breeze from the S. E. at 7 miles passed a white Clay marl or Chalk Bluff under this Bluff is extensive I discovered large Stone much like lime incrusted with a Clear Substance which I believe to be *Cabalt,* also ore is imbeded in the Dark earth, resembling Slate much Softer— above this Bluff we had the Prarie Set on fire to let the Souix See that we were on the river, & as a Signal for them to Come to it.

at 2 oClock passed the mouth of *River Jacque,* or Yeankton one Indian at the mouth of this river Swam to the Perogue, we landed and two others came to us, those Inds. informed that a large Camp of Soues, were on R. Jacque near the mouth. we Sent Sergt. Pryor & a Frenchman with Mr. Durioin the Souis interpeter to the Camp with derections to invite the Principal Chiefs to councel with us at a Bluff above Called the Calumet— two of those Indians accompanied them and the third continued in the Boat Showing an inclination to Continue, this boy is a Mahar, and inform that his nation, were gorn to the Parnias to make a peace with that nation.

We proceeded on about one and a half miles and in Camped on a bar makeing out from the S. S. the wind blew hard from the South. a Cool & Pleasent evening, The river has fallen verry Slowly and is now low.

Course and Dist & refrs. August 27.

N. 73° W.	7	miles to the upper part of a Calx or Chalk Bluff on the L. S. haveing passd. a large Sand bar on the L. S. and two on the S. S. also Some small bars in the R.
North	3	mes. to a tree in a bend to the S. S. pass 2 Sand bars in the river
West	2 ½	ms. to the mouth of River Jacque on the S. S. two large Sand bars on the L. S.
S. 80° W.	1 ½ 14	mes. on the Side of a large mud bar makeing out above the Rivr Jacques or Yeankton. This river about 85 or 90 yds. wide and is navagable for Perogues a Great distance, it heads with the St. Peters [Minnesota River], of the Mississippi & the *red River* which runs into Lake Winipeck & Hudsons Bay.[5] ⟨passing the head of Demoin River⟩

(*Point of Observation No. 34.*)

[Lewis]   *Monday August 27th*[6]

On the Stard. shore, opposite to the lower point, or commencement of the white Calk Bluff—

Observed Magnetic azimth. of by ☉ Circumftr.   S. 85° E.

	h	m	s
Time by Chronometer A. M.	7	41	52
Altd. of ☉ U. L. by Sextant.	60°	4′	″

☉'s magnetic Azimuth by circumferentr.   S. 84° E.

	h	m	s
Time by Chronometer A. M.	7	46	13
Altd. of ☉'s U. L. by Sextant	61°	57′	″

Observed time and altitudes of ☉ with Sextant

		Time			Altidue of		
		h	m	s			
A. M.		7	49	37	☉'s U. Limb	63°	8′ 15″
		″	51	3	☉'s Center	″	″ ″
		″	52	40	☉'s L. Limb.	″	″ ″

(*Point of observation No. 35*)

[Lewis]   [*ca. August 27 1804*][7]

On the Stard. shore opposite to the upper point of the white Chalk Bluffs.

Observed meridian Altd. U. L. with Sextant by the fore observation   115° — 45″

Latitude deduced from this observatn.   42 53 13

1. For *L'Eau qui Court,* or Niobrara River, see below, September 4, 1804.

2. Here Clark gets a good view of the Niobrara Formation, an impure chalk or marl, which later became famous for the fossil skeletons of marine reptiles and remains of foraminifera (one-celled animals) which it contains in abundance. The glassy substance is probably the coating of a concretion or nodule which is common in the Niobrara. Clark's references to cobalt and ore are wishful thinking as no metallic ores have been discovered here.

3. In Yankton County, South Dakota, between the mouth of the James River and the present town of Yankton. *Atlas* map 18; MRC map 30; MRR maps 82, 83.

4. The origin of the name Rivière aux Jacques is uncertain. It is now the James River, one of the principal streams of eastern North and South Dakota, locally known as "Jim River." *Atlas* map 18; MRC map 30.

5. The head of the James, in Wells County, North Dakota, is nowhere near the headwaters of the Mississippi, Red, or Minnesota rivers.

6. Lewis's observation from Codex O.

7. Lewis's undated observation from Codex O, immediately following the previous one; the location seems to be near the campsite of August 17.

[Clark]

28th August Tuesday, 1804 The wind blew hard last night   one Indian Stayed with us all night, Set out under a Stiff Breeze from S and proceedd on   passe a Willow Island at two miles   Several Sand bars   the river here is wide & Shallow full of Sand bars—   The High land appear to be getting nearer to each other   passed a Bluff containing Some white earth on the L. S.[1]   below this Bluff for Some mile the Plain rises gradually to the hight of the Bluff which is 70 or 80 foot, here the Indian boy left us for his Camp—   Capt Lewis & my Self much indisposed—   I think from the Homney w[e] Substitute in place of bread, (or Plumbs)   we proceeded on about 3 Miles higher and Camped below the Calumet Bluff in a Plain on the L. S.[2] to waite the return of Sergt Pryor & Mr. Durioun, who we Sent to the Soues Camp from the mouth of R: *Jacque,* before we landed the French rund a Snag thro: their Perogue, and like to have Sunk, we had her on loaded, from an examonation found that this Perogue was unfit for Service, & Deturmined to Send her back by the Party intended to Send back and take their Perogue,[3] accordingly Changed the loads, Some of the loading was *wet*   wind blows hard from the South. J Shields & J. Fields joined   they did not overtake Shannon with the horses who is a head of us.

$$\left.\begin{array}{l}\text{1st: }\langle\text{The}\rangle\text{ Polsey}^4\\ \text{2 White Crain}\\ \text{3 Little Bowl}\\ \text{4 red hand}\end{array}\right\}\text{ Bou Rouley gangue}^5$$

Cours Dist. &

S. 76° W.	4 ½	mes. to the lower part of a Bluff of white earth on the S. S haveing passd. Several large Sand bars on each Side of the water
S. 60 W.	4	mes. to the low part of the Calumet Bluff on the L. S. having
	8 ½	pass a point on east Side & Several Sand bars

[Clark]   28th *August Tuesday 1804.*

Set out under a Stiff Breeze from the South and proceeded on   passd.
a willow Island at 2 miles   Several Sand bars, the [river?] wide & Shallow   at 4 Miles passed a Short White Bluff of about 70 or 80 feet high,
below this Bluff the Prarie rises gradually from the water back to the
Hight of the Bluff which is on the Larboard Side   here the Indian who
was in the boat returned to the Sisouex   Camp on the R Jacque, Capt.
Lewis & my Self much indisposed owing to Some Cause for which we cannot account   one of the Perogues run a Snag thro her and was near Sink-
ing in the opinions of the Crew—   we came too below the *Calumet Bluff*
and formed a camp in a Butifull Plain near the foot of the high land which
rises with a gradual assent   near this Bluff I observe more timber in the
valey & on the points than usial—   The Perogue which was injurd I had
unloaded and the Loading put into the other Perogue which we intended
to Send back, the ⟨Perogue was mended the⟩ Perogue & changed the
Crew   after examoning her & finding that She was unfit for Service deturmined to Send her back by the party   Some load which was in the
Perogue much inju'd

The wind blew hard this after noon from the South—   J. Shields &
J. Fields who was Sent back to look for Shannon & the Horses joined us &
informed that Shannon had the horses a head and that they Could not
over take him   This man not being a first rate Hunter, we deturmined to
Send one man in pursute of him with Some Provisions.—[6]

Course Dis: & reffrs. 28th Augt. 1804

S. 76 W.	4 ½	mes. to the lower part of a Bluff of a Brownish red on S. S., passd. Sevl. Sand bars
S. 60° W.	4	me. to the lower part of the Calumet Bluff. L. S. passed a
	8 ½	pt. on each side and Several Sand bars.

[Lewis]   *Orders* August 28th 1804.[7]

The commanding officers direct that the two messes who form the
crews of the perogues shall scelect each one man from their mess for the
purpose of cooking and that these cooks as well as those previously appointed to the messes of the Barge crew, shall in future be exempted

from mounting guard, or any detail for that duty; they are therefore no longer to be held on the royaster.—

M. Lewis Capt.

1st U' S. Regt. Infty.

Wm Clark Cpt. &.

1. Again the Niobrara Formation with its chalk. This bluff is in Cedar County, Nebraska, in the vicinity of present Beaver Creek. *Atlas* maps 7, 18; MRC map 30; MRR map 83.

2. In Cedar County, just below the present Gavins Point Dam, which impounds Lewis and Clark Lake, and a mile west of the village of Aten. Calumet is a French term which has become common usage for the ceremonial Indian pipe, or "peace-pipe"; the etymology is complex. *Atlas* map 18; MRC map 30; MRR map 83; Mattison (GP), 53–55; Hodge, 1:191–95.

3. Evidently they intended to send back Corporal Warfington's party with dispatches, as planned earlier but not accomplished until April 1805.

4. Clearly a list of the most prominent men among the Sioux who arrived the next day. "The Polsey" was evidently the same man referred to elsewhere as "The Shake Hand." If Clark meant to write "palsey," we have the explanation for the other name. These may or may not be the chiefs listed by Ordway in his entries of August 30 and 31. See Quaife (MLJO), 119–23.

5. Here Clark identifies the group of Sioux, or Dakotas, as the Bois Brulé; they were actually Yankton Sioux. For discussion of these divisions, see below, August 31, 1804. Osgood (FN), 121 n. 2; Ronda (LCAI), 23–26.

6. Colter was sent in pursuit of Shannon, but could not overtake him. They finally caught up with the wanderer on September 11.

7. From the Orderly Book in Lewis's hand, except for Clark's own signature.

[Clark]

29th *August Wednesday* 1804— rained last night and Some this morning verry cloudy Set Some men to work to make a Toe rope of Elk Skin, and my Self to write, Sent one man to pursue Shannon a head with Some provisions, I am much engaged writeing a Speech at 4 oClock Sergt. Pryor & Mr. Durion the Soues interpeter with about 70 Soues arrived on the opposit Side of the river we Sent over for them, who came over Mr. D. & his Son[1] who was tradeing with the Indians Came over Mr. Durion informed that three Chiefs were of the Party, we Sent over Serjt. Pryor with young Mr. Durion, Six Kettles for the Indians to Cook the meat they Killed on the way from their Camp (2 Elk & 6 Deer) a bout a bucket of Corn & 2 twists of Tobacco to Smoke intending to Speak to them tomorrow— G. Drewyer Killed a Deer—. Sergt. Pryor[2] informs that when he approached the Indian Camp they Came to meet the[m] Supposeing Cap Lewis or my Self to be of the party intending to take us in a roabe to their Camp—[3] he approached the Camp which was hand-sum made of Buffalow Skins Painted different Colour, their Camps formed of a Conic form Containing about 12 or 15 persons each and 40 in number, on the River Jacque of 100 yds wide & Deep Containing but little wood, They had a fat dog Cooked as a feest; for them, and a Snug aptmt for them to lodge on their march they passed thro plains Covd. with game &. &. &.

[Clark]   *29th August Wednesday* 1804

Some rain last night & this morning, Sent on Colter with Provisions in pursute of Shannon, had a Toe roap made of Elk Skin, I am much en-gaged reriteing—[4] at 4 oClock P M. Sergt. Pryor & Mr. Dorion with 5 Chiefs and about 70 men &c. [boys?] arrived on the opposite Side we Sent over a Perogue & Mr. Dorrion & his Son who was tradeing with the Indians Came over with Serjt Pryer, and informed us that the Chiefs were there we Sent Serjt. Pryor & yound Mr. Dorion with Som Tobacco, Corn & a few Kittles for them to Cook in, with directions to inform the Chiefs that we would Speek to them tomorrow. Those Indians brought with them for their own use 2 Elk & 6 Deer which the young men Killed on the way from their Camp ⟨15⟩ 12 [*NB: 12*] miles distant.

Serjt. Pryor informs me that when Came near the Indian Camp they were met by men with a Buffalow roabe to Carry them, Mr. Dorion in-formed ["]they were not the Owners of the Boats & did not wish to be Carried"— the Sceouex Camps are handson of a Conic form Covered with Buffalow Roabs Painted different Colours and all Compact & hand Somly arranged, covered all round an orpen part in the Center for the fire, with Buffalow roabs each Lodg has a place for Cooking detached, the lodges contain 10 to 15 persons— a Fat Dog was presented as a mark of their Great respect for the party of which they partook hartily[5] and thought it good & well flavored

The River Jacque is Deep & is navagable for Perogues a long distance up at the mouth it is Shallow & narrow but above it is 80 or 90 yards

wide passing thro: rich Praries with but little timber   this river passes the
⟨Dumoin⟩ Souex River and heads with the St Peters and a branch of Red
river which which falls into Lake Winepik to the North[6]

1. Pierre Dorion, Senior, evidently had several sons by the wife he took among the
Yankton Sioux. The one met here is generally assumed to be Pierre, Junior, who later
joined the Astorians' overland trek to the Pacific and was killed by Indians in Idaho in
1811. An apparent reference to "Francis Durwain" earlier (see above, August 19, 1804),
suggests that another son had entered the picture earlier, perhaps during the second
council with the Otos. Clark's reference here, on August 29, seems to indicate that they
had just now met the son who was trading with the Sioux. Munnick (PD), 8:107–12;
Speck, 150–86; Irving (Astor), 97–100.

2. The following numerals are written under the August 29 entry about here on document 47 of the Field Notes: 125 64:64.

3. The custom of carrying a distinguished visitor to camp seated on a buffalo robe supported by several men was evidently widespread among the Sioux. The Blackfeet Sioux
(Sihasapa) greeted Father DeSmet thus in 1840. DeSmet, 1:253 and facing illustration.

4. Clark may have been copying his Field Notes into his notebook Codices A and B, in
anticipation of sending either the Field Notes or the notebooks back downriver with Corporal Warfington's party.

5. This word might be read as "hastily," but Biddle has "heartily." Coues (HLC), 1:91.

6. Clark repeats misinformation about the source of the James River. See above, August 27, 1804.

[Clark][1]

30th August Thursday 1804   A Foggeie morning   I am much en-
gagd.   after Brackfast we sent Mr. Doroun in a Perogue to the other Side
i'e' L S.[2] for the Chiefs and [w]arriers of the Soues, he returned at 10
oClock with the Chiefs, at 12 oClock I finished and we delivered a Speech
to the Indians expressive of the wishes of our government and explaining
of what would be good for themselves, after delivering the Speech we
made one grand Chief   1 2d Cheif and three third Chiefs and deliverd.
to each a few articles and a Small present to the whole   the grand Chief a
Parole [commission], Some wampom & a flag in addition to his present,
they with Drew and we retired to dinner, Mr. Durions Sun much displeased that he could not dine with Cap Lewis and my Self—   the number of Soues present is about 70 men—   Dressed in Buffalow roabes a
fiew fusees,[3] Bows and arrows, and verry much deckerated with porcu-

pine quills, a Society of which only four remains is present, this Society has made a vow never to giv back let what will happen, out of 22 only 4 remains, those are Stout likely men who Stay by them Selves, fond of mirth and assume a degree of Superiority—,[4] the air gun astonished them verry much   after night a circle was forrm around 3 fires and those Indians danced untill late, the Chiefs looked on with great dignity   much pleased with what they had, we retired late and went to bead.   wind hard from the South.

[Clark]   30th of *August Thursday* 1804

a verry thick fog this morning   after Prepareing Some presents for the Chiefs which we ⟨made⟩ intended make by giving Meadals, and finishing a Speech what we intend'd to ⟨mak⟩ give them, we Sent Mr. Dorion in a Perogue for the Chiefs & warreirs to a Council under an Oak tree near wher we had a flag flying on a high flag Staff   at 12 OClock we met and Cap L. Delivered the Speach & thin made one great Chiff by giving him a meadal & Some Cloathes one 2d. Chief & three third Chiefs in the Same way, They recvd. those thing with the goods and tobacco with pleasure   To the Grand Chief we gave a Flag and the parole [*NB: (certificate)*] & wampom with a hat & Chiefs Coat, we Smoked out of the pipe of peace, & the Chiefs retired to a Bo[*NB: war*]urey[5] made of bushes by their young men to Divide their presents and Smoke eate and Council   Capt Lewis & my Self retired to dinner and Consult about other measures—   Mr. Daurion Jr. much displeased that we did not invite him to dine with us (which he was Sorry for after wards)—   The Souix is a Stout bold looking people, (the young men hand Som) & well made, the greater part of them make use of Bows & arrows, Some fiew fusees I observe among them, not with Standing they live by the Bow & arrow, they do not Shoot So well as the Northern Indians[6]   the Warriers are Verry much deckerated with Paint Porcupin quils & feathers, large leagins & mockersons, all with buffalow roabs of Different Colours.   the Squars wore Peticoats & and a white Buffalow roabes with the black hair turned back over their necks & Sholders

I will here remark a Society which I had never before this day heard was in any nation of Indians—   four of which is at this time present and all who remain of this Band— Those who become members of this Society must be brave active young men who take a *Vow* never to give back let the danger be what it may; in War Parties they always go foward without Screening themselves behind trees or any thing else to this Vow they Strictly adheer dureing their Lives— an instanc which happened not long Since, on a party in Crossing the R Missourie on the ice, a whole was in the ice imediately in their Course which might easily have been avoided by going around, the foremost man went on and was lost the others wer draged around by the party— in a battle with the ⟨Crow⟩ [X: *Kite*] Indians who inhabit the *Coul Noir* or black mountain[7] out of 22 of this society 18 was Killed, the remaining four was draged off by their ⟨friends⟩ Party Those men are likely fellows the Sit together Camp & Dance together— This Society is in imitation of the Societies of the ⟨de Curbo or Crow⟩ [*NB: ⟨(de Corbeau)⟩ Kite*][8] Indians from whome they imitate—

(Point of Observation No. 36.)

[Lewis]   *Thursday August 30th*[9]

On the Lard. Shore at the lower point of Calumet Bluff.

Observed equal Altds. of the ☉, with Sextant

	h	m	s			h	m	s
A. M.	8	14	51		P. M.	2	49	24
	"	16	22			"	50	59
	"	18	3			"	52	38

Altd. given by Sextant at time of obstn. 70° 42' —"

1. Biddle's notation at the top of this sheet, document 48 of the Field Notes, reads, "Aug. 30 to Sept. 1st."

2. This appears to read "L S." but the camp was on the larboard (Nebraska) side of the river, so the "other side" must be the starboard (South Dakota) side.

3. "Fusils"—the French for "musket"—probably the smoothbore Indian trade gun variously known as the Hudson's Bay "fuke," the Northwest gun, and other names. The British trading companies in Canada sold it as one of their principal trade items, and American traders copied it almost exactly. Inaccurate compared with a rifle, it was simple, sturdy, and suited to the needs of an Indian hunter who might have little opportunity for having it repaired. Russell (GEF), 104–30; Russell (FTT), 64–70; Hanson.

4. One of the akicita, or warrior, societies which were a characteristic feature of Sioux

and plains Indian culture. Generally each society had certain special requirements dictated by its particular "medicine"—a supernatural source of power. These groups also acted as civil police in times of peace. Hassrick, 85.

5. A bower, or bowery, is a shelter made of brush. Indians often held councils in such structures, which provided shade on the treeless plains.

6. Perhaps the Great Lakes tribes, or those of the Old Northwest generally, the only "Northern" Indians he would have known well at this time.

7. The Crows (Corbeaux) had been driven from the Black Hills of South Dakota by the Sioux some time before this. However, the captains understood the term "Black Hills" as covering all the eastern outlying ranges of the Rockies which include the Laramie range as well. Allen, 240, 240 n. 18, 383; Hyde (IHP), 150.

8. Biddle has written his emendations in red in this entry and apparently crossed out the preceding four words.

9. Lewis's observation from Codex O.

[Clark]

31st of *August Friday* rose early   a fair Day—   a curioes *Society* among this nation worthey of remark, i,'e,' formed of their active deturmined young men, with a vow never to give back, let the danger or deficuelty be what it may, in war parties they always go forward, without Screening themselves behind trees or anything else, to this vow they Strictly adheer dureing their Lives, an Instance of it, is last winter on a march in Crossing the Missourei a hole was in the ice immediately in their Course which might easily be avoided by going around, the fore most man went on and was drowned, the others were caught by their party and draged around— in a battle with the Crow de Curbo Indians out of 22 of this Society 18 was killed, the remaining four was draged off by their friends, and are now here—   they assocate together Camp together and are merry fellows, ⟨to become one of the Society⟩   This Custom the Souex learned of the *de Carbours* inhabiting the *Cout Noie* or Black mountain   all the Chiefs Delivered a Speech agreeing to what we Said &. &. & beged which I answered from my notes. We made or gav a certificate to two Brave men the attendants of the Great Chief   gave them Some tobacco and prepared a Commission for Mr. Darion to make a peace with all the ⟨Chief⟩ nations in the neighbourhood, Mahas, Porncases [Ponca], Panie, Loups, Ottoes and Missouries—   & to take to the President Some of the Gt Chiefs of each nations who would accompany him   allso to do certain other things, and

26

wrot Instructions— gave him a flag and Some Cloaths— the Chiefs Sent all their young men home, and they Stayed for Mr. Dorion— in the evening late we gave the Comsn. [commission] & Instruction to Mr. Durion & he recved them with pleasa [pleasure?], & promised to do all which was necessary. I took a Vocabulary of the Seouex language, and a fiew answers to Some queries I put to Mr. Pitte Dorion respecting the War No. Situati[on] Trad &c. &. of that people which is divided into 20 tribes possessing Sepperate interest   they are numerous between 2 & 3000 men, divided into 20 tribes who view their interests[1] as defferent   Some bands at War with Nations which other bands are at peace— This nation call themselves—*Dar co tar.* The french call them Souex   Their language is not perculiar to themselves as has been Stated, a great many words is the Same with the *Mahas, Ponckais,* Osarge, Kanzies &c.   Clearly proves to me those people had the Same Oregean [origin]—[2]   this nations in-habit the *red river* of Hudson bay St. Peters [Minnesota River] Missippi, Demoin R. Jacque & on the Missourie   they are at War with 20 nations, and at piece with 8 only—   they recved their trade from the British ex-cept a few on the Missourie   they furnish Beaver Martain[3] Loues [loups, *i.e., wolves*] orter[4] [otter], Pekon[5] Bear and Deer and have forty Traders at least among them. The names of the Different bands of this nation are—[6]

1st   *Che che ree* or Bois ruley [Brulé] (the present band) Inhabit the Souex Jacque & Demoin Rivers—

2nd   *Ho in de bor to* or *poles.* They live on the head of the Suouex River—

3rd   *Me ma car jo* (or make fence on the river.)   the Country near the Big bend of the Missouri.

4th   *Sou on te ton* (People of the Prarie)   they rove North of the Mis-sourie in the Praries above.

5th   *Wau pa Coo do* (Beeds)   they live near the Prarie de Chaine [Prairie du Chien] on the Missippi—

6th   *Te tar ton* (or Village of Prarie) on the waters of the Mississippi above Prare de Chain (Dog Prarie)

7th   *Ne was tar ton* (Big Water Town) on the Mississippi above the mouth of the St. Peters River.

8th   *Wau pa to* (Leaf Nation). 10 Leagues up St. Peters

9th   *Cass car ba* (White man) 35 Lgs. up St Peters

10   *Mi ac cu op si ba* (Cut Bank) reside on the head of St. Peters river

11   *Sou on—*   on St. Peters in the Praries

12th   *Se si toons—*   40 Leagues up St Peters.

The names of the othe[r] tribes I could not get In

31st August Continud

The Distance of the Sun and moon   the moon West

Time			Distance		
H.	M	S.	d	'	"
11	12	18	41	51	00
11	14	23	"	48	00
"	15	49	"	46	00
"	16	42	"	45	30
"	17	52	"	46	30
"	19	32	"	46	30

31st August 1804 Speeches[7]

at 8 oClock the Chiefs and warriers met us in Council all with their pipes with the Stems presented towards us, after a Silence of abt. [*blank*] The great Chief Dressed himself in his fine Cloathes and two warriers in the uniform and armer of their Nation Stood on his left with a War Club & Speer each, & Dressed in feathurs.

The Shake hand 1st Chief Spoke

My Father. I am glad to here the word of my G. F. [great father, *i.e. the President of the United States*] and all my warriers and men about me are also glad.

My Father.—   now I see my two fathers th[e] Children, of my great father, & what you have Said I believe and all my people do believ also—.

My Father—   We are verry glad you would take pitty on them this Day, we are pore and have no powder and ball.

My Father.—   We are verry Sorry our women are naked and all our children, no petiecoats or cloathes—

My Father—   You do not want me to Stop the boats going up if we See,

I wish a man out of your [Dorion] boat to bring about a peace, betwe[en] all the Indians, & he can do So.

My Father— Listen to what I say   I had an English medal when I went to See them, I went to the Spanoriards   they give me a meadel and Some goods, I wish you would do the Same for my people.—

My Father.— I have your word   I am glad of it & as Soon as the Ice is don running I will go down & take with me, Some great men of the other bands of the Soues—

My Father— I will be glad to See My Grand Father but our Women has got no Cloathes and we have no Powder & Ball, take pity on us this day.

My Father— I want to listen and observe wath [what] you Say, we want our old friend (Mr. Durion) to Stay with us and bring the Indians with my Self down this Spring.

My Father— I opend my ears and all my yound men and we wish you to let Mr. Durion Stay, and a Perogue for to take us down in the Spring.[8]

The P[s]peach of th *White Crain Mar to ⟨Se⟩ ree* 2d Chief

My Fathr's listen to my word, I am a young man and do not intend to talk much, but will Say a few words.

My Father— my father was a Chief, and you have made me a Chief   I now think I am a chief agreeable to your word as I am a young man and inexperienced, cannot say much   What the Great Chief has Said is as much as I could Say—

Par nar ne Ar par be   Struck by the Pana [Pawnee] 3d Chief

My father's I cant Speek much   I will Speek a litle to you

My fathers.— ther's the Chiefs you have made high, we will obey them, as also my young men, the Pipe I hold in my hand is the pipe of my father, I am pore as you See, take pity on me   I believe what you have Said

My fathers— You think the great meadel you gave My great Chief pleases me and the small one you gave me gives me the heart to go with him to See my Great father. What the Great Chief has Said is all I could Say. I am young and Cant Speek.

A Warrier by name *Tar ro mo nee* Spoke

My father— I am verry glad you have made this man our great

Chief, the British & Spaniards have acknowledged him before but never Cloathed him.   you have Cloathed him, he is going to see our Great father, We do not wish to spear [spare?] him but he must go and see his great father

My Fathr's, my great Chief must go and See his Gd father, give him some of your milk [whiskey] to Speek to his young men,

My father. our people are naked, we wish a trader to Stop among us, I would be verry glad our two fathers would give us some powder and ball and some Milk with the flag.

Speech of *Ar ca we char chi the half man   3d Chief*

My fathr's   I do not Speak verry well, I am a pore man and [*one word illegible, crossed out*]

My Fathr's. I was on[c]e a Chiefs boy   now I am a man and a Chief of Some note

My Fathr's—   I am glad you have made my old Chief a fine and a great man, I have been a great warrier but now I here your words, I will berry my hatchet and be at peace with all & go with my Great Chief to see my great father.

My fath—s. When I was a young man I went to the Spaniards to see ther fassion, I like you talk and will pursue you advice, Since you have given me a meadal. I will tell you the talk of the Spaniards

My Father's.—   I am glad my Grand father has sent you to the read [red?] people on this river, and that he has given us a flag large and handsom the Shade of which we can Sit under—

My Fathr's.—   We want one thing for our nation very much   we have no trader, and often in want of good[s]

My Fathers—   I am glad as well as all around me to here your word, and we open our ears, and I think our old Frend Mr. Durion can open the ears of the other bands of Soux.   but I fear those nations above will not open their ears, and you cannot I fear open them—.

My Fathers. You tell us that you wish us to make peace with the Ottoes & M. [Missouri]   You have given 5 Medles   I wish you to give 5 Kigz [kegs?]with them—

My Fathers.—   My horses are pore running the Buffalow   give us

Some powder and ball to hunt with, and leave old Mr. Durion with us to get us a trader

My Father.— The Spaniards did not keep the Medal of the T[o]ken of our Great Chief when they gave him one   You have Dressed him and I like it   I am pore & take pitey on me—.

My fathers— I am glad you have put heart in our great Chief he can now speak with confidence, I will support him in all your Councils—

after all the chief presented the pipe to us

The *Half man* rose & spoke as follows viz.

My father— What you have Said is well, but you have not given ⟨me a paper⟩ any thing to the attendants of the Great Chiefs—

after which

from White river to the Isd. of Ceder in the Great Bend	
of the Missourie Called the Grand detour is about	30 Leajus[9]
from thence to Mo: of the Chien R: 1st Aricaras is ab.	28 do
& To R au (Morrow) [Moreau?] S. S.[10]	25 do
To the upper Aricaras Village[11]	64 Lgs
to the Mandins	10
to the Wanutaries[12]	3 do
	160
	3
	480 miles
	1140
	1620

In the evening late we gave Mr. Dorion a bottle of whiskey and himself with the Chiefs Crossed the river and Camped on the opposit bank   Soon after a violent Wind from the N W. accompanied with rain[13]

[Clark]   *31st of August*

We gave a Certificate to two Men of War, attendants on the Chief   gave to all the Chiefs a Carrot of Tobacco— had a talk with Mr. Dorion, who agreed to Stay and Collect the Chiefs from as many Bands of Soux as he coud this fall & bring about a pea[ce] between the Sciuex & their neighbours &. &c. &c.

31

after Dinner we gave Mr. Peter Darion, a Comission to act with a flag & some Cloathes & Provisions & instructions to bring about a peace with the Scioux Mahars, Panies, Ponceries, Ottoes & Missouries— and to employ any trader to take Some of the Cheifs of each or as many of those nations as he Could Perticularly the Sceiouex [*NB: down to Washn*]— I took a Vocabulary of the S10 Language— and the Answer to a fiew quaries Such a[s] refured to ther Situation, Trade, number War, &c. &c.— This Nation is Divided into 20 Tribes, possessing Seperate interests— Collectively they are noumerous Say from 2 to 3000 men, their interests are so unconnected that Some bands are at war with Nations which other bands are on the most friendly terms. This Great Nation who the French has given the nickname of Sciouex, Call them selves *Dar co tar* their language is not peculiarly their own, they Speak a great number of words, which is the Same in every respect with the Maha, Poncaser, Osarge & Kanzies. which Clearly proves that those nation at Some Period not more that a century or two past [once?] the Same nation— Those *Dar ca ter's* or Scioux inhabit or rove over the Countrey on the Red river of Lake Winipeck, St. Peter's & the West of the Missippie above Prarie De chain [*NB: Prairie de Chien*] heads of River Demoin, and the Missouri and its waters on the N. Side for a great extent. They are only at peace with 8 Nations, & agreeable to their Calculation at war with twenty odd.— Their trade Coms from the British, except this Band and one on Demoin who trade with the Traders of St Louis— The furnish *Beaver* Martain, ⟨Loues⟩ [*NB: Wolfs*] Pikon [*NB: pichon*],[14] Bear and Deer Skins—and have about 40 Traders among them. The *Dar co tar* or Sceouex rove & follow the Buffalow raise no corn or any thing else the woods & praries affording a Suffcency, the eat Meat, and Substitute the Ground potato which grow in the Plains for bread [15]

The names of the Different Tribes or Canoes of the Sceoux or Dar co tar Nation—

1st Che cher ree Yank ton (or bois ⟨rulay⟩ [*NB: brulé*]) now present inhabit the Sciouex & Demoin rivers and the Jacques. [*NB: 200 men*]

2nd Hoin de borto (Poles) they ⟨live⟩ rove on the heads of Souix & Jacqus Rivers—

3rd   Me ma car jo (make fence of the river) rove on the Countrey near the big bend of the Missouries—

4th   Sou on, Teton (People of the Prarie) the rove in the Plains N. of the Riv Missouries above this—

5th   Wau pa coo ⟨do⟩ tar (Leaf beds) the live near the Prare de Chain [*X: ien*] near the Missippi—

6th   Te tar ton (or village of Prarie) rove on the waters of the Mississippi above Prarie de Chain—

7th   Ne was tar ton (big water Town) rove on the Missippi above the St. Peters River—

8th   *Wau pa tow* (Leaf nation) live 10 Leagues up St Peters river—

9th   Cas Car ba (white man) live 35 Leagus up St Peters river—

10th   Mi ca cu op si ba (Cut bank) rove on the head of St. Peters—

11th   Sou on (—) rove on St peters river in the Prareis

12th   Sou si toons (—) live 40 Legus up the St peters river—

The names of the other bands neither of the Souex's interpters could inform me.   in the evening late we gave Mr. Dourion a bottle of whiskey, & he with the Cheifs & his Son Crossed the river and Camped on the Opposit bank—   Soon after night a violent wind from the N W. with rain   the rain Continud the greater part of the night   The river a riseing a little.

⟨1st September Satturday⟩

⟨Mr. Durion left his Kettle which was given him, we Sent it to him⟩ omited to put in the 31st of August in Place[16]

August the 31st 1804

after the Indians got their Brackfast the Chiefs met and arranged themselves in a row with elligent pipes of peace all pointing to our Seets, we Came foward and took our Seets, the Great Cheif *The Shake han* rose and Spoke to Some length aproving what we had Said and promising to pursue the advice.

Mar to ree 2d Cheif (White Crain [*NB: White Crane*]) rose and made a Short Speech and refured to the great Chief

Par nar ne Ar par be (Struck by the Pania) 3rd Cheif rose and made a Short Speech—

Ar ca we char che (the half man) 3d Chief rose & spoke at Some length. Much to the purpose.

The othe Cheif Said but little   one of the warreirs Spoke after all was don & promissed to Support the Chiefs, the promisd to go and See their Great father in the Spring with Mr. Dorion, and to do all things we had ⟨promised⟩ advised them to do.   and all Concluded by telling the distresses of ther nation by not haveing traders, & wished us to take pity on them, the wanted Powder Ball & a *little milk* [*NB:* (*rum milk of great father means Spirits*]

last night the Indians Danced untill late   in their dances we gave them [*NB: throw in to them as is usual*] Som knives Tobaco & belts & tape & Binding with which they wer Satisfied

[Lewis]   *Friday August 31st*[17]

Observed time and distance of ☉'s and ☽'s nearest limbs, with Sextant.   the ☉ West.

	Time			*Distance*		
	h	m	s			
A. M.	11	12	18	41°	51′	″
	″	14	23	″	48	
	″	15	49	″	47	45
	″	16	42	″	46	30
	″	17	52	″	46	30
	″	19	32	″	45	45

1. An astronomical table appears here at the top of document 49 of the Field Notes, after which the August 31 entry continues. Clark used asterisks to preserve continuity. The text is here brought together and the table placed at the end.

2. Clark's information undoubtedly came from the two Dorions and other traders. The Dakotas (Sioux), Poncas, Omahas, Osages, and Kansas all spoke languages belonging to the Siouan language family. However, these languages were not all mutually intelligible, and the separations must have occurred much earlier than he imagined. A summary of the linguistic relations among Plains Indians is Hollow & Parks.

3. The marten is *Martes americana*. Apparently the explorers saw no living specimen on the expedition. Burroughs, 73–74; Jones et al., 274–77.

4. The river otter is *Lutra canadensis*, first encountered on October 21, 1804. Jones et al., 307–9.

5. "Pekan" usually refers to the fisher, *Martes pennanti*, while the term "picou" seems to be for the lynx, *Lynx canadensis*. Criswell, 64; Burroughs, 73.

6. The divisional names recorded by Clark reflect the complex nature of what the whites called the "Sioux Nation." In historic times these people spread from western Minnesota through the Dakotas to western Nebraska, eastern Wyoming and Montana, and eventually to Colorado and Kansas. Calling themselves *Dak'ota* or *Lak'ota*, signifying "allies," they were the most numerous branch of the Siouan linguistic family. On the etymology of the word "Sioux" see Ives Goddard, "The Study of Native North American Ethnonymy," in *1980 Proceedings of the American Ethnological Society*, ed. Elisabeth Tooker (Washington, 1980) p. 105.

On linguistic grounds, the Dakotas may be classified in three regional divisions from east to west: Santee, Yankton-Yanktonai, and Teton. Later in the nineteenth century the Dakotas expressed their common kinship by referring to themselves as the "Seven Council Fires," although at no time are they known to have had a central government. Four of the seven "council fires" were Santee: Mdewakantons, Waḣpekutes, Sissetons, and Waḣpetons; the other three were the Yanktons, Yanktonais, and Tetons.

Throughout the eighteenth century the Tetons, Yanktons, and Yanktonais had been moving west, making the transition from a woodlands and prairie mode of life to that of high plains buffalo hunters. In Lewis and Clark's time the Tetons were still to be found on both sides of the Missouri; by mid-century they had moved almost entirely west of the river and had themselves subdivided into seven named groups.

The group names recorded by Clark here and in his "Estimate" (see Chapter 10) reflect the development of Dakota society at the beginning of the nineteenth century and differ significantly from the observations of later recorders. Clark's list of twelve names includes seven identifiable as Santee, three Yankton-Yanktonai, and two Teton. Names later associated only with the Teton ("Burned Thigh" and *Sa'oni*, numbers 1 and 11) are here given as Yanktonai and Yankton names, respectively. Certain group names transferred throughout historic times from one Dakota division to another, reflecting the fluid nature of the autonomous bands that collectively defined the structure of Dakota society.

The division names in Clark's list are here identified as far as possible, making comparative use of Clark's "Estimate" as well as of band name lists compiled by J. N. Nicollet in 1838–39. See DeMallie.

Che che ree [Yankton] (conjectural form: *sic'aŋgu ihaŋkt'uŋwaŋna*), "burned thigh little end village." According to Clark's "Estimate," this group was a subdivision of the Yanktonais.

Ho in de borto (conjectural form: *huŋkpat'ina*), "little campers at the opening of the circle." Clark's "Esimate" gives this group as a subdivision of the Yanktons. Regarding the name "poles," Nicollet recorded a Yanktonai band called "those who bring the poles of lodges." DeMallie, 256–57.

Me ma car jo (*mnik'owoju*), "planters by water." This group was a subdivision of the Tetons; Nicollet recorded the "Minikanye oju" as a band of the "Saones" group of the Tetons. DeMallie, 260.

Sou on te ton (*sa'oni t'íntat'uŋwaŋ*), "sa'oni prairie village." A subdivision of the Tetons. The meaning of *sa'oni* is uncertain.

Wau pa Coo do (*wahpe k'ute*), "leaf shooters." A subdivision of the Santees.

Te tar ton (*t'ínta t'uŋwaŋ*), "prairie village." Given on Clark's "Estimate" as a subdivison of the Mdewakanton group of Santees. Nicollet concurs. DeMallie, 256.

Ne was tar ton (conjectural form: *mde wak'aŋ t'uŋwaŋ*), "sacred lake village." A subdivision of the Santees. Clark's "Estimate" spells the name "Mindawarcarton"; assuming this is the name intended, Clark's writing here is very confused. However, spellings on the table are on the whole phonetically more accurate than those in this list.

Wau pa to (*wahpe t'uŋwaŋ*), "leaf village." A subdivision of the Santees.

Cass car ba (conjectural form: *kaskapa*), "strikers." From their location at the head of the Minnesota River they were apparently a subdivision of the Santees, although this name does not appear in the later literature. Clark's apparent translation, "white man," is not understandable. It is possible that Clark's Dakota spelling is again confused and is intended to represent the group he calls "Kee-uk-sah" on his "Estimate" (*k'iyuksa*), "break in two," a Mdewankanton band.

Mi ca cu op si ba (*maya kicaksa*), "bank cut in two." A subdivision of the Santees, given by Nicollet as a Sisseton band. DeMallie, 256.

Sou on (*sa'oni*), meaning uncertain. Clark's "Estimate" gives them as a subdivision of the Yanktons. Nicollet lists this group as a Yanktonai band and translates the name as "the people who whiten themselves." DeMallie, 257.

Se si toons (*sisit'uŋwaŋ*), etymology unknown. A subdivision of the Santees.

Since the Lewis and Clark journals are themselves used as primary sources by historians and anthropologists, it is not in every case possible to verify group names and locations. Much of the information in this list probably came from the Dorions. Hodge, 1:376–80; Hassrick; Abel (TN); Anderson (EDM); Hyde (RCF). The conference is ably covered in Ronda (LCAI), 23–16.

7. The speeches here recorded are on document 50 of the Field Notes, and are placed by date. "Augt. 31" and "White R" are at the bottom of the reverse of document 50, and "Shannon" in the lower right-hand corner, either Biddle or Clark. Also the following figures:

$$
\begin{array}{r}
1142 \\
6 \\
9\ \tfrac{1}{8} \\
\underline{26\ \tfrac{1}{4}} \\
1183\ \tfrac{1}{2} \\
\underline{30} \\
1214
\end{array}
$$

Some of the names may be identified linguistically:

Shake Hand (*nap'e škaŋ namna*), perhaps "shaking hand" (literally, "hand-moves-rips"). Clark's "Estimate" lists him as the principal chief of the "Yank-ton,-sa-char-hoo," a Yanktonai band.

White Crain Mar to Se ree (*mat'o ǧi*), "yellow (brown) bear." The name probably refers to the grizzly bear, often called in English, "white bear." "White Crain" may perhaps be a translator's error for "White Bear."

Par nar ne Ar par be (*p'anani ap'api*), "struck by the Ree (Arikara)."

Tar ro mo nee (conjectural form: *t'uŋk'aŋ hómni*), "turning rock."

Ar ca we char chi (*hanke wic'aša*), "half man."

8. The date "March 2" is written upside-down under this paragraph.

9. This table following the speeches may represent approximations based on traders' information, or Clark's own estimates after reaching the Mandan villages in October 1804. The points named will be noted on the appropriate dates.

10. The Moreau River is on the larboard side going upriver.

11. In Lewis and Clark's time the Arikara villages were by no means so widely separated as these figures indicate. The information may have been out of date or simply erroneous.

12. The "Wanutaries" are the Hidatsas (Minitaris).

13. This paragraph is at the beginning of document 51 of the Field Notes.

14. Biddle has made most of his emendations in red in this entry and also has crossed out some of Clark's words in order to substitute his own.

15. The first mention of *Psoralea esculenta* Pursh, breadroot. Fernald, 898. It is known by a variety of common names such as white apple, pomme blanche, pomme de prairie, and prairie turnip. McDermott (GMFV), 124–25; Steyermark, 897. Lewis describes it fully on May 8, 1805.

16. Clark started to write his entry of September 1, 1804, in Codex B, then realized that he had failed to include an account of the council under August 31.

17. Lewis's observation from Codex O, made at the same point as the observation for August 30, since they did not move on this date.

[Clark]

September 1st *Satturday* 1804   Mr. Durion left his Kettle which we gave him, which we Sent to him and Set out under a gentle Breeze from the South   (raind half the last night,) proceded on— pass Calumet Bluff of a ⟨redish⟩ yellowish read & a brownish white Hard clay,[1] this Bluff is about 170 or 180 foot high here   the high lands aproach the river on each Side with a jentle assent, opsd. the Bluff a large Island Covered with timber is Situated Close to the L. S.   we passed the Island opposit which the high land approach the river on both Side[2]   (river ros 3 Inchs last night) passed a large Island Covered with wood on the L. S.   Some rain, cloudy all day— the river wide & Hils close on each Side, Came to before night to go & See a Beaver house which is 1½ Miles to the L. S. of the riv   Cap

Lewis & my self with two men went to See this house which was represented as high & situated in a Small pond.   we could not find the Pon. Drewyer Killed a Buck Elk, it is not necessary to mention fish as we catch them at any place on the river, Camped at the lower point of Bonhomme Island—[3]

Course Distance & reffurence Septr. 1st 1804

N 88° W.	4	Mile to a high point of the Bluff on the S. S. haveing passed an Island on the (1) L. S. & Several Sand bars
S. 75 W.	2	to the low point of a large Island on the S. S. passd. a pt. on the L. S. and a Sand bar,
S 68 W	4	me. to a pt. on the L. S. haveing passed the upr pt. of the Isd. on the S S and some high banks 24 fee[t] abov the water, with bows & clare eviden[ce] of the land being made als[o] a tree, a Sand bar above Isd.
S 80 W	5 ―― 16 ══	m. to a tree on an Isld call Bonom [Bonhomme] on the S. S. haveing passed 1 pt. on the S. S. a Deep bend & a San & willow Bar on the L. S. water rose 3 Inches last night

[Clark]   *September 1st Satturday 1804*

Mr. Dourion left his Kettle & Sent back for it &c. We Set out under a jentle Breeze from the S. (It rained half the last night) proceeded on pass the Bluffs Compsd. of a yellowish red, & brownish [*WC?: &*] White Clay which is a hard as Chalk [*WC?: and much resemblig it*][4]   this Bluff is 170 or 180 feet high, here the High lands approach near the river on each Side, that on the S. S. not So high as that on the L. S.   opposit the Bluffs is Situated a large Island Covered with timber close under the L. S.   above the Isd the high land approach & form a ⟨Bluff⟩ Clift to the river on the S. S. this ⟨Bluff⟩ Clift is Called White Bear Clift[5] one of those animals haveing been killed in a whole in it

1st of *September Satturday 1804*[6]

Some hard wind and rain, Cloudy all day, the river wide & hills on each Side near the river, passd. a large (1) Island which appeared to be composed of Sand, Covered with Cotton wood[7]   close under the S. S. we landed at the Lower point of a large Island on the S. S. Called *bon homme* or *Good man,* here Capt Lewis & my Self went out a Short distance on the L. S. to See a Beave house, which was Said to be of Great hite & Situated in a Pond   we could not find the house and returned after night   Drewyer killed an Elk, & a Beaver.   numbers of Cat fish cought,[8] those fish is so plenty that we catch them at any time and place in the river

Course Dists. & refers. 1st Septr.

N. 88 W.	4	mes. to a high point of on the S. S. haveing pass an Isd. (1) on the L. S. & Several Sand bars
S. 75° W.	2	ms. to the lower pt. of a large Island on S. S. passed a pt. on the L. S. and a Sand bar.
S. 68° W.	4	mes to a pt. on L. S. passd. the upper pt. of the Isld. S S. and some land with bows and evident marks of being made 24 abov water.
S. 80 W.	5 / 16	mes. to a tree at the lower pt. of Bon homme Island on S S. haveing psd. a pt. on the S. S. a Deep bend of Sand and Willows on L S.

1. Niobrara Chalk somewhat weathered and stained with iron oxides.

2. The island is "I au Sigo" on Evans's map 1 (*Atlas* map 7), "Sego Island" on *Atlas* map 18, and "ile aux beufs" in Nicollet (MMR), 401. By the century's end it had evidently joined the Nebraska shore. The area where the bluffs narrow is at White Bear Cliffs (see n. 5, below). MRC map 30.

3. Bon Homme Island was still on maps in the 1890s, between Bon Homme County, South Dakota, and Knox County, Nebraska. It is now inundated by Lewis and Clark Lake. *Atlas* map 18; MRC map 31. A map on this sheet of the Field Notes (document 51) shows Bon Homme Island (fig. 1).

4. Perhaps it was Clark who has crossed through this passage and made his emendations in red.

5. The name has remained on the map in Bon Homme County. It is also known as Gavins Point, though Gavins Point Dam is some three miles below. The "white bear" is the grizzly, *Ursus horribilis,* here referred to for the first time in the journals, but not encountered until October 20. Mattison (GP), 56–57; Coues (HLC), 1 : 102–3 n. 11; *Atlas* map 18; MRC map 30.

6. For some reason Clark has two dated entries for September 1 in Codex B, one immediately following the other but on separate pages. Conceivably one or the other was inserted later on a space left blank.

7. The men may now be encountering a new variety of cottonwood, *Populus deltoides* Bartr. ex Marsh. ssp. monilifera (Ait.) Eckenwalder, plains cottonwood. Barkley, 101.

8. The catfish is probably *Ictalurus punctatus*, channel catfish, or perhaps *I. furtatus*, blue catfish. Lee et al., 446, 439.

[Clark]

2nd of Sept. Sunday 1804— Set out early & proceeded on   passed the Island & Came too above below ⟨under⟩ a yellow Bluff on the S S.[1]   the Wind being hard from the N W.   verry Cold   Some rain all day   much Thunder & lightning   G Drewyer R. Fields Howard & Newmon Killed four fat Elk on the Isld.   we had them Jurked & the Skins Stretched to Cover the Perogues   water riseing, I observe *Bear grass* & Rhue[2] in the Sides of the hills   at Sunset the [wind] luled and cleared up cool—   Aired the meet   all in high Spirits—   Shannon & the man Sent after him has not yet joind us—

Course Distance & reffurence Sept 2st 1804

N 75 W.   3   me. to the lower part of a antient foritifcation on the L: Side in a bend, passed over a prarie on the Island   This fortification (1)

N. 45 W. $\frac{1}{4}$ miles   me. on the L. pt. passing the head of the Island at ¾ a Mile   a bluff of yellow clay on S. S.   Hills at a Distc High on L S

2 Sepr. *description of a antient fortification*[3]

(1) From the river on the top of the antient fortification at this the 12 foot high 75 feet Base first Corse is from the river is S 76° W 96 yards. S 84° W. 53 yds.   at this angle a kind of ravilene [ravelin] covering a Saleport [sallyport], bearing East widing N 69 W 300 yds.   passed a gate way at 280 yds.   the bank lower & forming a right angle of 30 yards—   two wings or mounds running from a high nold to the West of the [Call?] way one 30 yards back of the other Covering the gate (at this place the mound is 15 feet 8 Inches higher than the plain forming a Glassee [glacis] outwards & 105 feet base   N. 32 W. 56 yards   N. 20 W. 73 yards   this part of the work is about 12 feet high, leavel & about 16 feet wide on the top)   at the experation of this course a low irregular work in a Direction to the river, out Side of which is several ovel mounds of about 16 feet high and at the iner part of the Gouge [gorge] a Deep whole across the Gauge   N.

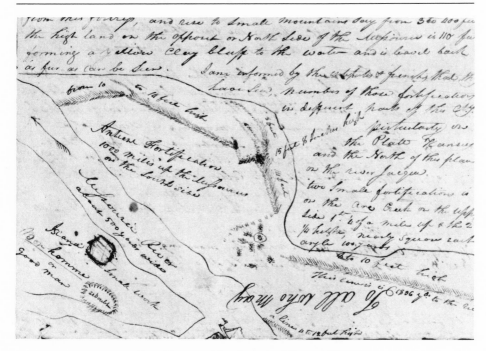

1. Bon Homme Island on the Missouri River,
ca. September 2, 1804, Field Notes, document 51

32 W 96 yds. to the Commencment of a wall of about 8 feet high   N. 81°
W. 533 yards to a Deep pond 73 yds in Deamuter, and 200 yards further
to a Saleport, where there is evident marks of its being Covered, the Same
Course Contined 1030 yards to the river bottom.

One half of the first part of the Fortification is washed into the river, a
Second line, has run from the Northrn extremity parrelel with the river
(as it appears to have run at that time[)] N. 56 W. this of different hith
from 4 to to 10 feet—   The high land is about 3 me. from this fortress,
and rise to Small mountains Say from 3 to 400 feet   the high land on the
opposit or North Side of the Missourie is 110 feet forming a yellow Clay
bluff to the water and is leavel back as fur as can be Seen. I am informed
by the inteperter & french, that they have Seen, numbers of those fortifications in different parts of this Cty. pirtcularly on the Platt Kansies
and the North of this place on the river Jacque.

two Small fortifications is on the *Arc* Creek on the upper side 1st ¼ of a
mile up & the 2d ¼ higher, nearly Square   each angle 100 yards

[Clark]   2nd *September Sunday 1804*

Set out early and proceeded on   Passed the Island and Landed on the
S. S above under a yellow Clay bluff of 110 feet high, the wind blew verry
hard a head from the N. W. with Some rain and verry Cold, G. Drewnyer
R. Fields Newman & howard Killed four fine Elk   w[e] had the meat all
jurked and the Skins Dried to Cover the Perogue, on the Side of the Bluff
I observed Bear Grass & Rhue, at Sun Set the wind luled and Cleared up
Cold, the high land on the L. S. is verry high, & uneaven, that on the S. S
from 80 to 120 foot & is leavel back   but fiew Small Streems falling into
the river.

Course Distance & reffs 2d Spr.

N. 75° W.	3	mes. to the lower part of an antient fortification (1) in a bend to the L. S. this Course passed ovr a pt. of the Isd & Sand
N. 45 W.	1	me. on the L pt. passed the head of the Island at ¾ of a mile opsd. a yellow bank S S.
	$\underline{4}$	

I went out and made a Survey of the antient works which is Situated in
a level plain about 3 miles from the hills which are high.

A Discription of the Fortification

(1) Commenceing on the river opsid the Good Mans Island, first Course from
the river is

S. 76d W.	96	yards thence
S. 84 W.	53	yards (at this angle a kind of angle or horn work[)]
N. 69 W.	300	yards to a high part, passing the gateway Covered by two half Circler works one back of the other lower than the main work the gate forms a right angle projecting inward
N. 32 W.	56	yards
N 20 W.	73	yards This part of the work appears to have either double,
	(578)	or a covered way. from this Some irregular works appear to have been on mounds between this and the river with a Deep round whole in the center of a gorge formed by another angle

42

This part of the work is from 10 to 15 feet 8 Inches— the mounds of various hights— the base of the work is from 75 to 105 feet, steep inward and forming a kind of Glassee out wards—

the Same Cours continued i e

N. 32° W.   96   yards to the Commencement of a wall from 8 to 10 feet high   this corse not on the wall but thro to the commencment of another detached

N. 81° W   1830   yards to the river & above where this bank Strikes the river is the remains of a Circular work

in this Course at 533 yards a Deep Pond of 73 yards Diameter perfectly round is in the Course of the bank which is about 8 feet high, from this Pond the bank it lowers gradually— a bank about the Same hight runs near the river, and must have joined the main work at a part which is now washed into the river, this is also perfectly Streight and widens from the main work, as the river above has washed in its banks for A great distance I cannot form an Idear How those two long works joined— where they Strike the river above, they are about 1100 yds apart, I am informed by our freench interpeters that a great number of those antint works are in Different parts of this Countrey, on the Platt River, Kansus, Jacque, Osarge Mine river &c.

⟨the⟩ Small one is on Island opposit the one I have Discribed, and two of our Party Saw two of those antient frtresses on the Pittiet *Arc* Creek on the upper Side near the mouth,[4] each angle of which were 100 yards and about 8 feet high—

1. In Bon Homme County, South Dakota. The site must now be inundated by Lewis and Clark Lake. It is called "yellow banks" on Evans's map 1 (*Atlas* map 7). *Atlas* map 18; MRC map 31.

2. Beargrass is an obsolete name for yucca. The species here is *Yucca glauca* Nutt., soapweed. Fernald, 437; Barkley, 546. "Rhue" is apparently a misspelling of "rhus" and could refer to *Rhus glabra* L., smooth sumac. Barkley, 223. If so, this is one of the few instances of Clark using a Latin term for identification. Both species are commonly found growing together on the hillsides of this area. Or Clark could mean rue.

3. Clark conducted an elaborate survey of these formations in Knox County, Nebraska, which the captains took to be artifacts comparable to those of the Mound Builders in the

Ohio valley. Descriptions appear in the Field Notes, Codex B, and Codex N. Clark made sketches of the area on document 51 of the Field Notes (fig. 1). Sketches in Codex N and additional notes were probably made on the return trip and will appear in a later volume. The captains' imaginations and their knowledge of military fortifications misled them; all these formations were natural sand ridges. See Lewis. Clark uses technical terms relating to fortifications in his description:

"ravilene"— a ravelin is a detached work of two lines forming an angle in front of the main fortification.

"Saleport"— a sallyport is an opening through which the defenders could make a sally, that is, a small, quick attack, and then retreat.

"Glassee"— a glacis is a natural or artificial slope in front of a fortification, on which the attackers would be exposed to fire from the defenders.

"gouge"— a gorge is the entrance into some outlying work.

"horn work"— a type of detached work joined to the main fortification by parallel walls.

4. Present Bow Creek, in Cedar County, Nebraska. The "fortifications" were again natural formations. Lewis.

[Clark][1]

3rd September Monday 1804. Set out at Sun rise, verry Cold morning clear and but little wind from the N W.   we proceeded on, the river wide, took an obsivation below Plumb Creek[2] which mouths on the S S.   this Creek is Small & coms in between 2 white banks, Great quantities of Plumbs of a most delisious flavour, I have collected the Seed of 3 Kinds which I intend to Send to my brother, also Som grapes of a Superior quallity large & well flavoured, the river is riseing a little, Several wild Goats[3] Seen in the Plains   they are wild & fleet   Elk & Buffalow is verry plenty, Scercely any timber in Countrey except a little on the river in the Points. Saw Some Signs of the 2 men who are a head, Colter has not over taken Shannon   Camped on the L. S. at the edge of a Plain—[4]

Course Distance and reffurences 3rd ⟨Aug⟩ Septr.

West	½	mile on the Point on the L. S. a Bluff of yellow Clay opsd.
S. 35° W.	3	me. to the upper pt. of Some wood at the foot of the high land in a bend on the L. S. passed a large Sand bar 400 yds. wide on L. S. & a pt. and Sand bar makeing out from the S. S.—
West	5 ½	mes. passed a pt & a deep bend on the S. S. and a large

		Sand bar from the L. S to an object in the bend to L. S. near the Hill
S. 45 W.	1	me. on the S. S. to the mouth of Plumb Creek passing under a white bank resembling Chalk, a Sand bar on L. S.
South	5	miles to a pt. on the S. S. passing a pt. on the L. S. & a Sand L. S. but little timber in this countrey— the hills on the S S. high at the end of this course
	15	

[Clark]   3rd of *September Monday 1804*

a verry Cold morning wind from N. W. we Set out at Sun rise, & proceeded on to a Bluff below the mouth of Plumb 12 yds. Creek on the S. S.
and took an obesvation of the Suns Altitude

This Creek is Small   it "abounds with blumbs of a Delicious flavour"
the River is wide and Crouded with Sand bars—   it is riseing a little   but
little timber in this Countrey   all that is, is on the river in the points.   we
Came too on the L. S in the edge of a Plain an Camped for the night—   we
Saw Some Signs of the two men Shannon & Colter, Shannon appeared to
be a head of Colter—   The White banks appear to Continu on both sides
of the river.   Grapes plenty and finely flavered—

Course Dists. & refrs 3rd Septr.

West	½	me. on the L. S. opsd. a Bluff
S. 35 W.	3	mes. to the upper point of Some wood at the foot of the high land on the L. S. in a bend of the river pass a large Sand bar 400 yds. wide on the L. S and a pt. & Sand bar from the L S.
West	5 ½	mes. to a objt. in a Deep bend to the S. S passed. a pt. S. S. and a large Sand bar on the L. S. +
S. 45 W.	1	me. to the mouth of Plumb Cr. on the S. S. psd. undr. white bank
South	5	mes. to a pt. on the S. S. passd. Several Sand bars & two pts. on the L. S.
	15	

1. Biddle added "& 7" after the date to indicate that this sheet of the Field Notes (reverse of document 51) carries entries through September 7.

2. Probably later Emanuel Creek, in Bon Homme County, South Dakota. *Atlas* maps 7, 19; Nicollet (MMR), 401; MRC map 31.

3. The first reference in the journals to the pronghorn, *Antilocapra americana*, described more fully on September 14. Cutright (LCPN), 81.

4. In Knox County, Nebraska, probably near the western boundary of the present Santee Sioux Indian Reservation. *Atlas* maps 18, 19; MRC map 31.

[Clark]

4th of September Tuesday 1804.   a verry Cold wind from South E. by S.   we Set out early   proceeded on to the mouth of a Small Creek in the bend to the L. S. Called ⟨Sand bar⟩ white *line* [lime]   at 1½ miles furthr passed the mouth of a R au platte or White paint Cr[1] about 25 yd. on Same Side Called, I walked on the top of the hill forming a Cliff Covd. with red Ceeder[2]   an extensive view from this hill, at 3 Miles from the Creek the high land jut the river forming a Bluff of Bluish Clay[3]   Continu 1½ miles   Came to at the mouth of Qui courre (rapid)[4]   this river Comes roleing its Sands whuch (is corse) into the Missouris from the S W by W.   this river is 152 yards across the water and not exeeding 4 feet Deep   it does not rise high when it Does it Spreds over a large Surface, and is not navagable   it has a Great many Small Islands & Sand bars   I went up this river 3 miles to the Spot the Panis[5] once had a large Village on the upper Side in a butifull extensive Plain riseing gradially from the river   I fel into a Buffalow road   joined the boat late at night at the Pania Island.[6]

Course Distance and refferences the 4th of September 1804—[7]

S. 5 W	1½	miles to the Mouth of a Creek on the L. S. th below a Seede[r] Clift
S. 35 W	1½	mes. to the mo: of a Creek on L. S. passing under a red Ceede[r] ⟨Bluff⟩ Clift
West	3	mes. to the upr. pt. of a wood on the L. S. opsd. a Bluff of bluwish Clay, several Sand bars L S
N. 72 W	1¼	me. to a mound on the L. Side bluff on the S. S. Several Sand bars in the river
West	¾ ⎯ 8	me. to the mo: of river Que courre on the L. S. (3) hills leave the river S S.

[Clark]   4th September Tuesday 1804

a verry Cold wind from the S. S. E, we Set out early and proceeded on the mouth of a Small Creek in a bend to the L. S. Called White lime, at 1 ½ miles higher up passed a large Creek on the L. S. Called ⟨*R. au platte*⟩ or *white paint*   between those two Creeks (the latter of which is abt. 30 yds. wide) we passed under a Bluff of ⟨white⟩ red Ceeder, at 4 mes. ½ passed the mouth of the River *Que Courre (rapid R*[)] on the L. S. and Came to a Short distance above, this River is 152 yards wide at the mouth & 4 feet Deep Throwing out Sands like the Platt (only Corser) forming bars in its mouth, I went up this river three miles to a butifull Plain on the upper Side where the Panias once had a Village   this river widens above its mouth and is devided by Sand and Islands, the Current verry rapid, not navagable for even Canoos without Great dificulty owing to its Sands; the colour like that of the Plat is light   the heads of this river is ⟨not known,⟩ [*NB: in the Black mountins*[8] *& waters a hilly country & indifferent soil*]   it Coms into the Missourie from the S. W. by West, and I am told that is Genl. Course Some distance up is parrelel with the Missourie

Course Dists & refrs: the 4th of Septr.

S. 5° W.	1 ½	mes. to the mo. of a Creek on the L. S. below a Ceeder Clift
S. 35°	1 ½	mes. to the mo. of White Paint River on the L. S. Passing under a Ceeder Clift
West	3	mes. to the upper pt. of wood on the L. S. opsd. a Bluff of bluish Clay, a Sd. bar L. S.
N. 72° W	1 ¼	mes. to a Mound on the L. S. a Bluff on the S. S. several Sand bars in the river—
West	¾	mes. to the mouth of the river *Que Courre* on the L. S. the
	8	hills leave the river on the S. S. river Crouded with Sand
	=	bars. & wind hard.

☞ *after this I will put the Course Distance & reffurencees of each day first and remks. after—*

1. Probably later Lost and Bazile creeks, in Knox County, Nebraska. Evans's map 1 (*Atlas* map 7) shows both creeks and names the second "grand R au pla." Below that designation and near the first creek someone, perhaps Clark, has added these words: "Pettite R

au platte or plate" and "R white white lime or Paint." The first appears without a name on *Atlas* map 18, while the second is named on *Atlas* map 19. MRC map 31. It was apparently Biddle who crossed out "*R. au platte*" in the second entry in red.

2. *Juniperus virginiana* L., red cedar. Barkley, 13. The observation of red cedars occurring on a steep cliff above the river is coincidental to the prairie fires which destoyed them at lower levels and restricted them to areas that could not be reached by the fires.

3. Either the upper part of the Niobrara Formation, which sometimes weathers to a bluish gray, or the lower part of the Pierre Shale, which grades into the Niobrara and is generally nearly black. The Pierre is the youngest Cretaceous unit in the region, and is a dark gray to black marine shale which makes up the bedrock on the valley walls of the Missouri River.

4. The Niobrara River, which runs through northern Nebraska and reaches the Missouri in Knox County. The French name, *L'Eau qui Court,* can be translated "the river that rushes." The Omaha name was *níubthatha,* "wide river." Link, 78–79; Fletcher & La Flesche, 1 : 93; *Atlas* map 19; MRC map 32.

5. Clark here seems to confuse the Pawnees with the Poncas, although his spelling may be to blame. This Ponca village would be in Knox County. See below, September 5, 1804.

6. Just above the mouth of the Niobrara, in Knox County, in or near present Niobrara State Park. *Atlas* map 19; MRC map 32.

7. Next to the total for this day's distance is the course "S 35 W."

8. Here again, in a notation added later, is the captains' use of the term Black Mountains (or hills) for outlying ranges of the Rockies. In fact, the Niobrara rises in the high plains in Niobrara County, in east-central Wyoming. Allen, 240, 240 n. 18; *Wyoming Guide,* 223; Brown, 101.

[Clark]

5th September 1804 Wednesday, Set out early   the wind blew hard from the South as it has for Some Days past, we Set up a jury mast & Sailed, I saw a large gangue of Turkeys, also Grous Seen[1] Passed a large Island of about 3 miles long in the Middle of the river   opposit the head of this Island the Poncarre River[2] Coms in to the Missourei on the L. S.—   the S. S is a Clift under which great numbers of Springs run out of mineral water, Saw Several wild goats on the Clift & Deer with black tales,—[3] Sent Shields & Gibson to the Poncas Towns,[4] which is Situated on the Ponca river on the lower side about two miles from its mouth in an open butifull Plain, at this time this nation is out hunting the biffalow   they raise no corn or Beens, Gibson killed a Buffalow in the Town, The two men which has been absent several Days is[5] ahead, we came to on the upper pt. of a large Island at 3 oClock to make a mast[6]   Sent out Some hunters on the Island (which I call no preserve Island, at this place we used the last of our Preservs)   They killed 3 bucks, & two Elk which we jurked—

Course Distance & reffurence the 5th of September

N: 85° W	2	mes. to a willow pt. S. S. ⟨under a bluff opsd.⟩ a ⟨Bluff⟩ Clift on the L. S. opsd.
N. 35° W.	3	mes. to a pt. on the Clift to S. S a large Island Call Pania Is. in the middle opsd.
N. 58 W	3 ½	me. to a ⟨pt on the Clift⟩ creek on the S. S[7] passed the head of the [island] at 1 mile & Sand bars making from it the mouth of Ponia river opposit
West	3 ½	mes. to the lower pt. of a large Island
N. 70 W.	1 ¾	mile on the right of the Isd. to the head. pass a Willow Isd. & Sand bar
	13 ¾	

[Clark]

Course Dists. & Refrs. Septr. 5th

N. 85° W	2	mes. to a willow pt. on the S. S. a Bluff opsd.
N. 35° W.	3	mes. to a high part of a Bluff on the S. S. a large Isld. Called pania Isd. in middle of the river
N. 58° W.	3 ½	to a Creek on the S. S. psd. the Isd. at 1 me. a Sand bar makeing from it Poncasar Rive opposit on the L. S. (1) 30 yds.
West	3 ½	mes. to the lower point of a large Island near the L. Side (1)
N. 70° W.	1 ¾	mes. to the right Side of the Sd. Island to the head, passed a willow Isd. & a Sand bar
	13 ¾	

⟨August⟩ *September 5th Wednesday 1804*

Set out early   the winds blew hard from the South, Goats turkeys Seen to day, passed a large Island (1)   opsd. this Island near the head the Poncasar River Coms into the Missourie from the West   this river is about 30 yards wide.   dispatched two men to the Poncaries Village Situated in a handsom Plain on the lower Side of this Creek about two miles from the

Missourie   (the Poncasars nation is Small and at this time out in the pra-ries hunting the Buffalow[)], one of the men Sent to the Village Killed a Buffalow in the town, the other, a large Buck near it, Some Sign of the two men who is a head.   ⟨*Shan*⟩[8]

above the Island on the S. S We passed under a Bluff of Blue earth, under which Seveal Mineral Springs broke out of the water of which had a taste like *Salts*,[9] we Came too on the upper point of a large Island (which I call *No preserves* Island)   here we made a Ceeder Mast, our hunters brought in three bucks, and two elks this evening which we had jurked

One of the hunter Shields, informed that he Saw Several black tailed Deer, near the Poncaser Village—

[Lewis]   Sept 5th[10]

saw some wild goats or antelopes on the hill above the Glauber Salts Springs   they ran off   we could not discover them sufficiently distinctly to discribe even their colour   their track is as large as a deer reather broader & more blont at the point—

This day one of our hunters brought us a Serpent beautifully varia-gated with small black spotts of a romboydal form on a light yellow white ground   the black pedominates most on the back the whiteis yellow on the sides, and it is nearly white on the belly with a few party couloured scuta on which the black shews but imperfectly and the colouring matter seems to be underneath the Scuta—   it is not poisonous   it hisses re-markably loud; it has 221 Scuta on the belly and 51 on the tale, the eyes are of a dark black colour   the tale terminates in a sharp point like the substance of a cock's spur—   Length 4 Ft. 6 I.

1. Perhaps the sharp-tailed grouse, *Tympanuchus phasianellus* [AOU, 308]. See Septem-ber 12, 1804.

2. Ponca Creek, in Knox County, Nebraska. *Atlas* map 19; MRC map 32.

3. The first notice in the journals of the mule deer, *Odocoileus hemionus*, described more fully on September 17, 1804, by Clark and on May 10, 1805, by Lewis. Burroughs, 128–33.

4. The Poncas were a Siouan-speaking tribe, whose language was nearly identical to the Omahas. They were horticulturists living in earth-lodge villages but made seasonal tribal hunting trips far out onto the plains; because of their absence on such a trip they did not meet Lewis and Clark. The village was on Ponca Creek, in Knox County, probably not far from the present village of Verdel. It is now known as Ponca Fort and was occupied in the

late eighteenth century and abandoned about 1800. *Atlas* map 19; Hodge, 2:278–79; Wood (TL); Wood (NPF).

5. Colter and Shannon, the former in pursuit of the latter. These last lines are split about here to go around the course and distance table; it is brought together for ease of reading.

6. The camp on the island lay between southeastern Charles Mix County, South Dakota, and northwestern Knox County, Nebraska. The island, nameless on *Atlas* map 19, is labeled "Isle des" on Nicollet with no further designation. *Atlas* map 19; Nicollet (MMR), 405; MRC map 32.

7. Goat Creek on *Atlas* map 19; present Chouteau Creek, the boundary between Bon Homme and Charles Mix counties, South Dakota. MRC map 32.

8. Clark evidently started to write "Shannon and Colter" and changed his mind.

9. Either Niobrara Formation or Pierre Shale (see the geology note of September 4). The salty taste of the mineral springs was caused by sulfate minerals, mostly gypsum. Modern wells here still yield water containing excessive amounts of sulfate, selenium, and other hardness-producing constituents. The bluff may be the later Chouteau Bluffs, in Charles Mix County. Coues (HLC), 1:110 n. 22; *Atlas* map 19; MRC map 32.

10. Lewis's natural history notes from Codex Q. The wild goats are pronghorn. In local, vernacular usage on the plains, the term goat is still applied. The snake is the bullsnake, *Pituophis melanolecus sayi*, first noticed on August 5, 1804. Benson, 89.

[Clark]

6th ⟨August⟩ Septr Thursday 1804, a Storm this morning from the N W. at day light which lasted a fiew minits, Set out after the Storm was over and proceeded on   a hard wind ahead   passed the [island] which is Seperated from the L. Side by a narrow Channel.   the morning is verry Cold.

Course W.	1 ½	me. to a pt. of wood on the Starboard Side opsd. a Bluff.
N. 85 W	7	me. psd. a pt. on the S. S. at 1 ½ mes. above which is large
	8 ½	Sand bars, on the L. S. high Clifts of Blue & redish Soft rock,[1] Colter joined us at this Clift—

Camped on S. Side before night[2]   no timbering in reach ahead, R. Fields killed 2 Deer   Saw Buffalow, & Goats this evening, the river riseing a little

[Clark]   6th Septr. 1804

Course Distance and reffeirencies

| West | 1 ½ | mes. to a pt. of wood on the S. S. opposit a Bluff |

N. 85° W.	7	mes. passed a pt. on the S. S. at 1 ½ mes. above which is a
miles	8 ½	large Sand bar. on L. S. a high Clift of Blue & redish
		Soft rock, Colter joined us

Septr. 6th Thursday 1804

a Storm this morning from the N. W. which lasted a fiew minits, we Set out and proceeded on   passed the head of the Isd. which is Seperated from the L. S by a narrow Channel, a hard wind from the N. W. a verry Cold day— we Camped on the S. S. at the upper point of Some timber, Some time before night, no timber, no timber being in reach.

I saw Several goats on the hills on the S. S. also Buffalow in great numbers—

1. The Niobrara Formation, overlain by Pierre Shale.
2. In Charles Mix County, South Dakota, probably a little below the Knox-Boyd county line, Nebraska, on the opposite shore. *Atlas* map 19; MRC map 32.

[Clark]

7th *September Friday* 1804.   a verry Cold morning   Set out at Day light

N. 60° W.[1]	3	mes. to the pt. of a Bluff on the S. S. opsd. a pt. on the L. S. below [w]hich there is a Sand bar
West	2 ½	mes to a Tree in the bend to the L. S. near a mountain
	5 ½	which is round formg a point on the riseing 70 feet higher than the high land from its Shape & Situation resembles a cupeleow [cupola][2] passed 2 small Islds. on the S. S,—

near the foot of this high Nole we discovered a Village of an annamale the french Call the Prarie Dog[3] which burrow in the grown & with the rattle Snake and Killed one & Caught one Dog alive   caught in a whole 2 frogs   near the hole Killed a Dark Rattle Snake with a P[rairie] do[g] in him[4]

The Village of those little dogs is under the ground a conisiderable distance   we dig under 6 feet thro rich hard clay without getting to their Lodges   Some of their wholes we ⟨pu throw⟩ put in 5 barrels of water without driveing them out, we caught one by the water forceing him out.   ther mouth resemble the rabit, head longer, legs short, & toe nails long   ther tail like a g[round] Squirel which they Shake and make chattering noise   ther eyes like a dog, their colour is Gray and Skin contains Soft fur

[Clark]   7th Septr. 1804

Course Distance & refeirencs 7.

N. 60° W.	3	mes. to the pt. of a Bluff on the S. S. opsd. a pt. on L. S.
West	2 ½	miles to a tree in a bend to the L. S. near the foot of a
	5 ½	round mountain resembling a Cupola (1) passed 2 Small Islds. S. S.

Septr. 7th Friday   a verry Cold morning   Set out at day light   we landed after proceding 5 ½ miles, near the foot of a round mounting which I saw yesterday resembling a dome.

Capt Lewis & my Self walked up, to the top which forms a Cone and is about 70 feet higher than [*WC: wind S. E.*][5] the high lands around it, the Bass is about 300 foot   in decending this Cupola, discovered a Village of Small animals that burrow in the grown (those animals are Called by the french Pitite Chien)   Killed one & Cought one a live by poreing a great quantity of water in his hole   we attempted to dig to the beds of one of thos animals, after diging 6 feet, found by running a pole down that we were not half way to his Lodges, we found 2 frogs in the hole, and killed a Dark rattle Snake near with a Ground rat [*X: or prarie dog*] in him, (those rats are numerous)   the Village of those animals Covs. about 4 acrs of Ground on a Gradual decent of a hill and Contains great numbers of holes on the top of which those little animals Set erect make a Whistleing noise and whin allarmed Slip into their hole—   we por'd into one of the holes 5 barrels of water without filling it, Those Animals are about the Size of a Small Squrel ⟨Shorter⟩ [*X: or larger longer*] & thicker, the head much resembling a Squirel in every respect, except the ears which is Shorter, his tail like a ground Squirel which thy Shake & whistle when allarmd.   the toe nails long, they have fine fur & the longer hair is gray, it is Said that a kind of Lizard also a Snake reside with those animals.   [*WC?: did not find this correct.*]   Camped[6]

1. This course is repeated and overwritten on the last lines of this page at the bottom of document 51 of the Field Notes.

2. Now called the Tower, in eastern Boyd County, Nebraska. On *Atlas* map 19 it is called the Steeple, a name perhaps given by American fur traders in the years after 1804. By the 1830s it was already the Tower on maps. Coues (HLC), 1:110 n. 23; Cutright (LCPN), 79; Nicollet (MMR), 406; MRC map 33.

3. Lewis and Clark deserve credit for the first scientific description of the prairie dog, *Cynomys ludovicianus,* and its characteristic colonies and burrows. Clark also notes the persistent legend that they share their holes with snakes, but correctly denies the truth of the fable. The following spring they sent a live specimen to Jefferson, which arrived safely. Lewis's more detailed description is dated July 1, 1806. Cutright (LCPN), 79–80, 121; Cutright (OMPD). The rattlesnake is probably the prairie rattler, *Crotalus viridis,* while the squirrel used for comparison is the gray squirrel, *Sciurus carolinensis.* Burroughs, 273–75; Jones et al., 148–52.

4. The September 7 entry continues from here with the next paragraph at the top of document 52 of the Field Notes. At the top of the sheet Clark has written "Wind S E"; Biddle's notation reads "Sept. 8 and 10 1804."

5. The bracketed phrase was inserted at the bottom of the page in Codex B. The remaining emendations are in red, but the writer is difficult to determine. Some of the scientific material has been crossed out lightly in red.

6. Near the foot of the Tower in Boyd County, Nebraska, roughly four miles downriver from the Nebraska-South Dakota boundary (43° N.) where it leaves the river and runs due west. *Atlas* map 19; MRC Map 33.

[Lewis and Clark][1]

8th of September 1804 Satturday. Set out early and proceeded on under a Gentle breese from the S. E.   at 3 mes passed the place where Trodow[2] wintered one winter [17]96 ⟨below the mouth of a creek on the L. S. at⟩

| N. 35 W. | 7 | me. a pt. L. S. opsd. Trodos house Situated in a wood on S S. no [number] of rabits. |
| N. 88 W. | 10 / 17 | Miles to a pont of woods Std. shore.   1 mile above the commencement of this course, the lower point of a willow Island commences, this Island 1¼ in length in the center of the river; a Small Sand Island at its upper extremity.   high bluff on Lard. begining at the upper point of the Island— much higher hills than usual appear to the ⟨West⟩ N, distant about [7 or 8?] miles, recently birnt—   three small islands commence five miles from the commencement of this course and continue about two miles lying on the Stard side of the main |

chanl.   here met with six buffaloe bulls of which we killed two— 1 ½ miles further an Island on the Lard about [*blank*] m in length—   came too at the lower point of this island and encamped, jerked the meet we had taken today consiting of two Buffaloe, one large buck Elk 1 Elk fawn, three fawn deer, three turkies & a Fox Squierel[3]

I went out to day on the S. S with a view to find Some of the little dogs, and Coats [goats], Traveled over a riged [ridged?] and mountanious Countrey without water & riseing to 5 or 600 hundred feet, Islands & Sands interveneing prevt. my getting to the boat untill after night, in my absent Capt. Lewis killed a Buffalow, I saw Greid many Buffalow & white wolves.[4] (Sailed all day)

[Clark]   8th Septr.

Course Distance & reffurences

| N. 35 W. | 7 | mes. to a pt. on L. S. opsd. the house of Mr. Troodo where he wintered in 96 & Seven Called the Pania hos. in a woo[d] to the S. S. (1) |
| N. 88° W | 10 / $\underline{\underline{17}}$ | mes to a pt. of woods S. S.   one mile above the Commencement of this course the Lowr. pt. of a willow Isld.   this Isld is 1 ¼ mes. in length, in the middle of the R: a Small Sand Isd. at its upper extremity |

8th of September Satturday

Set out early and proceeded on under a gentle Breeze from the S. E, at 3 mes. passed the house of Troodo where he wintered in 96. Called the Pania house, above is high hills on the S. S.   on the S. S. much higher hills than usial appear to the North distant 8 miles recently burnt—   pass 3 Small Islands at about 5 miles on this Course on the S. S.   here Capt. Lewis Killed a Buffalow in the river, and this men one other   Came to on the lower point of an Island in the midlle of the river Called Boat Island and incamped,[5] jurked the meet Killed to day Consisting of 2 buffalow, one large Buck Elk one Small, 4 Deer 3 Turkeys & a Squirel, I joined the boat at this Camp, The Countrey on the S S. is pore & broken.

[Lewis]   *Saturday September 8th*[6]

On the Lard. shore 3½ miles below Mr. Trudeau's House, Observed

☉'s Magnetic azimuth with Circumfertr	S. 85° E.

	h	m	s
Time by Chronometer A. M.	7	27	59
Altd of ☉'s U. L. by Sextant.	51°	4′	30″

☉'s Magnetic Azimuth by Circumferentr.	S. 84 E.

	h	m	s
Time by Chronometer A. M.	7	33	30
Alt. by Sextant of ☉'s U. L.	53°	2′	—″

Observed time and Altitudes of ☉, with Sextant

		Time				Altitude of
		h	m	s		
A. M.		7	33	30	☉'s U. L.	53° 2′ ″
		″	35	5	☉'s Center	″ ″
		″	36	41	☉'s L. L.	″ ″

I could not obtain the meridian altitude of sun this day in consequence of not being able to come too in time, without infinite danger of injuring the boat.   the evening was cloudy, which prevented my taking the altitude of any fixed star.

1. Lewis appears to have written the second entry in the course material to "in length."

2. Jean Baptiste Truteau came to St. Louis from Canada in 1774 and served as schoolmaster there for over half a century. In 1795 he stated that he had been making trips into the Indian country for twenty-six years. He could converse in the languages of several of the river tribes. In 1794 he headed the expedition of the Company of Explorers of the Upper Missouri in an attempt to reach the Mandan villages, having been appointed to the position by the Spanish lieutenant-governor, Zenon Trudeau, with whom his name has been confused. One would assume that the captains consulted him while in St. Louis, but records do not indicate this. Lewis and Clark apparently had portions of his journal of that trip with them. The Sioux blocked Truteau from reaching the Mandans, so he wintered at the post mentioned here. Clark's "Pania House" (or "Pawnee House") is more accurately named "Ponca House," being in the neighborhood of that tribe. It was located some thirty-four miles above the mouth of the Niobrara, in Charles Mix County, South Dakota. Truteau evidently wintered there in 1794–95, so Clark may have been in error in

writing "96." It could be either "Panca" or "Pania" on Evans's map 1 (*Atlas* map 7). *Atlas* map 19; Nasatir (JBT); Nasatir (BLC), 1:86–91, 259–94, 294–311; Jefferson to Lewis, November 16, 1803, Jefferson to Lewis, January 22, 1804, Nicholas Biddle Notes [ca. April 1810], Jackson (LLC), 1:136–39, 2:528, 739 n. 3; Abel (TD); Diller (MMR); Diller (PH); Allen, 68, 138–39.

3. The fox squirrel, *Sciurus niger.* Jones et al., 152–56.

4. The gray wolf, *Canis lupus nubilis,* which varies considerably in color. Burroughs, 84–88; Jones et al., 254–56.

5. Evidently on later Chicot, or Strehlow, Island, on the Gregory-Charles Mix county line, South Dakota, which follows the Missouri. They are now entirely within South Dakota. *Atlas* map 19; MRC map 33.

6. Lewis's observation from Codex O.

[Clark and Whitehouse][1]

9th ⟨Aug⟩ Septembr Sunday, Set out at Sunrise and proceeded on passed the Island   Several gangus of Buffalow on the Sides of the hils on the L. S. halted on L. Side   took breakfast. Capt. Clark walked on Shore, we proceeded on

N. 34 W.	3	miles to 2nd point of an Isl. L. S. a creek came in opposite lower point on N. S.[2] passed the Island Several Sand bars above, & a willow Isl. on L. S. halted on S. S. at 12 o.C. for m. observation, above the mouth of a Small creek[3] which came in close below a grove of cottonwood Timber.—
N. 40 W.	2 ½	miles to upper point of the grove of cottonwood. Several Sand bars above the willow Isl. at the bend of the river. the current verry rapid:
N. 83 W.	3 ¾	to a point of woods on Starbord Side passed Several Sand bars above the willow Isl. passed a high Bluff on L. S. about 100 feet high & of a dark coullour,[4] we took dinner at the mo. of a Small creek which came in between the Bluff. passed 2 more Small runs in the Same Bluff. G. Drewyer killed & put on bord the pearogue one Buck & 2 fauns.
N. 36 W.	4	miles to lower point of wood on L. Side in bend.
N 36 W.		to pt S. S. opposite passed a willow Isl. on S. S. Several Sand bars above. &c.

R. Fields came to the Boat   had killed one Buffalow.   passed red ceeder on the edge of the hills on bouth Sides of the river but most on the bluff on

57

L S. passed a handsome round knob on the hill on L. S. little abo. passed
a Smll Creek in bend at lower end of a Sand bar L. S. and Camped on a
Sand bar.[5] Capt Clak came in, Y.—k [York] killed a buffalow near the Boat
by the derections of the master, Capt Lewis wint out with R Fields & each
killed a buffalow, a fair Day wind from the S E Lattide 43° 11 N. Capt.
Clark did not get a Goat or a black taile deer the objects of his pursuite.
river fallinge.

[Clark]   9th Septr.

Course Distance & reffeirenc

N. 34° W.   3   mes. to a pt. on an Island on the L. S. of an the Isd. passed
                      Sand bars

N. 40 W.   3   mes. to an upper pt. of a wood in a bend S. S.

N. 83° W.   4 ¼   mes. to a pt. on S. S.

N. 44° W   4   mes. to the upper pt. of a wood L. S.
              ___
              14 ¼

9th September Sunday 1804

Set out at Sunrise and proceeded on passed the head of the Island on
which we Camped, passed three Sand & willow Islands, the Sand bars So
noumerous, it is not worth mentioning them, the river Shoal or Shallow
wind S E Came too and Camped on a Sand bar on the L. S. Capt Lewis
went out to Kill a buffalow. I walked on Shore all this evening with a view
to Kill a Goat or Some Prarie Dogs in the evening after the boat landed, I
Derected my Servent York with me to kill a Buffalow near the boat from a
numbr. then Scattered in the plains, I saw at one view near the river at
least 500 Buffalow, those animals have been in view all day feeding in the
Plains on the L. S. every Copse of timber appear to have Elk or Deer.
D[rouillard]. Killed 3 Deer, I Kiled a Buffalow Y. [York] 2, R. Fields one.

[Lewis]   Sept. 9th[6]

Capt. Clark found on the Lard shore under a high bluff issuing from a
blue earth a bittuminus matter resembling molasses in consistance, colour
and taste—

58

2. Missouri River near present Fort Randall Dam, South Dakota,
ca. September 9, 1804, Field Notes, reverse of document 53

(Point of observation No. 38.)

[Lewis]   *September 9th Sunday*[7]

On the Lard. Shore opposite to the upper point of boat Island.—
observed,

⊙'s Magnetic azimuth by Circumfert.   S. 89° E.

	h	m	s
Time by Chronometer A. M.	7	6	3
Altd. of ⊙'s U. L. by Sextant	43°	′	″

59

⊙'s Magnetic azimuth by Circumfetr.   S. 88° E.

	h	m	s
Time by Chronometer A. M.	7	12	3
Altd of ⊙'s U. L. by Sextant	44	57	15

Observed time; and Altd. of ⊙, with Sextant.

	Time				*Altitude of*		
	h	m	s				
A. M.	7	12	3	⊙'s U. L.	44°	57	15″
"	13	31		⊙'s Center	"	"	"
"	15	4		⊙'s L. L.	"	"	"

(Point of observation No. 39.)

[Lewis]   *[September 9, 1804]*[8]

On the Stard shore, near a point of woodland, being the extremity of the third course of this day.—

Observed meridian altd. of ⊙'s U. L. with Sextant fore observation   104° 51′ 30″

Latitude deduced from this Observatn.   43° 11′ 56.1″

1. From the word "halted" to "lower end of a Sand bar L. S." of this day's entry in the Field Notes (reverse of document 52) the writing appears to be in the hand of Private Joseph Whitehouse. Cf. Osgood (FN), 134 n. 2. The final entry (or entries) for White-house's course differ from Clark's in the codex. Other differences are also apparent.

2. Either Spring or Pease creeks, in Charles Mix County, South Dakota, both nameless on *Atlas* map 20. Martha's Island and Pease Island on MRC map 34, of about 1890, do not correspond well in their relative positions to the islands shown on *Atlas* map 20, although they are in the same stretch of the river. One could be the Spear Island shown on Evans's map 1 (*Atlas* map 7).

3. This point of observation is not marked on *Atlas* map 20. The creek may be Pease Creek or Campbell Creek, both nameless on the *Atlas* map. MRC map 34.

4. Pierre Shale. See also Lewis's note from Codex Q for this day.

5. From *Atlas* map 20 it appears the camp was in Gregory County, South Dakota, opposite Stony Point on the other shore. MRC map 34.

6. Lewis's notes from Codex Q, covering geology rather than the customary natural history. It is Pierre Shale, which Clark mentions in his entry. *Atlas* map 20 shows a "Molasses Spring."

7. Lewis's observation from Codex O.

8. Lewis's observation from Codex O, undated, but immediately following the one dated September 9, 1804.

[Clark]

10th September Monday a Cloudy morning   Set out early under a Gentle Breeze from the S E.   passed two Small Islands one on the L. S. & the other on the S. S. both in the first Course   at 10½ miles passed the lower pt. of Ceder Island¹ Situated in a bend to the L. S.   this Island is about 2 miles long Covered with red Ceder, the river is verry Shallow opsd. this Island—   below the Island on the top of a ridge we found a back bone with the most of the entire laying Connected for 45 feet   those bones are petrified,   Some teeth & ribs also Connected.²   at 3 mes. above ceder I passed a large Island on the S. S.   to this Island Several Elk Swam   above this Island on the ⟨L. S.⟩ Midle is Situated 2 Islands small one above the other, those Islands are Called mud Islands³ and camped on the upper Island of the[m]⁴   3 Buffalow 1 Elk &c. Killed to day, river falling

Course Distance & reffurence Sepr 10th 1804.⁵

North	5	mes. to a Small Island in a bend to S. S. undr. a bluff of hard black earth, passd. a Isd. on the L. S.
N. 65 W.	2	me. to a pt. on L. S. passed the Islands on each side
N. 80 W	½	mile on the L. Side, (1) a fish bones found on the top of a hill Petrefied 45 longuer in form
S 80 W	3	me. to Ceder Island in ⟨the middle⟩ L. S of this passed sand bars
N. 70 W.	8 ½	me. to the lower pt. of an Island in a bend to the L. S. haveing passed Ceder Island (2) and a large Island on the S S ⟨This Island is covered with Ceders⟩ Covered with timber (3) & many Sand bars water Shallow.
N. 35° W.	1 / 20	me. to the Lower pt. of a 2d Isd. Seprtd. from the first by a narrow Channel (one remarkable circumstance is 19/20th's of the buffalow seen is Bulls, ⟨but⟩ the Inds Kill the Cows.—[)]

a large Salt Spring of remarkable Salt water much frequented by Buffalow, Some Smaller Springs on the Side of the hill above less Salt, the water

excesiv Salt, and is 1 ½ miles from the river on the ⟨N⟩ S. W. or L. S. opposit Ceder Island—[6]

[Clark]   10th Septr

Course Distance & Reffeirenc

North	5	mes. to a Sml. Isd. undr. a Bluff to the S. S. passed a Isd. on L. S.
N. 65 W.	2	me. to a pt. on the L. S. passd. the Isd. on the L. S.
N. 80° W.	½	me. on the L. S.
S. 80 W.	3	mes. to Ceder Island in the middle of the R: found a fish back bone Pitrefied also the hd. just below the Isd. on the top of a hill Situated on the L. S.
N. 70° W.	8 ½	mes. to the Lowr. pt. of an Isd. is a bend to the L. S. pass the hd. of Ceeder Island at (2) ⟨miles⟩ and a large Isd. on the S. S. (3) & many Sand bars. Shallow
N. 35 W.	1 ____ 20	me. to the Lower pt. of a Small Island Seperated by a nar- row Channel.

10th September Monday 1804.

a Cloudy dark morning   Set out early, a Gentle breeze from the S. E,
passed two Small Islands on the L. S. and one on the S. S. all in the first
Course   at 10½ miles passed the lower point of an (2) Island Covered with
red Ceeder Situated in a bend on the L. S.   this Island is about 2 Moles
[miles] in length   (1) below this on a hill on the L. S. we found the back
bone of a fish, 45 feet long tapering to the tale, ⟨Some teeth⟩ &c.   those
joints were Seperated and all petrefied, opposit this Island 1 ½ miles from
the river on the L. S. is a large Salt Spring of remarkable Salt water.   one
other high up the hill ½ me. not So Salt.

we proceeded on under a Stiff Breeze.   three miles above Ceder Island passed a large Island on the S. S, no water on that Side (3)   Several
elk Swam to this Island   passed a Small Island near the Center of the
river, of a mile in length, and Camped on one aboav Seperated from the
other by a narrow Chanel, Those Islands are Called Mud Islands—   the

hunters killed 3 fuffalow & one Elk to day. The river is falling a little, Great number of Buffalow & Elk on the hill Sides feeding   deer Scerce

[Lewis]   Sept. 10th[7]

On the Lard. side of the river about 2 miles from the river Sergt. Pryor and Drewyer discovered a bold salt spring of strong water—

(*Point of Observation No. 40.*)

[Lewis]   *Monday September 10th*[8]

On the Lard. shore, under a high bluff, 2 miles below Ceder Island.—

Observed Meridian Altd. of ☉'s U. L. with Sextant by the fore observtn. 103 53 15

Latitude deduced from this observtn. [*blank*]

(*Point of Observation No. 41.*)

[Lewis]   [*September 10, 1804*][9]

On the Stard. shore 4 miles above the point of observation at noon—

Observed time and distance of ☉'s & ☽'s nearest limbs, the ☉ East.

	Time			*Distance*		
	h	m	s			
P. M.	4	31	15	76°	55′	15″
	"	34	5	"	56	—
	"	35	7	"	56	30
	"	36	14	"	57	15
	"	37	50	"	57	—
	"	38	54	"	57	30
	h	m	s			
P. M.	5	25	26	77°	9′	15″

1. Apparently later known as Little Cedar Island. *Atlas* maps 7, 20; Nicollet (MMR), 409; MRC map 34; MRY maps 31, 32.

2. This hill was in Gregory County, South Dakota, in the vicinity of the bend now called Mulehead Point. They had found the fossil remains of a pleisosaur, an aquatic dinosaur of the Mesozoic era. Some of the vertebra apparently are now in the Smithsonian Institution. Robinson, 553; Mattes, 501; *Atlas* map 20; MRC map 34.

3. These may include the later Hot Springs, Snag, and Pocahontas islands. Robinson, 553; MRC map 35.

4. On what was later Pocahontas, or Toehead, Island, between Gregory and Charles Mix counties, South Dakota. It is probably the "I au Vase" on Evans's map 2 (*Atlas* map 8). The area is now inundated by the Fort Randall Reservoir (Lake Francis Case). Robinson, 553; Mattes, 505–6; *Atlas* map 20; MRC map 35; MRY map 34.

5. Biddle added "& 13" to indicate that document 53 of the Field Notes goes through September 13.

6. The springs, in Gregory County, are shown on *Atlas* map 20 as "Salt Licks." Some letters begin this paragraph, apparently "St. P.—" which could be Sergeant Pryor who related the information. See Lewis's notes from Codex Q.

7. Lewis's notes from Codex Q, covering other items than the customary natural history. See n. 6 this day.

8. Lewis's observation from Codex O.

9. Lewis's observation from Codex O, undated, but evidently from the same date as the previous observation, which is probably the noon observation referred to here.

[Clark]

Course Distance & Refferenceis the 11th of September

N. 35° W.	4 ½	mes. to the lower pt. of a Island, haveing passed the Isld. on which we [camped?] & a large Sand bar from the upr. pt
N. 70° W.	2	mes. to the head of the Island on the L. S. of it
N. 45 W.	3	mes. to a pt. on the L. S. below an Island (1)
N. 50 W.	2	mes. to the upper pt. of an Isd. on the S. S. passed one on the L. S. ops: to which L. S. opsd. at ¼ of me. is a Village of littl dogs
West	4 ½ ⎯⎯ 16	mes. to a pt. on the S. S. passed an Island on the S S. just above the last. Several Sand bars.

we came too at the mouth of a Creek on the L. S.[1] at Dark in a heavy Shower of rain, it Continued to rain the greater part of the night, with a hard wind from the N W   Cold—

Septr. 11th *Tuesday* 1804   Set out early   a Cloudy morning   the river verry wide from one hill to the other, with many Sand bars   passed the Isd. on which we lay at a mile   passed three Isds.[2] one on the L. S. (¼ of a mile from it on the L. S. a village of little Dogs. I Killed four, this village is

800 yards wide & 970 yds. long on a jentle Slope of a hill in a plain, those animals are noumerous) the other two Islands are on the S. S. the river is verry Shallow & wide, the [boat?] got a ground Several times— The man G Shannon, who left us with the horses above the Mahar Village, and beleving us to be a head pushed on as long as he Could, joined us he Shot away what fiew Bullets he had with him, and in a plentifull Countrey like to have Starvd. he was ⟨9⟩ 12 days without provision, Subsisting on Grapes at the Same [time?] the Buffalow, would Come within 30 yards of his Camp, one of his horses gave out & he left him before his last belluts were Consumed— I saw 3 large Spoted foxes[3] to day a black tailed Deer, & Killed a Buck elk & 2 Deer, one othr Elk 2 Deer & a Porkipine[4] Killed to day at 12 oClock it became Cloudy and rained all the after noon, & night.

[Clark]

Course Distance & reffrs. 11th Septr.

N. 35° W.	4 ½	mes. to the lower pt. of an Island, passed the Isd. on which we Campd
N. 70° W.	2	mes. to the head of the Island on its L. S.
N. 45° W.	3	mes. to a pt. on the L S. below an Island (1)
N. 50° W.	2	mes. to the upper pt of an Island on the S. S. passed one on the L. S. opsd. to which at ¼ of a mile is a Village of the Barking Squirel L. S
West	4 ½	mes. to a pt. on the S. S. passed an Isd. on the S. S. just above the one mentioned in the last Course. 11th.
	16	

Sept. 11th Tuesday 1804

a cloudy morning, Set out verry early, the river wide & Shallow the bottom narrow, & the river Crouded with Sand bars, passed the Island on which we lay at one mile—, pased three Islands one on the L. S. and 2 on the S. S. opposit the Island on the L. S. I Saw a village of Barking Squriel 970 yds. long, and 800 yds. wide Situated on a gentle Slope of a hill, those anamals are noumerous, I killed 4 with a view to have their Skins Stufed.

here the man who left us [*NB: George Shannon*] with the horses 22 [*NB: 16*] days ago [*NB: He started 26 Augt.*] and has been a head ever Since joined, us nearly Starved to Death, he had been 12 days without any thing to eate but Grapes & one Rabit, which he Killed by shooting a piece of hard Stick in place of a ball—. This man Supposeing the boat to be a head pushed on as long as he Could, when he became weak and fiable detur-mined to lay by and waite for a tradeing boat, which is expected[5] Keeping one horse for the last resorse,— thus a man had like to have Starved to death in a land of Plenty for the want of Bulletes or Something to kill his meat we Camped on the L. S. above the mouth of a run a hard rain all the after noon, & most of the night, with hard wind from the N W. I walked on Shore the fore part of this day over Some broken Country which Continus about 3 miles back & then is leavel & rich all Plains, I saw Several foxes & Killed a Elk & 2 Deer. & Squirels the men[6] with me killed an Elk, 2 Deer & a Pelican[7]

1. Apparently just above the mouth of Rosebud, or Landing, Creek, in Gregory County, South Dakota. The area is now inundated by the Fort Randall Reservoir. *Atlas* map 20; MRC map 35; MRY map 37.

2. They appear on Evans's map 2 (*Atlas* map 8) and in Nicollet as "Les Trois Isles," and seem to have been in the vicinity of the later La Roche, or Colombs, and Hot Springs islands. The area is now inundated by the Fort Randall Reservoir. *Atlas* map 20; Nicollet (MMR), 410; MRC map 35; MRY map 35.

3. The cross fox, a color phase of the red fox, *Vulpes vulpes* (or *V. fulva*), has mixed colors, though "spotted" does not really describe it. Jones et al., 258–61.

4. The porcupine is *Erethizon dorsatum;* this specimen may have been the yellow-haired porcupine, *E. d. epixanthum,* a subspecies. It is described more fully in Lewis's natural his-tory notes on September 13. Burroughs, 119–20.

5. See below, September 15, 1804.

6. Ordway indicates that he was one of them, and Whitehouse names Pryor as another.

7. The American white pelican is *Pelecanus erythrorhynchos* [AOU, 125]. Lewis gave a lengthy description of the bird in Codex Q, under the date of August 8, 1804. Burroughs, 179–82.

[Clark]

Course Distance &c. 12th of Septr. 1804.

N. 45° W.   4   miles to a point of woods on the L. S.   passed an Isd Trouble-som Island[1] in the middle of the river   at the upper pt of this

Island the river was so crouded with Sand bars that we found great dificulty in getting the boat over, she turned on the Sand 4 times and was verry near turning over.   we camped on the L. S. near a village of Prarie Dogs

Some rain all day to day & Cold—

I walked on Shore   Saw Several foxes Several Villages of Prarie dogs, and a number of Grouse[2]

Septr. 12th Wednesday 1804   Set out early   a Dark Cloudey morning wind from the N W.   cold   passed, (a village of Little Squerals or Prarie dogs opsd. Camp on the N. Side.)[3]

[Clark]   (12th)

Course Distance & reffrs. Septr. 12th

N. 45° W.   4   miles to a point of wood on the L. S.   Passed an Island in the
               Center of the river and Several Sand bars (1) on which we
          4   found great dificuelty in passing the water being verry Shallow

Septr. 12th Wednesday 1804

a Dark Cloudy Day the wind hard from the N. W.   we passed (1) a Island the middle of the river at the head of which we found great dificuelty in passing between the Sand bars   the water Swift and Shallow, it took ¾ of the day to make one mile, we Camped on the L. S. opsd. a Village of Barking Prarie Squriels

I walked out in the morn:g and Saw Several Villages of those little animals, also a great number of Grous & 3 foxes, and observed Slate & Coal mixed,[4] Some verry high hills on each Side of the river.[5]   rains a little all day.

1. Evidently later Durex, or Hiram Wood, Island. *Atlas* map 20; MRC map 35; MRY map 37.
2. The sharp-tailed grouse, a Lewis and Clark discovery although they apparently never gave a full description of it. They sent a live specimen to Jefferson from Fort Mandan in April 1805, but it did not survive the journey. Cutright (LCPN), 81, 121, 375–77.
3. The prairie dog village, not the camp, was on the north side. The camp was in Brule County, South Dakota. *Atlas* map 20; MRC map 36.

4. Clark mistakes the Pierre Shale, which is very rich in organic matter and dark gray to black in color, for slate and coal.

5. Including the Bijou Hills in Brule County, east of the river. Nicollet (MMR), 411; MRC map 36.

[Clark]

Course Distance & remarks 13th Septr. Thursday 1804 [1]

N. 45° E	1 ½	me. on the L. S. wind N W. a Sand bar makeing out a Dark raining morning. G D. [Drouillard] Caught 4 remkby. large Bever
N. 30 E	1	me. on the L. S. verry Cold day or morning Hills high S. S.
N. 60 W.	1	me. on the L. Side to the Commencment of the black Bluffs
N. 64° W	2 ¾	to a wood on the L. S. passing under a Bluff L. S. and Sand bars all along on the S. S.
North	1 ¾	me. to a pt. of high Land on the S. S. pass Sand bars on both Sides (rains[)]
N. 10 W	4 ——— 12 ==	me. to the lower pt. of a timber on S. S. passing under a Bluff S. S. passing a large Sand Island on the L. S. & Sand bars and camped under a Bluff on the S. S. Musquitors verry bad, wors than I have Seen them, qts [quantities] of mud wash into the rivr from a Small rain

[Clark] Septr. 13th

Course Distance and reffeirencs

N. 45° E	1 ½	mes. on the L. S. a Sand bar makeing out
N. 30° E.	1	me. on the L. Side
N. 60° W.	1	me. on the L. S. to a Clift.
N. 64° W.	2 ¾	mes. on the L. S. to the Commencement of a wood passing under a Bluff of Slate & Coal,[2] & a Sand bar opposit
North	1 ¾	mes. to a pt. of high Land on the S. S. passd Sand bars on both Sides, Shallow
N. 10° W.	4 ——— 12 ==	mes. to the lower pt. of a timber passing under a Bluff, a Sand & Willow Island on the L. S.

13th Septr. Thursday 1804

a Dark Drizzley Day, G D Cought 4 Beaver last night   the winds from the N W. Cold   Set out early and proceeded on verry well   passed a number of Sand bars, Capt Lewis killed a Porcupin on a Cotton treee fieeding on the leaves & bowers of the Said tree, the water is verry Shallow [*X: in places*] being Crouded with Sand bars   Camped on the ⟨L⟩ S. Side under a Bluff.[3]   the Bluffs on the S. S. not So much impregnated with mineral as on the L. S.[4]   muskeetors verry troublesom—.

[Lewis]   September 13th[5]

Killed a *bluewinged teal* [*EC: Querquedula discors*] and a Porcupine [*EC: Erethizon dorsatum*]; found it [the porcupine] in a Cottonwood tree near the river on the Lard. Shore—   the leaves of the Cottonwood were much distroyed—   as were those of the Cottonwood trees in it's neighbourhood. I therefore supposed that it fed on the folage of trees at this season, the flesh of this anamal is a pleasant and whoalsome food—   the quills had not yet obtained their usual length—   it has four long toes, before ⟨and⟩ on each foot, and the same number behind with the addition of one short one on each hind foot on the inner side.   the toes of the feet are armed with long black nails particularly the fore feet—   they weigh from 15 to 20 lbs—   they resemble the *slowth* very much in the form of their hands, or fore feet.   their teeth and eyes are like the bever—

1. The courses and distances for September 13, 1804, on the reverse of document 53 of the Field Notes are written over a sketch map of part of the Missouri River (fig. 2). Though there are no names, it appears to show the river between the camps of September 8 and 9. See *Atlas* maps 19, 20. This area in Charles Mix and Gregory counties, South Dakota, is now inundated by Fort Randall Reservoir.

2. Pierre Shale (see the geology note of September 12).

3. In Brule County, South Dakota. *Atlas* maps 20, 21, 22; MRC map 36.

4. This portion of the Pierre Shale has less gypsum and other minerals.

5. Lewis's natural history notes from Codex Q. The bird is the blue-winged teal, *Anas discors* [AOU, 140]. Holmgren, 33. The porcupine is mentioned on September 11.

[Clark]   Septr 14th Friday 1804 Course Dists & rifur.[1]

Set out early   proceeded on   passed Several Sand bars   water wide & Shallow   N. 68° W. 2¾ mes. to a pt. of high Land on the L. S.   passed a

round Island on the ⟨L⟩ S S.—[2]   Caught 3 beaver last night, Some driz-
zeley rain   Cloudy & Disagreeable and Som hard Showers, I walked on
Shore with a view to find an old Volcano Said to be in this neghbourhood by
Mr. McKey[3]   I was Some distance out   Could not See any Signs of a Vol-
canoe, I killed a *Goat*,[4] which is peculier to this Countrey about the hite of a
Grown Deer Shorter, its horns Coms out immediately abov its eyes   broad
1 Short prong the other arched & Soft   the color is a light gray with black
behind its ears, white round its neck, no beard, his Sides & belly white,
and around its taile which is Small & white and Down its hams, actively
made   his brains on the back of its head, his noisterals large, his eyes like
a Sheep   only 2 hoofs on each foot no a[n]telrs (more like the antelope or
gazella of Africa than any other Specis of Goat). Shields Killed a *Hare*
weighing 6½ lb: verry pore, the head narrow and its ears 3 Inches wide
and 6 long, from the fore to the end of the hind foot; is 2 feet 11 Inch.
hite 1 foot 1¾ its tail long & thick white, clearly the mountain Hare of
Europe,[5] a rainy evening   all wett   The Soil of those Plains washes down
into the flats, with the Smallest rain & disolves & mixes with the water.[6]   we
See back from the river high hills in a leavel plain, evidently the remains
of mountains, what mud washed into the river within those few days has
made it verry mudy, passed two Small Creeks on the L. S. & Camped below a 3rd on the L. S.[7]   rained all evening

S. 70° W.	2 ½	me. to an object in the pt. on the L. S. passed the mo of a run L. S.
N. 4 W.	2 ½	mes. to the mo. of a Small Creek in the bend to the L. S.
N. 10 E	1 ¼	me. to the mo. of a Creek on the L. S., passed a bad Sand bar.
	<u>9 ¾</u>	

[Clark]   *Sept. 14*

Course Distance and refurences

N. 68° W.	2 ¾	mes. to a pt. of high Land on the L. S. passd. a round Island on the S. S.
S. 70° W.	2 ½	mes. to a tree in the pt. on the L. S. passed the Mo: of a run on the L. S.

N. 4° W.	2 ½	mes. to the mouth of a Small Creek in the bend to the L. S.
N. 10° E	1 ¼	mes. to to the mouth of a Creek on the L. S passed a bad Sand bar
	9̲	

14th Septr. Friday 1804.   Set out early proceeded on   passed Several Sand bars   the river wide and Shallow   3 beaver Caught last night, Drizeley rain in the forepart of this day, cloudy and disagreeable, I walked on Shore with a view to find an old Vulcanio, Said to be in this neighbourhood by Mr. J. McKey of St. Charles. I walked on Shore the whole day without Seeing any appearance of the Villcanoe, in my walk I Killed a Buck Goat of this Countrey, about the hight of the Grown Deer, its body Shorter, the Horns which is not very hard and forks ⅔ up   one prong Short the other round & Sharp arched, and is imediately above its Eyes   the Colour is a light gray with black behind its ears down its neck, and its Jaw white round its neck, its Sides and its rump round its tail which is Short & white   verry actively made, has only a pair of hoofs to each foot.   his brains on the back of his head, his Norstral large, his eyes like a Sheep—   he is more like the Antilope or Gazella of Africa than any other Species of Goat. Shields Killed a *Hare* like the mountain hare of Europe, waighing 6¼ pounds (altho pore) his head narrow, its ears large i, e, 6 Inches long & 3 Inchs wide one half of each white, the other & out part a lead grey   from the toe of the hind foot to toe of the for foot is 2 feet 11 Inches, the hith is 1 foot 1 Inche & ¾, his tail long thick & white.

The rain Continued the Greater part of the day   in My ramble I observed, that all those parts of the hills which was Clear of Grass easily disolved and washed into the river and bottoms, and those hils under which the river run, Sliped into it and disolves and mixes with the water of the river, the bottoms of the river was covered with the water and mud frome the hills about three Inches deep—   those bottoms under the hils which is Covered with Grass also [receves?] a great quantity of mud.

Passed 2 Small Creeks on the L. S and Camped below the third, (the place that Shannon the man who went a head lived on grapes)   Some heavy Showers of rain all wet, had the Goat & rabit Stufed   rained all night

September 14th 1804[8]

this day Capt. Clark killed a male *wild goat* [*EC: Antelope*] so called— it's weight 65 lbs.

	F	I
length from point of nose to point of tail	4	9
hight to the top of the wethers	3	—
do. behind	3	—
girth of the brest	3	1
girth of the neck close to the shoulders	2	2
do. near the head	1	7

Eye deep sea green, large percing and reather prominent, & at or near the root of the horn within one ¼ inches—

[Lewis] Sept. 14th 1804.[9]

Shields killed a *hare of the prarie*, [*EC: Lepus campestris*] weight six pounds and ¼

	F.	I.
Length from point of hind to extremity fore feet	2	11
hight when standing erect	1	1 ¾
length from nose to tale	2	1
girth of body	1	2 ¾
length of tale	—	6 ½
length of the year [ear]	—	5 ½
width of do. do.	—	3 ⅛
from the extremity of the hip to the toe of the hind foot	1	3 ½

the eye is large and prominent   the sight is circular, deep sea green, and occupyes one third of the width of the eye   the remaining two thirds is a ring of a bright yellowish silver colour.   the years ar placed at the upper part of the head and very near to each other, the years are very flexable, the anamall moves them with great ease and quickness and can contrat and foald them on his back or delate them at pleasure— the front outer foald of the year is a redis brown, the inner foalds or those which ly together when the years are thrown back and wich occupy two thirds of the width of the year is of a clear white colour except one inch at the tip of the year which is black, the ⟨lower or⟩ hinder foald is of a light grey— the head back sholders and outer part of the thighs are of a ledcoloured grey the sides as they approache the belly grow lighter becomeing gradually more white the belly and brest are white with a shad of lead colour— the furr is long and fine— the tale is white round and blounty pointed the furr on it is long and extreemly fine and soft when it runs it carry's it's tale strait behind the direction of the body— the body is much smaller and more length than the rabbit in proportion to it's height— the teeth are like those of the hair or rabbit as is it's upper lip split— it's food is grass or herbs— it resorts the open plains, is extreemly fleet and never burrows or takes shelter in the ground when pursued, I measured the leaps of one which I suprised in the plains on the 17th Inst. and found them 21 feet the ground was a little decending they apear to run with more ease and to bound with greater agility than any anamall I ever saw. ⟨they are extreemly fleet—⟩ this anamal is usually single seldom associating in any considerable numbers.

1. Biddle added "& 16" after the date to indicate that document 54 of the Field Notes goes through September 16.

2. Probably the later Dry Island. *Atlas* maps 20, 21, 22; MRC map 36.

3. There is no evidence of volcanic action in the area. Burning deposits of coal or lignite may have led Mackay to this belief, which would have been based on the testimony of Evans, since Mackay was never on this part of the Missouri. It is probably the same phenomenon as the Ionia Volcano of Nebraska (see August 24, 1804), that is, a zone where the oxidation of pyritic material yields sulfuric acid which, with the addition of water, produces a reaction so hot that the bituminous shale is ignited. Mackay's reference was probably to the "Burning Bluff" in Gregory County, South Dakota, which they had passed several days earlier. Robinson, 555; *South Dakota Guide*, 403.

4. The first scientific description of the pronghorn, often incorrectly called an antelope. Lewis and Clark continued to refer to it as a "goat," as do many persons on the plains; they also used the term "cabra." Cutright (LCPN), 81.

5. The first description of the white-tailed jackrabbit, *Lepus townsendii*, previously unknown to science. See Lewis's natural history notes for this day for more information. Ibid., 82–83; Jones et al., 114–16.

6. The soil is probably the dark, clayey soil of the grasslands which would make the water blackish. The White River, which they pass the next day, derives its name from white clay of western South Dakota.

7. As Clark notes in the Codex B entry, this third creek was where Shannon remained for some days while lost (see *Atlas* maps 20, 21, 22); they called it Shannon's River. Some-

one, perhaps Maximilian, has penciled additional names on *Atlas* map 21. It is apparently the stream later known as Ball or Bull Creek, in Lyman County, South Dakota. The September 14 camp was just below the mouth of the creek, in an area now inundated by Fort Randall Reservoir. Of the other two creeks, nameless on the *Atlas* maps, the second was Waterhole Creek. Mattes, 514–15; Nicollet (MMR), 412; MRC map 36; MRY map 41.

8. Lewis's natural history notes from Codex Q. The goat is the pronghorn, also described by Clark this day; see n. 4.

9. Lewis's second entry of natural history notes from Codex Q for this date. The white-tailed jackrabbit is also described by Clark this day; see n. 5.

[Clark]

Course Distance & reffurence 15th Septr. Satturday

N. 50° E	2	mes. to point of White River above on the L. S. above is a handsom Situation for a Town more timber than usial above the riv passed Several Sands
N. 26 E.	1 ½	me. to a pt. on the L. S. a Bluff. on the S. S.
N. 10 W.	½	me. on the L. S. to a Bluff of Black Slate
N. 30 W.	2	mes. to the ⟨upper⟩ Lower pt of an Island, on the L. S. this Island is covered with Ceeders & cald. Rabit Isd. (2)
North	2 — 9 =	mes. to the Mouth of a Creek on the L. S. a Point of high land opposit under which we camped, I Killed Elk & Deer to day White River is about 400 yds. Wide & like this R. [Missouri]

September the 15th Satturday 1804   Set out early   passed the Mouth of a [creek?] on the L S. where Shannon lived on grapes waiting for Mr. [Clintens?] boat Supposeing we had went on,[1] Capt Lewis and my Self halted at the mouth of White River[2] & wend up a Short   Crossed &, this river is about 400 yards, the water Confined within 150 yards, the Current regularly Swift, much resembling the Missourie, Sand bars makeing out from the points, Some Islands   we Sent up two men[3] to ⟨travers⟩ go up this river one Day and Meet us to morrow   we proceeded on   passed a Small Island Covered with Ceder timber, & great number of rabits, no game except rabits, and Camped on the S. S. opposit a large Creek,[4] on which there is more wood than usial on Creeks in this quaterr   this creek raised 14 feet last rain   I Killed a Buck elk & a Deer.

[Clark]   15th Septr.

Course Distance & reffurences

N. 50° E	2	mes. to the pt. mouth of White river (1) L. S. passed Sand bars &c.
N. 26° E	1 ½	mes. to a pt. on the L. S. a Bluff on the S. S.
N. 10° W.	½	mes. on the L. S. to the commencement of a Bluff of black Slate
N. 30° W.	2	mes. to the lower pt. of an Island Situated near the L. Side (2)
North	2	miles to the mouth of a Creek on the L. S. a point of high land opposit under which we camped
	8	
	=	

15th September Satturday 1804

Set out early   passed the mo of the Creek, and the mouth of White river; (1) Capt Lewis and my Self went up this river a Short distance and Crossed, found that this differed verry much from the Plat or que Courre, threw out but little Sand, about 300 yard wide, the water confind within 150 yards, the current regular & Swift much resemblig the Missourie, with Sand bars from the points   a Sand Island in the mouth, in the point is a butifull Situation for a Town   3 Gradual assents, and a much Greater quantity of timber about the mouth of this river than usial, we concluded to Send Some distance up this river   detached Sjt. Gass & R. Fields.   we proceeded on passed a Small (2) Island Covered with Ceeder on I Saw great numbers of Rabits & Grapes, this Island is Small & Seperated from a large Sand Isd. at its upper point by a narrow Channel, & is Situated nearest the L. Side. Camped on the S. S. opposit the mouth of a large Creek on which there is more timber than is usial on Creeks of this Size, this Creek raised 14 feet the last rains. I killed a Buck Elk & Deer, this evening is verry Cold, Great many wolves of Different Sorts howling about us.[5]   the wind is hard from the N W this evening

1. Obviously the expedition members assumed that some trader's boat was behind them. "Clinten" may have been Charles Courtin, who was trading with the Teton Sioux, the

Arikaras, and the Poncas in the next few years, and whom the party may have met on their return journey on September 14, 1806. Apparently Courtin and a party of trappers eventually reached the Three Forks and western Montana. Courtin was reported killed by Piegans near present Dixon, Montana, in 1809. Jackson (LLC), 2 : 437 n. 3; Osgood (FN), 136 n. 6; Josephy, 660–63.

2. White River still bears the name it derived from the clay of western South Dakota which gives a milky color. Rising in northwestern Nebraska, it curves across southwestern South Dakota and reaches the Missouri in Lyman County. *South Dakota Guide,* 323; Coues (HLC), 1 : 117 n. 43; *Atlas* maps 20, 21, 22; MRC map 36.

3. Gass and Reubin Field, as indicated in Codex B.

4. Clark named the island Rabbit Island on the maps covering this date. It was in the vicinity of later Bice Island. The camp in Brule County, South Dakota, was opposite the mouth of what he called Corvus Creek, later American Creek, or American Crow Creek, in Lyman County, just below the present town of Oacoma. Mattes, 521; *Atlas* maps 20, 21, 22; Nicollet (MMR), 421; MRC map 37; MRY maps 42, 45.

5. Probably they were hearing both the gray wolf and the coyote, the nocturnal serenades of the latter still being characteristic of the Great Plains. Cutright (LCPN), 85.

[Lewis]   Sunday September 16th 1804.[1]

This morning set out at an early hour, and come too at ½ after 7 A. M. on the Lard. Shore 1 ¼ miles above the mouth of a small creek which we named *Corvus,* in consequence of having kiled a beatiful bird of that genus near it[2]   we concluded to ly by at this place the ballance of this day and the next, in order to dry our baggage which was wet by the heavy showers of rain which had fallen within the last three days, and also to lighten the boat by transfering a part of her lading to the red perogue, which we now determined to take on with us to our winter residence wherever that might be;[3] while some of the men were imployed in this necessary labour others were dressing of skins washing and mending their cloaths &c.   Capt. Clark and myself kiled each a buck immediately on landing near our encampment; the deer were very gentle and in great numbers on this bottom which had more timber on it than any part of the river we had seen for many days past, consisting of Cottonwood Elm, some indifferent ash and a considerable quanty of a small species of white oak[4] which is loaded with acorns of an excellent flavor   very little of the bitter roughness of the nuts of most species of oak, the leaf of this oak is small pale green and deeply indented, [*NB: not copied for Dr Barton*] it seldom rises higher than thirty feet is much branched, the bark is rough and thick and of a light colour; the cup which contains the acorn is fringed on it's edges and imbraces the nut about one half; the acorns were now falling, and we concluded that the number of deer which we saw here had been induced thither by the acorns of which they are remarkably fond.   almost every species of wild game is fond of the acorn, the Buffaloe Elk, deer, bear, turkies, ducks, pigegians and even the wolves feed on them; we sent three hunters[5] out who soon added eight deer and two Buffaloe to our strock of provisions; the Buffaloe were so pour that we took only the tongues skins and marrow bones; the skins were particularly acceptable as we were in want of a covering for the large perogue to secure the baggage; the clouds during this day and night prevented my making any observations. Sergt. Gass and Reubin Fields whom we had sent out yesterday to explore the White river returnd at four oclock this day and reported that they had foll [*EC?: owed the*] meanders of that stream about 12 miles   r[iver]'s general course West, the present or principal channel 150 yards wide; the coulour of the water and rapidity and manner of runing resembled the Missouri presisely; the country broken on the border of the river about a mile, when the level planes commence and extend as far as the eye can reach on either side; as usual no timber appeared except such as from the steep declivities of hills, or their moist situations, were sheltered from the effects of the fire.   these extensive planes had been lately birnt and the grass had sprung up and was about three inches high.   vast herds of Buffaloe deer Elk and Antilopes were seen feeding in every direction as far as the eye of the observer could reach.

[Clark]

September 16th Sunday, we proceeded on 1¼ Miles and Camped ⟨for the⟩ on the L. Side in a butifull Plain Surounded with timber in which we Saw Severall Der, we delayed here for the purpose of Drying the articles which were wet & the cloathes   to Load the Perogue which we had intended to send back, finding the water too Shoal Deturmind to take on the Perogue also to make Some observations for Longitude &c.   the two men G. [Gass] & R. F. [Reubin Field] joined us and informed "that the river as far as they were up had much the Appearance of the river about the mouth, but little timber and that chiefly elm, the up land ⟨near⟩ between this river & the White river is fine, Great numbers of Goat, Deer of three kinds, Buffalow, & wolves, & Barking Squrels, The fallow Deer,[6] Cloudy, all day Cleaning out the boat examining & Drying the goods, & loading the Perogue, I killed 2 Deer Capt Lewis one & a Buffalow, one Buffalow & five other Deer Killed. I observed Pine Burs & Burch Sticks[7] in the Drift wood up white river which Coms in on the L. S. imedeately in the point is a butifull Situation for a town 3 Gentle rises, & more timber about the mouth of this river than usial

N. 72° E   1 ¼   to a pt on the L. S. and Camped in Some Timber round a
         1 ¼   plain   Grea numbers of plumbs near Camp, a Village of
              Barking Squirels near

from this date—   ☞ refur to the Book No. 2.[8]

[Clark]   16th Sept.

N. 72° E   1 ¼   Miles to a pt. on the L. S. and came too (1)

16th of September Sunday 1804

We Set out verry early & proceed'd on 1 ¼ miles ⟨thro⟩ between Sand bars and Came too on the L. S. (1)— deturmined to dry our wet thig and liten the boat which we found ⟨by⟩ could not proceed with the present load [NB: *as fast as we desired, owing to Sand bars*] for this purpose we Concluded to detain the Perogue we had intended to Send back & load her out of the boat & detain the Soldiers untill Spring & Send them from our winter quarters. We put out those articles which was wet, Clean'd the boat & perogus, examined all the Locker Bails &. &c. &.

This Camp is Situated in a butifull Plain Serounded with Timber to the extent of ¾ of a mile in which there is great quantities of fine Plumbs— The two men detachd up the White river joined us here & informed that the [river] as far as they were up had much the appearance of the Missourie Som Islands & Sands little Timber Elm, (much Signs of Beaver, Great many buffalow) & Continud its width, they Saw & well as my Self Pine burs & Sticks of Birch in the Drift wood up this river, They Saw also

Number of Goats Such as I Killed, also wolves near the Buffalow falling [fallow] Deer, & the Barking Squrels Villages   Capt. Lewis went to hunt & See the Countrey near the Kamp   he killed a Buffalow & a Deer

Cloudy all day   I partly load the empty Perogue out of the Boat. I killed 2 Deer & the party 4 Deer & a Buffalow ⟨who⟩ the we kill for the Skins to Cover the Perogus, the meet too pore to eat. Capt Lewis went on an Island[9] above our Camp, this Island is abt. one mile long, with a Great purpotion ceder timber near the middle of it

I gave out a flannel Shirt to each man, & powder to those who had expended thers

1. This Lewis entry and that of the next day are in the fragmentary Codex Ba; it contains Lewis's only known daily entries—as opposed to scientific notes in the specialized journals—between May 20, 1804, and April 7, 1805. For a discussion of this gap, see the Introduction to vol. 2.

2. The camp, where they remained until September 18, is near the town of Oacoma, Lyman County, South Dakota. They would stop there again on August 28, 1806, on the return trip. On that date Clark says that they had called it "Pleasant Camp" before, but in his Codex B entry for September 17, 1804, he calls it "Plumb Camp." Corvus Creek (American Creek) should not be confused with later Crow Creek, several miles above on the opposite side of the Missouri. The bird is the black-billed magpie, *Pica pica* [AOU, 475], described more fully on September 17. See also August 15, 1804, n. 7. Four living magpies were sent to Jefferson in April 1805, only one of which arrived alive. Cutright (OMPD). Mattes, 521–22; *Atlas* maps 20, 21, 22; MRC map 37.

3. As Clark notes below, they had now definitely decided not to send back Corporal Warfington's party in the red pirogue until next spring.

4. *Quercus macrocarpa* Michx., bur, or mossy-cup, oak. Fernald, 544; Barkley, 39; Cutright (LCPN), 88. Biddle has apparently marked through part of this scientific material.

5. According to Ordway, Drouillard, Deschamps, Roi, and Collins were among those who killed game on this date, besides the captains themselves.

6. Clark refers to the western white-tailed deer, *Odocoileus virginianus dacotensis*. Fallow deer is the name for the European species, *Cervus dama*, and used by the captains as a convenient word of differentiation without specific reference to the European animal. The captains were aware that this subspecies differed from the eastern white-tailed, *O. virginianus*, referred to as "common deer" by Clark on September 17. The men continued to apply these terms to the two deer. Burroughs, 124–25; Jones et al., 324–27, 346.

7. The pine burs are cones of *Pinus ponderosa* Laws., ponderosa pine, which had washed down the White River from its headwaters or tributaries. Paper birch (*Betula papyrifera* Marsh.), the only possibility for Clark's "Burch Sticks," is not known in this region. Barkley, 12, 43.

8. Clark's Book No. 2 was the notebook now designated Codex B. He may have had some thought of abandoning the Field Notes and keeping only the notebook journal. Osgood (FN), 139 n. 9, 144 n. 1.

9. Later known as American, or Cedar, Island, opposite present Chamberlain, Brule County, South Dakota. The area is now inundated by Fort Randall Reservoir. *Atlas* maps 20, 21, 22; MRC map 37.

[Lewis]   *Monday September 17th 1804.*

Having for many days past confined myself to the boat, I determined to devote this day to amuse myself on shore with my gun and view the interior of the country lying between the river and the Corvus Creek— accordingly before sunrise I set out with six of my best hunters,[1] two of whom I dispatched to the lower side of Corvus creek, two with orders to hunt the bottoms and woodland on the river, while I retained two others to acompany me in the intermediate country. one quarter of a mile in rear of our camp which was situated in a fine open grove of cotton wood passed a grove of plumb trees loaded with fruit and now ripe. observed but little difference between this fruit and that of a similar kind common to the Atlantic States.[2] the trees are smaller and more thickly set. this forrest of plumb trees garnish a plain about 20 feet more lelivated than that on which we were encamped; this plain extends back about a mile to the foot of the hills one mile distant and to which it is gradually ascending this plane extends with the same bredth from the creek below to the distance of near three miles above parrallel with the river, and is intirely occupied by the burrows of the *barking squril* hertefore discribed; this anamal appears here in infinite numbers, and the shortness and virdue [verdure] of grass gave the plain the appearance throughout it's whole extent of beatifull bowlinggreen in fine order. it's aspect is S. E. a great number of wolves of the small kind, halks and some pole-cats[3] were to be seen. I presume that those anamals feed on this squirril.— found the country in every direction for about three miles intersected with deep revenes and steep irregular hills of 100 to 200 feet high; at the tops of these hills the country breakes of as usual into a fine leavel plain extending as far as the eye can reach. from this plane I had an extensive view of the river below, and the irregular hills which border the opposite sides of the river and creek. the surrounding country had been birnt about a month before and young grass had now sprung up to hight of 4 Inches presenting the live green of the spring. to the West a high range of hills,[4] strech across the country from N. to S and appeared distant about 20 miles; they are not very extensive as I could plainly observe their rise and termination no rock appeared on them and the sides were covered with virdue similar to that of the plains this senery already rich pleasing and beatiful, was still farther hightened by immence herds of Buffaloe deer Elk and Antelopes which we saw in every direction feeding on the hills and plains. I do not think I exagerate when I estimate the number of Buffaloe which could be compreed at one view to amount to 3000. my object was if possible to kill a female Antelope having already procured a male; I pursued my rout on this plain to the west flanked by my two hunters untill eight in the morning when I made the signal for them to come to me which they did shortly after. we rested our selves about half an hour, and regailed ourselves on half a bisquit each and some jirk of Elk which we had taken the precaution to put in our pouches in the morning before we set out, and drank of the water of a small pool which had collected on this plain from the rains which had fallen some days before. We had now after various windings in pursuit of several herds of antelopes which we had seen on our way made the distance of about eight miles from our camp. we found the Antelope extreemly shye and watchfull insomuch that we had been unable to get a shot at them; when at rest they generally seelect the most elivated point in the neighbourhood, and as they are watchfull and extreemly quick of sight and their sense of smelling very accute it is almost impossible to approach them within gunshot; in short they will frequently discover and flee from you at the distance of three miles. I had this day an opportunity of witnessing the agility and superior fleetness of this anamal which was to me really astonishing. I had pursued and twice surprised a small herd of seven, in the first instance they did not discover me distinctly and therefore did not run at full speed, tho' they took care before they rested to gain an elivated point where it was impossible to approach them under cover except in one direction and that happened to be in the direction from which the wind blew towards them; bad as the chance to approach them was, I made the best of my way towards them, frequently peeping over the ridge with which I took care to conceal myself from their view   the male, of which there was but one, frequently incircled the summit of the hill on which the females stood in a group, as if to look out for the approach of danger. I got within about 200 paces of them when they smelt me and fled; I gained the top of the eminece on which they stood, as soon as possible from whence I had an extensive view of the country   the antilopes which had disappeared in a steep revesne now appeared at the distance of about three miles on the side of a ridge which passed obliquely across me and extended about four miles.   so soon had these antelopes gained the distance at which they had again appeared to my view I doubted at ferst that they were the same that I had just surprised, but my doubts soon vanished when I beheld the rapidity of their flight along the ridge before me   it appeared reather the rappid flight of birds than the motion of quadrupeds. I think I can safely venture the asscertion that the speed of this anamal is equal if not superior to that of the finest blooded courser.—   this morning I saw[5]

[Clark][6]

17th of Septr. Monday 1804   above White river   Dried all those articles which had got wet by the last rain, a fine day   Capt Lewis went hunting with a vew to see the Countrey & its productions, he was out all Day   Killed a Buffalow & a remarkable bird of the Spicies of Corvus, long tail of a Greenish Purple, Varigated   a Beck like a Crow   white round its neck comeing to a point on its back, its belley white   feet like a Hawk   abt. the size of a large Pigeon[7]   Capt Lewis returned at Dark. I took the Meridian & equal altitudes to day   made the Lattitude.

Colter Killed a Goat, & a Curious kind of Deer, a Darker grey than Common   the hair longer & finer, the ears verry large & long   a Small resepitical under its eye   its tail round and white to near the end which is black & like a Cow   in every other respect like a Deer, except it runs like a goat.   large.[8]

The hunters brought in 8 fallow Deer & 5 Common Deer to day, Great numbers of Buffalow in the Praries, also a light Coloured woolf Covered with hair & corse fur, also a Small wolf with a large bushey tail—[9]   Some Goats of a Different Kind Seen to day,—   Great many Plumbs, rabits, Porcupines & barking Squrels, Capt Lewis Killed a rattle Snake in a village of the Squirel's and Saw a Hair to day. Wind from the S. W.   we finished Drying our Provisions   Some of which was wet and Spoiled,[10]

White River 17th Septr. *Plomb Camp*
Course Distance & reffurence
17th of September Monday 1804

[Clark]

Dried all our wet articles this fine Day, Capt Lewis went out with a View to see the Countrey and its productions, he was out all day   he killed a Buffalow and a remarkable *Bird* [WC: *Magpy*] of the *Corvus* Species long tail the upper part of the feathers & also the wing is of a purplish variated Green, the black, [X: *back &*] a part of the wing feather are white edjed with black, white belley, white from the root of the wings to Center of the back is white, the head nake [neck] breast & other parts are black the Becke like a Crow. abt. the Size of a large Pigion.   a butifull thing (See Suplement in No. 3)[11]

I took equal altitudes and a meridian altitude. Capt. Lewis returned at Dark, Colter Killed a Goat like the one I killed and a curious kind of deer [WC: *Mule Deer*][12] of a Dark gray Colr. more so than common, hair long & fine, the ears large & long, a Small reseptical under the eyes; like an Elk, the Taile about the length of Common Deer, round (like a Cow) a tuft of black hair about the end, this Speces of Deer jumps like a goat or Sheep

8 fallow Deer 5 Common & 3 buffalow killed to day, Capt. Lewis Saw a *hare* & Killed a Rattle Snake in a village of B. squerels   The wind from S. W.   Dryed our provisions, Some of which was much Damaged.

[Lewis]   Sept. 17th[13]

one of the hunters killed a bird of the *Corvus genus* [EC: *Pica pica hudsonica*] and order of the pica & about the size of a jack-daw with a remarkable long tale.   beautifully variagated.   it ⟨has an agreeable note something like goald winged Blackbird⟩ note is not disagreeable though loud— it is twait twait twait, twait; twait, twait twait, twait.

	F	I
from tip to tip of wing	1	10
Do. beak to extremity of tale	1	8 ½

of which the tale occupys	1 1
from extremity of middle toe to hip	5 ½

it's head, beak, and neck are large for a bird of it's size; the beak is black, and of a convex and cultrated figure, the chops nearly equal, and it's base large and beset with hairs— the eyes are black encircled with a ⟨small⟩ narrow ring of yellowish black it's head, neck, brest & back within one inch of the tale are of a fine glossey black, as are also the short fathers of the under part of the wing, the thies and those about the root of the tale. the ⟨body⟩ belly is of a beatifull white which passes above and arround the but of the wing, where the feathers being long reach to a small white spot on the rump one inch in width— the wings have nineteen feathers, of which the ten first have the longer side of their plumage white in the midde of the feather and occupying unequal lengths of the same from one to three inches, and forming when the wing is spead a kind [of] triangle the upper and lower part of these party coloured feathers on the under side of the wing being of dark colour but not jut or shining black. the under side of the remaining feathers of the wing are darker. the upper side of the wing, as well as the short side of the plumage of the party coloured feathers is of a dark blackis or bluish green sonetimes presenting as light orange yellow or bluish ⟨tinge⟩ tint as it ⟨rise⟩ happens to be presented to different exposures of ligt— the plumage of the tale consits of 1 2 feathers of equal lengths by pai[r]s, those in the center are the longest, and the others on each side deminishing about an inch each pair— the underside of the feathers is a pale black, the upper side is a dark blueish green which like the ⟨upper and⟩ outer part of the wings is changable as it reflects differ-ent portions of light. towards the the extremety of these feathers they become of an orrange green, then shaded pass to a redish indigo blue, and again at the extremity assume the predominant colour of changeable green— the tints of these feathers are very similar and equally as beati-ful and rich as the tints of blue and green of the peacock— it is a most beatifull bird.— the legs and toes are black and imbricated. it has four long toes, three in front and one in rear, each terminated with a black sharp tallon from ⅜ths to ½ an inch in length.— these birds are seldom found in parties of more than three or four and most usually at this season single as the halks ⟨ravens⟩ and other birds of prey usually are— ⟨from it's appearance I believe to⟩ it's usual food is flesh— this bird dose not spread it's tail when it flys and the motion of it's wings when flying is much like that of a Jay-bird— ⟨it's note— tah, tah, tah, tah tah, tah, tah, tah⟩

The White turkey of the black hills from information of a french lad who wintered with the Chien Indians [*EC: rara avis in terris!*] About the size of the common wild turkey the plumage perfectly white— this bird is booted as low as the toes—

Point of Obstn. No. 42.

[Lewis]   *Monday* September 17th 1804.[14]

On the Lard. shore, one mile and a haf above the mouth of Corvus Creek observed equal Altitudes of ☉ with Sextant.—

	h	m	s		h	m	s
A. M.	7	46	49	P. M.	2	59	50
	"	47	25		3	1	30
	"	49	12		"	3	3

Altd. by sextant at the time of Observatn. 53° 17' 45"

Observed meridian Altitude of ☉'s L. L. with Octant by the back Observation 87° 31' 00"

1. They may have included Colter (see Clark's entry, below), and probably Drouillard, the premier hunter of the party.

2. These plums are the same species, the common wild plum.

3. Skunks, *Mephitis mephitis*. Cutright (LCPN), 93.

4. These may include the later Red Butte. *South Dakota Guide*, 403.

5. Codex Ba ends abruptly at this point.

6. Biddle has the notation "and 20" at the top of this document 55 of the Field Notes, indicating that the entries on this sheet go through that date.

7. Clark's, and Lewis's longer account in Codex Q for this date, are the first descriptions of the black-billed magpie. Magpies had not previously been known to exist in the New World; the American bird is a subspecies of the European magpie. They named Corvus Creek for this bird, one of the few uses of a Latin zoological term in the journals. Cutright (LCPN), 84–85.

8. The mule deer.

9. The latter was apparently their first specimen of the coyote, described in more detail on September 18. Cutright (LCPN), 85.

10. Clark evidently combined his September 17 and 18 entries in the Field Notes at this point. They are separated here and brought together in regular order.

11. Clark's "No. 3" is the notebook now called Codex C, but the reference here is probably to Lewis's lengthy description of the magpie in Codex Q under this date. See Appendix C, vol. 2.

12. Clark probably inserted the phrase "Mule Deer" later, when the captains had adopted that name for *Odocoileus hemionus,* based on its large ears. He used red ink for this and the previous emendation. Clark may also have lined out in red the passage about the magpie. Lewis's use of the term on April 23, 1805, is the first written use of today's common name of the animal, which Lewis and Clark were the first to describe. See also May 10, 1805.

13. Lewis's natural history notes from Codex Q. The bird is the black-billed magpie and the turkey may be the wild turkey, *Meleagris gallopavo* [AOU, 310], which Coues (in his interlineation) calls a rare bird in the area described. One authority suggests other possibilities, including the white-tailed ptarmigan, *Lagopus leucurus* [AOU, 304]. Holmgren, 34. The gold-winged blackbird mentioned for comparison of the magpie may be the red-winged blackbird, *Agelaius phoeniceus* [AOU, 498], or possibly some type of oriole (*Icterus* sp.).

14. Lewis's observation from Codex O.

[Clark]   Septr. 18

I Killed a prarie wolf to day about the Sise of a Gray fox with a bushey tail   the head and ears like a Fox wolf, and barks like a Small Dog—   The annimale which we have taken for the Fox is this wolf, we have seen no Foxes.[1]

18 *Septr. Tuesday*   Set out early   wind from the N W. Modrt.   our boat being much litened goes much better than usial

Course N. 45° E	1	me. to the lower point of a Island (1)
N. 25° E.	3	me. to a pt. on the L. S. passed the Isd. at 1 me. & Some Sand bars makeing from it a Creek opsd. on S. S.
N. 14° E	1 ½	mes. to a point of willows on the L. S.
N. 10 W.	1 ½	mes. to a point of wood on the L. S. hard wind
N. 22 W	1 ___ 8 =	me. to a pt. of wood on the L. S. and Came to at 5 oClock to jurke the meat killed to day and what was collected from what was Killed yesterday, i e 10 Deer to Day 4 & a Elk yesterday a Cole night for the Season

[Clark]   18th Septr.

Course Distance & reffurencs

N. 45 E	1	me. to the lower pt. of an Island (1)
N. 25° E	2	miles to a pt. on the L. S. passed the Isld. at one mile and Some Sand bars making from it, a Creek on the L. S. opsd. the upper point
N. 14° E	1 ½	mes. to a pt. of willows on the L. Side
N 10 W.	1 ½	mes. to a point of wood on the L S.
N. 22 W.	1	mile to a pt. on the L. S. and the upper part of the timber

$$\underline{\underline{7}}$$

September 18th Tuesday 1804

Wind from the N W.   we Set out early the boat much lightened, the wind a head proceed on verry Slowly   (1) Passed an I a Island about the middle of the river at 1 Mile   this Island is about a mile long, and has a great perpotion of red Cedir on it, a Small Creek comes in on the S. S. opposit the head of the Island,[2] proceeded on   passed many Sand bars and Camped on the L. S.[3]   before night the wind being verry hard & a head all Day.   the hunters Killed 10 Deer to day and a Prarie wolf, had it all jurked & Skins Stretchd after Camping

I walked on Shore Saw Goats, Elk, Buffalow, Black tail Deer, & the Common Deer, I Killed a Prarie Wollf, about the Size of a gray fox bushey tail head & ear like a wolf, Some fur   Burrows in the ground and barks like a Small Dog.

what has been taken heretofore for the Fox was those wolves, and no Foxes has been Seen; The large wolves are verry numourous, they are of a light Colr. large & has long hair with Corrs [X: *Coarse*] fur.[4]

Some Goats of a Different Kind Wer Seen yesterday   Great many Porcupin rabits & Barking Squirils in this quarter.   Plumbs & grapes.

[Lewis]   Sept. 18th[5]

this day saw the first brant on their return from the north—

1. Here and in his Codex B entry Clark gives a brief scientific description of the coyote,

one of the most widespread and characteristic mammals of the Great Plains. Lewis gives a more detailed description on May 5, 1805. Cutright (LCPN), 85.

2. The island was the later American, or Cedar, Island, and the creek is American Creek, at the site of present Chamberlain, Brule County, South Dakota. *Atlas* maps 20, 21, 22; MRC map 37. The fort shown on these maps as "Mr. Manuel's Fort" and "Cedar Fort," the site of which they passed a little below Cedar Island, was not there in 1804. It was one of the posts built by Manuel Lisa, probably the "Cedar Fort" his Missouri Fur Company established in 1809 to trade with the Sioux, which burned in 1810. The Lisa post has been thought to be either here or at the same site as Régis Loisel's Cedar Fort, or Fort aux Cedres (see below, September 22, 1804); the Maximilian maps suggest that the site here, in Lyman County, South Dakota, just below present Chamberlain, is correct. The notations on Maximilian's map were probably on the basis of later information inserted on Clark's originals. Mattes, 522–28; Oglesby, 83, 97; Chittenden, 1:145, 2:952–53; MRC map 37.

3. In Lyman County, a few miles northeast of present Oacoma. *Atlas* maps 20, 21; MRC map 37.

4. The "large wolves" are gray wolves. References to "prairie wolves" in the journals are probably to coyotes. Cutright (LCPN), 85; Burroughs, 88.

5. Lewis's natural history notes from Codex Q. The brant is probably the Canada goose, *Branta canadensis* [AOU, 172]. See the Weather Diary, March 1804.

[Clark][1]

Septr. 19th Wednesday 1804, Set out early.   a Cool morning clear & Still

Course

N. 50° W.	3	me. to a pt. of wood on the S. S. A Bluff on the L. S. opposit. here Commences a butifull Countrey on both Sides of the river
North	4	miles to the mouth of a River S. S. (1)—
N. 30 W.	2 ½	miles to the upper pt. of the Island S. S. ⟨in the middle of the river⟩ (2)
N. 43° W.	2	on the L. S. Passed a creek (3)
N. 54° W.	3	me. to a pt. of wood on the S. S.
N. 70 W.	5	mes. to a Bluff on the L. S. passed a creek (4)
West	3 ½	miles to some timber on the L. S. passed a creek (5)
	23 miles	Camped

(1) & (2) passed a large Island[2] Situated nearest the S. S. ½ a mile from the Lower pt. of this Island, the 1st of the 3 rivers mouths which is about

35 yards wide, running from the N E. one mile above the 2nd Comes in   this is Small not more that [than] 15 yards wide   a Short Distance above a 3d comes in scattering its waters thro a bottom. I walked on Shore to See this great Pass of the Sioux and Calumet ground, found it a handsom Situation, and Saw the remains of their Campt on the 2d river, for many years passed—   (3) passed a Creek on the L. S. 15 yds wide   we (4) passed a Creek 20 yds wide (5) passed a Creek 20 yd. wide on the L. S. I call Night C. as I did not get to it untill late at night, above the mouth of this Creek we camped,[3] the wind being favourable, for the boat   I Killed a fat Buffalow Cow, and a fat Buck elk, york my Servent Killed a Buck, the Huntes Killed 4 Deer,[4] & the boat Crew killed 2 Buffalow Swiming the river, handsom Countrey of Plains, I saw many trovs of Buffalow & a Gangue of 30 or 40 Elk and othr Scattering elk &c.   a find evening   I hurt my hands & feet last night—

[Clark] Sept. 19th

Course Distance & refferenc

N. 50° W.	3	miles to a pt. of wood on the S. S. opposit is a Bluff on L. S. (1)
North	4	miles to the Lower pt. of prospect Island opsd. the 3 rivers on the S. S. (2)
N. 30° W.	2 ½	miles to the upper pt. of the Island psd. the 3 rivers— (2)
N. 43° W.	2	miles on the L. S. passd. a Creek (3)
N. 54° W	3	mes. to a pt. on the S. S.
N. 70° W.	5	mes. to a Bluff on the L. S. passed a Creek (4)
West	3 ½	mes. to a timber on the L. S. passed a Creek (5)
N 50° W.	3 ¼	mes. to the upper pt. of an Island at (6) the Commencemt
	26 ¼[5]	of the Big bend

19th of September Wednesday 1804

Set out early, a Cool morning verry Clear the wind from the S. E   a Bluff on the L. S.—   here Commences a Butifull Countrey on both Sides of the Missourie, (2) passed a large Island Called Prospect Island   opposit this Isd. the 3 rivers Coms in, passing thro a butifull Plain, here I walked on Shore & Killed a fat Cow & Sent her to the boat and proceeded on to the first of the 3 rivers, this river is about 35 yards wide Contains a good deel of water, I walked up this river 2 miles & Cross, the bottom is high and rich Some timber, I crossed & returned to the mouth, & proceeded up one mile to the 2d river which is Small 12 yards wide, and on it but little timber, on this Creek the Seaux has frequently Camped, as appears by the Signs— the lands betwen those two Creeks in a purpindicular bluff of about 80 feet with a butifull Plain & gentle assent back— a Short distance above the 2nd a 3rd Creek Comes into the river in 3 places Scattering its waters over the large timbered bottom, this Creek is near the Size of the middle Creek Containing a greater quantity of water, those rivers is the place that all nations who meet are at peace with each other, Called the Seaux pass of the 3 rivers.

The boat proceeded on passd. the Island (3) passed a Creek 15 yds wide on the L. Side (4) passed a Creek on the L. S. 20 yards wide which I Call Elm Creek passing thro a high Plain (5) passed a Creek on the L. S. 18 yds. wide above which the boat Came too, I joined them late at night, and Call this Creek Night Creek the winds favourable all Day, I killed a fat buck Elk late and could only get his Skin and a Small part of his flesh to Camp. My Servent Killed a Buck, the Crew in the boat Killed 2 buffalow in the river— The Hunters on Shore Killed 4 Deer with black tails one of which was a Buck with two ⟨men⟩ [*NB: main*] Prongs on each Side forked equally, which I never before Seen. I saw Several large gangs of Buffalow 2 large Herds of Elk & goats &c. (6) pass a Small Island on the S. S. opposit to this Island on the L. S. a Creek of about 10 yards wide Coms in passing thro a plain in which great quantities of the Prickley Pear grows.[6] I call this Creek *Prickley Pear Creek,* This Isld. is Called the lower Island it is Situated at the Commencement of what is Called & Known by the *Grand de Tortu* [*NB: Detour*] or Big Bend of the Missourie.

Point of observation No. 43.

[Lewis]   *Wednesday September 19th 1804*[7]

On the Lard. shore opposite to the mouth of the lower of the two rivers of the Siouxs pass.

Observed Meridian Altd. of ☉'s U. L. with Sextant by the fore observation
95° 30′ 15

1. On September 19 the captains recorded temperature readings and other meteorological data for the first time since May 14, except for one reading in the Field Notes on
August 25. See Weather Diary, September 1804.

2. The island is the Prospect Island of the Codex B entry; evidently it retained that
name for some time—it appears by that name in Nicollet—but was also known as Des
Laurien's or Des laurier's. It is also "Prospect I" on Evans's map 2 (*Atlas* map 8), but may be
a later addition to the sheet. The three rivers are probably Crow, Elm (or Wolf), and
Campbell creeks. This place was called the "Sioux Pass of the Three Rivers" because the
Sioux commonly crossed the Missouri there. Clark's use of the term "Calumet ground" is
meant to relate to the pipestone quarry in present Minnesota, a neutral ground. See Au-
gust 21, 1804. The three streams are in Buffalo County, South Dakota, within the Crow
Creek Indian Reservation (Sioux). Just below the island, in Lyman County and within
Lower Brule Reservation, the Clark-Maximilian map (*Atlas* map 22) shows the location of
"U. S. Sioux Agency"; this was located at the American Fur Company post of Fort Lookout. Maximilian visited the place in 1833, and probably wrote in the notation then. The
location of the post has been in doubt, but this map would seem to settle the question.
Nicollet shows "Old Fort Lookout" and an unnamed site a little to the north of the first;
the latter, opposite the lower point of Prospect Island, appears to correspond to Maximilian's site. Mattes, 533–41, 548–49, 556–57; Coues (HLC), 1:122–23 and nn. 55, 56;
South Dakota Guide, 252; Nicollet (MMR), 413–14; MRC map 37.

3. The location of the creeks is not aided by various name changes over the years. The
fifteen-yard creek is perhaps a nameless stream that appears on *Atlas* map 22 and MRC
map 38, but it may be Good Soldier (Badger) Creek, with present Big Bend Dam just
above. Clark's Elm Creek may be Good Soldier Creek or possibly Counselor (Camel) Creek.
Night Creek may be Counselor or Fish (Brule) Creek. Adopting the latter solution in each
case leaves a problem in identifying the "Lower Island Creek" of *Atlas* map 22, "Prickly
Pear Creek" of Clark's journal, which might otherwise be Fish Creek. The camp was in
Lyman County, South Dakota. Mattes, 562–63; Mattison (BB), 249.

4. Ordway says that George Drouillard and Joseph Field were among them.

5. The shifting of the first and last distances over the next few days gives differences in
the totals of the entries.

6. Perhaps *Opuntia fragilis* (Nutt.) Haw., brittle prickly pear, a small, common species in
the area. Other possibilities include *O. polyacantha* Haw., plains prickly pear, or *O. mac-
rorhiza* Englem., bigroot prickly pear, both of which reach their northern and eastern
limit in this area. Barkley, 48–49.

7. Lewis's observation from Codex O.

[Clark]

September the 20th Thursday 1804 Detchd. 3 men[1] across the Big bend [(]Called the *Grand deTour*[2]) with the horse, to stay and hunt & jurk provisions untill we get around   (1) passed a Island on the S. S.[3]   the river Crouded with Sand bars,[4]

The Course

N. 50° W.	3 ¼	miles to the upper Point of an Island[5] on the S. S. about 2 me. long
North	4	mes. to a pt. on th L. S. passed one on the S. S. abov the Island—
N. 10° W	1 ½	mes. to a pt. of wood on the L. S.—
N. 22° W.	3	mes. to the L. S.
N. 60 W.	2	mes. to a Small timber on the L. S.—
West	3	mes. to a wood on L S.
S. 73 W.	3 ½	mes. to a pt of wood on L. S.—
South	4	miles to a tree on L. S. passed a Island (1) situated on the L. S. this Island[6] is Small with a large Sand
S. 74 E	3 ½	Miles to a point of wood on the L. S. pass Sands & Cpd. (2) &.
S. 56 E	3 ½	to a pt. on the S. S. opsd. a high hill on the L. S.
S. 28. E.	2 ——— 33 ¼	Mes. to a Ceder hill on the L. S in a bend opposit the Gorge of this bend where the river is only 1 ¼ mile across & 30 Miles around, the hills high with Some low land— This Day is refured to (1) (2) &c. for farth[er] explanition

20th of September 1804 Thursday (Continued[)]

(1) at the N W. extremity of this bend passed an Small Island on the L. S.   opposit the upper Point of this Solitary Island Came too[7] to [*one word illegible, perhaps* "pipit"] at the mouth of a Small run on the S. S. & Newmon & Tomson picked up Some Salt mixed with the Sand in the run,[8] Such as the ottoes Indians Collect on the Sands of the *Corn de Cerf* R.[9] & make use of, Camped on a Sand bar on the S. S. above the Island—   I went out to examine the portage which I found quit Short 2000 yards only, the Prarie below & Sides of the hills containing great quantites of

the Prickly Piar which nearly ruind my feet, I saw a hare, & I beleve he run into a hole, he run on a hill & disapeared, I Saw on this hill several holes. I Saw Several Goats Elk Ders &c. & Buffalow in every Derection feeding. R. Fields Killed a Deer & 2 Goats one a female, which differs from the male as to Size being Something Smaller, Small Straight horns without any black about the neck   Camped late

[Clark]   *20th Septr (Big Bend)*

Course Distance and reffurencs

From the lower Islands uppr pt.

North	4	mes. to a pt. on the L. S. Passed one on the S. S. above the island about one & ½ me.
N. 10° W.	1 ½	mes. on the L. Side
N. 22° W.	3	mes. on the L. Side pd. a Sd. Id.
N. 60° W.	2	mes. on the L. Side
West	3	mes. on the L. S. ⟨passed a Small Island on the L. S. a large Sand bar above & below.⟩
S. 73° W.	3 ½	mes. on the L. Side
South	4	mes. on the L. S. passed a Small Island on the L. S. a Small run opsd. S. S. (1)
S. 74° E	3 ½	mes. to a pt. of wood on the L. S. Camped (2)
S. 56° E	3 ½	mes. to a pt. on the S. S. opsd. a high hill (3)
S. 28° E	2	mes. to a Ceder Valey in a bend on the L. S. at this place the gorge is 2000 yds.
	30	

20th of September, Thursday 1804

a fair morning wind from the S E   detached 2 men to the 1st. Creek abov the big bend with the horse to hunt and wait our arrival   proceeded on passed the lower Island opposit which the Sand bars are verry thick & the water Shoal. I walked on Shore with a view of examining this bend Crossed at the narost part which is a high irregular hills of about 180 or 190 feet, this place the gorge of the Bend is 1 mile & a quarter (from river to river or) across, from this high land which is only in the Gouge, the bend is a Butifull Plain thro which I walked, Saw numbrs of Buffalow & Goats, I saw a Hare & believe he run into a hole in the Side of a hill, he run up this hill which is Small & has Several holes on the Side & I could not See him after, I joined the boat in the evening— passed a Small Island on the L. S. in the N. W. extremity of the bind Called Solitary Island, and Camped late on a Sand bar near the S. S.— R. Fields killed 1 Deer & 2 Goats one of them a feemale— She Differs from the mail as to Size being Smaller, with Small Horns, Stright with a Small prong without any black about the neck—

None of those Goats has any Beard, they are all Keenly made, and is butifull

[Clark]   [undated, ca. September 20, 1804][10]

		miles				
From River Dubois to St. Charles—		21	in Latitude	38°	54'	39"
from Do—	to the Mouth of Gasconade	104	do	38	45	35
do do—	to the Mouth of Osarge R:	138	do	38	31	16
do do	Mine river on the South	201	do			
do do	to Grand R. on the N. Side	254	do	38	47	54
do do	to Kanzies R on the South	366	do	39	5	25
do do	to Creek indepenanc at the Kanzies old village South	433	do	39	25	42
do do	Nodaway River N Side	481	do	39	39	22
do do	Nema har R. S. Side	511	do	39	55	56
do do	Bald pated Prarie N. Side	570	do	40	27	7
do do	the mo. of the Great River Plate on the South Side	632	do abt.	41	00	0
from the mouth of Missourie river to the Councel Bluffs opsd. the Ottoes		682	in Latd.	41°	17'	0"
to Little Sieoux River on N Side		766	do	41	42	34
to Mahar village S. Side 3 ms. off R.		864	do	42	13	41
to Mouth of the Great River Souex 3 miles west of Floyds river on N. Sd.		880	do	42	23	49

to Mo. of River Jacque on the N. Sd.	970	do	42	53	13
to mo. of River que Curre or the rapid river on the South Side	1020	do	—		
to *no preserves* Island 5 miles North of the Poncaries Village on the little river Pania on the S. Side—	1037	do	—		
To White River on the L. S. is	1142	do			
Grand de Touit [tour] or Big bend	1283	do	44	11	33³⁄10

[Lewis]   Septr. 20th[11]

on the lard. shore at the commencement of the big bend observed a clift of black porus rock which resembled *Lava* tho' on a closer examination I believe it to be calcarious and an imperfect species of the French *burr*— preserved a specemine, it is a brownish white, or black or yellowish brown—

1. Codex B says two men; Ordway confirms this and says they were Drouillard and Shields.

2. The Grand Detour or Big Bend of the Missouri is conspicuous on *Atlas* map 22 and was even more so in maps and in imaginations before Lewis and Clark. The land enclosed within the bend is in Lyman County, South Dakota. The waters of Lake Sharpe, impounded by the Big Bend Dam, have greatly widened the river in the area. MRC map 38.

3. Probably later Cadotte, or Skunk Island, but Clark's reference is unclear. The "(1)" here is probably misplaced. Mattison (BB), 254; *Atlas* map 22; MRC map 38.

4. Here Clark has inserted his courses and distances for September 20, to the bottom of the reverse of document 55 of the Field Notes. The text of the entry resumes at the top of document 56. A small piece in the corner of document 56 was missing from Osgood's facsimile but is restored today.

5. It is shown opposite Lower Island Creek on *Atlas* map 22.

6. Cadotte Island; see n. 3.

7. The island was later variously known as Cul de Sac, St. John's, and Jungle Island. The name "Solitary" may come from Evans's map 2 (*Atlas* map 8). The campsite was just above it, in Hughes County, South Dakota. The area is now inundated by the Big Bend Reservoir (Lake Sharpe). Mattes, 567–68; *Atlas* map 22; MRC map 38; MRY maps 56, 57.

8. The "Sand Salt" on the run is shown on a sketch of the Big Bend on this sheet (document 56) of the Field Notes, see fig. 3.

9. Clark refers to the Elkhorn River in Nebraska.

10. The following table of distances and latitudes is found on a small, undated sheet in the Field Notes (document 57) and is placed here by approximate date.

11. Lewis's note from the back page of Codex R, reading backward. Calcareous zones, sandy beds, and zones of concretions are present in the upper part of the Pierre Shale. Here Lewis probably views a weathered zone of the Pierre and it is unrelated to volcanic activity, that is, lava.

[Clark][1]

21st of September 1804 Friday 1804, last night or reather this morng at a half past one oClock the Sand bar on which we Camped began to give way, which allarmed the Serjt on guard[2] & the noise waked me, I got up and by the light of the moon observed that the Sand was giving away both above & beloy and would Swallow our Perogues in a few minits, ordered all hands on board and pushed off   we had not got to the opposit Shore before pt. of our Camp fel into the river.   we proceeded on to the Gorge of the bend & brackfast, the Distance of this bend around is 30 miles, and 1 ¼ miles thro:, the high lands extinds to the gauge [gorge] and is about 200 feet   the plain in the bend as also the two opposit Sides abov and below is delightfull plains with graduel assents from the river in which there is at this time Great number of Buffalow Elk & Goats feedg   The Course from the gauge on the L. S. is S. 70 W. 4½ Miles to the pt. of Ceder Timber on the L. S.   pass Sands.   worthy of remark the Cat fish not So plenty abov white river & much Smaller than usial, Great nunbers of Brant & plover, also goat and black tail Deer.

N. 50° W.	2 ½	passed a Willow Island on the L. S. a large Creek Called Tylors ⟨Creek⟩ R at 1 ½ me. about 40 yds wide above the Island on L. S.[3]
West	4 ½ 11 ½	mes. to a pt. of wood on the L. S. pass Sand bars & Shoal watr the river here is wide nearly a mile in width— Camped on the S. S. below the Mock Island, after passing a number of Stones of Different Sises on the Shore of the Same Side, huntes Killed a Deer, Bever, and a ⟨black⟩ white wolf and a Turkey, Saw many goats and Elk to day—

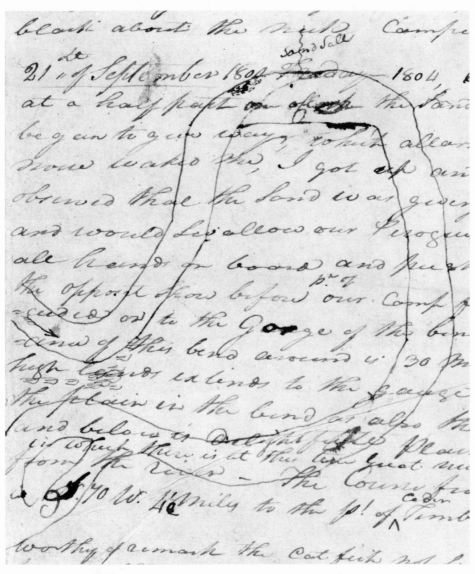

3. Big Bend of the Missouri River, ca. September 21, 1804,
Field Notes, document 56

[Clark]   21st Septr.

Course Distance and reffrs.

S. 70° W.   4 ½   Miles to the upper part of a Ceder bottom on the L. S.
                          passed Several Sand bars on both sides

N. 50° W.	2 ½	miles to a tree on the S. S. passing over a willow Island & a Creek on the L. S. (1)
West	4 ½	miles to a Point of timber on the L. S. Passed Sand bars
	11 ½	the river here is verry Shoal and about a mile wide. (2) Passed large hard Stone on the Shore on each Side, a Mock Island on the S. S.

[Clark]   *21st of September Friday 1804*

at half past one oClock this morning the Sand bar on which we Camped began to under mind and give way which allarmed the Sergeant on Guard, the motion of the boat awakened me; I get up & by the light of the moon observed that the land had given away both above and below our Camp & was falling in fast. I ordered all hands on as quick as possible & pushed off, we had pushed off but a few minets before the bank under which the Boat & perogus lay give way, which would Certainly have Sunk both Perogues, by the time we made the opsd. Shore our Camp fell in, we made a ⟨good⟩ 2d Camp for the remainder of the night & at Daylight proceeded on to the Gouge of this Great bend and Brackfast, we Sent a man to measure step off the Distance across the gouge, he made it 2000 yds. The distance arround is *30* mes. The hills extend thro: the gouge and is about 200 foot above the water—   in the bend as also the ⟨two⟩ opposite Sides both abov and below the bend is a butifull inclined Plain in which there is great numbers of Buffalow, Elk & Goats in view feeding & Scipping on those Plains   Grouse, Larks & the Prarie bird is Common in those Plains.   we proceeded on   passed a (1) willow Island below the mouth of a Small river called Tylors R[4] about 35 yds. wide which coms in on the L. S. 6 miles above the Gorge of the bend, at the mouth of this river the two hunters[5] a head left a Deer & its Skin also the Skin of a white wolf— we observe an emence number of Plover of Different kind Collecting and takeing their flight Southerly, also Brants which appear to move in the same Direction.

The Cat fish is Small and not So plenty as below

(2) The Shore on each Side is lined with hard rough Gulley [grittey?] Stones of different Sises,[6] which has roled from the hills & out of Small brooks, Ceder is comon here, This day is worm, the wind which is not

hard blows from the S. E, we Camped at the lower point of the Mock Island on the S. S.[7] this now Connected with the main land, it has the appearance of once being an Island detached from the main land Covered with tall Cotton wood— we Saw Some Camps and tracks of the Seaux which appears to be old three or four weeks ago— one frenchman I fear has got an abscess on his they [thigh], he complains verry much we are makeing every exertion to releiv him—

The Praries in this quarter Contains Great qts. of Prickley Pear.

1. This entry in the Field Notes (document 56) is written over a sketch map of the Big Bend (fig. 3).

2. Neither Gass nor Ordway mentions being sergeant of the guard at this time, but this is only slight proof that it was Sergeant Pryor's tour of duty.

3. Clark adds a note after this, "bt. fowd. 7," to keep his mileage accumulation correct as he goes to a different part of this sheet (document 56).

4. It is Tylor's River on Evans's map 2 (*Atlas* map 8) and on the day's route map (*Atlas* map 22). On the Indian Office map (*Atlas* map 5) it seems to be "R: de [vieux] Langlois" and "old Englishmans." The latter is probably a mistranslation of the French name Langlois. It became Turkey River on postexpeditionary maps (*Atlas* maps 125, 126). The stream is now Medicine River, or Creek, as in Nicollet, in Lyman County, South Dakota. The island below the mouth is later Medicine Island. Mattison (BB), 225; McDermott (WCS), 150; Nicollet (MMR), 416; MRC map 39; MRY map 58.

5. The hunters were Drouillard and Shields.

6. These stones are either slabs of the sandy beds or concretions out of the Pierre Shale or boulders and cobbles of the glacial till that are sometimes found in the Missouri River trench. The latter deposits are much younger than the Cretaceous age bedrock of the Pierre and date to the Pleistocene Period, from approximately two million to ten thousand years ago.

7. The island is shown on *Atlas* map 22 and may have gotten its name from Clark because it is connected to the shore. It is "halfmoon" island on Evans's map 2 (*Atlas* map 8). The camp was in Hughes County, South Dakota; the site is probably now inundated by Lake Sharpe. Judging by *Atlas* map 22, Clark overestimated the distance above Medicine Creek. Mattison (BB), 260; MRC map 39.

[Clark]   *22nd September Satturday 1804*

a thick fog this morning untill 7 oClock which detained us, Saw Some old tracks of the Indians on the S. S. proceeded on— one French man with a *abscess* on his thigh which pains him verry much for 10 or 12 Days a butifull Plain on both Sides low high land under which there is a number of lage Stone, we See great numbers of Buffalow feeding

S. 72° W.	5	miles to a pt. on the S. S. opsd. a High Bluff passed under a Bluff L. S. altitude at opsd. the Lower pt of 1st of the Isd. 3 Sisters with Sexton 92° 50′ 0″ Octt. 89° 47′ 0″—(1) The Lattitude produced from those obsevations is *44° 11′ 33″ ⁴/₁₀* North.
West	1	mile on the ⟨L⟩ S. S. a bottom Commences on the L. at the end of the course
N. 38 W.	4 ½	miles to a point of timber on the S. S. opposit Ceeder Island on which Louselle Wintered 1803 passed a Small Island at one & ½ miles, and a large Island 3 miles long above Called the 3 Sisters situated near the L. S. opposit this Island a large Creek Coms in on the L. S.
N. 30° W.[1]	3	Miles to a pt. on the S. S. passed Ceeder Island in the Middle of the river nearly in the form of a Dimond— (2)—the main Current on the L. Side Louisells ⟨Hous⟩ Fort of ceder 70 foot squar on the L. S. of it on the South Side of about the middle a number of Indian Camps, all the Cotton wood Cut down to feed their horses.
N. 22 E	2 ½ ——— 16 ==	mes. to the lower point of a timber on the S. S. below Cabid Islan (or Goat Isd). I walked out on the L. Side this evening & Killed a Deer, Camped late, great number of large Stone Some distance out from the Shore Camped on the S. S. at the end of this Course— The hunter Came in, Complain of their mockersons being burnt out by the Salts on the hills they killed only 1 Deer—

A continuation of notes taken assending the Missourie in 1804—by W. Clark[2]

Satturday the 22nd of September 1804—

A Thick fog this morning detained us untill 7 oClock, The plains on both Sides of the River is butifull and assends gradually from the river; noumerous herds of Buffalow to be Seen in every derections, (1) Took the altitude of the Sun & found the Lattitude to be 44° 11′ 33″ N— (2) passed a Small Island on the L. S. and one on the S. S. imediately above, & about 3 m: long, on the L. S. opposit this Island a Creek of about 15 yds wide mouthes, Called the Creek of the 3 Sisters[3] (3) passed Cedar Island 1½

M. long & 1 M. wide Situated a little above the last and nearest the S. S.— near the upper part of this Island on its S. Side a Tradeing fort is Situated built of Cedar—by a Mr. Louiselle of St Louis, for the purpose of Tradeing with the Teton Bands of Soues (*or "Sieux"*)[4] about this Fort I saw numbers of Indians Temporary Lodges, & horse Stables, all of them round and to a point at top,[5] I observed also numbers of Cotton Trees fallen for the purpose of feeding their horses on the Bark of the limbs of those trees which is Said to be excellent food for the horses— we came too on the S. S. below a Small Island called Goat Island,[6] passed a no: of large round Stones, Som distance in the river as also in the Sides of the hills,— I walked on the Shore this evening and Killed a verry large Deer— our hunters Killed 2 Deer & a Beaver, they Complain of the Mineral quallities of the high land distroying their mockersons—.[7]

Course Distance & rufferences 22d Sept

S. 72° W.	5	miles to a pt on the S. S— passing under a high Bluff on the L. S (1)
West	1	mile on the S. S.— ⟨to the⟩ Commencement of a bottom on the L. S.
N. 38° W.	4 ½	miles to a pt. of timber on the S. S. opsd. Cedar Isd. passed 2 Isds & a Creek opsd. L. S. (2)
N. 30° W.	3	miles to a pt. on the S. S— passed Cedar Island & Louisells Fort— (3)
N 22° E.	2 ½ (16)	miles to Some timber on the L. S. opposite a Small Island call Goat Isd.

[Clark]   22nd

Course Distance & reffuriences

S. 72° W.	5	miles to a point on the S. S. Passing under a high bluff on the L. Side (1)
West	1	mile on the S. S. a bottom Commenceing on the L. S. at the end of this Course
N. 38° W.	4 ½	miles to a pt. of timber on the S. S. opposit the Lower pt. of Ceder Island passed two Islands on the L. S. one ½ a

mile & the other 3 miles long called the 3 Sisters   opsd. a large Creek com in (2)

N. 30° W.	3	miles to a pt. on S. S. passed Ceeder Island Situated nearest the S. S. a trading house (3)
N. 22° E	2 ½	miles to a timber opposit the Lower L S pt. of a Small Island Called Goat Island (4)
	16	

22nd of September Satturday 1804

a thick fog this morning detained us untill 7 oClock   passed a butifull inclined Prarie on both Sides in which we See great numbers of Buffalow feeding—   (1) took the Meridean altitude of the Suns upper Leimb. 92° 50′ 00″ the SexSecnt the Latd. produced from this Obsivation is 44° 11′ 33″ ³⁄₁₀ North—

(2) passed a Small Island on the L. S.   imediately above passed a Island Situated nearest the L. S. abt. 3 miles long, behind this Isd. on the L. S. a Creek Comes in about 15 yards wide, this Creek and Islands are Called the 3 Sisters   a butifull Plain on both Sides of the river—

(3) passed a Island Situated nearest the S. S. imedeately above the last Called Ceder Island   this Island is about 1 ½ miles long & nearly as wide Covered with Ceder, on the South Side of this Island Mr. Louiselle a trader from St. Louis built a fort of Ceder & a good house to trate with the Seaux & wintered last winter; about this fort I observed a number of Indian Camps in a Conicel form,—   they fed their horses on Cotton limbs as appears.   here our hunters joined us havening killed 2 Deer & a Beaver, they Complain much of the Mineral Substances in the barren hills over which they passed distroying their mockersons.

(4) we proceeded on and Camped late on the ⟨L⟩ S. Side below a Small Island in the bend S. S. Called Goat Island. The large Stones which lay on the Sides of the banks in Several places lay Some distance in the river, under the water and is dangerous &c.

I walked out this evening and killed a fine Deer, the musquiters is verry troublesom in the bottoms

Point of observation No. 44.

[Lewis]   *Saturday Septr. 22nd 1804.*[8]

On the Stard. shore, about one mile below the lower Island of the three sisters.

Observed meridian Altd. of ☉'s U. L. with Sextant by the fore observation 92° 50′ ″

Latitude deduced from this observation   N 44° 11′ 33.4″

1. To the side of this course Clark has written: "Louisells Fort is 23 yards squa   each room is 20 feet Square and Sub Divided" and "Thermometer ⟨112⟩ abv o."

2. This September 22 entry is on document 58 of the Field Notes, the previous one being on document 56. Clark evidently began a second set of field notes with the intention of sending the previous ones back downriver with dispatches. See below, September 23, 1804, n. 3. Biddle's note "to 26" beside the entry date indicates that the entries on the sheet go to September 26.

3. Clark's "Three Sisters Creek" is later Cedar Creek, in Lyman County, South Dakota. Clark's name may be from Evans's map 2 (*Atlas* map 8). The island is the later "Dorion Isl. No. 1," or Cedar Creek Island. Mattison (BB), 261; *Atlas* map 22; MRC map 39; MRY maps 60, 62.

4. For a sketch of Régis Loisel, see above, May 25, 1804. He built *Fort aux Cedres* about 1800, or perhaps two years later, to trade with the Sioux. Sergeants Ordway and Gass made a record of its dimensions and layout. According to Ordway it was a cedar stockade, 65 to 70 feet square, with a "Sentery Box" at each of two opposite corners, the wall being 13½ feet high. Inside was a four-room cabin 45½ by 32½ feet. There were two presses for compacting pelts for shipment. Cedar Island was later known as Dorion Island No. 2, or Dores Island. The exact location of Loisel's fort was never determined and the island is now submerged by the Big Bend Reservoir. Mattison (BB), 241–63; Smith (BBHS), 47–54; *Atlas* map 22; MRC map 39; MRY map 62.

5. Clark may have seen the frameworks of tipis, "temporary" in the sense that they were portable, although the nomadic Sioux lived in them all the time. However, he may have been looking at the remains of some sort of brush shelter over which hides or blankets could be thrown.

6. There has been some confusion about this campsite, but *Atlas* map 22 clearly indicates that it was in Hughes County, South Dakota, nearly opposite the mouth of Loiselle Creek (named for Régis Loisel). Mattison (BB), 263. Goat Island appears to be a nameless sand bar on MRC map 39. Goat Island is "Cabri" (or some other spelling) on Evans's map 2 (*Atlas* map 8) and in some of Clark's references here. MRY map 63.

7. Sulphates in the weathered shale would decompose the leather more rapidly than usual. It also makes some of the land too acid to support vegetation.

8. Lewis's observation from Codex O.

[Clark]

23rd Septr. Sunday 1804 (*days and nights equal*)   Set out early under a gentle Breeze from the ⟨N E⟩ S E *N. 46° W* 3¾ Miles to the mo: of a Creek on the S. S.[1]   passd. a pt. on the L. S.   (1) a Small Island opsd. in the bend to the S. S.   This Island is Called goat Island, (1) this Creek is 10 yards wide.   passed bad Sand bars—   S. 46° W 2¾ mes. a wood at a Spring in the bend to the L. S.   Saw the Prarie a fire behind us near the head of Ceder Island L. S.   N. 80° W. 4½ to the lower pt of Elk Island[2]   pass 2 Willow Islands & Sand   I saw this morning 12 of those Black & white birds of the corvus Species.—

Capt Lewis went out to hund on the Island   a great number of Buffalow in Sight   I must Seal up all those Scrips & draw from my Journal at Some other time[3]   Wm Clark Cpt. [of E.?]

[Clark]   *Sunday the 23rd September 1804*[4]

Set out under a Gentle breeze from the S. E—   (1) passed Goat Island Situated in a bend to the S. S—   above passed a Small Creek 12 yards wide on the S. S.—   we observed a great Smoke to the S W. which is an In- dian Signal of their haveing discovered us, I walked on Shore and observed great numbers of Buffalows.   (2) passed 2 Small Willow Islands with large Sand bars makeing from their upper points   (3) passed Elk Island Situ- ated near the L. S. about 2½ mes. long & ¾ wide, Covered with Cotton wood, a red berry Called by the French "grise de buff,"[5]   Grapes &c.   the river is wide Streight & contains a great numr of Sand bars, (4) passed a Small Creek on the S. S. 16 yds wide   I call *Reubens* Cr.—[6]   R. Fields was the first who found it—   Came too & Camped on the S. S. in a Wood.[7] Soon after we landed three *Soues* boys Swam across to us, those boys in- formed us that a Band of Sieux called the *Tetons* of 80 Lodges wer Camped near the mouth of the next River, and 60 Lodges more a Short distance above them, they had that day Set the praries on fire to let those Camps Know of our approach—   we gave those boys two twists of Tobacco to carry to their Chiefs & Warriors to Smoke, with derections to tell them that we wished to Speak to them tomorrow, at the mouth of the next river—   Capt Lewis walked on Shore, R F. Killed a She Goat or ["]Cabbra."

Course distance & refferens 23rd Septr.

N. 46° W.	3 ¾	miles to the mouth of Smoke Creek in a bend S. S. passed Goat Isd. & Sand (1)
N. 46° W.	1 ¾	miles to a Coaps of wood at a Spring in a bend to the L. S.
N. 80° W.	4 ½	miles to the lower pt. of a Island passed 2 Small Islands, & Sand bars (2) (3)
N. 85° W.	5	miles to a pt. on the L. S— passd. the upper pt. of Elk Isd. at 2½ miles— (3)
West	5	miles to a pt. on the S. S— below a Creek L. S.— pass'd one on the S. S— (4)
	(26)[20?]	

[Clark]   *23rd Septr*

Course Distance & reffurencies

N. 46° W.	3 ¾	miles to a mouth of a Creek in the bend to the S. S. passed an Isld. on the S. S. (1) & Sands
S. 46° W.	1 ¾	miles to a Coaps of wood at a Spring in a bend to the L. S.
N. 80° W.	4 ½	miles to the lower pt. of a large Island (2) passed 2 ⟨Sand⟩ willow Islands & Several Bars.
N. 85° W.	5	miles to a pt. on the L. S. pass upper pt. of Elk Island at 2½ miles. Several Sands
West	5	miles to a pt. on the S. S. below a Creek on the L. S. passed a Creek on the S. S. (3)—
	20	

23rd of *September Sunday 1804*

Set out under a gentle breeze from the S. E, (1) passed a Small Island Situated in a bend to the L. S.   Called Goat Island, a Short distance above the upper point a Creek of 12 yards wide coms in on the S. S.   we observed a great Smoke to the S W.—   I walked on Shore & observed Buffalow in great Herds at a Distance   (2) passed two Small willow Islands with large Sand bars makeing out from them, passed (3) Elk Island about 2½ miles long & ¾ mile wide Situated near the L. S. covered with Cotton wood   the read Current Called by the French *Gres de Butiff* & grapes

&c. &c.   the river is nearly Streight for a great distance wide and Shoal. (4) passed a Creek on the S. S. 16 yards wide we Call Reubens Creek, as R Fields found it   Camped on the S. S. below the mouth of a Creek on the L. S.   three Souex boys Came to us Swam the river and informd that the Band of Soauex called the *Teton⟨gues⟩* of 80 Lodges were Camped at the next Creek above, & 60 Lodges more a Short distance above, we gave those boys two Carrots of Tobacco to Carry to their Chiefs, with derections to tell them that we would Speek to them tomorrow

Capt Lewis walked on Shore this evening, R. F Killed a Doe Goat,—

Point of observation No. 45.

[Lewis]   *Sunday September 23rd 1804.*[8]

On the Lard. Shore 3 miles below Elk Island.

Observed meridian altd. of ☉'s U. L. with Sextant by the fore observation   91° 48′ 45″

1. Smoke Creek on *Atlas* map 22, the reason for the name being found in the second Field Notes entry; later La Chapelle Creek, or Chapelle Creek, named for a French Canadian trader of later times, in Hughes County, South Dakota. Mattison (BB), 263–64; Nicollet (MMR), 416; MRC map 39.

2. Elk Island on *Atlas* map 23, where Maximilian or someone has penciled in "Simoneau's Island," presumably the name it had acquired by the 1830s. By about 1890 it had apparently joined the Hughes County mainland, unless it was the later Fort George Island. MRC map 40; MRY maps 64, 65.

3. It appears from this notation that Clark intended to seal up the sheets of the Field Notes to this point to be sent back down the river with dispatches. He had started separate entries on another loose sheet (document 58) for September 22 and 23. The captains had decided on September 16 to retain the pirogue under Corporal Warfington originally intended to carry these dispatches, but evidently they still hoped to encounter a trader's boat that could carry their messages for them. An address and notations appear on the back of document 56, which Clark apparently intended to use as the wrapper for the Field Notes to date, to be sent to his brother Jonathan for safekeeping until his return. In any event, none of the papers were sent back until the following spring. See also the Introduction to vol. 2 of this edition. Osgood (FN), 144 n. 1. The address (in Clark's hand) reads: Genl. Jona. Clark of Kentucky [*and*] To the 22nd of Septr. 1804 To the Care of Genl. Jona. Clark near Louisville Ky. To be opened by Capt. W. Clark or Capt: Meriwether Lewis. Someone other than Clark, perhaps Biddle, has written, "Septr 20th."

4. The second Field Notes entry, on document 58. The distance figures are different from the first entry but coincide with the codex figures. The latter two are correct.

5. Buffaloberry, *Shepherdia argentea* (Pursh) Nutt. Barkley, 203.

6. This stream is Little Medicine Creek on MRC map 40, was sometimes known as East Medicine Knoll Creek, and is the present Medicine Creek in Hughes County. Coues (HLC), 1:127 n. 66; Mattison (BB), 268–69; Nicollet (MMR), 417; *Atlas* map 23; MRY map 65.

7. In Hughes County, just below the mouth of Antelope Creek on the opposite side. Mattison (BB), 268–69; *Atlas* map 23; MRC map 40; MRY map 65.

8. Lewis's observation from Codex O.

[Clark]

Course & Distance & refferan 24th Septr

N. 80° W.	3	miles to a point on the Starboard Side, river wide Passed a Creek L. S.
West	2 ½	miles to the S. Side of an Island Situated near the L. Shore (1)
West	4	miles to a point on the S. S— passed the Island on the L. S. (1)
S. 85° W	4	miles to the mouth of *Teton* River on the L. S. Several
	(13 ½)	Inds (2)

Monday the 24th of September 1804

a fair morning   Set out early, wind from the East, passed the mouth of a Creek on the L. S. Called Creek in high water.[1]   passed a large (1) Island on the L. S.[2] about 2½ Miles long on which Colter had Camped & Killed 4 Elk.   the wind from the S. E.—   we prepared Some Clothes a few medal for the Chiefs of the Teton band of Sioux we expected to meet at the next River—   much Stone on the S. S. of the River, we Saw one hare to day—   our Perogues Called at the Island for the Elk, Soon after we passed the Island Colter ran up the bank & reported that the Sioux had taken his horse, we Soon after Saw five indians on the bank; who expressed a wish to come on board, we informed them we were friends, and wished to Continue So, we were not abraid any Indians—   Some of their young Men had Stolen a horse Sent by their Great Father to their great Chief, and we Should not Speak to them any more untill the horse was returned to us again—   passed a Island[3] about 1½ m. long on which we Saw maney elk & Buffalow, we Came too off the Mouth of a Small river,

The Teton of the burnt woods[4] is Camped 2 Miles up this river, this river we Call *Teton* is 70 Yds wide and coms in on the S W Side—[5] I went on Shore and Smoked with a Chief, Called Buffalow Medison,[6] who Came to See us here. The Chief Said he Knew nothing of the horse &c &. I informed them we would [c]all the grand Chiefs in Council tomorrow, all continued on board all night—

[Clark]   *24th Septr.*

Course Distance & reffurence

N. 80 W.	3	miles a pt. on the S. S.
West	2 ½	miles to the S. S. right of a Isld. Situated on the L. S. (1)
West	4	miles to a Point on the S. S. passed the Island on the L. S.
S. 85° W.	4	miles to the mouth of a River Called by Evens Little Missourie I call it the Teton river as the Teton Bands of the Soux reside on it—(2)
	13	

24th September Monday 1804

Set out early   a fair day the wind from the E, pass the mouth of Creek on the L. S.   called [*NB: High Water*] Creek *on* high water; passed (1) a large Island on the L. S. about 2 miles & ½ long on which Colter had Camped & Killed 4 Elk, the wind fair from the S. E.   we prepared Some Clothes and a fiew meadels for the Chiefs of the Teton's hand of Seaux which we expect to See to day at the next river, observe a Great Deel of Stone on the Sides of the hills on the S. S.   we Saw one Hare to day, prepared all things for action in Case of necessity, our Perogus went to the Island for the meet, Soon after the man on Shore run up the bank and reported that the Indians had Stolen the horse   we Soon after met 5 Inds. and ankered out Some distance & Spoke to them   informed them we were friends, & wished to Continue So but were not afraid of any Indians, Some of their young men had taken the horse Sent by their Great father for ther Chief and we would not Speek to them untill the horse was returned to us again.

passed (2) a Island on the S. S. on which we Saw Several Elk, about 1 ½ miles long Called Good humered [*NB: humoured*] Islds. Came to about

1 ½ miles above off the mouth of a Small river about 70 yards wide Called by Mr. Evins the Little Mississou [*NB: Missouri*] River,[7] The Tribes of the Scouix Called the Teton, is Camped about 2 miles up on the N W Side and we Shall Call the River after that nation, *Teton*   This river is 70 yards wide at the mouth of water, and has a considerable Current   we anchored off the mouth—

the french Perogue Come up early in the [*NB: ⟨morning⟩ day*], the other did not get up untill in the evening Soon after we had Came too. I went & Smoked with the Chief who Came to See us here   all well, we prepare to Speek with the Indians tomorrow at which time we are informed the Indians will be here, The French man who had for Some time been Sick, began to blead which allarmed him—   ⅔ of our party Camped on board The remainder with the Guard on Shore.

1. So named, probably by Clark, on Evans's map 3 (*Atlas* map 9). Now Antelope Creek in Stanley County, South Dakota. *Atlas* map 23; Nicollet (MMR), 417; MRC map 40.

2. Apparently the later Farm Island, some two miles below present Pierre, Hughes County, South Dakota. It is "Horse Island" on *Atlas* map 23. It is interesting that on Evans's map 3 (*Atlas* map 9), someone, perhaps Clark, has drawn a horse.

3. The captains called this Good Humored Island, but it is mislabeled "Bad humored Island" on *Atlas* map 23. It is correct (probably named by Clark) on Evans's map 3 (*Atlas* map 9). It is now La Framboise, or Leframboise, Island within the city of Pierre. See also entry for September 25. *South Dakota Guide*, 135; Mattison (OR), 17; MRC map 40; MRY map 67.

4. The word "Teton" derived from *t'íŋta t'uŋwaŋ*, "prairie dwellers" and was used to designate those Sioux who spoke the western or *Lak'ota* dialect. By mid-nineteenth century the Tetons lived entirely on the western side of the Missouri, although in Lewis and Clark's time they were still occupying both sides of the Missouri. By the middle of the century of the Tetons had developed seven named divisions: Brulés (*sic'aŋgu*, "burned thigh"); Oglalas (*oglala*, "scatter one's own"); Miniconjous (*mnik'owoju*, "planters by water"); Sans Arcs (*itazipco*, "without bows"); Blackfeet (*siha sápa*, "black soles"), not to be confused with the Algonquian speaking Blackfeet proper; Two Kettles (*o'ohenuŋpa*, "two boilings"); and Hunkpapas (*húŋkpap'a*, "camp circle head"). The captains' description makes it clear that the Tetons were by this time a classic plains people, dependent on the horse and the buffalo and living in tipis the year around. White (WW), 326–27 n. 17; Hodge, 1:736; Hassrick.

5. The captains' name was still used by Nicollet, in the 1830s; by 1855 it was called Bad River, the present name, derived from the Sioux name. It rises in western South Dakota and enters the Missouri in Stanley County, opposite Pierre. The camp for the day was just

above the river mouth, in or near present Fort Pierre. Appleman (LC), 351–52. Mattison (OR), 18–19; *Atlas* map 23; Nicollet (MMR), 418; Warren map 50; MRC map 40.

6. Buffalo Medicine's actual position as a chief is not clear. To Lewis and Clark he was the third chief in relation to Black Buffalo and the Partisan, whom they would meet the next day. Ronda (LCAI), 30–31. Clark gives his name as "Tar-ton-gar-wa-ker" which may be rendered *t'at'aŋka wak'aŋ*, "sacred buffalo bull."

7. Evans's map 3 (*Atlas* map 9) shows Bad River as the Little Missouri, but it should not be confused with the present Little Missouri in North Dakota.

Chapter Seven

From the Teton River to the Mandans

September 25–October 26, 1804

[Clark]   25th of September 1804 off *Teton River*

a fair Morning   the wind from the S. E.   raised a Flagg Staff and
formed an orning & Shade on a Sand bar in the Mouth of Teton R to
Council under, the greater portion of the party to Continue on board—
about 11 oClock the 1st & 2d Chief arrived, we gave them to eat; they
gave us Some meat, (we discover our interpeter do not Speak the language well)[1]   at 12 oClock the Councill Commenced & after Smokeing agreeable to the usial custom C. L. [Lewis] Delivered a written Speech
to them, I Some explinations &c.   all party Paraded, gave a Medal to
the grand Chief in Indian Un-ton gar-Sar bar, or Black Buffalow—[2]   2°
Torto-hongar, Partezon (Bad fellow)[3]   the 3d Tar-ton-gar-wa-ker, Buffalow medison—   we invited those Chiefs & a Soldier[4] on board our boat,
and Showed them many Curiossites, which they were much Surprised, we
gave they ½ a wine glass of whiskey which they appeared to be exceedingly fond of   they took up an empty bottle, Smelted it, and made maney
Simple jestures and Soon began to be troublesom   the 2d Chief effecting
Drunkness as a Cloak for his vilenous intintious (as I found after wards,)
realed or fell about the boat, I went in a perogue with those Chief who
left the boast with great reluctians, my object was to reconsile them and
leave them on Shore, as Soon as I landed 3 of their young ment Seased
the Cable of the Perogue, one Soldiar Huged the mast ⟨which was⟩ and

111

the 2d Chief was exceedingly insolent both in words and justures to me declareing I Should no go off, Saying he had not recived presents Suffient from us— ⟨his⟩ I attempted to passify ⟨him⟩ but it had a contrary effect for his insults became So personal and his intentions evident to do me injurey, I Drew my Sword ⟨and ordered all hands under arms⟩ at this motion Capt Louis ordered all in the boat under arms, the fiew men that was with me haveing previously taken up their guns with a full deturmination to defend me if possible— The grand Chief then took hold of the Cable & Sent all the young men off, the Soldier got out of the perogue and the 2nd Chief walked off to the Party at about 20 yards back, all of which had their bows Strung & guns Cocked— I then Spoke in verry positive terms to them all, ⟨but⟩ principaly addressing myself to the 1st Chief, who let the roape go and walked to the Indian, party about, 100— I again offered my hand to the 1st Chief who refused it— (all this time the Indians were pointing their arrows blank—[)][5] I proceeded to the perogue and pushed off and had not proceeded far before the 1st & 3r Chief & 2 principal men walked into the water and requested to go on board, I took them in and we proceeded on abot a Mile, and anchored near a Small Island, I call this Island Bad humered Island[6]

[Clark]   25th Septr[7]
    a fair morning   the wind from the S. E.   all well, raised a Flag Staff & made a orning or Shade on a Sand bar in the mouth of Teton River for the purpose of Speeking with the Indians under, the Boat Crew on board at 70 yards Distance from the bar   The 5 Indians which we met last night Continued, about 11 oClock the 1s & 2d Chief Came   we gave them Some of our Provsions to eat, they gave us great quantites of meet Some of which was Spoiled   we feel much at a loss for the want of an interpeter   the one we have can Speek but little.
    Met in council at 12 oClock and after Smokeing, agreeable to the usial Custom, Cap Lewis proceeded to Deliver a Speech which we oblige to Curtail for want of a good interpeter   all our Party paraded.   gave a medal to the Grand Chief Calld. in Indian *Un ton gar Sar bar* in French *Beefe nure* [*NB: Beuffle noir*] Black Buffalow Said to be a good man, 2 Chief *Torto hon*

gar— or the *Partisan*—or Partizan—*bad* the 3rd is the Beffe De Medison [*NB: Beuffle de Medecine*] his name is *Tar ton gar wa ker*

1. Contesabe [*NB: Considerable*] man *War zing go*

2. *do Second Bear = Ma to co que pan*

Envited those Cheifs on board to Show them our boat and Such Curiossities as was Strange to them, we gave them ¼ a glass of whiskey which they appeared to be verry fond of, Sucked the bottle after it was out & Soon began to be troublesom, one the 2d Cheif assumeing Drunkness, as a Cloake for his rascally intentions I went with those Cheifs [*NB: in one of the Perogues with 5 men 3 & 2 Ints.*] (which left the boat with great reluctiance) to Shore with a view of reconseleing those men to us, as Soon as I landed the Perogue three of their young men Seased the Cable of the Perogue [*NB: in which we had presents &c.*], the Chiefs Soldr. [*NB: each Chief has a Soldier*] Huged the mast, and the 2d Chief was verry insolent both in words & justures [*NB: pretended drunkeness & staggered up against us*] declareing I Should not go on, Stateing he had not recved presents Suffient from us, his justures were of Such a personal nature I felt my Self Compeled to Draw my Sword, [*NB: and made a Signal to the boat to prepar for action*] at this motion Capt. Lewis ordered all under arms in the boat, those with me also Showed a Disposition to Defend themselves and me, the grand Chief then took hold of the roop & ordered the young warrers away, I felt my Self warm & Spoke in verry positive terms

Most of the warriers appeared to have ther Bows Strung and took out their arrows from ther quves. as I [*NB: being surrounded*] was not permited [*NB: by them*] to return, I Sent all the men except 2 Inpt. [interpreters] to the boat, the perogu Soon returned with about 12 of our detumind men ready for any event this movement ⟨in the ls instance after Landing Pointed their arrows blank &c which⟩ caused a no: of the Indians to withdraw at a distance,— [*NB: leaving their chiefs soldiers alone with me*] Their treatment to me was verry rough & I think justified roughness on my part, they all left my Perogue and Councild. with themselves the result I could not lern and nearly all went off after remaining in this Situation Some time I offered my hand to the 1 & 2 Chief who refusd to recve it. I turned off & went with my men on board the perogue, I had not progd. more the 10 paces before the 1st Cheif 3rd & 2 Brave men waded in after me. I took them in & went on board ⟨prd on 1 me &⟩[8]

we proceeded on about 1 mile & anchored out off a willow Island placed a guard on Shore to protect the Cooks & a guard in the boat, fastened the Perogues to the boat, I call this Island bad humered Island as we were in a bad humer.

1. Apparently Pierre Cruzatte, who spoke the Omaha language, the tongue of his mother, and who may have been interpreting through some Omaha prisoners of the Tetons. Ordway says, "we had an old frenchman with us who could speak a little of the Souix language."

2. The chief, also known as Untongarabar (*t'at'aŋka sápa*, black buffalo bull) or Black Bull, was noted for a consistently friendly attitude toward whites, and is spoken of favorably by Pierre-Antoine Tabeau; he died in 1813. Ronda (LCAI), 27, 31; Abel (TN), 106 and n. 28, 108–9 and n. 38, 110 and n. 42, 111 and n. 45, 113–15, 131; Thwaites (EWT), 5 : 222–23.

3. His name may be rendered "war leader" (*blotahuŋka*). Tabeau echoes Clark's unfavorable judgement of this chief, giving instances of his obstreperousness. He may also have met in council with Zebulon Montgomery Pike in 1805. In 1815 he attended a council at Portage des Sioux to make peace with the United States. Ronda (LCAI), 30–31; Abel (TN), 106 and n. 29, 108 and n. 40, 110–11 and n. 45, 112–18, 134, 211 and n. 14, 214; Jackson (JP), 1 : 38.

4. The "soldiers," as the French traders called them, were warriors chosen to enforce order and discipline on certain occasions, such as hunts, when irresponsible individual behavior could not be tolerated. Sometimes the duty was assigned to the members of a particular warrior society. They punished offenders by flogging with horsewhips, killing the guilty party's dogs or horses, or by destroying his inanimate property. Since their appointment was temporary, the fear of retaliation sometimes inhibited them in the performance of their duties. Chiefs often appointed a soldier to protect a trader during his sojourn with the tribe. See below, September 26, 1804. Abel (TN), 116–20; Thwaites (EWT), 14 : 297; Hodge, 2 : 614–15.

5. Presumably Clark means that the Sioux warriors were pointing their arrows straight at him because they were at "point blank" range—so close that they did not need to elevate their aim to allow for dropping of the missile due to gravity. At such range men with muzzle-loading firearms such as the expedition carried would actually be at a disadvantage against bowmen, because of the amount of time required to reload. The whole Sioux confrontation is discussed in Ronda (LCAI), 27–41.

6. Probably later Marion Island, opposite the city of Pierre. *Atlas* map 23 shows Bad Humored Island below the mouth of Bad (Teton) River; this is probably a mistake of the copyist, working with Clark's original (now lost) in 1833. Maximilian appears to have penciled in the outline of Bad Humored Island in the correct place when he was in the area. MRC map 40.

7. All the emendations in this entry appear to be in Biddle's hand, but many could be by Clark. Most of the longer insertions are in red while the shorter are in dark ink.

8. This paragraph was misplaced in Codex B after the courses and distances for September 26. Clark may have missed this material in copying and when revising his Field Notes noticed his error and indicated the missing material by asterisks and a pointing hand.

[Clark]

26th S pt.

N. 28 W   4 ½   Miles to a pt. on L. S.

26th of Septr Set out early and proceeded on— the river lined with indians, came too & anchored[1] by the particular request of the Chiefs to let their Womin & Boys See the Boat, and Suffer them to Show us some friendship— great members [numbers?] of men womin & Children on the bank viewing us— Those people are Spritely Small legs ille looking Set men perticularly, they grease & Black themselves when they dress, make use of Hawks feathers about thier heads, cover with a Roab each a polecat Skin to hold their Smokeables, fond of Dress, Badly armed. ther women appear verry well, fin[e] Teeth, High Cheek [bones] Dress in Skin Peticoats, & a Roabe with the flesh Side out and harey ends turned back over their Sholdes, and look well— they doe all the Laborious work, and I may say are perfect Slaves to thier husbands who frequently have Several wives— Capt Lewis & 5 men went on Shore with the Chiefs, who appeared to wish to become friendly they requested us to remain one night & see them dance &c.— in the evening I walked on Shore, and Saw Several Mahar Womin & Boys in a lodge & was told they were Prisones lately taken in a battle in which they killed a number & took 48 prisoners— I advised the Chiefs to make peace with that nation and give up the Prisoners, if they intended to follow the words of their great father they promised that they would do So— I was in Several Lodges neetly formed, those lodges are about 15 to 20 feet Diametr Stretched on Poles like a Sugar Loaf, made of Buffalow Skins Dressed

about 5 oClock I was approached by 10 well Dressed young men with a neet Buffalow Roab which they Set down before me & requested me to get in they Carried me to ther Council Tents forming ¾ Circle & Set me

115

down betwn 2 Chefs where ⟨they had⟩ about 70 men were Seated in a circle, in front of the Chief   6 feet Square was cleared & the pipe of peace raised on forks & Sticks, under which was Swans down ⟨Spred⟩ Scattered, the Flags of Spane & the one we gave them yesterday was Displayed   a large fire was made on which a Dog was Cooked, & in the center about 400 wt of Buffalow meat which they gave us,—   Soon after, I took my Seat the young men went to the boat & brought Capt Lewis in the Same way & placed him by me   Soon after an old man rose & Spoke approveing what we had done.[2]   requesting us to take pitty on them &C. answered—   They form their Camp in a circle

The great Chief then rose in great State and Spoke to the Same purpos and with Solemnity took up the pipe of peace and pointed it to the heavens, the 4 quartrs and the earth, he made Some divistation [dissertation?], & presented the Sten [stem] to us to Smoke, after Smokeing & a Short Harrang to his people we were requested to take the meat, and the Flesh of the Dog gavin us to eat—   We Smoked untill Dark, at which time all was cleared away & a large fire made in the Center, Several men with Tamborens highly Decorated with Der & Cabra Hoofs to make them rattle, assembled and began to Sing & Beat—   The women Came forward highly decerated with the Scalps & Trofies of war of their fathes Husbands & relations, and Danced the war Dance, which they done with great chearfulness untill 12 oClock, when we informed the Chief we intended return on bord, (they offered us women, which we did not except)[3]   4 Chiefs accompanied us to the boat and Staid all night—   Those people have a Description of Men which they Call Soldiars, those men attend to the police of the Band, Correct all vices &.   I Saw one to day whip 2 Squars who appeared to have fallen out, when the Soldier approached all appeared [to] give way and flee ⟨with⟩   at night they Keep 4 or 5 men at different distances walking around their Camp Singing the acursenes [occurrences] of the night   all in Spirits this evening   wind hard from the S E

I saw 25 Squars & Boys taken 13 days ago in a battle with the Mahars, in which they destroyed 40 Lodges, Killed 75 men & boys, & took 48 prisones which they promised us Should be delivered to Mr. Durion now with the Yankton [two words illegible], we gave our Mahar interpeter a few alls [awls?] & &. to give those retched Prisonis, I saw Homney [hominy] of ⟨wild⟩

ground Potatos[4] a Spoon of the Big Horn animal[5] which will hold 2 quarts.

[Clark]   26th Septr. 1804 bad hd Isd.

Course Distance & reffurenc

N. 28° W.   4 ½   miles to a pt. on the L. S. passing a Small willow Island at 1 ½ miles & Several Sand bars the Water Shallow Come too ⟨1⟩

26th of September Wednesday 1804

Set out early proceeded on and Came to by the wish of the Chiefs for ⟨the⟩ to let their Squars & boys See the Boat and Suffer them to treat us well   great number of men women & Children on the banks viewing us, these people Shew great anxiety, they appear Spritely, generally ill look-ing & not well made thier legs & arms Small Generally—[*NB: high cheek bones—prominent eyes*]   they Grese & ⟨Black⟩ [*NB: paint*] themselves with coal when they dress, [*NB: the distingd men*] make use of a hawks feather [*NB: Calumet feather*[6] *adorned with porcupine quills & fastened to the top of the head & falls backwards*] about their heads   the men a robe & each a pole-cats Skins, for to hold ther *Bais roly* [*NB: Bois roule*][7] for Smokeing   fond of Dress & Show   badly armed with fuseis [fusils] &.   The Squaws are Chearfull fine lookg womin not handson, High Cheeks Dressed in Skins a Peticoat and roab which foldes back over thir Sholder, with long wool. doe all ther laborious work & I may Say perfect Slaves to ⟨all⟩ the men, as all Squars of nations much at war, or where the womin are more noumer-ous than the men—   after Comeing too Capt. Lewis & 5 men went on Shore with the Chiefs, who appeared desposed to make up & be friendly, after Captain Lewis had been on Shore about 3 hours I became uneasy for fear of Some Deception & sent a Serjeant[8] to See him and know his treatment which he reported was friendly, & thy were prepareing for a Dance this evening

The made frequent Selecitiation for us to remain one night only and let them Show their good disposition towards us, we deturmined to re-main, after the return of Capt. Lewis, I went on Shore ⟨on landing I was recved on a elegent painted B. robe & taken to the village by 6 men & was

not permited to touch the ground untill I was put down in the grand
Councl house on a White dressed robes—⟩   I saw Several Maha Prisoners and Spoke to the Chiefs   it was necessary to give those prisoners
up & become good friends with the Mahars if they wished to follow the
advice of their Great father   I was in Several Lodges neetly formed as
before mentioned as to the Bauruly [*NB: Bois brulé*] Tribe—   I was [*NB:
on landing from the boat*] met by about 10 well Dressd. yound men who
took me up in a roabe Highly a decrated and Set me Down by the Side of
their Chief on a Dressed robe in a large Council House   this house formed
a ¾ Cercle of Skins well Dressed and Sown together   under this Shelter
about 70 men Set forming a Circle in front of the Chiefs   a plac of 6 feet
Diameter was Clear and the pipe of peace raised on [*NB: forked*] Sticks
[*NB: about 6 or 8 inches from the ground*] under which there was Swans
down Scattered, on each Side of the Circle two Pipes, The [*NB: two*] flags
of Spain 2 & the Flag we gave them in front of the Grand Chief   a large
fire was near in which provisions were Cooking, in the Center about 400
wt. of excellent Buffalo Beif as a present for us—

Soon after they set me Down, the men went for Capt Lewis brough him
in the same way and placed him also by the Chief   in a fiew minits an old
man rose & Spoke approveing what we had done & informing us of their
Situation requesting us to take pity on them &c which was answered—
The Great Chief then rose with great State to the Same purpote as far as
we Could learn & then with Great Solemnity took up the pipe of peace
[*(NB: see 27 Septr in here)*]⁹ [*NB: this belongs to 26 Sepr*] whin the principal
Chiefs Spoke with the ⟨Knife⟩ pipe of Peace he took in one hand Some of
the most Delicate parts of the Dog which was prepared for the feist &
made a Sacrifise to the flag—   & after pointing it to the heavins the 4
quarter of the Globe & the earth, [*NB: then made a Speech*] ⟨he made Some
divistation⟩, lit it and prosist presented the Stem to us to Smoke, after a
Smoke had taken place, & a Short Harange to his people, we were requested to take the meal [*NB: & then put before us the dog which they had been
cooking, & Pemitigon¹⁰ & ground potatoe in Several platters. Pemn is buffo meat
dried or baked pounded & mixed with grease   raw Dog Sioux think great dish—
used on festivals.   eat little of dog   pemn & pote [potato] good*]   we Smoked
for an hour [*NB: till*] Dark & all was Cleared away   a large fire made in

the Center, about 10 misitions playing on tamberins [*NB: made of hoops &* *skin stretched*]. long sticks with Deer & Goats Hoofs tied So as to make a gingling noise and many others of a Similer kind, those men began to Sing, & Beet on the Tamboren, the women Came foward highly Deckerated in theire way, with the Scalps and Trofies of war of ther father Husbands Brothers or near Connection & proceeded to Dance the war Dance which they done with Great Chearfullness untill 12 oClock when we informed the Cheifs that they [*NB: must be*] were fatigued [*NB: amusing us*] &c. [*NB: women only dance— jump up & down. five or six young men selected accompanied with songs the tamborin— making the song extempore words & music— every now & then one of the men come out & repeat some exploit in a sort of song— this taken up by the young men and the women dance to it*] they then retired & we Accompd. by 4 Chiefs returned to our boat, they Stayed with us all night. Those people have Some brave men which they make use of as Soldiers those men attend to the police of the Village Correct all errors I saw one of them to day whip 2 Squars who appeared to have fallen out, when he approachd all about appeared to flee with great turrow at night thy keep two 3 4 or 5 men at deffinit Distances walking around Camp Singing the accurrunces of the night

all the men on board 100 paces from Shore wind from the S. E. moderate one man verry sick on board with a Dangerass abscess on his Hip. all in Spirits this eveninge

In this Tribe I saw 25 Squars and boys taken 13 days ago in a battle with the mahars in this battle they Destroyd 40 lodges, killed 75 men, & Som boys & children, & took 48 Prisones Womin & boys which they promis both Capt. Lewis and my Self Shall be Delivered up to Mr. Durion at the ⟨Bous roulee⟩ [*NB: Bois brulé*] Tribe, those are a retched and Dejected looking people the Squars appear low & Corse but this is an unfavourabl time to judge of them

we gave our Mahar inteptr. [Cruzatte] Some fiew articles to give those Squars in his name Such as alls needle &. &c.

I Saw & eat *Pemitigon* the Dog, Groud potatoe made into a Kind of homney, which I thought but little inferior— I also Saw a Spoon made of a horn of an animile of the Sheep kind [*NB: (the mountain ram or Argalia)*][11] the spoon will hold 2 quarts.

1. In Stanley County, South Dakota, about four miles north of Fort Pierre and two miles south of the present Oahe Dam. Appleman (LC), 351–52; *Atlas* map 23; MRC maps 40, 41.

2. The narrative continues on document 59 of the Field Notes. At the top of the page Biddle has "Sept 27," badly smudged, "Sept. 27 1804," and "& 28."

3. The offer of women was a combination of hospitality and diplomacy—a custom repeated by later tribes which the party met. See Ronda (LCAI), 36–37, 62–64.

4. *Apios americana* Medic., Indian potato, groundnut, or potato-bean, described more extensively by Lewis in an undated entry (at the end of Chapter 3). Fernald, 936. Cf. Criswell, cx, 67; Cutright (LCPN), 91. The reference to hominy indicates the approximate size of the small starch tubers which when cooked together resemble hominy. Present sources do not show the plant this far north along the Missouri River. Barkley, 159.

5. Their first mention of the bighorn sheep, *Ovis canadensis,* which they would not see alive until the following spring. A description had been published in Great Britain this same year (1804), based on a specimen obtained in the Canadian Rockies. Burroughs, 171–73.

6. The feather used most often in adorning the sacred pipe was that of the golden eagle, *Aquila chrysaetos* [AOU, 349]. The bird is described more fully on March 11, 1806. Coues (HLC), 1:138 n. 2; Burroughs, 205–8.

7. Bois roulé, otherwise kinnickinnick, comes from the Chippewa word, *kinikinigân,* "something mixed by hand." It was a mixture of bark, perhaps with some tobacco, used by many western tribes for smoking. Types of bark used varied from region to region. Hodge, 1:692; McDermott (GMVF), 29, 92.

8. Neither Ordway nor Gass mentions being sent on this mission; unless one of them simply omitted it, Pryor was the sergeant sent.

9. Biddle indicates that a few lines belonging with the Codex B entry for September 26 entry were somehow misplaced in the September 27 entry. They are placed here as indicated. His insertions are in red for the most part, faint and difficult to read.

10. Pemmican was meat dried and pulverized, mixed with melted fat and stored in sealed leather satchels; various kinds of berries might be added to improve the flavor. Other kinds of meat than buffalo might be used. Best results were obtained in a sunny, dry climate like that of the Great Plains. Pemmican was a basic travel ration with Indians and fur traders. The North West and Hudson's Bay companies carried on a considerable trade with the northern Plains tribes to obtain pemmican for their employees in the subarctic. Pemmican comes from the Cree word *pĭmĭkân,* "manufactured grease." Wentworth; Hodge, 2:223–24; Secoy, 49–50, 60.

11. Biddle is comparing the argali (*Ovis ammon*), a big-horned sheep of Asia, with the North American bighorn, either thinking them the same species or finding the argali the only known comparable animal.

[Clark]

27th of Septr. 1804— The Bank as usial lined with Sioux, gave the 2 principal Chiefs a blanket & a peck of Corn each, Capt Lewis accompanied the Chiefs to their Lodges, they informed us that a great part of their nation had not arrived, & would arrive to night and requested us to Delay one Day longer, that they might See us

I rote a letter to Mr. Durion, & prepared Some Commissions & a meadel & Sent to Captain Lewis— at 2 oClock Capt Lewis retuned with 4 chiefs & a Brave man named *War-cha pa*—[1] (when a[ny] of thos people Die they pierce ther flesh with arrows above & below ther elbows as a testimony of ther grief) after a delay of half an hour I went with them on Shore, they left the boat with reluctiance (we Suspect they are treacherous and are at all times guarded & on our guard) They again offered me a young woman and wish me to take her & not Dispise them, I wavered [waived?] the Subject, at Dark the Dance began as usial and performed as last night. womin with ther Husbands & relations cloths arms Scalps on poles &c. &c. Capt Lewis joined me & we continued untill about 11 oClock and 2 Chief accompaned us to the boat I with 2 Cheifs was in a Perogue going on board, by bad Stearing the parogu Struk the Cable with Such force as to brake it near the anchor (Cap Lewis) and 3 or 4 men on Shore, I had all hands up and was Compelled to Land— the Chief got allarmed & allarmed the Indians ⟨who⟩ the 1s Chief & about 200 men Came down in great hast armd and for action, and found it was false, about 20 of them Camped on Shore all night— this allarm Cap Lewis & well as my Self viewed as the Signal of their intentions, one half on guard, our misfortune of loseing our anchor obliged us to lay under a falling in bank much exposed to the Accomplishment of the hostile intentions of those *Tetons* (who we had every reason to believe from ther Conduct intended to make an attempt to Stop our progress & if possible rob us—[)] Peter Crusat who Spoke Mahar came in the night and informed me that the mahar Prisoners told him that the Tetons intended to Stop us— We Shew'd but little Sign of a knowledge of there intentions.

[Clark]   *27th of Septr. Thursday 1804*

I rose early aftr a bad nights Sleep   found the Chief all up, and the bank as usial lined with Spectators   we gave the 2 great Cheifs a Blanket a peace, or rethr they took off agreeable to their Custom the one they lay on and each one Peck of Corn   after Brackfast Capt. Lewis & the Chiefs went on Shore, as a verry large part of their nation was Comeing in, the Disposition of whome I did not know one of us being Suffcent on Shore, I wrote a letter to Mr. P. Durion & prepared a meadel & Some Comsns. [*NB: Certificates*] & Sent to Cap Lewis   at 2 oClock Capt. Lewis returned with 4 Chiefs & a Brave man [*NB: Conside man*] named *War cha pa* or *on his Guard.*   when the friends of those people [*NB: (the Scioux)*] die they run arrows through their flesh above and below their elbous as a testimony of their Greaf

after Staying about half an hour, I went with them on Shore, Those men left the boat with reluctience, I went first to the 2d Chiefs Lodge, where a Croud Came around   after Speeking on various Subjects I went to a princpal mans lodge from there to the grand Chiefs lodge, after a fiew minits he invited me to a Lodge within the Circle in which I Stayed with all their principal men untill the Dance began, which was Similer to the one of last night performed by their womn which poles [*NB: in their hands*] on which Scalps of their enemies were hung, Some with the Guns Spears & war empliments ⟨of⟩ [*NB: taken by*] their husbands [*NB: &c*] in their hands

Capt. Lewis came on Shore and we Continued untill we were Sleepy & returned to our boat, the 2nd Chief & one principal man accompanid us, those two Indians accompanied me on board in the Small Perogue, Capt. Lewis with a guard Still on Shore, the man who Steered not being much acustomed to Steer, passed the bow of the boat & peroge Came broad Side against the Cable & broke it ⟨our Cable broke I ordered⟩ which obliged me to order in a loud voice all hands ⟨up⟩ all hands up & at their ores, my preempty[2] order to the men and the bustle of their getting to their ores allarmd the Cheifs, togethr with the appearance of the men on Shore, as the boat turnd. The Cheif hollowered & allarmed the Camp or Town informing them that the Mahars was about attacting us. [*NB: them*]   in about 10 minits the bank was lined with men armed the 1st Cheif at their head, about 200 men appeared and after about ½ hour returned all but about 60 men who Continued on the bank all night, the Cheifs Contd. all night with us— This allarm I as well as Captn. Lewis Considered as the Signal of their intentions (which was to Stop our proceeding on our journey and if Possible rob us) we were on our Guard all night, the misfortune of the loss of our Anchor obliged us to Lay under a falling bank much exposd. to the accomplishment of their hostile intentions P. C [Cruzatte]—our Bowman who Cd. Speek Mahar informed us in the night that the Maha Prisoners informed him we were to be Stoped— we Shew as little Sighns of a Knowledge of their intentions as possible all prepared on board for any thing which might hapen, we kept a Strong guard all night in the boat no Sleep

1. War-cha pa's (*wac'ap'e*, "stabber") commission is now in the Huntington Library in San Marino, California; it seems to be the only extant specimen of a commission actually filled out and signed by Lewis and Clark. It bears the date August 31, 1804, suggesting that they first intended to issue it during their council with the Sioux at Calumet Bluff (see above), but had at least one left over from that occasion. Bakeless (LCPD), opposite p. 83; Osgood (FN), 150 n. 8.

2. Spelling unclear, but presumably Clark means "peremptory."

[Clark]

28th of Septr 1804 Friday I made maney attempts in defferent ways to find our anchor without Sukcess, the Sand had Covered her up, we De-turmined to proceed on to Day— and after Brackfast we with great Dificuelty got the Chiefs out of the boat, and when we were about Setting out the Class Called the Soldiars took possession of the Cable— the 1st Cheif [Black Buffalo] was Still on board and intended to go a Short distance up with us, was informed that the men Set on the Cable, he went out and told Capt Lewis who was at the Bow, they wanted tobacco The 2d Chief [Partisan] Demanded a flag & Tobacco which we refused to give, Stateing proper reasons to them for it, after much rangleing, we gave a ⟨twist⟩ Carrot of Tobacco to the 1st Cheif[1] and he to the men & jurked the Cable from them & proceeded on under a Breeze from the S E. we took in the 3rd Cheif [Buffalo Medicine] who was Sitting on a Sand bar 2 miles above— he told us the Rope was held by order of the 2d Chief who was a Double Spoken man— Soon after we Saw a man rideing full Speed up the bank, we brought him on board, & he proved to be the Sun of the 3d Cheif, by him we Sent a talk to the nation, explanitory of our hoisting the red flag under the white, if they were for Peace Stay at home and doe as we had Derected them and if they were for war or deturmined to attempt to Stop us, we were ready to defend our Selves (as I had before Said)— we Substituted large Stones in place of an Anchor, we came to at a Small Sand bar in the middle of the river and Stayed all night—[2] I am verry unwell I think for the want of Sleep—

Course & Distane 28th of Septr.

N. 33° W.   3   m. to the exty [extremity] of a Sand bar on the L. S.   passed a willow Isd L S

S. 80° W.   3   m. to a bend on the S. S. at a wood opsd. some high land L. S.
              6

[Clark]   *28th of September 1804 Friday*

Made many attemps in different ways to ⟨get up⟩ find our Anchor but could not, the Sand had Covered it, from the misfortune of last night our boat was laying at Shore in a verry unfavourable Situation, after finding that the anchor Could not be found we deturmined to proceed on, with great difficuelty got the Chiefs out of our boat, and when we was about Setting out the Class Called the Soldiers took possession of the Cable   the 1s Chief which was Still on board & intended to go a Short distance up with us, I told him the men of his nation Set on the Cable, he went out & told Capt Lewis who was at the bow the men who Set on the Roap was Soldiers ⟨they⟩ and wanted [*two words illegible, crossed out*] Tobacco ⟨& then we might proceed,⟩   Capt. L. Said would not agree to be forced into any thing, the 2d Chief Demanded a flag & Tobacco which we refusd. to Give Stateing proper reasons to them for it   ⟨*the necssity*⟩   after much difucelty—which had nearly reduced us to hostility   I threw a Carot of Tobacco to 1s Chief Spoke So as to touch his pride   took the port fire[3] from the gunner   the Chief gives the Tobaco to his Soldiers & he jurked the rope from them and handed it to the bows man   we then Set out under a Breeze from the S. E.   about 2 miles up we observed the 3rd Chief on Shore beckining to ⟨him⟩ us   we took him on board   he informed us the roap was held by the order of the 2d Chief who was a Double Spoken man, Soon after we Saw a man Comeing full Speed, thro: the plains left his horse & proceeded across a Sand bar near the Shore we took him on board & observed that he was the Son of the Chief we had on board   we Sent by him a talk to the nation Stateent the Cause of our hoisting the red flag undr. the white, if they were for peace Stay at home & do as we had Derected them, if the were for war ore were Deturmined to Stop us we were ready to defend our Selves, we halted one houre & ½ on the S. S. & made a Substitute of Stones for a ancher, refreshed our men and proceeded on about 2 miles higher up & came too a verry Small Sand bar in the middle of the river & Stayed all night, I am Verry unwelle for want of Sleep   Deturmined to Sleep to night if possible, the men Cooked & we rested well.

Course Distance & refr.

N. 33 W.	3	miles to the extmty of a Sand bar on the L. S. passed a ⟨Sand⟩ willow Isld. on the L. S at the Comse. of the course.
S. 80° W	3	mes. to an object on the bank in a bend to the S. S. at Some woods, opds. the High land on the L. S. Camped.
	6	

1. Clark later explained his action as attempting to touch the chief's pride and get him to use his influence to allay hostilities. See second entry for this day and Nicholas Biddle Notes [ca. April 1810], Jackson (LLC), 2:518.

2. *Atlas* map 23 erroneously shows the camp of September 26 and 27 as being also that of the twenty-eighth. The actual camp for this day was apparently at the site the map shows as the camp for September 29. It lay between Stanley and Hughes counties, South Dakota, perhaps three miles above the present Oahe Dam; the area is now inundated by Oahe Reservoir. Mattison (OR), 30–33; MRC map 41.

3. A portfire was a slow-burning fuse, probably a cord impregnated with gunpowder or some other flammable substance; the burning end could be touched to the touchhole of a cannon to fire the weapon. Ordway notes on September 25 that the swivel cannon was loaded with sixteen musket balls and the two smaller swivels (blunderbusses) with buckshot.

[Clark]   Capt. W. Clarks Notes Continued as first taken—[1]

29th of *September Satturday 1804*—   Set out early   Some bad Sand bars, at 9 oClock we observed the 2d Chief with 2 men and Squars on Shore, they wished to go up with us as far as the other part of their band, which would meet us on the river above not far Distant   we refused to let one more Come on board Stateing Suffient reasons, observd they would walk on Shore to the place we intended to Camp, offered us women   we objected and told them we Should not Speake to another teton except the one on board with us, who might go on Shore when ever he pleased, those Indians proceeded on untill later in the evening when the Chief requested that the Perogue might put him across the river which we agreed to—   Saw numbers of Elk on the Sand bars today, passed an old Ricara Village at the mouth of a Creek without timber[2]   we Stayed all night on the Side of a sand bar ½ a Mile from the Shore.[3]

Course & Distance &c.

South 60° W.	2	miles to a point on the S. S.
N. 80° W.	1 ¼	m. to a tree on the L. S.
N 16° E.	2 ½	m. to a point on the S. S.
N 80° W.	1 ¾	m. to the mouth of a Creek L. S.
N. 45° E.	2	M. to a point on the L. S.
N. 25° E.	1 ½	m. to a Willow Island.

[Clark]   29th *of Septr. Satturday 18[0]4*

Set out early   Some bad Sand bars, proceeded on   at 9 oClock we observed the 2d Chief & 2 principal men one man & a Squar on Shore, they wished to go up with us as far as the other part of their band, which they Said was on the river a head not far Distant   ⟨Cpt. Lewis⟩ we refused Stateing verry Sufficint reasons and was plain with them on the Subject, they were not pleased observed that they would walk on Shore to the place we intended to Camp to night, we observed it was not our wish that they Should for if they did we Could not take them or any other Tetons on board except the one we had now with us who might go on Shore when ever he pleased—   they proceeded on, the Chief on board askd. for a twist of Tobacco for those men   we gave him ½ a twist, and Sent one by them for that part of their band which we did not See, & Continued on   Saw great numbers of Elk at the mouth of a Small ⟨river⟩ Creek Called ⟨the⟩ No timber (—as no timber appeared to be on it.[)]   above the mouth of this Creek [*NB: a Ricara band of*] the Panies[4] had a Village 5 years ago,—   [*NB: no remains but the mound which surrounded the town*]   The 2d Chief Came on the Sand bar & requested we would put him across the

river, I Sent a Perogue & Crossed him & one man to the S. S. and proceeded on & Came too on a Sand bar on about ½ mile from the main
Shore & put on it 2 Sentinals   Continud all night at anchor (we Substitute large Stones for anchors in place of the one we lost[)]   all in high
Spirits &c

29 Septr.

Course Distance & reffens.

S. 60° W.	2	mes. to pt. on L. S. Passing Several Sand bars
N. 80° W.	1 ¼	to a tree on L. S.
N. 16° E.	2 ½	to a pt. on S. S.
N. 8° W	1 ¾	to the mouth of a Creek on the L. S. where the Panias had a Town
N. 45° E.	2	mes. to a pt. on the L. Side
N. 25° E	1 ½	miles to the Lower pt. of a willow Island in the middle of the river.
	11	

1. Document 60 of the Field Notes, unlike any of the other documents in that journal, is made up of several sheets pasted together. Osgood argues that the notes on this large sheet could not have been made in the field, but were copied from earlier notes now lost, which he believes true of the Field Notes after September 23, 1804. The notation at the top of the page, given here, appears to be in Clark's hand, and he could have added it at any time. The words "as first taken" could be interpreted as meaning that this document constitutes the original notes or that the sheet is an exact copy of the originals. Another notation, "to 24 Octo." (probably by Biddle) is just above the words "Set out" in the first entry. The entries on document 60 cover the last month of travel up the Missouri to the Mandan villages, from September 29 to October 24, 1804. Osgood (FN), xviii–xix, 152 n. 1.

2. Present Chantier Creek, in Stanley County, South Dakota. The Arikara village is believed to have been abandoned by 1794. Mattison (OR), 39–40; Robinson, 571; *Atlas* map 23; MRC map 41.

3. Not shown on *Atlas* map 23, the September 29 camp having been misplaced by the copyist (see above, September 28, 1804). The site was between Sully and Stanley counties, South Dakota, about 3½ miles above Chantier (No Timber) Creek; perhaps it was on the small island, in the location of later Okobojo Island, shown on *Atlas* map 23 near the mouth of Okobojo Creek (nameless on the map), the creek being on the starboard side in Sully County. Mattison (OR), 40; MRC map 41; MRY map 74.

4. Clark frequently refers to the Arikaras as "Panies" (Pawnees). Both peoples belong to the Caddoan language family; the Arikaras are believed to have separated from the

Skiri Pawnees. Archaeologists have not discovered any village remains at this location. Information of W. Raymond Wood.

[Clark]

30th of September Sunday 1804 had not proceeded far before we discovered an Indian running after us, he requstd to go with us to the *Ricaras,* we refused to take him, I discovered at a great Distanc a great number of men women & Children decending a hill towards the river above which the Chief with us told us was the other Band, Some rain & hard wind at about 10 oClock we anchored oppost the Camps of this band and told them we took them by the hand, and Sent to each Chief a Carrot of Tobacco & Some to the principal men and farth[er] Said that after Staying with the band below 2 days to See them we had been badly treated and Should not land again, as we had not time to Delay— refured then to Mr. Durion for a full account of us, and an explination of what had been Said, they appeard ansioes for us to eat with them and observed they were friendly we apoligised & proceeded on under a Double reafed Sale—[1] the Chief on board threw out to those that ran up Small pieces of Tobacco & told them to go back and open thier ears, We Saw great number of white guls— refresh the party with whiskey, in the evening we Saw 2 Indians at a Distance, The boat turned by accident & was nearly filling and rocked verry much, allarmed the Indian Chief on board who ran and hid himself, we landed & the Indian express a wish to return, we gave him a Blanket Knife & Some tobacco and advised him to keep his men away, we camped on a Sand bar.[2] verry Cold & windy—

Course & Distance

N. 30° W.	3	m. to the upper point of Some woods S. S.
N. 80° W	1 ½	m on the S. S—
N. 64° W.	3	m. to a Bush on the L. S.
N. 46° W.	1 ½	m. on the L. S.
N. 10° W.	3	m. to a pt. on the S. S. passed the 2nd Band of Tetons,
North	2	m. to a tree on the S. S.
N. 24° W.	4	m. to a point on the L. S.
N. 50° W.	2 ½	m to the Lower point of Pania Island.

[Clark]   *30th Septr.*

Course Distance & reffurenc

N. 30° W.	3	miles to a tree at the upper pt. of Some woods on the S. S.
N. 80° W.	1 ½	miles on the S. S.
N. 64° W.	3	ms. to a Bush on L. S.
N. 46° W.	1 ½	mes. on the L. S.
N. 10 W.	3	mes. to a pt. on the S. S. passed Several Sand bars & the Camp of a Band of Tetons (1)
North	2	miles to a tree on the S. S.
N. 24° W.	4	mes. to a pt. on the L. S.
N 50° W.	2 ½	mes. to the Lower pt. of Pania Island Situated in the Mide. of the river (2)
	20 ½	

30th of Septr. Sunday 1804.

Set out this morning early   had not proceeded on far before we discovered an Indn. running after us, he came up with us at 7 oClock & requested to come on bord and go up to the *recorees*   we refused to take any of that band on board   if he chose to proceed on Shore it was verry well Soon after I discovered on the hills at a great distance great numbers of Indians which appeared to be makeing to the river above us, we proceeded on under a Double reafed Sail, & Some rain   at 9 oClock observed a large band of Indians the Same which I had before Seen on the hills incamping on the bank ⟨of⟩ the L. S.   we Came too on a Sand bar Brackfast & proceeded on & cast the ancher opposit their Lodgs. at about 100 yards distand, and informed the Indians which we found to be a part of the Band we had before Seen, that [*NB?: we*] took them by the hand and Sent to each Chief a Carrot of tobacco, as we had been treated badly by Some of the band below, after Staying 2 days for them, we Could not delay any time, & refured them to Mr. Duron for a full account of us and to here our talk Sent by him to the Tetons, those were verry Selecitious for us to land and eate with them, that they were friendly &c. &.   we appoligised & proceeded on, Sent the peroge to Shore above with the Tobacco & Delivd. it to a Soldr. of the Chief with us   Several of them   ran up the river, the Chf. on board threw then out a Small twist of Tobacco & told them to go back & open ther ears.   they recved the Tobacco & returned to their lodges— we Saw great numbers of white guls   this day is cloudy & rainey— refresh the men with a glass of whisky after Brackfast.

we Saw about 6 miles above 2 Indians who came to the bank and looked at us a about ½ an hour & went over the hills to the S W.   we proceeded on under a verry Stiff Breeze from the S. ⟨W⟩ E, the Stern of the boat got fast on a log and the boat turned & was verry near filling before we got her righted, the waves being verry high, The Chief on board was So fritined at the motion of the boat which in its rocking caused Several loose articles to fall on the Deck from the lockers, he ran off and hid himself, we landed   he got his gun and informed us he wished to return, that all things were Cleare for us to go on we would not See *any* more Tetons &c.   we repeated to him what had been Said before and advised him to keep his men away, gave him a blanket a Knife & Some Tobacco, Smokd a pipe & he ⟨Dep⟩ Set out.   we also Set Sale and Came to at a Sand bar, & Camped, a verrey Cold evening, all on ou[r] guard

1. The sail was reefed, that is, folded or rolled, in two places to reduce the effect of the wind.

2. Clark clearly states that they camped on a sand bar, but the last course ends at "Pania Island," which from *Atlas* map 23 is apparently the later Cheyenne Island, just below the mouth of the Cheyenne River. It is unclear whether the camp was on the island or on a sand bar on the Sully County, South Dakota, shore, but Ordway says they camped on the north, that is, starboard, side. The area is now inundated by the Oahe Reservoir. Mattison (OR), 56–57; MRC map 42.

[Lewis and Clark]   [*Weather, September 1804*][1]

1804 Day of the month	Thermot. at ☉ rise	Weather	Wind at ☉ rise	thermotr. at 4 P. M.	Weather	Wind at 4 oC. P. M.
Septr. 19	46 a	f.	S. E.	71 a	f.	S. E.
20	51 a	f	S. E.	70 a	f	S. E
21	58 a	f.	S. W	88 a	f	S. W.
22	52 a	f	E.	82 a	f	S. E.

23	50 a	f	S E	86	f	S. E.
24th	54 a	f	E.	82	f	W.
25	50	f	S. W.	79	f.	W.
26th	54	f	W	78	f.	S. W.
27	52	f	W.	86	f.	S. W.
28	45	f	S. E	80	f.	S. E.
29th	45 a	f	S. E.	67	f.	S E
3oh	42 a	C a r	S. E.	52	C a r	S. E.

[Remarks][2]

September 19th the leaves of some of the cottonwood begin to fade. yesterday saw the first Brant passing from the N. W. to S. E.—

20th the antelope is now ruting, the swallow[3] has disappeared 12 days

21st Antilopes ruting, as are the *Elk*, the Buffaloe is nearly ceased— the latter commence the latter end of July or first of August.

22nd a little foggy this morning, a great number of green leged plove[4] passing down the river, also some geese & brant—

23rd aire remarkably dry-plumbs & grapes fully ripe— in 36 hours two Spoonfuls of water aveporated in a sauser

24th three tetons swam the river and came to our encampment this evening informed us that 30 longed [lodges] of their nation were near[by?]

[25] This day the Tetons and ourselves had nearly come to an open a ruptr [rupture]

27th Saw a large flock of white Gulls with wings tiped with black[5]

28th this day about 12 oCk. had a severe struggle to get away from the tetons[6]

29th ⟨the Tetons⟩ the 2nd Chief came on Lard. Shore[7] we

131

gave some tobacco and passed them over the river—
saw Indns.

30th passed the remainder of the band.[8] gave tobacco, the
chief left us[9]

1. Both captains resumed tabled weather observations, including two daily temperature readings, on September 19, 1804, having broken off after May 14, 1804. Neither
gives any explanation of the hiatus. Historian Doane Robinson has argued that the thermometer had been misplaced in packing and was found when the party dried and rearranged their baggage on September 16–17. Lewis's pre-expedition list of requirements
includes three thermometers. This seems a small number for such an enterprise, but it
appears unlikely that they could lose all three for four months, and the single August 25
reading disproves the theory. Robinson, 557; Lewis's List of Requirements, Jackson (LLC),
1:69, 75 n. 1. The table and remarks here follow Lewis's observations in his Weather
Diary, with a few variations in Clark's Codex C remarks being noted. Neither recorded
any information about the rise or fall of the river during the month, Lewis not even leaving a space for such observations in his table. See Weather Diary, January 1804, in Chapter 3 for further notes on the keeping of these weather tables.

2. Lewis's remarks in his Weather Diary were placed beside his tabled daily entries;
Clark's remarks in Codex C are on a separate page from his table. The two agree in substance, but a few variations by Clark are noted. The dates are Clark's, except on September 25; Clark repeats Lewis's note of that day on September 26.

3. Perhaps the barn swallow, *Hirundo rustica* [AOU, 613]. Holmgren, 33.

4. Perhaps the stilt sandpiper, *Calidris himantopus* [AOU, 233], or the pectoral sandpiper, *C. melanotos* [AOU, 239]. Ibid.

5. There are only two species of gulls likely to be on the upper Missouri: the herring
gull, *Larus argentatus* [AOU, 51], and the ring-billed gull, *L. delawarensis* [AOU, 54]; both
have black wingtips. Ibid., 30.

6. Clark, at the start of the entry, adds, "lost our Anchor last night."

7. Clark says, "The 2d Cheif came and offered women." See his Field Notes entry for
this date.

8. Clark says, "Passed 60 Lodges of Tetons."

9. Clark's September remarks in Codex C, from September 22 on, have been crossed
out.

[Clark]

1st of October Monday 1804   The wind blew hard from the S. E. all last
night, Set out early   passed a large Island in the middle of the river   opposit this Island the Ricaras lived in 2 Villages on the S W. Side,[1] about 2
Miles above the upper point of the Island the Chyenne River Coms in on

the L. S. and is about 400 yards wide dischargeing but little water for a R. of its Size, the Current jentle, and navagable, to the Black mountains [Black Hills]   we haule the Boat over a Sand bar, River wide & Shoal, pass'd a Creek at 5 mils we Call Sentinal Creek, a Small one above, but little timber about this river, the hills not So high as usial, the upper Creek I call lookout Creek,[2] Camped on a Sand bar, opposit a Tradeing house,[3] where a Mr. V [*V written over Leb*]alles & 2 men had Some fiew goods to trade with the Sioux, a boy came to us, This Mr. Vallie informed us he wintered last winter 300 Legus up the Chyemne River under the Black mountains, he Sais the River is rapid and bad to navagate, it forks 100 Leagus up   the N. fork enters the Black mountain 40 Leagues above the forks[4]   the Countrey like that on the Missouri less timber more Cedar, the Coat Nur or Black m. is high and Some parts retain Snow all Summer, Covered with timber principally pine, Great number of goats and a kind of anamal with verry large horns about the Size of a Small Elk,[5] White Bear   no bever on the chien [Cheyenne]   great numbers in the mountains, The Chyenne Nation has about 300 Lodges   hunt the Buffalow, Steel horses from the Spanish Settlements, which they doe in 1 month—[6]   the Chanal of this River is Corse gravel, Those mountains is inhabited also by the white booted Turkeys

worthy of remark that the Grouse or Prarie hen is Booted, the Toes of their feet So constructed as to walk on the Snow, and the Tail Short with 2 long Stiff feathers in the middle.[7]

Course & Distance

N. 80° W.	3	m. to the upper point of Pania Island.
N. 70° W.	2	m. to the Mouth of Chyenne River L. S.
N. 16° W.	2 ½	miles to a point on the S. S.
N. 50° E.	4	m. to willows on the L. S. passed 2 Creek.
S. 53° E.	4 ½	m to a pt. on the S. S. psd. a Bluff L. S.

[Clark]   1st October

Course Distance & reffurence

N. 80° W	3	mes. to the upper pt. of a large Island in the River
N 70° W.	2	mes. to the mouth of Chien or Dog River on the L. S. (1)

N. 16° W	2 ½	miles to a pt. on the S. S. passed verry bad Sand bar
N. 50° E.	4	mile to Some willows on the L. S. passed 2 Creek on the L. S. the upper Small— (2)
S. 53° E	4 ½	mes. to a pt. on the ⟨L.⟩ S. S. passing a Bluff on the L S.
	16	

Sand bars are So noumerous, that it is impossible to discribe them, & think it unnecessary to mention them.[8]

1st of October Monday 1804

The wind blew hard all last night from the S. E. verry Cold   Set out early   the wind Still hard   passed a large Island in the middle of the river (1)   opsd. the lower point of this Island the Ricrerees formerly lived in a large Town on the L. S. [*NB: remains only a mound circular walls 3 or 4 feet high*]   above the head of the Island about 2 miles we passed the (2) River ⟨Chien (or Dog River)⟩[9] [*NB: Chayenne*] L. S.   this river Comes in from the S W. and is about 400 yards wide, the Current appears gentle, throwing out but little Sands, and appears to throw out but little water the heads of this River is ⟨not known   a part of the nation of Dog⟩ [*NB: in the Second range of the Côte noir   its course generally about East. So called from the Chayenne*] Indians [*NB: who*] live ⟨Some distance⟩ [*NB: on the heads of it*] ⟨up this river, the presise distance I cant learn⟩,[10] above the mouth of this river the Sand bars are thick and the water Shoal   the river [Missouri] Still verry wide and falling a little   we are obliged to haul the boat over a Sand bar, after makeing Several attempts to pass.   the wind So hard we Came too & Stayed 3 hours   after it Slackened a little we proceeded on round a bend, the wind in the after part of the Day a head— (2) passed a Creek on the L. S. which we Call the Sentinal, this part of the river has but little timber, the hills not so high.   the Sand bars now noumerous, & river more than one mile wide including the Sand bars. (2) pass a Small Creek above the latter which we Call *lookout* C—.   Continued on with the wind imediately a head, and Came too on a large Sand bar in the middle of the river, we Saw a man opposit to our Camp on the L. S. which we discovd. to be a Frenchman, a little ⟨of⟩ [*NB: from Shore among*] the willows we observed a house, we Call to them to come over, a boy Came in a Canoo

& informed that ⟨three⟩ 2 french men were at the house with good to trade with the Seauex which he expected down from the rickerries everry day, Severl large parties of Seauex Set out from the *rics* for this place to trade with those men— This Mr. *Jon Vallie* informs us that he wintered last winter 300 Leagues up the Chien River under the Black mountains, he informs that this river is verry rapid and dificiult even for ⟨Perogues⟩ Canoos to assend and when riseing the Swels is verry high, one hundred Leagues up it forks one fork Comes from the S. the other at 40 Leagues above the forks enters the black Mountain. The Countrey from the Missourie to the black mountain is much like the Countrey on the Missourie, less timber & a greatr perpotion of Ceder. The black Mountains he Says is verry high, and Some parts of it has Snow on it in the Summer great quantities of Pine Grow on the mountains, a great noise is heard frequently on those mountains"—[11] ⟨no bever on Dog river⟩, on the mountains great numbers of ⟨an⟩ goat, and a kind of Anamale with large Circuler horns, This animale is nearly the Size of an Argalia Small Elk. White bear is also plenty— The ⟨Chien⟩ [*NB: Chayenne*] Inds. ⟨are about 300 lodges they⟩ inhabit this river principally, and Steel horses from the Spanish Settlements ⟨to the S W⟩ This excurtion they make in one month the bottoms & Sides of R Chien is Corse gravel. This frenchman gives an account of a white booted turkey an inhabitant of the Cout Noie— [*NB: (⟨Turke⟩ (Prairie Cock)*]

1st of ⟨September⟩ October Monday 1804

[Clark]   at the Mouth of River Chien or *Dog R*[12]

We proceeded now from the mouth of this river 11 miles and Camped on a Sand bar in the river opposit to a Tradeing house verry windy & Cold— *11 miles above the Chien R*

[Clark][13]

The red Berry is Called by the *Rees Nar-nis—(Choriser Grape)*[14]

The Ricares

Names of the nations who come to the Ricares to trafick and *bring Horses & robes*

1. * *Kun-na-nar-wesh* Gens de vash   Blue beeds

2. °	*Noo-tar-wau*	Hill Climbers
3. *	*Au ner-hoo*	the people who pen Buffalow to Catch them
4. *	*To-che-wah-Coo*	Fox Indians
5. *	*To-pah-cass*	White hair's
6. *	*Cat-tar kah*	Paducar
7. *	*Kie-wah*	Tideing Indians
8. *	*Too war Sar*	Skin pricks
9.	*Shar ha* (*Chien*)	the village on the other Side
10.	*We hee Shaw* (Chien)	The villages on this Side

Those nation all live on the praries from S W. by S. to West of the Ricaries, all Speek different languages and are numerous   all follow the Buffalow and winter in the mountains.

The Mandans Call a red berry common to the upper part of the Missouri *Ăs-sáy*   the engages call the Same berry grease de Buff—   grows in great abundance a makes a Delightfull Tart[15]

1. The island is apparently Clark's "Pania Island," later Cheyenne Island. The villages are marked on *Atlas* map 23 and are probably among the sites on or near what is called Black Widow Ridge, where there was almost a continuous series of late prehistoric and early historic Indian village sites. Lehmer, fig. 82.

2. Sentinal Creek, which bears that name on Evans's map 3 (*Atlas* map 9), is probably present McKenzie (Chicken) Creek, and Lookout Creek probably No Heart Creek, in Dewey County, South Dakota. Others have identified them, however, as Fox (Charlie) and McKenzie creeks, respectively. The hairpin bend they were going around ("horse shoe Bend" in *Atlas* map 9), divided between *Atlas* maps 23 and 24, was later called Lookout Bend. Mattison (OR), 59; MRC map 42; MRY map 83.

3. In present Dewey County, a few miles above the mouth of the Cheyenne River; the area must now be inundated by the Oahe Reservoir. The trader was Jean Vallé, probably a member of a prominent family of Ste. Genevieve, Missouri. He may be the "Vale" who was a clerk for Régis Loisel. Gass and Ordway note that he spoke English. Abel (TN), 78–80 and n. 21, 108, 133–34,150; Thwaites (LC), 1:176 n. 1; Nasatir (BLC), 1:111; MRC map 42.

4. The "Black Mountains," also "Cote noir" in Codex B for this date, are here the actual Black Hills of South Dakota. What little information whites had about this range came largely from Indian reports, and no one had any clear idea of its extent and location. At this point the captains applied the name to all the eastern outlying ranges of the Rockies. Vallé's north fork of the Cheyenne is the present Belle Fourche River, which

meets the Cheyenne in eastern Meade County, South Dakota. Taking a league to be three miles, Vallé's distance estimates are far too great. Allen, 190, 202, 239.

5. Bighorn sheep.

6. These Spanish settlements were probably in New Mexico, the traditional source of horses for the Plains tribes.

7. Perhaps the sharp-tailed grouse. Information of Paul Johnsgard, October 31, 1984. Cf. Cutright (LCPN), 95, and Holmgren, 29. For the turkey, see Lewis's natural history note, September 17, 1804.

8. Before these lines Clark crossed out the first two courses of the next day: S. 70 E 2 and S 80 E. 1.

9. At the time of writing this entry Clark evidently believed that the name "Cheyenne," for both the tribe and the river, derived from the French "*chien,*" for dog. It is, in fact, from the Sioux *Šhahiyena,* perhaps "red (alien) talkers." Having learned better later, he or Biddle evidently went back and crossed out some of the references to "dog," "*chien,*" and "nation of dogs." Hodge, 1:250.

10. Biddle has interlined and crossed out extensively here. Clark originally wrote, "the heads of this River is not known   a part of the nation of Dog Indians live some distance up this river, the presise distance I cant learn." Biddle's version becomes, "the heads of this River is in the Second range of the Côte noir   its course generally about East. So called from the Chayenne Indians who live on the heads of it." Biddle used information the captains acquired after Clark wrote this passage, in particular correcting the notion that the Cheyennes were "Chien," or dog, Indians. This is an indication that Clark wrote this Codex B entry on or soon after the given date. Compare with Biddle's published version in Coues (HLC), 1:146–47.

11. See below, June 20 and July 11, 1805.

12. Clark begins his notebook journal Codex C on October 1, 1804; Codices B and C have overlapping entries for October 1, 2, and 3. In this edition the Codex B entries are placed first, which seems the most likely order of composition. See the Introduction and Appendix C, vol. 2. Above this entry Clark wrote "From Journal No. 2" (which was Clark's designation for Codex B); the notation must refer to the overlap. Codex C was Clark's Journal No. 3.

13. Undated, miscellaneous information on the first two pages of Codex C, probably gathered among the Arikaras and Mandans and placed on the most convenient blank pages. All of the names seem to be in the Arikara language and designate either tribes or bands who came to the Arikaras to trade. Many of them can not be precisely identified today and conjecture beyond Clark's identifications seems pointless. This list at the very least indicates the extent of intertribal trade and the importance of the Arikara, Mandan, and Hidatsa villages as trading centers; these three tribes served as the middlemen of the northern Great Plains.

Kun-na-nar-wesh (*tUhkaNIhnaawiš*), "gray-stone village," the Arikara name for the Arapahoes; the term "gray stone" may have referred metaphorically to blue beads.

To-che-wah-coo (*tUhčiwáku'*), "fox village." This name probably indicated a band of some larger tribal group.

To-pah-cass (*tUhpAxkás*), "white head(ed) village." This is not a modern Arikara name for any group; it is possibly an old name for the Great Osages under their famous chief White Hair.

Cat-tar kah (*katAhká*). In modern Arikara the term refers to "white man"; however, the same term in the closely-related Pawnee language means "alien tribe" and was used to designate the Kiowa Apaches.

Kie-wah (*ka'íWA*), "Kiowa."

Too war Sar (*tuwaásA*). In modern Arikara the term designates a medicine society also named *neksaánu'*, "ghost." Inside the medicine bundle of the society is an image called *ka'íWA*, suggesting that it may have originated from that tribe. Clark's designation "Skin pricks," however, would seem to suggest the Wichitas.

Shar ha (*šaahé*), "Cheyennes."

We hee Shaw. This term is unclear although it may be related to *waahawiša*, "lying on its side." It is not a modern Arikara designation for any social group. Clark indicates that the term designated a division of the Cheyennes. "The other side" and "This side" may refer to the two sides of the Missouri River, indicating that the Cheyennes were still living, or had recently lived on both sides of the river. Later in the century they would be found entirely west of the river, ranging the plains from Montana to Oklahoma. Hodge, 1:71–74, 474, 698–701; 2:184, 705–7, 1158, 1037, 1172; Coues (NLEH), 1:384 and n. 6; 2:577–78; Hyde (IHP), 28–30, 130.

14. It is *naaní'Is* or "buffalo berry" in the Arikara language—the buffaloberry.

15. Again the buffaloberry, in the Mandan language it is *háŋse* or "bullberry."

[Clark]

2nd of October Tuesday 1804,   Mr. Vallie Came on board, Lat. 44° 19′ 36 N.   we observed Some Indians on a hill on the S. S.   one Came to the river & fired off his gun and asked us to come [*hole*] he wish us to go to his Camp near at hand[1]   we refused, passed a large Island[2] on the S. S., here we expected the Tetons would attempt to Stop us, and prepared for action, &c.   opposit this Island on the L. S. a Small Creek comes in, w[e] call this Caution Island, Camped on a Sand bar ½ mile from the main Shore[3]   the wind hard from the N W.   Cold, the current of the river less rapid, & retains less Sediment than below.

Course & Distance

S. 70° E.	2 ½	m. to a wood on the L. S.—
S. 80° E	1 ½	m. on the L. S.—
N 62° E.	2	m on the L. S.

N. 15° E	4	m. to the L. S. of an Island Situated near the S. S.—
N. 28 E.	2	m. to the upper pt. of the Sand bar abov the Island.

[Clark]   2nd of Octr.

Course Distance and refferuns

S. 70° E	2 ½	miles to a wood on the L. Side pass a large Sand bar in the middle & a willow Isd. close under the L. S.
S. 80° E	1 ½	me. on the L. S. ⟨a willow⟩
N. 62 E	2	miles on the L. S. a willow bottom opposit on the S S.
N. 15° E	4	miles to the L. Side of an Island Situated near the S S. & 1 me. above the lower point of the Sd. Island (1)
N. 28° E	2	miles to the pt. of a Sand bar makeing from the head of the Island & Camped (2)
	12	

2nd of *October Tuesday 1804*

a Violent wind all night from the S. E.   Slackened a little and we proceeded on. Mr. *Jon Vallee* Came on board and proceeded on 2 miles with
us, a verry Cold morning   Some black clouds flying   took a meridian
altitude & made the Lattitude   *44° 19′ 36″* North   this was taken at the
upper part of the gouge of the Lookout bend, the Sentinal heard a Shot
over the hills to the L. S. dureing the time we were Dineing on a large
Sand bar.   the after part of this day is pleasent, at 2 oClock opposit a
wood on the L. S. we observed some Indians on a hill on the S. S.   one
Came down to the river opposit to us and fired off his gun, & beckind. to
us to Come too, we payed no attention to him   he followed on Some distance, we Spoke a few words to him, he wished us to go a Shore and to his
Camp which was over the hill and Consisted of 20 Lodges, we excused
our Selves advised him to go and here our talk of Mr. Durion   he en-
quired for traders   we informed him one was in the next bend below &
parted, he returned— & we proceeded on (1) passed a large Island, ⟨on⟩
the S. S.   here we expected the Tetons would attempt to Stop us and
under that idear we prepared our Selves for action which we expected
every moment.   opsd. this Island on the L. S. a Small Creek Comes in,

This Island we call Isd. of *Caution* we took in Some wood on a favourable Situation where we Could defend our men on Shore & (2) Camped on a Sand bar ½ a mile from the main Shore.   the wind changed to the N. W. & rose verry high and Cold which Continud. The Current of the Missourie is less rapid & contains much less Sediment of the Same Colour.—

[Clark]   2nd of ⟨September⟩ *October Tuesday* 1804

Proceeded on as mentioned in Journal No. 2[4] *twelve* miles   *Camped* above a large Island on a Sand bar, verry windy and Cold the after part of this day, the mid day verry worm, The Lattitude as taken to day is *44° 19′ 36″*— observe great Caution this day expecting the *Seaux* intentions Some what hostile towards our progression, The river not So rapid as below the Chien, its width nearly the Same   1̲2̲ miles

Point of observation No. 46.

[Lewis]   *Tuesday October 2nd 1804.*[5]

On a large sand bar Lard. shore, opposite to the gorge of the bend *look-out*.

Observed the meridian altd. of ☉'s U. L. with Sextant by the fore observation. 84° 45′ 15″
Latitude deduced from this observation.   N. 44° 19′ 36.3″

1. Gass says the Indian "said he belonged to the Jonkta or Babarole band"—evidently meaning either the Yankton or Bois Brulé divisions of the Sioux.
2. On *Atlas* map 24 this appears as "Caution Island," as in the Codex B entry; probably the later Plum Island. MRC map 42; Mattison (OR), 62.
3. Just above Plum (Caution) Island, with Sully County, South Dakota, on the starboard shore and Dewey County on the larboard. The area is now inundated by Oahe Reservoir. *Atlas* map 24; MRC map 42.
4. Clark's Codex B; Clark is again referring to the longer entry for the day in that journal.
5. Lewis's astronomical observation from Codex O.

[Clark]

3rd of October Wednesday 1804   The N W. wind blew verry hard all night with Some rain, we Set out early, at 12 examoned our Stores & goods,

Several bags Cut by the mice[1] and Corn Scattered, Some of our Cloth also cut by them also papers &c. &c. at 1 oClock an Indian Came to the Bank S. S, with a turkey on his back 4 other soon joined him Some rain, Saw Brant & white guls flying Southerly

Course & Distance

N. 50° E.	2 ½	m. to a wood L. S.
N. 54° E	2	m. to a tree in a bend S. S.
N.	2	m to a point of high lands on the L. S.
N. 22° W.	1 ½	m. on the L. [S] under a Bluff (Sand bars So Common, impossible to Describe them)—

[Clark]   *3rd of October Wednesday 1804*

wind blew hard all night from the N W. Some rain and verry Cold. we Set out at 7 oClock & proceeded on

N. 50° E	2 ½	mes. to a pt. of wood on the L. S.
N. 54 E.	2	miles to a tree in a bend S. S.
North	2	miles to a pt. High Land on L. S wind hard a head Came too & Dined
N. 22° W.	4 ½	miles to the head of Good hope Island 2 Indians Came to the mouth of a Creek on the S. S. Shields[2]
	11	

[Clark]   3rd of *October Wednesday* 1804

The N. W. wind blew verry hard all night with Some rain a Cold morning, we Set out at 7 oClock and proceeded on at 12 oClock landed on a Bare L. S. examined the Perogus & factle[3] of the [*NB: boat*] to see if the mice had done any damage, Several bags Cut by them Corn Scattered &. Some of our Clothes also Spoiled by them, and papers &c. &. at 1 oClock an Indian Came to the bank S. S. with a turkey on his back, four others Soon joined him, we attempted Several Chanels and Could not find water to assend, landed on a Sand bar & Concluded to Stay all night, & Send out and hunt a Chanell, Some rain this after noon— Saw Brant & white gulls flying Southerly in large flocks—

3rd

Course Distance & reffurences

N. 50° E.	2 ½	miles to a point of wood on the Larboard Side—
N. 54° E	2	miles to a tree in the bend to the Larboard Side—
North	2	miles to a point of high Land on the Larboard Side—
N. 22° W.	1 ½	miles on the L. Side under a Bluff
	8	miles

1. Perhaps *Peromyscus* sp.

2. In the Field Notes and in Codex C this last distance is 1 ½ miles, giving a total mileage of 8. Good Hope Island—a name taken from Evans's map 4 (*Atlas* map 10)—is probably Pascal Island of later times. Clark usually refers to the upstream end of an island as the "head," but *Atlas* map 24 shows the campsite for this day below the downstream end of the island. Clark's and Ordway's entries for the next day indicate that they had failed to find the correct channel on October 3, and that they fell back three miles on October 4, then continued upriver past Good Hope Island. This still does not make it clear if they reached the head of the island on the third, then fell back to the sandbar where they camped that night; however, this would explain the mileage and other discrepancies for that day. If Clark's ambiguous entry means that they camped near the mouth of a creek which he intended to name for John Shields, it does not appear on the existing version of his map (*Atlas* map 24). Artichoke Creek may be "Shields." It enters the Missouri from the east in present Potter County, South Dakota, at about the proper distance below the island, and at that point is a bluff corresponding to that under which Ordway indicates they camped. The campsite was on a sandbar near the line of present Potter and Dewey counties, South Dakota. The area is now inundated by the Oahe Reservoir. MRC map 43.

3. Biddle tried to improve Clark's spelling by adding letters in red to yield "forecastle" or something approaching that.

[Clark]

4th of October Thursday— the Wind blew all night from the N W. Some rain we were obliged to drop down 3 miles to get a Channel Sufficient Deep to pass Several Indians on the bank, Call'd to us frequently to Land, one gave 3 yels & Sciped a Ball before us,[1] we payed no attention to them, while at Brackfast one Swam across to us, beged for Powder, we gave him a Small piece of Tobacco & put him over on a Sand bar, passed a large Island in the middle of the river Good hope I.[2] Passed a small Creek L. S.[3] passed a creek L S[4] Camped on a Sand bar at the upper

point of an Island on which is the remains of an old ricara Village fortified Called *La hoo call*[5]   It was circular, this Village appears to have been
deserted about 5 or 6 years, 17 houses yet remain, the Island Contains
but little timber, the evening verry Cold and wood Scerce, make use of
Drift wood

Course & Distance

N. 18° W.	8 ½	m. to a point on the S. S.— passed good hope Island
N. 12° E.	1 ½	m. on the S. S. passd. a Creek L. S.
N. 45° E.	2	m. on the S. point passed *Le hoo calls* Island—

[Clark]   4th of *October Thursday* 1804

the wind blew all night from the NW. Some rain, we were obliged to
Drop down 3 miles to get the Chanel Suft. deep to pass up, Several In-
dians on the Shore viewing of us Called to us to land   one of them gave 3
yels & Sciped [X: *Skipped*] a ball before us, we payed no attention to him,
proceeded on and Came too on the L. S. to brackft   one of those Indians
Swam across to us beged for Powder, we gave him a piece of Tobacco &
Set him over on a Sand bar, and Set out, the wind hard a head   (1) passed a
Island in the middle of the river about 3 miles in length, we call *Good*hope
Island, (2) at 4 miles passed a (2) Creek on the L. S. about 12 yards wide
Capt. Lewis and 3 men walked on Shore & crossed over to an (3) Island
Situated on the S. S. of the Current & near the Center of the river   this
Isld. is about 1 ½ miles long & nearly ½ as wide, in the ⟨S. S. nearly op-
posit⟩ Center of this Island was an old Village of the rickeries Called *La ho
catt*   it was Circular and walled Containing 17 lodges and it appears to
have been deserted about five years, the Island Contains but little timber.   we Camped on the Sand bar makeing from this Island, the day
verry Cool.

4th Octr.

Course Distance & reffurence—

N. 18° W.	8 ½	miles to a pt. on the S. S. passed an Island Goodhope in the middle of the river (1)
N. 12° E.	1 ½	miles on the S. S. passed a Creek on the L. S. (2)

N. 45° E.   2   miles on the S. pt.   passed an Island ⟨and place⟩ on which
                    there was a village ⟨3⟩ of Ricreries in the year 1797.   La
             12   hoo-catt
             ==

1. The Indian fired his musket and sent the ball skipping over the water.

2. Probably later Pascal Island. See above, October 3, 1804; *Atlas* maps 10, 24; MRC map 43.

3. Nameless on *Atlas* map 24; probably later Pascal Creek. MRC map 43.

4. On *Atlas* map 24 this stream is Teel Creek, presumably from a teal duck. It is the later Stove, or Cherry, Creek, in Dewey County, South Dakota. MRC map 43.

5. The island was the later Dolphees, or Lafferty, Island, lying between Dewey and Potter counties, South Dakota. The village appears clearly in *Atlas* map 24. The name of the village appears on Evans's map 4 (*Atlas* map 10). The area is now inundated by Oahe Reservoir. Mattison (OR), 63; Ronda (LCAI), 43; MRC map 43; MRY map 91. The word, *NAhuukaátA* or "by the water," comes from the name of an Arikara band. Parks (BVAP), 225.

[Clark]

5th of October Friday 1804   Frost this morning, Set out early   passed a Small Creek on the L. S.   saw 3 Tetons on the S. S.   they beged Some Tobacco, we proceed on   passed a Creek on the S. S.[1]   I Saw a white brant in a gangue on the Sand bar[2]   Saw a large herd of Cabra or antelopes Swiming the River, we Killed four of them   passed a Small Island on the L. S.   a large Creek on the L. S. at the head of the Island White Brant Creek,[3] I walked on the Island which is covered with wild rye,[4] I Killed a Buck & a Small wolf this evening, Clear pleasant evening, Camped on a mud bar S. S.[5]   refreshd the men with whiskey.

Course Distance &c.

N 63° E	1 ½	miles to high land on the L. S.
East	3	m. to a pt. of Timber on the L. S. passed a Creek L. S.
N. 80° E	1 ½	m to a tree in a bend to S. S.
N. 36° W.	2	m. to a pt. of high Land on the L. S. passed a Creek on the S. S.
N. 50° W.	3	m. to a pt. on the S. S.
N. 17° W.	3	to a tree on the S. S. passed an Island and Creek L. S.
N. 16° E	6	m. to a point on the L. S. opposit a willow Isd.

[Clark]   5th of *October Friday* 1804

Frost this morning, we Set out early and proceeded on   (1) passed a Small Creek on the L. S.   at 7 oClock heard Some yels   proceeded on Saw 3 Indians of the Teton band, they called to us to Come on Shore, beged Some Tobacco, we answd. them as usial and proceeded on,   passed (2) a Creek on the S. S.   at ⟨the⟩ 3 mes. abov the mouth we Saw one white ⟨goose⟩ Brant in a gang of about 30, the others all as dark as usial, a Discription of this kind of Gees or Brant Shall be given here after   Saw a Gang of Goats Swiming across the river out of which we killed four   they were not fatt.   in the evening passed a Small (3) Island Situated Close to the L. Side, at the head of this Isd. a large Creek coms in on the L. S.   Saw white ⟨Gees⟩ or Brants, we Call this Creek white ⟨gees⟩ Brant Creek—   I walked on the Isd.   found it Covered with wild rye, I Shot a Buck, Saw a large gang of Goat on the hills opposit, one Buck killed, also a Prarie wolf this evening, the high Land not So high as below, river about the Same width, the Sand bars as noumerous, the earth Black and many of the Bluffs have the appearance of being on fire,[6] we Came too and Camped on a mud bar makeing from the L. S.   The evening is Calm and pleasant, refreshed the men with a glass of whiskey—

                                                          5th October

Course Distance & reffurences.

N. 63° E.	1 ½	under Some high land on the S. S.
East	3	miles to a point of Timber on the L. S. passed a Creek on the L. S. (1) high land on the S. S.
N. 80 E	1 ½	mes. to a Tree in the bend to the S. S.
N. 36° W.	2	mes. to a pt. of high land on the L. S. passed a Creek on the S. S. (2)
N. 50° W	3	miles to a Point to the S. S.
N. 17° W.	3	mes. to a tree on the S. S. passd a Small Island Close on the L. S. above the Sd. Island a Creek comes in on the L. S.
N. 16° E.	6	mes. to a pt. on the L. Side opposit a willow Island Situated near the S. Shore
	20	

145

1. Now the Little Cheyenne River, otherwise Cheyenne Creek, reaching the Missouri in Potter County, South Dakota. It appears as "Hidden Creek" on *Atlas* map 24. MRC map 43; MRY map 92.

2. The captains' references to "brant" are often obscure, especially since brant and geese often migrate in mixed flocks. The white brant here may be the snow goose, *Chen caerulescens* [AOU, 169]. The darker birds mentioned in Codex C, below, may be the brant, *Branta bernicla* [AOU, 173]. Coues (HLC), 1:154 n. 22; Burroughs, 192–93.

3. This creek, in Dewey County, South Dakota, retained the same name late in the nineteenth century, according to MRC map 43; more recently it was Swift Bird Creek. *Atlas* map 24; MRY map 93.

4. *Elymus canadensis* L., Canada wild rye. Barkley, 489.

5. In Potter County, in an area now inundated by Oahe Reservoir. *Atlas* map 24; Mattison (OR), 71–72; MRC map 43.

6. Pierre Shale (see entries of August 24 and September 14, 1804, for a discussion of "fire").

[Clark]

6th of October Satturday 1804   Cold Wind from the N.   Saw many large round Stones near the middle of the River   passed an old Ricara village of 80 Lodges Picketed in   those lodges in nearly an octagon form, 20 to 60 feet Diameter   Specious [spacious] Covered with earth and as Close as they Can Stand,[1] a number of Skin Canoes[2] in the huts, we found Squashes of 3 different Kinds growing in the Village   Shields Killed an Elk Close by—   The Magpy is common here, we Camped off the mouth of Otter Creek on the S. S.[3]   this Creek is 22 yds. wide & heads near the R. Jacque,—   contains much water.

Course & Distance

N. 4° E.	8	m. to a wood pt. on the L. S.
N. 8° W.	1	m. on the L. S.
N. 32° W	3	m. to a pt. on the S. S.
N. 40° W	2	m. to Otter Creek S. S.[4]

[Clark]   6th *October Satturday* 1804

a cool morning wind from the North   Set out early   passed a willow Island (1) Situated near the S. Shore at the upper point of Som timber on the S. S.   many large round Stones near the middle of the river, those Stones appear to have been washed from the hills   (2) passed a village of about 80 neet Lodges covered with earth and picketed around, those loges are Spicious of an Octagon form as close together as they can possibly be placed and appear to have been inhabited last Spring, from the Canoes of Skins Mats buckets[5] & found in the lodges, we are of appinion they were the recrereis   we found Squashes of 3 Different Kinds growing in the Village,[6] one of our men killed an Elk Close by this Village, I saw 2 wolves in persute of another which appeared to be wounded and nearly tired, we proceeded on   found the river Shole   we made Severl. attempts to find the main Channel between the Sand bars, and was obliged at length to Drag the boat over to Save a league which we must return to get into the deepest Channel, we have been obgd to hunt a Chanl. for Some time past the river being devided in many places in a great number of Chanels, Saw Gees, Swan, Brants, & Ducks of Different kinds on the Sand bars to day, Capt Lewis walked on Shore Saw great numbers of Prarie hens,[7] I observe but fiew Gulls or Pleaver in this part of the river, The *Corvos* or Magpye is verry Common in this quarter

We Camped on a large Sand bar off the mouth of ⟨Beaver or⟩[8] Otter Creek on the S. S.   this Creek is about 22 yards wide at the mouth and contains a greater perpotion of water than Common for Creeks of its Sise

6th Octr

Course Distance and Reffurencies—

N. 4° E	8	miles to a point of wood land on the L. S. passed a willow Isd. S. S.
N. 8° W.	1	me. on the L. Side
N. 32 W.	3	mes. to a point on the S. S. passed an old village of the Rickorreis at the Comst. of this Course (2)
N. 40° W.	2⟨½⟩	miles the mouth of Beaver Otter Creek on the S. S. a large Sand bar opposit
	14 ½	

1. Clark is describing the earth lodge characteristic of the sedentary tribes of the Missouri. The area is shown on *Atlas* map 25.

2. Probably "bullboats," buffalo skins stretched over a hemispherical frame. Though hard to steer, they were handy for crossing the river and could be carried by one person.

3. Later known as Swan Creek, in Walworth County, South Dakota. There is an Otter

Creek a few miles farther down the Missouri, but its location does not correspond with that shown on *Atlas* map 25. The campsite would now be inundated by the Oahe Reservoir. Mattison (OR), 76–77; MRC map 44.

4. In Codex C the distance is 2½ miles, with the fraction possibly crossed out.

5. Biddle apparently added the letters "uc" in red in the middle of this word, blotting out Clark's first spelling.

6. Varieties of *Cucurbita pepo* L., pumpkins and squashes, and possibly *C. maxima* Duchesne, hubbard and turban squashes. Fernald, 1349. Gilmore lists eight types of pumpkins and squashes among the Omahas. Gilmore (UPI), 65–66.

7. Perhaps the same as the "grouse" of October 7, below, that is, the sharp-tailed grouse. See April 15, 1805, below, where Lewis notes that grouse are also called "prairie hens."

8. Biddle apparently crossed out "Beaver or" with his usual red ink.

[Clark]

7th of October Sunday 1804   frost last night, passed a River 90 yds. wide the *Ricaras* Call *Sur-war-kar-ne*[1]   all the water of this river runs in a chanel of 20 yards, the Current appears jentle, I walked up this River a mile, Saw the tracks of white bear, verry large, also a old Ricara village partly burnt, fortified   about 60 Lodges built in the Same form of those passed yesterday, many Canoes & Baskets about the huts—   about 10 oClock we Saw 2 Indians on the S. S.   they asked ⟨cours⟩ for Something to eat & told us they were Tetons of the band we left below on ther way to the *Ricaras* we gave them meat & wind hard from the South, passed a large open Island covered with grass and wild rye, I walked on the Isd & 4 men they ⟨our⟩ Killed a Braroe & a Black tale Doe with a black breast, the largest Deer I ever saw, the great numbers of Grous on it, we call it Grous Island,[2] Camped opposit the Island near the S. Side.[3]

Course Distanc & reffurence

N. 42° W.	2	m. to the mouth of Sur-war-kar-ne river L. S.
N. 30° E.	3 ½	miles to a Bend S. S.
N 30° W.	2	m. to a pt. of high land L. S.
N. 35° W.	7	m. on the L. S.
N. 10° W.	1	m. on the L. S. to a pt.—.
N. 80° W.	3	m. to the left Side of Grous Island
N. 45° W.	1	m. to the head of Sd Isd.

148

| West | 2 ½ | M to a point on the main S. S. [High open?] lands on both Sides |

[Clark]   7th of *October Sunday 1804*

a Cloudy morning, Some little rain frost last night, we Set out early proceeded on 2 ⟨½⟩ miles to the mouth of a (1) river on the L. S. and brackfast   this river whin full is 90 yards wide   the water is at this time Confined within 20 yards, the Current appears jentle, this river throws out but little Sand   at the mouth of this river we Saw the Tracks of White bear which was verry large, I walked up this river a mile— below the (2) mouth of this river, is the remains of a Rickorrie Village or Wintering Camp fortified in a circular form of a bout 60 Lodges, built in the Same form of those passed yesterday   This Camp appears to have been inhabited last winter, many of their willow & Straw mats, Baskets & Buffalow Skin Canoes remain intire within the Camp, ⟨we passed⟩ the Ricares Call this river *Sur-war-kar-na* or Park [*NB: Rr.*][4]   from this river [*NB: which heads in the 1st black mountains*] we proceeded on under a gentle Breeze from the S. W.   at 10 oClock we Saw 2 Indians, on the S. S.   they asked for Something to eate, & informed us they were part of the *Beiffs De Medisons* [*NB: Beuffles de Medecines*] Lodge on their way to the Rickerreis, passed (3) a willow Island in a bind to the S. S.   (4) at 5 miles passd. a willow Island on the S. S.— wind hard from the South   in the evening I walked on an (5) Island nearly the middle of the river Called ⟨Shaved⟩ Grous Island, [*NB: (the wall of a village on this island)*] one of the men killed a Shee Brarrow, another man killed a Black tail Deer, the largest Doe I ever Saw (Black under her breast[)]   this Island is nearly 1 ¼ ms. Squar no timbr high and Covered with grass wild rye and Contains Great numbers of Grouse, we proceeded on a Short distance above the Island and Camped on the S. S.   a fine evening.

7th October

Course Distance & Reffurence

| N. 42° W. | 2 | miles to the mouth of a River Caled *Sur war car notre* a bend to the S. S. (1)   a village at Mo: (2) |

149

N. 30° E	3 ½	me to a Clump of bushes in a bend to the S. S. passing for ¾ mile on the L. S.
N. 30° W.	2	miles to a pt. of high land on the L Side, passed a willow Island (3)
N. 35° W.	7	on the L. Side passed a Sand bar on the S. S. (4).
N. 10° W.	1	mile on the L. S. to a pt.
N. 80° W.	3	miles to the left Side of an Island (5) in the mid river
N. 45° W.	1	mile to the head of the ⟨timbered la⟩ willows at the head of the Sd. ⟨Shaved⟩ Grouse Isld.
West	2 ½	to a point on the main S. S. a large Sand bar from the upper point of the Island high land on both Sides op-posit this Island.
	22	

1. The Moreau River reaches the Missouri in Dewey County, South Dakota. The Arikara village appears on *Atlas* map 25. Mattison (OR), 78; MRC map 44.

2. Grouse Island is the later Blue Blanket Island, between Dewey and Walworth counties, South Dakota; it is now inundated by Oahe Reservoir. Clark noted the walls of an abandoned village on the island on *Atlas* map 25, but did not comment on it in the text, although there is an interlineation reference in the codex journal. The village appears to have been a short-lived Arikara site probably occupied during the 1780s to 1790s. Stephenson. The grouse are probably the sharp-tailed grouse. Burroughs, 211–12; Cutright (LCPN), 81.

3. Just above Blue Blanket (Grouse) Island, in Walworth County, near the present town of Mobridge. Mattison (OR), 85; *Atlas* map 25; MRC map 45.

4. The text of the entry is interrupted here by the courses and distances; the two parts are brought together for ease of reading.

[Clark]

8th of October Monday 1804   a cool Morning   wind from the N. W. passed the mouth of a Small Creek on the L. S.[1] about 2½ Miles above the Isd.   Passed the Mouth of a River on the L. S. called by the *Ricaries* We-tar-hoo.[2]   this river is 120 yards wide, the water Confined within 20 yards, throws out mud with little Sand, great quanties of red Berries, resembling Currents[3] near the mouth of this river   Latd. 45° 39′ 5′ N. this river heads in the 1s Black Mountain,[4] 2 Miles higher up passed a Small River on the L. S. Called *Maropa*[5] 25 yards wide Chocked up with mud—   our hunters discovered a Ricara village on an Island a fiew miles above[6] we passed the 1s Ricara Village[7] about the center of the Island, in presence of Great numbers of Spectators and Camped above the Island on the L. S. at the foot of Some high land. (Mr. Gravotine a French man joined us as an interpeter)[8] The Island on which 1s Ricara Village is Situated, is about 3 miles long Seperated from the Main L. Side by a Narrow Deep Channel, those Indians Cultivate on the Island Corn Beens Simmins,[9] Tobacco &c &c.   after Landing Capt. Lewis with Mr. Gravelin and 3 men went to the Village, I formd a Camp on Shore[10] with the Perogue crew & guard, with the Boat at Anchor, Capt Lewis returned late, a french man and a Spaniard accompanied him[11]

Course Distance &c

N. 70° W.	2	m. to a Tree in a bend to the L. S. passed a Small creek L. S.
N. 10° W	1	M. to a point on the S. S.
N 15° E	2 ½	m. to the mouth of We terhoo River in a Bend to the L. S.
N. 40° E	1	m. on the L. S.
N. 30 E	1	m to the mouth of Maropa River on the L. S.
N 15° E	1	m. to the lower point of an Island
North	3 ½	m to a pt. on the L. S passed the 1s Ricara V. & the Island.

[Clark]   8th of *October Monday* 1804

a Cool morning   Set out early   the wind from the N. W.   proceeded on   passed the mouth of a Small Creek on the L. S. about 2½ miles above Grouse Island, (3) passed a willow Island which Divides the Current equilly.   (2) passed the mouth of a River called by the ricares *We tar hoo* on the L. S.   this river is 120 yards wide, the water of which at this time is Confined within 20 yards, dischargeing but a Small quantity, throwing out mud with Small propotion of Sand, great quantities of the red Berries, ressembling Currents, are on the river in every bend— 77° 33′ 0″ Lattitude from the Obsevation of to day at the mouth of this river [*NB: heads in the Black mountn*] is 45° 39′ 5″—North—   proceeded on passed a (3) Small river of 25 yards wide Called (4) ⟨*Rear par*⟩ or Beaver Dam R   this river [*WC: Maropa*] is intirely Chocked up with mud, with a Streem of 1 Inch Diamiter passing through, discharging no Sand, at 1 (5) mile passed

151

the lower pint of an Island close on the L. S. 2 of our men discovered the reckerrei village, about the Center of the Island on the L. Side on the main Shore. this Island is[12] about 3 miles long, Seperated from the L. S. by a Channel of about 60 yards wide verry Deep, The Isld. is covered with fields, where those people raise their Corn Tobacco Beens &c. &c. Great numbers of those People came on the Island to See us pass, we passed above the head of the Island & Capt. Lewis with 2 interpeters & 2 men went to the Village   I formed a Camp of the french & the guard on Shore, with one Sentinal on board of the boat at anchor, a pleasent evening   all things arranged both for Peace or War, This Village (6) is Situated about the Center of a large Island ⟨on⟩ near the L. Side ⟨at the⟩ & near the foot of Some high bald uneaven hills, Several french men Came up with Capt Lewis in a Perogue, one of which is a Mr. Gravellin a man well versed in the language of this nation and gave us Some information relitive to the Countrey naton &c

8th Octr

Courses Distance and reffurences

N. 70° W	2	miles to a tree in the bind to the L. Side, passed a small Creek L. S. (1)
N. 10° W.	1	miles to the pt. on the S. S.
N. 15° E.	2 ½	to the Mo: of a River We ter hoo in the bend to the L. S., (2) passing over a ⟨low [Bluff?] of Soft Slate Stone⟩ 120 yds wide ⟨passd⟩ a willow Island (3)
N. 40° E.	1	mile on the L. Side
N. 30 E	1	mile on the L. S. to the mouth of a Small river *Ma-ro-pa* (4)
N. 15° E	1	mile to the lower pt. of an Isd. (5)
North	3 ½	miles to a pt. on the S. S. passd. the head of the Isd. and the 1st. reckorrees Village (6) opsd. a Creek we Call after the 1st. Chief Kakawissassa Creek. L. S.
	12	

Orders

[Clark]   October the 8th 1804[13]

Robert Frazer being regularly inlisted and haveing become on of the

Corps of *Vollenteers* for *North Western Discovery,* he is therefore to be viewed & respected accordingly; and will be anexed to Sergeant Gass's mess.

Wm Clark Cpt &.

Meriwether Lewis

Capt. 1st U' S. Regt. Infty

River Marapa

Point of Observation No. 47.

[Lewis]

Monday October 8th 1804.[14]

On the Lard. shore, in the point fromed [formed] by the junction of the Weterhoo river with the Missouri.

Observed meridian Altd. of ☉'s U. L. with Sextant by the fore observation. 77° 35′ ″

Latitude deduced from this observation   N. 45° 39′ 5″

1. Bellsman, or Deadmans, Creek, in Corson County, South Dakota. *Atlas* map 25 shows it as "Slate Run." MRC map 45; MRY map 106.

2. Present Grand River, in Corson County. Maximilian has penciled in the present name on *Atlas* map 25. MRC map 45. The word may actually be the Mandan term *witahu,* "place characterized by oaks."

3. Buffaloberry.

4. The sources of the two principal forks of the Grand are in northwest South Dakota, to the north of the Black Hills as presently defined.

5. Later Rampart, or Oak, Creek, in Corson County. Mattison (OR), 88; *Atlas* map 25; MRC map 45. The word may be *mirapa,* which is Hidatsa for "beaver."

6. Later Ashley Island, with its village, Sawa-haini. Maximilian would later note that it was abandoned and it may have been he who scribbled across the site pictured on *Atlas* map 25. Ronda (LCAI), 53; Mattison (OR), 93–94; MRC map 45.

7. The Arikaras belonged to the Caddoan language family, most closely related to the Skiri Pawnees; they called themselves *sahnis* (people) or Star-rah-he (as Lewis and Clark termed it). As indicated by the many abandoned villages seen by Lewis and Clark, they moved a great deal within the Missouri valley. The Corps of Discovery found them in four villages, in Corson and Campbell counties, South Dakota, above the mouth of the Grand River. Most of the area is now inundated by the Oahe Reservoir.

The Arikaras were sedentary farmers in earth-lodge villages. Their social and political structure was distinctly hierarchical, with hereditary chiefs. Like the other village tribes of the upper Missouri, they were middlemen in intertribal trade. They had by 1804 been in contact with traders for several years, and venereal disease was already a problem.

The friendly relations between whites and Arikaras did not continue. The death of their chief who went to Washington at the captains' invitation apparently antagonized them, and they prevented the return of the Mandan chief Sheheke to his people in 1807.

During the fur-trade days of the 1820s and 1830s they were openly hostile to whites. This hostility must have influenced the unfavorable judgements of many later white traders and travelers, who emphasized the "Rees'" various deviations from Anglo-American mores. Eventually declining numbers, caused by disease and war with the Sioux, forced them to move to Like-a-Fishhook village in North Dakota with the Hidatsas and Mandans. This event, about 1845, finally brought about an alliance suggested by Lewis and Clark. The tribe now resides at Fort Berthold Reservation, North Dakota. Meyer; Denig; Holder; Parks (BVAP); Ronda (LCAI), 43–53; Thwaites (EWT), 5:127–41, 167–81, 6:111–31, 142–46, 23:386–95; Hodge, 1:83–86; *Atlas* map 25.

8. Joseph Gravelines was an associate or employee of Régis Loisel and Pierre-Antoine Tabeau, reported in 1811 as having lived among the Arikaras for more than twenty years. The captains found him useful as an Arikara interpreter, and in 1805 he accompanied the Arikara chief who journeyed to Washington. He had to return alone, bearing the news of the chief's death; the Arikaras gave him an unpleasant reception. The government later employed him as its representative among the Arikaras, an indication of the captains' high opinion of him. Henry Dearborn to James Wilkinson, April 9, 1806; Lewis to Pierre Chouteau, June 8, 1809, Jackson (LLC), 1:137 n. 71, 303–5 and n. 1, 2:431 n. 19, 437 n. 1, 455; Graveline; Thwaites (EWT), 4:127 and n. 84; Abel (TN), 41, 106 n. 28, 133 n. 101, 138 n. 109, 140.

9. Apparently Clark's version of "simlin" or "simnel," a term used in the Southern states for summer squashes. Criswell, 78. Probably cultivated varieties of pumpkins and squashes, including possibly *Cucurbita moschata* Duchesne, crookneck squash. Fernald, 1349.

10. The camp, where they would remain until October 11, was in Corson County, between Rampart (Maropa) Creek and Cathead Creek (Clark's Kakawissassa Creek), above Ashley Island. The area is now inundated by Oahe Reservoir. Mattison (OR), 95; *Atlas* map 25; MRC map 45; MRY map 107.

11. The Spaniard does not appear in the Codex C version. Possibly he was Joseph Garreau, who had lived with the Arikaras since 1793, and who has been variously described as a Spaniard or a Frenchman. An "old Spaniard" who was living with the Arikaras in 1807 acted as interpreter for Nathaniel Pryor's unsuccessful expedition to return the Mandan chief Sheheke to his home. Pryor's report to Clark on the venture indicates that the latter was already acquainted with the man. See below, March 16, 1805. The Frenchman, if he was not Gravelines, was probably Pierre-Antoine Tabeau. Pryor to Clark, October 16, 1807, Jackson (LLC), 2:434, 438 n. 4; Loos, 809.

12. The text of the entry is interrupted here by the courses and distances; the two parts are brought together for ease of reading.

13. From the Orderly Book in Clark's hand, except for Lewis's own signature.

14. Lewis's astronomical observation in Codex O.

[Clark]

9th *of October Tuesday 1804*   a windey night   Some rain, and the [wind] Continued So high & cold We could not Speek in Council with the Indians, we gave them Some Tobacco and informed them we would Speek tomorrow, all the grand Chiefs visited us to day also Mr Taboe,[1] a trader from St. Louis— Many Canoes of a Single Buffalow Skin made in the form of a Bowl Carrying generally 3 and Sometimes 5 & 6 men, those Canoes, ride the highest Waves— the Indians much asstonished at my Black Servent and Call him the big medison, this nation never Saw a black man before, the wind verry high, I saw at Several times to day 3 Squars in single Buffalow Skin Canoes loaded with meat Cross the River, at the time the waves were as high as I ever Saw them in the Missouri—

[Clark]   *9th of October* 1804 Tuesday

a windey rainey night, and Cold, So much So we Could not Speek with the Indians to day   the three great Chiefs and many others Came to See us to day, we gave them Some tobacco and informed them we would Speek on tomorrow, the day Continued Cold & windey   Some rain   Sorry Canoos of Skins passed down from the 2 villages[2] a Short distance above, and many Came to view us all day, much asstonished at my black Servent, who did not lose the oppertunity of his powers Strength &c. &.   this nation never Saw a black man before.

Several hunters Came in with loads of meat, I observed Several Canoos made of a Single buffalow Skin with 2 & 3 Thre Squars Cross the river to day in Waves as high as I ever Saw them on this river, quite uncomposed   I have a Slite Plurise this evening   Verry Cold &c. &.

  1st Chiefs name *Ka kawissassa* (lighting Crow.)[3]

  2d   do   do   *Pocasse* (or Hay)[4]

  3d   do   do   *Pia he to* (or Eagles feather)[5]

1. Pierre-Antoione Tabeau was born in Lachine Parish, near Montreal, and received an unusually good education in Montreal and Quebec; by 1776 he had gone west as an *engagé* in the fur trade. He lived for some years in the Illinois country, took an oath of fidelity to the United States in 1785, and moved to Missouri some time before 1795, when he first went up the Missouri River. He was an employee of Régis Loisel in 1802–1804, spending much of his time among the Arikaras. He was a major source of information for the captains on the Upper Missouri tribes, besides serving as an interpreter and general intermediary; the numerous journal entries that mention him suggest their good opinion of the man. His *Narrative* of his experiences, not published until 1939, is a major source

for the history and culture of the river tribes in the late eighteenth and early nineteenth centuries, although he is accused of inflating his own role and reducing that of Loisel. Abel (TN), 32–46 passim; Nasatir (BLC), 1 : 114, 354.

2. The two villages on the larboard side (which Clark may have considered as one) are known as the Leavenworth site. Going upriver, the first village was Rhtarahe with Pocasse as chief, and the second was Waho-erha with Piaheto as chief. Settled in the late 18th century, they were occupied by the Arikaras at various times and finally abandoned in 1832. The single village opposite was long ago destroyed by channel migration of the river and no remains were ever discovered. The villages are in Corson County (two villages) and Campbell County (the single village), South Dakota. Strong, 366–70; Krause, 15; Ronda (LCAI), 53–54. All the sites are shown on *Atlas* map 25. See also October 11, below.

3. His name may be rendered as *kaakaawiisisa'*, "crow going across." Tabeau recalled this chief as one who gave him much trouble, constantly demanding gifts and stirring up difficulties when disappointed. Abel (TN), 125, 141 and n. 116, 143 and n. 119, 144.

4. Tabeau's "Pacosse—The Straw" (*La Paille*) which may be *pákUs*, "straw"; he gave Tabeau an unpleasant reception in 1803. Ibid., 125, 139–40.

5. His name may be given as *pi'a' hiítu'*, "eagle feather." He may be the same person as "Too ne," or Whip-poor-will, otherwise called Ar ke tar na shar, or Chief of the Town (*akitaaneešaánu'*, "band chief"), the latter perhaps a title rather than a proper name. Toone was the chief who accompanied the expedition to the Mandans and Hidatsas to make peace and seek an alliance against the Sioux. If Piaheto and Toone are the same person, then he may also be the chief who died in Washington in 1806, to the detriment of United States-Arikara relations. Jefferson, in writing condolences to the tribe on the man's death, was uncertain which of the above names was the correct one, finally settling on "Arketarnawhar chief of the town" after writing and crossing out "Piaketa" and "Toone" with their English versions. Osgood (FN), 158–59 n. 9; Foley & Rice (RMC), 7; Abel (TN), 125; Jefferson to the Arikaras, April 11, 1806, Jackson (LLC), 1 : 306 and n. 2.

[Clark]

10th of October 1804   at 11 oClock the wind Shifted from S. E to N W. Mr. Taboe visited us—   we hear that Some jealousy exists as to the Chiefs to be made—   at 1 oclock the Cheifs all assembled under an orning near the Boat, and under the American Flag.   we Delivered a Similar Speech to those delivered the Ottoes & Sioux, made three Chiefs, one for each Village and gave them Clothes & flags—   1s Chief is name *Ka-ha-wiss assa* lighting ravin   2d Chief *Po-casse* (Hay) & the 3rd *Piaheto* or Eagles Feather—   after the Council was over we Shot the Air gun, which astonished them, & they all ⟨Departed⟩ left us, ⟨we⟩ I observed 2 Sioux in the Council one of them I had Seen below, they Came to interceed with the Ricaras to Stop us as we were told—   the Inds. much astonished at my black

Servent, who made him Self more turrible in thier view than I wished him to Doe as I am told telling them that before I cought him he was wild & lived upon people, young children was verry good eating   Showed them his Strength &c. &c.—[1]   Those Indians are not fond of Licquer of any Kind—[2]

[Clark]   10th of *October Wednesday* 1804.[3]

a fine forming wind from the S. E   at about 11 oClock the wind Shifted, to the N. W.   we prepare all things ready to Speak to the Indians, Mr. Tabo & Mr. Gravolin Came to brackfast with us   the Chiefs &. came from the lower Town, but none from the 2 upper Towns, which is the largest, we Continue to delay & waite for them   at 12 oClock Dispatchd Gravelin to envite them to Come down, we have every reason to believe that a jellousy exists between the Villages for fear of our makeing the 1st Cheif from the lower Village, at one oClock the Cheifs all assembled & after Some little Cerrimony the Council Commenced, we informd them what we had told the others before i' e' Ottoes & Seaux.   made 3 Cheif 1 for each Village.   gave them presents.

after the Council was Over we Shot the air guns[4] which astonished them much, the[y] then Departed and we rested Secure all night,

Those Indians wer much astonished at my Servent, They never Saw a black man before, all flocked around him & examind. him from top to toe, he Carried on the joke and made himself more turibal than we wished him to doe.   (Thos Indians were not fond of Spirits Licquer. of any kind[)]

1. Legends grew up about York among the Arikaras and also certain stereotypes were added by later writers because of such episodes. Betts (SY), 16–18, 58, 65–66, 69–70.

2. According to Biddle's account the captains offered the Arikaras whiskey, as was customary in such negotiations, but the chiefs refused, "with this sensible remark that, they were surprised that their father should present to them a liquor which would make them fools." See October 18, 1805. Coues (HLC), 1:160.

3. On this date Ordway writes, "we left one of our frenchman with Mr Tabbow & took his Soon in his place." It is unclear whether this is the son of Tabeau (who is not known to have had a son) or the son of the unnamed *engagé*. Nor is it clear whether the Frenchman intended to remain at the Arikara villages, leaving the expedition, or was only left at the lowest village temporarily. If the former, he was probably paid off in cash, like others discharged that fall, leaving no written record of his departure. Nothing further appears

about the son. On February 28, 1805, Ordway notes that a "Mr Roie" came up to Fort Mandan from the Arikara villages with Gravelines. This could be Peter Roi, an expedition *engagé*, who may be the man left at the Arikaras. Roi could have been discharged at Fort Mandan, however—the lack of a record of his discharge indicating payment in cash in the fall of 1804—and then have gone down to the Arikara villages.

4. This is the only indication that there may have been more than one air gun with the party, and it is very likely a slip of the pen.

[Clark]

11th *of October Thursday 1804*   wind S. E.   at 11 oClock met the 1s Chief in Council,[1] he Thanked us for what we had given him & his people promised to attend to our advise, and Said the road was open for us and no one Dar[e] Shut it &c. &.   we took him and one Chief on board and Set out, on our way took in the 2d Chief at the mo of a Small Creek,[2] and Came too off the 2d village which is 3 miles above the Island, we walked up with the 2 & 3 Chiefs to their villages which is Situated on each Side of a Small Creek,[3] the[y] gave us Something to eat in thier way, after Conversations on various Subjects & Beareing the civilities of those people who are both pore & dirtey we informed the Chiefs we would here what they had to Say tomorrow and returned on board about 10 oClock P M. Those people gave us to eat Corn & Beans, a large well flavoured Been which they rob the Mice of in the Plains and is verry nurishing—[4]   all tranquillity—

[Clark]   11th *October* Thursday 1804

a fine morning the wind from the S. E.   at 11 oClock we met the Grand Chief in Council & and he made a Short Speech thanking us for what we had Given him & his nation promisseing to attend to the Council we had given him & informed us the road was open & no one dare Shut it, & we might Departe at pleasure, at 1 oClock we Set out for the upper villages 3 miles distant, the Grand Chief & nephew on board, *proceeded on*   at 1 mile took in the 2d Chief & Came too off the first Second village Seperated from the 3rd by a Creek   after arrangeing all matters we walked up with the 2d Chief to his village, and Set talking on various Subjects untile late   we also visited the upper or 3rd Village each of which gave us Something to eate in their way, and a fiew bushels of Corn Beens &. &c.

after being treated by everry civility by those people who are both pore & Durtey we returned to our boat at about 10 oClk. P M.   informing them before we Departed that we would Speek to them tomorrow at there Seperate Villages. Those people gave us to eate bread made of Corn & Beens, also Corn & Beans boild. a large Been, [*NB: of*] which they rob the mice of the Prarie [*NB: who collect & discover it*] which is rich & verry nurrishing also [*NB: S*]quashes &c.   all Tranquillity.

[Clark][5]

(*Ricares*)

October the 11th Thursday 1804   we met in Council to hear what the Grand Chief *Ka kaw issassa* had to Say in answer to the Speech of yesterday

The Grand Chief rose and spoke as follows i, e',—

My Fathers—!   My heart is glader than it ever was before to See my fathers.—   a *repetition*.

If you want the road open no one Can provent it   it will always be open for you.

Can you think any one Dare put their hands on your rope of your boat. No!   not one dar

When you Get to the mandans we wish you to Speak good words with that Nation for us.   we wish to be at peace with them.

It gives us pain that we do not Know how to work the Beaver, we will make Buffalow roabs the best we Can.

when you return if I am living you will See me again the same man

The Indian in the prarie know me and listen to my words, when you [come] they will meet to See you.

We Shall look at the river with impatienc for your return.   Finished

Point of observation No. 48.

[Lewis]   *Thursday October 11th 1804.*[6]

At our camp on the Lard. shore a small distance above the upper pooint of an Island on which the lower village of the Ricaras is situated.

Observed Equal Altitudes of the ☉ with Sextant.

	h	m	s		h	m	s
A. M.	9	8	7	P. M.	3	41	49
"	10	1		"		42	36
"	11	57		"		44	40

Altitude by Sextant at the time of observtn.   42° 16′ 45″

1. See below with this day's entries for the speech.

2. Possibly Clark's Kakawissassa Creek, later Cathead Creek. *Atlas* map 25; MRC map 45.

3. The second village may be the one on the starboard shore, in Campbell County, South Dakota. They camped on the opposite side, in Corson County, near the two neighboring villages on that side, which Clark seems alternately to regard as either one or two. The small creek is apparently one which appears nameless on MRC map 45 and MRY maps 113, 114 but not on *Atlas* map 25. The area is now inundated by Oahe Reservoir. Mattison (OR), 97–98.

4. The bean is the product of the hog peanut or ground bean plant, *Amphicarpa bracteata* (L.) Fern. Fernald, 938–39. The Arikaras obtained them from the underground stores of the meadow mouse or vole, *Microtus pennsylvanicus*. It is said that they always left some other food in its place for the mice. Cutright (LCPN), 100; Gilmore (UPI), 43–44.

5. This material is on a loose sheet in the Voorhis Collection, Missouri Historical Society. See Indian Speeches, Appendix C, vol. 2.

6. Lewis's astronomical observation from Codex O.

[Clark]

12th of October Friday   after Brackfast we joined the Chiefs & Indians on the bank who wer waiting for us, and proseeded to the 1st village[1] and Lodge of the *Pocasse,* This man Spok[2] at Some lengths, to the Sam[e] purpote of the 1s Chief, & Declareing his intentions of visiting his great father, Some Doubts as to his Safty in Passing the Sioux, requested us to take a Chief of their nation and make a good peace with the Mandan for them, that they Knew that they were the Cause of the war by Killing the 2 Mandan Chiefs— this Chief & people gave us about 7 bushels of Corn, Some Tobacco of their own make,[3] and Seed Legins & a Robe We proceeded to the 3rd Chiefs Village which is the largest,[4] after the usial Seremoney of Eating Smokg. &. he Spoke to near the Same amount of the last Chief, & more pleasently, he gave us 10 bushels of Corn, Some Beens & Simmins, after he had Spoken, and [I] gave Some Sketches of the Power & Magnitude of Our Countrey, we returned to our Boat, I have the rhumetism on my neck [*blot*]   the Chiefs accompanied us on board, w[e] gave them Some Sugar Salt and a Sun Glass each, and after eating a little they returned on Shore leaveing one to accompany us to the Mandans, and we Set out viewed by men womin & children of each village   proceeded on about 9½ miles and Camped on the S S.[5]   Clear & Cold—   The Ricaras Are about 500 men   Mr. Taboe say 600   able to bear arms, and the remains of ten different tribes of Panias   reduced by the Small Pox & wares [wars] with the Sioux, they are tall Stout men corsily featured, their womin Small & industerous   raise great quantites of corn beans &c also Tobacco for the men to Smoke, they collect all the wood and doe the Drudgery common amongst Savages—   Their language is So corrupted that many lodges of the Same village with dificuelty under Stand all that each other Say—   They are Dirty, Kind, pore, & extravegent; possessing natural pride, no begers, rcive what is given them with pleasure, Thier houses are close together & Towns inclosed with Pickets, thier Lodges are 30 to 40 feet in Diamute[r] Covered with earth on Neet Poles Set end wise resting on 4 forks Supporting Beems Set in a Square form near the Center, and lower about 5 feet high   other forks all around Supt. Strong Beems, from 8 to 10 of those, with a opening at top of about 5 to 6 feet Square, on the Poles which pass to the top, Small Willow & grass is put across to Support the earth—[6]   The Sioux exchange, Some merchndze of Small value which they get from Mr. Cameron[7] of St. Peters for Corn &c and have great influence over this people   treat them roughly and keep them in contineal dread—   The Ricaras are at war with the Crow Indians and Mandans—&c. &—   The Ricaras, have a custom Similar to the Sioux in maney instances, they think they cannot Show a Sufficient acknowledgement without [giving?] to their guest handsom Squars and think they are despised if they are not recved

The Sioux followed us with women two days   we put them off.   the Ricarries we put off dureing the time we were near their village—   2 were Sent by a man to follow us, and overtook us this evening, we Still procisted in a refusial—[8]   The Dress of the Ricara men is Simpally a pr. of Mockersons & Legins, a flap, and a Buffalow Robe—   Their Hair is long and lais loose   their arms & ears are decerated with trinkets—

The womin Dress Mockersons & Legins & Skirt of the Skin of the Cabre or Antelope, long fringed & [roab?] to the fringes & with Sleaves, verry white, and Roabes— all were Dressed to be without hare in the Summer

Those people make large Beeds of Diferrent colours, out of glass or Beeds of Dift colours, verry ingeniously

Course & Deistance &c.

N. 45° E.	2	m. To the Mouth of a Creek between the two upper Ricara villages
S. 75 E.	1 ½	m. to a Point on the L. S.
N 45° E	2	m to a pt of wood L. S.
N. 45° E	2	m. to a pt. of wood on the L S[9]
N. 20° W.	2 ½	m to a pt. on the L. S.
N. 8° W	1 ½	m to a pt. on the L S. river narrow and large wooded points

[Clark]   12th *October Friday* 1804

I rose early   after brackfast we joined the Indians who were waiting on the bank for us to come out and go and Council, we accordingly joined them and went to the house of the 2nd Chief *Lassil* [Pocasse] where there was many Chief and warriers & about 7 bushels of Corn, a pr Leagins a twist of their Tobacco & Seeds of 2 Kind of Tobacco we Set Some time before the Councill Commenced   this man Spoke at Some length declareing his dispotion to believe and prosue our Councils, his intention of going to Visit his great father   acknowledged the Satisfaction ⟨which he⟩ in receiveing the presents &c.   rais'g a Doubt as to the Safty on passing the nations below particularly the Souex.   requested us to take a Chief of their nation and make a good pact with Mandins & nations above.   after answering[10] those parts of the 2d Chiefs Speech which required it, which appeared to give General Satisfaction we went to the Village of the 3rd Chief and as usial Some Serimony took place before he Could Speek to us on the Great Subject. This Chief Spoke verry much in the Stile on nearly the Same Subjects of the other Chief who Set by his Side, more Sincear & pleasently, he presented us with about 10 bushels of Corn Some beens & quashes all of which we acksepted with much pleasure, after we had ansd. his Speech & give them Some account of the Magnitude & power of our Countrey which pleased and astonished them verry much we returned to our boat, the Chiefs accompanied us on board, we gave them Some Sugar a little Salt, and a Sun Glass, & Set 2 on Shore & the third proceeded on with us to the Mandens by name _____,[11] at 2 oClock we Set out the inhabitints of the two Villages Viewing us from the banks, we proceeded on about 9½ miles and Camped on the S. S. at Some woods passed, the evening Clear & pleasent Cooler

The Nation of the Rickerries [*NB: Rickaras*] is about [*WC: ⟨450 men⟩ Mr. Taboe says, I think 500 men*] 600 men able to bear arms [*NB: Mr Tabat is right*]   a Great perpotion of them have fusees   they appear to be peacefull, their men tall and perpotiend, womin Small and industerous, raise great quantities of Corn Beens Simmins &c. also Tobacco for the men to Smoke   they Collect all the wood and do the drugery as Common amongst Savages.

Thise ⟨nation is⟩ [*NB: two villages are*] made up of ⟨10⟩ [*NB: nine*] Different Tribes of the Pania [*NB: Panies*],[12] who had formerly been Seperate, but by Commotion and war with their neighbours have Come reduced and compelled to Come together for protection,[13] The Curruption of the language of those different Tribes has So reduced the language that the Different Villages do not understade all the words of the others.—   Those people are Durtey, Kind, pore, & extravigent pursessing ⟨Pride⟩ national pride.   not beggarley reive what is given with great pleasure, Live in worm houses large and built in an oxigon [octagon] form forming a Cone at top which is left open for the *Smoke* to pass, those houses are generally 30 or 40 foot Diamiter. Covd. with earth on poles willows & grass[14] to prevent the earths passing thro',

Those people express an inclination to be at peace with all nations— The Seaux who trade the goods which they get of the British Traders for their corn, and great influence over the Rickeres, poisen their minds and keep them in perpetial dread.

I Saw Some of the ⟨Chien or Dog⟩ [*NB: Chyenne*] Indians, also a ⟨fiew⟩ man of a nation under the *Court new*—[15]   This nation is at war with the Crow Indians & have 3 Children prisoners.

a curious Cuistom with the Souix as well as the reckeres is to give handsom Squars to those whome they wish to Show Some acknowledgements to—   The Seauix we got Clare of without taking their Squars, they followed us with Squars 13th[16] two days. The Rickores we put off dureing the time we were at the Towns but 2 Handsom young Squars were Sent by a man to follow us, they Came up this evening and peresisted in their Civilities.

Dress of the men of this nation is Simply a pr. mockerson, Leagins, flap in front & a Buffalow roabe, with ther [their?] arms & ears Deckorated

The women, wore Mockersons leagins fringed and a Shirt of Goat Skins, Some with Sleaves.   this garment is longe & Genlry. White & fringed, tied at the waste with a roabe, in Summer without hair.

12th Octr.

Course Distance & reffurence

N. 45 E	2	Miles to the mouth of a creek between the 2 upper villages of the Rickeres L. S. (1)
S. 75° E.	1 ½	miles the point on the L. S. passed the Village (2)
N. 45° E.	2	mes. to a point of wood on the L. S.
N. 20° W.	2 ½	miles to a pt. on the S. S.
N. 8° W.	1 ½	miles to a pt. on L. S. passed a Sand bar.
	9 ½	

[Clark]   [*undated, October 12, 1804*][17]

2nd Chief Ricaras

My Father, I am glad to See this is a fine Day to here the good Councils & talk good talk

I am glad to See you & that your intentions are to open the road for all we See that our Grand father has Sent you to open the road   we See it

Our Grand father by Sending you means to take pity on us

Our Grand father has Sent you with tobacco to make peace with all nations, we think

The first nation who has recomended the road to be clear and open.

You Come here & have Directed all nations which you have met to open & clear the road.

[If?] you come to See the water & roads to Clear them as Clear as possible

164

you just now Come to See us, & we wish you to tell our Grand ftar that we wish the road to be kept Clear & open.

I expect the Chief in the next Town will tell you the Same to move on & open the road

I think when you Saw the nations below the[y] wish you to open the road— (or something to that amount:

when you passd. the Souex they told you the Same I expect. we See you here to day we are pore our women have no Strouds & Knives to Cut their meat take pitty on us when you return.

you Come here & Derect us to Stay at home & not go to war, we Shall do So, we hope you will when you get to the *Mandins* you will tell them the Same & Cleer the road, no one Dar to Stop you, you go when you please,—

The you tell us to go Down, we will go and See our grand father & here & receve his Gifts, and think fully that our nation will be covered after our return, our people will look for us with the same impatience that our Grand father looks for your return, to Give him

If I am going to See my grand father, many bad nations on the road, I am not afraid to Die for the good of my people (all Cried around him.)

The Chief By me will go to the Mandans & hear what they will Say. (we agree'd.)

The verry moment we Set out to go down we will Send out my Brother to bring all the Nation in the open prarie to See me part on this Great mission to See my Great father.

our people hunting Shall be glad to here of your being here & they will all Come to See, as you Cannot Stay they must wate for your return to See you, we are pore take pity on our wants

The road is for you all to go on, who do you think will injure a white man when they come to exchange for our Roabes & Beaver

after you Set out many nations in the open plains may Come to make war against us, we wish you to Stop their guns & provent it if possible. Finished

3d Chief of Ricares

My fathers I will see the Indians below & See if they have the hart as they tell you

The nation below is the ⟨Mandan⟩ Mahas & Ottes & but one nation, (the Souix[)] has not a good heart.

I always look at the 1t Chief & the 2d whin they go & will also follow ther example & go on also

You See those 2 men they are chiefs, when I go they will take Care, they beleve your words.

Mabie we will not tell the trooth, as to the Child   perhaps they will not wish to go.

My Children the old women & men whin I return I can then give them, Some a Knife Some powder & others Ball &c. What is the matter if we was to go for nothing   my great Chief wish to go, I wish to go also.

when I go to See my Grand father I wish to return quicke for fear of my people being uneasy.

my Children are Small & perhaps will be uneasy whin I may be Safe

I must go, I also wish to go, perhaps I may when I return make my people glad

I will Stay at home & not go to War even if my people are Struck

we will believ your word but I fear the Indians above will not believe your word.

I will think that ½ of the men who will return will Stay in this Village ½ below in the other villages

what did the Seaus tell you—   (we informd them)

1. Evidently they walked, which would mean that this village (Rhtarahe) was the nearer to their camp of the two on the larboard side of the Missouri in Corson County, South Dakota. *Atlas* map 25.

2. For his speech and that of the next chief see below in this day's entry.

3. *Nicotiana quadrivalvis* Pursh. Goodspeed, 451; Gilmore (SCAT); Cronquist et al., 72.

4. The other village on the larboard shore (Waho-erha), just upstream from the one they had already visited. *Atlas* map 25.

5. In Campbell County, South Dakota, in an area now inundated by the Oahe Reservoir. *Atlas* map 25; Mattison (OR), 108–9; MRC map 45.

6. Gass gives an excellent description of an Arikara earth lodge on October 10.

7. Murdoch Cameron, a Scotsman, was a trader on the St. Peters, or Minnesota, River, whom Lewis and Clark believed to have a bad influence on the Indians. They never met him, but in 1805 Zebulon Montgomery Pike warned him against trading liquor to the Sioux. Cameron died in 1811, reportedly from being poisoned by a Sioux. See below, February 28, March 18, 1805, and Lewis's Summary of Rivers and Creeks, Chapter 10. Clark

to Hugh Heney, July 20, 1806, Observations and Reflections of Lewis [August 1807], Jackson (LLC), 1:312–13 and n. 1, 2:703 and n. 8; Jackson (JP), 1:33 and n. 61, 34, 37, 39, 62 and n. 104, 120, 122.

8. Or perhaps the party did not refuse. See Ronda (LCAI), 62–64. Cultural explanations for this seemingly promiscuous practice are given in ibid. and in Kehoe. It was sanctioned for purposes of trade, for hospitality, and, most importantly, it was a means by which power was transferred from older or more powerful men to aspiring young men via their wives.

9. The line is probably a repeat of the preceding.

10. The text of the entry is interrupted at this point by the courses and distances; the two parts are joined together for ease of reading.

11. If this man was the same as Piaheto, whose name was already recorded, it is hard to see why Clark left a blank, unless he had become aware that the man had a multiplicity of names and was waiting to decide which to use.

12. *Atlas* map 25 indicates that the village on the starboard side of the Missouri, in Campbell County, was the one composed of nine separate groups of people, and says "The other two villages are Ricaries proper." The reference to "Panias" (Pawnees) refers to their being of the same Caddoan language family as the Pawnees. This shows the diversity of language and culture often found among Indians classed by whites as belonging to the same "tribe." Hodge, 1:83–86; Parks (NCL).

13. Clark here ignores the predominant role played by smallpox in reducing the population of the river tribes. Elsewhere he notes the devastation wrought by the disease. White (WW), 325–27; Stearn & Stearn.

14. Possibly *Andropogon gerardi* Vitman, big bluestem, or *Spartina pectinata* Link, prarie cordgrass or sloughgrass. Gilmore (UPI), 16, 14.

15. The Cheyennes were a small tribe of the Algonquian language family, who moved from Minnesota into the Dakotas in the eighteenth century, ahead of the Sioux. In the early 1800's, having adopted the nomadic hunting life of the plains, they became allies of the Sioux. Their role in the wars later in the nineteenth century won them a fame out of proportion to their numbers. The identity of the "nation under the *Court new*"—that is, Côte Noir, Black Hills—is not readily apparent. Possibly they were Kiowas, some of whom were still near the Black Hills near the end of the eighteenth century, or possibly Arapahoes. Hyde (IHP), 144, 151–52.

16. "13th" here may mean that the two Arikara women mentioned below continued to follow them on October 13 as they had on the twelfth.

17. This material is on loose sheets in the Voorhis Collection, Missouri Historical Society. See Indian Speeches, Miscellaneous Documents of Lewis and Clark, Appendix C, vol. 2. The date was established from references in the regular entry.

[Clark]

13th of October Satturday 1804   Newmon Confined for Mutinous expressions,[1] proceeded on   passed a Camp of *Sioux* on the S. S.   those people did not Speak to us.   passed a Creek on the S. S. 18 miles above the Ricaras I call Stone Ido[l] Creek, this Creek heads in a Small lake at no great distance,[2] near which there is a Stone to which the Indians ascribe great virtue &. &c.   at 21 Miles passed a Creek 15 yds wide on the L. S I call Pocasse,[3] we observed great quantites of grapes, a fine Breez from S E   Camped on the L. S.[4]   Some rain thus evening, we formed a Court Martial of 7 of our party to Try Newmon, they Senteenced him 75 Lashes and banishment from the party—   The river narrow current jentle & wood plenty on the Bottoms   the up land is as usial Open divircified plains, generally rich & leavel.

Course & Distance

N. 60° W.	3	m. to a pt on the S. S.
N. 40° W.	2	m. to a point of timber on the L. S.
N. 10° W.	2	m to a point on L. S.
N. 53° W.	1 ½	m to a point on the S. S.
North	2	m to a point on the L. S. opposit a Creek on the L. S.
N. 18° E.	3	miles to the upper point of Some timber on the S. S. & Camped

[Clark]   13th Octr.

Course distance & reffurence

N. 60° W.	3	miles to a pt. on the S. S.
N. 40 W.	2	miles to a pt. of timber on L. S
N. 10° W.	2	miles to the pt. on the L. S.
N. 53 W.	1 ½	mes. to a pt. on the S. S.
North	2	mes. to a pt. on the L. S. opsit the mouth of a Creek on the ⟨L⟩ S. S. (1)
N. 70° W.	4 ½	miles to a pt. on the S. S. passing a Island (2) and opsd. a Creek L. S. (3)[5]
N. 18° E	3	mes. to the upper point of some wood on the S. S. and Camped
	18	

13th of October Satturday 1804

one man J. Newmon Confined for mutinous expression   Set out early proceeded on, passd. a Camp of Seauex on the S. S.   those people only viewed us & did not Speak one word—   The visiters of last evening all except one returned which is the Brother of the Chief we have on board passed (1) a Creek on the S. S. 13 yds. at 18 me. above the Town heading in Some Ponds a Short Diste. to the N. E we call Stone Idol C. (well to observe here that the Yankton or R Jacque heads at about 2 Days March of this place Easterly, the R de Seauex one Day further, the *Chien* [*NB: Chayenne (the Chays formerly there*] a branch of R. Rouche [*NB: Rouge*] Still beyend, and the River *St. Peters* 4 Days March from this place on the Same direction   Informtn. of the Rickores).[6]   passed 2 large willow (2) & Sand Islands above the mouth of the last Creek—   at 21 miles above the Village passed a (3) Creek about 15 yards wide on the L. S. we Call after 2d Chief Pocasse (or Hay)   nearly opposit this creek a fiew miles from the river on the S. S. 2 Stones resembling humane persons & one resembling a Dog is Situated in the open Prarie, to those Stone the Rickores pay Great reverance make offerings [*NB: (votive dress [or press?] &c*] whenever they pass (Infomtn. of the Chief & Intepeter)   those people have a Curious Tredition of those Stones, one was a man in Love, one a Girl whose parents would not let marry, [*NB: The man as is customary went off to mourn, the feamale followed.*] the Dog went to mourn with them   all turned to Stone gradually, Commenceing at the feet. Those people fed on grapes untill they turned, & the woman has a bunch of grapes yet in her hand   on the river near the place those are Said to be Situated, we obsd. a greater quantity of fine grapes than I ever Saw at one place.

The river about the Island on which the lower Rickores Village is Situated is narrow and Conts. a great propotion of Timber than below, the bottoms on both Sides is Covered with timber   the up lands naked   the Current jentle and Sand bars Confined to the points Generally

We proceeded on under a fine Breeze from the S.E. and Camped late at the upper part of Some wood on the ⟨L⟩ Starboard Side, Cold & Some rain this evening.   we Sent out hunters   Killed one Deer.

We Tried the Prisoner Newmon last night[7] by 9 of his Peers[8] they did "Centence him 75 Lashes & Disbanded the party."

Orders

[Lewis and Clark]   13th of October 1804[9]

A court Martial to Consist of nine members will set to day at 12 oClock for the trial of John Newman now under Confinement   Capt. Clark will attend to the forms & rules of a president without giveing his opinion

Detail for the Court Martial

Sert. John Ordaway
Sergeant Pat. Gass
Jo. Shields
H. Hall
Jo. Collins
Wm. Werner
Wm. Bratten
Jo. Shannon
⟨P Wiser⟩
Silas Goodrich

Meriwether Lewis Capt.
1st U' S. Regt. Infty.
Wm Clark Capt
or [on?] E. N W D[10]

In conformity to the above order the Court martial convened this day for the trial of John Newman, charged with "having uttered repeated expressions of a highly criminal and mutinous nature; the same having a tendency not only to distroy every principle of military discipline, but also to alienate the affections of the individuals composing this Detachment to their officers, and disaffect them to the service for which they have been so sacredly and solemnly engaged."— The Prisonar plead *not guilty* to the charge exhibited against him. The court after having duly considered the evidence aduced, as well as the defense of the said prisonor, are unanimously of opinion that the prisonar John Newman is guilty of every part of the charge exhibited against him, and do sentence him ⟨under the articles of the [*blank*] Section of the⟩ agreeably to the rules and articles of war, to receive seventy five lashes on his bear back, and to be henceforth discarded from the perminent party engaged for North Western discovery; two thirds of the Court concurring in the sum and nature of the punishment awarded. the commanding officers approve and confirm the sentence of the court, and direct the punishment take place tomorrow between the hours of one and two P. M.— The commanding officers further direct that John Newman in future be attatched to the mess and crew of the red Perogue as a labouring hand on board the same, and that he be deprived of his arms and accoutrements, and not be permited the honor of mounting guard untill further orders; the commanding officers further direct that in lue of the guard duty from which Newman has been exempted by virtue of this order, that he shall be exposed to such drudgeries as they may think proper to direct from time to time with a view to the general relief of the detachment.—

1. The incident may actually have occurred on October 12, since Ordway notes Newman's confinement in his entry for that day. He also notes that Moses B. Reed, the erstwhile deserter, was confined at the same time. No other record or journal mentions Reed's connection with the affair, and there is no indication of what his offence was. See sketches of Reed and Newman in Appendix A, vol. 2. See also Chuinard (CMML) for an assessment of this incident.

2. The stream has no name on *Atlas* map 26, but the lake from which it flows is clearly shown. It is later Spring, or Hermaphrodite, Creek, reaching the Missouri in Campbell County, South Dakota. Its actual source is much farther east, in McPherson County, South Dakota. MRC map 46.

3. Named after the second Arikara chief; later Hunkpapa Creek, in Corson County, South Dakota, named after a Teton Sioux division. Just above the mouth of the creek Manuel Lisa later erected his trading post, Fort Manuel (1812–13). It was there, according to the best evidence, that Sacagawea, the expedition's Shoshone interpreter and only woman member, died on December 20, 1812. The fort site is now inundated at high water by Oahe Reservoir. Mattison (OR), 111–16; Appleman (LC), 352; Anderson (CFP), 60–61; *Atlas* map 26; MRC map 46.

4. In Campbell County, about a mile south of the present North Dakota state line; their last camp in present South Dakota on the westbound journey. *Atlas* map 26; Coues (HLC), 1:166 n. 35; MRC map 46.

5. This course is missing from the Field Notes entry.

6. The Jacques is the James River. The "R de Seauex" may be the Bois des Sioux River, between Minnesota and the Dakotas, rather than the Big Sioux; either is difficult to fit into this description. The "Chien" is the Sheyenne River in eastern North Dakota, rather than the Cheyenne River in western South Dakota. Biddle has made some spelling changes here (not shown) as well as interlineations. The "Rouche" (Rouge) is the Red River of the North. The St. Peters is the Minnesota River.

7. Newman was tried on October 13. Clark's reference to "last night" indicates that he

wrote this Codex C entry the following day. At this time, it would appear, he was copying and expanding his Field Notes in his notebook journal soon after the former were written.

8. The Field Notes entry, above, says that there were seven men on the court; the numeral is quite distinct. The Orderly Book's record of the trial lists nine members.

9. The first portion of this order in the Orderly Book is in Clark's hand, except for Lewis's own signature. The remainder, after the signatures, is in Lewis's hand.

10. "N W D" probably stands for "northwest discovery." The "E" may stand for "engineer," since Clark had expected to be commissioned a captain in the Corps of Engineers, and the captains were concealing from the men the fact that he had actually only been commissioned a second lieutenant in the Artillery. Alternatively, "E" might stand for "expedition."

[Clark]

14th of October Sunday 1804   Some rain last night   we Set out in the rain which continued all day   passed a Creek on the L. S. *Piaheto* 15 yds Wide,[1]   halted on a Sand bar and had the punishmt inflicted on New-mon, which caused the indian Chieif to cry untill the thing was explained to him   Camped opposit an antient fortification which is on the L. S,[2] when I explained to the Chief the Cause of whipping N—   he observed that examples were necessary & that he himself had made them by Death, but his nation never whiped even from their bearth.

Course & Distance

S. 70° W	3[3]	m to a ⟨point on the L. S.⟩ Bend on the L. S
N. 63° W	2	m. to a point on the S. S. passed a Creek L. S
N. 30° W.	1 ½	to a Tree on the L. S.
N 40° E.	1 ½	to Some trees on the S. S.
N 60° W	3	m to ⟨Some trees⟩ a pt. on the L S
N. 70°	3	m to a point on the S. S.— passed an Antient fortification.

[Clark]   14th *of October Sunday* 1804.

Some rain last night all wet & Cold,   we Set early the rain contind ⟨untill⟩ all ⟨oClock⟩[4] Day   at [*blank*] miles we passed a (1) Creek in the L. S. 15 yards wide   this Creek we Call after the 3rd Chief *Piaheto* (or Eagles feather)   at 1 oClock we halted on a Sand bar & after Dinner executed the Sentence of the Court Martial So far a[s] giveing the Corporal punishment, & proceeded on a fiew miles, the wind a head from N. E.   Camped in a Cove of the bank on the S. S.   imediately opposit our Camp on the L. Side I observe an antient fortification the walls of which appear to be 8 or 10 feet high, [*NB: most of it washed in*]   the evening wet and disagreeable, the river Something wider more timber on the banks

The punishment of this day allarmd. the Indian Chief verry much, he Cried aloud (or effected to Cry)   I explained the Cause of the punishment and the necessity [*NB: of it,*] ⟨which⟩ He [*NB: also*] thought examples were also necessary, & he himself had made them by Death, his nation never whiped even their Children, from their burth.

14th

Courses & Distance & reffurencs.

S. 70° W.	1	mes. to a pt. on the L. S. the Same course continud 2 me. to a bend L. S.
N. 63° W.	2	mes. to the pt. on the S. S. passd. a creek on the L. S. (1)
N. 30° W.	1 ½	me. to a large Tree in the L. S.
N. 40° E	1 ½	mes to Some trees on the S. S.
N. 60° W.	3	mes. to a pt. on the L. S. Passing
N. 70° W.	3	miles to a point on the S. S. passed an antient fortification on the L. S.
	12	

1. In Codex C and on *Atlas* map 26 Clark has used both the Indian name of the Arikara chief for whom he named the creek and the English version, "Eagles Feather." Eagle Feather Creek, in Corson County, South Dakota, appears on MRC map 46; later it became Bald Head Creek. It enters the Missouri about a mile downstream from the state line. MRY map 119.

2. On the starboard side, in Emmons County, North Dakota, their first camp in that state; Fire Heart Butte is roughly opposite on the other side. The campsite and the "antient fortification" are now inundated by Oahe Reservoir. *Atlas* map 26; MRC map 47.

3. This distance is one mile in Codex C.

4. Clark wrote "untill [*blank*] oClock," then put "all" in the blank and interlined "Day."

[Clark]

15th of October   Rained all last night, passed a Ricara hunting camp on the S. S. & halted at another on the L. S, Several from the 1t Camp visited us and gave meat as also those of the Camp we halted at, we gave them

fish hooks Some beeds &c. as we proceeded on we Saw a number of indians on both Sides all day, Saw L. S some Curious Nnobs high and much
the resemblance of a hiped [hipped] rough [roof] house, we halted at a
Camp of 10 Lodges of Ricaras on the S. S.,[1] we visited thier Lodges &
were friendly recved by all— their women fond of our men— &c.

Course Distance

West	2 ½	m to a Creek on the L. S.
North	4	m. to a wood point on the L. S.
N 34° W.	3 ½	m. to a pt S. S. ⟨passed an Old Chyenne Village on the L. S. below a Creek on⟩ the L. S.[2] a Camp of Ricaras on the S. S.

[Clark]   15th of *October Monday* 1804

rained all last night, we Set out early and proceeded on at 3 Miles
passed an Ind. Camp [*NB: of hunters Ricaras*] on the S. S. we halted above
and about 30 of the Indians came over in their Canoos of Skins, we eate
with them, they give us meat, in return we gave fishhooks & Some beeds,
about a mile higher we came too on the L. S. at a Camp of *Ricres* [*NB:
ricaras*] of about 8 Lodges, we also eate & they gave Some meat, ⟨here we
found the relation of⟩ we proceded on Saw numbers of Indians on
both Sides passing a Creek,[3] Saw many Curious hills, high and much the
resemblance of a house [*NB: like ours*] with a hiped roof, at 12 oClock it
Cleared away and the evening was pleasent, wind from the N. E.— at
Sunset we arrived at a Camp of Ricares of 10 Lodges on the S. S. we
Came too and Camped near them ⟨I⟩ Capt Lewis & my Self went with
the Chief who accompanis us, to the Huts of Several of the men all of
whome Smoked & gave us Something to eate also Some meat to take away,
those people were kind and appeared to be much plsd. at the attentioned
paid them.

Those people are much pleased with my black Servent— Their womin
verry fond of carressing our men. &.

15th Octr

Course Distance & Reffurencs

West	2 ½	miles to a Creek on the L. S. passing over a Sand bar make-ing from the S. pt.
North	4	miles to a point of wood on the L. S. passing over a Sand point on the S. S.
N. 34° W.	3 ½	miles to a point of wood on the S. S. passing old Village of the *Shár há* or Chien Indians on the L. S below a Creek on the Same Side.[4] passed a Camp of Ricares on S. S.
	10	

1. The party's camp was above the last Arikara camp in Emmons County, North Dakota, below present Fort Yates, on the opposite shore. The three Arikara camps are shown on *Atlas* map 26. The site is now inundated by Oahe Reservoir. MRC map 47.

2. The passage about the Cheyenne village also appears in the Codex C courses and distances for October 15, but there it does not appear to be crossed out. Entries for October 16, below, clearly indicate that they passed the village on that date. *Atlas* map 26 shows the village site almost exactly opposite the October 15 camp, and this may explain why Clark had some confusion about which day he should give as the one when they "passed" the spot.

3. Later Four Mile Creek, nameless on *Atlas* map 26, in Sioux County, North Dakota. MRC map 47.

4. Sharhá Creek on *Atlas* map 26. This is a very difficult stretch of the river to locate with any precision. It has been identified as modern Porcupine Creek by some authorities but could just as easily be Long Soldier Creek, both in Sioux County. Wood (BS), 63–64; MRC map 47; MRY map 122.

[Clark]

16th of October Tuesday 1804   Some rain this morning   2 Squars verry anxious to accompany us   we Set [out] with our Chief on Board by name *Ar ke tar nar shar* (or Chief of the Town)[1]   a little above our Camp on the L. S.   passed an old Shyenne Village,[2] which appears to have been Se-rounded with a wall of earth; this is the retreat & first Stand of this nation after being reduced by the Sioux and drove from their Countrey on the heads of red River of L Winipic[3] where they Cultivated the lands— passed a Creek I call *So-harch* or Girl Creek L. S.[4]   2 miles higher passed Woman Crreek or *Char-part*[5]   passed an Island Situated in a bend to the S. S.   at the lower point of this Island a Creek comes in Called *Kee-tooch*

Sar-kar-nar- or the place of Beaver[6]   above the Island a Small River on the Same S. Side Called *War-re-Con nee* Elk shed their horns,[7] this river is 35 yards wide & heads near the River au Jacque, Carp Island[8]   wind hard a head from the N W.   Saw great numbers of goats or Antelope on Shore, Capt Lewis one man & the Ricara Chief walked on Shore, in the evening I discovered a number of Indians on each Side and goats in the river or Swiming & on Sand bars, when I came near Saw the boys in the water Swiming amongst the goats & Killing them with Sticks, and then hauling them to the Shore   those on Shore Kept them in the water, I saw 58 Killed in this way and on the Shore, the hunter with Cap Lewis Shot 3 goats   I came too and Camped above the Ricara Camp on the L. S.[9]   Several Indians visited us duereing the night Some with meat, Sang and were merry all night.—

Cours & Distance 16

North	4	m to a point on the S. S. passed 2 Creeks L. S.
N. 10° E	6	m. to the upper pt. of Some timber on the L. S. opsd. a Creek haveing passed an Isld. on the S. S a Creek at its lower point
N.	½	a m on the L. Side
N. 30° W	1	m on the L. point
N 38° W.	3	m. to a point on the S. S.—

[Clark]   *16th October Tuesday 1804*

Some rain this morning,   2 young Squars verry anxious to accompany us, we Set out with our Chief on board by name *Ar ke tar na Shar* or Chief of the Town, a little above our Camp on the L. S. passed a Circular work, where the, *Shār há* (*or Chien*, or Dog Indians[)]] formerly lived, a Short distance abov passed a Creek which we Call Chien [*NB: Chayenne or Sharha Mr Hayley says not Chien*][10] Creek, above is a willow Island Situated near (1) the L. Side a large Sand bar above & on both Sides   (2) passed a Creek above the Island on the L. S. call *So-harch* (or Girls) Creek, at 2 miles higher up (3) passed a Creek on L. S. call *Char part* (or womins) Creek   passed (5) an Island Situated in a bend to the S. S.   this Isd. is about 1½ miles long, Covered with timber Such as Cotton wood, opsd. the lower point a creek coms in on[11] the S. S. called by the Indians *Kee tooch Sar kar nar* (or place [*NB: place*] of Beavr[)] above the Island a ⟨large Creek⟩ Small river about 35 yards wide coms in Called *War re con ne* or (Elk Shed their horns). The Island is Called Carp Island by Ivens.[12] wind hard from the N. W. Saw great numbers of Goats on the Shore S. S. proceeded on Capt. Lewis & the Indian Chief walked on Shore, Soon after I discovered Great numbers of Goats in the river, and Indians on the Shore on each Side, as I approached or got nearer I discovered boys in the water Killing the Goats with Sticks and halling them to Shore, Those on the banks Shot them with arrows and as they approachd. the Shore would turn them back of this Gangue of Goats I counted 58 of which they had killed & on the Shore, one of our hunters out with Cap Lewis killed three Goats, we passed the Camp on the S. S. and proceeded ½ mile and Camped on the L. S. many Indians came to the boat to See, Some Came across late at night, as they approach they hollowed and Sung, after Staying a Short time 2 went for Some meat, and returned in a Short time with fresh & Dried Buffalow, also goat, those Indians Strayed all night, They Sung and was verry merry the greater part of the night ⟨wind hard from N W.⟩

16th Octr

Course Distance & reffurences

North	4	miles to a pt. on the S. S. Passed a willow Island L. S. (1) a Creek (2) above the Isd. & one at 2 miles furthr (3)
N. 10° E.	6	miles to the upper point of Some Timber on the L. S. opsd. the mouth of a Creek on the S. S. (4). passed a Isld. on the S. S. (5). opsd. the Lower pt. of which comes in a Creek (5).
North	½	mile on the L. Side
N. 30° W.	1	me. on the L. point High Ld.
N. 38° W.	3	miles to a point on the S. S.
	14 ½	

[Lewis]   October 16th[13]

This day took a small bird [*EC: Phalaenoptilus nuttalli*] alive of the order of the [*blank*] or goat suckers. it appeared to be passing into the dormant state. on the morning of the 18th the murcury was at 30 a[bove] o. the bird could scarcely move.— I run my penknife into it's body under the wing and completely distroyed it's lungs and heart— yet it lived upwards of two hours this fanominon I could not account for unless it proceeded from the want of circulation of the blo[o]d.— the recarees call this bird to'-na it's note is at-tah-to'-nah'; at-tah'to'-nah'; to-nah, a nocturnal bird, sings only in the night as does the whipperwill.— it's weight— 1 oz 17 Grains Troy

1. See above, October 9, 1804.

2. In Sioux County, North Dakota, between present Four Mile and Long Soldier or Porcupine creeks. The site, probably now inundated by Oahe Reservoir, represents a period when the Cheyennes were relatively sedentary, before they had adopted a completely nomadic way of life in the latter part of the eighteenth century. *Atlas* map 26; Hyde (IHP), 47–48 and n. 15; Grinnell, 1 : 23–24; Berthrong, 9–13; MRC map 47. Other authorities disagree with Grinnell that it is a Cheyenne site. Wood (BS), 63–64.

3. Osgood interprets these words as "Levenispice," and suggests that it may mean that the Cheyennes were deprived of "living space." However, Clark spells Lake Winnipeg "Winipic" on his 1805 map (*Atlas* maps 32*a*, 32*b*, and 32*c*), and since the Red River of the North flows into that lake, it is likely that he is here identifying the river more fully. The exact spelling is not clear. Osgood (FN), 161 and n. 3.

4. Perhaps later Porcupine or Battle Creek, in Sioux County, nameless on *Atlas* map 27. Clark is apparently applying Arikara names learned from the chief accompanying them to this and other streams passed. It may be rendered as *suúnatš*, "girl" in Arikara. MRC map 47; MRY map 123.

5. The second nameless stream on the larboard side on *Atlas* map 27, perhaps later Battle Creek, in Sioux County. It is *sápat*, "woman" in Arikara. MRC map 47; MRY map 123.

6. Presently Little Beaver Creek, in Emmons County, North Dakota. It is *čítUx sAhaánu'*, "beaver creek" in Arikara. *Atlas* map 27; MRC map 47.

7. The Arikara words *wah* for "elk" and *arika* for "horn" may coincide with Clark's rendition. Now Beaver Creek, in Emmons County. *Atlas* map 27; MRC map 47.

8. As Clark notes in Codex C, he derived the name of the island from Evans's map 5 (*Atlas* map 11). It seems to have joined the starboard shore by the late nineteenth century. *Atlas* map 27; MRC map 47.

9. In Sioux County, roughly two miles above the mouth of Beaver Creek. *Atlas* map 27; MRC map 48.

10. "Mr. Hayley" is probably Hugh Heney, whom the party met at Fort Mandan (see below, December 16, 1804). Apparently it was he who informed the captains that "Cheyenne" was not derived from the French "*chien*," for dog.

11. At this point the text of the Codex C entry is interrupted by the courses and distances; here the two parts are brought together for ease of reading.

12. Shown on *Atlas* map 11, see n. 8 above.

13. Lewis's natural history notes from Codex Q. The bird is the common poorwill, *Phalaenoptilus nuttallii* [AOU, 418], as noted interlineally by Coues. Burroughs notes that it was not until the 1940s that zoologists discovered the bird's tendency to hiberate. Burroughs, 236, 327 n. 7. The poorwill is a close relative of the whip-poor-will (*Caprimulgus vociferus* [AOU, 417]) that Lewis uses for comparison.

[Clark]

17th of October 1804 Wind S. W. I walked on Shore with the Ricara Chief and an Inteprieter,[1] the[y] told me maney extroadenary Stories, I Killed 3 Dear & a Elk, the Chief Killed a Deer and our hunters Killed 4 Deer, in my absenc the wind rose So high that the Boat lay too all Day; Latd 46° 23′ 57″ N, I caught a Small uncommon whiperwill[2] we observe emence herds of Goats, or Antelopes flocking down from the N E Side & Swiming the River, the Chief tels me those animals winter in the Black Mountain, and in the fall return to those mounts from every quarter, and in the Spring disperse in the planes, those emence herds we See all of which is on the N E Side of the River is on their way to the mountain, and in the Spring they will be as noumeroes on their return (some ganges winter on the Missouri)— camped on the L. S.[3]

Course Distance &c.

N. 10° E.	1 ½	m to a pt. on the L. S.
N.	½	a m on the L. S.
N. 10° W.	½	a m. on the L. S.
N 33° W.	3 ½	m. to Some wood on the L. S.

[Clark]   17th Octr.

Course Distance & reffurenc.

N. 10° E.	1 ½	miles to a pt. on the L. S.
North	½	me. on the L. S.

N. 10° W.   ½   me. on the L. S.

N. 33° W.   3 ½   mes. to the Commencement of Some woods on the ⟨L⟩ S. S.

             6
             =

☞ note from the *Ricares* to the River Jacque near N. E. is about 40 mes. to the ⟨Souex 20⟩ Chien a fork of R Rogue 20 [*NB: further*] passing the Souix River near the Chien   this from information of Mr. Graveline who passed through this Countrey[4]

17th *October* ⟨*Friday*⟩ Wednesday 1804.

Set out early   a fine morning the wind from the N W.   after brackfast I walked on Shore with the Indian Chief & Interpeters,[5] Saw Buffalow Elk and Great numbers of Goats in large gangues   (I am told by Mr. G. that those Animals winter in the Black mountains [*NB: to feed on timber &c*] and this is about the Season they Cross from the East of the Missouris to go to that Mountain, they return in the Spring and pass the Missourie in Great numbers[)] [*NB: to the plains*]. This Chief tells me of a number of their Treditions about Turtles, Snakes, &. and the power of a perticiler rock or Cave on the next river which informs of everr thing[6]   none of those I think worth while mentioning—   The wind So hard a head the boats Could not move aftr 10 oClock, Capt Louis Took the altitude of the Sun Latd. *46° 23′ 57″*   I Killed 3 Deer and the hunters with me killed 3 also   the Indian Shot one but Could not get it—   I Scaffeled up the Deer[7] & returned & met the boat after night on the L. S. about 6 miles above the place we Camped last night—   one of the men Saw a number of Snakes, Capt Lewis Saw a large Beaver house S. S.   I Cought a Whipprwill Small & not Common—.   the leaves are falling fast—.   the river wide and full of Sand bars,—.   Great numbers of verry large Stone on the Sides of the hills & Some rock of a brownish Colour in the Ld. Bend below this—.[8]

Great numbers of Goats are flocking down to the S. Side of the river on their way to the Black Mountains where they winter   those animals return in the Spring in the Same way & Scatter in different directions.

Point of Observation No. 49.

Wednesday October 17th 1804.[9]

[Lewis]

On the Stard. shore, opposite to a high projecting Bluff; which from the great number of rattlesnakes found near it, we called the *rattlesnake Bluff.*

Observed meridian altd. of ⊙'s U. L. with Sextant by the fore observation 69° 17′

Latitude deduced from this observation   N. 46 23 57.1

1. The interpreter was probably Joseph Gravelines, but see below, n. 5.

2. The common poorwill. See Lewis's natural history note, October 16, 1804.

3. In Sioux County, North Dakota, a mile or two south of the present village of Cannon Ball. On *Atlas* map 27 it is erroneously labeled "7th of October." MRC map 48.

4. See above, October 13, 1804, n. 6.

5. The word appears to be plural in Codex C, but in the Field Notes entry it is apparently singular. Later entries refer to "interpreters." Gravelines was certainly with them as interpreter for the Arikara chief. Pierre-Antoine Tabeau could have served in that capacity, but there is no evidence that he accompanied them upriver. Sergeant Ordway's entry of October 10, 1804, says, "we left one of our frenchman with Mr Tabbow & took his Soon in his place." Obviously this person could be either the son of Tabeau, or the son of the unnamed French *engagé.* If he had been living at the Arikara villages he could have served as a supplementary interpreter, but it is not clear that he actually accompanied the party upriver rather than simply attending the council held October 10.

6. See below, February 21, 1805.

7. He placed the carcass on a improvised scaffold to keep wolves and coyotes from getting it.

8. Upper Cretaceous Fox Hills Formation, mostly sandstones, crops out in this region, which is just within the glacial boundary. The very large stones are probably glacial erratics.

9. Lewis's astronomical observation from Codex O.

[Clark]

18th of October 1804.   at 6 miles passed the mouth of *La Bullet* or Cannon Ball River[1] on the L. Side about 140 yards Wide, and heads near the Black Mountains   above the mouth of this River, in and at the foot of the Bluff, and in the water is a number of round Stones, resembling Shells and Cannon balls of Different Sises, and of excellent grit for Grindstons—   the Bluff continus for about a mile, The water of this River is confined within 40 yards—   we met 2 french men in a Canoe,[2] who informed us they wer trapping near the mandans and were robed of 4 Traps, & part of their

Skins and Several other articles by Indians he took to be Mandans   those men return with us, Saw emence numbers of Goats all Day S. S.   our hunters Kill Sevral   passed a large Creek Called *Che wah* or fish Creek on the S. S. 28 yds. wide,[3] passed a Small Creek at 2 m on the L. S.[4]   Camped on the L. S.[5]   Saw a no of Buffalow, & in one gangue 248 Elk   our hunters Killed 6 Deer & 4 Elk this evening, The Countrey is leavel and fine   Some high Short hills, and ridges at a Distance, Bottoms fine and Partially timbered with Cotton wood principally Some ash & Elm.[6]

Course Distance &c.

N. 50° W.	3	m. to Cannon ball River L. S.
N. 20° W.	2	m to a pt. of wood on the S. S. passing Can Ball Bluff L S
North	2 ½	m to a pt of wood on the L. S.
N. 15° W.	½	m on the L. S. opsd. a Creek.
N. 10° E.	2 ½	to a point on S S passd. a Small Creek L. S.
N. 20° E.	3	m to a point of wood on the L. S.

[Clark]   18th of *October* ⟨*Satturday*⟩ Thursday 1804

Set out early   proceeded on   at 6 mes. passed the mouth of (1) la Boulet [*NB: Le boulet*] (or Cannon Ball River) about 140 yards wide on the L. S.   this river heads in the *Court noi* or Black mountains)   (a fine Day) above the mouth of this river Great numbers of Stone perfectly round with fine Grit are in the Bluff and on the Shore, the river takes its name from those Stones which resemble Cannon Balls.—   The water of this river is Confined within 40 yards. We met 2 french men in a perogue Desending from hunting, & complained of the Mandans robing them of 4 Traps ther fur & Seeveral othr articles   Those men were in the imploy of our Ricaree interpeter Mr. Gravelin   the[y] turned & followered us.

Saw Great numbers of Goats on the S. S. Comeing to the river   our hunters Killed 4 of them   Some run back and others crossed & prosceed on their journey to the *Court Noir*, at (3) passed a Small River Called *Che wah* or fish river on the S. S.   this river is about 28 yards wide and heads to the N. E, passed a Small creek on the L. S. 1 mile abov the last, and Camped on a Sand bar on the L. S.   opposit to us we Saw a Gangue of Buffalow bulls which we did not think worth while to kill—   our hunters

Killd. 4 Goats 6 Deer 4 Elk & a pelican & informs that they Saw in one Gang 248 Elk, (I walked on Shore, in the evining with a view to See Some of those remarkable places mentioned by evens, none of which I could find,)[7]   The Countrey in this quarter is Generally leavel & fine   Some high Short hills, and some ragid ranges of Hills at a Distans

(18th Octr)

Course Distanc & Refferens

N. 50° W.	3	miles to the mouth of a River (1) *Cannon ball* L. S.
N. 20° W.	2	miles to a point of wood land on the S. S. passing a Bluff in which theres round Stone (2)
North	2 ½	miles to a point of wood land on the L. S.
N. 15° W.	½	mile on the L. S. opsd. a Creek on the S. S. (3).
N. 10° E.	2 ½	miles to a point on the L. S. passing a Small Creek on L. S.
N. 20° E	3	miles to a point of woods on the L. S. passing over a Sand bar
	13	

☞ The ricara Indians inform us that they find no black tail Deer as high up as this place, those we find are of the fallow Deer Kind[8]

☞ The *Ricareis* are not fond of Spiritous liquers, nor do they apper to be fond of receiveing any or thank full for it [*NB: they say we are no friends or we would not give them what makes them fools.*][9]

1. The Cannonball at this point is the boundary of Sioux and Morton counties, North Dakota. It rises in the Badlands of southwestern North Dakota, which Lewis and Clark as usual consider part of the "Black Mountains." The round stones which are the origin of both the French and English names are the result of moisture acting on sandstone. *North Dakota Guide*, 297; Mattison (OR), 139–40; *Atlas* map 27; MRC map 48.

2. The identification of these two has become somewhat involved. Quaife's conclusion that they were François Rivet and Phillippe Degie seems doubtful in both cases. Rivet was an expedition *engagé* from the start; the presence of Degie apparently has no basis except that he was in later years an associate of Rivet. One of the two men was probably Grenier, an employee of Joseph Gravelines and evidently the "Greinyea" Clark notes on August 21, 1806, as having wintered with the party at Fort Mandan in 1804–1805. He may have been Francis Fleury *dit* Grenier of St. Louis, but there are other possibilities. Quaife (MLJO), 191 nn. 1, 3; Osgood (FN), 162 n. 7; Munnick (FR), 237–43; Abel (TN), 168 n. 22; Thwaites (LC), 5:350 n. 1; Clarke (MLCE), 114; Jackson (LLC), 1:305 n. 1, 2:429 n. 9.

3. Later Long Lake, or Badger, Creek, in Emmons County, North Dakota. In Arikara it is *čiwáhtš*, "fish." *Atlas* map 27; MRC map 48.

4. Nameless on *Atlas* map 27, it is later Long Knife, or Rice, Creek in Morton County. MRC map 48; MRY map 130.

5. In Morton County, just below modern Livona on the opposite shore, and a little above Rice Creek. *Atlas* map 27; MRC map 48; MRY map 130.

6. The ash is probably green ash, *Fraxinus pennsylvanica* Marsh. var. *subintegerrima* (Vahl) Fern., and the elm is probably the American elm, *Ulmus americana* L. Barkley, 299, 33.

7. Evans's map 5 (*Atlas* map 11), shows such features as "Jupiters fort," "Jupiters house," and "the Hermitt" on the west bank. It is not clear whether these refer to natural features or remains of Indian villages. They may be poor translations of French or Indian names or Evans's own inventions. "Jupiters house" might be the "Old fortification" shown on *Atlas* map 27, in the vicinity of the later Fort Rice Historic Site. There is nothing remarkably different from the rest of the river valley in the area today. The captains may have had notes by Evans or James Mackay giving information not on the map. We have replaced Clark's square brackets around this passage with parentheses. Wood (JE); MRC map 48; MRY map 130.

8. The black tail deer is the mule deer and the fallow deer is the white-tailed deer. See note at September 16, 1804. The mule deer was not so limited in range as Clark suggests. Coues (HLC), 1:172 n. 46; Cutright (LCPN), 85–86, Burroughs, 124–33.

9. Cf. the similar phrasing in Biddle's history. Coues (HLC), 1:160.

[Clark]

19th of October Friday 1804. Set out early under a gentle Breeze from the S. E. more timber than Common in the bottoms passed a large Pond on the S. S. I walked out on the high land L. Side and observed great numbers of Buffalows, I counted in view at one time 52 gangues of Buffalow & 3 of Elk, besides Deer & goats &c. all the Streems falling from the hills or high lands So brackish that the water Can't be Drank without effecting the person making use of it as Globesalts—,[1] I saw in my walk Several remarkable high Conocal hills, one 90 feet, one 60 and others Smaller—[2] the Indian Chief Say that the Callemet Bird[3] live in the hollows of those hills, which holes are made by the water passing from the top & &. I also Saw an old Village fortified Situated on the top of a high Point, which the Ricarra Chief tels me were Mandans,[4] we Camped on the L. S. I Killed a Deer & Saw Swans &c. our hunters Killed 4 Elk and 6 Deer to Day

Course Distance &.

N. 60° W.   2 ½   m. to a pt. on the S. S.   passed a Creek S. S.

N. 40° W.	2	m to Some wood in a bend to the L. S.
N. 10° E.	1 ½	m to a pt on the L S.
N. 20° W.	2	m. to a tree in the bend S. S.
N 83° W.	3	m to the point S. S.
N. 44° W.	1	m. to a Willow pt. on the L. S. opsd a Lake S. S.
N. 30° W.	2	m. to a tree in bend S. S.
N. 80° W.	3	m. to a pt. on the S. S[5]

[Clark]   19th October Friday 1804.

a fine morning   wind ⟨hard⟩ from the S. E.   we Set out early under a gentle Breeze and proceeded on verry well, more timber than Common on the banks on this part of the river—   passed a large Pond on the S. S.—   I walked out on the Hills & observed Great numbers of Buffalow feedeing on both Sides of the river   I counted 52 Gangues of Buffalow & 3 of Elk at one view, all the runs which come from the high hills which is Generally about one or 2 miles from the water is brackish and near the Hills (the Salts are)[6] and the Sides of the Hills & edges of the Streems, the mineral salts appear   I saw Som remarkable round hills forming a Cone at top one about 90 foot one 60 & Several others Smaller, the Indian Chief Say that the Callemet bird live in the holes of those hills, the holes form by the water washing thro Some parts in its passage Down from the top—   near one of those noles, on a point of a hill 90 feet above the lower plane I observed the remains of an old village, [*NB: high, strong, watch-tower &c.*] which had been fortified, the Indian Chief with us tels me, a party of Mandins lived there, Here first saw ruins of Mandan nation   we proceeded on & Camped on the L. S.[7] opposit the upper of those Conocal hills—

our hunters killed 4 Elk 6 Deer & a pelican, I saw Swans in a Pond & Killed a fat Deer in my walk, Saw above 10 wolves. This day is pleasent

19th Octr.

Course Destance & reffurence

N. 60° W.	2 ½	mes. to a pt. on the S. S. Passed a Creek on the S. S.
N. 40° W.	2	mes. to Some wood in a bend on the L. S.

N. 10° E	1 ½	mile to the point on L. S.
N. 20° W.	2	miles to a tree in the bend S. S.
N. 83° W.	3	miles to the point on the S. S.
N. 44° W	1	mile to a willow point on the L. S. pd. a Lake S S.
N. 30° W	2	miles to a tree in the bind to the S. S.
N. 80° W.	3 ½	miles to a point on the S. S. (2) opposit a round nole on the L. S. a Deep bend to the L. S. & pond
	17 ½	

1. Glauber's Salts, the decahydrate form of sodium sulfate, used as a laxative.

2. They appear on *Atlas* map 28 in Morton County, North Dakota; the highest is probably the "Sugarloaf" of Evans's map 5 (*Atlas* map 11), present Sugarloaf Butte. MRC map 49; MRY map 133.

3. The golden eagle.

4. The village may be the Eagle Nose site set atop a flat-topped eminence known today as Eagle Nose Butte or Birds Bill Hill, in Morton County. It figures prominently in Mandan folklore. *Atlas* map 28 calls it a "hunting camp fortifed on a hill." Mattison (OR), 148; Will, 313; Bowers (MSCO), 162, 197 199, 252; MRC map 49. The location of the camp is discussed in n. 7.

5. The location of the camp is discussed in n. 7. The distance is 3½ in Codex C.

6. We have changed Clark's square brackets around this passage to parentheses.

7. The letters are uncertain in Codex C, but are clearly "L. S." in the Field Notes. *Atlas* map 28 seems to indicate a campsite a little above the upper hill; aside from possible error by the map copyist, Clark's use of the word "opposite" is not always precise. The camp would be in Morton County, a few miles upstream from the village of Huff; it is now inundated by Oahe Reservoir. MRC map 49.

[Clark]

20th of October 1804   wind from the S E, I walked out to view those remarkable places pointed out by Evens,[1] and continud all day   Saw an old Village of the Mandans below the Chess chi ter R.[2]   appear to have been fortified   above the village on the Same L. S. is a coal bank where we Campd.[3]   passed a Small Creek on the S. S. and an Island on the L. S[4] Covered with willows Small Cotton[wood]   the Countrey thro which I passed this day is Delightfull, Timber in the bottoms, Saw great nos. of Buffalow Elk Goats & Deer   as we were in want of them I Killed 3 Deer, our hunters 10 Deer and wounded a white Bear,[5] I Saw Several fresh tracks of that animal double the Sise of the largest track I ever Saw, great numbers of wolves, those animals follow the buffalow and devour, those that die or are Killed, and those too fat or pore to Keep up with the gangue

Course Distance &c

N. 30° W.	2	m to Some timber in a bend to the S. S. at a Creek
N. 10° W.	1	m on the S. S.
N. 54° W.	3	m to a pt. on L S
N.	2	miles to Some trees in a bend to the S. S. opposit an Island
N. 70° W	2	m. to a point on the S S. passed the Island
N. 50° W	2	m to the upper part of a Coal Bluff L S. pass an old Mandan V[illage]. L S

[Clark]   20th October

Courses Distance *& Reffers.*

N. 30° W	2	miles to Some timber in a bend to the S. S. at a Creek (1)
N. 10° W.	1	mile on the S. S
N. 54° W.	3	miles to a pt. on the L. S. Isd passing over a Sand bar S. S.
N.	2	miles to Some high trees in a bend on the S. S. passing the lowr. pt. Isd. (2)
N. 70° W.	2	miles to a pt. on the S. S. passing the upper pt. of the Island on the L. S.
N. 50° W	2 12 =	mes. to the upper part of a Bluff in which there (3) is Stone Cole on the L. S. passing the 1st old Mandin Village on the L. S. (4)

20th of October Satterday 1804

Set out early this morning and proceeded on   the wind from the S. E after brackfast I walked out on the L. Side to See those remarkable places pointed out by Evins, I saw an old remains of a villige [*NB: covering 6 or 8 acres*] on the Side of a hill which the Chief with us *Too né* tels me that nation [Mandans] lived in ⟨2⟩ a number villages on each Side of the river and the Troubleson Seauex caused them to move about 40 miles higher up where they remained a fiew years & moved to the place they now live, (2) passed a Small Creek on the S. S. (3) and one on the L. S.[6]   passed (4) a Island Covered with willows laying in the middle of the river   no current on the L. S.   Camped   on the L. S. above a Bluff containing Coal (5) of an inferior quallity,[7] this bank is imedeately above the old village of the Mandans—   The Countrey is fine, the high hills at a Distanc with gradual assents, *I Kild 3 Deer*   The Timber Confined to the bottoms as usial which is much larger than below. Great numbers of Buffalow Elk & Deer, Goats.   our hunters killed 10 Deer & a Goat to day and wounded a white Bear   I saw Several fresh track of those animals which is 3 times as large as a mans track—, The wind hard all Day from the N. E. & East, great numbers of buffalow Swiming the river

I observe near all large gangues of buffalow wolves and when the buffalow move those Anamals follow and feed on those that are killed by accident or those that are too pore or fat to Keep up with the gangue.

[Lewis]   20th October[8]

Peter Crusat this day shot at a white bear   he wounded him, but being alarmed at the formidable appearance of the bear he left his tomahalk and gun; but shortly after returned and found that the bear had taken the oposite rout.—   soon after he shot a buffaloe cow broke her thy, the cow pursued him he concealed himself in a small raviene.—

1. See above, October 18, 1804.

2. This village and a number of others are conspicuous on both sides of the river on *Atlas* map 28. The one mentioned here is called On-a-Slant (or simply Slant) village, now marked by several modern replicas of earth lodges. The river is now Heart River, passed the next day. Mattison (OR), 153; Strong, 360–65; MRC map 49.

3. About five miles south of present Mandan, Morton County, North Dakota, and within Fort Lincoln State Park, commemorating Fort Abraham Lincoln (1873–91). Bismarck, the capital of North Dakota, is nearly opposite in Burleigh County. Appleman (LC), 344–45; Mattison (OR), 149–52; *Atlas* map 28; MRC map 49.

4. The creek is Apple Creek, called "Shepherds Creek" on *Atlas* map 28, in Burleigh County, and the island is probably later Sibley's Island. MRC map 49.

5. This was their first encounter with the grizzly bear and they did not get a specimen. Lewis's natural history note and weather remarks for this date show that Pierre Cruzatte shot the animal and had to beat such a hasty retreat that he left his gun behind. Burroughs, 57–68. For difficulties in nomenclature, see Jones et al., 266–67, and Hall, 951–58.

6. Clark does not mention this stream in the Field Notes; nameless on *Atlas* map 28, it is later Little Heart Creek, or River, in Morton County. MRC map 49.

7. Lower Tertiary rocks that contain lignite (low grade coal) crop out in this area.

8. Lewis's natural history notes from Codex Q. See n. 5, above.

[Clark]

21t of October Sunday 1804   a verry Cold night   wind hard from the N. E.   Some rain in the night which feesed [froze] as it fell, at Day began to *Snow* and Continued all the fore part of the day, at ¼ of a mile passed the Mouth of Chess-che tar (or Heart) River L. S. 38 yards wide, this river heads near Turtle mountain with Knife River[1]   on this River is a Smothe Stone which the Indians have great fath in & Consult the Stone on all great occasions which they Say Marks or Simblems [*symbol + emblems*] are left on the Stone of what is to ⟨pass⟩ take place &c.   an old mandan Village above the mouth of this Little River,[2] I saw a Single tree in the open Plains which the Mandans formerly paid great Devotion to   run Cords thro their flesh & tie themselves to the tree to make them brave,[3]   passed an old Village on a Small run on the S S.   one on the bank L. and Camped,[4] I Killed a fat Buffalow this evening—   Little gun all my hunting[5]

Course Distance &c

S. 80° E	2	mi. to bend on S. S. 2d Vig [village] passed Chess-che-tar River
N. 16° W.	1 ½	m to a wood S. S.
N. 40° W	3 ½	m. to a pt. on the S. S. River wider & more Sand than Common.

[Clark]   21st *October Sunday 1804*

a verry Cold night   wind hard from the N. E   Some rain in the night which frosed up it fell   at Day light it began to *Snow* and Continud all the fore part of the Day   passed just above our Camp (1) a Small river on the L. S. Called by the Indians *Chiss-Cho-tar*   this river is about 38 yards wide Containing a good Deel of water   Some Distance up this River is Situated a Stone which the Indians have great fath in & Say they See painted on the Stone, ["]all the Calemites & good fortune to hapin the nation & partes who visit it"—   a tree (an oak[)] which Stands alone near this place about 2 miles off in the open prarie which has with Stood the fire they pay Great respect to, make Holes and tie Strings thro the Skins of their necks ⟨Skin⟩

and around this tree to make them brave [*NB: Capt. Clarke saw this tree*] (all this is the information of Too ne is a whipper will) the Chief of the Ricares who accompanied us to the Mandins, at 2 miles (2) passed the 2nd Villages of the Manden, which was in existance at the Same time with the 1st   this village is at the foot of a hill on the S. S. on a butifull & extensive plain [*NB: nearly opposite is another village in a bottom the other side of Missouri*]—   at this time Covered with Buffalow—   a Cloudy afternoon, I killed a fine Buffalow, we Camped on the L. S.   [*NB: below an old Mandan village having passed another up a Creek 3 miles below on S. S*]   verry Cold ground Covered with Snow.   one orter Killd.[6]

21t Oct.

Course Distance & reffus.

S. 80° E	2	miles to the place the Mandan had a village formerly at the foot of a [*several words interlined, illegible*] on the S. S. passed a river
N. 16° W.	1 ½	miles to a grove on the S. S.
N. 40° W.	3 ½	miles to a pt. on the S. S. river wide and Sand bars, a large willow Island
	7	

1. Clark's "Chess-che tar" or "*Chiss-Cho-tar*" is the Arikara word *čisčítA*, "fork (of a river)." Heart River reaches the Missouri at present Mandan, Morton County, North Dakota, opposite Bismarck. Clark's "Turtle Mountain" is the present Killdeer range in western North Dakota. While the range can be considered the source of Knife River, the sources of Heart River in Stark County would more properly be associated with the Badlands. Coues (HLC), 1:174 n. 51; *Atlas* map 28; MRC map 49.

2. There are a number of prehistoric villages in the area just above the camp for this date. The various villages mentioned in the journals are shown on *Atlas* map 28, in the vicinity of present Bismarck, North Dakota. None have been investigated in the detail necessary to identify them with Clark's words or map. See Will & Hecker, 81–82.

3. Clark is apparently describing a version of the Sun Dance, practiced by many Great Plains tribes. Endurance of such physical pain was part of the ritual practiced by several, but not all, tribes. George Catlin has left a vivid record of such ceremonies among the Mandans. Catlin (NAI), 1:192–99 and pl. 66; Catlin (OKP); Liberty.

4. In or near present Mandan, North Dakota. Mattison (GR), 11; *Atlas* map 28; MRC map 50.

5. Clark evidently means that he did all his hunting with a relatively small-caliber "Kentucky" long rifle, or "squirrel gun," probably his own property. Russell (FTT), 38.

6. Their first encounter with the river otter, an animal already known to science. Bur-roughs, 75.

[Clark]

22nd of October 1804   last night at about 1 oClock I was violently at-tacked with Rhumetism in my neck, which was so violently I could not move, Cap L. applied a hot Stone raped in flannel which gave temperry ease, we passed a War party of Tetons on their way as we Supposed to the Mandans of 12 men on the L. S.   we gave them nothing and refused to put them across the river, passed 2 old Villages at the mouth of a large Creek L. S[1] and a Small Island at the head of which is a bad place, an old Village on the S. S. and the upper of the 6 Villages the Mandans occupied about 25 years ago[2]   this village was entirely cut off by the *Sioux* & one of the others nearly, the Small Pox distroyed great Numbers

Course & Distanc

N. 50° W.	3	m to a pt. on the S. S.
N 34° W.	3	m. to the Lower pt. of an Island on the L. S.
N. 34 W	3	to a pt. on L. S. passed old vig S S & a Bad riffle
N.	1	m to a pt. on the L. S,
N. 24° W.	2	m to a pt. on the S. S.—

[Clark]   22nd *October Monday 1804*

last night at 1 oClock I was violently and Suddinly attacked with the Rhumitism in the neck which was So violent I could not move   Capt. [Lewis] applied a hot Stone raped in flannel, which gave me some tem-porry ease,—.   we Set out early, the morning Cold   at 7 oClock we Came too at a Camp of Teton Seaux on the L. S.   those people 12 in number were naikd and had the appearanc of war, we have every reason to believ that they are going or have been to Steel horses from the Mandins, they tell two Stories, we gave them nothing   after takeing brackfast proceeded on—   my Neck is yet verry painfull at times Spasms. [*NB: Passed old Man-dan village near which we lay, another at 4 miles one at 8 miles (4 miles further) at mouth of large creek all on Larboard Side.*]

Camped on the L Side,[3] passed an Island Situated on the L. Side at the head of which & Mandans village S. S. [*NB: 2 miles above*] we passd a bad place— [*NB: ⟨above the island 2 miles from last village⟩*] The hunters killed a buffalow bull, they Say out of about 300 buffalow which they Saw, they ⟨only⟩ did not See one Cow. Great Deel of Beaver Sign. Several Cought every night.

22d Octr

Course Distance & reffurence

N. 50° W	3	miles to a pt. on the S. S.
N. 34° W.	3	miles to the lower point on an Island on the L. S.
N. 34° W.	3	miles to a pt. on the S. S.[4] passed a bad ripple on bar
North	1	mile to a point on the L. S. a deep bend to S. S.
N. 24° W	2	miles to a point on the S. Side.—
	12	

[*NB: The mounds, 9 in number along river within 20 miles the fallen down earth of the houses, some teeth and bones of men & animals mixed in these villages, human Skulls, are Scattered in these villages*]

1. Most of these villages, in Morton and Burleigh counties, North Dakota, are marked on *Atlas* map 28. The creek—Hunting Creek on the *Atlas* map—is Square Butte Creek, in Morton County. MRC map 50; MRY map 142. The most conspicuous village in this locale is the Boley site, which appears to be a late eighteenth century Mandan site. It lies half-way between the camp of October 21 and the mouth of Square Butte Creek. Will & Hecker, 103–6.

2. The village is today's Double Ditch Mandan site, now a North Dakota State Historic Site. Will & Spinden, 82 passim.

3. Probably in southeast Oliver County, North Dakota, just above the Morton County line. *Atlas* map 28; MRC map 50.

4. "L. S." in the Field Notes. "S. S." is probably correct; see *Atlas* map 28.

[Clark]

23rd of October 1804 Some Snow, passed 5 Lodges ⟨of⟩ fortified   the place the two french men were robed[1]   Those are the hunting Camps of the mandans, who has latterly left them.   we camped on the L. S.[2]

Course Distanc &c.

N. 45° E.	2	m. bend S. S.
N. 18° W	1 ½	m to a High land S. S.
N. 65° W.	3	m to a tree in a bend to the L S.
N 33° W	2 ½	m. to a pt. on the L. S.
N. 18° W.	1	m on the L. S.
N 45° W.	3	m. to a point on the S. S.—

[Clark]   23rd of *October Tuesday 1804*

a cloudy morning Some Snow   Set out early   pass five Lodges ⟨of India⟩ which was Diserted, the fires yet burning   we Suppose those were the Indians who robed the 2 french Trappers a fiew days ago   those 2 men are now with us going up with a view to get their property from the Indians thro us.   cold & Cloudy camped on The L. S. of the river [*NB: saw at 12 miles   passed old village on S. S. of Maharha* Indns, a band of Minnetarrées who now live ⟨with⟩ between Mands & Minnetarres   *Ah na ha wa's   see note 10 May, 1805*][3]

                                                              23rd Octr

Course Distance & reffurencs

N. 45° E	2	miles to a Tree in the bend S. S.
N. 18° W.	1 ½	mes. to High land on the S. S.
N. 65° W.	3	mes. to a tree in the bend L S.
N. 33 W.	2 ½	mes. to a pt. on the L S.
N. 18° W.	1	mile on the L S.
N. 45° W	3	miles to a point on the S. S. passing as common many
	13	Sand bars

1. This site, in Oliver County, North Dakota, does not appear on Clark's maps, since the Mandan hunting camp marked on *Atlas* map 29 is upstream from the October 23 camp of the party.

2. Near present Sanger, Oliver County. *Atlas* map 29; MRC map 51.

3. On *Atlas* map 29 this appears as "Old village of Ah na ha was band," probably the

Molander site, in Oliver County. The former inhabitants were the Awaxawis, who became a division of the Hidatsas, or Minitaris, who occupied the area about 1760, before moving to the mouth of the Knife River. The bracketed material was added later, perhaps by Biddle in 1810. The reference date is in error; it is to a brief note on the tribe in Clark's entry for March 10, 1805. Wood & Moulton, 384–85; MRC map 51.

[Clark]

24th of October   Cloudy   Some little Snow   (my Rhumetism Continue, not So bad as the 2 last days,) a butufull Countrey on both Sides, bottoms covered with wood, we See no game to day, passed an old [village] of a Band of Me ne tarres Called *Mah har ha* where they lived 40 year ago on the L. S.[1]   Came too on an Island Caused by the river cutting through a narrow point 7 years ago,[2] on this Island we wer visited by the grand Chief of the mandans a 2d Chief and Some other, who wer Camped on the Island, those Chief met our Ricarra Chief with great Corduallity, & Smoked together   Cap Lewis Visited the Camps 5 Lodges, and proceeded on & Camped near a 2d Camp of Mandans on the S. S. nearly opposit the old *Ricara* & Manden Village which the Ricarras abandaned in the year 1789[3]

Course & Distanc &c.

N. 20° W	1 ½	m to a pt. on the S. S.[4]
N. 10° W.	2	m. to a pt. on the L. S. opsd. to new mandan Island— Cut point—
N. 34°[5] W.	2	m to S S.
N. 64° W.	2	m to a point of high land on which the Mandans & after them the Ricaras formrley lived.

[Clark]   24th Octr

Course Distance and reffurencs

N. 20° W.	1	mile to a pt. on the S. S.
N. 10 W.	2	miles to a pt. on the L. S. at this place the river has laterly Cut thro forming a large Island to the S. S. (1)
N. 35° W.	2	miles to an Object on the S. S.
N. 64° W.	2	miles to a point of high land on which the Mandins formerly lived (2)
	7	

24th *October Wednesday 1804*

Set out early   a Cloudy day   Some little Snow in the morning   I am Something better of the Rhumutim in my neck—   a butifull Countrey on both Sides of the river. The bottoms Covd. with wood, we have Seen no game on the river to day a prof of the Indians hunting in the neighbourhod   (1) passed a Island on the S. S. made by the river Cutting through a point, by which the river is Shortened Several miles—   on this Isld. we Saw one of the Grand Chiefs of the Mandins, with five Lodges hunting, this Cheif met the Chief of the *Ricares* who accompanied us with great Cordiallity & Sermony   Smoked the pipe & Capt. Lewis with the Interpeter went with the Chiefs to his Lodges at 1 mile distant, after his return we admited the Grand Chief & his brother for a few minits on our boat.   proceeded on a Short distance and Camped on the S. S. below the old Village of the Mandins & ricares.—   Soon after our landg. 4 Mandins Came from a Camp above, the Ricares Chief went with them to their Camp,

1. The only old village of this group of Indians on *Atlas* map 29 is the one mentioned in Codex C on October 23; the map clearly indicates that the twenty-third was the day they passed the site. The reference in Codex C, however, was clearly inserted later, placed by what Clark knew to be the correct date. MRC map 51.

2. Indicated clearly on *Atlas* map 29, this cutoff left an "oxbow" lake, later called Painted Woods Lake, on the McLean County, North Dakota, side of the Missouri, just above present Sanger. MRC map 51; MRY 151.

3. Perhaps two miles below present Washburn, McLean County. *Atlas* map 29 shows some six old villages in present Oliver County, below Hensler, some of them indicated as having been abandoned nine years, that is, since 1795.

4. The distance is one mile in Codex C.

5. This bearing is 35° in Codex C.

[Clark][1]

Course and Distance &c the 25 of October

N. 80° W.	3	M. to a pt. on the L. S. pass old Ricara village (1)
W.	1	m on the L. S.
S. 80° W.	1	m on the L. S.
S. 60° W	2	m. to a pt. on the L S. opsd. the old mandan Villages (2)

S. 30° W   2   m. to a tree on the L. S.

S. 33° W.   2   m. to a point on the S. S. opsd. a hill.

25th of October Thursday 1804.   a Gentle Breeze from the S. E by E passed an (1) old Village on a high Plain where the Mandans onced lived & after they lef[t] the Village & moved higher the Ricaras took possession & live until 1799 when they abandoned it & flew from the just revenge of the Mandans, a verry extensive Bottom above the Village above the Center of which (2) the Mandans lived in the 2 villages on the L. S.,[2] but little timber— Several parties of Indians on each Side of the River going up. in view in every directions— we are informed that the Sioux has latterly taken horses from the Big Bellies or *Minitaries*[3] and on their way homerwards the[y] fell in with the Assinniboins who killed them and took the horses & a frenchman *Menard*[4] who resided with the Mandan for 20 years past was Killed a fiew days ago on his way from the Britishment astablishments on the Assineboin River,[5] 150 miles N. of this place to the mandans by the assinniboin Indians— we were frequently Called to by parties of Indians & requested to land & talk, passed a verry bad place & Camped on a Point S S. opposit a high hill[6]   Several Indians visit us this evening   the Sun of the late great Chief of the Mandans who had 2 of his fingers off and appeared to be pearced in maney places   on inquiring the reason, was informed that it was a testimony to their grief for Deceased freinds, they frequently Cut off Sevral fingers & pierced themselves in Different parts, a Mark of Savage effection, wind hard from the S. W.   verry Cold   R Fields with a Rhumitisum in his Neck   one man R. in his hips[7]   my Self much better, Those Indians appear to have Similar Customs with the Ricaras, their Dress the Same   more mild in their language & justures &c. &c.

[Clark]   25th of October

Course Distance & Reffurences

N. 80° W.   3   miles to a pt. on the L. Side   passed an old Village (1)

West   1   mile on the L. Side

S. 80° W.   1   mile on L. Side

S. 60 W.   2   miles to a pt. on the L. Side

S. 30° W.	2	miles to a Tree on the Larboard Side
S. 33° W.	2	miles to a point on the Starboard Side opposit a high hill
	11	

[Clark]   25th *of October Thursday 1804*

a Cold morning   Set out early under a gentle Breeze from the S. E. by E   proceeded on, passed (1) the 3rd old Village of the Mandans which has been Desd. for many years, This village was Situated on an eminance of about 40 foot above the water on the L. S.   back for Several miles is a butifull plain   (2) at a Short distance above this old village on a Continuation of the Same eminance was Situated the ⟨Ricares Village⟩ [*NB: two old villages of ricaras one on top of high hill the 2d below in the bottom.*] which have been avacuated only Six [*NB: five*] years, above this village a large and extensive bottom for Several miles in which the Squars raised ther Corn, but little timber near the villages, [*NB: about 3 or 4 miles above Ricaras villages are 3 old villages of Mandans near together—here they lived when the R's came for protection   afterwards moved where they now live.*]   on the S. S. below is a point of excellent timber, and in the point Several miles above is fine timber, Several parties of Mandins rode to the river on the S. S. to view us   indeed they are *continuelly* in Sight Satisying their Curiossities as to our apperance &c.   we are told that the Seaux has latterly fallen in with & Stole the horses of the *Big belley,* on their way home they fell in with the Ossiniboin who killed them and took the horses—   a frenchman has latterly been killed by the Indians on the Track to the tradeing establishment on the Ossinebine R. in the North of this place (or British fort) This frenchman has lived ⟨20⟩ many years with the Mandins—   we were frequently called on to land & talk to parties of the Mandins on the Shore, wind Shifted to the S. W at about 11 oClock and blew hard untill 3 OCk. clouded up   river full of Sand bars & we are at a great loss to find the Channel of the river, frequently run on the Sand bars which Detain us much   passed a verry bad riffle of rocks in the evining by takeing the L. S. of a Sand bar and Camped on a Sand point on the S. S. opposit a high hill on the L. S.   Several Indians Come to See us this evening, amongst others the Sun of the late great Cheif of the Mandins, [*NB: mourning for his father*] this man has his two little fingers off—; on inqureing the Cause, was told it was Customary for this nation to Show their greaf by Some testimony of pain, and that it was not uncommon for them to take off 2 Smaller fingers of the hand [*NB: at the 2d joints*] and Some times more with ther marks of Savage effection

The wind blew verry hard this evening from the S. W. verry Cold

R. Fields with the rhumitim in his neck, P. Crusat with the Same Complaint in his Legs— the party other wise is well, as to my Self I feel but Slight Simptoms of that disorder at this time,[8]

1. The courses and distances of October 25 and 26 are at the bottom of document 60 of the Field Notes, while the narrative entries are on document 61. Here they are placed together on appropriate dates. At the head of document 61 are the words "continued" (probably by Clark) and "& 27" (probably by Biddle).

2. The first village passed this day is probably the Bagnell site, a very large late prehistoric Mandan or Hidatsa site. It is shown on *Atlas* map 29 almost directly across from the camp of October 24. Two other villages are also shown in close proximity. The one on the point (the middle one) is the Greenshield site, which appears to be an old Mandan village which was re-occupied by the Arikara during visits to the locale in the later eighteenth century. The third village has not been located. Clark's codex entry for the date says the place was evacuated about six years, while the *Atlas* map gives it as nine years. Will & Hecker, 109–10; Lehmer, Meston, & Dill, 160–66.

3. Names for the Hidatsas.

4. Ménard, a French Canadian possibly bearing the Christian name Pierre and otherwise known as "Manoah" and "old Menard," had lived with the Mandans and Hidatsas since the 1770s. He told Jean Baptiste Truteau that he had been on the Yellowstone River some time before 1795, making him possibly the first white man to have seen that stream. Different sources attribute his death to the Assiniboines, the "Gros Ventres," and the Mandans. Abel (TN), 167–68 and n. 21; Wood & Thiessen, 43–44, 166 n. 27, 180 n. 62; Nasatir (BLC), 1 : 82, 89, 90, 91, 93, 161, 304, 331, 332, 2 : 381, 390; Glover, 170, 172, 174; Coues (NLEH), 1 : 311–12.

5. The Assiniboine River of southeastern Saskatchewan and southern Manitoba is a major tributary of the Red River of the North. The North West and Hudson's Bay companies had several trading posts on the Assiniboine and its tributaries.

6. In the vicinity of present Fort Clark, Oliver County, North Dakota. Because of shifts in the river, the campsite may be in either Oliver or McLean County. *Atlas* map 29; MRC 51.

7. If "R." stands for "rheumatism," the man may be Pierre Cruzatte, noted in Codex C for this date as having the ailment in his legs. If "R." is the man's initial, it could be Reed, Rivet, or Roi.

8. At this point Clark inserted material belonging under the October 26 entry; see below, October 26, 1804.

[Clark]

Course Distance & 26th of October

N. 45° W	1	m. bend L. S.
N. 70° W	1	m. to a pt S. S.—
S 26° W.	2	m. to a camp of mandans L. S.—
West	1	m L S.—
N. 27° W.	3	miles [*WC: Fort Mandan Stands*]¹ to S. S. passed Bluff L
N. 55° W.	1	m. to a pt. on L. S.
S. 60° W.	2	m to the 1st mandan village on the L. S

26th of October 1804   wind from the S. E   we Set the Ricara Chief on Shore with Some Mandans, many on each Side veiwing of us, we took in 2 Chiefs (Coal and Big Man)² and halted a feiw minits at their Camps,³ on the L. S. fortified in their way, here we Saw a trader from the Ossinniboin River Called McCracken,⁴ this man arrived 9 day ago with goods to trade for horses & Roabs   one other man with him—   we Camped on the L. Side a Short distanc below the 1st mandan village on the L. S.⁵   many men women & Children flocked down to See us—   Capt Lewis walked to the Village with the Chief and interpeters, my Rheumitism increasing prevented me from going also, and we had Deturmined that both would not leave the boat at the Same time untill we Knew the Desposition of the Nativs, Some Chieef visited me & I Smoked with them—   they appeared delighted with the Steel Mill⁶ which we were obliged to use, also with my black Servent, Capt Lewis returned late—

[Clark]   26th *of October Friday 1804*

Set out early   wind from the S W   proceeded on   Saw numbers of the Mandins on Shore, we Set the Ricare Chief on Shore, and we proceeded on to the Camp of two of their Grand Chiefs where we delayed a fiew minits, with the Chiefs and proceeded on takeing two of their Chiefs on board & Some of the heavy articles of his house hole, Such as earthen pots & Corn, proceeded on, at this Camp Saw a [*NB: Mr*] McCracken Englishmon from the N. W [*NB: Hudson Bay*] Company   this mana Came nine Days ago to trade for *horses & Buffalo* robes,—   one other man Came with him.   the Indians Continued on the banks all day— but little wood on this part of the river, many Sand bars and bad places, water much devided between them—

for the 26th. Octr.[7] we came too and Camped on the L. S. about ½ a mile below the 1st. Manddin Town on the L. S.   Soon after our arrival many men womin & Children flocked down to See us, Capt Lewis walked to the village with the principal Chiefs and our interpters, my rhumatic Complaint increasing I could not go— if I was well only one would have left the Boat & party untill we new the Disposition of the ⟨party⟩ Inds. I Smoked with the Cheifs who Came after. Those people apd much pleased with the Corn mill which we were obliged to use, & was fixed in the boat.

26th Ocr.

Course Distance & reffrs.

N. 45° W.	1	me. to a tree in the bend to the Larboard Side
N. 70° W.	1	me. to a pt. on the S. S.
S. 26 W.	2	mes. to a wood in the bend Camp of Mandan L. S.
West	1	mes. to to a tree in bind L. S. passed a Small Creek
N. 27° W.	_3_	mes. to the pt. Fort Mandan Stard Passing a bluff of indft.
	8	Coal L. S.
N. 55° W.	1	me. to a pt. on the L. S.
S. 60° W.	_2_	me. to the 1st Village of the Mandins Situated on the L. Side
	11	in an open Plain

1. Obviously Clark interlined the note about Fort Mandan's location later, after the fort was constructed.

2. The Coal, whose name in the Mandan tongue Clark renders as Sho-ta-har ro-ra (*šotaharore,* "it's a white cloud"), was apparently an Arikara by birth, and had been adopted by the Mandans. He was a rival of Black Cat, considered by the captains to be head chief of the Mandans. Big Man, Oh-he-nar (*óhiŋr,* "to be full"), also called "Le Grand," was according to Clark an adopted Cheyenne prisoner. Such adoption was not uncommon; with males it usually occurred in childhood. Both these men were chiefs of the first Mandan village. Coues (NLEH), 1:332; Thwaites (EWT), 5:128, 132, 6:111, 23:231–32 and n. 189.

3. *Atlas* map 29 shows this hunting camp, in Mercer County, North Dakota. MRC map 52.

4. In Codex C, below, Clark writes that Hugh McCracken worked for the North West Company, then corrects it to "Hudsons's Bay." In fact, he appears to have been a free trader working for neither firm. McCracken had been to the Mandans and had resided there several times before he guided David Thompson of the North West Company there in 1797. Lewis and Clark entrusted him with their message to Charles Chaboillez, North West Company factor on the Assiniboine River. In 1806 he accompanied Chaboillez and Alexander Henry the Younger to the Mandan villages. Henry characterizes him as "an old Irishman formerly belonging to the [Royal?] artillery." David Thompson reports him killed by the Sioux on a journey to the Mandans, but the date is certainly wrong. Lewis and Clark to Chaboillez, October 31, 1804, Jackson (LLC), 1:213–14 and n. 1; Tyrrell, 160, 177, 180 and n.; Coues (NLEH), 1:304.

5. The first Mandan village, shown on *Atlas* map 29, was Matootonha (or Mitutanka), on or near the later site of the now defunct village of Deapolis, Mercer County. See fig. 4. The word is not identifiable, although it apparently includes the Mandan word *máŋtu*, "mud." Archaeologists have labeled the site Deapolis; it was destroyed by gravel pit operations in the 1950s. Thompson. Because of river shifts the camp may have been in modern McLean County. The Mandans were an agricultural people who have lived on the Missouri River since they were first known to Europeans. Cultural traits and ancient village sites have suggested an origin far to the southeast in the Mississippi valley. Europeans first mentioned them in 1719, but the first account by a visitor comes from Pierre Gaultier de Varennes, Sieur de La Vérendrye, who encountered them in 1738. They may have been living with the Hidatsas even then, but outsiders did not distinguish the two tribes until later. Lewis and Clark found them in two villages, Matootonha (noted here) and Rooptahee (Ruptáre, Nuptadi). The presence among them of certain unusually light-complexioned and fair-haired persons led to speculations about European origins, a persistent notion being that they were the fabled Welsh Indians, the story that brought John Evans up the Missouri in 1796. All such theories have proved illusory.

In addition to their farming and hunting, the Mandans were important as middlemen in intertribal trade. They were generally peaceful and accommodating in their relations with whites, as with Lewis and Clark, and were less aggressive in their relations with other Indians than their allies the Hidatsas. The presence among them of prominent men of Cheyenne and Arikara birth suggests a relatively low degree of ethnocentrism. They had a rich ceremonial and religious life, of which Lewis and Clark saw only a small part.

The tribe had suffered in the smallpox epidemic of the 1780s; the epidemic of 1837 reduced them to a handful. Thereafter they lived by necessity with the Hidatsas and intermarried with them. At the present time there are believed to be no full-blooded Mandans, though they are counted as one of the Three Affiliated Tribes (Mandan-Hidatsa-Arikara) at Fort Berthold Reservation, North Dakota. Hodge, 1:796–99; Ronda (LCAI), 67–132; Bowers (MSCO); Tyrrell, 171–80; Meyer; Catlin (NAI), 80–184, 203–7; Williams; Masson, 1:327–93; Abel (CJ); Coues (NLEH), 1:323–403.

6. Lewis had purchased three hand-operated mills for grinding corn while gathering equipment in Philadelphia in 1803. Supplies from Private Vendors [June 30, 1803], Jackson (LLC), 1:84.

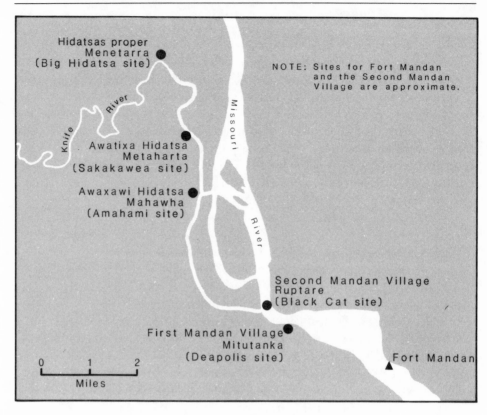

4. Knife River Indian Villages

7. The remainder of this Codex C passage of October 26 appears at the end of the October 25 entry, with Clark's interlined note giving the correct date. Asterisks also served to establish the connection. There is considerable space between the end of the October 26 entry, as written, and the courses and distances for that day. Apparently Clark wrote these courses first, leaving space for the narrative, then found that he had not left sufficient space, so utilized space at the end of the October 25 entry.

Chapter Eight

Among the Mandans

October 27–December 27, 1804

[Clark]

27th of October Satturday 1804 we Set out early and Came too at the village [Matootonha] on the L. S. where we delayed a few minits, I walked to a Chiefs Logg [lodge] & Smoked with them, but Could not eat, which did displease them a little, here I met with a Mr: Jessomme,[1] who lived in this nation 18 [13?] years, I got him to interpet & he proceedd on with us we proceeded on to a Central point opposit the Knife River, & formed a Camp on the S. S. above the 2d Mandan village[2] & opsd. the Mah-har-ha village—[3] and raised a flag Staff—[4] Capt Lewis & the Intepeters walked down to the 2d Village of Mandans, & returned in about an hour, we Sent 3 Carrotes of tobacco to the other villages & enviting them to come down and Council with us tomorrow,— we endeaver to precure Some Knowledge of the principal Chiefs of the Different nations &.— well to give my ideas as to the impression thais man [Jusseaume] makes on me is a Cunin artfull an insoncear [insincere?]— he tels me he was once empld. by my brother in the Illinois & of his description I conceve as a Spye upon the British of Michillinicknac & St Joseph,[5] we think he may be made use full to us & do employ him as an interpeter— no. of Indians bring their wives &c. to the campes of our party on Shore &c.

Course distanc &c

West	2	m. to a bend on the L. S. passed a Coal bank on the L. S.
N. 10° W.	2	m to a wood on the S. S. passed the 2d Mandan V. on the S. S. to the place we counciled & Stayed untill the 1st Nov.—

Cours & Distance. up the Missouri abov the Mandans[6]

N. 12° W.	3	m. to a Bluff 30 feet high above the wooded bottom S. Side
N. 20° W.	2	m. to a tree under a Bluff of about 20 feet high on the S. S.
N. 30° W.	1 ½	m. to a pt of the Same Bluff 30 feet high in which is Coal
N. 45° W.	1 ½	m. to the lower point of an Island, the Current on the L. S.

Mandans

[Clark]   *27th of October Satturday 1804*

we Set out arly   Came too at this Village on the L. S.   this village is Situated on an eminance of about 50 feet above the Water in a handson Plain   it Containes houses in a kind of Picket work.   the houses are round and Verry large Containing Several families, as also their horses which is tied on one Side of the enterance, a Discription of those houses will be given hereafter, I walked up & Smoked a pipe with the Cheifs of this Village   they were anxious that I would Stay and eat with them, my indisposition provented my eating which displeased them, untill a full explination took place, I returned to the boat and Sent 2 Carrots of Tobacco for them to Smoke, and proceeded on, passed the 2d Village and Camped opsd. the Village of the *Weter Soon* or ah wah har ways which is Situated on an eminance in a plain on the L. S.   this Village is Small and Contains but fiew inhabitents.   above this village & also above the Knife river[7] on the Same Side of the Missouri the Big bellies Towns are Situated[8]   a further Discription will be given here after as also of the Town of Mandans on this Side of the river i' e' S. Side—

a fine worm Day   we met with a french man by the name of *Jassamme* which we imploy as an interpeter   This man has a wife & Children in the Village—   Great numbers on both Sides flocked down to the bank to view us as wee passed.

Capt. Lewis with the Interpetr. walked down to the village below our Camp   After delaying one hour he returned and informed me the Indians had returned to their village &c., &c., we Sent three ⟨twists⟩ Carrots of Tobacco by three young men, to the three Villages above inviting them to come Down & Council with us tomorrow.   many Indians Came to view us   Some Stayed all night in the Camp of our party—   we procured Some information of Mr. Jessomme of the Chiefs of the Different Nations

Course Distance 27th

West	2	Miles to a bind on the L. S. passing a Cole Bank
N. 10° W	2	miles to a wood on the S. S. passd. the 2 Village on S. S.
	4	

1. René Jusseaume, or Jessaume, was a free trader who in 1804 had lived with the Mandans for about fifteen years, drawing his goods on credit from the North West Company. He told Clark he had been a spy for George Rogers Clark in the Illinois country during the Revolutionary War. He acted as Mandan interpreter for many persons, but apparently was not considered a good one. He seems to have participated fully in the social and ceremonial life of the Mandans, which may account for some of the low opinions whites expressed of him. Evans thought that Jusseaume planned his murder in 1796, when Evans tried to exclude him from the Indian trade. David Thompson, whom he accompanied to the Mandans in 1797, was not impressed with his character, and Alexander Henry the Younger called him "that old sneaking cheat." Lewis and Clark also found him "assumeing and discont'd." Nevertheless they hired him to accompany Sheheke (Big White), the Mandan chief, to Washington as interpreter in 1806. During the attempted return of that chief in 1807, which was stopped by the Arikaras, Jusseaume suffered a crippling wound and petitioned Jefferson for a pension. In 1809 he apprenticed his thirteen-year old son to Lewis, to provide for the boy's education. He was still alive at the time of Maximilian's visit to the Mandans in 1833–34, and was still not considered a really good interpreter. Coues (NLEH), 1:333, 401; Glover, 160, 162, 171–72, 180; Masson, 1:294, 303, 376 and n., 377–78; Nasatir (BLC), 1:102–5, 496–97, passim.; Thwaites (EWT), 5:156–59, 167; Luttig, 74, 77; Williams; Speck, 71–78; Nathaniel Pryor to Clark, October 16, 1807, Jackson (LLC), 2:436, 438 n. 8.

2. Rooptahee (Ruptáre, Nuptadi), in McLean County, North Dakota. It has been destroyed by river changes and no trace of it can be found today. It is called the Black Cat site, after the village chief. The camp was on the same side of the river, north of Rooptahee and opposite the present site of Stanton, Mercer County, North Dakota. See fig. 4. Appleman (LC), 342; Wood (OHI), 10–11; Ronda (LCAI), 67–132; *North Dakota Guide*, 317; *Atlas* map 29; MRC map 52.

3. Mahawha (apparently a Mandan name, *maŋxáxa*, "spread out place"), on the site of present Stanton; see *Atlas* map 29. It is called the Amahami site but is largely destroyed by buildings in Stanton, principally the Mercer County Courthouse. See fig. 4. Its inhabitants were the members of one of the three commonly recognized divisions of the Hidatsa, or Minitari, tribe. The captains recognized that the people of this village were somewhat distinct from the Minitaris, though allied with them. This small group had a multitude of names; Clark at various times called them Ahnahaways, Ahwahaways, Gens de Soulier, Mahaha, Maharhar, Shoe Indians, Soulier Noir (Black Shoe), and Watersoons, among other names. The last may come from an Arikara designation, *wiitatshaánu'*. The name Amahami ("mountainous country") gained acceptance from Washington Matthews's ethnographic studies; Alfred Bowers calls them the Awaxawi. The different spellings reflect

two orthographic systems; the term may be related to the Hidatsa word *awaxáawi*, "mountain." Their dialect was distinct from that of the other two Hidatsa village groups, though all three understood each other readily; all belonged to the Siouan language family. The Awaxawi said they came to the Missouri River from eastern North Dakota. Hodge, 1 : 47, 547–49; Bowers (HSCO); Wood (OHI); Ronda (LCAI), 67–132; Meyer; Matthews.

4. With this line the Field Notes entry of October 27 continues on document 62. Biddle's note at the top of the page reads "Octo. part of 27 & 29 Octo. 1804."

5. Michilimackinac Island, at the Straits of Mackinac between Lake Michigan and Lake Huron, and St. Joseph, on the St. Joseph River in southern Michigan, were British posts in the Old Northwest during the Revolutionary War.

6. These courses are for Clark's trip above the villages on October 30, repeated in Codex C (for that date).

7. Knife River reaches the Missouri in Mercer County. *Atlas* map 29; MRC map 52.

8. "Big Bellies" is a literal translation of the French *gros ventres*, otherwise known as the Minitaris, and now called the Hidatsas. The term Hidatsa may come from *hiráaca* with an uncertain etymology. Minitari is from *miɲintari* (literally, "water ford"), the Mandan designation for the Hidatsas based on a loan word borrowed from the Hidatsa language. Clark uses all the first three names, in various spellings. The name Gros Ventres apparently derived from the Plains sign language designation for these people, which used both hands to indicate an expanded stomach. Travelers' accounts made the point that the tribe had no larger stomachs than others. The name has been a fruitful source of confusion, since "Gros Ventres" was a name also applied to the Atsinas, a nomadic tribe of Algonquian language stock who apparently broke away from the Arapahoes and lived well to the west of the Hidatsas. Nineteenth-century writers attempted to resolve the confusion by distinguishing between the "Gros Ventres of the Missouri" (Hidatsas) and the "Gros Ventres of the Prairie" (Atsinas). The Hidatsas were of Siouan language family and lived in sedentary farming villages of earth lodges in North Dakota. Lewis and Clark found the Hidatsas in three villages near the mouth of Knife River, in Mercer County. The first was that of the Amahami, or Awaxawi, described in a separate note above. Second going upstream was Metaharta, also called the Sakakawea site from its association with Sacagawea, the captains' Shoshone interpreter. The third village was Big Hidatsa site, home of the Hidatsas proper. The captains frequently referred to the Mandan and Hidatsa villages by numbers from south to north; the Mandan villages were numbers 1 and 2, so the Awaxawi village was number 3, Metaharta number 4, and Big Hidatsa number 5. See *Atlas* maps 29, 46, 55, and fig. 4. While ethnologists speak of one people called Minitaris or Hidatsas, there were at least three divisions within these people, corresponding roughly to the three villages, each conscious of being somewhat different in language, culture, and antecedents. In the southernmost village were the Awaxawi. The other two groups, distinct yet more closely allied in culture and language than were the Awaxawi, were the Hidatsas proper at Big Hidatsa, the northern village, and the Awatixa, at Metaharta, the middle village. Awatixa is a Hidatsa name, *awatixáa*, "high village," while Metaharta is a Mandan term, *miɲ'tixata*, "village spread out." The Awatixa claimed that they had always lived on the Missouri, which suggests residence there beyond traditional memory. The Hidatsas proper,

like the Awaxawi, said they came from eastern North Dakota, the former being the last to arrive. Apparently the Awaxawi and Hidatsas proper lived near the mouth of Heart River before moving north to the Knife River, where all three groups were established by 1787. A further complication is that archaeologists cannot distinguish between prehistoric Hidatsa sites and those of the Mandans on the basis of artifacts. This suggests long association and close cultural connections between the two peoples, in spite of their own awareness of distinctiveness. All of these groups suffered from the great smallpox epidemic of the 1780s and from Sioux attacks. Reduction of population and the need for a defensive alliance were no doubt responsible, at least in part, for the five Mandan and Hidatsa villages drawing closer together in the late eighteenth century. All of these groups were sedentary farmers in permanent earth lodge villages who hunted to supplement their agricultural products. However, the Hidatsas proper are said to have learned corn growing from the Mandans after they reached the Missouri, and even at the time of Lewis and Clark were apparently semi-nomadic. All the Hidatsas seem to have had a stronger military tradition than the Mandans. John Bradbury noted in 1809 that the Awaxawi had only fifty warriors, yet they, like the others, carried out raids against the Shoshones and Flatheads in the Rockies. It was in one of these Hidatsa raids that Sacagawea was captured. The smallpox epidemic of 1837 further reduced the Hidatsas; Metaharta and the Awaxawi village were destroyed by the Sioux in 1834. After the epidemic the Hidatsas absorbed the remnants of the Mandans and moved to Like-a-Fishhook village, near the Fort Berthold trading post, in 1845. The Arikaras joined them there and the defensive alliance of the three tribes, proposed by Lewis and Clark, was finally consummated. The "Three Affiliated Tribes" still live at Fort Berthold Reservation, North Dakota. Hodge, 1 : 47, 547–49; Bowers (HSCO); Wood (OHI); Ronda (LCAI), 67–132; Smith (LAFV); Meyer; Thwaites (EWT), 5 : 163; Catlin (NAI), 1 : 185–202; Matthews; Clark, 193–97.

[Clark]

28th of October 1804   the wind So hard from the S. W.   We could not meet the Indians in Councils, those who visited us we Sent to the nearest village, Consulted the Black Cat M Chief[1] about the Chiefs of the Different Villages, who gave his Oppinion to us.

[Clark]   *Sunday 28th of October 1804*

a windey Day, fair and Clear   many of the *Grosvantres* [(]or Big Bellies) and Watersons Came to See us and hear the Council   the wind being So violently hard from the S. W. provented our going into Councel, (indeed the Chiefs of the Manodans from the lower Village Could not Cross, we made up the presents and entertained Several of the Curious Cheifs whome, wished to See the Boat which was verry Curious to them viewing it as great medison, [*NB: (whatever is mysterious or unintelligible is called great medicine)*] as they also viewed my black Servent   The Black Cat Grand Chief of the Mandans, Capt Lewis & my Self with an Interpeter walked up the river about 1 ½ miles   our views were to examine the Situation & Timbers for a fort, we found the Situation good but the Timber Scerce, or at least Small timbr Such as would [*NB: not*] answer us—,

we Cunsulted the Grand Chief in respect to the other Chiefs of the Defferent Villages   he gave the names of 12—   George Drewyer Cought 2 Beaver above our Camp last night, we had Several presents from the Woman of Corn boild homney, Soft Corn &c. &c.   I prosent a jar [*NB: earthern jar glazed*] to the Chiefs wife who recved it with much pleasure our men verry Chearfull this evening—   we Sent the Cheifs of the Gross Vantres to Smoke a pipe with the Grand Chef of the Mandins in his Village, & told them we would Speek tomorrow.

1. His Indian name was Posecopsahe, variously spelled. It is from the Mandan term, *púskapsi*, "black cat." The captains were impressed with this chief's intelligence and friendliness, and thought he would be useful to American interests. British traders found him equally hospitable and helpful, but he made a point of displaying the American flag Lewis and Clark had given him when visited by North West Company traders in 1806. He and The Coal were supposed to be rivals, so perhaps Black Cat's authority was not as supreme as the captains imagined. His residence was at Rooptahee village. Masson, 1 : 366–67; Coues (NLEH), 1 : 324–29; Wood & Thiessen, 137 n. 13, 265–66; Ronda (LCAI), 81–90, 115–16; Thwaites (EWT), 23 : 231–32.

[Clark]

29th of October 1804   a fine morning   after Brackfast we were Visited by the Old Chief of the Big Bellies or *me ne tar res,*[1]   this Man has Given his power to his Son who is now on a war party against the Snake Indians who inhabit the Rockey Mountains,[2] the S W wind verry high—   we met in Council under an orning and our Sales Stretched round to keep out as much wind as possible & Delivered a long Speach Similar to what had been Said to the nations below, the old Chief was restless before the Speech was half ended, observed his Camp was exposed & could wait no longer &c.   at the Conclusion of the Speach we mentioned the Ricaras & requested them to make a peace & Smoke out of the Sacred Stem with their Chief which I intreduced and gave him the pipe of peace to hand around, they all Smoked with eagerness out of the pipe held by the Ricara Chief *Ar-ke-tar-na-Shar* we mentioned our hands that were to be discharged here, also the roberrey commited on th 2 french men below, & requested them to answere us tomorrow, gave the Chief Small preasents and a fiew presents for each village Shot the air gun which both Surprised and astonished the nativs, and Soon dispersed—

our Ricara Chief Came told me he wished to return to his nation tomorrow I put him off & Said we would Send a talk by him after the Chiefs had Spoken to us— we gave a Steel mill[3] to the mandans which was verry pleasing to them

The Chief who recved Medals to Day are as follows viz—in Council[4]

1s Mandan village Ma-too-ton ka—
  1s Chief *Sha-ha-ka* Big White[5]
  2nd *Ka-goh-ha-me* little Crow[6]

2 do village *Roop tar-hee*
  1s & grand Chief Poss-cop-sa-he Black Cat—
  2d Chief *Car-gar-no-mok-she* raven man Chief—

Mah har-ha village
  1s Chief *Ta-tuck-co pin re has,* white Buffalow Skin unfolded

Little Menetarre village
  1s Chief Omp-Se-ha-ra Black mockerson.[7]
  2d Chief *Oh-harh* little Fox.

The Grand village of Manetarres, The One Eye is the principal Chief and he is out on a hunting party.[8] we Send by the Grape all the articles for this grand Chief and all the Village what goods was intended for that Village—[9] The Prarie got on fire and went with Such Violenc & Speed as to Catch a man & woman & burn them to Death, Several escapd. among other a Small boy who was Saved by getting under a green Buffalow Skin, this boy was half white, & the Indians Say all white flesh is medisan, they Say the grass was not burnt where the boy Sat &c. &. this fire passed us at 8 oClock, and lookd truly tremendious.

[Clark]   29th *October Monday 1804.*

a fair fine morning   after Brackfast we were visited by the old Cheaf of
the *Big bellies* or [*blank*]   this man was old and had transfered his power
to his Sun, who was then out at war against the Snake Indians who inhabit
the rockey mountains—   at 10 oClock the S W. wind rose verry high, we
Collected the Chiefs and Commened a Council ounder a Orning and our
Sales Stretched around to Keep out as much wind as possible, we delivered
a long Speech the Substance of which Similer to what we had Delivered to
the nations below.   the old Chief of the Grossanters was verry restless
before the Speech was half ended   observed that he Could not wait long
that his Camp was exposed to the hostile Indians, &c. &.   he was rebuked
by one of the Chiefs for his uneasiness at Such a time as the present, we at
the end of the Speech mentioned the *Ricare* who Accompanied us to make
a firm peace, they all Smoked with him (I gave this Cheaf a Dollar of the
American Coin as a Meadel with which he was much pleased)   In Councel we prosented him with a Certificate of his Sincrrity and good Conduct
&c.   we also Spoke about the fur which was taken from 2 french men by
a Mandan, and informd of our intentions of Sending back the french
hands—   after the Coun[c]i[l] we gave the presents with much Seremoney, and put the Meadels on the Cheifs we intended to make viz. one
for each Town to whome we gave Coats hats & flags, one Grand Cheif to
each nation to whome we gave meadels with the presidents likeness   in
Councel we requested them to give us an answer tomorrow or as Soon as
possible to Some points which required their Deliberation—   after the
Council was over we Shot the Air gun which appeared to assonish the
nativs much, the greater part them retired Soon after—

The *Ricare* Cheaf *Ar-ke-tar-na-shar* Came to me this evening and tells
me that he wishes to return to his Village & nation, I put him off Saying
tomorrow we would have an answer, to our talk to the Satisfaction & Send
by him a String of wompom informing what had passed here.   a Iron or
Steel Corn Mill which we gave to the Mandins, was verry Thankfully recived—   (☞ The Prarie was Set on fire (or Cought by accident) by a young
man of the Mandins, the fire went with Such velocity that it burnt to death
a man and woman, who Could not Get to any place of Safty, one man a
woman & Child much burnt and Several narrowly escaped the flame—   a

boy half white was Saved un hurt in the midst of the flaim, Those igne-
rent people Say this boy was Saved by the great Spirit medisin because he
was white— The Cause of his being Saved was a Green buffalow Skin
was thrown over him by his mother who perhaps had more fore Sight for
the pertection of her ⟨self⟩ Son, and [l]ess for herself than those who escaped the flame, the Fire did not burn under the Skin leaving the grass
round the boy

This fire passed our Camp last about 8 oClock P. M. it went with great
rapitidity and looked Tremendious

The following Chiefs were made in Councel to day

Mar-too-ton-ha or Lower Village of the Mandans
    1st Cheif *Sha-ha-ka* or Big White
    2 do *Ka-goh-ha-mi* or *Little raven*

Roop-tar-hee or Second Village of the Mandans
    1st and Grand Cheif—Pass-cop-sa-he or *black Cat*
    2nd Cheif *Car-gar-no-mok-She* raven man Cheaf

Mah-har-ha 3rd Village
    Chief Ta-tuck-co-pin-re-ha (white Buffalow robe unfolded)
    ⟨*Man resse-sar-ra-ree* or Neighing horse⟩

Me-ne-tar-re Me-te har-tar
    1st Cheif—*Omp-se-ha-ra*. Black Mockersons
    2 do. *Oh-harh* or *Little fox*

we Sent the presents intended for the Grand Chief of the *Mi-ne-tar-re*
or Big Belley, and the presents flag and wompoms by the Old Chief and
those, and those intended for the Cheif of the Lower Village by a young
Cheif—

The following Cheifs were recommended in addition to those Viz.—

1st Village
    Oh-hee-nar Big Man— [*NB: a Cheyenne prisoner adopted by them*] a
        Chien
    Sho-ta-har ro-ra

2d Village

Taw nish-e-o—   Bel-lar sa ra[10]

Ar-rat-ta na-mock-She—   Wolf Man Chief[11]

3rd Village

⟨*Te-tuck-co-pin-re-ha—*   white Buffalow Skin unfolded⟩[12]

Min-nis-Sur-ra-ree (Neighing horse[)]

Lo-tong-gar-ti har—   old woman at a distance

4th Village

Mar-noh-tah   the big Steeler ⟨(out at war)⟩[*NB: (who was then out at war & was killed afd*)]

Man-se-rus-se—   tale of Callumet bird

5th Village

Shā hakó ho pin nee   Little Wolfs medisons

Ar-rat-toe-no mook-gu   (man wolf Chief[)] (*at war*[)][13]

Cal-tar cō tá—   (*Cherry* grows [*NB: ing*] on a bush) old Chief and father to the above mentd.

Chief Maw-pah'-pir-re-cos-sa too—[14]   This chief is near this hunting and a verry Considerable man

To the 1st Chiefs we gave a medal with the Imp. of the President of the U S.

To the 2d Chiefs a medal of weaveing & Domestic animals.

To the 3rd Chiefs a medal with the impression of a man Sowing wheat.[15]

4th Village

⟨*War-ka-res-so-ra*⟩

1 *Ea pa no pa—*   Two taled Calumet bird young Chief

2 *War he ras sa*   the red Shield young Chief of Big belley—big town[16]

Point of Observation No. 50

[Lewis]   *Monday October 29th 1804.*[17]

On the stard. shore at council camp, about half a mile above the upper Mandan Village.

Observed meridian Altd. of ☉'s U. L. with Sextant by the fore observation 58° 55' 15"

Latitude deduced from this observation   N. 47° 22' 56.7"

☞ The Chronometer ran down today. I was so much engaged with the Indians, that I omited winding her up.—

1. Variously called Caltarcota, Cherry Grows on a Bush, Chokecherry, Cerina Grape, and The Grape, this elderly Hidatsa chief had supposedly turned over his authority to his son, Man Wolf Chief. Nevertheless, he appears prominently in accounts by visitors to the tribe at this period. Coues (NLEH), 1:367–68, 376–78, 388–89, 390, 395; Wood & Thiessen, 166–67 and n. 29; Ronda (LCAI), 82–84. An undated copy by Clark of a "Speech of the Cherry" (perhaps from this date) is on a loose sheet in the Voorhis Collection, Missouri Historical Society. See Indian Speeches, Miscellaneous Documents of Lewis and Clark, Appendix C, vol. 2. It is badly mutilated, with many words unclear or missing, and is not reproduced here. The council of this day is discussed in Ronda (LCAI), 82–84.

2. Shoshonean tribes living about the headwaters of the Missouri and just across the Continental Divide.

3. A steel corn mill, which Alexander Henry the Younger later found broken up to be used for arrow barbs and other purposes. Coues (NLEH), 1:329.

4. Some of these names (also from the codex entry) may be identified linguistically:

Sha-ha-ka (*šáhaka*), etymology uncertain, possibly related to *ha*, "cloud"

Ka-goh-ha-me (*kéka x^amanhe*), "little raven"

Car-gar-no-mok-she (*kékanuŋmaŋkši*), "chief raven" (literally, "raven good man")

Ta-tuck-co pin re has, possibly a compound of Dakota *t'at'aŋka,* "buffalo bull" and Mandan *xop^iníŋrehas,* "the holy separated thing"

Man resse-sar-ra-ree (*m^iníŋs^arare*), "neighing horse"

Omp-Se-ha-ra (*húŋpsih^ara*), "blackens moccasin"

Oh-harh (*óxa*), "fox"

Oh-hee-nar (*óhiŋr*), "to be full"

Sho-ta-har ro-ra (*šotaharore*), "it's a white cloud"

Bel-lar sa ra (*w^eros^ara*), "bellowing bull"

Ar-rat-ta na-mock-She (*x^arate núŋmaŋkši*), "chief wolf"

Lo-tong-gar-ti har (*rókaŋkatiŋxa*), "old woman appears over the horizon"

Mar-noh-tah (*máŋnuŋxta*), "thief" (literally, "big stealer")

Man-se-rus-se (*máŋsiruše*), "grasps the yellow eagle-like bird"

Sha hako ho pin nee (*sehékoxop^iriŋ*), "medicine coyote"

Ar-rat-toe-no mock-gu (*x^arate núŋmaŋke*), "wolf man"

Maw-pah'-pir-re-cos-sa too (*máŋhpapirakaŋsetu*), "there are some horned weasels"

Ea pa no pa (*ípanunpa*), "two bird tails"

War he ras sa (*wó'kire sa*), "red shield"

5. Principal chief of the lower Mandan village, Matootonha; his proper name (Sheheke), variously spelled, is commonly translated "Coyote." The name Big White, or Big White Man, was given by whites because of his supposed resemblance to whites and his size—he was notably obese. He accompanied Lewis and Clark to Washington on their return journey in 1806. Returning him to his people became a major problem to the captains in their later capacities as governor and Indian superintendent; because of Sioux and Arikara

hostility he did not reach home until 1809. The Mandans did not believe his tales of the wonders he had seen, and he lost much of his prestige and influence; perhaps his long absence had in any case allowed rivals to supplant him. He is reported as expressing a desire to return to the whites and live among them, but he was killed in a Sioux raid on his village in 1832. Hodge, 2 : 518–19; Clark to Toussaint Charbonneau, August 10, 1806, Lewis to Jefferson, September 23, 1806, Jackson (LLC), 1 : 315, 323–25 and n. 7; Ronda (LCAI), 87–88, 247–50; Thwaites (EWT), 5 : 151, 162–64, 6 : 137, 152; Coues (NLEH), 1 : 330–31, 333; Thompson, 171, 179–80; Abel (CJ), 20; Foley & Rice (RMC).

6. Clark ranks him as second chief of the lower Mandan village, Matootonha; he was also called Little Raven. He was to have accompanied Big White to Washington in 1806, but he changed his mind. He was still prominent among the Mandans nearly thirty years later. Thwaites (EWT), 24 : 22 and n. 14; Ronda (LCAI), 69, 246–47.

7. The captains considered Black Moccasin head chief of the second Hidatsa village, Metaharta. In 1833, at a great age, he recalled them fondly; sitting for a portrait by George Catlin, he asked the painter to carry his regards to Clark in St. Louis. Thwaites (EWT), 5 : 167; 6 : 140; Ronda (LCAI), 70, 91–92; Catlin (NAI), 1 : 186–87 and n., plate 72.

8. For the formidable One Eye, or Le Borgne, see below, March 9, 1805.

9. With this sentence the Field Notes entry of October 29 continues on document 63. Biddle's note at the top of the page reads "Octo. 29 and nov. 13 1804."

10. It is not clear in the journals whether these two names represent one man or two. Biddle's *History* indicates two, the translations of whose names the captains were unable to learn. Coues (HLC), 1 : 183.

11. Since he appears as a chief at the Mandan village of Rooptahee, he is apparently not the Hidatsa leader Man Wolf Chief. There may have been an error on the part of Clark or an interpreter. Mandan chiefs with similar names occur in writings thirty years later; the name may have been common, or possibly it was a title rather than a proper name. Abel (CJ), 127; Catlin (NAI), 1 : 92, plate 49; Bowers (HSCO), 224; Thwaites (EWT), 22 : 345 n. 318, 24 : 17; Bowers (MSCO), 137.

12. It apparently was Biddle who crossed out this line with red ink.

13. This young chief of the Hidatsas was the son of Cherry Grows on a Bush, who had reportedly turned over most of his power to the younger man. Other sources call him Wolf Chief or Chief of the Wolves. He was a noted warrior and war leader. This same fall a war party under his direction killed some Canadian traders on the Saskatchewan River, allegedly because they mistook them for enemy Indians. Coues (NLEH), 1 : 368, 379; Thwaites (EWT), 5 : 163 and n. 99; Masson, 1 : 306–7, 342–43, 344; Wood & Thiessen, 166–67 n. 29, 233, 243–44.

14. The "Horned Weasel" who was "not at home" to Lewis on November 27, 1804.

15. The medals "with the Imp. of the President" were, of course, Jefferson portraits. The others were the so-called "Washington Season Medals" designed by the artist John Trumbull during Washington's administration but not completed until John Adams's term of office. Struck in both silver and copper, with a 45 mm. diameter, they portrayed domestic scenes that presumably represented the civilization to which the government wished to

convert the Indians. As Clark indicates, one showed a woman weaving on a loom, another pictured cattle and sheep, and another a man sowing wheat. Prucha (IPM), 17, 89–95.

16. Clark's "4th Village" was Metaharta (see *Atlas* map 29). At a later date Red Shield reportedly killed Le Borgne, or One Eye. Thwaites (EWT), 5:162, 15:97, 23:219–20, 24:23.

17. Lewis's observation from Codex O.

[Clark]

30th of October Tuesday 1804   many Indian Chief visit us to day   I went in th Perogou to the Island 7 miles above[1] to look out a proper place for to winter, it being near the tim the ice begins to run at this place, and the Countrey after a few leagues high is Said to be barron of timber, I found no place Soutable, & we concluded to drop down to th next point below & build a fort to winter in   the Party Danced which Delited the ⟨Savages⟩ Indians.

[Clark]   30th *October Tuesday 1804*

Two Chiefs came to have Some talk   one the princapal of the lower Village the other the one who thought himself the principal mane, & requested to hear Some of the Speech that was Delivered yesterday   they were gratified, and we put the medal on the neck of the Big White to whome we had Sent Clothes yesterday & a flag, those men did not return from hunting in time to ⟨here⟩ join the Counell, they were well pleased (2d of those is a Chien)[2]   I took 8 men in a Small perogue and went up the river as far as the 1st Island about 7 miles to See if a Situation Could be got on it for our Winter quarters, found the wood on the Isd. as also on the pt. above So Distant from the water that, I did not think that we Could get a good wintering ground there, and as all the white men here informed us that wood was Sceres, as well as game [*NB: game*] above, we Deturmined to drop down a fiew miles near wood and game

Course to the Island

N. 12° W.	3	me. to a Bluff 30 feet high above the point of wood S. S.
N. 20° W	2	mes. to a tree under the bank about 20 feet high— S. S. butifull plain

N. 30° W.	1 ½	mes. to a pt. of the Same Bluff 30 feet high under which There was Coal S. S.
N. 45° W.	1 ½	me. to the Lower point of an Island Current on the L. S. this Isd. abt. 1 mile long.
	<u>7</u>	

on my return found maney Inds. at our Camp, gave the party a dram, they Danced as is verry Comn. in the evening which pleased the Savages much.   Wind S. E

[Clark][3]

Mandans

Ka gar no mogh ge the 2d Chief of the 2d Village of Mandins Came the 30t of Octr. and Spoke to us as follows.   Viz

Will you be So good as to go to the Village   the Grand Chief will Speek & give Some Corn, if you will let Some men take bags it will be well. I am going with, the Chief of the ricares to Smoke a pipe with that nation—   I concluded to go down

Mockerson Indians[4]

The principal Chief of the *Wau te Soon* Came and Spoke a fiew words on Various Subjects not much to the purpose.   we Smoked and after my Shooting the air gun he departed, Those nations know nothing of reagular Councils, and know not how to proceed in them, they are restless &c—

At the same place.

[Lewis]   *Tuesday October 30th 1804.*[5]

Wound up the Chronometer, and observed equal Altitudes of the ☉ with Sextant.

A. M.	8	4	44	P. M.	lost in consequence
	"	7	31		of the sun's being
	"	10	31		obscured by clouds.

Altitude given by Sextant at the time of Obstn.   44° 53′ 15″

1. Probably the island which is prominent above the last Hidatsa village on *Atlas* map 29, surrounded by a sandbar. It appears later to have joined the McLean County, North Dakota, shore. Warren map 89; MRC map 52.

2. Big Man, the adopted Cheyenne.

3. This transcript is on a loose sheet in the Voorhis Collection, Missouri Historical Society. See Indian Speeches, Miscellaneous Documents of Lewis and Clark, Appendix C, vol. 2. Included on this sheet is the following (see also October 1, 1804):

Ricare Name for Dift. Nations

Shar ha or Dog Indians	in the open Prarie West
Ki a wah	
Kun na war wih	
Wa na tar wer	all those nations live the West &
War too che work koo	South West of the Rickaries Nation
An *nah* hose	
Te pah cus	
Car tar kah	

4. This transcript immediately follows the previous speech on the same sheet, suggesting that it was made on the same day.

5. Lewis's observation from Codex O, made at the same place as that of October 29.

[Clark]

31st of October Wednesday 1804   The main Chief of the mandans Sent 2 Cheifs for ⟨us⟩ to envite us to Come to his Lodge, and here what he has to Say   I with 2 interpetes walked down, and with great Cerimony was Seated on a Robe by the Side of the Chief; he threw a Robe highly decoraterd over my Sholders, and after Smokeing a pipe with the old men in the Circle, the Chief Spoke   "he belived all we had told him, and that peace would be genl. which not only gave himself Satisfaction but all his people; they now Could hunt without fear & their women could work in the fields without looking every moment for the ememey, as to the Ricaras addressing himself to the Chief with me   you know we do not wish war with your nation, you have brought it on your Selves, that man Pointing to the 2d Chief and those 2 young warriers will go with you & Smoke in the pipes of peace with the Ricaras—   I will let you see my father addressing me that we wish to be at peace with all and do not make war upon any—["]   he continud to Speak in this Stile (refer to notes)[1]   he delivered 2 of the Traps to me which was taken from the french men, gave me 2 bushels of Corn,

I answered the Speech which appeared to give general Satisfaction—and returned to the boat, In the evening the Chief Visited us Dressed in his new Suit, & delayed untill late   the men Dancd untill 10 oClock which was common with them   wrote to the N W Copanys agent on the Ossinniboin River[2] by a Mr. McCruckin.

[Clark]   31st *of October Wednesday 1804*

a fine morning, the Chief of the Mandans Sent a 2d Chief to invite us to his Lodge to recive Some Corn & here what he had to Say   I walked down and with great ceremoney was Seeted on a roab by the Side of the Chief, he threw a handsom Roabe over me and after smokeing the pipe with Several old men arround, the Chief Spoke

Said he believed what we had told them, and that peace would be general, which not only gave him Satisfaction but all his people, they now Could hunt without fear, & ther womin Could work in the fields without looking everry moment for the Enemey, and put off their mockersons at night, [*NB: sign of peace undress*] as to the *Reares* we will Show you that we wish peace with all, and do not make war on any without Cause, that Chief pointing to the 2d and Some brave men will accompy. the Ricare Chief now with you to his village & nation, to Smoke with that people, when you Came up the Indians in the neighbouring Villages, as well as those out hunting when they heard of you had great expectations of reciving presents   they those hunting imediately on hearing returned to the Village and all was Disapointed, and Some Dessatisfied, as to himself he was not much So but his Village was—   he would go and See his great father &c. &c.

he had put before me 2 of the Steel traps which was robed from the french a Short tim ago.   about 12 bushels of Corn which was brought and put before me by the womin of the Village   after the Chief finished & Smoked in great cerrimony, I answered the Speech which Satisfied them verry much and returned to the boat.   met the princapal Chief of the 3d Village and the Little Crow both of which I invited into the Cabin and Smoked & talked with for about one hour. Soon after those Chiefs left us the Grand Chief of the Mandans Came Dressed in the Clothes we had given with his 2 Small Suns, and requested to See the men Dance which they verry readily gratified him in,— the wind blew hard all the after part of the day from the N E and Continud all night to blow hard from that point, in the mornig it Shifed N W. Capt Lewis wrote to the N W Companys agent [*NB: fort &c there*] on the Orsineboine River [*NB: about 150 miles hence*] abt. ⟨9 Days march⟩[3] North of this place

[Clark]   [*undated, October 31, 1804*][4]

black Cat or Pose-cop-sa-he 1st Chief of the Mandans & 2d Village

"I believe what you have told us in Council, & that peace will be general, which not only givs me pleasure, but Satisfaction to all the nation, they now Can hunt without fear, and our womin Can work in the fields without looking every moment for the enimey—" as to the *Ricares* we will Show you that we wish piace with all, and do not make [war] on any with out Cause, that Chief pointing to the 2d of the Village and Some young men will accompany the Ricrea Chief home to his Nation to Smoke with that people— When the Indians of the Different Villages heard of your Comeing up they all Came in from hunting to See, they expected Great presents. they were disapointed, and Some dissatisfied— as to my Self I am not much So, but my Village are— he believed the roade was open; and he would go and See his great father— he Delivered up 2 Traps which had been taken from the french, & gave me a roabe & about 12 bushels of Corn— & smoked &c

I answered the Speech it explained, many parts which he Could not understand—of the Speech of yesterday.

[Lewis]   *Wednesday October 31st 1804.*[5]

The river being very low and the season so far advanced that it frequently shuts up with ice in this climate we determined to spend the Winter in this neighbourhood, accordingly Capt. Clark with a party of men reconnoitred the countrey for some miles above our encampment; he returned in the evening without having succeed in finding an eligible situation for our purpose.—

1. Clark evidently refers to notes of speeches by Indian chiefs which are printed here under their proper dates. This meeting is discussed in Ronda (LCAI), 85–87.

2. Charles Chaboillez, born in Montreal, entered the service of the North West Company in 1793, and at this time was in charge of the company's operations on the Assiniboine River, as *bourgeois* of Fort Assiniboine. He visited the Mandans and Hidatsas himself in 1806, but was not enthusiastically received. Lewis and Clark to Chaboillez, October 31, 1804 (the letter referred to here), Jackson (LLC), 1:213–14; Masson, 1:300, 307, 328, 340, 383–85, 391; Coues (NLEH), 1:60–61 n. 61, 202; Wallace, 432.

3. It was apparently Biddle who crossed out these words with red ink.

4. This transcript is on a loose sheet in the Voorhis Collection, Missouri Historical Society. See Indian Speeches, Miscellaneous Documents of Lewis and Clark, Appendix C, vol. 2. The date was established from remarks in this day's regular entry.

5. Lewis's note from Codex O, but not the customary astronomical observations.

[Lewis and Clark]   [*Weather, October 1804*][1]

1804 Day of the month	Thermot. at ☉ rise	Weather	Wind at ☉ rise	thermotr. at 4 P. M.	Weather	Wind at 4 oC. P. M.
Octr. 1st	40	c.	S E.	46	c.	S E
2nd[2]	39	f	S E	75	C.	N. W
3rd	40	c.	N W	45	c. a r & f	N W
4th	38	c a r	N. W	50	c.	N. W.
5th	36	f.	N W.	54	f	N. W.
6th	43	f.	N W.	60	f	N W.
7th	45	c	S. E.	58	f	S E
8th	48	f	N. W.	62	f	N W
9th	45	c.	N. E	50	c. a. r.	N.
10th	42	f. a r	N W	67	f.	N. W
11th	43	f	N. W.	59	f.	N. W.
12th	42	f	S	65	f.	S. E.
13th	43	f.	S W.	49	c a r	N E
14th	42	r.	S E	40	r.	S E
15	46	r.	N.	57	f. a. r.	N. W.
16	45	c.	N. E	50	f	N. E.
17	47	f	N. W	54	f.	N. W
18	30	f	N. W.	68	f.	N W
19	43	f	S E.	62	f	S
20	44	f	N. W.	48	f	N.

21	31	s	N. W.	34	s	N W
22	35	c. a. s	N. E	42	c	N E
23	32	s	N W	45	c	N E
24	33	s a f	N. W.	51	c a s	N W
25	31	c	S E	50	c	S E.
26	42	f	S E	57	f	S E
27th	39	f	S W	58	f	S W.
28	34	f	S W	54	f	S W
29	32	f	S W	59	f	S. W.
30	32	f	S W	52	f	S W.
31	33	f	W	48	f	W.

[*Remarks*][3]

October 1st the leaves of the ash popular & most of the shrubs begin to turn yellow and decline came too this evening near the habitation of a Frenchman—[4]

      3rd the earth and sand which form the bars of the river are so fully impregnated with salt that it shoots and adhers to the little sticks which appear on the serface it is pleasent & seems niterous.—

      5th slight white frost last night— brant & geese passing to South

      6th frost as last night saw teal, mallard,[5] & Gulls large.

      8th arrived at Recare vilage, visited the Chief on the Island[6]

      9th wind blew hard this morning drove the boat from her anker, came to Shore, some brant & geese passing to the south, ⟨spoke to them recares⟩

    10th had the mill erected shewed the savages its operation, spoke to them shot my airgun. the men traded some articles for robes, the savages much pleased, the French chief lost his presents by his canoe overseting

    11th no fogg or dew this morning nor have we seen either for many days (i e) since the 21st of Septr.— received the answer at the 1st Chief, set out

12th   receved the ⟨answer and⟩ present of corn from the 3rd Cheif and the answers from both ⟨of these⟩ the 2d & 3rd. recieved the corn from 2d last evening obtained 20 bushe[l]s.   set out at 2 in the evening.

13th   tried Newman at 12 oCk for mutiny—   cottonwood all yellow and the leaves begin to fall, abundance of grapes and red burries—[7]

14th   the leaves of all the trees as ash, elm &c except the cottonwood is now fallen—   punished newman—[8]

17th   saw a large flock of White geese with Black wings,[9] Antilopes are passing to the black hills to winter, as is their custom

18th   hard frost last night, the clay near the water edge was frozen, as was the water in the vessels exposed to the air.

19th   no *Mule* deer seen above the *dog river*[10] none at the *recares*

20th   much more timber than usual—   Saw the first black haws[11] that we have seen for a long time—   Pier Crusat shot a white bear left his gun and tomahalk

22nd   the snow ½ inch deep.[12]   some Souixs 14 in number came to us on the Lard. this morning—[13]   beleive them to be a war party—   they were naked except their legings—.

24th   arrived at a mandane hunting camp   visited the lodge of the chief

25th   this evening passed a rapid and sholde place in the river were obliged to get out and drag the boat—   all the leaves of the trees have now fallen—   the snow did not lye.

27th   camp for the purpose of speaking to the five villages, arrived at ½ past 12 at the place we intended to fix our [camp][14]   sent runners to invite them to council tomorrow with tobacco—   an article indispensible in those cases—

28th   wind so heard that we could not go into council[15]

29th   we Spoke to the Indians in council—   tho' the wind was so hard that it was extreemly disagreeable. the sand was blown on us in clouds—

30th   Capt. Clark visited the island above to look out a place for winter encampment, but did not succeed [16]

31st   this day the Mandanes of the 2nd or upper vilage gave us an answer and some corn

1. Lewis's weather observations for this month are in his Weather Diary and are followed here; some significant variations in Clark's version in Codex C are noted. As in September, neither noted the rise or fall of the river.

2. Clark gives the 4:00 p. m. wind direction for October 2 and 3 as "N."

3. The remarks are from Lewis's Weather Diary, with substantial variations in Clark's Codex C noted.

4. Clark says they came to at "a trading house of 3 french men."

5. Probably the blue-winged teal, first mentioned on September 13, 1804; the mallard, which the captains frequently called the "duckinmallard," is *Anas platyrhynchos* [AOU, 132]. Holmgren, 30, 32, 33.

6. Most of Clark's remarks for October 8 to 31 appear to have been crossed out, though it is not always clear which were intended to be marked out and which not.

7. Clark placed these observations about plants under October 14. The "red burries" are the buffaloberry.

8. Clark added, "& to be Discharged."

9. The snow goose. Holmgren, 28, 30.

10. Here again is a mistranslation of the name of the Cheyenne River.

11. *Viburnum lentago* L., nannyberry. This more northerly species is different from the "black haws" found on the lower Missouri River (*V. prunifolium* L. and *V. rufidulum* Raf.). See June 19, 1804. All three species have similar leaves and black fruits. Barkley, 329–30; Fernald, 1340.

12. Clark notes the depth of snow on October 21.

13. Clark says the Sioux came "on the L. S. with their guns cocked."

14. Lewis left out the word "camp," which Clark included.

15. Clark adds, "maney of the Indians of different villages visit us."

16. Clark's version reads, "Examoned the Country in advance for Several Leagues for a place for winter encampment without finding a Spot Calculated for one."

[Clark]

1 November 1804   Visited by Several Chiefs of the lower Village who requested we would call on them &c.   Spoke to the Same purpote [purport] with the Grand Chief.   we Set out in the evening & I with the Party droped down to the place we intended to winter[1] & Cap Lewis called at the Village 3 miles above &. &.

[Clark]   1st *of November Thursday* 1804

the wind hard from the N W.   Mr. McCrackin a Trader Set out at 7 oClock to the fort on the Ossiniboin   by him Send a letter, (incloseing a Copy of the British Ministers protection)[2] to the principal agent of the Company—   at about 10 OClock the Cheifs of the Lower Village Cam and after a Short time informed us they wished they would us to call at their village & take Some Corn, that they would make peace with the *Ricares*   they never made war against them but after the *rees* Killed their Chiefs they killed them like the birds, and were tired [*NB: of killing them*] and would Send a Chief and Some brave men to the *Ricares* to Smoke with that people   in the evening we Set out and fell down to the lower Village where Capt. Lewis got out and continud at the Village untill after night   I proceeded on & landed on the S. S. at the upper point of the 1st Timber on the Starboard Side after landing & Continuinge—   ⟨Some⟩ all night droped down to a proper place to build[3]   Capt Lewis Came down after night, and informed me he intended to return the next morning by the perticular Request of the Chiefs.

We passed the Villages on our Decent in veiw of Great numbers of the inhabitents

[Clark]   The 1st of Novr. *Mandins 1s Village*[4]

the Main Chief Big White & 2 others i e the Big Man or *Sha-ha-ca* and [*blank*] Came early to talk, and Spoke as follows, after Smoking, Viz.

Is it Certain that the ricares intend to make good with us   our wish is to be at peace with all, we will Send a Chief with the pania Chief and Some young men to Smoke and make good peace—?   are you going to Stay abov or below this Cold [season?].—   answer by C. L   We are going down a few miles to look a place   we can find no place abov proper.

The panias know's we do not begin the war, they allway begin, we Sent a Chief and a pipe to the Pania to Smoke and they killed them—, we have killed enough of them   we kill them like the birds, we do not wish to kill more, we will, make a good peace

We were Sorry when we heard of your going up but now you are going down, we are glad, if we eat you Shall eat, if we Starve you must Starve also,   our village is too far to bring the Corn to you, but we hope you will Call on us as you pass to the place you intend to Stop

C[aptain] L[ewis] answered the above—!

[Lewis]   *Thursday November 1st 1804*[5]

The wind blew so violently during the greater part of this day that we were unable to quit our encampment; in the evening it abated;—   we droped down about seven miles and land on N. E. side of the river at a large point of Woodland.

1. This passage is misleading; as Clark indicates in the Codex C entry, the party did not go as far as the future site of Fort Mandan this day. The camp is not shown on *Atlas* map 29, but was between, and somewhat north of Matootonha, the lower Mandan village, and the fort site, on the McLean County, North Dakota, side (starboard). Note how the river bends between the two places on the *Atlas* map. MRC map 52.

2. Edward Thornton, later Sir Edward, entered the British diplomatic service in 1791. He served in various posts in the United States from then until 1804, being chargé d'affaires and acting minister in Washington from 1800. In February, 1803, he issued Lewis a passport, requesting all subjects of His Majesty to permit Lewis to pass and to render all aid and protection possible, on a mission he declared to be purely scientific. Lewis's British Passport [February 28, 1803], Jackson (LLC), 1 : 19–20.

3. Clark here refers to events of November 2, indicating that the Codex C entry of November 1 was composed later.

4. This transcript is on a loose sheet in the Voorhis Collection, Missouri Historical Society. See Indian Speeches, Miscellaneous Documents of Lewis and Clark, Appendix C, vol. 2. The talk is covered in Ronda (LCAI), 87–88.

5. Lewis's note from Codex O, though not concerned with astronomy.

[Clark]

2nd Novr. 1804 Friday—   Capt Lewis returned to the Village & I fixed on a place for to build a fort and Set to work[1]   Cap Lewis returned in the eveng with 11 bushels of Corn, the Ricarre Chief Set out for his Village accompanied by Several mandans—

[Clark]   *2nd November Friday 1804*

This morning at Day light I went down the river with 4 men to look for a proper place to winter   proceeded down the river three miles & found a place well Supld. with wood, & returned, Capt. Lewis went to the village to here what they had to Say & I fell down, and formed a camp near where a Small Camp of Indian were huntig   Cut down the Trees around our Camp, in the evening Capt. Lewis returned with a present of 11 bushe[l]s of Corn, our recaree Chief Set out acccompanied by one Chief [*NB: of Mandans ⟨& Minetarees⟩*] and Several Brave men, [*NB: of Minitarees & Mandans*]   he Called for Some Small article which we had ⟨given⟩ [*NB: promised*] but as I could not understand him he Could not get [*NB: (afd he did get it*] [*NB: leave out this*][2]   the wind from the S. E. a fine day— many Indians ⟨to view us⟩ to day

[Lewis]   *Friday November 2nd 1804*[3]

This morning early we fixed on the site for our fortification which we immediately set about.

This place we have named Fort Mandan in honour of our Neighbours.

1. The site of Fort Mandan, where the Corps of Discovery remained until April 1805, is in McLean County, North Dakota, about fourteen miles west of Washburn. The actual site has been washed away by the Missouri and lies at least partially underwater. Appleman (LC), 341; *North Dakota Guide*, 204; *Atlas* map 29; Warren map 88; MRC map 51.

2. Biddle has made considerable emendations here to get it to read differently, perhaps for his *History*. He finally concluded: "leave out."

3. Lewis's note from Codex O, though not concerned with astronomy.

[Clark]

3rd of November Satturday 1804   wind hard from the west   Commence building our Cabins,[1] Dispatched 6 hunters in a perogue Down the River to hunt, Discharged the french hands,[2] Mr. Jessomme his Squar & child moved to camp, the little Crow loaded his Squar with meat for us also a Roabe, we gave the Squar an ax & &.   Cought 2 bever near Camp

[Clark]   *3rd of November Satterday 1804*

a fine morning   wind hard from the *West*   we commence building our Cabins, Send Down in Perogue 6 men to hunt   Engaged one man,[3] [*NB: Canadian Frenchman who had been with the Chayenne Inds on the Cote noir & last summer descended thence the little Missouri—he was of our permanent.*]   Set the french who intend to return to build a perogue, many Indians pass to hunt, Mr. Jessomme [*NB: Jesseaume*] with his Squar & Children.   come Down to live, as Interpter, we recive [*NB: hired*] a hors for our Sirvice, in the evening the *Ka goh ha mi* or little ravin Came & brought us on his Squar [*NB: who carried it on her back*] about 60 Wt. of Dried Buffalow meat a roabe, & Pot of Meal &.   they Delayed all night— we gave his Squar an ax & a fiew Small articles & himself a piece of Tobacco, the Men were indulged with a Dram, this evening

two Beaver Cought This morning— and one Trap Lost [*NB: The Frenchmen 9 engaged thus far now returning.   but 2 or 3 volunteered to remain with us the winter which they did & in the Spring left us.*]⁴

1. Sergeant Gass, who being a carpenter probably had a major part in building the structure, describes Fort Mandan as a roughly triangular stockade, with two converging rows of huts and some sort of bastion in the angle opposite the gate. This accords with the description given by François-Antoine Larocque. According to Gass, the outer walls were 18 feet high; no other measurements are known. A small sketch on *Atlas* map 29 confirms the triangular shape. Masson, 1:307–8.

2. Some of the discharged *engagés* wintered with the permanent party at Fort Mandan; others seem to have spent the winter at the Mandan, Hidatsa, or Arikara villages. Those who wished to stay among the Indians, perhaps trading and trapping on their own, apparently received their pay in cash at this time; there is no record of their being paid, which complicates the effort to determine their identities. Five men received their pay from Lewis's agent in St. Louis in 1805: Baptiste Deschamps, Jean Baptiste La Jeunesse, Etienne Malboeuf, Charles Pineau (otherwise Peter Pinaut), and François Rivet. These five probably returned with the keelboat sent down the Missouri in April 1805. It is likely but not certain that among them were the ones who wintered at Fort Mandan. See also n. 4, below, and weather remarks for November 6, 1804. Jackson (LLC), 1:237 n. 7.

3. Jean Baptiste Lepage took the place of the discharged John Newman and went with the permanent party to the Pacific and back. Most of what is known of him is in this entry and elsewhere in the journals. The information in Clark's interlineation indicates that he had been to the Black Hills and on the Little Missouri River, in country that few, if any, other whites had seen. He probably contributed some information to the Western map Clark prepared during this winter (*Atlas* maps 32a, 32b, 32c). Lewis's record dates his enlistment from November 2 and describes him as of "no particular merit." Lewis to Henry Dearborn, January 15, 1807, Jackson (LLC), 1:368; Clarke (MLCE), 147.

4. Biddle apparently added this bracketed material, perhaps to aid him in sorting out the number of *engagés* who stayed for the winter. Biddle's account says that some of the discharged men built a pirogue—probably a dugout canoe—to return to Missouri. See also weather remarks, November 6, 1804. Coues (HLC), 1:189.

[Clark]

4th of Novr.   a french man by Name Chabonah,[1] who Speaks the Big Belley language visit us, he wished to hire & informed us his 2 Squars were Snake Indians,[2] we engau him to go on with us and take one of his wives to interpet the Snake language   The Indians Horses & Dogs live in the Same Lodge with themselves

Fort Mandan

[Clark]   4th November Sunday 1804

a fine morning   we Continued to Cut Down trees and raise our houses, a Mr. Chaubonée, [*NB: Chaboneau*] interpeter for the *Gross Vintre* nation Came to See us, and informed that he came Down with Several Indians from a Hunting expedition up the river, to here what we had told the Indians in Councl   this man wished to hire as an interpeter, the wind rose this evining from the East & Clouded up—   Great numbers of Indians pass hunting and Some on the return—

1. Toussaint Charbonneau is, of course, one of the best-known members of the Corps of Discovery, thanks to his association with Sacagawea. He was a French Canadian, born about 1758, who had worked for the North West Company and had apparently lived among the Hidatsas as an independent trader for several years by 1804. He appears, of course, in all accounts of the expedition and in the various biographies of Sacagawea, but relatively little has been written on the man himself. Estimates of his character have generally been unfavorable, many historians portraying him as a coward, a bungler, and a wife-beater. Lewis described him as "A man of no peculiar merit" who "was useful as an interpreter only"; nonethless, his services in that capacity, together with his wife's, were virtually indispensable, to say nothing of his considerable ability as a cook. Clark evidently had a higher opinion of Charbonneau, for he saw to the education of the couple's son, offered to set Charbonneau up as a farmer or trader, and saw to it that his old associate had employment in the fur trade and government service until his own (Clark's) death. After the expedition Charbonneau worked for Manuel Lisa in the Missouri Fur Company, then carried out diplomatic errands among the Missouri River tribes for the United States during the War of 1812. He joined an expedition to Santa Fe in 1815, where the Spanish briefly imprisoned him, and worked as an interpreter for Major Stephen H. Long, Prince Paul of Wurttemburg, and Prince Maximilian, in addition to serving various fur-trading firms. During Clark's long tenure as superintendent of Indian affairs in the trans-Mississippi West, Charbonneau was on the government payroll much of the time as Mandan and Hidatsa interpreter. He was discharged in 1839, about a year after Clark's death, and thereafter disappears from the record; evidently he was dead by 1843. A prob-

able likeness of him is found in Karl Bodmer's painting "The Travelers Meeting with Minataree Indians near Fort Clark," which shows someone, perhaps Charbonneau, interpreting for Maximilian in 1833–34, when he was probably in his seventies. Clark to Charbonneau, August 20, 1806, Lewis to Henry Dearborn, January 15, 1807, Jackson (LLC), 1:315–16, 368; Anderson (CFP); Clarke (MLCE), 147–48; Speck, 96–148; Hafen (TC); Luttig, 135–41 and passim.; Abel (CJ), 270–71 n. 258, 276–82 n. 280 and passim.

2. One of them was, of course, Sacagawea, destined to be the most famous member of the Corps of Discovery after the captains themselves. In spite of the multitude of words written about her, most of what we know about her life and personality is to be found in the expedition journals and a few other papers of Clark. A Lemhi Shoshone from the region of the Continental Divide in Idaho and Montana, probably born around 1788, she was taken prisoner by a Hidatsa raiding party near the Three Forks of the Missouri about 1800 and was apparently living at Metaharta, the middle Hidatsa village (now called the Sakakawea site), when purchased by Charbonneau, probably in 1804. Many writers have referred to her as the guide of the expedition, but Lewis and Clark hired her and Charbonneau as interpreters. Her services in that capacity among the Shoshonean-speaking people in the Rockies were indispensable, while her presence with a baby calmed the fears of many tribes that the party was a war expedition. She did provide valuable assistance as a guide in the region of southwestern Montana in which she had spent her childhood. Clark seems to have had a high opinion of her, as he did of Charbonneau and the couple's son, but romantic fantasies concerning the two have no foundation in the record. There is some controversy about whether the name by which we know her was Shoshone or Hidatsa, and the appropriate spelling and pronunciation remain in doubt. All of the captains' attempts to render the name indicate a hard "g" sound in the third syllable. Lewis understood the name to mean "Bird Woman." (See below, May 20, 1805.) On her subsequent life there is also little information. The best evidence is that she died at Manuel Lisa's trading post, Fort Manuel, on the Missouri River in Corson County, South Dakota, in 1812. (See above, October 14, 1804.) Certainly Clark recorded her as having died by 1825–28. Assertions that she lived to be nearly one hundred, dying in 1884 on the Wind River Shoshone Reservation in Wyoming, rest on shaky evidence. Anderson (CFP); Anderson (SSS); Howard; Hebard; Clark to Charbonneau, August 20, 1806, Clark's List of Expedition Members [ca. 1825–28], Jackson (LLC) 1:315–16, 2:638; Luttig, 106, 132–35; Ronda (LCAI), 256–59. Anderson and Ronda will lead readers to numerous other sources on Sacagawea and the interpretations on these points.

[Clark]   5th *November Monday 1804*[1]

I rose verry early and commenced raising the 2 range of Huts ⟨proe⟩ the timber large and heavy   all to Carry on Hand Sticks, Cotton wood & Elm Som ash Small, our Situation Sandy, great numbers of Indians pass to and from hunting   a Camp of Mandans, A fiew miles below us Cought within two days 100 Goat, by Driveing them in a Strong pen, derected by a Bush fence widening from the pen &c. &.   the Greater part of this day Cloudy, wind moderate from the N. W.   I have the Rhumitism verry bad, Cap Lewis writeing all Day—   we are told by our interpeter[2] that 4 Ossiniboin Indians,[3] have arrived at the Camps of the Gross Venters & 50 Lodges are Comeing

1. There is no entry for November 5 in the Field Notes.

2. As with some other references to an unnamed interpreter during the winter at Fort Mandan, it is not clear whether the man referred to is Jusseaume or Charbonneau.

3. The Assiniboines called themselves *Nak'ota* and spoke a dialect of the Sioux language. Although closely related, the two groups maintained distinct identities from their first mention by whites in 1640. By the time of Lewis and Clark the Assiniboines, like the Sioux, were nomadic buffalo hunters, ranging north of the Missouri on both sides of the present United States-Canadian border, in northeastern Montana, northwest North Dakota, and southern Saskatchewan. Their linguistic relationship with the Sioux did not preclude hostilities between the two. Hodge, 1:102–5; Denig, 63–98; Lowie(TA); Kennedy; Coues (NLEH), 2:516–23.

[Clark]

6th of Nov.   Mr. Gravolin our Ricara Interpreter & 2 of our french hands & 2 boys Set out in a Canoe for the Ricaras   Mr. ravelli[n] is to accompany the Ricaras Chiefs to the City of Washington in the Spring,[1] Great numbers of Geese pass to the South which is a certain approach of ice—

Fort Mandan

[Clark]   6th *November Tuesday* 1804

last night late we wer awoke by the Sergeant of the Guard to See a nothern light, which was light, [*NB: light but*] not red, and appeared to Darken and Some times nearly obscered [*NB: about 20 degrees above horizon—various Shapes*], and ⟨open⟩ [*NB: divided*], many times appeared in light Streeks, and at other times a great Space light & containing floating Collomns which appeared ⟨to⟩ opposite each other & retreat leaveing the lighter Space at no time of the Same appeerence[2]

This morning I rose a Day light   the Clouds to the North appeared black   at 8 oClock the [wind] begun to blow hard from the N W. and Cold, and Continud all Day   Mr. Jo Gravilin our ricare interpeter Paul *premor, Lajuness* & 2 french Boys,[3] who Came with us, Set out in a Small perogue, on their return to the ricaree nation & the Illinois, Mr. Gravilin has instructions to take on the recarees in the Spring &c.— Continue to build the huts, out of Cotton Timber, &c. this being the only timber we have.—

1. Arketarnashar, or Piaheto, the chief Gravelines accompanied, died in Washington in 1806. See above, October 9, 1804.

2. The aurora borealis. See above, April 1, 1804.

3. Paul Primeau and Jean Baptiste La Jeunesse. The two "French boys" were presumably expedition *engagés* also, but it is not clear whether they are ever listed in the records or whether they are regarded as supernumeraries.

[Clark]   7th *November Wednesday* 1804[1]

a termperate day   we continued to building our hut, Cloudy and fogging all day

1. There are no entries in the Field Notes after November 6 until November 13. Entries become irregular and generally quite brief from this point; all those from November 19, 1804, to April 3, 1805 (the last dated entry in the Field Notes) are on one sheet, document 64, except for those on document 65 for November 30 and December 1, 1804. Clark's Codex C entries are continuous through this period, except for a hunting trip in February 1805, filled in by Lewis. It appears that Clark kept Codex C as his only journal during the Fort Mandan winter, except for scattered Field Notes entries. See the Introduction, vol. 2.

[Clark]   8th *Novr. Thursday 1804*

a Cloudy morning   Jussome our [*NB: Mandan*] interpreter went to the Village, on his return he informed us that three English men had arrived from the Hudsons Bay Company,[1] and would be here tomorrow, we Contd. to build our huts, many Indians Come to See us and bring their horses to Grass near us

1. See below, November 19, 1804.

[Clark]   9th *Novr. Friday* 1804

a verry hard frost this morning   we Continue to build our Cabens, under many disadvantages, Day Cloudy wind from the N W.   Several Indians pass with flying news, [*NB: reports*] we got a ⟨Squar⟩ White weasel, (Taile excepted which was black at the end)[1] of an Indian Capt Lewis walked to the hill abt. ¾ of a mile— we are Situated in a point of the Missouri North Side in a Cotton wood Timber, this Timber is tall and heavy Containing an imence quantity of water Brickle & Soft ⟨fine⟩ food for Horses to winter (as is Said by the Indians)[2] The Mandans Graze their horses in the day on Grass, and at night give them a Stick [*NB: an arm full*] of Cotton wood [*NB: boughs*] to eate, Horses Dogs & people all pass the night in the Same Lodge or round House, Covd. with earth with a fire in the middle[3]

great number of wild gees pass to the South, flew verry high

1. The long-tailed weasel, *Mustela frenata*, then unknown to science. Burroughs, 81–82; Cutright (LCPN), 122.

2. From "we are Situated" on, the passage is crossed out in red, apparently by Biddle. He has also made other slight spelling changes, not shown.

3. From "Horses Dogs . . ." on, the passage is crossed out in red, apparently by Biddle.

[Clark]   10th *November Satturday* 1804

rose early continued to build our fort numbers of Indians Came to See us a Chief Half Pania[1] Came & brought a Side of a Buffalow, in return We Gave Some fiew small things to himself & wife & Son, he Crossed the river in the Buffalow Skin Canoo & and, the Squar took the Boat [*NB: on her back*] and proceeded on to the Town 3 miles the Day raw and Cold wind from the N W, the Gees Continue to pass in gangues as also brant to the South, Some Ducks also pass

1. Probably The Coal, elsewhere described as an Arikara by birth. Clark again refers to the Arikaras as Pawnees.

Fort Mandan

[Clark]   11th November Sunday 1804

a Cold Day Continued at work at the Fort Two men Cut themselves with an ax, The large Ducks pass to the South an Indian gave me Several roles of parched meal two Squars of the Rock Mountain, purchased from the Indians by ⟨2⟩ a frenchmen [*NB: Chaboneau*] Came down ⟨and⟩   The Mandans out hunting the Buffalow—

Point of Observation No. 51

[Lewis]   *Fort Mandan, Sunday November 11th 1804*[1]

Observed Meridian altitude of ☉'s U. L. with Sextant by the fore observation 51° 4′ 52″

Latitude deduced from this observation   N. 47° 21′ 32.8″

1. Lewis's astronomical observation from Codex O.

[Clark]   12th *November Monday* 1804

a verry Cold night   early this morning the Big White princapal Chief of the lower Village of the Mandans Came Down, he packd about 100 W. of fine meet on his Squar for us, we made Some Small presents ⟨on⟩ to the Squar, & Child   gave a Small ax which She was much pleased—   3 men Sick with the [*blank*][1]   Several, Wind Changeable verry cold evening, freesing all day   Some ice on the edges of the river.

Swans passing to the South, the Hunters we Sent down the river to hunt has not returned

The interpeter Says that the Mandan nation as they old men Say Came out of a ⟨Small lake⟩ [*NB: Subterraneous village & a lake*] where they had Gardins,[2] maney years ago they lived in Several Villages on the Missourie low down, the Smallpox destroyed the greater part of the nation and reduced them to one large Village and Some Small ones, all ⟨the⟩ nations before this maladey was affrd. [*NB: afraid*] of them   after they were reduced the Sioux and other Indians waged war, and killed a great maney, and they moved up the Missourie, those Indians Still continued to wage war, and they moved Still higher, untill they got in the Countrey of the Panias, whith this ntn. [nation] they lived in friendship maney years, inhabiting the Same neighbourhood untill that people waged war, They moved up near the *watersoons* & *winataree* where they now live in peace with those nations, the mandans Specke a language peculial to themselves ⟨verry much⟩

they can rase about 350 men, the Winatarees [*NB: ⟨or⟩ the ⟨600, 700⟩*

Wittassoons or Maharha 80] about 80 and the Big bellies *[NB: or Minitarres]* about 600 or 650 men. the mandans and Seauex [*X: ⟨Shoe Tribe of Minataras⟩*] have the Same word for water—[3] The Big bellies *[NB: or]* Winitarees & ravin *[NB: & Wattassoons, as also the Crow (or Raven)]* Indians Speake nearly the Same language and the presumption is they were origionally the Same nation   The Ravin Indians[4] "have 400 Lodges & about 1200 men, & follow the Buffalow, or hunt for their Subsistance in the plains & on the Court noi & Rock Mountains, & are at war with the Sioux Snake Indians["]

The Big bellies & Watersoons are at war with the Snake Indians & Seauex, and were at war with the *Ricares* untill we made peace a fiew days passd.—   The Mandans are at War with all who make war on them, at present with the Seauex only, and wish to be at peace with *all* nations, Seldom the agressors—

1. Probably venereal disease, about which they would be more frank in later entries. The passage has been crossed out in red, apparently by Biddle.

2. Mandan creation accounts are found in Beckwith, 1–17. Clark later gave Biddle more information. See Nicholas Biddle Notes [ca. April 1810], Jackson (LLC), 2:520.

3. The Mandan word for water is *miniŋ;* the Hidatsa term is *miri.* The similarity of pronunciation would be striking to Lewis and Clark.

4. Generally known as the Crows, from the French traders' term *gens de corbeaux,* they called themselves Absaroke, variously translated as crow, sparrowhawk, or bird people, or "anything that flies." They separated from the Hidatsas proper and the Awatixa in the eighteenth century, hence the similarity in language; their tongue was of the Siouan family. Although Clark here places them in the Black Hills, by the beginning of the nineteenth century they had been driven west from the hills of South Dakota by their enemies and were centered in the Yellowstone basin, including the valleys of the Powder, Tongue, and Bighorn rivers; Clark places them in the Yellowstone region in his "Estimate of Eastern Indians," prepared at Fort Mandan. Since they visited the Hidatsas regularly, white traders at that tribe's villages had seen them, and the Canadian Ménard (see above, October 25, 1804) claimed to have visited them on the Yellowstone before 1795; however, François-Antoine Larocque's account of his trip to the Yellowstone in 1805 is the earliest first-hand written account of them. Nasatir (BLC), 2:381; Hodge, 1:367–69; Wood (OHI), 4; Wood & Thiessen, 156–220; Lowie (TC); Denig, 137–204; Thwaites (LC), 6:103–4.

[Clark]

13th   The Ice begin to run   we move into our hut, visited by the Grand Chief of the Mandans, and *Che chark* Lagru[1] a Chief of the Assinniboins & 7 men of that Nation, I Smoke with them and gave the Chief a Cord & a Carrot of Tobacco—   this Nation rove in the Plains above this and trade with the British Companes on the Ossinniboin River, they are Divided into Several bands, the decendants of the Sioux & Speak nearly their langguage   a bad disposed Set & Can raies about 1000 men in the 3 bands near this place, they trade with the nations of this neighbourhood for horses Corn &   Snow all Day   Capt. L. at the village.[2]

[Clark]   *13th Novr. Tuesday* 1804

The Ice began to run in the river ½ past 10 oClock P. M   we rose early & onloaded the boat before brackfast except, the Cabin, & Stored away in a Store house—   at 10 oClock A M the Black Cat the Mandin Chief and *Lagru* [NB: Fr: name] *Che Chark* ⟨Christans a⟩ ⟨Ossiniboin⟩ Chief[3] & 7 men of note visited us at Fort Mandan, I gave him a twist of Tobacco to Smoke with his people & a Gold Cord with a view to Know him again, The nation [NB: bands] [NB: *This Chief was one of 3 bands of Assns who rove between the Missouri & Assn river. The 3 consist   here describe all Asns*] Consists of about 600 men, hunt in the Plains & winter and trade on the Ossiniboin River, they are Decendants of the Siaux and Speake their language, they Come to the nations to this quarter to trade or (make preasthts) for horses ⟨& robes⟩ the method of this Kind of Trafick by addoption Shall be explained hereafter &,[4] Snow'd all day, the Ice ran thick and air Cold.[5]

1. This Assiniboine chief's name may be the Cree word *otchitchâk*, "crane," and his French name *La Grue*, also translates "The Crane." He owed his life, in 1806, to Le Borgne (One Eye) of the Hidatsas, who protected him, as a guest, from the Cheyennes. Coues (NLEH), 1:385; Baraga, 62.

2. The number "19" (apparently written by Clark) appears at the bottom of this sheet (document 63), probably a direction to the next entry in the Field Notes, November 19, on a new sheet.

3. Apparently Clark first identified La Grue as a "Kristinaux," that is, a Cree (see below, November 14, 1804), then crossed this out because the chief was actually an Assiniboine, which designation he also lined through.

4. The adoption ceremony allowed enemies to become temporary fictional relatives and trade in peace. Ronda (LCAI), 89, 130.

5. From "Speake their language" on, the remainder of the passage is crossed out in red, apparently by Biddle.

Fort Mandan

[Clark]   *14th of November Wednesday 1804*

a Cloudy morning, ice runing verry thick   river rose ½ Inch last night Some Snow falling, only two Indians visit us to day Owing to a Dance at the Village last night in Concluding a Serimoney of adoption, and interchange of property, between the Ossiniboins, ⟨Christinoes⟩ [*NB: Knistenaux*][1] and the nations of this neighbourhood— we Sent one man by land on hors back to know the reason of the Delay of our hunters, this evening 2 french men who were traping below Came up—with 20 beaver we are compelled to use our Pork which we doe Spearingly for fear of Some falur in precureing a Sufficiency from the Woods.

our Interpeter informs that 70 Lodges one of 3 bands of Assinniboins & Some Crestinoes, are at the Mandan Village. The Crrirstinoes are abt. 300 [*NB: 240*] men   Speak the Chipaway—Language, the live near Fort De peare[2] [*NB: on Assiniboin & Apaskashawan*][3] [*NB: they are bands of the Chippaways*]

1. The name Cree was an abbreviated form of Kristinaux, the French version of a Cree name for themselves, *Kenistenoag*. They were of the Algonquian language family. The Plains Crees were buffalo-hunting nomads whose range was almost entirely in Canada, north of the Assiniboines and the Sioux. Clark's statement that they "Speak the Chipaway" refers to the Chippewas, or Ojibways, who also spoke an Algonquian tongue. The adoption Clark refers to was apparently to insure good treatment of the visitors during trading. Hodge, 1:359–62; Denig, 99–136; Coues (NLEH), 2:510–16. It was apparently Biddle who crossed out Clark's spelling in red and substituted his own.

2. There were several North West Company posts called Fort des Prairies; this one was probably on the South Saskatchewan River. Wood & Thiessen, 82 n. 13, 84 n. 16.

3. The Saskatchewan River, one of the major streams of the Canadian Great Plains.

[Clark]   15th of November Thursday 1804

a Cloudy morning, the ice run much thicker than yesterday   at 10 oClock G Drewyer & the frenchman we Dispatched yesterday came up from the Hunters, who is incamped about 30 miles below—   after a about one hour we Dispatched a man with orders to the hunters to proceed on without Delay thro the floating ice, we Sent by the man Tin, to put on the parts of the Perogue exposed to the ice & a toe roape— The wind Changeable— all hands work at their huts untill 1 oClock at night— Swans passing to the South— but fiew fowls water to be Seen— not one Indian Came to our fort to day

[Clark]   16th   November Friday 1804

a verry white frost   all the trees all Covered with ice, Cloudy, all the men move into the huts which is not finishd   Several Indians Come to Camp to day, The *Ossiniboins* is at the Big bellie Camp, Some trouble like to take place between them from the loss of horses &c. as is Said by an old Indian who visited us with 4 buffalow robes & Corn to trade for a pistol which we did not let him have, men imployed untill late in dobing their huts,[1] Some horses Sent down to Stay in the woods near the fort, to prevent the Ossniboins Steeling them

1. Daubing, that is, coating the walls with clay to close the chinks between the logs.

[Clark]   17th *November Satturday* 1804

a fine morning, last night was Cold, the ice thicker than yesterday, Several Indians visit us, one Chief Stayed all day   we are much engaged about our huts.

[Clark]   18th *Novr. Sunday 1804*

a Cold morning   Some wind   the Black Cat, Chief of the Mandans Came to See us, he made Great inquiries respecting our fashions.   he also Stated the Situation of their nation, he mentioned that a Council had been held the day before and it was thought advisable to put up with the resent insults of the Ossiniboins & Christonoes untill they were Convinced that what had been told thim by us, ⟨untill⟩ Mr. Evins had deceived them & we might also, he promised to return & furnish them with guns & amunitiion, we advised them to remain at peace & that they might depend upon Getting *Supplies* through the Channel of the Missouri, but it requred time to put the trade in opperation. The Assiniboins &c have the trade of those nations in their power and treat them badly as the Soux does the *Ricarees* and they cannot resent for fear of loseing their trade &.[1]

1. For the Mandan point-of-view of this meeting see Ronda (LCAI), 89–90.

[Clark][1]

19th *of November 1804*   our hunters return with 32 Deerr, 12 Elk & a Buffalow   Ice ran which detained the huntes much   Cap lewis visit the *Me ne tar rees*, the 25th and returned the 27th of Nov. with 2 Chiefs &c. &c. and told me that 2 Clerks & 5 men of the N W Company & Several of the hudsons Bay Company had arrived with goods to trade with the indians   a Mr. *La Roche* & Mc Kinzey are the Celerks   (Distanc 150 Miles across)

[Clark]

19th Novr. Monday   a Cold day   the ice Continue to ⟨sine⟩ run   our Perogue of Hunters arrive with 32 Deer, 12 Elk & a Buffalow, all of this meat we had hung up in a Smoke house, a timeley supply—   Several Indians here all day—   the wind bley hard from the N. W. by W.   our men move into their huts, Several little Indian aneckdts. [anecdotes] told me to day

1. Biddle's notation after the first date on this document 64 of the Field Notes reads "to 3d April 1805." Clark seems to have run the entries for several days together in the same paragraph; for notes on November 25 and 27, see under those dates.

[Clark]   20th *November Tuesday 1804*

Capt Lewis & my Self move into our huts, a verry hard wind from the W.   all the after part of the day   a temperate day   Several Indians Came Down   to Eat fresh meat, three Chiefs from the 2d Mandan Village Stay all Day, they are verry Curious in examining our works. Those Chiefs informs us that the Souix settled on the Missourie above Dog [*NB: Chayenne*] River, threten to attacked them this winter, and have treated 2 Ricares who Carried the pipe of peace to them Verry roughly.   whiped & took their horses from them &c. &c. & is much displeased with Ricares for makeing a peace with the Mandans &. &. through us, &.   we gave them a Sattisfactory answer. &c. &c.

[Clark]

21st Novr. Wednesday. a fine Day   dispatched a perogu and Collected Stone for our Chimnys, Some wind from the S. W.   arrange our different articles—   maney Indians visit us to day, G D [Drouillard] hurd his hand verry bad—   all the party in high Spirits—   The river Clear of ice, & riseing a little—

[Clark]   22nd *of November Thursday* 1804

a fine morning   Dispatched a perogue and 5 Men under the Derection of Sergeant Pryor to the 2nd Village for 100 bushels of Corn in ears which Mr. Jessomme, let us have   did not get more than 80 bushels—   I was allarmed about 10 oClock by the Sentinal, who informed that an Indian was about to Kill his wife in the interpeters ⟨hut⟩ fire about 60 yards below the works, I went down and Spoke to the fellow about the rash act which he was like to commit and forbid any act of the kind near the fort—[*NB: he might lawfully have killed her for running away.*]   Some missunderstanding took place between this man & his fife about 8 days ago, and She came to this place, & Continued with the Squars of the interpeters, 2 days ago She returned to the Villg.   in the evening of the Same day She came to the interpeters fire appearently much beat, & Stabed in 3 places—   We Derected that no man of this party have any intercourse with this woman under the penelty of Punishment—   he the Husband observed that one of our Serjeants Slept with his wife & if he wanted her he would give her to him, We derected the Serjeant Odway[1] to give the man Some articles, at which time I told the Indian that I believed not one man of the party had touched his wife except the one he had given the use of her for a nite, in his own bed, no man of the party Should touch his Squar, or the wife of any Indian, nor did I believe they touch a woman if they knew her to be the wife of another man, and advised him to take his Squar home and live hapily together in future,—   at this time the Grand Chief of the nation [Black Cat] arrived, & lecturd him, and they both went off apparently dis [*NB: dissatisfied*]

The grand Chief continued [*NB: with us*] all day   a warm Day fair afternoon— many Indian anickdotes   one Chief & his familey Stay all night.

1. Clark interlined "Odway"; Ordway has nothing to say about the episode in his journal.

[Clark]

23rd   a fair warm Day, wind from the S. E.   Send after Stone   Several men with bad Colds, one man Sheilds with the Rhumitism   the river on a Stand haveing rose 4 Inches in all

[Clark]   24th of *November Satturday 1804*

a warm Day   Several men with bad Coalds   we continue to Cover our Huts with hewed punchens,[1] finishd. a Cord to draw our boat out on the bank, this is made 9 Strans of Elk Skin,—   the wind from the S. E.—

1. Puncheons are split logs with one side roughly flattened.

[Clark]   *25th of Novr. Sunday 1804*

a fine day warm & pleasent   Capt. Lewis 2 Interpeters & 6 men Set out to See the Indians in the different Towns & Camps in this neighbour hood, we Continu to Cover & dob our huts, two Chiefs Came to See me to day one named Wau-ke-res-sa-ra,[1] a Big belley and the first of that nation who has visited us Since we have been here, I gave him a Handkerchef Paint & a Saw band, and the other Some fiew articles, and paid a perticular attention which pleased them verry much, the interpeters being all with Capt. Lewis I could not talk to them.   we Compleated our huts— Several men with bad Colds, river fall 1½ inch

1. Apparently Red Shield. See Ronda (LCAI), 91, for a discussion of the meeting and the day's events.

[Clark]   26th of *Novr. 1804* Monday *Fort Mandan*

a little before day light the wind shifted to the N. W. and blew hard and the air Keen & Cold all day, Cloudy and much the appearance of Snow; but little work done to day it being Cold &c.

[Clark]   *27th of November Tuesday 1804*

a cloudy morning after a verry Cold night, the River Crouded with floating ice   wind from the N W.   finished Dobing   Capt. Lewis returned
from the Villages with two Chiefs Mar-noh toh & Man-nes-sur ree & a
Considerate man with the party who accompanied him, The Menitares,
(or Big bellies) were allarmed at the tales told them by the Mandans Viz:
that we intended to join the *Seaux* to Cut off them in the Course of the
winter, many Circumstances Combind to give force to those reports i' e'
the movements of the interpeters & their families to the *Fort*, the strength
of our work &. &.

all those reports was contridicted by Capt Louis with a Conviction on
the minds of the Indians of the falsity of those reports— the Indians in
all the towns & Camps treated Capt Lewis & the party with Great respect
except one of the principal Cheifs *Mar par pa par ra pas a too* or (Horned
Weasel) who did not Chuse to be Seen by the Capt. & left word that he
was not at home &.

Seven Traders arrived from the fort on the Ossinaboin from the N W
Companey   one of which Lafrances[1] took upon himself to speak un-
favourably of our intentions &.   the princpal Mr. *La Rock,*[2] (& Mr. McKen-
sey)[3] was informed of the Conduct of their interpeter & the Consiquinces
if they did not put a Stop to unfavourable & ill founded assursions &c. &.

The two Chiefs much pleased with their treatments & the Cherefullness
of the party, who Danced to amuse them &c. &c.

The river fall 2 Inches   verry Cold and began to Snow at 8 oClock P M
and Continued all night— Some miss understanding with Jussomm &
his woman— at Day the Snow Seased

1. Baptiste Lafrance, interpreter for the North West Company, seems to have accompanied René Jusseaume to the Mandans as early as 1793. Evans, meeting him there in
1796, had as poor an opinion of him as did Clark. Coues (NLEH), 1:50 n. 56, 301–02,
329, 332; Nasatir (BLC), 1:105, 106, 2:502 and n. 4; Masson, 1:299, 327–28, 351–52.
2. François-Antoine Larocque, born in L'Assomption parish, Quebec, received part of
his education in the United States, where he learned English, which he afterwards pre-
ferred to French. He joined the XY Company in 1801, and the North West Company
when the two merged in 1804, serving as a clerk in the Upper Red River Department. At
the time of this trip to the Mandans he was only twenty. He denies, in his account of the
trip, the accusations of Lewis and Clark that he attempted to win over the Missouri tribes

to the British. Although frustrated in his desire to accompany Lewis and Clark west, he made a trip to the Yellowstone and Bighorn country in 1805, accompanying the Crows from the Hidatsa villages. His is the first European account of the Yellowstone, and of the life and culture of the Crows. He was an observant and literate man, and his accounts of his journeys are valuable in themselves and as complements to those of Lewis and Clark. A successful businessman in Montreal, he spent his last years in religious retreat and study. Wallace, 460; Masson, 1 : 299–313; Wood & Thiessen, 129–220.

3. Charles McKenzie, born in Scotland, joined the North West Company in 1803, and the Hudson's Bay Company when the two firms merged in 1821. He was not particularly successful and was still a clerk when he retired in 1854. His various accounts of his journeys to the Mandans are important sources on the Missouri tribes and on Lewis and Clark. He found Clark agreeable but judged Lewis to be a strong Anglophobe. Wallace, 476; Masson, 1 : 299–313, 317–93; Wood & Thiessen, 221–96.

[Clark]   28th *Novr. Wednesday 1804*

a cold morning wind from the N. W   river full of floating ice, began to Snow at 7 oClock *a' m* and continued all day   at 8 oClock the *Poss-cop-so-he* or Black Cat Grand Chief of the Mandans Came to See us, after Showing Those Chiefs many thing which was Curiossities to them, and Giveing a fiew presents of Curioes Handkerchiefs arm bans & paint with a twist of Tobaco they departed at 1 oClock much pleased, at parting we had Some little talk on the Subject of the British Trader Mr. Le rock Giveing Meadils & Flags, and told those Chiefs to impress it on the minds of their nations that those Simbells were not to be recved by any from them, without they wished incur the displieasure of their Great American Father— a verry disagreeable day— no work done to day   river fall 1 Inch to day

[Clark]   29th *November Thursday* 1804

A verry Cold windey day wind from the N. W by W. Some Snow last night   the Detpt of the Snow is various in the wood about 13 inches, The river Closed at the Village above and fell last night two feet   Mr. *La Rock* and one of his men Came to visit us   we informed him what we had herd of his intentions of makeing Chiefs &c. and forbid him to give meadels or flags to the Indians, he Denied haveing any Such intention, we agreeed that one of our interpeters Should Speak for him on Conditions he did not Say any thing more than what tended to trade alone— he gave fair promises &.

Sergeant Pryor in takeing down the mast put his Sholder out of Place, we made four trials before we replaced it[1]   a Cold after noon wind as usial N W.   river begin to rise a little—

1. The treatment was apparently imperfect. Pryor would suffer repeated dislocations of the shoulder during the expedition, and in 1827 Clark reported him as disabled by the injury. Chuinard (OOMD), 257–58 and n. 5; Clark to James Barbour, August 4, 1827, Jackson (LLC), 2:646.

[Clark]

30h of Nov.   an Indian Chief Came and informed us that five Men of the Mandans Nation was on a hunting party to the S W, distance about Eight Leagues, they were Surprised   one man Killed two wounded and nine horses taken, Severale others men wer on hunting partes & were to have returned Several days ago & had not yet returned, & that they expected to be attacked by an army of *Sioux*   I took 23 men and went to the Village deturmined to Collect the warriers of the Different Villages and meet the Sioux—   The village not expecting Such Strong aid in So Short a time was a little alarmed of the formable appearance of my party— The principal Chiefs met me at 200 yards Distance from the Town, and envited me to his Lodge. I told the Nation the Cause of Comeing &c. was to assist in Chastiseing the enimies of my Dutifull Children—   I requested great Chief to repeat the Cercunstance of the Sioux attack as it realy happined which he did—   I told them to Send runners to the other villages & assemble the warriers & we Would go and Chastize the Sioux for Spilling the Blood of my Dutifull Children—   after a Conversation of a few minits amongst themselves, a Chief Said that they now Saw that what we had told them was the trooth and we were ready to protect them and Kill those who did not listen to our Councils (and after a long Speech) he concluded   Said ["]the Sious who Spilt our Blood is gorn home—   The Snow is deep and it is Cold, our horses Cannot Travel thro the plains in pursute—   If you will go and conduct us in the Spring after the Snow is gorn, we will assemble all the warriers & Brave men in all the villages and go with you." I answered the Speach at Some length, explained to them their Situation declareing our intentions of Defending them at any time dureing the time we Should Stay in ther nieghbourhood, explained the Situation of the Ricaras & told them not to get angrey with them untill they were Certain of their haveing violated the treaty &c. &. I crossed the River on the Ice and returned to the *fort*[1]

[Clark][2]

⟨We Promiss⟩ 30th   in the morning early a Indian Came to the river opposit & requsted to be brought over, that he had Some thing to Say from his nation   we Sent for him, and after he had Smoked—   he Said he thought the river was frosted across here & expected to Cross on the ice—

7 or 8 Mandans out hunting in a S. W, Derection from this place about 8 Leagues, after they had made their hunt and on their return was attackted by a large Party of Seaux, one of the party a young Chief was Killed 2 wounded & 9 horses taken, the men who made their escape Say the one half of the party who attacked them was *Panias*—[3]

The two Panias who Came here a fiew days ago was imediately Sent home, for fear of their being [pu]t to death by the party Defeated—

Tw[o of th]e attacting party was Known to be Panies. The man who was killed mentioned that after he was wounded, ⟨men⟩ that he had been at *war* & been wounded, "this day I shall die like a man before my Enimies,!   tell my *father* that I died bravely, and do not greive for me—["]

4 of the Big bellies who were Camped near thos is missing, and Searching for him in their Camps above—   no one Dare to go to the ground where the battle was for fear of the Sioux being noumerous—.

[Clark]   30th *of November Friday* 1804

This morning at 8 oClock an Indian Calld from the other Side and informed that he had Something of Consequence to Communicate.   we Sent a perogue for him & he informed us as follows. Viz: "five men of the Mandan Nation out hunting in a S. W. derection about Eight Leagues was Suprised by a large party of *Sceoux* & Panies, one man was Killed and two wounded with arrows & 9 Horses taken, 4 of the We ter Soon nation[4] was missing, & they expected to be attacked by the Souix &c. &.["]   we thought it well to Show a Disposition to ade and assist them against their enimies, perticularly those who Came in oppersition to our Councils, and I Deturmined to go to the town with Some men, and if the Sceoux were comeing to attact the nation to Collect the worriers from each Village and meet them, thos Ideas were also those of Capt Lewis, I crossed the river in about an hour after the arrival of the Indian express with 23 men including the interpeters and flankd the Town & came up on the back part— The Indians not expecting ⟨not⟩ to receive Such Strong aide in So Short a time was much Supprised, and a littled allarmed at the formadable appearance of my party—   The principal Chiefs met me Some Distance from the town (Say 200 yards) and invited me in to town, I ord my pty into dft. lodges &

I explained to the nation the cause of my comeing in this formadable manner to their Town, was to asst and Chastise the enimies of our Dutifull Children,—   I requested the Grand Cheif to repeat the Circumstancies as they hapined which he did as was mentioned by the *Express* in the morning—   I then informed them that if they would assemble their warrers and those of the different Towns I would to meet the Army of Souix & Chastise thim for takeing the blood of our dutifull Children &c.   after a conversation of a fiew minits amongst themselves, one Chief the *Big Man Cien* [*NB: (a Chayenne)*] Said they now Saw that what we hade told them was the trooth, whin we expected the enimies of their Nation was Comeing to attact them, or had spilt their blood were ready to protect them, and Kill those who would not listen to our Good talk—   his people had listened to what we had told them and Cearlessly went out to hunt in Small parties believing themselves to be Safe from the other Nations—   and have been killed by the *Panies* & *Seauex.* "I knew Said he that the Panies were liers, and told the old Chief who Came with you (to Confirm a piece with us) that his people were *liers* and bad men and that we killed them like the Buffalow, when we pleased, we had made peace Several times and you Nation ⟨& They⟩ have always Commened the war, we do not want to Kill you, and will not Suffer you to Kill us or Steal our horses, we will make peace with you as our two fathers have derected, and they Shall See that we will not be the Ogressors, but we fear the Ricares will not be at peace—long—["]   "My father those are the words I Spoke to the Ricare in Your presents—   you See they have not opened their ears to your good

Councils but have Spuilt our blood." two Ricarees whome we Sent home
this day for fear of our peoples Killing them in their greaf—informed us
when they Came here Several days ago, that two Towns of the *Ricares*
were makeing their Mockersons, and that we had best take care of Our
horses &."— a number of Sieuex were in their Towns, and they believed
not well disposed towards us— four of the *Wetersoons* are now absent
they were to have been back in 16 days they have been out 24 we fear
they have fallen. my father the Snow is deep and it is cold our horses
Cannot travel thro the the plains,— those people who have Spilt our
blood have gorn back? if you will go with us in the Spring after the Snow
goes off we will raise the Warriers of all the Towns & nations around about
us, and go with you."

I told this nation that we Should be always willing and ready to defend
them from the insults of any nation who would dare to Come to doe them
injurey dureing the time we would ⟨Stay⟩ remain in their neighbourhood,
and requstd. that they would inform us of any party who may at any time
be discovered by their Patroles or Scouts;

I was Sorry that the Snow in the Plains had fallen So Deep Sence the
Murder of the young Chief by the Scioux as prevented, their horses from
traveling I wished to meet those Scioux & all others who will not open
their ears, but make war on our dutifull Children, and let you See that
the Wariers of your great father will Chastize the enimies of his dutifull
Children the Mandans, wetersoons & Winitarees, who have opend. their
ears to his advice— you Say that the Panies or Ricares were with the
Sciaux, Some bad men may have been with the *Sciaux* you know there
is bad men in all nations, do not get mad with the racarees untill we know
if those bad men are Counternoncd. by their nation, and we are Convsd.
those people do not intend to follow our Councils— you know that the
Sceaux have great influence over the ricarees and perhaps have led Some
of them astray— you know that the Ricarees, are Dependant on the
Sceaux for their guns, powder, & Ball, and it was policy in them to keep
on as good terms as possible with the Siaux untill they had Some other
means of getting those articles &c. &. you know your Selves that you are
Compelled to put up with little insults from the *Christinoes & Ossinaboins*

(or Stone Inds.) because if you go to war with those people, they will provent the traders in the north from bringing you Guns Powder & Ball and by that means distress you verry much, but whin you will have Certain Suppliers from your Great American father of all those articls you will not Suffer any nation to insult you &c.   after about two hours conversation on various Subjects all of which tended towards their Situation &c. I informed them I Should return to the fort, the Chief Said they all thanked me verry much for the fatherly protection which I Showed towards them, that the Village had been Crying all the night and day for the death of the brave young man, who fell but now they would wipe away their tears, and rejoice in their fathers protection—and Cry no more—

I then Paraded & Crossed the river on the ice and Came down on the N. Side   the Snow So deep, it was verry fatigueing   arrved at the fort after night, gave a little Taffee,[5] [*NB: dram to my party*]   a Cold night   the river rise to its former hite—   The Chief frequently thanked me for Comeing to protect them—   and the whole Village appeared thankfull for that measure

1. The events of the day, particularly the Indian point-of-view, are discussed in Ronda (LCAI), 95–98.

2. The second entry in the Field Notes for November 30 is on document 65.

3. Here again Clark is referring to the Arikaras as "Pawnees" because of the linguistic kinship between the two.

4. The Awaxawi Hidatsas.

5. Probably tafia, an inferior grade of rum made from molasses. Thwaites (LC), 1:232 n. 1.

[Lewis and Clark]   [*Weather, November 1804*][1]

1804 Day of the Month	Ther. at ☉ rise	Weather	Wind at ☉ rise	Thert. at 4 P. M.	Weather	Wind at 4 P. M.	River raise or fall	Feet	Inches
Novr. 1	31	f	N. W.	47	f	N. W.			
2	32	f	S E	63	f	S E			
3	32	f	N. W.	53	f	N. W.			
4	31	f	N W	43	c	W.			

5	30	c	N. W	58	c	N W			
6	31	c	S W	43	c	W			
7	43	c	S	62	c	S			
8	38	c	S	39	c	W.			
9th	27	f	N W	43	f	N W			
10th	34	f	N W	36	c	N. W			
11th	28	f	N W	60	f	N W			
12	18	f	N.	31	f	N E			
13	18	s	S E	28	c a s	S E	f²	1	½
14	24	s	S E	32	c a s	S E	r	1	
15	22	c³	N W	31	c a s	N W	r		½
16	25	c	N W	30	f	S E	r		¼
17	28	f	S. E	34	f	S E	r		¼
18	30	f	S E	38	f	W	r		¼
19	32	f	N W	48	f	N W	r	1	
20	35	f	N. W.	50	f	W	r	1	¼
21	33	c	S	49	f	S E	r		
22	37	f	W	45	f	N W	r		½
23	38	f	W	48	f	N W			
24	36	f	N W	34	f	N W			
25	34	f	W	32	f	S W			
26	15	f	S W	21	f	W			
27	10	f	S E	19	c	S E	f	3	
28	12	s	S E	15	s	E	f	4	
29	14	c a s	N E	18	f	W	f	2	½
30	17	f	W	23	f	W	f		

[*Remarks*][4]

Novr. 1st   the winds blue so heard this day that we could not decend the river[5] untill after 5 P. M. when[6] we left our

2nd   the boat droped down to our winter station & formed a camp I ⟨went⟩ ascended to the lower mandane vilage

3rd   wind blew hard all day—Mr. Jessome arrived with his Squaw[7] employed a Frenchman— sent out 6 hunters in a Perogue—[8]

[4]   wind hard this evening.[9]

5th   drew Mr. Gravlins instructions &c. and discharged two of my hands

6th some little hail about noon— Mr. Gravlin received his instructions and departed in a perogue with Premo;[10] Lajuness and two french boys for the recares.

7th a few drops of rain this evening— saw the arrora. borialis at 10 P. M. it was very briliant in perpendiculer collums frequently changing position—

8th Since we have been at our present station the River has fallen about nine inches

9th very head frost this morning—

10th many Gees passing to the South— saw a flock of the crested cherry birds passing to the south[11]

13th large quanty of drift ice running this morning   the river has every appearance of closing for winter

16th very hard frost this morning[12] attatched to the limbs and boughs of the trees—

17th the frost of yesterday remained on the trees untill 2 P. M. when it descended like a shower of snow—   swans passing from the N.

19th the hunters arrived with a perogue loaded with fine meat— the runing ice had declined

20th little soft ice this morning; that from the board[er] of the river came down in such manner as to endanger the boat.

21st Mr. Charbona arrived, we got into our hut yesterday evening.—

25th set out with Charbono and Jessome to visit the Indian hunting camps.   spent the evening with the black mockersons the Prince. Cheif of the little Vilage grosventres.[13]

26th wind bleue verry hard, visited the upper camp of the big bellies and returned to the lower camp[14] where I had slept the preceeding night—

27th much drift ice running in the river—   returned to ⟨camp⟩ the fort in company with two chiefs and a warrior[15]

28th the Indians left us late in the evening on their return

29th the snow fell 8 inches deep— it drifted in heeps in the open growns— visited by Mr. La Rock,[16] a trader.—

30th the indians pass over the river on the ice— Capt Clark visits the Mandanes with a party of men.[17]

1. Lewis's weather table comes from his Weather Diary; Clark's table is in Codex C. Lewis is followed here, with some variations by Clark being noted.

2. Lewis here resumes noting the fall and rise of the river, which was only possible while they remained in one place during the day.

3. From this point through the rest of the month and into December Lewis has transposed his "Weather" and "Wind at ☉ rise" columns, putting the information in the wrong place. The information has been rearranged to avoid confusion.

4. The remarks are from Lewis's Weather Diary, with substantial variations in Clark's Codex C noted. The dates are Clark's, since he wrote his remarks separately and Lewis placed his beside his weather table. Someone has crossed out Clark's remarks, except those for the first, seventh, eighth, ninth, and thirteenth.

5. Clark inserts "to a proper place to camp" here.

6. Here Clark has "the Boat droped down."

7. Here Clark adds "& child."

8. Clark adds "wind hard this evening."

9. Clark has no remarks for this date.

10. This must be Paul Primeau. It is not clear if the two French boys were listed as *engagés*, were with the expedition as unlisted choreboys, or were encountered at the Mandan villages. Primeau and La Jeunesse were probably the two hands discharged on November 5.

11. Probably cedar waxwings, *Bombycilla cedrorum* [AOU, 619]. Lewis calls them "cherry or cedar birds" in his weather remarks for April 6, 1805, giving a brief description. The species was not named until 1807. Burroughs, 254–55.

12. Clark's remark ends here.

13. Clark notes that Lewis set out, and has "Big Bellies" instead of "grosventres."

14. From here Clark has "& passed a Second night," apparently writing in the first person although he is clearly describing Lewis's activities.

15. Clark again writes as if in the first person, although describing Lewis's activities.

16. From here Clark writes, "a Clerk of the N W Company."

17. From here Clark, writing of himself in the third person, says "to assit them in defenc of the Sioux who had killed one man wounded 2 & taken maney horses. returned in the evening on the ice."

[Clark][1]

1s Decr.   a young Chief arrived

7 Chiens Came to the Village with a pipe & the 3 Ricares who Came here a fiew days ago & Sent off yesterday have returned and Say that the Sieaux & ricares are Camped together

[Clark]   1st of *December Satturday* 1804

wind from the N W.   all hands ingaged in gitting pickets &. at 10 oClock the half brother of the man who was killed Came and informd. us that after my ⟨arrival⟩ departure last night *Six Chiens* So Called by the french ⟨Chat⟩ Shar ha Indians had arrived with a pipe and Said that ⟨their nation was at one days march and intended to Come & trade &c.   three Panies had also arrived from the nation⟩ [*NB: their nation was then within 3 days march & were coming on to trade with us.   ⟨to be inserted this⟩   Three Pawnees accompd these Chayennes—   The Mandans call all ricaras Pawnees; don't ⟨know⟩ use the name of rics. but the rics call themselves Rics*][2]   The mandans apprehended danger from the *Shar has* as they were at peace with the Seaux; and wished to Kill them and the Ricarees (or Panies) but the Cheifs informed the nation ["]it was our wish that they Should not be hurt, and forbid being Killed &c."   we gave a little Tobacco &c. & this man Departed well Satisfied with our councils and advice to him

in the evening a Mr. G Henderson[3] in the imploy of the *hudsons bay* Company Sent to trade with the *Gros ventre—*or *big bellies* So Called by the french traders

1. On one side of this document 65 of the Field Notes are entries for November 30 and December 1, 1804. Below the latter entry is this column of figures: 3, 21, 2, and a total of 26. On the other side are the notations "Notes at Wood River 1803–4," and "Genl. Jonathan Clark Near Louisville Kentucky," and "Nothing." It would appear that Clark intended at some point to wrap his River Dubois notes in this piece of paper to send to his brother Jonathan. See Introduction, vol. 2; Osgood (FN), xvi–xvii.

2. "Rics" is obviously an abbreviation for "Arikara." Clark also uses "Rees," later a common abbreviation for "Arikaree." Biddle is noting the fact that the Mandans called the Pawnees and Arikaras by the same name.

3. George Henderson was in charge of a party of Hudson's Bay Company men who had come from the Assiniboine River to compete with the North West Company traders. The

exact date of his arrival is not clear, since Clark refers to the coming of men of both companies in his Field Notes for November 27 (see above under November 19, 1804). The December 1 entry may only refer to Henderson's visiting Fort Mandan that day, but Larocque notes the arrival of a Hudson's Bay man on the first. Masson, 1:299, 306.

[Clark][1]

2d of Decr. 1804   Visited by Several Mandan Chiefs and 4 Chyannes Inds. who Came with a pipe to the Mandans, Sent a Speech to ther Nation a flag & Some tobacco, also written a Speech to the Ricaras & Sioux, informe them what they might depend on if they would not open their ears, & &.

[Clark]   *2nd of December Sunday 1804*

The latter part of last night was verry warm and Continued to thaw untill [*blank*] oClock when the wind Shifted to the North   at 11 oClock the Chiefs of the Lower village of the Mandans with maney of theire young men and 4 of the *Shar-ha's* who had come to Smoke with the pipe of Peace with the Mandans, we explained to them our intentions our views and advised them to be at peace, Gave them a flag for theire nation, Some Tobacco with a Speech to Deliver to their nation on theire return, also Sent by them a letter to Mrs. Tabbo & Gravoline, at the Ricares Village, to interseid in proventing Hostilities, and if they Could not effect those measures to Send & informe us of what was going on, Stateing to the Indians the part we intend to take if the Rickores & Seauex did not follow our Derections and be at peace with the nations which we had addopted— We made Some fiew Small presents to those *Shar ha's* and also Some to the Mandans & at 3 oClock they all Departed well pleased, haveing Seen many Curisossties, which we Showed them—.   river rise one inch

1. This entry returns to document 64 of the Field Notes.

[Clark]   3rd *December Monday 1804.*

a fine morning   the after part of the day Cold & windey   the wind from the N W.   The Father of the Mandan who was killed Came and made us a present of Some Dried Simnens [*NB: Pumpkins*] & a little pemicon

[*NB: pemitigon*], we made him Some Small preasents for which he was much pleased

[Clark]   4th *of December Tuesday 1804*

a Cloudy raw Day   wind from the N. W.   the Black Cat and two young Chiefs Visit us and as usial Stay all Day   the river rise one inch   finish the main *bastion,* our interpetr. [*NB: Jesseaume*] we discover to be assumeing and discontent'd—

[Clark]   5th *December Wednesday 1804*

a Cold raw morning   wind from the S. E. Some Snow, two of the N W. Companey Came to See us, to let us Know they intended to Set out for the establishment on the osinniboin River in two Days—& their party would Consist of 5 men, Several Indians also visited us   one brought Pumpkins or Simmins as a preasent   a little Snow fell in the evening at which time the wind Shifted round to N. E.

                                                              Fort Mandan
[Clark]   6th *of December Thursday 1804*

The wind blew violently hard from the N, N W. with Some Snow   the air Keen and Cold. The Thermometer at 8 oClock A, M, Stood at 10 dgs. above o—   at 9 oClock a man & his Squar Came down with Some meat for the inturpeter   his dress was a par mockersons of Buffalow Skin ⟨a⟩ Pr. Legins of Goat Skin & a Buffalow robe, 14 ring of Brass on his fingers, this metel [*NB: ornaments*] the Mandans ar verry fond off—   Cold after noon   river rise 1½ Inch to day

[Clark]   at Fort mandan[1]

7th of December 1804, we were informed by a Chief that great numbers of Buffalow were on the hills near us   Cap Lewis with a party went out & Killed 11 three in view of our fort, The weather so excesive Cold & wolves plenty, we only saved 5 of them, I with a party turned on the 8th out and found the Buffalow at 7 ms. distant   Killed 8 & a Deer, I returned with 2 Cows leaving men with remaining meat—   Several men badly frost bit— The Themormeter Stood this morning at 44 d. below Breizing [freezing].

Capt Lewis went out 9th & Stayed all night out Killed 9 buffalow— maney of the Buffalow Killed were So meager that they not fit for use— Collected by the ade of Some horses the best of the meat in fact all we could Save from wolves & I went on a hunting party the 14 & 15 of Decr.— much Snow verry cold 52° below freesinge. N W. & H Bay Clerks Visit us ⟨on⟩ the 16th also Mr Hainey, Cold Tem: 74° below freesing—

I visit the Mandans on the 1s of January Capt Lewis the 2nd—

[Clark]   7th *of December* ⟨*Wednesday*⟩ *Friday* 1804

a verry Cold day wind from the N W. the Big White Grand Chief of the 1s Village, Came and informed us that a large Drove of Buffalow was near and his people was wating for us to join them in a Chase Capt. Lewis took 15 men & went out joined the Indians, who were at the time he got up, Killing the Buffalows on Horseback with arrows which they done with great dexterity, his party killed 14 Buffalow, *five* of which we got to the fort by the assistance of a horse in addition to what the men Packed on their backs— one Cow was killed on the ice after drawing her out of a vacancey in the ice in which She had fallen, and Butchered her at the fort— those we did not get in was taken by the indians under a Custon which is established amongst them 'i 'e. any person Seeing a buffalow lying without an arrow Sticking in him, or Some purticular mark takes posse- sion, many times (as I am told) a hunter who Kills maney Buffalow in a chase only Gets a part of one, all meat which is left out all night falls to the Wolves which are in great numbers, always in the Buffalows— the river Closed opposit the fort last night 1½ inches thick The Thermometer Stood this morning at 1 d. below 0— three men frost bit badly to day

1. Here again Clark has run together brief entries for various dates under one heading on document 64 of the Field Notes, indicating a perfunctory keeping of his Field Notes while the notebook journal, Codex C, was kept each day. For notes, see the appropriate dates.

[Clark]   8th *December ⟨Thursday⟩ Satturday* 1804

a verry Cold morning, the Thermometer Stood at 12 d. below o which is 42 d.[1] below the freesing point, wind from the N W   I with 15 men[2] turned out [*NB: Indians joined us on horseback   shot with arrows   rode along side of buffaloe*] and killed 8 buffalow & one Deer, one Cow and Calf was brought in, two Cows which I killed at 7 miles Dst. I left 2 men to Skin & Keep off the wolves, and brought in one Cow & a calf, in the evening on my return to the fort Saw great numbers of Buffalow Comeing into the Bottoms on both Sides of the river   This day being Cold Several men returned a little frost bit; one of men with his feet badly frost bit   my Servents feet also *frosted* & his P—s a little, I feel a little fatigued haveing run after the Buffalow all day in Snow many Places 10 inches Deep, Generally 6 or 8, two men hurt their hips verry much in Slipping down—   The Indians kill great numbers of Buffalow to day—   2 reflectings Suns to day[3]

1. The correct figure is 44, which Clark has in the Field Notes.

2. Ordway says he was one of them.

3. The sun dog, or parhelion, is produced by the sun's rays reflecting off ice crystals in the very high atmosphere. It is commonly associated with advancing frontal systems and was thus used by natives and modern inhabitants as a harbinger of an approaching storm. Allen, 218. See also entry of December 11.

[Clark]   9th *December ⟨Friday⟩ Sunday 1804*

The Thermometer Stood this morning at 7° above o, wind from the E.   Capt Lewis took 18 men & 4 horses [*NB: 3 hired 1 bought*] and went out   Send in the meet killed yesterday and kill more, the Sun Shown to day Clear, both interpeters went to the Villages to day   at 12 oClock two Chiefs Came loaded with meat   one with a dog & Slay also loaded with meat, Capt. Lewis Sent in 4 Hors's loaded with meat, he continued at the hunting Camp near which the[y] killed 9 buffalow.

[Clark]   10th *Monday Decr.* 1804 *Fort Mandan*

a verry Cold Day The Thermometer to day at 10 & 11 Degrees below o., Capt. Lewis returned, to day at 12 oClock leaveing 6 men at the Camp to prepare the meat for ⟨the⟩ to pack 4 Horse loads Came in, Capt Lewis had a Cold Disagreeable night last in the Snow on a Cold point with one Small Blankett   the Buffaloe Crossed the river below in emence herds without brakeing in.   only 2 buffalow killed to day one of which was too pore to Skin, The men which was frost bit is gitting better.   the rise 1½ inch   wind North

[Clark]   11th *December Tuesday 1804*

a verry Cold morning   Wind from the north   The Thermomettr at (4 oClock A M at 21°)[1] Sunrise at 21°   See list.[2] below 0 which is 53° below the freesing point and getting colder, the Sun Shows and reflects two imigies, the ice floating in the atmespear being So thick that the appearance is like a fog Despurceing—

Sent out three horses for meat & with Derections for all the hunters to return to the fort as Soon as possible   at 1 oClock the horses returned loaded   at night all the hunters returned, Several a little frosted, The Black Cat Chief of the Mandans paid us a Visit to day   continue Cold all day   river at a Stand

1. Clark seems to have bracketed this passage; we have used parentheses.
2. Perhaps a reference to the Weather Diary for this date.

[Clark]   *12th December Wednesday 1804*

a Clear Cold morning   wind from the *north*   the Thormometer at Sun rise Stood at 38° below 0, moderated untill 6 oClock at which time it began to get Colder. I line my Gloves and have a cap made of the Skin of the *Louservia* (*Lynx*) (or wild Cat of the North)[1] the fur near 3 inches long   a Indian Of the *Shoe* [*NB: Maharha or Mocassin*] nation Came with the half of a *Cabra* ko kâ[2] or Antilope which he killed near the Fort, Great numbers of those animnals are near [*NB: so that they do not all return to rock mountain (goat*] our fort but the weather is So Cold that we do not think it prudent to turn out to hunt in Such Cold weather, or at least untill our Consts.[3] are prepared to under go this Climate. I measure the river from bank to bank on the ice and make it 500 yards

1. Clark refers to the *loup cervier,* the French name for the Canada lynx. Alternatively, the pelt may have belonged to a northern bobcat, *Lynx rufus.* One skin of a "louservia,"

probably not the one Clark used in his gloves and cap, was sent to Jefferson in the spring of 1805. Reid, 102 n. 34; Burroughs, 92.

2. *Kóke* is the Mandan word for pronghorn.

3. Probably "constitutions."

[Clark]   *13th December Thursday 1804*

The last night was verry Clear & the frost which fell Covered the ice old Snow & thos parts which was naked ⅙ of an inch, The Thermotr. Stands this morning at 20° below 0, a fine day.   find it imposible to make an Observation with an artifical Horsison[1] Joseph Fields kill a Cow and Calf to day one mile from the fort   river falls

1. See November 19, 1803, and Lewis's note, July 22, 1804.

[Clark]   *14th December Friday 1804*

a fine morning.   wind from the S. E.   the murckerey Stood at 'o' this morning   I went with a party of men down the river 18 miles to hunt Buffalow, Saw two Bulls too pore to kill, the Cows and large gangues haveing left the River, we only killed two Deer & Camped all night with Some expectation of Seeing the Buffalow in the morning, a verry Cold night, Snowed.

[Clark]   *15th of December 1804 Satturday*

a Cold Clear morning, Saw no buffalow, I concluded to return to the Fort & hunt on each Side of the river on our return which we did without Success—   the Snow fell 1½ inches deep last night.   wind North—   on my return to the fort found Several Chiefs there

Fort Mandan

[Clark]   *16th December, Sunday 1804*

a clear Cold morning, the Thermtr. at Sun rise Stood at 22° below 0, a verry Singaler appearance of the Moon last night, as She appeared thro: The frosty atmispear—   Mr. *Henny*,[1] from the Establishment on River Ossinnniboin, with a letter from, Mr Charles Chaboillez[2] one of the *Cos* arrived in 6 Days, Mr. C in his letters expressed a great anxiety to Serve us in any thing in his power—

a root Discribed by Mr. Henny for the Cure of a Mad Dog[3]

Mr. Le rock a Clerk, of the N W Company and Mr. George Bunch[4] a Clerk of the Hudsons bay Compy accompanied Mr. Henny from the Village—

1. Hugh Heney, or Hené, was supposedly an employee of Régis Loisel on the Missouri from 1800; in 1804 he entered the service of the North West Company. At some point he traded with the Minniconjou Sioux near the mouth of Cheyenne River in South Dakota; the captains questioned him extensively about this tribe. They later sought his aid in persuading Teton Sioux chiefs to go to Washington. Wallace, 455–56, gives a sketch of a man supposed to be the Heney known to Lewis and Clark, but the birth date given (1789) seems incompatible with other information about him. Coues (NLEH), 1:424 n. 1, 425, 526; Masson, 1:307–9; Abel (TN), 24–25 nn. 57 and 59, 26, 31, 231–34; Nasatir (BLC), 1:112–14, 2:622, 628, 636; Clark to Heney, July 20, 1806, Jackson (LLC), 1:309–13.

2. The name seems to have been squeezed into this space later.

3. A space was left here for a description of the root that was never filled in. Clark describes its use from information of Heney on February 28, 1805. Lewis also gives a detailed account of its uses and application in a letter to Jefferson and it is mentioned in a list of goods being returned from Fort Mandan (see April 3, 1805). Jackson (LLC), 1:220–21. It is *Echinacea angustifolia* DC. var. *angustifolia,* narrow leaf purple coneflower, a plant used for many ailments including toothache, snakebites, other venomous bites and stings, and several poisonous conditions. Gilmore (UPI), 79; Foster; Cutright (LCPN), 122. Clark describes its use in detail on February 28, 1805.

4. Larocque calls him "Budge." He could speak the Hidatsa language well, an indication that he had been to their villages before. This gave him an advantage in trading over Larocque, whose journal indicates that the two were more concerned with competing with each other than with spreading British influence among the Indians, as Lewis and Clark may have feared. Wood & Thiessen, 144, 144 n. 23.

[Clark]   17th *December Monday 1804*

a verry Cold morning   the Thrmt. Stood a 43° [*WC: 45*] below 0. We found Mr. Henny a verry intelligent man from whome we obtained Some Scetches of the Countrey between the Mississippi & Missouri,[1] and Some Sketches from him, which he had obtained from the Indins. to the *West* of this place   also the names and charecktors of the Sceoux &c   about 8 oClock P M. the thermometer fell to 74° below the freesing pointe—   the Indian Chiefs Sent word that Buffalow was in our neighbourhood, and if we would join them, in the morning they would go and kill them—

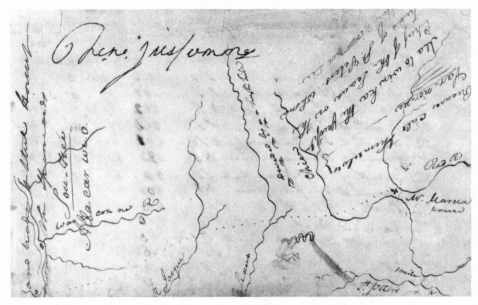

5. Country between the Missouri and Red Rivers, ca. December 17, 1804,
Field Notes, reverse of document of 66

1. The sketches may be a map, fig. 5, on the reverse of document 66 of the Field Notes. See Chapter 10, part 1, for a discussion of the map and also Osgood (FN), 184 n. 6.

[Clark]   18th December Tuesday 1804

The Themometer the Same as last night   Mr. Haney & La Rocke left us for the Grossventre Camp, Sent out 7 men to hunt for the Buffalow   They found the weather too cold & returned, Several Indians Came, who had Set out with a veiw to Kill buffalow, The river rise a little   I imploy my Self makeing a Small map of Connection &. Sent Jessomme to the Main Chief of the mandans to know the Cause of his detaining or takeing a horse of *Chabonoe* our big belly interpeter, which we found was thro: the rascallity of one Lafrance a trader from the N W. Company, who told this Cheif that Chabonah owd. him a horse to go and take him   he done So agreeable to an indian Custom—   he gave up the horse

[Clark]   *19th December Wednesday* 1804

The wind from S. W. the weather moderated a little, I engage my self in Connecting the Countrey from information.   river rise a little

[Clark]   *20th December Thursday 1804*

The wind from the N W   a moderate day, the Thermometr 37° [*WC:* 24°] above o, which givs an oppertunity of putting up our pickets next the river, nothing remarkable took place to Day   river fall a little

[Clark]   *21st December Friday 1804*

a fine Day worm and wind from the N W by W, the Indian whome I stoped from Commiting murder on his wife, thro jellousy of one of our interpeters, Came & brought his two wives and Showed great anxiety to make up with the man with whome his joulassey Sprung—   a womin brought a Child with an abcess on the lower part of the back, and offered as much corn as She Could carry for Some medison, Capt Lewis administered &c.

[Clark]   *22nd December Satturday 1804*

a number of Squars womn & men Dressed in Squars Clothes[1] Came with Corn to Sell to the men for little things, we precured two horns of the animale the french Call the rock mountain Sheep [bighorn]   those horns are not of the largest kind—   The mandans Indians Call this Sheep *Ar-Sar-ta*   it is about the Size of a large Deer, or Small Elk, its Horns Come out and wind around the head like the horn of a Ram and the teckere [*NB: texture*] not unlike it   much larger and thicker perticelarly that part with which they but or outer part which is [*blank*] inchs thick, the length of those horns, which we have is[2]

[Lewis]   *Saturday December 22nd 1804.*[3]

Observed Equal altitudes of ☉ with Sextant

	h	m	s			h	m	s
A. M.	9	6	43		P. M.	1	25	39
	"	9	52			"	28	57
	"	13	9			"	32	10

		h	m	s
Cronometer too slow on Mean time		o	39	37.6

1. Male transvestites were to be found among a number of plains tribes. The Anglo-Americans called them by the French traders' term "berdache," from the French *bardache,* a homosexual male, which Clark later and somewhat incorrectly explained to Biddle that they were. Nicholas Biddle Notes [ca. April 1810], Jackson (LLC), 2:531. Ronda (LCAI), 130–31, discusses the spiritual nature of this phenomenon, while Whitehead looks at the larger institution of gender-crossing.

2. See below, May 25, 1805, for a description by Lewis based on observation. Clark's "*Ar-Sar-ta*" is probably the Mandan term, *áŋse xte,* "big horn."

3. Lewis's astronomical observation from Codex O.

[Clark]   *23rd December Sunday 1804*

a fine Day   great numbers of indians of all discriptions Came to the fort many of them bringing Corn to trade, the *little Crow,* loadd. his wife & Sun with corn for us, Cap. Lewis gave him a few presents as also his wife, She made a Kettle of boild Simnins, beens, Corn & Choke Cherris[1] with the Stones which was paletable

This Dish is Considered, as a treat among those people, The Chiefs of the Mandans are fond of Stayin & Sleeping in the fort

1. The choke cherry is *Prunus virginianus* L. Barkley, 148.

[Clark]   *24 December Monday 1804*

Several Chiefs and members of men womin and Children at the fort to day, Some for trade, the most as lookers on, we gave a fellet of Sheep Skin (which we brought for Spunging) to 3 Chiefs one to each of 2 inches wide, which they lay great value (priseing those felets equal to a fine horse[)], a fine Day   we finished the pickingen [*NB: Riqueting*] around our works

[Clark]   25th *December Christmass* Tuesday

I was awakened before Day by a discharge of 3 platoons[1] from the Party and the french, the men merrily Disposed, I give them all a little Taffia and permited 3 Cannon fired, at raising Our flag, Some men went out to hunt & the Others to Danceing and Continued untill 9 oClock P, M, when the frolick ended &c.

1. Here "platoon" is used in its old sense of volleys, or a group of men firing in unison.

[Clark] 26th *Decr. Wednesday* 1804

a temperate day   no Indians to day or yesterday. A man from the N W Company Came Down from the Gross Vintres to Get one of our inter-peters to assist them in trade[1]   This man informed that the Party of Gross Ventres who persued the Ossinboins that Stold their horses, has all re-turned in their usial way by Small parties, the last of the party bringing 8 horses which they Stole from a Camp of Asniboins which they found on Mouse river—[2]

1. Larocque was seeking Charbonneau's services. Wood & Thiessen, 144–45.

2. The Souris (Mouse) River rises in southeastern Saskatchewan, curves into North Da-kota and then into Manitoba, and finally runs into the Assiniboine River.

[Clark] 27th *December 1804 Thursday*

a little fine Snow   weather something Colder than yesterday   Several Indians here to Day, much Surprised at the Bellos & method of makeing Sundery articles of Iron[1]   wind hard from the N W.

1. The Corps had a small forge, complete with bellows and fueled by charcoal, on which they could work iron and other metals. Shields and Willard were the smiths. Besides re-pairing expedition equipment, they made tomahawk heads and other articles to trade to the Indians for food. Russell (FTT), 358–61; Ronda (LCAI), 102–4.

Chapter Nine

Among the Mandans

December 28, 1804–April 6, 1805

[Clark][1]   28th of *December Friday 1804*

blew verry hard last night, the frost fell like a Shower of Snow, nothing remarkable to day, the Snow Drifting from one bottom to another and from the leavel plains into the hollows &c

1. This entry is from Codex C. The Field Notes entries are quite irregular from November 19, 1804, to April 3, 1805. See note at November 7, 1804.

[Clark]   *29th December Satturday 1804*

The frost fell last night nearly a ¼ of an inch Deep and Continud to fall untill the Sun was of Some hite, the Murcurey Stood this morning at 9 d below o which is not considered Cold, as the Changes take place gradually without long intermitions

a number of Indians here

[Clark]   30th *December Sunday 1804*

Cold the Termtr. at 20 d below o   a number of Indians here to day the[y] are much Supprised at the Bellows   one Deer Killed

Fort Mandan

[Clark]   31st of December Monday 1804

a fine Day   Some wind last night which mixed the Snow and Sand in the bend of the river, which has the appearance of hillocks of Sand on the ice, which is also Covered with Sand & Snow, the frost which falls in the night continues on the earth & old Snow &c. &c.— a Number of indians here every Day our blckSmitth mending their axes hoes &c. &c. for which the Squars bring Corn for payment

[Lewis and Clark]   [*Weather, December 1804*][1]

1804 Day of the Month	Ther. at ☉ rise	Weather[2]	Wind at ☉ rise	Thert. at 4 P. M.	Weather	Wind at 4 P. M.	River raise or fall	Feet	Inches
Dec. 1	1 b o	f.	E.	6	f	S E	r	1	
2	38 a	f	N. W.	36	f	N W	r		1
3	26 a	f	N W.	30	f	N. W.	r		1
4	18	f	N.	29	f	N.	r		1
5	14	c	N E.	27	s	N E			
6th	10 a	s	N W	11	c a s	N W			
7	a o[3]	f.	N. W	1	c.	N W	r	2	½
8	12 b	s.	N W	5	f a s	N W			
9	7 a	f	E	10	f	N W			
10	10 b	c	N	11	c	N	r		1½
11	21 b	f.	N	18	f	N	f		½
12	38 b	f	N	16	f	N			
13	20 b	f.	S. E.	4	c	S. E.			
14	2 b	c.	S E	2	s	S E	f		1
15	8 b	c. a. s.	W.	4	c a s	W.			
16	22 b	f.	N. W.	4	f	N W	f		1
17	43 b[4]	f	N	28	f	N.	r		3
18	32 b	f	W	16	f	S W	r		1
19	2 b	c	S W	16	f	S.	r		1
20	24 a	c[5]	N. W.	37	f	N W	r		3½
21	22 a	f	N W	22	c	W.	r		2
22	10 a	f	N W	23	f	N W	r		2½
23	18 a	c	S. W.	27	c	W	f		1
24	22 a	s	S W	31	c a s	W	f		2½
25	15	s	N W	20	c a s	N W	f		1
26	18	c.	N W	21	f	N. W.			
27	4 b	c	N W	14	c	N W			
28	12 a	f	N	13	f	N. W.	r.		2½
29	9 b.	f	N.	3	f	N	r		1
30	20 b	f.	N.	11	f	N	r		½
31	10 b	f	S E.	12	c	S W	r		1½

[Remarks]⁶

1st Ice thick.
     wind hard

5th Wind blew excessively hard this ⟨morning⟩ night from N W.

6th Capt. Clark was hunting the Buffaloe this day with 16 Men— sev-
     erall of the men frosted   killed 3 buffaloe himself and the party
     killed 5 others.[7]

7th last night the river blocked up[8] with ice which was 1 ½ inches thick
     in the part that had not previously frosen—   The Buffaloe appear
     go out with a party in quest of them kill 14.   the mandanes take
     two—the reasen—

8th The ice 1 ½ inch thick on the part that had not previously frosen.
     The Buffaloe appear   Capt Lewis with 15 men Kill 14[9]

[9] went hunting with a party of fifteen men   killed 10 Buffaloe and 1
     deer   staid out all night[10]

14th Capt. Clark sets out with a hunting party on the ice with three small
     sleds—

15   snow fell one ½ inch—[11]   visited by the big man & the big white
     inform me that many buffaloe have visited the Grosventers on the
     opposite side of the river   they came from the West.

16   Mr. Haney and Mr. La Roche visits us.[12]

17th at 8 P. M. this evening the Thertr. stood at 42 b. o.

19   ⁄began to Piquet the Fort on the river side—

24th Snow verry inconsiderable[13]   complete the fort

[25] Do   do

26th played at the good old game of backgammon n—i s—h[14]

27th The trees all this day with the white frost which attached itself to
     their boughs

28th the [wind] blue verry hard last night.   the frost fell like a shower
     of snoe

1. The weather table is drawn from Lewis's Weather Diary; there are a few discrepancies in Clark's tables in Codex C and Voorhis No. 4, which are noted in their proper place.

2. As in his November observations (see above), Lewis had transposed the notations in his "Weather" and "Wind at ⊙ rise" columns through December 6; after that date, shifting to another page, he resumes doing them correctly. The columns are printed correctly here to avoid confusion.

3. Clark has "o ⟨a⟩."

4. Clark has "45 b" here in Codex C and "43 b" in Voorhis No. 4.

5. There are several discrepancies between Lewis and Clark on this date; in Codex C Clark's sunrise weather is "f"; his 4 p. m. temperature is "22 a"; his 4 p. m. weather is "C"; his 4 p. m. wind is "W"; his river rise is 2 inches. His table in Voorhis No. 4 agrees with Lewis.

6. These remarks follow Lewis's in his Weather Diary; the dates are taken from Clark's Codex C. Clark has remarks for December 1 and 2 in Voorhis No. 4 that are not found in the other two notebooks.

7. Clark appears to have crossed out this remark in his Codex C.

8. From here Clark writes "opposit Fort Mandan." The remainder of the information in this remark is in Clark's remark for December 8. Lewis has no remarks for that date.

9. Clark's remarks in Codex C; Lewis has no remarks for this date. In Voorhis No. 4 Clark writes "I hunt   3 men frosted."

10. Clark notes this hunting trip in Voorhis No. 4 (and not in Codex C) and adds "no blanket" after referring to Lewis's remaining out all night.

11. Clark's Codex C remarks end at this point.

12. Clark has no Codex C remarks for this date; in Voorhis No. 4 he writes "W C. huntig" for December 16 and 17.

13. Clark's remarks in Codex C for December 24 and 25 agree with Lewis's; in Voorhis No. 4, however, he has "Snow very much" and "do" for the two dates. In that notebook he places "Complete the Fort" under December 23.

14. One of the few indications of how they passed their time at Fort Mandan. It is unclear whether they brought a backgammon board and dice along or improvised them on the spot. The letters may have some reference to the game, but they do not resemble the modern system of scoring. Clark has nothing on this date.

Fort Mandan on the N E bank

of the Missouries 1600 miles up *Tuesday*

[Clark]   *January the 1st 1805*

The Day was ushered in by the Discharge of two Cannon, we Suffered 16 men [1] with their musick to visit the 1st Village for the purpose of Danceing, by as they Said the perticular request of the Chiefs of that village, about 11 oClock I with an inturpeter & two men walked up to the Village (my views were to alay Some little miss understanding which had taken place thro jelloucy and mortificatiion as to our treatment towards them[)]

I found them much pleased at the Danceing of our men, I ordered my black Servent to Dance which amused the Croud verry much, and Some what astonished them, that So large a man Should be active &c. &.

I went into the lodges of all the men of note except two, whome I heard had made Some expressions not favourable towards us, in Compareing us with the trabers from the north— Those Cheifs observed [*NB: to us that*] what they Sayed was in just [*NB: in jest*] & lafture.— just as I was about to return the 2d Chief and the Black man, also a Chief returnd from a mission on which they had been Sent to meet a large party 150 of *Gross Ventres* who were on their way down from their Camps 10 Miles above to revenge on the *Shoe* tribe an injurey which they had received by a Shoe man Steeling a *Gross Venters Girl,* those Chiefs gave the pipe turned the party back, after Delivering up the girl, which the Shoe Chief had taken and given to them for that purpose. I returned in the evening, at night the party except 6 returned, with 3 robes, an 13 Strings of Corn which the indians had given them, The Day was worm, Themtr. 34° abov 0, Some fiew Drops of rain about Sunset, at Dark it began to Snow, and Snowed the greater part of the night, (the temptr for Snow is about 0) The Black Cat with his family visited us to day and brought a little meet

1. These included Ordway, and probably François Rivet, who earlier had "danced on his head" for the Indians.

[Clark]   2nd of *January Wednesdey 1805*
a Snowey morning a party of men go to Dance at the 2nd Village to Dance, Capt Lewis & the interptr visit the 2d Village, and return in the evening, Some Snow to Day verry Cold in the evining

[Clark]   3rd *of January Thursday 1805*
Soome Snow to day; 8 men go to hunt the buffalow, killed a hare & wolf Several Indians visit us to day & a Gross Ventre came after his wife, who had been much abused, & come here for Protection.

Fort Mandan

[Clark]   4th of *January Friday 1805*

a worm Snowey morning, the Themtr. at 28° abov 0, Cloudy, Sent out 3 men to hunt down the river, Several Indians Came to day   the little Crow, who has proved friendly Came   we gave him a handkerchf & 2 files, in the evening the weather became cold and windey, wind from the N W.   I am verry unwell the after part of the Daye

[Clark]   5th of *January Satturday 1805*

a cold day   Some Snow, Several Indians visit us with thier axes to get them mended, I imploy my Self drawing a Connection of the Countrey from what information I have recved—[1]   a Buffalow Dance (or Medison) [*NB: medecine*] for 3 nights passed in the 1st Village, a curious Custom the old men arrange themselves in a circle & after Smoke a pipe, which is handed them by a young man, Dress up for the purpose, the young men who have their wives back of the circle ⟨Com⟩ go to one of the old men with a whining tone and [*NB?: request*] the old man to take his wife (who presents necked except a robe) and—(or Sleep with him)   the Girl then takes the Old man (who verry often can Scercely walk) and leades him to a Convenient place for the business, after which they return to the lodge, if the Old man (or a white man) returns to the lodge without gratifying the man & his wife, he offers her again and again; it is often the Case that after the 2d time ⟨he⟩ without Kissing the Husband throws a nice robe over the old man & and begs him not to dispise him, & his wife

(we Sent a man to this Medisan ⟨Dance⟩ last night, they gave him 4 Girls)

all this is to cause the buffalow to Come near So that They may kill thim[2]

1. Clark was probably at work on some version of his map of the West sent back to Jefferson in April 1805 (*Atlas* maps 32*a,* 32*b,* and 32*c*), based on information from Indians and traders.

2. In the delicate fashion of the era Biddle rendered Clark's account of the ceremony into Latin, with a few additional details, in his *History.* Even Coues, or his publisher, did not see fit to translate the passage from Latin in 1893. The purpose here was the passing of the spiritual power of the old men to the younger generation through their wives. The white visitors also received such offers because they were also thought to possess great

power. Nicholas Biddle Notes [ca. April 1810], Jackson (LLC), 2:538 (the English version of Biddle's notes on the ceremony, from Clark's recollections); Thwaites (EWT), 24:30 (Maximilian's brief description of the same ceremony); Coues (HLC), 1:221–22. Ronda (LCAI),131–32, discusses the ceremony in its cultural setting. For a modern translation, see Marx.

[Clark]   6th of *January Sunday 1805*

    a Cold day   but fiew indians to day   I am ingaged as yesterday

                                                      Fort Mandan

[Clark]   7th of *January Monday 1805*

    a verry Cold clear Day, the Themtr Stood at 22 d below o wind N W., the river fell 1 inch   Several indians returned from hunting, one of them the Big White Chef of the Lower Mandan Village, Dined with us, and gave me a Scetch of the Countrey as far as the high mountains, & on the South Side of the River Rejone,[1] he Says that the river rejone recves [*NB: receives*] 6 Small rivers on the S. Side, & that the Countrey is verry hilley and the greater part Covered with timber, Great numbers of beaver &c.— the 3 men returned from hunting, they kill'd 4 Deer & 2 wolves, Saw Buffalow a long ways off, I continue to Draw a connected plote from the information of Traders, Indians & my own observation & idea— from the best information, the Great falls is about [*NB?: 800*] miles nearly west,—[2]

[Lewis]   Monday January 7th 1805[3]

    Observed time and distance of ⊙'s and ☽'s nearest limbs, with Sextant. ⊙ West.

		Time			*Distance*		
		h	m	s			
A. M.	2	21	—		79°	25′	45″
	″	23	55		″	26	15
	″	25	3		″	26	30
	″	26	3		″	27	—
	″	27	47		″	27	15
	″	29	29		″	28	—
		h	m	s			
P. M.	2	38	12		79°	30′	15″

"	39	22		"	31	—
"	40	19		"	31	45
"	41	36		"	32	15
"	42	33		"	32	45
"	43	25		"	33	—

1. Clark was receiving information about the Yellowstone, or Roche Jaune, River. The Canadian trader Ménard (see above, October 25, 1804) claimed to have been on the river some time before 1795 and gave a description of it to Jean Baptiste Truteau. In any case, the French traders of St. Louis had received enough information from Indians before Lewis and Clark's time to have given it a name, perhaps derived from the yellow rocks in the river's upper canyon in present Yellowstone National Park. The information given by Big White was incorporated into "Big White's map," (*Atlas* maps 31*a* and 31*b*) and Clark's 1805 map of the West (*Atlas* maps 32*a*, 32*b*, and 32*c*). The Great Falls of the Missouri, as the Indians told him, were roughly due west of the Mandan villages. Nasatir (BLC), 2 : 381; Allen, 173, 242–43, 259 and n. 21.

2. This last sentence has been crossed out in red, apparently by Biddle who may also have added "800" in red to a blank space.

3. Lewis's astronomical observation from Codex O.

[Clark]   8th *of January Tuesday* 1805

a Cold Day   but fiew indians at the fort to day   wind from the N, W, one man at the Village[1]

1. Ordway says it was himself in his entry for this day.

[Clark]   9th of *January Wednesday 1805*

A Cold Day   Themometer at 21° below o, Great numbers of indians go to Kill *Cows*, [*NB: Cn Clark accd them with 3 or 4 man   killed a number of cows near the fort.*] the little Crow Brackft. with us, Several Indians Call at the Fort nearly frosed, one man reported that he had Sent his Son a Small boy to the fort about 3 oClock, & was much distressed at not finding him here, the after part of this day verry Cold, and wind Keen

[Clark][1]

10th Of January 1805   This morning a boy of 13 years of age Came to the fort with his feet frozed, haveing Stayed out all night without fire, with no other Covering than a Small *Robe* goat skin leagens & a pr. Buffalow Skin mockersons— The Murcery Stood at 72° below the freesing point— Several others Stayed out all night not in the least hurt, This boy lost his Toes only—[2]

[Clark]   10th *of January Thursday 1805*

last night was excessively Cold   the murkery this morning Stood at 40° below 0 which is 72° below the freesing point, we had one man out last night, who returned about 8 oClock this morning   The Indians of the lower Villages turned out to hunt for a man & a boy who had not returnd from the hunt of yesterday, and borrowd a Slay to bring them in expecting to find them frosed to death   about 10 oclock the boy about 13 years of age Came to the fort with his feet frosed and had layen out last night without fire with only a Buffalow Robe to Cover him, the Dress which he wore was a pr of Cabra [*NB: Antelope*] Legins, which is verry thin and mockersons— we had his feet put in Cold water and they are Comeing too— Soon after the arrival of the Boy, a man Came in who had also Stayed out without fire, and verry thinly Clothed, this man was not the least injured—

Customs & the habits of those people has ancered to bare more Cold than I thought it possible for man to indure—

Send out 3 men to hunt Elk below about 7 miles—

1. One of Clark's sporadic entries on document 64 of the Field Notes.

2. Since the boy did not actually lose his toes until January 27 (see below), Clark must have written at least the last sentence of this Field Notes entry some time after the given date.

[Clark]   *11th January Friday 1805*

verry Cold, Send out 3 men to join 3 now below & hunt,[1]

Pose-cop se ha or Black Cat came to See us and Stay all night

Sho sa har ro ra or Coal also Stayd all night, the inturpeter oldst wife Sick,[2] Some of our men go to See a war medison ⟨Dance⟩[3] made at the village on the opposit Side of the river, this is a

1. Among these six men, judging from Ordway's entry of January 14, were Joseph and

Reubin Field, George Shannon, John Collins, and Joseph Whitehouse. Whitehouse's journal records events at the fort during this time, but he was probably copying from others. See also below, January 12, 1805.

2. One of Charbonneau's wives, which one is not clear. Sacagawea was about eight months pregnant at this time.

3. This may refer to the wolf ceremony which was designed to ensure success for one about to embark on the warpath. Beckwith, 249; personal communication from Jeffery R. Hanson, October 18, 1985. Clark ended the entry in mid-sentence and left nearly a half-page blank.

Fort Manden

[Clark]   12th of *January Satturday* 1805

a verry Cold Day   three of our hunters J. & R *Fields* withe 2 Elk on a Slay   Sent one more hunter out.

[Clark]   13th of January Sunday (1805)

a Cold Clear Day (great number of Indians move Down the River to hunt) those people Kill a number of Buffalow near their Villages and Save a great perpotion of the meat, their Custom of makeing this article of life General [*NB: see note common*][1] leaves them more than half of their time without meat   Their Corn & Beans &c they Keep for the Summer, and as a reserve in Case of an attack from the Soues, which they are always in dread, and Sildom go far to hunt except in large parties, about ½ the Mandan nation passed this to day to hunt on the river below, they will Stay out Some Days, Mr. Chabonee (our inturpeter) and one man that accompanied him[2] to Some loges of the Minatarees near the Turtle Hill[3] returned, both frosed in their faces.

Chaboneu informs that the Clerk of the Hudsons Bay Co.[4] with the *Me ne tar res* has been Speaking Some fiew expressns. unfavourable towards us, and that it is Said the N W Co. intends building a   fort at the *Mene tar re's*—   he Saw the Grand Chief of the *Big bellies* who Spoke Slightly of the Americans, Saying if we would give our great flag to him he would Come to See us.

[Lewis]   Sunday January 13th 1805[5]

Observed Meridian altitude of ☉ U. L. with Sextant and glass artifical Horizon.   43° 18′ 30″

Latitude deduced from this observation.   N. 47° 20′ 52.6″

1. Biddle's interlined "common" was intended to amplify "General." What Clark meant was that all meat was shared in common among all members of the tribe, instead of being the property of the man who killed it and his family. Coues (HLC), 1 : 224. Apparently it was also Biddle who crossed through this passage with red ink.

2. Whitehouse identifies Charbonneau's companion as a "Frenchman."

3. Probably the present Killdeer Mountains, in Dunn County, North Dakota, shown as "Turtle Hill" on the copy of David Thompson's 1798 map in the captains' possession. However, the present Turtle Mountain is on the Manitoba-North Dakota border. Allen, 92.

4. Presumably George Bunch, or Budge, who would have seen Le Borgne, "Grand Chief of the *Big Bellies*."

5. Lewis's astronomical observation from Codex O.

[Clark]   14th of *January 1805 Monday*

This morning early a number of indians men womin children Dogs &c & passed down on the ice to joine those that passed yesterday, we Sent Sergt Pryor and five men with those indians to hunt   ⟨(Several men with the Venereal cought from the Mandan women)⟩   one of our hunters[1] Sent out Several days arived & informs that one Man (Whitehouse) is frost bit and Can't walk home—

[Lewis]   Monday January 14th astronomical 1805[2]

Observed an Eclips of the Moon. I had no other glass to assist me in this observation but a small refracting telescope belonging to my sextant, which however was of considerable service, as it enabled me to define the edge of the moon's immage with much more precision that I could have done with the natural eye. The commencement of the eclips was obscured by clouds, which continued to interrupt me throughout the whole observation; to this cause is also attributable the inacuracy of the observation of the *commencement of total darkness*. I do not put much confidence in the observation of the middle of the Eclips, as it is the wo[r]st point of the eclips to distinguish with accuracy. The two last observations (i. e.) the *end of total darkness,* and the *end of the eclips,* were more satisfactory; they are as accurate as the circumstances under which I laboured would permit me to make them.—

	h	m	s
Commencement of total darkness	12	28	5
Middle of the Eclips	12	57	24
End of total darkness	13	41	30
End of the eclips	14	39	10

1. Ordway notes the man was Shannon.
2. Lewis's astronomical observation from Codex O.

Fort Mandan

[Clark]   15th *January Tuesday 1805*

between 12 & 3 oClock this morning we had a total eclips of the moon, a part of the observations necessary for our purpose in this eclips we got which is at 12h 57m 54s   Total Darkness of the moon   @ 1 44 00   End of total Darkness of This moon   @ 2 39 10   End of the eclips—[1]

This morning not So Cold as yesterday   wind from the S. E.   wind choped around to the N W.   Still temperate   four Considerate men of the Minetarre Came to See us   we Smoked in the pipe, maney mands. [Mandans] present also, we Showed [*NB: attentions*] to those men who had been impressed with an unfavourable oppinion of us. [*NB: which satisfied them*]

[Lewis]   *Tuesday January 15 1805*[2]

Observed equal Altitudes of the ☉ with sextant and Glass artifical horizon adjusted with a sperit level

	h	m	s			h	m	s
A. M.	8	26	32		P. M.	—	—	—
	"	29	14			—	—	—
	"	32	1			1	49	46

Altitude given by the sextant at the time of obtn.   26° 6′ 15″

	h	m	s
Chronomerter too slow on mean time—	1	1	57.7

Chronometer's daily rate of going, as deduced from this observation, and that of the 22nd of December 1804 is too slow on mean time   s 55.8

☞ I do not place much confidence in this observation in consequence of loosing the observation of the Altitude of the ☉'s L. L. and center P. M. and that his U. L. was somewhat obscured by a cloud. the weather was so could that I could not use water as the reflecting surface, and I was obliged to remove my glass horizon from it's first adjustment lest the savages should pilfer it.

1. The captains discussed their observations with Larocque on January 30. As he recalled it, they asserted that David Thompson had placed the Mandan and Hidatsa villages much too far west on his 1798 map, and that they had now corrected this by their observations of the eclipse. In fact, Thompson's longitude for the villages (101° 14′ 24″ W. for Matootonha) is relatively close to the actual position (101° 27′ W.). The captains' observation from the eclipse gave a position about two degrees east of the true one (99° 26′ 45″ W.). However, Lewis actually did not place too much confidence in some of these observations, because of the slowness of the chronometer and meteorological difficulties. On Clark's Fort Mandan map (*Atlas* maps 32*a*, 32*b*, and 32*c*), the villages appear west of 101° W. longitude. Since the captains had a version of Thompson's map, they may have abandoned their own observations, in which they had less confidence than Larocque suggests, and followed Thompson. Larocque may have misunderstood what he was told. Wood & Thiessen, 151–52; Allen, 87–93, 117 n. 19, 142, 162; Thompson, 179; Nicholas Biddle to John Vaughn, [ca. October 13, 1810], Jackson (LLC), 2 : 560–61; Diller (MMR), 517–18.

2. Lewis's astronomical observation from Codex O.

[Clark]   16th *January Wednesday 1805*

about thirty Mandans Came to the fort to day, 6 Chiefs. Those Me ne ta rees told them they were liars, had told them if they came to the fort the whites men would kill them, they had been with them all night, Smoked in the pipe and have been treated well and the whites had danced for them, observing the Mandans were bad and ought to hide themselves— one of the 1st War Chiefs of the big belles nation[1] Came to See us to day with one man and his Squar [*NB: (his wife handsome)*] to wate on him [*NB: requested that she might be used for the night*] we Shot the Air gun, and gave two Shots with the Cannon which pleased them verry much, the little Crow 2d Chf of the lower village came & brought us Corn &. 4 men of ours who had been hunting returned one frost'd ⟨but not bad⟩[2]

This war Chief gave us a Chart in his way of the Missourie,[3] he informed us of his intentions of going to war in the Spring against the Snake Indians   we advised him to look back at the number of nations who had been distroyed by war, and reflect upon what he was about to do, observing if he wished the hapiness of his nation, he would be at peace with all, by that by being at peace and haveing plenty of goods amongst them & a free intercourse with those defenceless nations, they would get on easy terms a great Number of horses, and that nation would increas, if he went to war against those Defenceless people, he would displease his great father, and he would not receive that pertection & Care from him as other nations who listened to his word—   This Chief who is a young man 26 yr. old replied that if his going to war against the Snake indians would be displeasing to us be would not go, he had horses enough.

we observed that what we had Said was the words of his Great father, and what we had Spoken to all the nations which we Saw on our passage up, they all promis to open their ears and we do not know as yet if any of them has Shut them   (we are doubtfull of the Souxs)   if they do not attend to what we have told them their great father will open their ears—   This Cheif Said that he would advise all his nation to Stay at home untill we Saw the Snake Indians & Knew if they would be friendly, he himself would attend to what we had told him—

1. He may be the same as Mar-book She-a-O-ke-ah, or Seeing Snake, who visited the fort again on February 1, in pursuit of his runaway wife. He could also be the Rattle Snake known to Charles McKenzie and Alexander Henry the Younger as a noted warrior; if so, he was apparently another son of Cherry Grows on a Bush, and a younger brother of Man Wolf Chief. The woman mentioned here was evidently his wife, not that of the other man. Masson, 1:374–78; Coues (NLEH), 1:368, 387, 399; Coues (HLC), 1:226.

2. Whitehouse. See above, January 14, and Whitehouse's entry for that same date.

3. Indian cartography is discussed in Ronda (IC).

[Clark]   17th *January Thursday 1805*

a verry windey morning hard from the North   Thermometer at 0, Several Indians here to day

[Clark]   18th *January Friday 1805*

a fine worm morning, Mr. La Rock & McKinzey Came down to See us with them Several of the Grosse Venrees.

[Clark]   19th *January Satturday 1805*.

a find Day   Messrs. Larock & McKinzey returned home, Sent three horses down to our hunting Camp for the meet they had killed, Jussoms Squar, left him and went to the Village

[Clark]

20th   a Cold fair day   Several Indians at the fort to day   a miss understanding took place between the two inturpeters on account of their Squars, one of the Squars of Shabownes Squars being Sick, I ordered my Servent to, give her Some froot Stewed and tee at dift Tims which was the Cause of the misundstd

[Lewis]   Sunday January 20th 1805[1]

Observed Equal altitudes of the ☉, with Sextant & glass horizon.

	h	m	s			h	m	s
A. M.	8	40	20		P. M.	1	21	55
	"	47	15			"	24	47
	"	50	10				lost by a cloud	

Altitude given by Sextant at the time of obstn.   31° 40° 15″

	h	m	s
Chronometer too slow on mean time—	1	15	20.3

☞ the horizon was removed from it's first adjustment.

1. Lewis's astronomical observation from Codex O.

                                                      Fort Mandan

[Clark]   21st *Monday January 1805*

a number of Indians here to day   a fine day   nothing remarkable   one ban [man] verry bad with the ⟨pox⟩[1]

1. The pox is syphilis, not smallpox.

[Clark]   *22nd January 1805 Tuesday*

a find warm Day   attempted to Cut the Boat & the perogues out of the
Ice, found water at about 8 inches under the 1st Ice, the next thickness
about 3 feet

[Clark]   23rd January 1805 Wednesday

a Cold Day   Snow fell 4 Inches deep, the occurrences of this day is as is
common—

[Clark]   24th *January Thursday 1805*

a fine day, our inturpeters appear to understand each others better
than a fiew days past   Sent out Several hunters, they returned without
killing any thing, Cut Coal wood—

[Clark]   *25th of January 1805 Friday*—

we are informed of the arrival of a Band of Asniboins at the Villages
with the Grand Cheif of those Tribes call the (Fee de petite veau) [*NB: Fils
de Petit Veau*][1] to trade, one of our interpeter & one man Set out to the Big
Belley Camp opposit the Island   men employ'd in Cutting the Boat out
of the ice, and Collecting Coal wood.

1. *Fils de Petit Veau* would be French for "Son of the Little Calf." Clark calls him "Grand
Chief of those Tribes"—that is, the Assiniboines. Larocque, who gives his name as *Petit
Vieux,* does not indicate that his status was so exalted. Wood & Thiessen, 146, 150.

[Clark]   *26th of January Satturday 1805*

a verry fine warm Day   Several Indians Dine with us and are much
Pleased—   one man taken violently Bad with the Plurisee, Bleed & apply
those remedeis Common to that disorder.[1]

[Lewis]   Saturday January 26th 1805[2]

Observed Meridian Altitude of ☉'s U. L. with sextant and artificl. Horzn. of
water   48° 50' —

Latitude deduced from this observatn.   N. 47 21 47

1. The remedies probably included purging and greasing the chest. Chuinard (OOMD), 266–67.

2. Lewis's astronomical observation from Codex O.

[Clark]   27th of *January Sunday* 1804[1]

a fine day, attempt to Cut our Boat and Canoos out of the Ice, a deficuelt Task I fear as we find waters between the Ice, I Bleed the man with the Plurisy to day & Swet him, Capt Lewis took of the Toes of one foot of the Boy who got frost bit Some time ago,[2] Shabonoe our interpeter returned, & informed that the Assiniboins had returned to their Camps, & brough 3 horses of Mr. Laroches to Stay here for fear of their being Stolen by the Assiniboins who are great rogues— Cut off the boy toes—

1. Clark has been correcting the year for his January entries, here he missed one.

2. Removal of more toes was necessary on January 31. For the probable procedure, see Chuinard (OOMD), 267–69.

[Clark]   28th *January Monday* 1805

attempt to cut through the ice &c get our Boat and Canoo out without Suckcess, Several Indians here wishing to get war hatchets made [*here a drawing*] this shape[1] the man Sick yesterday is getting well Mr. Jessome our interpeter was taken verry unwell this evening warm day

[Lewis]   *Monday January 28th 1805*[2]

Observed Equal altitudes with Sextant and artifical Horizon on the construction recommended by Mr. Andrew Ellicott, in which sperits were substituted for water, it being to could to use the latter.

A. M.	8	7	29	P. M.	1	52	34
"		9	51	"		54	58
"		12	20	"		57	26

Altd. by Sextant at the time of observation   33° 25′ —″

	h	m	s
Chronometer too slow on mean time	1	11	12.2

			s
her daily rate of going on M. T. too slow	—	—	51.2

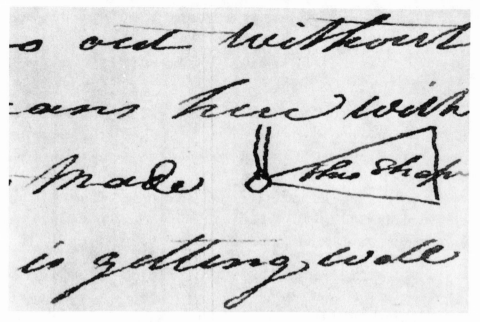

6. War Hatchet, January 28, 1805, Codex C, p. 158

☞ the accuracy of this observation may be depended on.

Longitude of Fort Mandan as deduced from the observation of the end of toal darkness when the eclips of the moon tok place the 14th of January Astronocl. 1805

	h	m	s				
W. from Greenwich	6	37	31.2	or	99°	22′	45.3″

Longitude of Fort Mandan as deduced from the *end* of the same eclips

	h	m	s				
	6	37	47	or	99°	26′	45″

1. Clark sketched the form of tomahawk head the Indians desired. See fig. 6. Lewis described it in detail on February 5, 1805. It was apparently Biddle who wrote "Qu" in red across this passage.

2. Lewis's astronomical observation from Codex O.

[Clark]   29th *January Tuesday* 1805

Gave Jassome a Dost of Salts   we Send & Collect Stones and put them on a large log heap to heet them with a View of warming water in the

Boat and by that means, Sepperate her from the Ices, our attempt appears to be defeated by the Stones all breaking & flying to peaces in the fire, a fine warm Day, we are now burning a large Coal pit,[1] to mend the indians hatchets, & make them war axes, the only means by which we precure Corn from them—

1. They were making charcoal in a pit to fuel the forge. Criswell, 25.

[Clark]   30th *January Wednesday* 1805

a fine morning, Clouded up at 9 oClock, Mr. La Rocke paid us a Visit, & we gave him an answer respecting the request he made when last here of accompanying us on our Journey &c. [*NB: refused*][1]

1. The captains had no intention of helping Larocque to acquire, at United States government expense, geographical knowledge that would be of advantage to the North West Company and the British government.

[Clark]   31st January Thursday, 1805

Snowed last night, wind high from the N W.   Sawed off the boys toes Sent 5 men down the river to hunt with 2 horses, our interpeter Something better, George Drewyer taken with the Ploursey last evening   Bled & gave him Some Sage tea, this morning he is much better—   Cold disagreeable

[Lewis and Clark]   [*Weather, January 1805*][1]

Day of the Month	Ther. at ☉ rise	Weather	Wind at ☉ rise	Thert. at 4 P. M.	Weather	Wind at 4 P. M.	River raise or fall	Feet	Inches
Jany. 1	18 a	s	S E	34 a	f	N W	r	1	
2	4 b	s	N W	8 b	f a s	N.			
3	14 b.	c	N.	4 b	s	S E			
4	28 a	c a s	W.	4 b	c	N W	r		2½
5	20 b	c	N. W.	18 b	s	N. E.	r		2
6	11 b	c a s	N W	16 b	f	N W	r		3
7	22 b	f	N W	14 b	f	W	f		1

8	20 b	f	N W	10 b	f	N W	r	1
9	21 b	f	W	18 b	f a c	N W	r[2]	1
10	40 b	f	N W	28[3]	f	N W	r[4]	1[5]
11	38 b	f	N W	14 b	f	N W	f	½
12	20 b	f	N W	16[6]	f	N W	r	1
13	34 b	f	N W	20[7]	f	N W	r[8]	2[9]
14	16 b	s	S E	8 b	c a s	S E		
15	10 b	f	E	3 a	c[10]	S W	r	1
16	36 a	c	W	16 a	f	S W	r	2½
17	2 b	c	W	12 b	f	N W		
18	1 b[11]	f	N W	7 a	f a c	N W	f	1
19	12 a	c	N E	6 b	f	N W	r	1
20h	28[12]	f	N E	9 b	c	S E	r	¾[13]
21	2 b	c	N E	8 a	f	S E	r[14]	
22	10 a	f a h	N W	19 a	c	N W	r	1¾
23	2 b	s	E	2 b	c a s	N	f	2½
24	12 b	c	N. W.	2 b	f	N. W.	r	¼
25	26 b	f	N W	4 b	f a c	W		
26	12 a	c	N E	20 a	f a c	S E		
27	20 a	c	S E	16 a	c	N W	r	2
28	2 b	f	N W	15 a	f	S W		
29	4 a	f	S W	16 a	f	W	r	½
30	6 a	c	N W	14 a	c	N W	r	1
31	2 b	c a s	N W	8 a	f a c	N W	f	1

[*Remarks*][15]

[2]   visit the Mandans with a party of the men, who danced for their amusement in the lodge of the Black Cat—[16]

January   3rd the Snow was not considerable   the ground is now covered 9 inches deep—

6th at 12 oC. today two Luminous spots appeared on either side of the sun extreemly bright

8th the snow is now ten inches deep.[17]

12th singular appearance of three distinct *Halo* or luminus rings about the moon appeared this evening at half after 9 P. M. and continued one hour.   the moon formed the center of the middle ring, the other two which lay N & S. of the moon & had each of them a limb passing through the Moons Center and projecting N & S a simidiameter beyond the middle ring to which last they were equal in dimentions, each ring appearing to subtend an angle of 15 degrees of a great circle[18]

15th an eclips of the moon total last night, visible here but partially obscured by the clouds.

[18] at Sun rise 12° below o.[19]

19th Ice now 3 feet thick on the most rapid part of the river—

[22] mist the afternon observation.[20]

23rd the snow feel about 4 inches deep last night and continues to snow

25th it frequently happens that the ☉ rises fair and in about 15 or 20 minutes it becomes suddonly ⟨cloudy⟩ turbid, as if the had some chimical effect on the atmosphere.—

31st the Snow feel 2 Inches last night.

1. This weather table follows Lewis's in his Weather Diary; some discrepancies with those of Clark in Codex C and Voorhis No. 4 are noted.

2. This "r" is found in Clark's Voorhis No. 4.

3. In Codex C Clark gives this temperature as "28 b."

4. Clark has a blank here in Codex C.

5. Here Clark has a blank in Codex C.

6. Clark has "16 b" in Codex C.

7. In Codex C Clark has "20 b."

8. Clark has a blank here in Codex C.

9. Clark has a blank here in Codex C.

10. From the fifteenth through the rest of the month Lewis has reversed his "Weather" and "Wind at 4 P. M." columns; Clark follows this in Voorhis No. 4 but not in Codex C. The error has been corrected here to avoid confusion.

11. In Voorhis No. 4 Clark gives this as "20 b."

12. In Codex C Clark gives this as "28 a."

13. Clark has "½" in Codex C but agrees with Lewis in Voorhis No. 4.

14. The "r" is only in Clark's Voorhis No. 4.

15. The remarks follow Lewis's in the Weather Diary, noting variations in Clark's Codex C. The dates are Clark's. Clark's remarks in Voorhis No. 4 are few and very brief.

16. Clark has no remarks for January 2.

17. Clark adds "accumolateing by frosts" in Codex C.

18. Clark's brief remarks of this phenomenon in Voorhis No. 4 appear to be intended for either the tenth or the eleventh. One might interpret Lewis's remark as placed under the thirteenth, but Clark's Codex C version is clearly dated the twelfth. The captains are actually seeing an atmospheric event caused by the refraction of light by ice crystals. Neiburger, Edinger, & Bonner, 426.

19. Clark has no remarks for this date.

20. Clark has no remarks for this date.

[Clark]   1st *of February Friday 1805*

a cold windey Day   our hunters returnd. haveing killed only one Deer, a war Chief of the *Me ne tar ras* Came with Some Corn   requested to have a War hatchet made, & requested to be allowed to go to war against the Souis & Ricarres who had Killed a mandan Some time past— we refused, and gave reassons, which he verry readily assented to, and promised to open his ears to all we Said   this man is young and named (*Seeing Snake— Mar-book, She-ah-O-ke-ah*[)])[1]   this mans woman Set out & he prosued her, in the evening

1. This seems to be from the Hidatsa words *maapúkša*, "snake" and *kía*, "to fear," perhaps translating to "fears the snake."

[Clark]   2nd *of February* Satturday 1805

a find Day   one Deer Killed   our interpeter Still unwell, one of the wives of the Big belley interptr taken Sick—   Mr. Larocke leave us to day (this man is a Clerk to the N W Company, & verry anxious to accompany us)

[Lewis]   3rd *of February* Sunday 1805.[1]

a fine day; the blacksmith again commences his opperations.   we were visited by but few of the natives today.   the situation of our boat and perogues is now allarming, they are firmly inclosed in the Ice and almost covered with snow. The ice which incloses them lyes in several stratas of unequal thicknesses which are seperated by streams of water.   this peculiarly unfortunate because so soon as we cut through the first strata of ice the water rushes up and rises as high as the upper surface of the ice and thus creates such a debth of water as ⟨had⟩ renders it impracticable to cut away the lower strata which appears firmly attatched to, and confining the bottom of the vessels.   the instruments we have hitherto used has been the ax only, with which, we have made several attempts that proved unsuccessfull from the cause above mentioned.   we then determined to attempt freeing them from the ice by means of boiling water which we purposed heating in the vessels by means of hot stones, but this expedient proved also fruitless, as every species of stone which we could procure in the neighbourhood partook so much of the calcarious genus[2] that they burst into small particles on being exposed to the heat of the fire.   we now determined as the dernier resort to prepare a parsel of Iron spikes and attatch them to the end of small poles of convenient length and endeavour by means of them to free the vessels from the ice.   we have already prepared a large rope of Elk-skin and a windless by means of which we have no doubt of being able to draw the boat on the bank provided we can free from the ice.—

[Clark]

3rd of February 1805   our provisions of meat being nearly exorsted I concluded to Decend the River on the Ice & hunt, I Set out with about 16 men 3 horses & 2 Slays   Descended nearly 60 miles Killed & loaded the horses back, & made 2 pens which we filed with meat, & returned on the 13th   we Killed 40 Deer, 3 Bulls 19 Elk, maney So meager that they were unfit for use

1. Clark was absent from Fort Mandan from February 4–13, during which time Lewis kept daily entries in Codex C. Clark's Field Notes entry for February 3 (next) seems to have been written after his return; he summarized the trip in Codex C in brief entries covering the ten days, perhaps from some sort of brief notes kept on the trip, which have not been found. Lewis's writing of lengthy entries in Clark's journal during the latter's absence may indicate that Lewis was keeping no daily journal of his own during the period; otherwise, Clark could have copied Lewis's journal on his return, a practice he later picked up. See the Introduction, vol. 2.

2. When rocks containing calcium carbonate are heated the CO_2 is driven off, leaving a powder of CaO. Trapped moisture when heated to steam will also cause rocks to break.

[Lewis]   *4th February, Monday 1805.*

This morning fair tho' could   the thermometer stood at 18° below Naught, wind from N. W.   Capt Clark set out with a hunting party consisting of sixteen of our command and two frenchmen[1] who together with two others, have established a small hut and resided this winter within the vicinity of Fort Mandane under our protection.   visited by many of the natives today.   our stock of meat which we had procured in the Months of November & December is now nearly exhausted; a supply of this articles is at this moment peculiarly interesting as well for our immediate consumption, as that we may have time before the approach of the warm season to prepare the meat for our voyage in the spring of the year. Capt. Clark therefore deturmined to continue his rout down the river even as far as the River bullet unless he should find a plenty of game nearer—   The men transported their baggage on a couple of small wooden Slays drawn by themselves, and took with them 3 pack horses which we had agreed should be returned with a load of meat to fort mandane as soon as they could procure it.   no buffaloe have made their appearance in our neighbourhood for some weeks [*NB: time (shorter)*]; and I am informed that our Indian neighbours—suffer extreemly at this moment for the article of *flesh*.   Shields killed two deer this evening, both very lean—   one a large buck, he had shed his horns.

   1. Gass and Joseph Field were among the hunters. The Frenchmen may have been the two met at the mouth of the Cannonball River (here called "River bullet") on October 18, 1804.

[Lewis]   *5th February Tuesday 1805.—*

Pleasent morning wind from N. W. fair; visited by many of the natives who brought a considerable quanty of corn in payment for the work which the blacksmith had done for them—   they are pecuarly attatched to a *battle ax* formed in a very inconvenient manner in my opinion.[1]   it is fabricated of iron only, the blade is extreemly thin, from 7 to nine inches in length and from 4¾, to 6 Inches on it's edge, from whence the sides proceed nearly in a straight line to the eye where it's width is generally not more than an inch. The eye is round & about one inch in diameter.   the

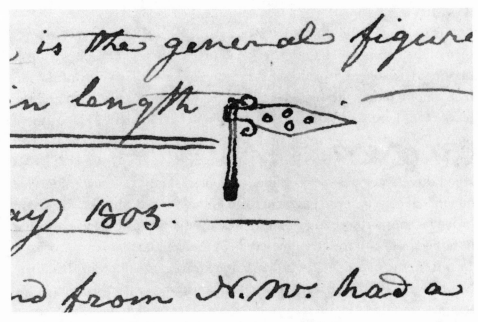

7. Battle Ax, February 5, 1805, Codex C, p. 165

handle seldom more than fourteen inches in length, the whole weighing about one pound— the great length of the blade of this ax, added to the small size of the handle renders a stroke uncertain and easily avoided, while the shortness of the handel must render a blow much less forceable if even well directed, and still more inconvenient as they uniformly use this instrument in action on horseback. The oalder fassion is still more inconvenient, it is somewhat in the form of the blade of an Espantoon but is attatchd to a helve of the dementions before discribed the blade is sometimes by way of ornament purforated with two three or more small circular holes— the following is the general figure it is from 12 to 15 inces in length   [*drawing*]²

1. Clark sketched this form of tomahawk in his entry of January 28, 1805. See fig. 6. The type, later known as the "Missouri war hatchet," was favored by various tribes on the Great Plains, the Missouri River, and the eastern verge of the plains. Lewis's entry is a major source of information on this tomahawk. Russell (FTT), 284–86.

2. See fig. 7. The blade was shaped like the head of a spontoon, or espontoon, for which, see below, May 3, 1805. The style, in spite of Lewis's disapproval, was popular among many tribes across North America. Ibid., 275–78; Woodward, 54.

[Lewis]   *6th February Wednesday 1805.—*

    Fair morning   Wind from N. W.   had a sley prepared against the re-
turn of the horses which Capt Clark had promised to send back as soon as
he should be able to procure a load of meat.   visited by many of the natives among others the Big white, the Coal, big-man, hairy horn and the
black man, I smoked with them, after which they retired, a deportment
not common, for they usually pester us with their good company the ballance of the day after once being introduced to our apartment. Shields
killed three antelopes this evening.   the blacksmiths take a considerable
quantity of corn today in payment for their labour.   the blacksmith's have
proved a happy resoce to us in our present situation as I believe it would
have been difficult to have devised any other method to have procured
corn from the natives.   the Indians are extravegantly fond of sheet iron
of which they form arrow-points and manufacter into instruments for
scraping and dressing their buffaloe robes—   I permited the blacksmith
to dispose of a part of a sheet-iron callaboos [*NB: camboose/Stove*][1] which
had been nearly birnt out on our passage up the river, and for each piece
about four inches square he obtained from seven to eight gallons of corn
from the natives who appeared extreemly pleased with the exchange—

[Lewis]   *Wednesday February 6th 1805*[2]

    Observed equal altitude of the ☉ with Sextant artifical horizon with water

	h	m	s			h	m	s
A. M.	7	59	31		P. M.	1	49	31
	8	1	36		"		51	24
	"	3	5		"		53	41

Altitude given by Sextant at the time of Obstn.   32° 11′ 15″

    Observed time and distance of ☉'s and ☽'s nearest limbs with Sextant the ☉
West.

		Time			*Distance*	
P. M.	2	8	32	87	28	15
	"	12	16	"	30	—
	"	15	58	"	30	45
	"	18	48	"	32	—
	"	20	—	"	33	—
	"	22	25	"	34	—

	Time			Distance		
	h	m	s			
P. M.	2	26	15	87°	35′	15″
	″	29	40	″	35′	45
	″	31	37	″	36	30
	″	33	27	″	36	45
	″	35	3	″	37	30
	″	36	38	″	38	—

I do not place great confidence in these observations, as the person who took the time was not much accustomed to the business. Capt. Clark was absent

1. Also called a "caboose," apparently from a Dutch sailors' term for a galley stove or an oven. Criswell, 20.

2. Lewis's astronomical observation from Codex O.

[Lewis]   *7th February Thursday 1805.*

This morning was fair   Thermometer at 18° above naught much warmer than it has been for some days; wind S. E.   continue to be visited by the natives. The Sergt. of the guard reported that the Indian women (wives to our interpreters[)] were in the habit of unbaring the fort gate at any time of night and admitting their Indian visitors, I therefore directed a lock to be put to the gate and ordered that no Indian but those attatched to the garrison should be permitted to remain all night within the fort or admitted during the period which the gate had been previously ordered to be kept shut which was from sunset untill sunrise.—

[Lewis]   *8th February Friday 1805.*

This morning was fair wind S. E.   the weather still warm and pleasent— visited by the *black-Cat* the principal chief of the Roop-tar-he, or upper mandane vilage.   this man possesses more integrety, firmness, inteligence and perspicuety of mind than any indian I have met with in this quarter, and I think with a little management he may be made a usefull agent in furthering the views of our government. The black Cat presented me with a bow and apologized for not having completed the shield he had promised alledging that the weather had been too could to permit his making it, I gave him som small shot 6 fishing-hooks and 2 yards of ribbon   his squaw also presented me with 2 pair of mockersons for which in return I gave a small lookingglass and a couples of nedles.   the chief dined with me and left me in the evening.   he informed me that his people suffered very much for the article of meat, and that he had not himself tasted any for several days.—

[Lewis]   *9th February Saturday 1805.*

The morning fair and pleasant, wind from S. E.— visted by Mr. McKinzey one the N. W. Company's clerks.   this evening a man by the name of Howard whom I had given permission to go the Mandane vilage returned after the gate was shut and rether than call to the guard to have it opened scaled the works   an indian who was looking on shortly after followed his example. I ⟨told⟩ convinced the Indian of the impropryety of his conduct, and explained to him the riske he had run of being severely treated, the fellow appeared much allarmed, I gave him a small piece of tobacco and sent him away   Howard I had comitted to the care of the guard with a determineation to have him tryed by a Courtmartial for this offence. this man is an old soldier which still hightens this offince—[1]   ⟨visited to⟩

1. Ordway records that Howard was tried the next day (February 10) for "Setting Such a pernicious example to the Savages." If any hostility developed with the local Indians, the knowledge that the walls were so easily scaled would be dangerous. Howard was found guilty and sentenced to fifty lashes, but the court recommended mercy and Lewis forgave him the punishment. For some reason the trial was not recorded in detachment orders. As far as the record goes, this was the last serious disciplinary problem of the expedition, or at least the last meriting trial by court-martial.

[Lewis]   *10th February Sunday 1805.*

This Morning was Cloudy after a slight snow which fell in the course of the night   the wind blue very hard from N. W.   altho' the thermometer stood at 18° Above naught the violence of the wind caused a degree of could that was much more unpleasent than that of yesterday when thermometer stood at 10° only above the same point. Mr. McKinzey left me this morning. Charbono returned with one of the Frenchmen and informed that he had left the three Horses and two men with the meat which Capt. Clark had sent at some distance below on the river— he told me that the horses were heavy loaded and that not being shod it was impossible for horses to travel on the ice. I determined to send down some men with two small slays for the meat and accordingly I gave orders that they should set out early the next morning. two men were also sent to conduct the horses by way of the plain.

[Lewis]   *11th February Monday 1805.*

The party that were ordered last evening set out early this morning. the weather was fair and could wind N. W. about five oclock this evening one of the wives of Charbono was delivered of a fine boy.[1] it is worthy of remark that this was the first child which this woman had boarn and as is common in such cases her labour was tedious and the pain violent; Mr. Jessome informed me that he had freequently adminstered a small portion of the rattle of the rattle-snake, which he assured me had never failed to produce the desired effect, that of hastening the birth of the child; having the rattle of a snake by me I gave it to him and he administered two rings of it to the woman broken in small pieces with the fingers and added to a small quantity of water. Whether this medicine was truly the cause or not I shall not undertake to determine, but I was informed that she had not taken it more than ten minutes before she brought forth perhaps this remedy may be worthy of future experiments, but I must confess that I want faith as to it's efficacy.—

1. Jean Baptiste Charbonneau would have a varied and lengthy career on the frontier, starting with his role as the youngest member of the Corps of Discovery. Clark nicknamed him "Pomp" or "Pompy," and named Pompey's Pillar (more properly Clark's "Pompy's Tower") on the Yellowstone after him in 1806. Clark offered to educate the boy as if he were his own son, and apparently took him into his own home in St. Louis when the child was about six. In 1823 he attracted the notice of the traveling Prince Paul of Wurttemburg, who took him to Europe for six years. On his return to the United States he became a mountain man and fur trader, and later a guide for such explorers and soldiers as John C. Frémont, Philip St. George Cooke, W. H. Emory, and James Abert. He eventually settled in California and died in Oregon while traveling to Montana in 1866. Hafen (JBC); Clarke (MLCE), 148–49; Anderson (CFP).

[Lewis]   *12th February Tuesday 1805.*

The morning was fair tho' could, thermometer at 14° below naught wind S. E.   ordered the Blacksmith to shoe the horses and some others to prepare some gears in order to send them down with three slays to join the hunting party and transport the meat which they may have pocured to this place—   the ⟨horses and⟩ the men whom I had sent for the meat left by Charbono did not return untill 4 OClock this evening. Drewyer arrived with the horses about the same time, the horses appeared much fatieged   I directed some meal brands given them moisened with a little water but to my astonishment found that they would not eat it but prefered the bark of the cotton wood which forms the principall article of food usually given them by their Indian masters in the winter season; for this purpose they cause the trees to be felled by their women and the horses feed on the boughs and bark of their tender branches.   the Indians in our neighbourhood are freequently pilfered of their horses by the Recares, Souixs and Assinniboins and therefore make it an invariable rule to put their horses in their lodges at night.[1]   in this situation the only food of the horse consists of a few sticks of the cottonwood from the size of a man's finger to that of his arm. The Indians are invariably severe riders, and frequently have occasion for many days together through the whole course of the day to employ their horses in pursuing the Buffaloe or transporting meat to their vilages during which time they are seldom suffered to tast food; at night the Horse returned to his stall where his food is what seems to me a scanty allowance of wood.   under these circumstances it would seem that their horses could not long exist or at least could not retain their flesh and strength, but the contrary is the fact, this valuable anamall under all those disadvantages is seldom seen meager or unfit for service.—   A little after dark this evening Capt. Clark arrived with the hunting party—   since they set out they have killed forty Deer, three buffaloe bulls, & sixteen Elk, most of them were so meager that they were unfit for uce, particularly the Buffaloes and male Elk—   the wolves also which are here extreemly numerous heped themselves to a considerable proportion of the hunt—   if an anamal is killed and lyes only one night exposed to the wolves it is almost invariably devoured by them.

1. From "but prefered" to here Biddle has apparently crossed through the passage with red ink.

[Lewis]   *13th February Wednesday 1805.*

The morning cloudy   thermometer 2° below naught   wind from S. E.   visited by the Black-Cat   gave him a *battle ax* with which he appeared much gratifyed.—

[Clark]¹

I returned last night from a hunting party much fatigued, haveing walked 30 miles on the ice and through of wood land Points in which the Snow was nearly Knee Deep

The 1st day [*EC?: Feb. 4*] I left the fort   proceeded on the ice to *new Mandan* Island,² 22 miles & Camped   Killed nothing, & nothing to eat,

The 2d day   the morning verry Cold & Windey, I broke thro the ice and got my feet and legs wet, Sent out 4 hunters thro' a point to Kill a Deer & Cook it by the time the party Should get up, those hunters killed a Deer & 2 Buffalow Bulls   the Buffalow too Meagur to eate, we eate the Deer & proceeded on to an old Indian Lodge,³ Sent out the hunters & they brought in three lean Deer, which we made use of for food,—   walking on uneaven *ice* has blistered the bottom of my feat, and walking is painfull to me—

3rd day   Cold morning the after party of the Day worm, Camped on a Sand point near the mouth of a Creek on the S W. Side we Call hunting Creek,⁴ I turned out with the hunters, I Killed 2 Deer the hunters killed an Elk, Buffalow Bull & 5 Deer.   all Meager

4th Day   hunted the two bottoms near the Camp   Killed 9 Elk, 18 Deer, brought to camp all the meat fit to eate & had the bones taken out.   every man ingaged either in hunting or Collecting & packing the meat to Camp

5th Day   Dispatched one of the party our Interpeter & 2 french men with the 3 horses loaded with the best of the meat to the fort 44 miles Distant, the remaining meat I had packed on the 2 Slays & drawn down to the next point about 3 miles below, at this place I had all the meat Collected which was killed yesterday & had escaped the wolves, Raven⁵ & Magpie, (which are verry noumerous about this Place) and put into a close pen made of logs to secure it from the wolves & birds & proceeded on to a large bottom nearly opposit the Chisscheter (heart) River,[6] in this bottom we found but little game, Great No. of wolves, on the hills Saw Several parsels of Buffalow.— Camped. I killed a Buck

6th Day   The Buffalow Seen last night provd to be Bulls.   lean & unfit for to make uce of as food, the Distance from Camp being nearly 60 miles, and the packing of meat that distance attended with much difficulty deturmined me to return and hunt the points above, we Set out on our return and halted at an old Indian lodge 40 miles below Fort Mandan[7]   Killed 3 Elk & 2 Deer—.

7th Day   a cold Day   wind blew hard from the N. W.   J Fields got one of his ears frosed   deturmined to lay by and hunt to day   Killed an Elk & 6 deer, * this meat I had Boned & put onto a Close pen made of logs—   * all that was fit for use—

8th day   air keen   halted at the old Camp we Stayed in on the 2d night after we left the Fort,[8] expecting to meat the horses at this Place, killed 3 Deer, Several men being nearly out of Mockersons & the horses not returning deturmind me to return to ⟨Camp⟩ the Fort on tomorrow

9th day.   Set out early, Saw great numbers of *Grouse* feeding on the young willows, on the Sand bars   one man[9] I sent in persute of a gangue of Elk killed three near the old Ricara Village and joined at the fort, Sent him back to Secure the meat one man with him—   The ice on the parts of the River which was verry rough, as I went down, was Smothe on my return, this is owing to the rise and fall of the water, which takes place every day or two, and Caused by partial thaws, and obstructions in the passage of the water thro the Ice, which frequently attaches itself to the bottom.—   the water when riseing forses its way thro the cracks & air holes above the old ice, & in one night becoms a Smothe Surface of ice 4 to 6 Inchs thick,—   the river falls & the ice Sink in places with the water and attaches itself to the bottom, and when it again rises to its former hite, frequently leavs a valley of Several feet to Supply with water to bring it on a leavel Surfice.

The water of the Missouri at this time is Clear with little Tinges.

I saw Several old Villages near the Chisscheta River   on enquirey found

they were Mandan Villages destroyed by the Sous & Small Pox, they noumerous and lived in [*NB: 9*] 6[10]   Villages near that place.

1. Having returned from his hunting trip, Clark resumed keeping Codex C. He gives a
brief summary of the trip, detailed enough to suggest his keeping some brief notes while
traveling, notes that are unknown today.

2. Shown on *Atlas* map 29 as Mandan Island, in McLean County, North Dakota, four to
five miles below Washburn and a little above Sanger. The camp might have been on the
island, on the starboard side, or on the larboard side, in Oliver County, since the Missouri
could be crossed on the ice, as the hunting party clearly did on subsequent days. MRC
map 51.

3. Probably an earth lodge in one of the abandoned villages shown on *Atlas* maps 28
and 29, downriver from Mandan Island.

4. Shown on *Atlas* map 28, evidently Square Butte Creek in Oliver County, North Dakota, its mouth a little below the Morton County line. The party had passed it the previous
October 22, but Clark probably bestowed the name during this hunting trip. MRC map 50.

5. The common raven, *Corvus corax* [AOU, 486], evidently, with which the captains
were familiar. Burroughs, 248. The meat cache was apparently near Mandan, Morton
County. MRC map 50.

6. Opposite the mouth of Heart River they would be in or near present Bismarck, Burleigh County, North Dakota. *Atlas* map 28; MRC map 50.

7. Again he may mean an earth lodge in one of the abandoned villages in the area
between Heart River and Fort Mandan. *Atlas* maps 28, 29.

8. Presumably below Mandan Island, where they stayed the first night out (see n. 2,
above), but *Atlas* maps 28 and 29 show no hunting camps in the area. Probably Clark refers to another abandoned village, since he indicates that they stayed at "an old Indian
lodge" on the second night out (see above). MRC maps 50, 51.

9. Probably Drouillard; see Lewis's entry for February 12, above.

10. Eight old Mandan villages and an old hunting camp can be counted in the Heart
River area on *Atlas* map 28.

[Clark]

14th   Sent 4 men[1] with the Horses Shod & 2 Slays down for the meat I
had left, 22 miles below those men were rushed on by 106[2] *Sioux* who
robed them of 2 of their horses—   & they returned

[Clark]   14th of *February Thursday* 1805

The Snow fell 3 inches Deep last night, a fine morning, Dispatched
George Drewyer & 3 men with two Slays drawn by 3 horses for the meat
left below—

1. As indicated the next day in Codex C, they were Drouillard, Frazer, Goodrich, and Newman.

2. Codex C for February 15 says "105"; it is hard to see how such precision would be possible under the circumstances in any case.

[Clark]

15th   Capt. Lewis with a party of men[1] & 4 Indians went in pursute of the Sioux, the Indians returned the next Day & informed me that the Sioux had Burnt all my meat & gorn home (they Saw me but was afraid to attact me)   Capt Lewis returned the 21st with 2400 l[bs]. of meat, haveing Killed 36 Deer & 14 Elk, the Sioux burnt one of my meet houses; they did not find the other

[Clark]   15th of *February Friday* 1805

at 10 oClock P M. last night the men that dispatched ⟨last night⟩ yesterday for the meat, returned and informed us that as they were on their march down at the distance of about 24 miles below the Fort "about 105 Indians which they took to be *Souis* rushed on them and Cut their horses from the Slays, *two* of which they carried off in great hast, the 3rd horse was given up to the party by the intersetion of an Indian who assumd Some authority on the accasion, probably more thro' fear of himself or Some of the Indians being killed by our men who were not disposed to be Robed of all they had tamely, they also forced 2 of the mens knives & a tamahawk, the man obliged them to return the tamahawk   the knives they ran off with

G Drewyer Frasure, S Gutterage, & Newmon with a broken Gun

we dispatched two men to inform the mandans, and if any of them chose to pursue those robers, to come down in the morning, and join Capt Lewis who intended to Set out with a party of men verry early, by 12 oClock the Chief of the 2ed Village Big white Came down, and Soon after one other Chief and Several men— The Chief observed that all the young men of the 2 Villages were out hunting, and but verry fiew guns were left,— Capt. Lewis Set out at Sunrise with 24 men, to meet those *Soues* &c.   Several Indians accompanied him Some with Bows & arrows Some withe Spears & Battle axes, a ⟨fiew⟩ 2 with fusees [*NB: fusils*]— the morning fine the Thermometer Stood at 16° below o, *Nought*, visited by 2 of the *Big Bellies* this evening,— one Chief of the Mandans returned from Capt Lewises Party nearly blind— this Complaint is as I am infomd. Common at this Season of the year and caused by the reflection of the Sun on the ice & Snow, it is cured by "jentilley Swetting the part affected by throweng Snow on a hot Stone"[2]

verry Cold part of the night— one man Killed a verry large Red Fox to day[3]

1. They included Ordway and Gass, all volunteers according to Ordway.

2. Snowblindness is the result of the sun's reflecting off snow causing serious irritation to unprotected eyes. David Thompson reports essentially the same cure, the application of hot steam to the eyes, among Indians far to the north of the Mandans on Hudson's Bay. He calls it "the only efficient cure yet known." Maximilian, however, claims that in his time (1833–34) the Mandans and Hidatsas treated the affliction with a solution of gunpowder and water. Thompson, 36; Thwaites (EWT), 23 : 360. Biddle underlined part of this passage in red: "this complaint . . . of the year."

3. The red fox was already known to science. Burroughs, 91.

[Clark]   16th *of February Satturday 1805*

a fine morning, visited by but fiew Indians to day, at Dusk two of the Indians who wint down with Capt. Lewis returned, Soon after two others and one man (Howard) with his feet frosted, and informed that the Inds. who Commited the roberry of the 2 horses was So far a head that they could not be overtaken, they left a number of pars of Mockersons which, the Mandans knew to be Souix mockersons,— This war party Camped verry near the last camp I made when on my hunting party, where they left Some Corn, as a deception, with a view to induc a belief that they were Ricarras.

Capt Lewis & party proceeded on down   the meat I left at my last Camp was taken.

[Clark]   17th of *February Sunday* 1805

this morning worm & a little Cloudy, the Coal & his Son visited me to day with about 30 w. of Drid Buffalow meat, & Some Tallow   Mr. McKinsey one of the N W. Compys. Clerks visited me (one of the hoses the Sous

robed a fiew Days past belonged to this man)   The after part of the day
fair,

[Clark]   18th of *February Monday 1805*

   a cloudy morning   Some Snow, Several Indians here to day Mr. McKinsey leave me, the after part of the day fine   I am much engaged makeing
a discriptive List of the Rivers from Information[1]   our Store of Meat is
out to day

   1. Clark refers to a list entered in Codex C of rivers and other geographical features
above Fort Mandan, with estimated distances. The material is in Chapter 10, this volume.
The Mandans and Hidatsas would have been the only source for most of this. Clark listed
tributaries of the Missouri and of the Yellowstone, and some mountain ranges, as far west
as "a large river on the west of the mountain," probably a stream such as the Lemhi or the
Salmon River in Idaho, or the Bitterroot or Clark's Fork in Montana, immediately beyond
the continental divide. Distance estimates would have been based on the time it took the
Hidatsas to travel to these points on horseback on their raids. Allen, 210–25, 241–50.

[Clark]   19th of *February Tuesday 1805*

   a fine Day   visited by Several of the Mandans to day, our Smiths are
much engaged mending and makeing Axes for the Indians for which we
get Corn

                                                                      Fort Mandan
[Clark]   20th *February Wednesday 1805*

   a Butifull Day, visited by the Little raven verry early this morning   I am
informed of the Death of an old man whome I Saw in the Mandan Village.   this man, informed me that he "was 120 winters old, he requested
his grand Children to Dress him after Death & Set him on a Stone on a
hill with his face towards his old Village or Down the river, that he might
go Streight to his brother at their old village under ground["][1]   I observed Several Mandan ⟨of⟩ verry old Chiefly men

   1. The man's wish that his spirit go downriver is apparently related to the Mandans'
belief that the spirits of deceased persons traveled south to spirit villages at the mouth of
the Heart River. There was also a belief that an underground village was located near the
mouth of the Mississippi River from which the precursors of the Mandans surfaced.
These two ideas may become garbled in Clark's rendition. The man's reference to meeting

his brother may relate to the Mandans' idea that life after death was more or less the same as life before death. Bowers (MSCO), 98–99, 183–84; Thwaites (EWT), 23:360–62; personal communication from Jeffery Hanson, October 18, 1985.

[Clark]   21st *February Thursday* 1805

a Delightfull Day   put out our Clothes to Sun—   Visited by the big white & Big man   they informed me that Several men of their nation was gorn to Consult their Medison Stone about 3 day march to the South West [1] to know What was to be the result of the insuing year—   They have great confidence in this Stone and Say that it informs them of every thing which is to happen, & visit it every Spring & Sometimes in the Summer— "They haveing arrived at the Stone give it Smoke and proceed to the wood at Some distance to Sleep   the next morning return to the Stone, and find marks white & raised on the Stone representing the piece or war which they are to meet with, and other changes, which they are to meet"   ["]This Stone has a leavel Surface of about 20 feet in Surcumfrance, thick [*NB: thick*] and pores," and no doubt has Some mineral qualtites effected by the Sun.

The Big Bellies have a Stone to which they ascribe nearly the Same Virtues

Capt Lewis returned with 2 Slays loaded with meat, after finding that ⟨they⟩ he could not overtake the Souis war party, (who had in their way distroyd all the meat at one Deposit which I had made & Burnt the Lodges) deturmined to proceed on to the lower Deposit, which he found had not been observed by Soux   he hunted two day   Killed 36 Deer & 14 Elk, Several of them So meager, that they were unfit for use, the meet which he killed and that in the lower Deposit amounting to about 3000 wt was brought up on two Slays, one Drawn by 16 men had about 2400 wt on it

1. This stone is on Medicine Hill, in Medicine Rock State Historic Site in Grant County, North Dakota, south of Elgin. A sandstone outcrop at the site is covered with pictographic paintings and petroglyphic carvings. Thwaites (EWT), 15:57–58, 23:339–40; information of Lawrence L. Loendorf.

Fort Mandan

[Clark]   22nd *of February Friday* 1805.

a Cloudy morning, at about 12 oClock it began to rain and Continud for a fiew minits, and turned to Snow, and Continud Snowing for about one hour, and Cleared away fair   The two hunters left below arrived, They killed two Elk, and hung them up out of the reach of the wolves—   The Coal a Ricara who is a considerable Chief of the Mandans visited us to day, and maney others of the three nations in our neighbourhood.—

[Clark]   *23rd of February 1805 Satturday—*

All hands employed in Cutting the Perogus Loose from the ice, which was nearly even with their top; we found great difficuelty in effecting this work owing to the Different devisions of Ice & water   after Cutting as much as we Could with axes, we had all the Iron we Could get & Some axes put on long poles and picked throught the ice, under the first water, which was not more the 6 or 8 inches deep—   we disengaged one Perogue,[1] and nearly disingaged the 2nd in Course of this day which has been warm & pleasent   vised by a no of Indians, Jessomme & familey went to the Shoes Indians Villag to day

The father of the Boy whose feet were frose near this place, and nearly Cured by us took him home in a Slay—

[Lewis]   Saturday February 23rd 1805[2]

Observed time and distance of $\odot$'s and $\mathbb{D}$'s nearest limbs with Sextant, $\odot$ East.

		Time			*Distance*		
	h	m	s				
A. M.	6	12	15	66°	24'	15"
	"	14	17	"	23	43
	"	16	14	"	22	45
	"	17	51	"	22	—
	"	20	23	"	21	25
	"	22	18	"	21	—
	h	m	s				
A. M.	6	25	56	66°	20'	—"
	"	28	5	"	19	15
	"	29	6	"	19	—
	"	30	58	"	18	—
	"	32	38	"	17	45
	"	34	59	"	17	15

Immediately after the Lunar observations observed Equal altitudes of the ⊙ with Sextant and artificial Horizon with water.

	h	m	s			h	m	s
A. M.	6	41	5	P. M.	—	46	20
"		43	9	"		48	30
"		45	19	"		50	35

Altitude given by Sextant at the time of observation   40° 15′ 45″

	h	m	s
Chronometer too slow Mean Time	2	28	14.9

Preperation for Lunar Calculation.

[Lewis]   Febr. 23rd 1805 Fort Mandan[3]

Latitude of the place of observation   47° 21′ 47″

	h	m	S
Time by Chronometer of Obstn. A. M.	6	23	45
	h		
Chronometer too Slow Apt. T at noon	2	14	25.7
	h	m	S
True time of observtn. as Shewn by the Chrotr. A. M.	8	38	10.7

	h	m	S
True apparent time of observation A. M. as deduced from Mean Time by the application of the Equation of time with its sighn changed—	8	38	18

Distance of ⊙'s and ☽'s nearest linbs at the time of this observation. ⊙ East   66° 20′ 31.7″

	h	m	S
Estimated Greenwich time of the Observation	15	15	57.7

⊙'s Declination corrisponding with the Greenwich time of this observation   9° 52′ 6.8″ South

	h	m	S
True mean time of Observation at this place A. M.	8	51	59.5

Hour ∠ of the A M. observation   50° 25′ 3″

Altitude of the ⊙'s Center at time of Obsert. by Mr. Elicot's formula—   17° 24′ 00″

By Mr. Patterson's Altd. ⊙'s Center at time of observation—   18° 30′ 56″

[Lewis]   [*undated, February 23, 1805*][4]

F.	width	
12	30	N.
10	30	N.

⟨Description⟩
Place of their entrances
width of their mouths
sources and connexion with other streams
peculiar or distinctive characters, how far navigable
face and description of the country through which they pass
⟨how far⟩
Salt river branch of the Republican, alter to W.

1. The white pirogue; see Weather Diary remarks for this date.
2. Lewis's astronomical observation from Codex O.
3. This collection of astronomical data is on document 35 of the Field Notes and is placed here according to the date given. Note the references to Andrew Ellicott and Robert Patterson, from whom Lewis learned navigation.
4. This material is on document 35 of the Field Notes, upside-down to the preceding astronomical data, and is placed according to the date on that material. Most of it appears to be a list of data to be noted about rivers, similar to Jefferson's instructions to Lewis and similar to the captain's survey of rivers and creeks. The last line appears to be a note about a map correction. There are also a number of other wordings, jottings, and doodles on this sheet which are not transcribed here.

[Clark]   *24th February Sunday* 1805

The Day fine, we Commenced very early to day the Cutting loose the boat which was more difficuelt than the perogus with great exertions and with the assistance of Great prises we lousened her and turned the Second perogue upon the ice, ready to Draw out, in Lousening the boat from the ice Some of the Corking drew out which Caused her to Leake for a few minits untill we Discovered the Leake & Stoped it— Jessomme our inter-peter & familey returned from the Villages   Several Indians visit us to day

[Clark]   25th *of February Monday 1805*

we fixed a Windlass and Drew up the two Perogues on the upper bank and attempted the Boat, but the Roap which we hade made of Elk Skins proved too weak & broke Several times night Comeing on obliged us to leave her in a Situation but little advanced— we were Visited by the Black mockerson Chief of the little Village of Big Bellies, the Cheif of the Shoe Inds and a number of others those Chiefs gave us Some meat which they packed on their wives, and one requested a ax to be made for hies Sun, Mr.[1] Bunch, one of the under traders for the hudsons Bay Companey— one of the Big Bellies asked leave for himself & his two wives to Stay all night, which was granted, also two Boys Stayed all night, one the Sun of the Black Cat.

The Day has been exceedingly pleasent

1. At this point the circled word "Root" appears at the top of p. 186 in Codex C; it must be a reference to the root described on the following notebook page, on February 28.

[Clark]

26th of Feby 1805 Drew up the Boat & perogus, after Cutting them out of the ice with great Dificuelty—& trouble

[Clark]   *26th February Tuesday 1805*

a fine Day Commencd verry early in makeing preparations for drawing up the Boat on the bank, at Sunset by repeated exertions the whole day we accomplished this troublesom task, just as we were fixed for having the Boat the ice gave away near us for about 100 yds in length— a number of Indians here to day to See the Boat rise on the Bank—

[Clark]   27th of *February* Wednesday 1805

a fine day, prepareing the Tools to make perogues all day— a feiw Indians visit us to day, one the largest Indian I ever Saw, & as large a man as ever I Saw, I commence a Map of the Countrey on the Missouries & its waters &c. &c.—[1]

1. Perhaps the original of the 1805 map (*Atlas* maps 32*a*, 32*b*, 32*c*), if that had not been started long before.

[Clark]

28th of February 1805 Thursday   Mr. Gravilin 2 frenchmen[1] and 2 Ricaras arrived from the Ricaras with letters from Mr. Taboe &c. informing us of the Deturmination of the Ricaras to follow our councils— and the threts & intintions of the Sioux in Killing us whenever they again met us— and that a party of Several bands were formeing to attacke the Mandans &c. &c.

we informed the Mandans & others of this information & ⟨answered⟩ also the wish the Ricars had to live near them & fite the Sioux &c. &c. &c.

despatched 16 Men 5 Miles abov to build 6 Canoes for the voyage, being Deturmend to Send back the Barge—

[Clark]   28th of *February Thursday* 1805

a fine morning, two men of the N W Compy arrve with letters and Sacka comah[2] also a Root[3] and top of a plant presented by Mr. Haney, for the Cure of mad Dogs Snakes &c, and to be found & used as follows vz: "this root is found on high lands and asent of hills, the way of useing it is to Scarify[4] the part when bitten to chu or pound an inch or more if the root is Small, and applying it to the bitten part renewing it twice a Day.   the bitten person is not to chaw nor Swallow any of the Root for it might have contrary effect."

Sent out 16 men to make four Perogus   those men returned in the evening and informed that they found trees they thought would answer.—

Mr. Gravelin two frenchmen & two Inds. arrive from the Ricara Nation with Letters from Mr. Anty Tabeaux, informing us of the peaceable dispositions of that nation towards the Mandans & Me ne ta res & their avowed intentions of pursueing our Councils & advice, they express a wish to visit the Mandans, & Know if it will be agreeable to them to admit the Ricaras to Settle near them and join them against their common Enimey the *Souis* we mentioned this to the mandans, who observed they had always wished to be at peace and good neighbours with the *Ricaras,* and it is also the Sentiments of all the Big Bellies, & Shoe Nations

Mr. Gravilin informs that the *Sisetoons* and the 3 upper bands of the *Tetons,* with the Yanktons of the North intend to come to war in a Short time against the nations in this quarter, & will Kill everry white man they

See— Mr. T. also informes that Mr. Cameron of St peters has put arms into the hands of the Souis to revenge the death of 3 of his men Killed by the Chipaways[5] latterly— and that the Band of tetons which we Saw is desposed to doe as we have advised them— thro the influenc of their Chief the Black Buffalow—

Mr. Gravilin further informs that the Party which Robed us of the 2 horses laterly were all Sieoux 100 in number, they Called at the Ricaras on their return, the Ricares being displeased at their Conduct would not give them any thing to eate, that being the greatest insult they could peaceably offer them, and upbraded them.

1. Ordway says "Mr Gravelleen and Mr Roie 2 frenchmen." Codex C and Lewis's Weather Diary (see below) indicate two Frenchmen besides Gravelines. Roie was probably Peter Roi, one of the expedition *engagés,* who had perhaps gone down to the Arikara villages after being discharged at Fort Mandan in the fall, although he could have been the man mentioned by Ordway as having been left with Tabeau at the Arikaras on October 10, 1804. The captains usually reserved the title "Mister" for French traders, not for French boatmen. Coues (HLC), 1:239.

2. More commonly written saccacommis, the word derives from a Chippewa word, *saga'komĭnagûnj'.* Lewis gives an incorrect etymology of the word on January 25, 1806. Hodge, 2:407. It is *Arctostaphylos uva-ursi* (L.) Spreng., bearberry or kinnikinick. Fernald, 1126; Barkley, 126. Bearberry was often mixed with *Cornus sericea* L., red osier dogwood, referred to as kinnikinick, and smoked ceremonially by the Indians of the plains. Gilmore (UPI), 56; Densmore, 287.

3. Purple coneflower. See December 16, 1804.

4. Several lines were crossed out here, from "a Root and . . . to Scarify," with red ink and apparently by Biddle.

5. The Chippewas, or Ojibways, are an Algonquian-language people. They formerly lived north of Lake Huron and around Lake Superior, and as far west as Turtle Mountain on the North Dakota-Manitoba border. Swanton, 260–64; Hodge, 1:277–81.

[Lewis and Clark]   [*Weather, February 1805*][1]

1805 Day of the Month	State of the Ther. at ⊙ rise	Weather	Wind at ⊙ rise	Thermt. at 4 oCk. P. M.	Weather[2]	Wind at 4 oCk. P. M.	State of the River at ⊙ rise raise or fallen	Feet	Inches
Febr 1	6 a	c	N W	16 a	f	N W	r		2½
2	12 b	f	N W	3 a	f.	S.	f		1
3d	8 b	f	S W	2 a	f	W.			

4	18 b	f	N W	9 b.	f	W.		
5	10 a	f	N W	20 a	f	N W	r.	1
6	4 b	f	N W	12 a	f	W	r	½
7	18 a	f	S E	29³	c	S	r	½
8	18 a	f	N W	28 a	c	N E	f	1
9	10 a	f	S E	33 a	c.	S E		
10	18 a	c a s	N W	12 a	c	N W		
11	8 b	f	N W	2 b	f	N W		
12	14 b	f	S E	2 a	f	W.		
13	2 b	c	S E	10 a	c	N W	f	1
14	2 a	c a s	N W	2 b	f	N W		
15	16 b.	f	S. W.	6 b.	f	W.		
16	2 a	f	S. E	8 a	f	W	f	1
17	4 a	c	S. E	12 a	f	N W	f⁴	½
18	4 a	s	N E	10 a.	f	S.		
19	4 a	f	S. E	20 a	f	S		
20	2 a	f	S.	22 a	f	S		
21	6 a	f	S	30 a	f	S		
22	8 a	c	N	32 a	c. a r & s	N W⁵		
23	18 a	f	N W	32 a	f	W	r	½
24	8 a	f	N W	32 a	f	W.		
25	16 a	f	W.	38 a	f	N. W		
26	20 a	f	N. E	31 a	f	N.		
27	26 a	f	S E	36 a	f	E	f	½
28	24 a	f	E	38 a	c	S E		

[Remarks]⁶

[4]   Capt. Clark set out on a hunting party with 18 men

[5]   visited by many of the savages today.—

February   8th   visited by the black Cat who dined with me   the Black &
white & Speckled woodpecker⁷ has returned—

[9]   visited by Mr. McKinsey, very little snow

[10]   Mr. Mckinsey leaves me   Charbono returns with out
horses or meat

[12]   Capt. Clark and party returned from hunting

14th   The Snow fell 3 Inches deep last night

[15] Lewis Set out in pursute of a party of Souis who forced 2 horses from a party (Dispatched after meat on the river below) with 24 men

[17] the Indians who went with Capt Lewis returned last night— Visited by Mr. McKinsey

[18] Mr. McKinsey liave me

[21] Cap Lewis return with about 3, 1⟨oo⟩ w of meat

[23] got the poplar perogue out of the ice.[8]

[24] loosed the boat & large perogue from the ice.

[25] Visited by the principall Chiefs of the Mar-har-ha & the Min-ne-tar-re—Matehartar.— also Mr. Bunch, engage of the H B Copy

[26] got the Boat and perogus on the bank

27th got the Boat and Perogues on the bank.

[28] Mr. Gravlin arrived with some Ricaras & two frenchmen

1. This weather table follows Lewis's in his Weather Diary, with discrepancies between it and Clark's table in Codex C being noted. Clark wrote the remarks in the Weather Diary for Februrary 15–21 and probably also the table for those dates.

2. Lewis reversed the "Weather" and "Wind at 4 oCk. P. M." columns, as he had done with the latter part of January 1805 on the same pages, through February 24. The error is corrected here to avoid confusion.

3. This temperature is "29 a" in Clark's Codex C table.

4. Lewis has no indication of rise or fall, but gives the figure "½"; Clark gives neither rise nor fall nor a figure.

5. Clark's wind direction here is either blank or illegible.

6. The remarks here follow Lewis's Weather Diary; Clark evidently wrote those for February 15, 17, 18, and 21. In Codex C Clark wrote remarks only for the eighth and fourteenth; his dates are used there.

7. The yellow-bellied sapsucker, *Sphyrapicus varius* [AOU, 402], has been suggested. Holmgren, 33.

8. Perhaps the only evidence of what sort of wood either pirogue was made of; from the remark of the next day this would be the smaller, or white, pirogue. See Saindon (WP). Since it is unclear when the captains obtained the white pirogue, it can not be determined what sort of "poplar" is meant. It may have been a variety of *Populus*, but could have been constructed in the East from a variety of *Liriodendron*, tulip-poplar. Maximilian

called attention to the use of the tulip-poplar for carpentry work in Ohio in 1833 and noted that it was locally known as "poplar." Maximilian Journal, January 4, 1833, The InterNorth Art Foundation Collection, Center for Western Studies, Joslyn Art Museum, Omaha. See also September 4, 1803. Moulton (NWP). On March 27 (given as March 28) Clark mentions cottonwood in connection with the pirogues, but it is unclear whether he means the construction of the vessels or the additions being made to them. In fact, he may have been referring only to the newly constructed canoes.

[Clark]   March 1st Friday 1805

    a fine Day   I am ingaged in Copying a map, men building perogus, makeing Ropes, Burning Coal, Hanging up meat & makeing battle axes for Corn

[Clark]   2nd of *March 1805 Satturday*

    a fine Day   the river brake up in places   all engaged about Something   Mr. *La Rocque* a Clerk of the N W Company visit us, he has latterly returned from the Establishments on the Assinniboin River with Merchindize to tarade with Indians—   Mr. L informs us the N, W. & X Y Companies have joined, & the head of the N W. Co. is Dead Mr. McTavish of Monteral,—[1]   visted by the Coal & Several Indians

    1. Simon McTavish came to America from Inverness-shire, Scotland, before 1772, and was a fur trader in Albany, New York, moving to Montreal in 1775. He was one of the original partners of the North West Company in 1779, becoming head of the company "in fact, if not in name," and perhaps the richest man in Montreal. The X Y, or New North West Company was founded in part by North West men who broke with the old company in 1798–1800, because of disagreement with McTavish's policies. His death in 1804 apparently made the merger of the two firms possible. Wallace, 15–17, 485–86; Davidson, 69–91, passim.

[Clark]   3rd of *March Sunday* 1805

    a fine Day   wind from the W, a large flock of Ducks pass up the River— visited by the black Cat, Chief of the Mandans 2d Cheif and a Big Belley, they Stayed but a Short time   we informed those Chiefs of the news recved from the Ricaras, all hands employd

Fort Mandan

[Clark]   4th *March Monday 1805*

a Cloudy morning   wind from the N W   the after part of the day Clear, visited by the Black Cat & Big White, who brought a Small present of meat, an Engage of the N W Co. Came for a horse, and requested in the name of the woman of the princapal of his Department[1] Some Silk of three Colours, which we furnished—.   The Assinniboins who visited the Mandans a fiew Days ago returned and attempted to take horses of the Minetarres & were fired on by them—

1. The "principal" may have been Charles Chaboillez, in charge of the Company's operations in the Assiniboine River. See above, October 31, 1804.

[Clark]   5th *March Tuesday* 1805

A fine Day   Themometer at 40° abo o.   Several Indians visit us to day   one frenchman cross to join a Indian   the two pass through by Land to the Ricaras with a Letter to Mr. Tabbow

[Clark]   6th of *March Wednesday 1805*

a Cloudy morning & Smokey all Day from the burning of the plains, which was Set on fire by the *Minetarries* for an early crop of Grass as an endusement for the Buffalow to feed on—[1]   the horses which was Stolen Some time ago by the Assinniboins from the *minetarries* were returned yesterday—   visited by *Oh-harh* or the Little fox 2d Chief of the lower Village of the Me ne tar ries—   one man *Shannon* Cut his foot with the ads[2] in working at a perogue, George[3] & Graviline go to the Village, the river rise a little to day—

1. This mention of early spring prairie fires set intentionally to improve the growth of prairie grasses and attract the buffalo to graze was only one of the several reasons for purposefully setting the fires. See July 20, 1804. Some authorities believe the fires account largely for the lack of woody vegetation on the plains. Pyne; White (RD), 184–86, 374–75 n. 17; Moore.

2. An adze, a tool for rough-shaping wood.

3. George Drouillard seems to have been the only man in the Corps that Clark commonly referred to by his first name, although George Gibson is a possibility. George Shannon is the least likely, since he had just cut his foot.

[Clark]   7th of *March Thursday* 1805

a little Cloudy and windey N E.   the *Coal* visited us with a Sick child, to whome I gave Some of rushes Pills—   Shabounar returned this evening from the Gross Vintres & informed that all the nation had returned from the hunting—   he our menetarre interpeter had received a present from Mr. Chaboilleiz of the N. W. Company of the following articles 3 Brace[1] of Cloath 1 Brace of Scarlet a par Corduroy Overalls ⟨Coats⟩ 1 Vests 1 Brace Blu Cloth 1 Brace red or Scarlet with 3 bars, 200 balls & Powder, 2 bracs Tobacco, 3 Knives.—

1. The brace as a measure of length equaled the span of the two extended arms; the French *brasse* was about sixty-four inches.

[Clark]   8th of *March Friday 1805*

a fair morning Cold and windey, wind from the East, visited by the Greesey head & a Riarca to day, those men gave Some account of the Indians near the rockey mountains

a young Indian same nation & Differnt Village Stole the Doughter of the Black man [*NB: Mandan (Minetarie)*], he went to his Village took his horse & returned & took away his doughter

[Clark]

on the 9th of March we were Visited by the Grand Chief of the Minetarres,[1] to whome we gave a medal & Some Cloths & a flag. Sent a French Man & a Indian with a letter to Mr. Tabboe informing them the Ricarras of the desire the Mandans had to See them &. &.—

[Clark]   9th *of March Satturday* 1805

a Cloudy Cold and windey morning   wind from the North—   walked up to See the Party that is makeing Perogues, about 5 miles above this, the wind hard and Cold   on my way up I met The [*NB: The Borgne*] Main Chief of the Manitarres with four Indians [*NB: see note of 9 March after*] on Thier way to [*NB: 10th March 1805*] See us, I requested him to proceed on to the fort where he would find Capt. Lewis   I should be there my Self in corse of a fiew hours, Sent the interpeter back with him and proceeded on my Self to the Canoes   found them nearly finished, the timber verry bad,[2] after visiting all the perogues where I found a number of Indans I wind to the upper mandan Village & Smoked a pipe the greatest mark of friendship and attention with the Chief and returned   on my return found the Manitarree Chief about Setting out on his return to his village, having recieved of Captain M. Lewis a *medel* Gorget[3] armbans, a *Flag* Shirt, Scarlet &c. &c. &c. for which he was much pleased   Those Things were given in place of Sundery articles Sent to him which he Sais he did not receive   2 guns were fired for this Great man

1. Le Borgne, or One Eye, was easily the most notorious chief—among whites—on the upper Missouri at this period. He had a formidable, and largely bad, reputation. Traders' and travelers' accounts agree in describing him as ugly, brutal, lecherous, bad-tempered, and homicidal, while generally acknowledging his leadership ability and prowess in war. Alexander Henry the Younger seems one of the few to have given a positive evaluation of him. He was less than cordial to Lewis and Clark but was far more favorable toward the British traders, being particularly helpful to François-Antoine Larocque, when the rest of the tribe opposed the trader's proposed trip to the Yellowstone in 1805. When he chose to accept someone as his guest, he protected that person with all the force of his character and reputation. The Hidatsas finally threw him out of power in 1813, after which he withdrew and established a separate village of only a few lodges. Some time later he was reportedly killed by another Hidatsa chief, Red Shield. Wood & Thiessen, 116 n. 28 and passim.; Thwaites (EWT), 5:161–62, 167, 6:140–41, 15:97; Coues (NLEH), 1:379–80 and passim.; Masson, 1:343–92; Pierre Chouteau to William Eustis, December 14, 1809, Nicholas Biddle Notes [ca. April 1810], Jackson (LLC), 2:482, 505, 539; Luttig, 73, 121–22.

2. Here is a short interlineation in red, "Qut" for question, probably by Biddle.

3. Originally a piece of armor to protect the throat, by the eighteenth century the gorget had become a purely ornamental plate hung around the neck to symbolize officer status. It was also used as merchandise in the Indian trade and as a gift to chiefs. Criswell, 43; Woodward, 25–26, 30–37.

[Clark]   10th of *March Sunday* 1805.

a Cold winday Day.   we are visited by the Black mockersons, Chief of the 2d Manetarre Village and the Chief of the Shoeman [*NB: Shoe or Mocassin Tr:*] Village or Mah hâ ha V. [*NB: Wattassoans*]   those Chiefs Stayed all day and the latter all night and gave us man[y] Strang accounts of his nation &c   this Little tribe or band of Menitaraies Call themselves Ah-nah-hâ-way or people whose village is on the hill. [*NB: Insert this Ahnahaway is the*

nation Mahhaha the village]   nation formerleyed lived about 30 miles below this but beeing oppressed by the Asinniboins & Sous were Compelled
to move ⟨near⟩ 5 miles the Minitaries, where, the Assinniboins Killed the
most of them   those remaining built a village verry near to the Minitar-
ries at the mouth of Knife R where they now live[1] and Can raise about 50
men, they are intermixed with the Mandans & Minatariers— the Mandans formerly lived in 6 [*NB: nine*] large villages at and above the mouth
of *Chischeter* or Heart River   five [*NB: six*] Villages on the West Side [*NB:
of the Missouri*] & two [*NB: three*] on the East   one of those Villages on the
East Side of the Missouri & the larges was intirely Cut off by the Sioux &
the greater part of the others and the Small Pox reduced the others.

1. The first location was the Molander Site (see above, October 23, 24, 1804; *Atlas* map
29). If Clark's statement means that they moved to a spot five miles below the Knife River,
then this could be the Mahhaha Site, within present Fort Clark, Oliver County, North
Dakota. Wood (OHI), 11–14, 20.

Fort Mandan

[Clark]   11th of *March Monday 1805*

A Cloudy Cold windey day, Some Snow in the latter part of the day, we
deturmin to have two other Perogues made for us to transport our Provisions &c.

We have every reason to believe that our Menetarre interpeter, (whome
we intended to take with his wife, as an interpeter through his wife to the
Snake Indians of which nation She is) has been Corupted by the [*blank*]
Companeys &c.[1]   Some explenation has taken place which Clearly proves
to us the fact, we give him to night to reflect and deturmin whether or not
he intends to go with us under the regulations Stated.

1. The captains may have assumed that the Hudson's Bay and North West companies
wished to sabotage their expedition in the interests of securing the Indian trade to themselves. To this they attributed Charbonneau's decision to quit (see March 12, 1805, below).
Larocque and McKenzie make no reference to such maneuvers, and Larocque gives the
impression that he and Bunch (or Budge), the Hudson's Bay man, were far more inter-
ested in competing with each other than in forestalling the Americans. It is hard to say
whether the captains' suspicions were more than mere Anglophobia. See Wood & Thiessen,
137, 238, and passim.

[Clark]

12th   a fine day   Some Snow last night   our Interpeter Shabonah, detumins on not proceeding with us as an interpeter under the terms mentioned yesterday   he will not agree to work let our Situation be what it may not Stand a guard, and if miffed with any man he wishes to return when he pleases, also have the disposial of as much provisions as he Chuses to Carrye.

in admissable and we Suffer him to be off the engagement which was only virbal[1]   wind N W

1. Ordway notes on March 14 that Charbonneau "has pitched a lodge outside of the Garrison and moved out," and that Gravelines had been hired in his place, whether for the journey or only while they were at Fort Mandan is not indicated.

[Clark]   13th *of March Wednesday 1805*

a fine day   visited by Mr. Mckinsey one of the Clerks of the N W Companey, the river riseing a little—   maney Inds. here to day all anxiety for war axes   the Smiths have not an hour of Idle time to Spear   wind S W

[Clark]   *14th March Thursday 1805.*

a fine day   Set all hands to Shelling Corn &c.   Mr. McKinsey leave us to day   maney Indians as usial.   wind west   river Still riseing

[Clark]   15th *of March Friday 1805*

a fine day   I put out all the goods & Parch meal Clothing &c to Sun, a number of Indians here to day   They make maney remarks respecting our goods &c.   Set Some men about Hulling Corn &c.[1]

1. Perhaps they were stripping the husks from the ears, more commonly called "shucking," but more likely they were removing the outer skin of the kernels.

[Lewis]   March 16th, 1804.[1]

Mr. Gurrow[2] a Frenchman who has lived many years with the Ricares & Mandans shewed us the process used by those Indians to make beads.   the discovery of this art these nations are said to have derived from the Snake Indians who have been taken prisoners by the Ricaras.   the art is kept a secret by the Indians among themselves and is yet known to but few of them.

the Prosess is as follows,— Take glass of as many different colours as you think proper, then pound it as fine as possible puting each colour in a seperate vessel. wash the pounded glass in several waters throwing off the water at each washing. continue this opperation as long as the pounded glass stains or colours the water which is poured off and the residium is then prepared for uce. You then provide an earthen pot of convenient size say of three gallons which will stand the fire; a platter also of the same materials sufficiently small to be admitted in the mouth of the pot or jar. the pot has a nitch in it's edge through which to watch the beads when in blast. You then provide some well seasoned clay with a propertion of sand sufficient to prevent it's becoming very hard when exposed to the heat. this clay must be tempered with water untill it is about the consistency of common doe. of this clay you then prepare, a sufficient number of little sticks of the size you wish the hole through the bead, which you do by roling the clay on the palm of the hand with your finger. this done put those sticks of clay on the platter and espose them to a red heat for a few minutes when you take them off and suffer them to cool. the pot is also heated to cles it perfectly of any filth it may contain. small balls of clay are also mad of about an ounce weight which serve each as a pedestal for a bead. these while soft ar distributed over the face of the platter at su[c]h distance from each other as to prevent the beads from touching. some little wooden paddles are now provided from three to four inches in length sharpened or brought to a point at the extremity of the handle. with this paddle you place in the palm of the hand as much of the wet pounded glass as is necessary to make the bead of the size you wish it. it is then arranged with the paddle in an oblong form, laying one of those little stick of clay crosswise over it; the pounded glass by means of the paddle is then roped in cilindrical form arround the stick of clay and gently roled by motion of the hand backwards an forwards until you get it as regular and smooth as you conveniently can. if you wish to introduce any other colour you now purforate the surface of the bead with the pointed end of your little paddle and fill up the cavity with other pounded glass of the colour you wish forming the whole as regular as you can.   a hole is now made in the center of the little pedestals of clay with the handle of your shovel sufficiently large to admit the end of the stick of clay arround which the bead is formed.   the beads are then arranged perpindicularly on their pedestals and little distance above them supported by the little sticks of clay to which they are attatched in the manner before mentioned. Thus arranged the platter is deposited on burning coals or hot embers and the pot reversed with the apparture in it's edge turned towards coverd the whole.   dry wood pretty much doated[3] [*NB: doughted*] is then plased arron the pot in sush manner as compleatly to cover it is then set on fire and the opperator must shortly after begin to watch his beads through the appar- ture of the pot le[s]t they should be distroyed by being over heated.   he suffers the beads to acquire a deep red heat from which when it passes in a small degree to a pailer or whitish red, or he discovers that the beads begin to become pointed at their upper extremities he ⟨throws⟩ removes the fire from about the pot and suffers the whole to cool gradually.   the pot is then removed and the beads taken out.   the clay which fills the hollow of the beads is picked out with an awl or nedle, the bead is then fit for uce. The Indians are extreemly fond of the large beads formed by this process.   they use them as pendants to their years, or hair and some- times wear them about their necks.—

[Clark]   *16th of March Satturday 1805*

    a Cloudy day   wind from the S. E   one Indian much displeased with whitehouse for Strikeing his hand when eating with a Spoon for behave- ing badly. Mr. Garrow Shew'd us the ⟨method⟩ way the ricaras made their large Beeds

1. Lewis placed this lengthy version of Garreau's account in Codex C after Clark's entry of March 21, 1805. It is placed here by date.

2. Joseph Garreau first visited the Arikaras with Jacques D'Eglise's expedition in 1793, and remained with the tribe. Described as either a Frenchman or a Spaniard, he has been called the first white settler in South Dakota. He was an interpreter and trader among the Arikaras and Mandans for various concerns for some forty years. Various witnesses gave a low estimate of his character. He may have been the Spaniard the captains met at the

Arikara villages on October 8, 1804, and the "Old Spaniard" who interpreted for Nathaniel Pryor's expedition in 1807. Nathaniel Pryor to Clark, October 16, 1807, Jackson (LLC), 2:434, 438 n. 4; Abel (TN), 138–39 n. 109, 140–41 n. 114, 144; Nasatir (BLC), 1:81, 95, 101 n. 103, 103, 109, 195, 233–35, 242, 248–50, 267, 297, 298, 234, 2:479, 503; Thwaites (EWT), 24:35, 58–61, 68–69; Luttig, 64, 68, 84, 90, 92–94, 97, 104, 107, 117, 158.

3. A variant of "doted," meaning decayed inside, or unsound—probably with dry rot in this case. Criswell, 33.

[Clark]

17th of March Sunday   a windey Day   attempted to air our goods &. Mr. Chabonah Sent a french man of our party that he was Sorry for the foolissh part he had acted and if we pleased he would accompany us agreeabley to the terms we had perposed and doe every thing we wished him to doe &c. &c.   he had requested me Some ⟨time⟩ thro our French inturpeter[1] two days ago to excuse his Simplicity and take him into the cirvise, after he had taken his things across the River we called him in and Spoke to him on the Subject, he agreed to our terms and we agreed that he might go on with us &c &c.   but fiew Indians here to day; the river riseing a little and Severall places open.

1. Probably François Labiche, whose services in translating between French and English Lewis later deemed worthy of extra pay, unless "French" here refers only to the man's origin and not to the language from which he translated. Charles McKenzie refers to a "mulatto who spoke bad French and worse English" who was interpreter between Charbonneau and the captains at Fort Mandan. This man is sometimes identified as York, but there is no evidence that Clark's servant knew French. Labiche seems the most likely person to be the "mulatto," although his ancestry is commonly given as half-French and half-Omaha. He may have had some black ancestry, or Mackenzie may have used the word "mulatto" in some sense other than the usual one. Charbonneau spoke little English at this time and needed an interpreter himself. Labiche may also be the Frenchman of the party mentioned above as Charbonneau's intermediary. Lewis to Henry Dearborn, January 15, 1807, Jackson (LLC), 1:367; Masson, 1:336–37. See also Appendix A in vol. 2 of this edition.

[Clark]

18th of March 1805   a cold cloudy Day   wind from the N.   I pack up all the merchindize into 8 packs equally devided So as to have Something of every thing in each Canoe & perogue   I am informed of a Party of

Christanoes & assinniboins being killed by the Sioux, 50 in Number near the Estableishments on the assinniboin R. a fiew days ago (the effect of Mr. Cammeron, revenge on the Chipaway for Killing 3 of his men) Mr. Tousent Chabono, Enlisted as an Interpreter this evening, I am not well to day.

[Clark]

19th of March 1805 Cold windey Day Cloudy Some little Snow last night Visited to Day by the *big white* & Little Crow, also a man & his wife with a Sick Child, I administer for the child I am told that two parties are gorn to war from the Big bellies and one other party going to war Shortly.

[Clark]

I visited the Mandans on the 20th & have the canoes taken to the River, ready to Decend to the fort when the River Clears,

Fort Mandan

[Clark]   *20th March Wednesday 1805.*

I with all the men which could be Speared from the Fort went to ⟨Perogues⟩ Canoes, there I found a number of Indians the men carried 4 [canoes] to the River about 1 ½ miles thro the Bottom, I visited the Chief of the Mandans in the Course of the Day and Smoked a pipe with himself and Several old men. cloudy wind hard from N.

[Clark]

I return on the 21st and on my return I passed on the points of the high hills S. S. where I saw an emence quantity of Pumice Stone, and evident marks of the hills being on fire I collected some Pumice Stone, burnt Stone & hard earth and put them into a furnace, the hard earth melted and glazed the other two a part of which i, e, the Hard Clay became a Pumice-Stone,[1] I also collected a Plant the root of which is a Cure for the Bite of a mad dog & Snake which I shall Send— Mr. Haney (I think it grows in the Blue R Barrens)[2] ⟨Mr. I.⟩[3] the Indians make large Beeds of Different Colours—

[Clark]   *21st March Thursday 1805*

a Cloudy Day   Some snow, the men Carried the remaining the 2 remained Canoes to the River, all except 3 left to take care & complete the
Canoes, returned to the fort with their baggage, on my return to day to
the Fort I came on the points of the high hills, Saw an emence quantity of
Pumice Stone on the Sides & foot of the hills and emence beds of Pumice
Stone near the Tops of the [hills] with evident marks of the Hill haveing
once been on fire, I collected Some the differnt i e Stone Pumice Stone &
a hard earth and put them into a furnace   the hard earth melted and
glazed the others two and the hard Clay became a pumice Stone Glazed. I
collected Some plants &c.

1. Pumice is frothy volcanic glass. When heated in a furnace it will fuse; some clays,
when heated to about 2000° F, expand and resemble somewhat the frothy volcanic rock.

2. If Clark is referring to a stream which he knows, it may be the Big Blue or the Little
Blue in Missouri. The plant is the purple coneflower. See December 16, 1804.

3. The letters crossed out here can be read as "Mr J" or even "Mr G"; the sentence that
follows is about the Indians' manufacture of glass beads, a subject they learned about
from Joseph Garreau. "Mr J" or "Mr G" might therefore stand for his name.

[Clark]

22nd of March 1805[1]   Visited by the 2nd Chief of the Grand Village
of the Minetarrees to whome we gave a medal & Some Clothes acknowledging him as a 2d Chief,[2] he Delayed all night, & Saw the men Dance,
which is common amusement with the men   he returned the 23rd with
Mr. La Rocque & McKinsey two of the N W. Companys Clerks—   Some
few Drops of rain this evening for the first time this Winter   visited by
many Indians to day—

[Clark]   *[March 22, 1805][3]*

23rd of March   Friday 1805   a Cloudy Day visited by Mrs. Lack [La-
rocque] McKinsey & the 2d Chief of the Bigbellies, the white wolf and
many other Menataries, we gave a Medal Some Clothes and wampoms to
the 2 Chief and Delivered a Speach, which they all appeared well pleased
with   in The evening the men Danced   Mr. Jessomme displeased

1. The date is in red ink with some overwriting of usual ink.

2. The Codex C entry (misdated March 23) refers to "the 2d Chief of the Big Bellies, the white wolf and many other Minataries," making it unclear whether the second chief and White Wolf are the same or not. White Wolf is presumably Man Wolf Chief, son of Cherry Grows on a Bush. The Grand Village is Big Hidatsa, the northernmost village (see *Atlas* map 29). If the second chief is not White Wolf, he could be the brother of Le Borgne who visited on March 23, since the second chief returned that day. The Field Notes entry implies that the second chief was acknowledged by the captains on March 22, rather than on October 29, 1804, when the grand council was held. Since Man Wolf Chief was absent on a war party at the time of this council, this could be the reason for the delay, if the two are the same.

3. From March 22 through March 31, 1805, Clark has misdated his Codex C entries. Biddle has corrected them in red ink, but his numbers are not included here.

[Clark]   *[March 23, 1805]*
                         24th *of March Satturday 1805*

after Brackfast Mr. La Rocke and Mr. McKinsey and the Chiefs & men of the Minetarras leave us—   Soon after we were visited by a Brother of the Burnia [*NB: of the Borgne, ⟨gro⟩ or one eyed chief of the Minitarees*] who gave us a Vocabulary of his Language—   the Coal & many other Mandans also visit us to Day.   a find Day in the fore part   in the evening a little rain & the first this winter—

[Clark]   *[March 24, 1805]*[1]

25h of March 1805   prepareing to Set out   Saw *Swan* passing N E.

[Clark]   *[March 24, 1805]*
                         25th *of March Sunday 1805*

a Cloudy morning   wind from the N E   the after part of the Day fair, Several Indians visit us to day, prepareing to Set out on our journey   Saw Swans & wild Gees flying N E this evening

1. Clark's entries in the Field Notes from this date are misdated, like his Codex C entries, through March 30, 1805.

[Clark]   *[March 25, 1805]*

26h   The ice broke up in Several places in the evenig   broke away and was nearly takeing off our new Canoes   river rise a little

[March 25, 1805]

[Clark]   26th of March Monday 1805

a find Day   wind S. W.   but fiew Inds visit us to day the Ice haveing broken up in Several places, The ice began to brake away this evening and was near distroying our Canoes as they wer decnding to the fort, river rose only 9 Inches to day   prepareing to Depart

[Lewis]   Monday March 25th 1805[1]

Observed ☉'s magnetic Azimuth with Circumferenter   S. 60° W.

	h	m	s
Time by Chronometer P. M.	5	7	49

Altitude of ☉'s L. L. by Sextant   32° 2' 0"

☉'s Magnetic Azimuth by Circumferenter   S. 61° W.

	h	m	s
Time by Chronometer P. M.	5	11	31

Altitude of ☉'s L. L. by Sextrand   30° 49' 15"

☉'s Magnetic Azimuth by Circumferentr.   S. 63° W

	h	m	s
Time by Chronometer P. M.	5	19	30

Altd. by Sextant of ☉'s L. L.   28° 13' 30"

1. Lewis's astronomical observation from Codex O.

[Clark]   [March 26, 1805]

27th   river choked up with ice opposit to us and broke off in the eveng

[March 26, 1805]

[Clark]   27th of March Tuesday 1805

The river choked up with ice opposit to us and broke away in the evening   raised only ½ Inch   all employed prepareing to Set out

[Clark]   [March 27, 1805]

28th   had all the Canoes, the ⟨B &⟩ Perogus corked pitchd & lined oover the Cotton Wood, which is win Shaken[1]   (the Mandans feed their horses on the cotton wood Sticks in places of corn).

[*March 27, 1805*]

Fort Mandan

[Clark]   28th of March Friday 1805

a windey Blustering Day   wind S W   ice running the [river] Blocked
up in view for the Space of 4 hours and gave way leaveing great quantity
of *ice* on the Shallow Sand bars.   had all the canoes corked pitched &
tirred [tarred] in and on the cracks and windshake which is universially in
the Cotton wood

1. Windshakes are cracks in wood caused by the strain of force of wind. Criswell, 92.

[Clark]   [*March 28, 1805*][1]

29th   the ice Stoped running owing to Some obstickle above   all prepareing to Set out   but few Indians visit us to day   they are watching to
catch the floating Buffalow which brake through the ice in Crossing,[2]
those people are fond of those animals ta[i]nted and Catch great numbers every Spring

[*March 28, 1805*]

[Clark]   *29th of March Satturday 1805*

The ice has Stoped running owing to Som obstickle above, repare the
Boat & Perogues, and prepareing to Set out   but few Indians visit us
to day   they are now attending on the river bank to Catch the floating
Buffalow

[Lewis]   Thursday March 28th 1805[3]

Observed Equal altitudes of the ☉ with Sextant & water articl. Horizon.

	h	m	s		h	m	s
A. M.	8	45	28.5	P. M.	4	17	4
	"	47	9		"	18	51.5
	"	48	5		"	20	43

Altitude by Sext. at time of Observation   48° 50′ —″

1. Under this entry and the next in the Field Notes (reverse of document 64) is a drawing in red crayon (see fig. 8), showing a man smoking a pipe and holding a firearm.

2. The carcasses of buffalo drowned in the river were an important source of meat for the tribes of the upper Missouri, and a fairly advanced state of decomposition added to the attraction. Denig, 49–50; Abel (TN), 75.

3. Lewis's astronomical observation from Codex O.

[Clark]   [*March 29, 1805*]

30th of March.   The Ice is passing in great quantites, river ran a little, The Plains are on fire on both Sides of the river   it is common for the indians to Set those Plains on fire near their village for the advantage of early Grass for the hors & as an inducement to the Buffalow to visit them—

[*March 29, 1805*]

[Clark]   *30th of March Sunday 1805*

The obstickle broke away above & the ice came dow in great quantites the river rose 13 inches the last 24 hours   I observed extrodanary dexterity of the Indians in jumping from one Cake of ice to another, for the purpose of Catching the buffalow as they float down   maney of the Cakes of ice which they pass over are not two feet Square. The Plains are on fire in view of the fort on both Sides of the River, it is Said to be common for the Indians to burn the Plains near their villages every Spring for the benifit of ther horse, and to induce the Buffalow to come near to them.

[Clark]   [*March 30, 1805*]

31h of March Monday 1805   Cloudy   Several gangus of Ducks and Gees pass up   not much ice floating. All the party in high Spirits, but fiew nights pass without a Dance   they are helth. except the—vn. [venereal]—which is common with the Indians and have been communicated to many of our party at this place—   those favores bieng easy acquired. all Tranquille

[*NB: 30th Saturday. See Ordway here*][1]

[Clark]   *31t of March Monday 1805*

Cloudy Day   Seven Gangs of Gees and Ducks pass up the river—   but a Small portion of ice floating down to day—   but fiew Inds visit us to day   all the party in high Spirits   they pass but fiew nights without amuse-

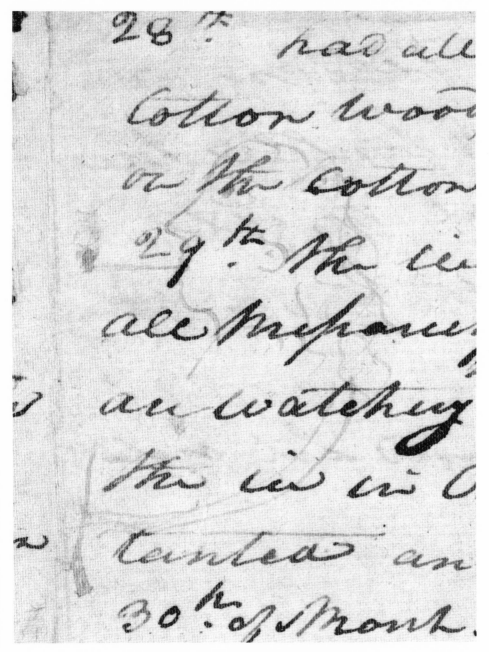

8. Profile of a Man with Pipe, ca. March 29, 1805,
Field Notes, reverse of document 64

ing themselves danceing possessing perfect harmony and good understanding towards each other   Generally healthy except venerials complains which is verry Commion amongst the natives and the men Catch it
from them [*NB: Qu:*][2]

[Lewis]   Saturday March 30th 1805[3]

Observed Equal Altitudes of the ☉, with Sextant and artificial Horzn. of Water.

A. M.	8	42	46	P. M.	4	17	33
	"	44	27		"	19	15
	"	46	10		"	20	59

Altd. by Sextant at the time of observt.   49° 45′ 00″

1. Biddle inserted this red-inked note to himself to consult Sergeant Ordway's journal,
which he was using in preparing his *History*. Possibly this enabled him to detect the misdating of entries by Clark. Clark had no March 31 entry in either his Field Notes or Codex
C, probably due to this same misdating, and Biddle's note may mean that he would have to
consult Ordway for the events of that day, which the entry in his *History* shows that he did.
Cutright (HLCJ), 136; Coues (HLC), 1:250.

2. A red-inked note by Biddle to ask Clark for more information about venereal disease among the Mandans and Hidatsas. See Nicholas Biddle Notes [ca. April 1810], Jackson (LLC), 2:506, 521.

3. Lewis's astronomical observation from Codex O.

[Lewis and Clark]   [*Weather, March 1805*][1]

Day of the Month 1805	State of Ther. at ☉ rise	Weather	State of wind at ☉ rise	State of Thermt. at 4 OClock	Weather at 4 Ock	Wind at 4 OClock	State of the River at ☉ rise raise or fallen	Feet	Inches
March 1st	28 a	c	W	38 a	f	N W			
2nd	28 a	f	N E.	36 a	f	N E	r		1½
3	28 a	c	E	39 a	f	N W			
4	26 a	f	N W	36 a	f	N W			
5	22 a	f	E	40 a	f	N W			
6	26 a	c	E	36 a	f	E	r		2
7	12 a	f	E	26 a	c	E	r		2

8	7 a	c	E	12 a	f	E	r		2½
9	2 a	c	N.	18 a	f	N W	r		2
10	2 b.	f	N W	12 a	f	N W	r		3½
11	12 a	c	S E	26²	f a c	N W	r		4½
12	2 b	f a s	N.	10 a	f	N W	r		5
13	1 b	f	S. E	28 a	f	S W	r		3½
14	18 a	f	S E	40 a	f	W.			
15	24 a	f	S E	38 a	f	W	f		1
16	32 a	c	E	42 a	c	W	f		3
17	30 a	f	S E	46 a	f	S. W.	r		2
18	24 a	c	N	34 a	c	N	f		1
19h	20 a	c a s	N.	31³	f	N W	r		1
20	28 a	c	N W	28⁴	f	N W	r		3
21	16 a	c	E	26 a	s & h	S			
22	22 a	f a s	S	36 a	f	S W	f		4
23	34 a	f	W.	38 a	c a r	N W	f		4
24	28 a⁵	c a s	N. E	30 a	c a. s.	N.	r		1
25	16	f	E.	32 a	f.	S.	r		5
26	20	f	S E	46 a	f	W	r		4½
27	28	f	S E	60 a	f	S W	r		9
28	40	f	S. E	64 a	f	S W	r		1
29	42	f	N W	52 a	f	N W	f		11
30	28	f	N W	49 a	f	N W	r	1	1
31	35	c a r	S E	45 a	c	S E	r		9

[Remarks]⁶

March 2d the snow has disappeared in many places the river partially broken up—⁷ Mr. Larocque visits us—

3rd a flock of ducks pased up the river this morning—

[9] wind hard all day. visited by the Birn the great Chief of the Big bellies⁸

12th snow but slight disappeared to day

[18] collected Some herbs pla[n]ts in order to send by the boat. paticularly the root said to cure the bites of the mad dog and rattlesnake.—⁹

19th But little snow not enough to cover the ground

[20] one of the men informed that the Menetares have plenty of artichokes.—[10]

21st some ducks seen to light in the river opposit the fort

[23] but little rain.[11]

24th but little Snow.

25th a gang of *swan* return to day   the ice in the river has given way in many places and it is with some difficulty it can be passed—

26th the ice gave way in the river about 3 P. M. and came down in immense sheets very near distroying our perogues—[12] some *gees* pass today.

27th the first insect I have seen was a large black knat today— the ice drifting in large quantities.—

28th it [river] raised 13 inch and fell 12.   wind hard, ice abates in quantity

29th a variety of insects make their appearance, as flies bugs &c.   the ice ceases to run   supposed to have formed an obstruction above.—

30th ice came down in great quantities   the Mandans take Some floating Buffaloe

31st ducks and Gees passing ice abates in quantity

1. This weather table follows Lewis's Weather Diary, with some discrepancies in Clark's table in Codex C being noted.

2. This temperature in Codex C is "26 a."

3. In Codex C this temperature is "31 a."

4. Clark has "28 a" in Codex C.

5. Codex C has "28 a" here.

6. These remarks follow Lewis's in the Weather Diary, with exceptions noted. The dates follow Clark's in Codex C.

7. Clark's remark ends here.

8. Clark has no remarks for this date.

9. In Clark's Codex C these remarks are placed, undated, after his remarks for March 19. The root is the purple coneflower which Clark mentioned in his regular entries as having collected on March 21, that date probably being correct.

10. Clark's undated version of this remark reads "The Indians raise a kind of artechokes which they Say is common in the praries. well tasted." The artichokes are *Helianthus tuberosus* L., Jerusalem artichoke. Barkley, 380. Lewis gives a more detailed description on April 9, 1805.

11. Clark has no remarks for this date.

12. Clark has "new canoes" instead of "perogues."

[Clark]

April 1st 1805[1]   we have Thunder lightning hail and rain to day   the first rain of note Sinc the 15 of October last, I had the Boat Perogus & Canos put in the water, and expect to Set off the boat with despatches   in her will go 6 Americans 3 frenchmen, and perhaps Several ricarra Chief imediately after we Shall assend in 2 perogus & 6 canoes, accompanied by 5 french who intends to assend a Short distance to trap the beavr which is in great abundance highr up   our party will consist of one Interpter & Hunter,[2] one French man as an interpreter with his two wives[3] (this man Speaks Minetary to his wives who are L hiatars[4] or Snake Indians of the nations through which we Shall pass, and to act as interpretress thro him[)]—   26 americans & french my servant and an Mandan Indian and provisions for 4 months—

Fort Mandan

[Clark]   *April the 1st Tuesday 1805*

The fore part of to day haile rain with Thunder & lightning, the rain continued by intimitions all day, it is worthey of remark that this is the 1st rain which has fallen Since we have been here or Since the 15 of October last, except a fiew drops at two or three defferent times—

had the Boat Perogus & Canoes all put into the water.

1. Clark seems to have no entries for March 31, 1805, in either his Field Notes or Codex C, probably due to his misdating of the last few days in March. Clark may have neglected either Field Notes or Codex C or both for several days during this busy time, and in resuming on or after April 1, was misled by his wrong dates and failed to realize there was no March 31 entry. The resumption of daily entries in the Field Notes on March 24 (March 25 by Clark's reckoning) after months of skimpy and irregular writing in them suggests that he was using them once more as the basis for Codex C during this hectic period, and that in transferring into Codex C he repeated the dating error. From April 1 his dates

appear to be correct, but he still has the days of the week wrong up through the April 7 entry in Codex C. Biddle has corrected them in red, but we do not carry his emendations.

2. George Drouillard served as both hunter and interpreter.

3. Apparently the captains intended to take both of Charbonneau's wives along, but something unrecorded happening in the last few days at Fort Mandan resulted in Sacagawea's being the only one actually to make the trip.

4. The word is difficult to read, but it is clearly a reference to the Shoshones, the people of Sacagawea and Charbonneau's other wife. However spelled, it is apparently a variation of "Ietan," also L'Iatan, Aliatan, and many other variants. In the captains' "Estimate of the Eastern Indians," sent back to Jefferson from Fort Mandan, the word is "Alitans" or "Aliatans." This name was applied loosely by Plains tribes and traders to the Utes, the Shoshones, or the Comanches (all "Snakes" in the sign language), depending on the context. The derivation is perhaps from the Utes' name for themselves. Hodge, 1:594–95; 2:556–57; Hyde (IHP), 99–100, 183–84, 200–02.

[Clark]

April the 2nd   a Cold rain day   we are writeing and prepareing dispatches all day—   I conclude to Send my journal to the President of the United States in its original State for his own perusial, untill I call for it or Some friend if I should not return, an this journal is from the 13th of May 1804 untill the 3rd of April 1805.[1]   wrote untill verry late at night but little time to devote to my friends,[2] the river is falling fast.

[Clark]   *April the 2nd* Friday   1805

a cloudy day rained all the last night   we are preparing to Set out   all thing nearly ready. The 2d Chief of the 2d Mandan Village took a miff at our not attending to him perticelarely after being here about ten [*NB: ten*] day and moved back to his village

The mandans Killed twenty one elk yesterday 15 miles below this, they were So meager that they Scercely fit for use

1. See the Introduction, vol. 2, for a discussion of which journal Clark means here.

2. Clark presumably means that he had little time to write letters to family and friends to be sent with the downriver party.

[Clark]

3rd of April   we Shall pack up to day and Set out tomorrow.[1]

[Clark]   *April the 3rd Thursday 1805*

a white frost this morning, Some ice on the edge of the water, a fine
day   Pack up and prepare to load

observed equal allitudes of the ☉ with Sextant and artificial horizen

	H	m	s			h	m	s
A M	7	51	15	P M		5	1	22
"		52	52.5			5	3	3
"		54	30		"		5	41

altitude producd from this observation is   36° 31″ 15″
Chronometer too fast 32 minets

observed Time and Distance of ☉s & ☽s nearest limbs withe Sextant and
Chromometer—   Sun west

		Time			*Distance*		
	H	M	S				
P M	5	15	50	43°	27′	15″
"		18	24	"	30	0
"		20	5	"	30	30
"		31	29	"	34	0
"		36	47	"	36	30
"		39	7	"	37	15
"		40	55	"	37	30

Mrs. La Roche & McKinsey Clerk to the N W. Compy. visit us. Mr.
McKinzey wishes to get pay for his horse lost in our Service this winter
and one of ⟨Horse⟩ which ⟨was⟩ [*ML: our men were*] robed ⟨of our men⟩
this winter by the Tetons, we Shall pay this man for his horse.   we are all
day ingaged packing up Sundery articles to be Sent to the President of
the U. S.[2]

Box No. 1, contains the following articles i e'
In package No. 3 & 4 Male & Female antelope, with their Skelitons.
    "   No. 7 & 9 the horns of two mule or Black tailed deer.   a Mandan

bow an quiver of arrows—with some Ricara's tobacco seed [3]

" No. 11 a Martin Skin,[4] Containing the tail of a Mule Deer, a ⟨white⟩ weasel and three Squirels from the Rockey mountains.

" No. 12. The bones & Skeleton of a Small burrowing wolf of the Praries the Skin being lost by accident.

" No. 99 The Skeliton of the white and Grey *hare*.

Box No. 2, contains 4 Buffalow *Robes*, and a ear of Mandan Corn.

The large Trunk Contains a male & female *Brarow* [*ML: or burrowing dog of the Prarie*] and female's Skeliton.

a Carrote of Ricaras *Tobacco*

a red fox Skin Containing a *Magpie*.

No. 14 Minitarras Buffalow robe Containing Some articles of Indian dress.

No. 15 a Mandan *robe* containing two burrowing Squirels, a white *weasel* and the Skin of a Loucirvea.   also

13 red fox Skins.

1 white Hare Skin &.

4 horns of the mountain ram

1 Robe representing a battle between the Sioux & Ricaras, [*ML: against the*] Minetarras and Mandans.[5]

In Box No. 3.

nos. 1 & 2 The Skins of the Male & female Antelope with their Skelitons.   & the Skin of a yellow *Bear* which I obtained from the *Scious*

No. 4. Box Specimens of plants numbered from 1 to 67.[6]

Specimens of Plants numbered frome 1 to 60.

1 Earthen pot Such as the Mandans Manufacture and use for culinary purposes.[7]

Box No 4 Continued

1 Tin box, containing insects mice[8] &c.

a Specimine of the fur of the antelope.

a Specimon of a plant, and a parcel of its roots highly prized by the natives as an efficatious remidy in Cases of the bite of the rattle Snake or Mad Dog.[9]

In a large Trunk

Skins of a Male and female Braro, or burrowing Dog of the Prarie, with the Skeliton of the female.

1 Skin of the red fox Containing a Magpie.

2 Cased Skins of the white hare.

1 Minitarra Buffalow robe Containing Some articles of Indian Dress

1 Mandan Buffalow robe Containing a dressed Lousirva Skin, and 2 Cased Skins of the Burrowing Squirel of the Praries.

13 red fox Skins

4 Horns of the Mountain Ram or big horn.

1 Buffalow robe painted by a mandan man representing a battle fought 8 years Since by the Sioux & Ricaras against the mandans, *menitarras* & Ah wah har ways (Mandans &c. on horseback[)]

Cage No. 6.

Contains a liveing burrowing Squirel of the praries

Cage No. 7.

Contains 4 liveing magpies

Cage No. 9.

Containing a liveing hen of the Prarie [10]

a large par of Elks horns containing by the frontal bone—[11]

1. This is the last daily entry in the Field Notes (document 64). Since they intended to leave on April 4, Clark undoubtedly sealed up the Field Notes sheets to be sent back with the return party. Delays not mentioned in the journals kept them at Fort Mandan until April 7. During that time Clark did not add to the Field Notes but did add entries in Codex C through the seventh.

2. A similar list of goods is found in an enclosure with Lewis to Jefferson, April 7, 1805, Jackson (LLC), 1:234–36. Someone, perhaps Biddle, has drawn red lines through the list.

3. The tobacco seed is discussed in the botany section of Chapter 10. This line appears to be in Lewis's hand.

4. Not a bird but the marten, a mammal of the weasel family. It is an inhabitant of evergreen forests, and some Mandan or Hidatsa had probably obtained the skin in trade. The journals do not indicate that the captains saw any live specimens on the expedition. Jones et al., 274–77; Burroughs, 73–74.

5. On the possible fate of the buffalo hide, see Jackson (LLC), 1:241 n. 29, 2:734 n. 1.

6. Lewis is probably confused here and means the mineralogical specimens that were sent back from Fort Mandan which are not noted as being packed anywhere else in this list. Cf. Jackson (LLC), 1:235. A further possible error is that the receiving list (the Donation Book at the American Philosophical Society, see Appendix C, vol. 2) numbers sixty-eight items. Hurried preparations for leaving in the final days at Fort Mandan could easily account for the errors. See Chapter 10 for the list. Cutright (LCPN), 357 n. 21.

7. Fragments of Mandan pottery said to be from the expedition are discussed in Wedel (PV).

8. Perhaps the northern short-tailed shrew, *Blarina brevicauda*. If so, the species is another expedition discovery. Cutright (LCPN), 439; Jones et al., 53–56.

9. Purple coneflower.

10. Of the live animals shipped, only the prairie dog and one of the magpies reached Jefferson alive. Cutright (LCPN), 375–78.

11. This list is crossed out in Codex C.

[Clark]   April the 4th 1805 Wednesday

a blustering windey Day   the Clerks of the N W. Co. leave us   we are arrangeing all things to Set out &c.

[Clark]   *April the 5th* 1805 Thursday

we have our 2 perogues & Six Canoes loaded with our Stores & provisions, principally provisions.   the wind verry high from the N W.   a number of Mandans visit us to day

[Clark]   *April the 6th Friday* Saturday *1805*

a fine day   visited by a number of mandans, we are informed of the arrival of the whole of the *ricarra* nation on the other Side of the river near their old village.   we Sent an interpreter to See with orders to return imediately and let us know if their Chiefs ment to go down to See their great father.[1]

1. Probably they were near the sites of the old Arikara villages shown on *Atlas* map 29, in Oliver County, North Dakota, roughly opposite present Washburn. Gravelines was probably the interpreter sent across the river. MRC map 51.

Chapter Ten

Fort Mandan
Miscellany

Introduction

The end of the winter at Fort Mandan marked an important stage in the expedition; difficult and potentially dangerous as the route had so far been, all the men's efforts had been directed to reaching a point where other whites had ventured before them, on a route already mapped. From Fort Mandan on, they would enter country for which they had only Indian information and the conjectural maps based on that information and on geographical speculation.

All along the captains had distinguished between their "permanent party" and the others, boatmen and soldiers, who would return from some point up the Missouri. The heavy keelboat would become less useful as the river became shallower in its upper reaches, while the hired boatmen would be less necessary when the keelboat went back. They had designated Corporal Richard Warfington's squad from the start as the group that would return from some point during the first year carrying dispatches and specimens to President Jefferson. The original plan was that this return party would leave, probably in a pirogue, before the first winter; Jefferson would thus receive early word of the progress of the expedition, would have their first journals to peruse, and would receive their first plant, animal, and mineral specimens. Even if disaster later overtook the Corps of Discovery, something would be saved to add to knowledge of the West. The captains finally decided not to send this return party back before winter, but to wait for the following spring.

Among the items sent back were the journals completed to date; while there may still be room for some discussion here (see the Introduction to vol. 2), it seems clear that most of the daily journal material was Clark's, including the Field Notes and Codices A, B, and C. Lewis's Codex O, also sent back, is a collection of astronomical observations made during the first eleven months of the journey and "A Summary view of the Rivers and Creeks, which discharge thems[elves] into the Missouri. . . ." A more condensed, tabular list of rivers, creeks, and "remarkable places" by Clark is in Codex C; both men include lists of tributaries of the Missouri above Fort Mandan and of the Yellowstone, based on Indian information. There are also a number of miscellaneous documents that nearly repeat these summaries; they are discussed in the pages which follow. Lewis's and Clark's summaries form part 1 of this chapter. A list which identifies Lewis and Clark's points by their modern names is also a part of this section.

Some of Lewis and Clark's observations (such as astronomical notes and weather data) are dated and can be placed in the journals by date, as is done in this edition. Many of the other miscellaneous materials, however, cannot be dated with any precision, except that they clearly belong to the period ending with the departure from Fort Mandan. For this reason they appear together in this chapter as a miscellany of observations covering the first phase of the expedition and sent back from Fort Mandan. One such item is an extensive separate document by Clark listing and describing Indian tribes east of the Rockies, his "Estimate of Eastern Indians." From this, supplemented by other journal material, Jefferson prepared "A Statistical View of the Indian Nations Inhabiting the Territory of Louisiana and the Countries Adjacent to its Northern and Western Boundaries," which he presented to Congress and which was published in 1806. Again miscellaneous documents duplicate this material and they are discussed below. The Indian material, along with a list identifying the tribes by modern designation, makes up part 2 of the chapter.

On the trip to Fort Mandan Lewis took extensive notes on the fauna and flora of the Missouri River valley. These he copied into special notebooks, Codices Q and R. The zoological material in Codex Q is placed in these volumes by date, as are astronomical and weather data. The botanical information from Codex R presents a different situation. The material is presented in the journal as a list, similar to the captains' summaries of rivers and creeks. Moreover, since many of the items are undated they appeared more appropriate for this chapter. Botanical specimens that were sent back from Fort Mandan with Warfington's party were eventually received by the American Philosophical Society and are listed in the Donation Book there. Part 3 of the chapter contains the lists from Codex R and the Donation Book. Since so many of these plants are not mentioned in the captains' daily journals, a table has been added to match the lists and to give modern identifications of the plants as far as possible.

A list of mineral specimens sent back from Fort Mandan is also a part of the Donation Book, apparently a copy of a list prepared by the captains themselves, done by persons at the society. It appears as part 4 of this chapter. Part 5 is a section of miscellaneous items that were apparently drawn up at Fort Mandan, while part 6 is lists of Indian presents and "necessary stores" for the expedition from Codex C.

Part 1: Affluents of the Missouri River

Lewis's extensive geographical treatise of the Missouri River, which is printed first in this section, is found in his Codex O (pp. 69–128); it is in a sense a complement to Clark's 1805 map of the West (*Atlas* maps 32*a*, 32*b*, 32*c*), and like it was prepared at Fort Mandan. It combines the captains' actual observations of these tributaries where they entered the Missouri with information received from traders and Indians about the upper reaches of these streams and their own tributaries. Lewis has filled in the gaps in his information—and his misunderstanding of some of it—with speculation. As might be expected, the picture becomes more sketchy and inaccurate the farther one goes from the Missouri and the homes of his Indian informants. The most interesting part is perhaps the conjectural picture of the Missouri above Fort Mandan and the Yellowstone, all of it based on Indian information. Lewis was ready to pronounce on the importance of the junction of the Missouri and the Yellowstone before he had seen it.

In a few instances it is clear that Lewis has drawn on earlier notes. His description of St. Charles, Missouri, at the beginning of the document reproduces almost verbatim his entry for May 20, 1804, in Codex Aa. The description of the Platte is a revised version of the material on document 35 of the Field Notes, dated July 21, 1804. Other geographical notes of the same sort, now apparently lost, undoubtedly went into the present document, and Lewis would also have consulted Clark's journals.

Some other items that he may have drawn on were done by Clark at an unknown time. Or, these items may have post-dated Lewis's summary and may even be postexpeditionary documents that were prepared for Nicholas Biddle as he worked with the journals in 1810. Two items are from the papers discovered in Biddle's estate by his grandsons in 1913 and deposited with the American Philosophical Society some time later. They were the first and third pieces of the material known as the "seven manuscript items" (see Appendix B, vol. 2) and have never been published. They may, in fact, be one document that was separated at some point with their apparent order reversed in their present arrangement. Believing them to be preliminary drafts or copies of Lewis's material, made either during or after the expedition and differing from the main document only in style and wording, we do not print the Clark pieces here. Likewise, two small tables from a larger document at the Missouri Historical Society, mentioned below as Clark's "A Summary Statement . . . in the year 1804," closely follows Lewis's lists of affluents of the Kansas and Platte rivers. Notes to Lewis's summary will mention areas of substantial differences with these sources.

Clark's table covering nearly the same information as Lewis's summary appears in his Codex C (pp. 248–53, reading backward). It is a tabular version of Lewis's descriptive narrative, and it too includes the conjectural depiction of the Missouri above Fort Mandan and of the Yellowstone. This document also has its counterparts and they too are unclear as to timing or date of composition. Two items are similar to it in form and content: (1) Clark's "Names of remarkable places Rivers Creeks Empping into the Missouri," and (2) Clark's "A Summary Statement of the Rivers, Creeks & most remarkable places, their Distances &c. &c. from the mouth of the Missouri, as high up that River as was explored in the year 1804." Both items are loose, letter-size sheets at the Missouri Historical Society. Clark also made what appear to be postexpeditionary copies in two other notebooks, Codex N and Voorhis No. 4. Both cover not only the material gathered up to Fort Mandan, but also continue their tables through the rest of the journey. Since no significant differences have been discovered among these documents, only Clark's summary from Codex C is printed here.

A final historic document is included in this section. Clark made an undated table of distances in his Field Notes (documents 66 and 67) in which he added the latitudes of prominent points along the Missouri besides giving the mileage figures which correspond to his summary in Codex C. Similar material is also found in Codex C, p. 247, but much abbreviated, and in Voorhis No. 4, also less detailed.

The final item in this section is a combined table of Lewis and Clark's lists of the Missouri's affluents together with their modern equivalents. On the left is a combination of all the streams and points mentioned by the men in their various lists, while the material on the right identifies the places by their modern names. In some instances it has been difficult to determine the exact river, creek, or island to which the captains refer, therefore the date of the expedition's passing of the site is noted. The same is done for points that are disputed or for those which involve considerable discussion. At the relevant date and in the journal entry's notes readers will find a full discussion of the locale. The identifications are taken from the annotation to the daily entries, where readers will find sources for these determinations. Locations given for streams refer to their mouths.

[Lewis]   [*undated, winter 1804–5*][1]

A Summary view of the Rivers and Creeks, which discharge thems[elves] into the Missouri; containing a discription of their characters and peculiarities, their sources and connection with other rivers and Creeks, the quality of the lands, and ther apparent face of the country through which they pass, and the width, and distance of their entrances from each other; to which is also added a short discription of some of the most remarkable points and places on the Missouri; taken from the information of Traders, Indians & others; together with our own observations, from the junction of that river with the Mississippi, to Fort Mandan.—

The confluence of the Mississippi and Missouri Rivers is situated in 89° 57′ 45″ Longitude West from Greenwich, and 38° 55′ 19.6″ North Latitude. Ascending the Missouri from hence, at the distance of 21 miles, you arrive at the Village of St. Charles, situated on the North bank of the river, in a narrow tho' elivated plain, which is bounded in the rear by a range of small hills; hence the appellation of *Petit cote*, a name by which, this village is better known to the inhabitants of the Illinois, than that of St. Charles. The village is bisected or divided into two equal parts by one prinsipal streed about a mile in length, runing nearly parallel with the river. It contains a Chapple, one hundred dwelling houses and about 450 inhabitants. the houses are generally small and but illy constructed. a great majority of the inhabitants are miserably poor, illiterate, and when at home, excessively lazy; tho' they are polite, hospitable and by no means deficient in point of natural genious. they live in great harmony among themselves, and place as implicit confidence in the doctrines of their speritual pastor, (the Roman Catholic priest) as they yeald passive obedience to the will of their temporal master, the Commandant. A small garden of vegetables is the usual extent of their cultivation. this labour is commonly imposed on the old men and boys;— those in the vigor of life view the cultivation of the soil as a degrading employment, and in order to gain the necessary subsistence for themselves and families, either under take hunting voyages on their own account, or engage themselves as hirelings to such as posses sufficient capital to extend their traffic to the natives to the interior parts of the country. on those voyages on their own account, or engage themselves as hirelings to such as possess sufficient capital to extend their traffic to the natives of the interior parts of the country. on those voyages in either case, they are frequently absent from their families or homes, the term of six, twelve, or eighteen months, during which time they are always subjected to severe and incessant labour, exposed to the ferosity of the lawless savages, the vicissitudes of weather and climate, and dependant on chance and accedent alone, for food, raiment, or relief in the event of malady; yet they undertake those voyages with cheerfullness, and prefer the occupation of the hunter, or engage, to that of the domestic, and independent farmer.—

Ascending the Missoury at the distance of 12 miles, *Bonhomme* Creek discharges itself on the S. side. it is 23 yards wide at it's entrance, is of no great length, & passes through a fertile well timbered country, inhabited by American emigrants principally.—

at the distance of 9 miles higher up we pass the mouth of the *Osage woman's* river, which discharges itself on the N. side; it is 30 yards wide at it's entrance, heads with two small streams which discharge themselves into the Mississippi a small distance above the mouth of the Illinois River, is navigable for perogues some miles during the spring season, and waters a fertile well timbered country inhabited by about fifty American families. this part of the country is generally called Boon's settlement, having derived it's name from it's first inhabitant Colo. Daniel Boon, a gentleman well known in the early settlement of the state of Kentuckey.

About 9^2 miles higher up, and 69, from the Mississippi, Chaurette Creek falls in on the N. side. it is 20 yards wide at it's mouth, waters a tolerable country well covered with timber, but is of no great extent. it heads with the waters of the River O cuivre[3] a branch of the Mississippi.— immediately below the mouth of this creek five French families reside, who subsist by hunting and a partial trade w[h]ich they mantain with a few detatched Kickapoos who hunt in their neighbourhood. this is the last settlement of white persons which we meet with in ascending the Missouri.

At the distance of 34 miles high up the *Gasconade* disembogues on the S. side behind a small Island covered with willow. at it's entrance it is 157 yards wide, but is much narrower a little distance up, and is not navigable, (hence the name *gasconade*)[4] this river is of no great length, heads with the Marameg & St. Francis rivers. the country watered by this river, is generally broken, thickly covered with timber and tolerably fertile. the hills which border on the Missouri near the mo[u]th of this river are about

300 feet high, containing excellent limestone in great abundance. I have observed in ascending the Missouri to this place, that whenever the river washes the base of the hills on either side, it discloses large quarries of this stone, lying in horizontal stratas, from ten to 40 feet in thickness. this stone is of light brown colour, with a smal tint of blue; fracture imperfect conchoidal; when broken it presents the appearance of a variety of small shells and other marine substances, of which it seems to be entirely composed. in this solid and massive rock, are inclosed stones of yellowish bron flint, of bulbous and indeterminate shapes, from an ounce to ten or twelve pounds weight. these stratas of limestone are not unusually found overlaying a strata of freestone, or soft sandstone, from two to twenty feet in thickness. this stone produces lime of an excellent quality, and is the same—with that, which makes it's appearance on the Mississippi from Cape Gerrardeau, to the entrance of the Missouri.[5]

Ffteen[6] miles higher up pass *Muddy River* which falls in on the N side. this river waters a most delightfull country; the land lies well for cultivation, and is fertile in the extreem, particularly on the Missouri, both above and below this river for many miles; it is covered with lofty and excellent timber, and supplyed with an abundance of fine bould springs of limestone water. this river is 50 yards wide several miles above it's mouth.—

2 miles higher up *Muddy creek* discharges itself; it is 20 yards wide at it's mouth, heads with cedar Creek, and the branches of Muddy river. the country through which it passes is similar to that last mentioned.—

At the distance of 19 miles higher up, you arrive at the mouth of the *Osage River;* being 137 miles from the junction of the Missouri and Mississippi. it is 397 yards wide at it's mouth, opposite to which, the Missouri is 875 yards wide. it disembogues on the S. side just above a cluster of small Islands. it takes it's rise in an open country of Plains and Praries, with some of the Northern branches of the Arkansas; some of it's tributary streams on it's North side, also have their souces in a similar country, with the Southern branches of the Kanzas river. The rivers Arkansas and Kanzas circumscribe the length of this river, and interlock their brances to the West of it. The country watered by this river, is generally level & fertile, tho' it is more broken on the lower portion of the river; the bottom lands are wide, well timbered, and but partially liable to inundation; the soil consists of a black rich loam many feet in debth. the uplands also consist of a dark loam overlaying a yellow or red clay;[7] a majority of the country consist of plains intersperced with groves of timber. the timber still diminishes in quantity as you proceed Westwardly with the river. on the South side of this river 30 leagues below the Osage Village, there is a large lick, at which some specimenes of the bones of the Mammoth have been found; these bones ar said to be in considerable quantities, but those which have been obtained as yet, were in an imperfect state.[8] Mr. Peter Chouteau, a gentleman of St. Louis, mande an attempt some years since to explore this lick, but was compelled to desist from his labour, in consequence of the quantity of water discharged into the lick from a neighbouring spring, which he had not the means or the leasure to divert; since which time, no further attempt has been made. The specimens obtained by Mr. Couteau were large; but much mutilated. the Osage river is navigable 120 leages for boats and perogues of eight or ten tons burthen, during the fall and spring seasons; in winter it's navigation is obstructed by ice, and during the Summer months it experiences an unusual depression of it's waters, a characteristic of most streams, which have their sources in an open plain country, or which, in their courses pass through a majority of that discription of lands. the bed of the river is generally composed of mud, gravel and sand, and is but little obstructed by rocks or driftwood.—

At the distance of five miles above the mouth of the Osage river, *Murrow* Creek falls in on the S side, 20 yards wide at it's mouth and navigable for perogues a few miles. it takes it's rise with the waters of the Osage river and those of Salt river (branch of the Missouri) it traverses in it's course to the Missouri, a tolerable country, well timbered and waterd. the mouth of this creek is the point at which the Saukes, Foxes, and Ayauways usually pass this river wars with the Osages.—

7 miles higher up, *Cedar Creek* falls in on the N. side, above an Island, on which there is Cedar, hence the name of the creek. it heads with muddy creek, and passes through a delightfull country in it's course to the Missouri. it is well timbered and abounds in springs of excellent water.—

at the distance of ten miles further you pass the mouth of *Good-woman's*

Creek, about 20 yards wide. opposite to the entrance of this creek the Missouri washes the base of a high hill which is said to contain lead ore, our surch for this ore however pruved unsuccessfull and if it does contain ore of any kind, it must be concealed. this Creek takes it rise in the highlands with Split rock Creek and passes through a fertile country well timbered and watered. in the last nine miles of it's course it passes through an extensive fertile bottom nearly parallel with the Missouri.—

Nine miles higher you pass the mouth of *Manitou* Creek on the S. Side. it is but a small creek head a few miles back in an open country; the land abut it's entrance on the Missouri are of an excellent quality and covered with good timber.—

Nine miles further *Split rock* Creek discharges itself on the N. side, twenty yards wide and navigable for perogues some miles. it waters a well timbered country; the land about the mouth, appears to be of the second quality, or a least inferior to that heretofore seen in ascending the Missouri.—

at the distance of 3 miles, still ascending, *Salt* river disembogues on the S. side; being 180 miles from the entrance of the Missouri. it is 30 yards wide and navigable for perogues 40 or 50 miles; passes through a delightfull country, intersperced with praries. so great is the quantity of salt licks and springs on this river that it's waters are said to be brackish at certain seasons of the year. one large lick and spring are situated on it's S. E. bank about nine miles from the Missouri. this river heads with the waters of the Osage river, Murrow Creek, and Mine river.—

Ascending the Missouri ten miles further we arrive at the entrance of Manitou river, which disembogues on the N. side, just below a high clift of limestone rock, in which we found a number of rattle snakes of large size. this stream is about 30 yards wide, and is navigable for perogues some miles. about three miles from the Missouri on the lower side of this river there are three small springs of salt water which do not appear to be of the best quality. the country about the mouth of this river, particularly on it's lower side, is a charming one; the soil fertile in the extreme, and well covered with excellent timber. the country on the upper portion of this river is but little known.—

At the distance of nine miles further, *Good-woman's* river falls in on the

N side; it is 35 yards wide at it's entrance; meanders through an extensive rich bottom nearly parallel with the Missouri for some miles before it discharges itself.   it is navigable for perogues 15 or 20 miles, waters a fine farming country interspeced with open plains and praries, and heads with the little Shariton river.—

At the distance of nine miles *Mine river* discharges itself on the S. side. it derives it's name from some lead mines which are said to have been discoved on it, tho' the local situation, quality, or quantity of this ore, I could never learn.   this river is 70 yards wide at it's entrance, navigable for perogues 80 or 90 miles, and through the greater part of it's course runs parellel with the Missouri; at the distance of 70 miles up this river it is only 5 leagues distant from the Missouri.   it takes it's rise in an open hilly country with Bluewater river and some of the Northern branches of the Osage river.   the courant of this river is even and gentle. The country through which it passes is generally fertile, and consists of open plains and praries intersperced with groves of timber.   near it's entrance, the country is well timbered and watered, and the lands are of a superior quality.

Twenty two miles higher up the two Shariton rivers discharge themselves on the N. side, the smaller falling into the larger on it's lower side at a small distance from the Missouri.   the little Shariton river heads with Good-woman's river, and is 30 yards wide at it's entrance; this country has not been much explored, the portion of it which is known is fertile, and consists of a mixture of praries and woodlands. The larger Shariton is 70 yards wide above the entrance of the smaller, and is navigable for perogues nearly to it's source.   it takes it's rise near the Red Cedar river a Western brance of the river Demoin.   the country through which it passes is level, and fertile, consisting of an irregular mixure of woodlands and praries, each alternately predominating in different parts.

Twenty two miles higher up, the *Grand river* disembogues on the N. side just above a beatifull and extensive prarie in which the ancient village of the Missouris was situated. Old Fort Orleans is said to have stood on the lower point of an Island a few miles below this place, no traces of that work are to be seen.[9]   this river is 90 yards wide at it's entrance and is said to be navigable for boats and perogues a ⟨very⟩ considerable distance.   it heads with the Rackoon river a branch of the Demoin. The country through which it passes is similar to that discribed on the large Shariton river. about the entrance of this river the lands are extreemly fertile; consisting of a happy mixture of praries and groves, exhibiting one of the most beatifull and picteresk seens that I ever beheld.—

At the distance of eight miles *Snake creek* falls in on the N. side. 18 yards wide at it's entrance. it runs parallel with the Missouri nearly it's whole extent, passing through a delightfull country, well timbered and watered.—

Thirty seven miles higher up Tigers Creek falls in on the N. side, opposite to the upper point of a large island. some excellent bottom lands in the neighbourhood of it's mouth; interior country not known.—

Fifteen miles higher up *Eubert's* river and Creek fall in on the S. side, opposite to an island, which concealed their entrances from our view. they are but small streams, head with the Mine river, and water an excellent country, consisting of a mixture of praries and woodlands.—

Twenty six miles further *Hay Cabbin* Creek falls in on the S. side. it heads near the Bluewater river and passes through a good country. the land is very fine and well timbered near it's mouth.—

Seventeen miles above, *Bluewater river* falls in on the S. side; 36 yards wide at it's entrance; and navigable but a short distance. it has one considerable fall, and several rappids well situated for water-works. it heads in an open country with Mine river, and passes through a roling country. the lands are tolerably good; it's bottom lands are wide, fertile and sufficiently covered with good timber; some beatifull natural meadows are also seen on it's borders.—

Still assending the Missouri, at the distance of 9 miles the Kanzas river disembogues itself on the South side; being 364 miles from the junction of the Missouri and Mississippi. This river takes it's rise not very distant from the principal branch of the Arkanas in a high broken sandy country, forming the Southern extremity of the *black hills*. from hence it takes it's course nearly East about 300 leagus through fertile and leavel, plains & praries, intersperced with groves of timbered land; it then enters a country equally fertile and well timbered, through which it meanders about 20 leagues further and discharges itself into the Missouri. it has been navigated 200 leagues and there is good reason to believe from the appearance of the river and country at that point that it is navigable for perogues much further perhaps nearly to it's source. The rivers Platte and Arkansas interlock their branches West of this stream. there are no obstructions to the navigation of the Kanzas, it's current is gentle, and the bed of the river composed of soft loam, gravel and sand; in the summer and autumn it's waters are transparent. about ¾ of a mile from the entrance of this river on it's North side there is a handsome bluff about 100 feet high, which furnishes an excellent situation for a fortication; there is an abundance of excellent timber for the purpose immediately at the place.— The Colateral branches of this river, and the most remarkable places on the same so far as we have been enabled to inform ourselves are as follow—[10]

Names of Creeks rivers & remarkable places	distances from each other	distances of each from the Mouth of the Kanzas	width in yards	the side of the Kanzas into which they fall
The three rivers, near each other and about the same size		10	20	N.
The Stanger's wife river	5	15	35	N.
Bealette's Creek	3	18	22	N.
Wor-rah-ru za river	1	19	40	S.
Grasshopper Creek	2	21	25	N.
Heart river	10	31	30	N.
The old Kanzas Village	9	40		N.
Full river	5	45	50	S.
Black-paint river	27	72	38	N.
Bluewater river and the present village of the Kanzas just below	8	80	60	N.
Me-war-ton-nen-gar Creek	5	85	18	N.
War-ho-ba Creek	3	88	15	S.
Republican river	15	103	200	N.

Solomon's Creek	12	115	30	N.
Little salt Creek	10	125	30	N.

On the West side of the Republican river, about sixty leagues above it's junction with the Kanzas, a small creek falls in on the S. W. side, called *Salt creek,* the water of this creek is excessively salt. salt in it's dry and granulated state, is to be found in large quantities on the borders of this stream throughout it's whole extent; the earth on which it forms, is remarkably furm, and the salt can be readily collected, free from any extranious substance, by sweeping with a brush of feathers.—

Ten miles higher up the Little river Platte falls in on the N. side, 60 yards wide at it's entrance. it heads in open plains between the Nadawa and grand rivers, and through the principal part of it's course passes through high open plains interspersed with groves of timber. 6 or seven leagues before it discharges itself into the Missouri, it meanders through a high fertile well timbered bottom nearly parallel with that river, and receives in it's course severall handsom creeks, which discharge themselves into it from the hills. at the distance of 12 leagues it's navigation is obstructed by a considerable fall, above which, it is shallow and interrupted by such a number of rappids, that it is no further practicable. This fall, and many of the rapids afford excellent situations for gristmills, and other waterworks.—

Twenty five miles further *Turkey Creek* falls in on the S. side. this creek is but small, passes through open bottoms nearly parallel with the Missouri, and in rear of an Old Kanzas Village. This creek once furnished water to an old French garrison situated near it's mouth.—[11]

Thirty three miles further *Independance* creek falls in on the S. side, a little below the second old village of the Kansas; is 22 yards wide at it's mouth; it possesses some excellent bottom lands, and waters a beatifull and fertile country consisting of high open plains and praries principally; on it's borders, and about it's entrance there is a sufficient quantity of timber. it takes it's rise with the *Stranger's wife* river, and the waters of Woolf river. we knew of no name by which this creek was called, and therefore gave it that of *Independance,* from the circumstance of our having arrived at it's mouth on the 4th of July 1804.—

At the distance of 48 miles higher up *Nodaway* river discharges itself on the N. side nearly opposite to the upper point of a large Island, which bears it's name. it is 70 yards wide some miles above it's mouth, and is navigable for perogues a very considerable distance. it takes it's rise with grand River, Nish-nah-ba-to-na, and the waters of the river Demoin; and passes in it's course to the Missouri through a fine fertile country, consisting of a mixture of woodlands and plains; the lands about it's mouth are well timbered and waterd.—

Fourteen miles further up the Missouri, Woolf river discharges itself on the S. side. it is 60 yards wide at it's entrance, and navigable for perogues a considerable distance; takes it's rise with the waters of the Kanzas and Ne-ma-haw rivers, and in it's course to the Missouri passes through a level fertile country principally open plains and praries, tho' generally well watered and possesses a sufficient quantity of timber on it's borders and near it's mouth. great quantities of grapes, plumbs & raspberries are found in the neighbourhood of this stream.—

Sixteen miles higher up, *Big Ne-ma-har* falls in on the S. side, opposite to an Island covered with willows; it is 80 yards wide, and navigable for large boats some distance, and for perogues nearly to it's source. it heads with Blue-water river, branch of the Kanzas, and throught it's whole course, passes through rich, and level plains, and praries. there is some timber on it's borders, and about it's entrance, it's tributary streams are also furnished with some timber. the country is well watered.

Three miles further the *Tarkio Creek* falls in on the N. side; twenty three yards wide at it's entrance; it is navigable for perogues a short distance. it heads with the Nadiway and passes through a tolerable country of plains and woodlands.—

Twenty five miles higher up The *Nish-nah-ba-to-na* River discharges itself opposite to the lower point of an Island on the N. Side, and is 50 yards in width at it's entrance. it heads with the Nadawa river and passes through a fertile country deversifyed with plains meadows and woodlands; considerable bodies of the latter appear in some parts of this country. at the *Bald-pated prarie,* it enters the Missouri bottom and approaches that river within 300 paces, when it returns again to the highlands, and continues it's course along the foot of the same about 30 miles before it discharges itself. at the Bald pated prarie it is 40 yards wide, possesses considerable debth of water, and is navigable many miles; the country lying between the Missouri and this river from the Balld pated prarie nearly to it's mouth, is one of the most beautiful, level and fertile praries that I ever beheld; it is from one to three miles in width. there is a considerable quantity of timber on the banks of the Missouri, and but little on the Nishnabatona.—

At the distance of eight miles higher up, the Little Ne-ma-har River falls in on the S. side, 40 yards wide. it heads with salt River branch of the River Platte, and passes through an open fertile country inersperced with groves of timber. it is navigable some miles for large perogues.— there are several handsome streams of fine water, which fall into the Missouri both above and below the mouth of this river in it's neighbourhood.—

Fifty two miles higher up, *Weeping water* Creek falls in on the S. side. it is 25 yards wide at it's entrance, heads in high broken plains near Salt river, and passes through a roling country, mostly uncovered with timber and not very fertile there is a scant proportion of timber on it banks and some clumps of trees are scattered over the face of the country. there is some handsom bottom lands on this stream, and the country is generally well wartered.—

Thirty two miles higher up, and distant 630 [*blank*] from the confluence of the Missouri and Mississippi, the great river *Platte* disembogues on the S. side. The steady, regular, and incessant velocity of this stream, is perhaps unequaled by any on eath; notwithstanding it's great rapidity the surface of the water continues smooth, except when occasionally interrupted by a boiling motion, or ebullition of it's waters. this motion of the water, is also common to the Missouri, and Mississippi, below the mouth of that river and always takes place in the most rapid part of the current; in this manner the water, is seen to rise suddenly many inches higher than the common surface, then breaking with a rappid and roling motion extends itself in a circular manner in every direction arround interrupting the smooth, tho' rappid surface of the water for many yards. this ebullition of the water of those rivers, is a singular phenomenon, nor do I know to what cause to attribute it, unless it be, the irregular motion of large masses of sand and mud at their bottoms, which are constantly changing their positions. The bed of the river Platte is composes almost entirely of white sand, the particles of which, are remarkably small and light; these collecting, from large masses, which being partially buoyed up, are hurryed along at the bottom by this impetuous torrent, with irresistible force; sometimes obstructed by each other, suddonly stop; and form large sandbars in the course of a few hours, which are again as suddenly dissipated to form others, and to give place perhaps to the deepest channel of the river. From the experiments and observations we are enabled to make, with rispect to the comparitive velocity of the currents of the Mississippi, Missouri and Platte rivers, it results, that a vessel will float in the Mississippi below the mouth of the Missouri, at the rate of four mils an hour; in the Missouri from it's junction with the Mississippi to the entrance of Osage river at the rate of 5½ to 6 miles an hour; from thence to the Kanzas, from 6½ to 7; from thence to the Platte, from 5½ to 6 miles an hour, while that of the Platte is at least 8. The current of the Missouri above the entrance of the Platte is equal to about 3½ miles an hour as far as the mouth of the Chyenne river, when it abates to about 3 miles an hour, with which it continues as far as we have yet ascended it, and if we can rely on the information of the Indians, it's current continues about the same to the falls of the Missouri, situated five hundred miles above Fort Mandan.

The river Platte does not furnish the Missouri with it's colouring matter, as has been asserted by some; but it throws into it immence quanties of sand, and gives a celerity to it's current, of which it does not abate untill it joins the Mississippi. The water of the Platte is turbid at all seasons of the year, but it is by no means as much so, as that of the Missouri; the sediment it deposits consists of small particals of white sand, while that of the Missouri is composed principally of a dark rich loam in much greater quantity.— This river has in some few instances been navigated as high as the Pania Village with perogues, but is attended with infinate labour and risk. Hunters have also ascended this river in small canoes as high as the Woolf river, a distance of 35 leagues; and the savages sometimes decend in small leather canoes made of a Buffaloe's skin. When the Plat enters the Missouri it's superior force changes and directs the current of the latter aginst it's Northern bank, compressing it [*blank*] within a channel of not more than one fifth of the width it had just before occupied. this river is 600 yards wide at it's entrance; and when we passed it, on the 21st of July, it's greatest debth of water was five feet. we were informed by one of our engages, who is well acquainted with this river for a considerable distance, that in many places it was from two to three miles wide, containing great numbers of small islands and sandbars, and that the navigation became wose, the higher he ascended. the banks of this river are very low, yet it is said, that it very seldom overflows them, or rises more than about 6 feet perpendicular above it's lowest tide.—

The position of the head of the Southern, or main branch of this river is not well asscertained; on connecting the sources of the rivers better known, it appears most probable, that it takes it's rise in the Rockey, or shineing Mountains with the Bravo or North river [Rio Grande], and the Yellow stone river, branch of the Missouri; from whence it takes it's course nearly East, passing the heads of the Arkansas at no great distance from Santa Fee, continues it's rout to the Missouri, through immence level and fertile plains and meadows, in which, no timber is to be seen except on it's own borders and those of it's tributary streams. commencing at the Missouri and ascending this river, it's principal subsidiary streams are first the *Salt river,* seven leagues distant, falls in on the S. side, and is 50 yards in width. this stream is however more remarkable for the excellency of it's salt licks and springs than for it's magnitude. the whole courant of this river is brackis in the Summer season quite to it's mouth. There are three principal salines on this stream; the first at the distance of 50 miles from it's mouth, and the others at no great distance above; two of these furnis considerable quantities of salt in it's dry and granulated state, the other furnishes Salt both granulated, and in compact masses. the granulated salt is found on the surface of a compact and hard earth composed of fine sand with a small proportion of clay producing no vegitable substance of any kind and is easily collected by sweeping it together with a soft broom or brush of feathers. the massive salt is formed by concretion, and is found either on the surface of the earth over which the water passes, or adhering to stones sticks or other furm substances washed by the salt water in it's passage. I have obtained no satisfactory account of any fossil salt being found in Louisiana, altho' repeated enquiries have been made off such as possess the best information of the interior parts of the country; I am therefore disposed to believe, that those travellers who have reported it's exhistance, must have mistaken this massive salt, formed by concretion, for that substance. saltpetre has been found in it's crystallized state in some limestone caverns near the head of this river.—

Thre leagues above the salt river a beatifull clear and gentle stream called *Corne des Cerfe*, or *hart's horn* river discharges itself on the N. side. it is about sixty yards wide. it takes it's rise in some sandy plains between the Wolf River and the Quecurre; thence runing Eastwardly approaches the Missouri within a few leagues opposite to the entrance of the Sioux river, thence veering about the S. E. passes through a fertile level country, parallel with the Missouri to the River Platte. it is navigable a considerable distance for canoes and light perogues. there is but little timber in the country though which it passes.—

Ascending the Platte five leagues further you pass the village of the Ottoes and Missouris situated on the S. side. 15 leagues higher up and on the same side, the Panias Proper, and Republican Panias reside in one large village.[12] five leagues further still ascending, the Wolf river falls in on the N. side. 400 hundred yards wide, and is navigable for Perogues between 4 and 500 miles, and for large boats a very considerable distance. This stream takes it's rise in a remarkable large fountain, situated in a level plain, equadistant between the rivers Quicurre and Plat, at some little distance below the *Cote noir* or Black Hills; from whence it passes through level and fertile plains and meadows in which there is scarcely a tree to be seen except on it's own borders, and those of it's tributary streams. the current of this river is gentle and sufficiently deep; it's bed is composed principally of a brown sand, unbroken by rocks or drift wood, and has no rappids worthy of notice from it's source to it's mouth.—

At the distance of seventy five leagues higher up, *Ringing Water* river falls in on the S. side about 300 yards wide. heads in the Black hills near the source of the Kanzas, and passes through an open tho' broken country about half it's course; it then descends into a level and fertile country composed almost entirely of open plains and meadows through which it passes to the Platte.—

Just above the black hills, though which the Platte passes, a large river said to be nearly as large as the South fork, falls in on the N. side, after haveing continued it's rout along the Western side of the Black hills for a very considerable distance. the distance from the entrance of this river to the mouth of the Platte is not well asscertained. This is usually called the Paducas fork; it heads with the Bighorn river, branch of the Yellow Stone, in some broken ranges of the Rockey mountains. it's upper portion passes through a hilly, broken and Mountanous country, possessing considerable quantities of timber; it then descends to a plain open and level country lying between the Rockey Mounts and the black hills, through which it passes to join the Platte. there are some considerable bodies of woodland on and near this stream.—

The smaller branches of the rivers Platte & Wolf so far as they are known to us are as follows; they uniformly water a level open country generally fertile.—[13]

Names of streams falling into the *Platte*	distances from the Missouri in leagues	width in yards	side of the river on which they discharge
Shell river	27	30	N.
Short Leg river	40	30	S.
The Falling Creek	70	20	S.
Tose of the Loups, or Wolf River			
Little willow Creek	42	25	N.
Mustle shell Creek	45	20	N.
Elk Creek	49	26	S.
Gravley Creek	54	20	S.
White Bluff creek	64	20	S.
Deepwater Creek	79	25	S.

[Ed: Here is placed Clark's fuller table of affluents of the Platte and Loup rivers from an undated document at the Missouri Historical Society. Lewis's narrative resumes immediately after the table.]

The names of Rivers, Creeks and the most Remarkable places on the Platt River, from information

	Distances from one place to the other in Leagues	Distance from the Missouri by water, in Leagues	The Width of the Rivers & Creeks in yards—	The side on which they mouth or are Situated either N or S
To the mouth of the Salene or Salt River	7	7	50	S E
" " " Corne des Cerfe or Harts				
Horn River	3	10	60	N. W.
To the Ottoes Village	5	15	—	S.
To the Panies Creek	10	25	20	S
To the mouth Coque, or Shel River	2	27	30	N
To the Grand Ponia Village	3	30	—	S.
To the Fork of the River or mouth of Loup or Wolf River	5	35	400	N
" " mouth of Short Leg River up the plate	5	40	30	S.
" " " Deer Creek do	12	52	28	S.
" " " falling Creek	18	70	20	S
To the forks River called Ringing Water about Up the Wolf Fork	40	110	300	S
To the pt. *Saule* or little Willow Creek	7	42	25	N.
" " Mustle Shell Creek	3	45	20	N
" " Elk ⟨River⟩ Creek	4	49	26	S
" " Graveley Creek	5	54	20	S
" " White Bluff Creek	10	64	25	S.
To the Loups or Wolf Villages on this River	7	71	—	N
" " Deep Water Creek	8	79	25	S

Three miles above the entrance of the river Platte Butterfly Creek falls in on the S. side, 18 yards wide, heads in the plains between the Hart's Horn river and the Missouri; the courntry fertile with but little timber.—

7 miles higher Musquetoe Creek falls in on the N. side; it is 22 yards wide and heads with the Nishnahbatona river in an open country. the Missouri bottom through which it passes is about 6 miles wide, level, extreemly fertile and about one half well covered with timber.

20 miles further *Indian Creek* falls in opposite to the lower point of an Island on the N. side, three miles above an old Ayouway's village.[14] it heads in the highlands a few miles back; passes through the Missouri bottom and approaches the river within 20 feet, 6 miles above it's entrance; at this point it is 5 feet higher than the water of the Missouri. it is 15 yards wide.—

8 miles higher up Bowyer's river falls in on the N. side. it is 25 yards wide, and navigable for perogues some distance; passes through a country tolerably fertile, with but little timber.—

Twelve miles above the mouth of Bowyer's river we arrive at the *Council Bluff* on the S. side. this is one of the points, which in our statistical view of the Indian Nations of Louisiana, we have recommended as an eligible position for a trading establishment. it is a delightfull situation for a fortification, & commands a view of the river both above and below for a considerable distance. the base of the Bluff is washed by the river about a mile; it is about 60 feet high & nearly perpendicular; as it's lower extremity it leaves the river nearly at right angles, descending with a handsome and regular declivity on it's lower side about forty feet to a high, level, fertile and extensive bottom, lying between itself and the river. the top of the bluff is a level plain from one to two miles in width, and about five miles in length. This place would be sufficiently convenient for the Ottoes, Missouris, Panias Proper, Panias, Loups, Panias Republican, Poncaras, Mahas, & the Yanktons Ahnah.[15] if peace is established between the various tribes of Indians inhabiting this immence country, it is more than probable, that this post would also be visited by manty of those wandering bands, who inhabit the country west of the black hills. The principal difficulty which will attend the erection of a fortification at this place is the want of proper timber with which to build. there is a sufficient quantity of a species of poplar common to all the bottom lands of the Missouri, called by the French inhabitants of the Illinois—Liard, and by the Americans Cotton-wood. it is a soft white wood, by no means dureable, and of which it is extreemly difficult to make plank or scantling. There is some oak in the neighbourhood but it is of an inferior quality. I concieve that the cheepest and best method would be to build of brick, the eath appears to be of an excellent quality for brick, and both lime and sand are convenient. The drift wood of the Missouri will always supply a sufficient quantity of fuell independant of that in the neighbourhood. with rispect to quality and quantity of timber, this bluff is better situated than any other for upwards of a thousand miles above it, and equal to any below it for many miles.—

Leaving the council Bluff and ascending the Missouri 39 miles we arrive at the mouth of Soldier's river 30 yards wide. it heads with the river Demoin, and passes to the Misouri through an open, level and fertile country. is navigable for Perogues a considerable distance.

44 miles further up *Ye-yeau War da-pon* or *stone river* falls in on the N. side. this river is known to the traders of the Illinois by the name of little *Sioux river,* but as they have given the appellation of Sioux to four distinct streams we thought it best to adopt the name given it by the Siouxs, to whos country it's entrance forms the lower boundary on the Missouri. this stream is 80 yards wide at it's entrance; takes it's rise in a small lake nine miles distant from the River demoin, with which, it communicates in high water through a small channel; the river demoin is but shallow at this point tho' it is 70 or 80 yards wide, and said to be navigable. this stream is navigable from it's souce to the Missouri for perogues or canoes, passes through a broken country with but little timber. the land is tolerably fertile. an Easterly and most navigable fork of this river is formed by the discharge of Lake Dispree [d'Esprit], 22 leagues in circumference; this lake is long not very wide and approaches the river demoin within 15 miles. the country between the Demoin and Lake Dispree is level, with but little timber, and interrupted with a number of small lakes or ponds.—

From the entrance of the *ye-yeau War-da-pon,* to the Old Maha Village, a distance of 100 miles, there is not a single stream which discharges itself into the Missouri, that is worthy of notice.[16] *The Maha creek,* on which the last village occupied by that nation was situated at some little distance from the Missouri, discharges itself on the S. side through several channels. this creek is but small, takes it's rise in some level and fertile praries near the Hart's Horn river and passes through a delightfull country in it's course to the Missouri. the distance from the old Maha village to the Council Bluff is 90 miles by land.

16 miles higher up Floyds river falls in on the N. side 38 yards wide. This river is the smallest of those called by the trades of the Illinois the *two rivers of the Sioux,* but which with a view to discrimination, we have thought proper to call Floyd's river in honor of Sergt. Charles Floyd, a worthy and promising young man, one of our party who unfortunately died on the 20th of August 1804, and was buried on a high bluff just below the entrance of this stream. This river takes it's rise with the waters of the rivers Sioux and Demoin; from whence it takes it's course nearly S. W. to the Missouri, meandering through level and fertile, plains and meadows, intersperced with groves of timber. it is navigable for perogues nearly to it's source.

3 miles above Floyds river, The river Sioux disembogues on the N. side above a bluff; it is one hundred and ten yards wide at it's entrance, and navigable nearly to it's source; with the exception of one fall of about twenty feet high, situated 70 leagues from it's mouth. it takes it's rise with the St. Peter's and Vulter rivers, in a high broken and woody country called the *Hills of the prarie.* it waters a deversifyed country, generally level fertile and uncovered with timber; in some parts particularly near the falls, it is broken & stoney, and in others, intersected by a great number of small lakes which possess some timber generally on their borders. at no great distances below the falls and in a remarkable bend of the river, three handsom streams fall in on it's East Side at no great distance from each other; the 1st ascending is the *Prickley Pear* river, which takes it's rise in some small lakes near the Demoin. the 2nd *The River of the Rock,* passes the head of the River Demoin, and takes it's rise in small lakes. the third is called *red pipe Stone river,* which heads with the waters of the River St. Peters.[17] the country watered by this last river is remarkable for furnishing a red stone, of which the savages make their most esteemed pipes. the

Indians of many nations travel vast distances to obtain this stone, and it is asserted, tho' with what justice I will not pretend to determine, that all nations are at peace with each other while in this district of country, or on the waters of this river.—

Sixty miles above the Sioux river the *White Stone river* discharges itself on the N. side.   it is 30 yards wide at it's entrance, heads in a chain of Nobs West of the bend of the Sioux river, and passes in it's whole course through level beautifull and fertile plains and meadows entirely destitute of timber.   it is not navigable.

20 miles higher up *little* bow creek falls in on the S side, below an old Maha village.   it is 20 yards wide and waters a beautifull, fertile, plain, and open country.   the remains of two small ancient fortifications, are found on this creek at a short distance from it's entrance.[18]

12 Miles higher up, and distant 974 from the junction of the Missouri and Mississippi, the *river James* discharges itself; it is 90 yards wide, and navigable for perogues a very considerable distance; it's current is gentle and it's bed composed of mud and sand.   it takes it's rise with Chyinme river, branch of Red river which discharges itself into Lake Winnipic. This steam passes through an open country of plains and meadows through it's whole course.   the land is generally fertile, and a scant proportion of timber is found on the banks of the river. The Siouxs annually hold a fair[19] on some part of this river, in the latter end of May.   thither the Yanktons of the North, and the Sissitons, who trade with a Mr. Cammaron[20] on the head of the St. Peter's river, bring guns, pouder & balls, Kettles, axes, knives, and a variety of European manufactures, which they barter to the 4 bands of *Tetons* and the *Yanktons Ahnah,* who inhabit the borders of the Missouri & upper part of the River Demoin, and receive in exchange horses, leather lodges, and buffaloe robes, which they have either manufactured, or plundered from other Indian nations on the Misouri and west of it. This traffic is sufficient to keep the Siouxs of the Missouri tolerably well supplyed with arms and amunition, thus rendering them independant of the trade of the Missouri, and enableing them to continue their piratical aggressions on all who attempt to ascend that river, as well as to disturb perpetually the tranquility of their Indian neighbours. I am perfectly convinced that untill such measures are taken

by our government as will effectually prohibit all intercourse or traffic with the Siouxs by means of the rivers Demoin and St. Peters, that the Citizens of the United States can never enjoy, but partially, those important advantages which the navigation of the Missouri now presents. it appears to me that with the assistance of the garrisons of St. Louis, and Chicargoo, with the establishment of two others, the one at or near the entrance of the Oisconsin and the other on the Mississippi at Sand lake, that the passages of the trades to the rivers Demoin and St. Peters ⟨might⟩ would be sufficiently guarded. by prohibiting the trade with the Siouxs through the St. Peters and Demoin for a few years, they will be made to feel their dependance on the will of our government for their supplies of merchandize, and in the course of two or three years, they may most probably be reduced to order without the necessity of bloodshed. in the mean time the trade of the Missouri will be acquiring a strength, and regularity within itself, and an influence among other indian nations, which dould not be easily interrupted by the Siouxs, when the government should hereafter tink proper to reestablish an intercourse with them, through the channels of the St. Peter's and Demoin rivers.—

At the distance of 38 miles higher up *Plumb Creek* falls in on the N. side. this creek is but small, heads in the highlands a few miles back, and passes through beatifull level and fertile praries in it's course to the Missouri.—

8 miles higher up *white Paint Creek* falls in on the S. side, 28 yards in width. it takes it's rise in a broken Hilly and open country between the Quicurre and Hart's horn rivers. passes through a broken country with some handsome plains an[d] praries, it is not navigable. but possesses many excellent situations for grist mills and other waterworks.

6 miles above this creek and at the distance of 1026 from the entrance of the Missouri, the *River Quiccurre* [X: *Qui-court*] or *rappid river*, discharges itself on the S. side; where it is one hundred and fifty two yards wide. this river takes it's rise in the Black hills, about one hundred leagues West of it's mouth, and passes through a variagated country. at it's source and for seventy five leagues below the country is mountanous rockey and thickly covered with timber, principally pine; the bed of the river is interrupted by immence quanties of loose and broken rocks, many ledges of

rocks also lie acoss this stream over which it tumbles perpendicularly from 6 to 15 feet. in this country the Indians as well as some of the French hunters report the existence many mines. some of lead, others of a metal resembleing lead, but of a lighter colour more dense & equally malleable; it is not stated to be silver. this metal is said to be readily extracted from it's ore which is a loose earth, with the heat of a common fire of wood. there are said to be some sand plains of considerable extent lying between the upper portion of this river and the Hart's Horn river. the country on it's lower portion for 25 leagues consists of open plains and meadows, with but a very small proportion of timber; the bed of the river here consists entirely of a coarse brown sand. the velocity of it's current is nearly or quite equal to that of Platte. it is not navigable a single mile.—

8 mile above the rappid rive, the *Poncar* river disembogues on the S side, 30 yards wide. Three miles from the moth of this river on it S. side the Poncars resided a few years since in a fortifyed village, but have now joined the Mahas and become a wandering people. Poncar river heads in the open plains not far from the mouth of White river, and runs nearly parallel with the Missouri passing through some tolerably fertile plains and meadows.—

At the distance of 114 miles higher up, White river discharges itself on the S. side. it is 300 yards wide at it's entrance, and is navigable for boats and perogues for many leagues. this river is perfectly the Missouri in miniture, resembleing it in every particular. it takes it's rise short of the black hills, with the waters of the Cyenne and rappid rivers, in an open country; from whence it passes through level and fertile plains & meadows, in which there is scarsely any timber to be seen. some pine most probably grows on it's borders, I discovered several sticks of that timber among the driftwood at it's entrance.

22 Miles higher up, the Three rivers of the Siouxs pass discharge themselves, on the N. side, opposite to a large Island well covered with timber. the 1st of these streams which we meet with as we ascend is 35 yards wide, and is navigable for perogues some distance, with a few obstructions of rappids or shoals. it heads with James's river, and possesses but little timber on it's borders. the country on the upper side of this river is a

high level and fertile plain of many leagues in exten the lower side generally broken Praries, neither possessing any timber worthy of mention.   the
other two streams are small, extending only about 8 miles back, and water
a country of high handsome and fertile plains, with but little timber.—

From hence to the commencement of the *big bend* is twenty miles; in
this distance you pass four small Creeks, which discharge themselves on
the S. side, and one on the N. side; these creek take their rise at the distance
of 6 or 7 miles in the open plains, and possess but little timber.   the bottoms of the Missouri are generally wide and but badly timbered.   the big
bend of the Missouri lies in a circular form, and is 30 miles around, while
it is only one mile and a quarter across the gorge.—

5 miles above the uper extremity of this bend *Tylor's river* falls in, on the
S. side.   this river is about 35 yards wide, and is navigable some miles for
perogues.   it takes it's rise in an open country between the White river
and river Teton, and passes through a level fertile and open country.   below the mouth of this river on the Missouri there is an extensive bottom
well covered with timber, consisting principally of red cedar.

55 miles higher up, the Teton River discharges itself on the S. side.   this
river is seventy yards wide, and is navigable for perogues many leagues.
it heads with the waters of the Chyenne and White rivers, and passes
through open and fertile plains and meadows.   possesses some timber
on it's borders, as do also it's tributary streams.   in these plains there is
rarely an instance of a tree to be seen.—

47 miles above the entrance of the Teton river and 1327 from the Mouth
of the Missouri, the rive Chyenne disembogues on the S. side, and is about
400 yards wide at it's entrance, and is navigable for perogues to it's forks
near the black hills, a distance of 200 Miles by land, nearly due west from
it's entrance. The Northern branch of this river penetrates the Black hills,
and passes through a high broken well timbered country to it's source, the
Southern fork takes it's rise in the Black hills, on their E side, and passes
through a broken country covered with timber, to it's junction with the N
fork; from whence united, they take their course through a woody and
broken country fror some few leagus, then entering an open fertile and
level country it continues it's rout to the Missouri   the timber of the Black
hills, and on this river near them, consists of pine and Cedar principally;

on it's lower portion Cottonwood and Cedar, of which however there is but a scant proportion and that confined immediately to the river hills and bottoms. about the entrance of this river we have recommended an establishment for the purpose of trading with the Indians. it's position is central and sufficiently convenient for a number of Nations and tribes; but the difficulty of procuring timber for the purpose of building is very considerable, tho' in this particular it is equal to any other for an emence distance both above and below it. a difficulty also arises with rispect to lime of which there is none in it's neighbourhood. large quantities of tar may be procured on the river near the Black hills, and may be readily brought down the river. tar and sand in the proportion of one gallon to the Bushel, make a furm and strong cement. if an establishment is made at this place, the work must of necessity be principally formed of brick; there being no stone and but little timber. the drift-wood of the Missouri will supply an ample quantity of fuell.—

78 miles higher up, *Otter Creek* falls in on the N. side, 22 yards wide, navigable a few miles in high water. it takes it's rise in open plains nearly E. of it's entrance, and passes through a similar country; very little timber in it's vicinity.—

3[21] miles higher up, and on the S. side, the *Sar-war-car-na* river discharges itself, 90 yards wide. it is navigable for perogues 40 or 50 leagues; takes it's rise short of the Black Hills with the waters of the Chyenne; from whence it meanders through fertile and level plains and meadows, almost entirely destitue of timber.—

22[22] miles above, *We-ter-hoo* river discharges itself on the S. side. this stream is 120 yards wide; and may be navigated nearly to it's source in the Black Hills. It passes through a country simalar to that discribed on the *Sar-war-kar-na*.

2 miles higher up, and the same distance below an island on which the lower village of the Ricaras, the river *Ma-ro-pa* falls in, on the the S. side; it is 25 yards wide at it's entrance; takes it's rise about 5 leagues west of the entrance of the *war-re-con-ne* river, in open plains. it passes through an uneven roling country, without timber, and but badly watered, for the distance of about 50 miles, nearly parallel to the Missouri, before it discharges

itself.— The Ricaras obtain a red and black earth on the borders of this stream, which they use for the purpose of painting their skins, or ornamenting their Buffaloes robes, which at all seasons of the year constitutes a principal article of their dress.—

Leaving the mouth of this river and ascend the Missouri, at the distance of 2½ miles you pass the 1st Ricara village, from 3½ to 4 miles further, you pass two others situated on the South side near the river.[23]   still ascending at the distance of 24 miles above the entrance of *Ma-ro-pa* river, the *Stone Idol Creek* falls in on the N. side; 18 yards wide.   it heads in a small lake a few leagues distant and passes through a rich level plain; the land is fertile but without timber.   a canoe can pass from the river to this lake.

37 miles higher up, *Sar-kar-nah* or *Beaver Creek* falls in on the N. side, at the lower point of an Island.   about 20 yards wide, heads in some small lakes a few miles from the river, and passes through a level fertile and open country.

3 Miles further still ascending, and at the distance of 1498 miles from the entrance of the Missouri, *War-re-con-ne* river falls in on the N. side just above an island.   it is 35 yards wide at it's entrance, and is navigable in high water to it's source.   takes it's rise in an assemblage of small lakes, in level and open plains, not very distant from the head of James's river.   in it's course to the Missouri it passes through extensive, level and fertile, plains and meadows, in which scarsely a tree is to be seen.—

13 miles higher up, the *Cannon Ball* river falls in on the S side, and is 140 yards wide.   it is navigable for boats a considerable distance, with a few interruptions of rappids, and for perogues and Canoes nearly to it's source.   it takes it's rise in a level country with the Chesschetar and the waters of the Wetarhoo rivers, from whence in it's course to the Misouri it passes through a variety of country, some broken & partially timbered, near it's source; other parts broken, hilly and bare of timber, and in others beautifull and extensive plains and meadows, with but little timber, all sufficiently fertile, and some extreemly so.   there is some Cottonwood, Ash and Elm on it's borders.

5 miles higher up the *Fish Creek* discharges itself on the N Side; 28

yards wide. it takes it's rise in small lakes, in the open plains, and passes through handsome plains and meadows, in it's course to the Missouri; but little timber on it's borders.—

35 miles higher up, *Ches-che-tar,* or heart river falls in on the S. W. side; 38 yards wide; not navigable except in high water, and then but a short distance. it heads with the waters of the Knife river in open plains S. W. of the turtle mountain. in it's course to the Missouri it passes through open plains and meadows, generally fertile, and always untimbered. there is some Ash, Cottonwood, and Elm on it's borders.

14 miles higher up, Hunting creek discharges itself on the S. side. it's bottom lands are wide and fertile with but little timber, takes it's rise in, and passes through an open country of high plains.—

50 miles higher up at the distance of 1,615 miles from the junction of the Missouri and Mississippi, the Knife river falls in near the Village of the Ahwahharways on the S. side—a little above the Mandans. this river is about 80 yards wide, but is not navigable, except for a few days in the spring of the year. It takes it's rise in the turtle Mountains about 90 Miles N. W. of it's mouth, and passes through an open fertile country. there is a considerable quantity of timber on the upper part of this river, and much more on it's borders generally, than is met with on streams of the same size in this open country. The Minetares, Ahwahharways, and Mandans hunt principally on this river, and many of Minetares pass the winter on it, in small parties, of 5 ore six families.—

As we have only ascended the Missouri, a few miles above the Mouth of Knife river, the subsequent discription of this river, and it's subsidiary streams are taken altogether from Indian Information. the existence of these rivers, their connection with each other, and their relative positions with rispect to the Missouri, I conceive are entitled to some confidence. information has been obtained on this subject, in the course of the winter, from a number of individuals, questioned seperately and at different times. the information thus obtained has been carefully compared, and those points only, in which they generally agreed, have been retained, their distances they give, by days travel, which we have estimated at 25 miles pr. day.—[24]

About fifteen miles above the mouth of Knife river, the *E-pe,-Âh-zhah,* or *Miry river* discharges itself on the N. Side.   it is but an inconsiderable stream as to width, but extends itself through level and open plains about 30 miles N. E. of it's entrance, taking it's rise in some small lakes, strongly impregnated with Glauber Salts.   not navigable.[25]

Ascending the Missouri about one hundred miles further, the *E-mâh-tark', Ah'-zhah* or Little Missouri discharges itself on the S. side.   about the width of Knife river.   takes it's rise in the Nothern extremity of the Black-hills.   and passes through a broken country with but little timber.   it passes near the turtle mountain in it's course to the Missouri.   it is said not to be navigable in consequence of it's rappidity and shoals.—

About 117 miles higher up, the *Ok-hah-Âh-zhâh*, or *White earth river*, discharges itself on the N. side.   it is said to be about the size of the Cannon-ball river; takes it's rise N. Westwardly from it's mouth in level open plains with the waters of the S. fork of the Saskashawin river, and passes through an open and level country generally without timber some timber on the borders of this stream.   it is navigable nearly to it's source, which is said not to be very distant, from the establishment of the N. West Company on the S. branch of the Saskashawin.   if this information be correct it is highly probable that a line drawn due West from the lake of the Woods, in conformity to our treaty with Great Britain; would intersect the waters of this river, if so the boundary of the United States would pass Red river between the entrance of the Assinniboin and Lake Winnipic, including those rivers almost entirely, and with them the whole of the British trading establishments on the red Lake, Red river and the Assinniboin.   should the portage between the Saskashawin and *White earth* river, prove not to be very distant or difficult, it is easy to conceive the superior advantages, which the Missouri offers as a rout to the Athabasca country, compared with that commonly traveled by the traders of Canada.—

About 3 miles above the mouth of *White Earth* river the Meé,-ah'-zah, or *Yellowstone river* discharges itself on the S. side.   this river is said to be nearly as large as the Missouri, but is more rappid.   it takes it's rise in the Rocky mountains, with the waters of a river on which the Spaniards reside; but whether this stream be the N. *river,* or the waters of the Gulph of California, our information dose not enable us to determine.   from it's source it takes it's course for many miles through broken ranges of the

Rocky mountains, principally broken, and stoney, and thickly timbered. the vallies said to be wide in many places and the lands fertile. after leaving the Rocky mountains it descends into a country more level, tho' still broken, fertile and well timbered. this discription of country continues as far down as the *Oke-tar-pas-ah-ha,* where the river enters an open level and fertile country through which it continues it's rout to the Missouri; even in this open country it possesses considerable bodies of well timbered land. there are no stream[s] worthy of notice which discharge themselves into this river on the N. side, the country between this river, and the Missouri being watered by the *Mussle shell* river. the yellow Stone river is navigable at all seasons of the year, for boats or perogues to the foot of the Rocky Mountains, near which place, it is said to be not more than 20 miles distant from the most southernly of the three forks of the Missouri, which last is also navigable to this point. if Indian information can be relied on, this river waters one of the fairest portions of Louisiana, a country not yet hunted, and abounding in animals of the fur kind. The bed of this river is formed of sand gravel and yellow rock. from the great rapidity of this stream after it enters the rocky mountains, it is said not be navigable. we are informed that there is a sufficiency of timber near the mouth of this river for the purpose of erecting a fortification, and the necessary buildings. in point of position, we have no hesitation in declaring our belief, of it's being one of the most eligible and necessary, that can be chosen on the Missouri, as well in a governmental point of view, as that of affording to our citizens the benefit of a most lucrative fur trade. this establishment might be made to hold in check the views of the British N. West Company on the fur-trade of the upper part of the Missouri, which we believe it is their intention to panopolize if in their power. They have for several years maintained a partial trade with the Indian nations on the Missouri near this place, over land from their establishment at the entrance of Mouse river on the Assinniboin, unlicenced by the Spanish government, then the sovereigns of the country. But since the U' States have acquired Louisiana, we are informed, that relying on the privilege extended to them by our treaty with Great Britain, they intend fixing a permanent establishment on the Missouri near the mouth of Knife river, in the course of the present summer. if this powerfull and ambitious company, are suffered uninterruptedly to prosecute their trade with the nations inhabiting the upper portion of the Missouri, and thus acquire an influence with those people; it is not difficult to conceive the obstructions, which they might hereafter through the medium of that influence, oppose to the will of our government, or the navigation of the Missouri. whether the privileges extended to British subjects, under existing treaties with that power, will equally effect a territory not in our possession at the time those treaties were entered into, is not for me to determine; but it appears to me, that in this rispect Liouisiana is differently situated, from the other territory of the United States.—

The tributary streams of the Yellow stone river so far as we have been enabled to inform ourselves are as follow.—

Names of the subsidiary streams of the Yellow Stone river, ascending from it's entrance	distance from each other & of the 1st from the mouth of the river	Side on which they discharge
	Miles	
Oke-tar-pas-ah-ha	75	S.
War-rah-sash, or powder river	75	S.
Le-ze-ka, or tongue river	50	S.
Mar-shas-kap river	100	S.
Ark-tar-ha river	125	S.
Ar-sar-ta, or big-horn	75	S.
Stinking cabbin creek [26]	175	S.

About one hundred fifty miles on a direct line, a little to the N. of West, a river falls in on the N. side called by the Minetares *Ah-mâh-tâh, ru-shush-sher* or the river which scolds at all others. this river they state to be of considerable size, and from it's position and the direction which they give it, we believe it to be the channel through which, those small streams, on the E side of the Rocky Mountain, laid down by Mr. Fidler,[27] pas to the Missouri. it takes it's source in the Rocky mountains S. of the waters of the Askow or bad river. and passes through a broken country in which, there is a mixture of woodlands and praries. it is worthy of remark, that the Missouri in it's course from the mouth of the yellow stone river to the

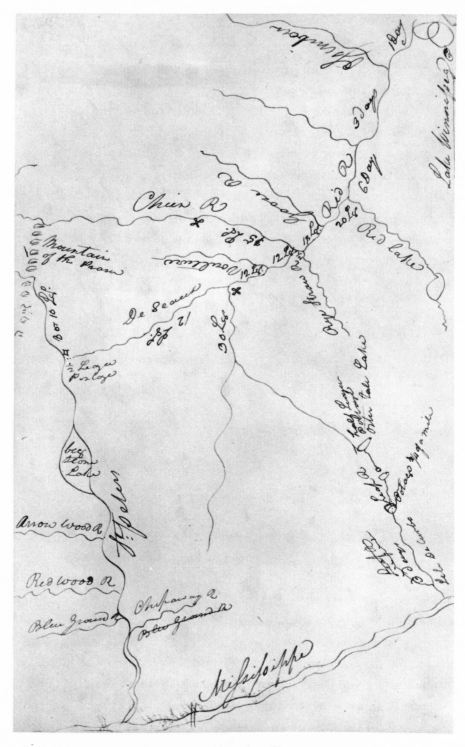

9. Mississippi River and Tributaries in Present Minnesota,
undated (winter 1804–5), Codex C, p. 155

entrance of this rivr. passes considerably further to the North than the mouths of either of these rivers; this information we have received since our map has been completed. it will be observed by reference to the map, that there are no streams falling into the Askow on it's S. side, from which, it is probable, that the country nearly to it's borders, is watered by the streams of some other river, and as the Missouri runs considerably N. above the Mouth of the Yellow stone river, and that on it's nothern border no stream of any magnitude discharges itself except the scolding river, the probability is that the country very near to the Askow is watered by the little rivulets of the Missouri, and the branches of the s[c]olding river. I have scarsely a doubt, but that a line drawn due West from the Lake of the Woods, in conformity to our treaty with Great Britain, will intersect the waters of the Missouri, if not the main body of that river itself.

About 120 miles on a direct line, nearly S. W. the Mah-tush,-ah-zhah, or Muscle shell river falls in on the S. side. this river is about the size of the Cannonball river, heads in a range of mountains which commence about the falls of the Missouri, and extending themselves nearly South terminate near the yellow stone river. this stream passes through a broken and woody country. The woody country commences on the Missouri just above the mouth of this river.—

About 120 miles further a little to the S. of West, on a direct line, the great falls of the Missouri are situated. this is discribed by the Indians as a most tremendious Cataract. they state that the nois it makes can be heard at a great distance. that the whole body of the river tumbles over a precipice of solid and even rock, many feet high; that such is the velocity of the water before it arrives at the precipice, that it projects itself many feet beyond the base of the rock, between which, and itself, it leaves a vacancy sufficiently wide for several persons to pass abrest underneath the torrent, from bank to bank, without weting their feet. they also state that there is a fine open plain on the N. side of the falls, through which, canoes and baggage may be readily transported. this portage they assert is not greater than half a mile, and that the river then assumes it's usual appearance, being perfectly navigable.—

About 15 miles further on a direct line a little to the S. of W. a large stream called *Mah-pah-pah,-ah-zhah,* or *Medecine river* falls in on the N.

side. this river heads in the rocky Mountains opposite to a river which also takes it's rise in the same mountains and which running West discharges itself into a large river, which passes at no great distance from the Rocky mountains, runing from N to South. it passes through a mountanous, broken and woody country. not navigable in consequence of it's rapidity and shoals.

About 6o miles further on a direct line nearly S. W. the Missouri passes through the first connected chain of the Rocky mountains. and is said to be rapid and shoaly from hence to the second chain of the rocky Mountains a distance of 75 miles further, about the same course last mentioned. above this second range of mountains the current of the Missouri is said to be smoth even and gentle; here two small rivers fall in on the S. side, receiving their waters from the west side these mountains between the Missouri and the Yellow stone river.

Still proceeding S. W. about 75 miles further the Missouri divides itself into three nearly equal branches just above a third chain of very high mountains, all these streams are navigable for some distance. the most Nothern is the largest, and is navigable to foot of chain of high mountains, being the ridge which divides the waters of the Atlantic from those of the Pacific ocean. the Indians assert that they can pass in half a day from the foot of this mountain on it's East side to a large river which washes it's Western base, runing from S to N. at no great distance below the *Flat head* Indians live in one considerable village on the western border of this river. this is the utmost extent of the war exurtions of the Minetares and we have therefore been unable to acquire any information further West than the view from the top of thes mountains extend. The Indians inform us that the country on the Western side of this river consists of open & level plains like those they themselves inhabit, with a number of barren sandy nobs irregularly scattered over the face of the country; the E. side of the river, betwen it and the mountains is broken, and thickly covered with pine. they state that there are no buffaloe west of the second range of the Rockey mountains, and that the Flat heads live principally on a large fish, which they take in the river on which they reside. The Snake Indians also frequently visit this Western river at certain seasons of the year, for the purpose of taking fish which they dry in the sun and transport on horses to their vilages on the three forks of the Missouri. This river we suppose to be the S. fork of the Columbia, and the fish the Salmon, with which we are informed the Columbia river abounds.— this river is said to be rapid but as far as the Indian informants are acquainted with it is not intercepted with shoals. it's bed consists principally of sand and gravel.

The waters of the Missouri are transparent at all seasons of the year above the falls.

With rispect to other rivers, their Subsidiary streams, and their connection with other rivers and streams, the map which is herewith forwarded, will give you a more perfict idea, than a detaled discription of them would do. the mountains, salines, trading establishments, and all the other remarkable places, so far as known to us, are also laid down on this map.—

Meriwether Lewis Capn.

1st U' S Regt. Infty.

[Clark]   *[undated, winter 1804–5]*[28]

A Summary Statement of the Rivers, Creeks and most remarkable places; their Distances &c. from the mouth of the Missouri as high up that River as was explored in the year 1804 by Captain's Lewis and Clark.

Common Names	Distance from one place to the other on the River, in miles	Distancies from the Mouth of the Missouri	The width of the Rivers and Creeks at their mouths, comptd. in yards	The Side of the Missouri on which they are Situated,—
	miles	*miles up*	*yards*	*Side*
To the village of St. Charles	21	21	—	N. E
" Bon-homme Creek	12	33	—	S W.
" Osage Womans River	9	42	30	N. E

" a Cave Called the Tavern	5	47	—	S W.
" the Chaurette above a Small village	22	69	20	N E
" Shepherdess Creek	15	84	—	S W.
" Gasconnade River	19	103	157	S W
" Muddy River	15	118	50	N E
" Osage River	19	137	397	S W.
" Murrow Creek	5	142	20	S W.
" Cedar Island & Creek	7	149	20	N. E
" the Lead Mine Hill	10	159	—	S W.
" Manitou Creek	9	168	20	S W.
" Split Rock Creek	9	177	20	N. E.
" Saline or Salt River	3	180	30	S. W.
" Manitou River	10	190	30	N. E.
" Good womans River	9	199	35	N. E.
" Mine River	9	208	70	S W.
" the Arrow Prairie	8	216	—	S. W.
" " Two Charliton Riv's	14	230	30 [&] 70	N. E.
To the Antient Village of the Missouri nation, near which place Fort Orleans Stood	18	248	—	N. E
To the mouth of *Grand River*	4	252	90	N. E
" Snake Creek	8	260	18	N. E.
To the antient village of the Little Osage Indians	12	272	—	S. W.
To Tigers Creek & Island	25	297	25	N. E.
" *Eueberts* Isld. Creek & River	15	312	—	S. W.
" Fire Praire Creek	14	326	Small	S W
" Hay Cabin Creek	12	338	20	S. W.
" the *Coal banks*	7	345	—	S. W.
" Blue water River	10	355	30	S. W.
" Kanzas River	9	364	230	S. W.

" Little River Platte	10	374	60	N. E.
To the Wau-car-ba, War-con-da Island opposit the 1st Antient Kanzas Village on the S. W. Side	30	404	—	—
To the Indipendance Creek a mile below the 2nd old Kanzas village on the S W. Side	28	432	22	S. W.
To St. Michaels Prairie	28	460	—	N. E
To Nadawa River	20	480	70	N. E.
" Wolf or 'Loup' River	14	494	60	S W.
" Big *Ne-ma-har* River	16	510	80	S W
" *Tar-ki-o* Creek	3	513	23	N E.
" *Neesh-nah-ba-to-na*, R	25	538	50	N. E
Little *Ne-ma-har* River	8	546	40	S. W.
To the Bald-pated prarie at which place the *Neesh-nah-ba-to-ne* within 300 yards of the Missouri	23	569	—	N. E
To the Weepingwater Creek	29	598	25	S W
" " Platte River	32	630	600	S W
" " 'Papillion' or Butterfly Creek	3	633	18	S. W.
" " Musquetor Creek	7	640	22	N. E.
" " Antient Ottoes Village	11	651	—	S. W.
To a Bluff above an antient Ayauwais Village	6	657	—	N. E.
To Bowyers Creek	11	668	25	N. E.
To the *Council Bluffs*	12	680	—	S. W.
" Soldiers River	39	719	40	N. E.
To 'Pitite River de Sioux" *Ea-neah-wau-de pon* or Stone River	44	763	80	N. E.
Wau-can-da Bad Spirit Creek	55	818	Small	S. W.
Around a bend of the Missouri to the N. E. the gorge of which is 974 yd.	21	839	—	—

To an Island 3 miles N. E. of the Mahar Old Village, S W.	27	866	—	S. W.
To Floyds River (above a Bluff)	13	879	38	N. E.
" Grand Sioux River	3	882	110	N. E.
To the Commencement of the Coperas, Cobalt, perites, & alum Bluffs	24	906	—	S. W.
To the *Hot* or *Burning* Bluffs	30	936	—	S. W.
" White Stone Creek	6	942	30	N. E.
To pitite Arc, an Old Mahar Villg. at the mouth of little Bow Creek	20	962	15	S. W.
" River Jacque	12	974	90	N. E.
" the Calumet Bluffs	10	984	—	S W.
" an Antient Fortification	18	1002	—	S. W. pt.
To White paint Creek	18	1020	28	S W.
" *"Quicurre"* or Rapid River	6	1026	152	S. W
" Poncar River	8	1034	30	S. W.
" the Dome & Burrow (or village) of Barking Squirels	20	1054	—	S. W.
To the Island of Cedar	42	1096	—	
" White River (*handsom Spot*)	52	1148	300	S W.
To the thre Rivers of the Sioux Pass opposit an Island	22	1170	{ 1.35 2.8 3.6 }	N E
To an Island in the comencement of the big bend	20	1190		N. E
To the upper part of the big bend or "Grand de tourte," the gorge of which is one mile & a quatr.	30	1220	—	bend to the N. E.
To the Mouth of Tylors R.	5	1225	35	S. W.
To the fort on Cedar Island	18	1243	—	—
To Teton River	37	1280	70	S. W.
" Antient Ricara Village	42	1322	—	S. W.

" Chyanne River	5	1327	400	S W
" an old Ricaras Village on *Lahoocatts* Island	43	1370	—	—
" Otter Creek	35	1405	22	N. E.
" *Sar-war-kar-na* River	2	1407	90	S W.
" *We-ter-hoo* River	25	1432	120	S W
" *Ma ro pa* River	2	1434	25	S. W.
" the 1st Ricara Village	2	1436	—	—
" 2d & 3d Ricara Village	4	1440	—	S. W.
" Stone Idol Creek	18	1458	18	N. E
" *War-re-con-ne* River	40	1498	35	N. E
" Cannon Ball River	13	1511	140	S W
" *She-wish* or Fish Crek	5	1516	28	N. E
To the mouth of "Ches-che-tar" or heart River	35	1551	38	S. W.
" " Hunting Creek	14	1565	25	S W
" New mandan Island near their old villages	21	1586	—	N. E
" the Old Ricara Village avacuated in the Summer 1798	3	1589	—	S. W.
" Fort Mandan	20	1609	—	N E
" Mandan Villages 1st is	3	1612	—	S W & N E.
" The Mouth of Knife River near the Mi-ne-tar-ra Villgs.	3	1615	80	S. W.
To Miry Creek	15	1630	22	N. E.

The Missouri and it's Subsidiary Streams higher up; are taken altogether from information Collected dureing the Winter 1804, 5 of Indians &c.—

	about miles	miles	near yds	
To the Mouth of the little Missouri or *E-wâh-tark', Ah-zhah*	100	1730	100	S. W.

To Ok-hah, Âh zhah, or the White Earth River	117	1847	100	N W
To the mouth of *Mee, Ah-zhah* or *Yellow Stone* River	3	1850	400	S W
To the mouth of *Ah-mâh-tâh, ru-shush sher,* or the River which Scolds at all others—	150	2000	abt. 100	North
To the Mouth of the *Mah-tush, ah-zhah* or the Muscle Shell River	120	2120	140	South
" the Great Falls	120	2240	—	—
" *Mah-pat-puh, Ah-zhah* or Medison River	15	2255	150	N. W
To the 1st Chain of Rockey mountains about	60	2315	—	—
To the 2nd Chain of Rockey mountains about	75	2390	—	—
To the *three* forks of the Missouri above the 3rd Chain of mountains	75	2465	—	—
To the foot of the next mountain nearly West		2515	—	N. W.
To a large River on the west of the mountain	15	2530	—	—

The Yellow Stone River and it's Subsidiary Streams &c.—

	miles	miles	yards		
To the mouth of *Oke-tar-pas-ah-ha*	75	1705	abt.	30	S. E
" *War-rah-Sash* or Powder R	75	1780	"	40	S. E.
" *Le-ze-ka* or Tongu River	50	1830	"	100	S. E
" *Mar-Shas-kap* River	100	1930	"	40	S. E.
" Little Wolf mountain Creek	55	1985	"	20	N W
" *Ark-tar-ha* River	70	2055	"	30	S. E.
" *Ar-Sar-ta,* or Bighorn R	75	2130	"	150	S. E.
" To the Rockey or Shineing Mountains	200	2330	—		N. W.

[Clark] [*undated, winter 1804–5*][29]

The Distances of the following places as estimated from the mouth of the Missourie, with Lattitude anexed—1806

	miles				
To St. Charles Situated on the North Side	21	in Lattitude	38°	54′	39″
″ The mouth of Gasconade River S. S.	103	ditto	38°	44	35
″ The mouth of Osarge River S. S.	137	do	38	31	16
″ The mouth of Grand River N. S.	252	do	38	47	54
″ The mouth of *Kenzas* River S. S.	364	do	39	5	25
″ The mouth of Independence Creek S. S.	432	do	39	25	42
″ The mouth of Nodawa River N. S.	480	do	39	39	22
″ The mouth of the Gd. *Nemaha* R. S. S.	510	do	39	55	56
″ The Bald pated prarie N. S.	569	do	40	27	7
″ The Mouth of River Platt S. Side	630	do	40	54	35
″ The Council Bluff on the S. S.	680	do	41	17	0
″ The mouth of the Little *Seaus* R. N. S.	763	do	41	42	34
″ The Camp opsd. the *Maha* Village S. S.	866	do	42	13	41
″ The mouth of Seaux River on the N. S.	882	do	42	23	49
″ The mouth of River Jacque on the N. S.	974	do	42	53	13
To the mouth of the River *Que courre* S. Side (rapid) is	1020	in Latd.			
″ The mouth of white River on the South Side	1148	do			
″ The Island in the Grand de tortu or Big bend of the Missourie is	1200	do			
″ The fort on the Island of Ceders is	1243	do	44°	11′	33″
″ The mouth of the Teton River on the So. Side	1280	do			

ʺ The mouth of the Chien (or Dog River[)] So. Side	1327	do	44°	19ʹ	36ʺ
ʺ The mouth of the *Sur-war-kar-na* River So. Side	1407	do			
ʺ The mouth of the *We-ter-hoo* River So. Side	1432	do	45	39	5
ʺ The Ricara Villages 3 on the S. S.	1440	do			
ʺ The River *Boulet* or Cannon Ball R.	1511	do	46	29	00
ʺ The River *Chiss-che-tar* & old Village L. S.	1551	do			
ʺ The 1st Village of the Mandens L. S.	1612	do			
ʺ *Fort Mandan* on the N. Side is	1609	do	47	21	47
ʺ Knif River & Shoemans village S S	1616				
ʺ The Mouth of Muddey Creek N S	1630				

LEWIS AND CLARK'S POINTS ON THE MISSOURI RIVER TO FORT MANDAN

Lewis and Clark's Name	Present Name and Location
Camp Dubois (Camp Wood)	Probably beneath Missouri River
St. Charles	St. Charles, St. Charles County, Missouri
Bonhomme Creek	Bonhomme Creek, St. Louis County, Missouri
Osage Woman's River	Femme Osage River, St. Charles County, Missouri
Tavern Cave	Tavern Rock, Franklin County, Missouri (see entry for May 23, 1804)
Chaurette Creek	Charette Creek, Warren County, Missouri
Shepherds Creek	Big Berger Creek, Franklin County, Missouri
Gasconnade River	Gasconade River, Gasconade County, Missouri
Muddy River	Auxvasse River, Callaway County, Missouri
Muddy Creek	Muddy Creek, Callaway County, Missouri
Osage River	Osage River, Osage-Cole county line, Missouri

Murrow Creek	Moreau River, Cole County, Missouri
Cedar Creek	Cedar Creek, Callaway County, Missouri
Good Woman's Creek	Bonne Femme Creek, Boone County, Missouri
Lead Mine Hill	Cole County, Missouri
Manitou Creek	Moniteau Creek, Cole County, Missouri
Split Rock Creek	Perchee Creek, Boone County, Missouri
Salt River	Petite Saline Creek, Moniteau County, Missouri
Manitou River	Moniteau Creek, Howard-Boone county line, Missouri
Good Woman's River	Bonne Femme Creek, Howard County, Missouri
Mine River	Lamine River, Cooper County, Missouri
Arrow Prarie	Vicinity of Arrow Rock State Park, Saline County, Missouri
Two Shariton Rivers	Little Chariton and Chariton rivers, Chariton County, Missouri
Ancient village of the Missouri nation	See entries for June 13, 15, and 16, 1804
Grand River	Grand River, Carroll-Chariton county line, Missouri
Snake Creek	Wakenda Creek, Carroll County, Missouri
Ancient village of the Little Osage	See entry for June 15, 1804
Tigers Creek	Crooked River, Ray County, Missouri
Eubert's River	Sniabar River, Lafayette County, Missouri (see entry for June 21, 1804)
Fire Prarie Creek	See entry for June 22, 1804
Fort point	See entry for June 23, 1804
Hay Cabbin Creek	Little Blue River, Jackson County, Missouri
Coal Bank	Jackson County, Missouri (see entry for June 25, 1804)

Bluewater River	Big Blue River, Jackson County, Misouri
Kanzas River	Kansas (Kaw) River, Wyandotte County, Kansas
Little River Platte	Platte (Little Platte) River, Platte County, Missouri
Turkey Creek	Corral Creek, Leavenworth County, Kansas
Waucarba Warconda Island	Kickapoo Island, between Leavenworth County, Kansas, and Platte County, Missouri (see entry for July 2, 1804)
Independance Creek	Independence Creek, Atchison-Doniphan county line, Kansas
St. Michaels Prarie	Vicnity of St. Joseph, Buchanan County, Missouri
Nodaway River	Nodaway River, Holt-Andrew county line, Missouri
Wolf or Loup River	Wolf Creek, Doniphan County, Kansas
Big Ne-ma-har River	Big Nemaha River, Richardson County, Nebraska
Tarkio Creek	Tarkio River (Big Tarkio Creek), Holt County, Missouri (see entry for July 13, 1804)
Nish-nah-ba-to-na River	Nishnabotna River, Atchison County, Missouri (see entries for July 14 and 17, 1804)
Little Ne-ma-har River	Little Nemaha River, Nemaha County, Nebraska
Bald-pated Prarie	Vicinity of Waubonsie State Park, Fremont County, Iowa
Weeping Water Creek	Weeping Water Creek, Otoe County, Nebraska
Platte River	Platte River, Cass-Sarpy county line, Nebraska
Butterfly or Papillion Creek	Papillion (Big Papillion) Creek, Sarpy County, Nebraska
Musquetoe Creek	Mosquito Creek, Pottawattamie County, Iowa (see entry for July 22, 1804)
White Catfish Camp	Near Mills-Pottawattamie county line, Iowa

Ancient village of the Ottoes	Omaha, Douglas County, Nebraska (see entires for July 27 and 28, 1804)
Ancient Ayauways (Iowa) village	North of Council Bluffs, Pottawattamie County, Iowa (see entry for July 28, 1804)
Indian or Indian Knob Creek	Pigeon Creek, Pottawattamie County, Iowa
Bowyers Creek	Boyer River, Pottawattamie County, Iowa
Council Bluff	Vicinity of Fort Calhoun, Washington County, Nebraska
Soldiers River	Soldier River, Harrison County, Iowa
Ye-yeau War-da-pon, Stone River, or Little Sioux River	Little Sioux River, Harrison County, Iowa
Hill where the late king of the Mahars was buried	Blackbird Hill, Thurston County, Nebraska
Wau-can-da or Bad Spirit Creek	Blackbird (South Blackbird) Creek, or North Blackbird Creek, Thurston County, Nebraska (see entry for August 11, 1804)
Camp Fish	Dakota County, Nebraska, or Woodbury County, Iowa (see entry for August 13, 1804)
Floyds River	Floyd River, Sioux City, Woodbury County Iowa
Sioux River	Big Sioux River, South Dakota-Iowa state line
Hot or burning bluffs	Dixon County, Nebraska (see entry for August 24, 1804)
White Stone River	Vermillion River, Clay County, South Dakota
Little Bow Creek	Bow Creek, Cedar County, Nebraska
James River	James River, Yankton County, South Dakota
Calumet Bluffs	Near Gavins Point Dam, Cedar County, Nebraska
Ancient fortification on Good Mans Island	Between Bonhomme County, South Dakota and Knox County, Nebraska (see entries for September 1 and 2, 1804)
Plumb Creek	Emanuel Creek, Bonhomme County, South Dakota

White Paint Creek	Bazile Creek, Knox County, Nebraska (see entry for September 4, 1804)
Quiccurre or Rappid River	Niobrara River, Knox County, Nebraska
Poncar River	Ponca Creek, Knox County, Nebraska
The Dome	The Tower, Boyd County, Nebraska
Island of Cedar	Little Cedar Island, between Gregory and Charles Mix counties, South Dakota
White River	White River, Lyman County, South Dakota
Three rivers of the Sioux pass	Crow Creek, Elm (Wolf) Creek, and Campbell Creek, Buffalo County, South Dakota
Big Bend, or Grand de Tourte	Big Bend of the Missouri River, Lyman, Hughes, and Buffalo counties, South Dakota
Tylor's River	Medicine River (Creek), Lyman County, South Dakota
Fort on Cedar Island	Dorion Island No. 2 (now submerged), between Hughes and Lyman Counties, South Dakota (see entry for September 22, 1804)
Teton River	Bad River, Stanley County, South Dakota
Ancient Ricara village	Stanley County, South Dakota (see entry for October 1, 1804)
Cheyenne River	Cheyenne River, Stanley-Dewey county line, South Dakota
Old Ricaras village on Lahoocatts Island	Dolphees (Lafferty) Island, between Dewey and Potter counties, South Dakota (see entry for October 4, 1804)
Otter Creek	Swan Creek, Walworth County, South Dakota
Sar-war-car-na River	Moreau River, Dewey County, South Dakota
We-tar-hoo River	Grand River, Corson County, South Dakota
Ma-ro-pa River	Rampart (Oak) Creek, Corson County, South Dakota
1st Ricaras village on an island	Ashley Island, between Corson and Campbell counties, South Dakota (see entry for October 8, 1804)

2d and 3d Ricaras Villages	Corson and Campbell counties, South Dakota (see entry for October 9, 1804)
Stone Idol Creek	Spring (Hermaphrodite) Creek, Campbell County, South Dakota
Sar-kar-nah or Beaver Creek	Little Beaver Creek, Emmons County, North Dakota
War-re-con-ne River	Beaver Creek, Emmons County, North Dakota
Cannon Ball River	Cannonball River, Sioux-Morton county line, North Dakota
Fish Creek	Long Lake (Badger) Creek, Emmons County, North Dakota
Ches-che-tar or Heart River	Heart River, Morton County, North Dakota
Hunting Creek	Square Butte Creek, Morton County, North Dakota (see entry for February 13, 1805)
Fort Mandan	Vicinity of Fort Mandan State Park, McLean County, North Dakota
Mandan villages	Mercer County, North Dakota
Knife River	Knife River, Mercer County, North Dakota

At Fort Mandan both Lewis and Clark made up lists from Indian information giving tributaries and other points on the Missouri above the fort and on the Yellowstone. Since they are based solely on Indian information and distance estimates, not on the captains' observation, their identifications and locations are necessarily conjectural. Correct names of actual Lewis and Clark sightings will be given in future chapters. Translations are placed in a note at the end of this section.

AFFLUENTS OF THE MISSOURI RIVER ABOVE FORT MANDAN

Lewis and Clark's Name	*Present Name and Location*
Miry River or E-pe,-Âh-zhah	Snake Creek, McLean County, North Dakota
Little Missouri River or E-mâh-tark',-Ah'-zhah	Little Missouri, Dunn County, North Dakota

White Earth River or Ok-hah-, Âh-zhâh	White Earth River, Mountrail County, North Dakota (see entries for April 16 and 21, 1805)
Yellowstone River or Meé, ah'-zah	Yellowstone River, McKenzie County, North Dakota
River which scolds at all others or Ah-mâh-tâh, ru-shush-sher	Milk River, Valley County, Montana
Muscle shell River or Mah-tush,-ah-zhah	Musselshell River, Petroleum-Garfield county line, Montana
Great Falls	Great Falls of the Missouri, Cascade County, Montana
Medicine River or Mah-pah-pah, ah-zhah	Sun River, Cascade County, Montana
1st Chain of Rocky Mountains	Cascade and Lewis and Clark counties, Montana
2d Chain of Rocky Mountains	Lewis and Clark County, Montana
Three Forks of the Missouri	Three Forks of the Missouri (Jefferson, Madison, and Gallatin rivers), Madison-Broadwater county line, Montana
A large river on the west of the mountain	Lemhi and Salmon Rivers, Lemhi County, Idaho, or Bitterroot and Clark Fork rivers, Ravalli and Missoula counties, Montana

AFFLUENTS OF THE YELLOWSTONE RIVER

Lewis and Clark's Name	*Present Name and Location*
Oke-tar-pas-ah-ha	O'Fallon Creek, Prairie County, Montana
War-rah-sash or Powder River	Powder River, Prairie County, Montana
Le-ze-ka or Tongue River	Tongue River, Custer County, Montana
Mar-shas-kap River	Rosebud Creek, Rosebud County, Montana
Little Wolf Mountain Creek	Big Porcupine Creek, Rosebud County, Montana

Ark-tar-ha River	Sarpy Creek, Treasure County, Montana
Ar-sar-ta or Bighorn River	Bighorn River, Treasure-Yellowstone county line, Montana
Stinking Cabbin Creek	Boulder River, Sweetgrass County, Montana

NOTES FOR PART 1

1. This document is found in Codex O, pp. 69–128. Other Clark documents, either preliminary drafts or copies of this one, will be compared for substantial differences. Clark's long title on the item at the American Philosophical Society is very similar to Lewis's, but is interesting in that it has a date of February 20, 1805, scored out. The date does not give a clue to the timing of the document, whether it preceded or postdated Lewis's, but does confirm what has been known for some time, that the summaries were made during the winter at Fort Mandan. Since the term "summary statement" was an overused title for the documents in this section, Clark's summaries used here for comparison will be called "Clark's No. 3" and "Clark's No. 1" corresponding to their numbers in the seven manuscript items at the American Philosophical Society. The two documents at the Missouri Historical Society also used for comparison will be called "Clark's table of the Kansas River" and "Clark's table of the Platte River."

2. Clark's No. 3 gives "27" which is probably more accurate as most other sources give a figure in the 20s.

3. Probably stands for "aux Cuivre." Today's Cuivre River which falls into the Mississippi River northwest of St. Charles, Missouri.

4. "Gasconade" means bragging or boasting; the river appears greater than it actually is.

5. See geology notes at November 24, 1803, and June 7, 1804.

6. Clark's No. 3 has "16."

7. See geology notes at June 7 and July 7, 1804.

8. For the Osage villages, see entry for June 15, 1804. For the fossils, see Mehl; McMillan.

9. See entries for June 15 and 16, 1804.

10. Clark's table of the Kansas River also adds his French equivalents for: Stranger's Wife, "famme étrangére"; Grasshopper, "jauterelle"; Heart, "du cour"; Full, "Plein"; Black Paint, "vermillion noir"; and Bluewater, "de l'eau Bleu." Clark does not have the Little Salt Creek on his chart but has the phrase "Several streams fall in higher up." There are also a few minor differences in the mileage figures and spelling of Indian names for streams. The locations named may be identified as:

Three Rivers	uncertain
Stranger's Wife River	Big Stranger Creek
Bealette's Creek	Captain Creek
Wor-rah-ru za River	Wakarusa River

Grasshopper Creek	Delaware River
Heart River	Big Soldier Creek?
Full River	Buck (Mill) Creek
Black Paint River	Vermillion River
Bluewater River	Big Blue River
Me-war-ton-nen-gar Creek	Wildcat Creek
Republican River	Republican River
Little Salt Creek	Saline River

The word "Wor-rah-ru za" is identifiable as a Siouan name, possibly from Omaha or Iowa-Oto, and indicates "where they gather wor-rah," a kind of edible plant. "Me-war-ton-nen-gar" is also Siouan, with the likely meaning "wildcat." "War-ho-ba" is Siouan, *waxóbe,* "sacred."

11. For the first old Kansas village and French garrison, see entry for July 2, 1804. For the second village, below, see also the entry for July 2, 1804.

12. For these Indian villages, see entry for July 20, 1804.

13. Because Clark's table of the Platte River is more extensive it is included here following Lewis's shorter table. The locations named may be identified as:

Salt River	Salt Creek
Corne des Cerfe River	Elkhorn River
Panies Creek	Skull Creek
Shell River	Shell Creek
Wolf River	Loup River
Short Leg River	Dry Creek
Deer Creek	Dry Creek (repeated name)
Falling Creek	Plum Creek
Ringing Water	South Platte River
Little Willow Creek	Beaver Creek
Mustle Shell Creek	Plum Creek
Elk Creek	Cedar River
Graveley Creek	Horse Creek
White Bluff Creek	Spring Creek
Deep Water Creek	North Loup River

14. See entry for July 28, 1804.

15. The Yanktonais, one of the seven major divisions of the Sioux or Dakota. See entry for August 31, 1804.

16. Clark's No. 3 mentions another intervening stream, the "*War-car-da* or Bad Spirit Creek." It is also listed in other sources and all note it as being about fifty-five miles above the Little Sioux River. It is Blackbird (South Blackbird) Creek, or North Blackbird Creek, Thurston County, Nebraska. See entry for August 11, 1804.

17. These affluents of the Big Sioux River may be identified as Broken Kettle Creek, Rock River, and Pipestone Creek.

18. See entries for June 26 and September 2, 1804.

19. The Dakota Rendezvous is discussed in Ewers 17–18, 17–8 n. 3, and Wood (PT).

20. For Cameron, see entry for October 12, 1804.

21. Clark's No. 3 says two miles.

22. Clark's No. 3 says twenty-five miles.

23. See entries for October 8–11, 1804.

24. At Fort Mandan both Lewis and Clark made up lists from Indian information giving tributaries and other points on the Missouri above the fort and on the Yellowstone. The present names of the streams are given in the pages immediately preceding these notes. Here the Indian words are given transliterations and translations as far as possible. The following are in Hidatsa (the word *awáat^hi*, "river," was their name for the Missouri River:

E-pe,-Âh-zhah (*apée áaši*, "coiling creek")

E-mâh-tark',-Ah'-zhah (*awáat^hi áaši*, "[Missouri] river creek")

Ok-hah-,Âh-zhâh (*oxáati áaši*, "white creek")

Meé,ah'-zah (*mí'i áaši*, "stone creek")

Ah-mâh-tâh, ru-shush-sher (*awáat^hi arušaša*, "[Missouri] river forks")

Mah-tush,-ah-zhah (*matóoki áaši*, "mussel shell creek")

Mah-pah-pah, ah-zhah (*máapiwiri áaši*, "sun creek")

The remaining names are in Mandan (only part of them have been identified):

Oke-tar-pas-ah-ha (*pasáŋh*, "creek"); the meaning of oke-tar is not known.

War-rah-sah (*w^hrašuŋte*, "powder")

Le-ze-ke (*résik*, "tongue")

Ar-sar-ta (*áŋsexte*, "bighorn")

25. Clark's No. 3 breaks its duplication of Lewis's summary here and then ends after summarizing the area to the north of the Mandan-Hidatsa villages. From this point Clark's No. 1 follows Lewis's summary, but giving distances in leagues rather than miles.

26. This may be either Boulder River in Sweetgrass County, Montana, as we give it on our list and as shown on *Atlas* map 107 or Shoshone River, Park County, Wyoming, an affluent of the Bighorn and known historically as Stinking Water. The latter is shown on Drouillard's map of 1808. Both possibilities are speculative because the river's name was received before the party had reached the area. Allen, 378–79, 378–79 n. 57, 380–81, fig. 43.

27. For Fidler, see entry for June 8, 1805.

28. This document is Clark's tabular summary of rivers and creeks and is found in Codex C, pp. 248–53, reading backward. Someone has drawn lines vertically across the pages. Other, similar items are noted in the introduction to this part. Preceding this entry is a map (fig. 9) on p. 255 of Codex C. It shows the Mississippi, Minnesota (Clark's St. Peters), Red River of the North, and subsidary streams in modern Minnesota. It was probably made during the winter of 1804–5 from information of traders.

29. This table of distances and latitudes begins on document 66 of the Field Notes and continues after the "River Jacque" entry on the reverse of document 67. Clark must have prepared it at Fort Mandan. Someone has added the figures "1806" after the heading, but the date is not appropriate here. On the reverse of document 66 is a fairly detailed sketch

map (see fig. 5) of the country between the Missouri and the Red River of the North, in eastern North and South Dakota. Shown are "War re con ne R" (Beaver Creek), "R Jacque" (James River), "R Seaux" (Big Sioux River), "St Peters" (Minnesota River), and Red River. On the portage between the Sheyenne and Red rivers is "Mr. Marcia House," presumably a trading post. It is difficult to determine the date of this sketch, since the information could have come from various sources. "Rene Jussomme" in large letters may indicate that Jusseaume was a source for the map. However, Hugh Heney definitely gave the captains information about the country between the Mississippi and the Missouri (see above, December 17, 1804), and this map may embody his knowledge. See *Atlas*, 8, 18 n. 81. Clark's "S. S." in this table means south rather than starboard side. A similar table appears in Codex C, p. 247, probably copied from the one given here, but leaving out some points in the table reproduced. The Little Sioux River of the printed table is the "*Ea-neah, Wau-de-pon*" of the shorter table. A short table giving only latitudes and not strictly in order proceeding up the Missouri appears in Voorhis No. 4. It includes the following points, some of them not on the Missouri River, that do not appear in the list printed here: the mouth of the Missouri, Dimond Island, Old Kanzas Village, Good Island, 15 July Island, 19 July, above River Plate, 4 August, 5 August, Mahar Kings hill (Blackbird Hill), mouth of the Ohio, Philadelphia, Nootka Sound (giving also longitude for these last three), and North Winipeg River. Latitudes for points along the Missouri can be found in the daily journal entries.

Part 2: Estimate of the Eastern Indians

This document, in Clark's hand, consists of seven sheets of letter paper pasted together to form one large sheet about 35″ x 28″. Apparently there were two copies, one sent to the secretary of war and now lost, and the present copy, now in the archives of the American Philosophical Society, where it was deposited by Biddle in 1818 (see Introduction and Appendix C, vol. 2). The material is arranged in a large table providing information about the tribes living east of the Rocky Mountains, although a few mountain tribes, such as the "Snakes" (Shoshones), Crows, and Flatheads, are included. The captains must have obtained their data from traders and Indians in St. Louis and on up the Missouri. The copy sent to the secretary of war evidently contained information not found in the existing document, as indicated by a memorandum by Clark on the back of the latter, which reads as follows:

additional Remarks made on the Copy Sent to the Secretary at War

1st   the boundaries of the Countrey which they Claim—   the quantity of land & face of the Countrey

2d   their Ancient residence if Known.

3   the State of their Trade whether it Can be expected to increase and in what proportion.

4th   their Trafick with other Indian nations, in what it Consists, and where Carried on

5th   their Disposition towards the whites, and their conduct to their Traders

6   to what place they might be provailed on to remove to make room for other nations

7   whether they cultivate or not

8   whether Stationary or roveing

9   whether the nations is increasing or Demenishing

Genl. remarks on the Trade & remittences and amt. Esimtated # of Establishments in a Govtmt pt. of view—   Notations on Indian Names Sub Divisions of the Sioux Bands & names of the principal Chiefs.

Also on the reverse of the document are the words: "To Genl. Jno Clark Kentucky," "Wetepehatoes," and "WC." The final column of the table, here given as category "*s*," is also found on the back of the sheet.

Jefferson used the secretary of war's copy to prepare his *Message* for Congress in which the document was titled "A Statistical View of the Indian Nations Inhabiting the Territory of Louisiana and the Countries Adjacent to its Northern and Western Boundaries," and published in 1806. The published version, to avoid the difficulties of printing so large a table, placed the information under lettered headings corresponding to the columns of the original. Thwaites followed this procedure in his edition, and the same is done here. Clark occasionally used ditto marks or the letters "do." under columns of repeating information. Since this would be unclear in the present arrangement, we have repeated the information. Otherwise Clark's words are given as he wrote them. The information given in the printed report exceeds that in the manuscript version, and from its appearance may well have been drawn verbatim, or nearly so, from the secretary of war's copy. Therefore material in category "*s*" from the printed document of 1806 is given here in paragraphs separate from the tabulated material; these paragraphs follow the "*s*" tabular material under each tribe. Certain phrases in the lettered material found in the printed document and not in the manuscript appear here in parentheses and italics. The printed document also places the manuscript material here given as letter "*r*" under the letter "*i*," thus displacing all subsequent material to letter "*s*" by one letter. This only becomes confusing if one attempts to compare the two. Bracketed material in italics is that of the editor, as usual.

There are at least three documents of a roughly similar nature in Clark's hand. Some were probably preliminaries to this compilation, prepared either on the journey up the Missouri or at Fort Mandan, while others may have been made for Nicholas Biddle after the expedition. One document is part of the "seven manuscript items" (item five) at the American Philosophical Society (see Appendix B, vol. 2). It is a table very similar to Clark's "Estimate." Two documents at the Missouri Historical Society, both loosely titled "Names of Nations," are abbreviated versions of the "Estimate."

A List of the Names of the different Nations & Tribes of Indians Inhabiting the Countrey on the Missourie and its Waters, and West of the Mississippi (above the Missourie) and a line from its head in Latd. 47° 38′ N. & Longt. 95° 6′ W. to the N W extremity of the Lake of the Woods, in Latd. 49° 37′ N. and Longd. 94° 31′ W. and Southerley & Westerley, of a West line from the Said Lake of Wood, as far as is known Jany. 1805. Expressive of the Names, Language, Numbers, Trade, water courses & Countrey in which they reside Claim & rove &c. &c. &c.

Explanatory References [*found as column headings on manuscript*]

a. The Names of the Indian Nations, as usially Spelt and pronounc'd by the English

b. Primitive Indian names of Nations & *Tribes,* English orthography, the syllables producing the Sounds by which the Inds themselves express the Names of their respective Nations

c. Nick names or those which have Generally obtained among the Canadian Traders

d. The Language they Speak if primitive marked *, otherwise derived from & approximating to

e. Nos. of Villages

f. Nos. of Tents or Lodges of the roveing Bands

g. Number of Warriours

h. The probable Number of Souls   of this Numbr. deduct about ⅓ generally

i.   The Names of the Christian Nations or the Companies with whome they Maintain their Commerce and Traffick

j.   The places at which the Traffick is usially Carried on

k.   The estimated Amount of Merchindize in Dollars at the St. Louis & Mickilimackanac, prices for their Anual Consumption [*there are separate columns, one for St. Louis and one for Michilimackinac; only the St. Louis column has figures*]

l.   The estimated amount of their returns, in Dollars, at the St. Louis & Michilimacknac prices—[*there are separate columns, one for St. Louis and one for Michilimackinac; only the St. Louis column has figures*]

m.   The ⟨estimated qty and⟩ Kind of ⟨Furs and⟩ pelteries & Robes which they Annually supply or furnish

n.   The defferant kinds of Pelteres, Furs, Robes Meat Greece & Horses which each Could furnish for trade

o.   The place at which it would be mutually advantageous to form the principal establishment in order to Supply the Several nations with Merchindize.

p.   The Names of the Nations with whome they are at War

q.   The names of the Nations with whome they maintain a friendly alliance, or with whome they may be united by intercourse or marriage

r.   The particular water courses on which they reside or rove

s.   The Countrey in which they usially reside, and the principal water Courses ⟨They Cultivate Corn Beans &c &c⟩ on or near which the Villages are Situated, or the Defferant Nations & tribes usially rove & *Remarks*

Notations [*found only in the printed document*]

⁻   over *a*, denotes that *a* sounds as in caught, taught, &c.

^   over *a*, denotes that it sounds as in dart, part, &c.

a, without notation has its primitive sound as in ray, hay, &c. except only when it is followed by *r* or *w*, in which case it sounds as *â*.

˛   set underneath denotes a small pause, the word being divided by it into two parts.

The Indian Trade [*found only in the printed document*]

The sums stated under and opposite [*k*] are the amounts of merchandise annual furnished the several nations of Indians, including all incidental

expenses of transportation, &c. incurred by the merchants which generally averages about one third of the whole amount. The merchandise is
estimated at an advance of 125 per cent. on the sterling cost. It appears to
me that the amount of merchandise which the Indians have been in the
habit of receiving annually, is the best standard by which to regulate the
quantities necessary for them in the first instance; they will always con-
sume as much merchandise as they can pay for, and those with whom a
regular trade has been carried on have generally received that quantity.

The amount of their returns stated under and opposite [*1*] are estimated by the peltry standard of St. Louis, which is 40 cents per pound for
deer skins; (i. e.) all furs and peltries are first reduced by their comparative
value to lbs. of merchantable deer skins, which are then estimated at 40
cents per lb.

These establishments are not mentioned as being thought important at
present in a governmental point of view.

1. a. Grand Osarge
   b. Bar-har-cha
   c. Grand Ose or zo
   d. *Osarge
   e. 2
   f. [*blank*]
   g. 1200
   h. 7000 [or] 5000
   i. a Co: at St Louis
   j. at their Village & the 3 forks of the Arkansaw River
   k. 15,000
   l. 20,000
   m. Skins of the small Deer, Some Beaver a fiew Bear, & otter Skins
   n. Beaver, otter, Small Deer, Black Bear, & racoons Skins
   o. at the 3 forks of the Arkansaw 600 Miles up

that river and 60 Lg S. West of their Village

p. With all Nations of Indians (*except the Little Osage*) untill the United States took possession of Louisiana

q. (*With the Little Osage only*)

r. Osarge Riv (*At the three forks of the Arkansas river, and eighty leagues up the Osage river, on the south side*)

s. Their villages are [*blank*] Leagues up the Osarge River on the S. E. Side, they Claim all the Coun-trey included in the following boundrey. Viz beginning at a S E. branch of the Osarge Called *Niangua* R up that

390

river to the head from
thence Southerley to the
Arkansaw 100 miles be-
low the three forks up
the Arkansaw and a
Southerly fork Some Dis-

tance above the Great Sa-
line, & the Ctry nearly to
the Kanzus river—
Cultivate Corn, Beens &c
&c

Claim the country within the following limits, viz. commencing at the mouth of a south branch of the Osage river, called *Neangua,* and with the same to its source, thence southwardly to intersect the Arkansas about one hundred miles below the three forks of that river; thence up the principal branch of the same, to the confluence of a large northwardly branch of the same, lying a considerable distance west of the Great Saline, and with that stream nearly to its source; thence northwardly, towards the Kansas river, embracing the waters of the upper portion of the Osage river, and thence obliquely approaching the same to the beginning. The climate is delightful, and the soil fertile in the extreme. The face of the country is generally level, and well watered; the eastern part of the country is covered with a variety of excellent timber; the western and middle country high prairies. It embraces within its limits four salines, which are, in point of magnitude and excellence, unequalled by any known in North America: there are also many others of less note. The principal part of the Great Osage have always resided at their villages, on the Osage river, since they have been known to the inhabitants of Louisiana. About three years since, nearly one half of this nation, headed by their chief the *Big-Track,* emigrated to the three forks of the Arkansas, near which, and on its north side, they established a village, where they now reside. The Little Osage formerly resided on the S. W. side of the Missouri, near the mouth of Grand river; but being reduced by continual warfare with their neighbors, were compelled to seek the protection of the Great Osage, near whom they now reside. There is no doubt but their trade will increase: they could furnish a much larger quantity of beaver than they do. I think two villages, on the Osage river, might be prevailed on to remove to the Arkansas, and the Kansas, higher up the Missouri, and thus leave a sufficient scope of country for the Shawnees, Dillewars, Miames, and Kickapoos. The Osages cultivate corn, beans, &c.

2. a. Little Osarge
   b. ooed-za-tar
   c. Petite ose or zo (or little zo[)]
   d. *Osarge
   e. 1
   f. [*blank*]
   g. 300
   h. 2000 [or] 1300
   i. a Co: at St Louis
   j. near their Village
   k. 5000
   l. 8000
   m. Skins of the small Deer, Some Beaver a fiew Bear, & otter Skins
   n. Beaver, otter, Small Deer, Black Bear, & racoons Skins
   o. at the 3 forks of the Arkansaw 600 Miles up that river and 60 Lg S. West of their Village ⟨at their village on the Osage⟩
   p. With all Nations of Indians untill the United States took possession of Louisiana (*except the Great Osages*)
   q. (*With the Great Osage only*)
   r. Osarge Riv (*Near the Great Osages*)
   s. Their villages are [*blank*] Leagues up the Osarge River on the S. E. Side, they Claim all the Countrey included in the following boundrey. Viz beginning at a S E.

branch of the Osarge Called *Niangua* R up that river to the head from thence Southerley to the Arkansaw 100 miles below the three forks up the Arkansaw and a Southerly fork Some Distance above the Great Saline, & the Ctry nearly to the Kanzus river—Cultivate Corn, Beens &c &c

3. a. Kanzas
   b. Kar sea
   c. Kah
   d. *Osarge
   e. 1
   f. [*blank*]
   g. 300
   h. 2000 [or] 1300
   i. the Merchants of St Louis
   j. at their Village and on the Missouri about the mouth of the Kanzes River (*not stationary*)
   k. 5000
   l. 8000
   m. Skins of the small Deer, Some Beaver a fiew Bear, & otter Skins (*with buffaloe grease and robes*)
   n. Beaver otter, Deer, Bear & ⟨fox⟩ Muskrat Skins
   o. 1 Mile up on the N Side above the Mouth of the Kanzas R
   p. with all nations

q. (*They are sometimes at peace with the Ottoes and Missouris, with whom they are partially intermarried*)

r. on Kanzes R. (*Eighty leagues up the Kansas river, on the north side*)

s. their village is 80 Leagues up the Kanzes River, they Hunt high up the Kanzes and Arkansaws   they Cultivate Corn Beans &c. &c Great robers

The limits of the country they claim is not known. The country in which they reside, and from thence to the Missouri, is a delightful one, and generally well watered and covered with excellent timber: they hunt on the upper part of Kanzas and Arkanzas rivers: Their trade may be expected to increase with proper management. At present they are a dissolute, lawless banditti; frequently plunder their traders, and commit depredations on persons ascending and descending the Missouri river: population rather increasing. These people, as well as the Great and Little Osages, are stationary, at their villages, from about the 15th of March to the 15th of May, and again from the 15th of August to the 15th of October: the balance of the year is appropriated to hunting. They cultivate corn, &c.

4. a. Ottoes
   b. War-doke-tar-tar
   c. ⟨Les Ottoe⟩ la Zoto
   d. *Missouri, & Some words of Osarge
   e. 1 [*with the Missouris*]
   f. [*blank*]
   g. 120
   h. 500
   i. the Merchants of St Louis
   j. at their Village and at tradeing houses, at different Places between the Grand Ne ma har and Platt rivers (*not stationary*)
   k. 4000 (*including the Missouris*)

l. 6000 (*8000, including the Missouris*)
   m. Beaver, otter, racoons, Deer & Black Bear Skins
   n. Beaver, otter, Muskat racoon, wolves Deer, bear, Skins bears oil & Buffalow tallow Elk
   o. Council Bluffs 50 miles by water above R. Platt or there abouts, and about
   p. with all nations generally   Partially at peace with the Panias and Kanzies nations
   q. with the Missouries (*With*)

393

> the Panis proper, Saukees
> and Renars)
> r. 18 Lg up the platt (*South
> side of the river Platte, fif-
> teen leagues from its mouth*)
> s. The Village is 18
> Leagues up the Platt
> River, S E. Side they
> hunt up the Saline and
>
> grand Ne-ma-har Rivers
> &. they cultivate Corn
> Beans &c. &c. This na-
> tion formerley lived on
> the Missoure river above
> the Plate river, they
> Speake Some words of
> the Osarge & Mahar
> (bad[)]

They have no idea of an exclusive possession of any country, nor do they assign themselves any limits. I do not believe that they would object to the introduction of any well disposed Indians: they treat the traders with respect and hospitality, generally. In their occupations of hunting and cultivation, they are the same with the Kanzas and Osage. They hunt on the Saline, Nimmehaw rivers, and west of them in the plains. The country in which they hunt lies well; it is extremely fertile and well watered; that part of which borders on the Nimmehaw and Missouri possesses a good portion of timber: population rather increasing. They have always resided near the place their village is situated, and are the descendants of the Missouris.

5. a. Missouries
   b. New-dar-cha
   c. Missourie
   d. *Missoure, & Some words of Osarge
   e. 1 [*with the Otoes*]
   f. [*blank*]
   g. 80
   h. 500 [or] 300
   i. the Merchants of St Louis
   j. at their Village and at tradeing houses at differ-ent Places between the Grand Ne ma har and Platt rivers
   k. 4000 [*included with the Otos*]
   l. 6000 [*included with the Otos*]
   m. Beaver, otter, racoons, Deer & Black Bear Skins
   n. Beaver, otter, Muskrat racoon, wolves Deer, bear, Skins bears oil & Buffalow tallow Elk
   o. Council Bluffs 50 miles by water above R. Platt or there abouts, and about
   p. with all nations gener-ally Partially at peace

with the Panias and Kan-
zies nations

q. with the Ottoes (*With the
Panis proper, Saukees and
Renars*)

r. with the Ottoes

s. with the Ottoes and
hund also above the Plate
near the Missourie near

the Corn Des cerf River;
they Cultivate Corn
Beans &c. This nation
formerley lived below the
grand River, and was
noumerous, they Speake
Some words of the Os-
arge (bad[)]

These are the remnant of the most numerous nation inhabiting the Missouri, when first known to the French. Their ancient and principal village was situated in an extensive and fertile plain on the north bank of the Missouri, just below the entrance of the Grand river. Repeated attacks of the small pox, together with their war with the Saukees and Renars, has reduced them to their present state of dependence on the Ottoes, with whom they reside, as well in their village as on their hunting exur-sions. The Ottoes view them as their inferiors, and sometimes treat them amiss. These people are the real proprietors of an extensive and fertile country lying on the Missouri, above their ancient village for a consider-able distance, and as low as the mouth of the Osage river, and thence to the Mississippi.

6. a. Pania proper
   b. Parnee
   c. Grand par
   d. *Pania
   e. ½ (*One*)
   f. [*blank*]
   g. 400
   h. 2000 [or] 1600
   i. the Merchants of St Louis
   j. at their Village
   k. 3200
   l. 5000
   m. Beaver otter & racoons Skins & Buffalow Robes

   n. Beaver, otter, racoon, Cabra & a fiew Deer Skins, roabs, Buffalow meat & greas & Horses
   o. Council Bluffs 50 miles by water above R. Platt or there abouts, and about
   p. Ossar[ge]s, Kanzes, Pania Pickey, Padouces, *A-li tans* & La-plays
   q. republickin Pania Loup & Mahas
   r. 30 Lgs up the Platt (*South side*)

s. Their Village is 30
   Leagus up the river plate
   on the S E. Side, they
   Hunt on the heads of the
   Kanzes, and its N W

waters and high up the
Platt   they Cultivate
Corn, Beans &c &c.
(mild well disposed)

With respect to their idea of the possession of soil, it is similar to that of the Ottoes: they hunt on the south side of the river Platte, higher up and on the head of the Kanzas. A great proportion of this country is open plains, interspersed, however, with groves of timber, which are most generally found in the vicinity of the water courses. It is generally fertile and well watered; lies level, and free of stone. They have resided in the country which they now inhabit, since they were known to the whites. Their trade is a valuable one, from the large proportion of beaver and otter which they furnish, and it may be expected yet to increase, as those animals are still abundant in their country. The periods of their residence at their village and hunting, are similar to the Kanzas and Osages. Their population is increasing. They are friendly and hospitable to all white persons; pay great respect and deference to their traders, with whom they are punctual in the payment of their debts. They are, in all respects, a friendly, well disposed people. They cultivate corn, beans, melons, &c.

7. a. Pania Loup (or Wolves)
   b. ⟨Ea⟩ Skee-e-ree
   c. La Loup (or Lou) Pania
      Maher
   d. *Pania
   e. ⟨1⟩
   f. [*blank*]
   g. 280
   h. 1600 [or] 1000
   i. the Merchants of St
      Louis
   j. at the Pania Vilage
   k. 2400
   l. 3500
   m. Beaver otter & racoons
      Skins & Buffalow Robes
   n. Beaver, otter, racoon,

   Cabra & a fiew Deer
   Skins, roabs, Buffalow
   meat & greas & Horses
   ⟨and the Skins of the Big
   horned animal⟩

   o. Council Bluffs 50 miles
      by water above R. Platt
      or there abouts, and
      about
   p. Ottoes & Missouries, and
      the Same as the Panias
   q. The Same as the Panias
   r. on the Loup R. (*N. E.
      side, 36 leagues from its
      mouth*)
   s. Their Village is 40
      Leagus above the Panias

on the right of the R
Loup which empties into
the Plate 8 Lgs. above the
Panias, they hunt on the

rivers *platt* & Loup above
their Village   they Cultivate Corn Beens &c. &c
[(]mild & well disposed)

These are also a branch of the Panias proper, who separated themselves from that nation many years since, and established themselves on a
north branch of the river Platte, to which their name was also given: these
people have likewise no idea of an exclusive right to any portion of country.
They hunt on the Wolf river above their village, and on the river Platte
above the mouth of that river. This country is very similar to that of the
Panias proper; though there is an extensive body of fertile well timbered
land between the Wolf river below their village and the river Corn de
Cerf, or Elkhorn river. They cultivate corn, beans, &c. The particulars
related of the other Panias is also applicable to them. They are seldom
visited by any trader, and therefore usually bring their furs and peltry to
the village of the Panias proper, where they traffic with the whites.

8. a. Pania Republicans
   b. Ar-rah-pa-hoo
   c. Republick
   d. *Pania
   e. ½ (*Pānias proper and
       Pānias Republican live in
       the same village*)
   f. [*blank*]
   g. 300
   h. 2000 [or] 1400
   i. the Merchants of St
       Louis
   j. at the Pania Vilage
   k. 3200
   l. 5000
   m. Beaver otter & racoons
       Skins & Buffalow Robes
   n. Beaver, otter, racoon,
       Cabra & a fiew Deer
       Skins, roabs, Buffalow
       meat & greas & Horses

⟨and the Skins of the Big
horned animal⟩ ⟨The
Same except the Big
horn⟩
o. Council Bluffs 50 miles
    by water above R. Platt
    or there abouts, and
    about
p. the Same as the Panias
q. The same as the Panias
r. with the Panias
s. Their village is with the
    Pania on the River Plate,
    they hunt on a branch of
    the Kanzus Called the
    Republican fork, and
    near the Kanzes river
    also with the Panias
    Cultivate Corn Beens &c.
    &c.   (mild & well
    disposed)

Are a branch of the Pānia proper, or, as they are frequently termed, the *Big Paunch*. About ten years since they withdrew themselves from the mother nation, and established a village on a large northwardly branch of the Kanzas, to which they have given name: they afterwards subdivided and lived in different parts of the country on the waters of Kanzas river; but being harassed by their turbulent neighbors, the Kanzas, they rejoined the Panias proper last spring. What has been said with respect to the Panias proper is applicable to these people, except that they hunt principally on the Republican river, which is better stocked with timber than that hunted by the Panias.

9. a. Mahar
   b. Oh Mar-ha
   c. La Mar
   d. *Mahar with Some words of the Osarge, & Souix
   e. [*blank*]
   f. 80 (*60*)
   g. 200 [or] 150
   h. 1200 [or] 600
   i. the Merchants of St Louis
   j. on the Missourie at different places between the old Mahar Village and River Platt
   k. 3000 (*4,000, including the Pon´ cârs*)
   l. 5000 (*7,000, including the Pon´ cârs*)
   m. Beaver, otter & racoons Skins & Buffalow Robes & B Bear
   n. Beaver, otter, racoon, wolves Deer, Bear & Cabra Skins, & Buffalow robes, g[r]ees & oil
   o. Council Bluffs 50 miles by water above R. Platt or there abouts, and about
   p. Ottoes & Missouries, ⟨Tetons⟩ all the Bands of Sieux, except the Yanktons of the burnt woods
   q. Panias, Loup, republicks, Poncarer
   r. rove on River Quicure (*and head of the Wolf river*)
   s. Their Village was 1 League from the Missourie on the S W Side, about 4 Leagues below ⟨the Grand R⟩ Floyds river & 5 below the Grand R Sieux, They now rove (haveing been reduced by the Small pox and war with the Soues) on rapid river or Quicure   No Corn Beens to Cultivate at present, lost all in the late maladey with the Small pox—

They have no idea of exclusive possession of soil. About ten years since, they boasted 700 warriors. They have lived in a village, on the west bank of the Missouri, 236 miles above the mouth of the river Platte, where they cultivated corn, beans, and melons: they were warlike, and the terror of their neighbors. In the summer and autumn of 1802, they were visited by the small-pox, which reduced their numbers to something less than 300; they burnt their village, and have become a wandering nation, deserted by the traders, and the consequent deficiency of arms and ammunition has invited frequent aggressions from their neighbors, which have tended to reduce them still further. They rove principally on the waters of the river Quicurre, or Rapid river. The country is generally level, high, and open: it is fertile, and tolerably well watered. They might easily be induced to become stationary: they are well disposed towards the whites, and are good hunters: their country abounds in beaver and otter, and their trade will increase and become valuable, provided they become stationary, and are at peace. The Tetons Bois brûlé killed and took about 60 of them last summer.

10. a. Poncare
    b. Poong-car
    c. La Pong
    d. *Mahar with some words of the Osarge, & Souix
    e. [blank]
    f. 20
    g. 50
    h. 300 [or] 200
    i. the Merchants of St Louis
    j. on the Missourie at different places between the old Mahar Village and River Platt (*No place of trade latterly*)
    k. 3000
    l. 5000
    m. Beaver, otter, racoons
    Skins & Buffalow Robes & B Bear
    n. Beaver, otter, racoon, wolves Deer, Bear & Cabra Skins, & Buffalow robes, g[r]ees & oil
    o. Council Bluffs 50 miles by water above R. Platt or there abouts, and about
    p. Ottoes & Missouries, ⟨Tetons⟩ all the Bands of Sieux, except the Yanktons of the burnt woods
    q. the Mahars only
    r. with the Mahas
    s. Their Village was 1 League up a Small river

above the quicure
Called Poncerres River,
they being reduced by
the Small pox, and their
war with the Soues rove
in the plains with the

Mahars   bad fellows (a
tribe of Mahars)   No
Corn Beens to Cultivate
at present, lost all in the
late maladey with the
Small pox—

The remnant of a nation once respectable in point of numbers. They formerly resided on a branch of the Red river of lake Winnipie: being oppressed by the Sioux, they removed to the west side of the Missouri, on Poncar river, where they built and fortified a village, and remained some years; but being pursued by their ancient enemies the Sioux, and reduced by continual wars, they have joined, and now reside with the Mahas, whose language they speak.

11. a. Ricaras 8 tribes
    b. Star rah he
    c. Ree
    d. Pania Corrupted
    e. 3
    f. [*blank*]
    g. 500
    h. 3000 [or] 2000
    i. a Co: at St. Louis
    j. at their Villages
    k. 2500
    l. 6000
    m. Buffalow roabes, Greese
       & a fiew fox Skins, and
       a little Beaver
    n. Buffalow robes, Tallow
       Grece de mele, large &
       Small fox Skins, wolves
       Beaver otter & Small
       furs, also Cabre, a few
       Deer & a fiew White
       Bear Skins
    o. ⟨Fort Mandan⟩ Those
       four nations [*Ricaras,
       Mandans, Shoes, and Big*

Bellies] would move to
the River Yellowstone at
or about that place
would be a proper place
for the establishment
for them
    p. with the Gens des Ser-
       pent or Snake Indians
    q. the Tetons in their
       neighbourhood   the
       Chyennes & nations to
       the S. West
    r. on the Missouri (*On the
       S. W. side of the Missouri,
       1,440 miles from its
       mouth*)
    s. Their Villages   one in
       an Island in the Mis-
       souries above the
       Maropa River 1430
       Miles up, two others
       near each other 4 miles
       above on the S W Side,
       those villages are the re-
       mains of Eight different

tribes of the Pania Na-
tion who have become
reduced by the *Soues*
and compelled to live
together in fortified
towns for their protec-
tion, their villages on
Different parts of the
Missouries from the
Teton river to near the

Mandans they may be
Stiled gardners for the
Soues they raise Corn
Beans &c & hunt in
their Neighborhood
Those people have a
partial exchange with
the Soues for guns pow-
der Ball &c for Horses
& corn &c &c

Are the remains of ten large tribes of Panias, who have been reduced, by the small pox and the Sioux, to their present number. They live in fortified villages, and hunt immediately in their neighborhood. The country around them, in every direction, for several hundred miles, is entirely bare of timber, except on the water courses and steep declivities of hills, where it is sheltered from the ravages of fire. The land is tolerably well watered, and lies well for cultivation. The remains of the villages of these people are to be seen on many parts of the Missouri, from the mouth of Tetone river to the Mandans. They claim no land except that on which their villages stand, and the fields which they cultivate. The Tetons claim the country around them. Though they are the oldest inhabitants, they may properly be considered the farmers or *tenants at will* of that lawless, savage and rapacious race the Sioux *Teton,* who rob them of their horses, plunder their gardens and fields, and sometimes murder them, without opposition. If these people were freed from the oppression of the Tetons, their trade would increase rapidly, and might be extended to a considerable amount. They maintain a partial trade with their oppressors the Tetons, to whom they barter horses, mules, corn, beans, and a species of tobacco which they cultivate; and receive in return guns, ammunition, kettles, axes, and other articles which the Tetons obtain from the Yanktons of the N. and Sissatones, who trade with Mr. Cammeron, on the river St. Peters. These horses and mules the Ricaras obtain from their western neighbors, who visit them frequently for the purpose of trafficking.

12. a. Mandans
   b. Ma-too-tonka 1st Vilg &

    Roop-tar ha 2nd Vil.
  c. Mandan

d. *Mandan (Some words
like the Osarge &
Sieux[)]

e. 2

f. [*blank*]

g. 350

h. ⟨1,500⟩ 1250

i. Hudsons Bay, N W. &
X. Y, Companies from
Assinniboin R. over
Land N. 150 ms.

j. at their Villages

k. 2000

l. 6000

m. Buffalow robes, wolves
a fiew Beavers Elk Skins
& a fiew Horses Foxes &
Corn

n. The same as the above
and white Hars, & large
foxes

o. ⟨at Fort Mandan on the
Missouri near their vil-
lage 16000 [1600] miles
up in Lat. 47 N.
Longtd. 101° 2′, West⟩;
Those four nations
[*Ricaras, Mandans, Shoes,
and Big Bellies*] would
move to the River Yel-
lowstone at or about
that place would be a
proper place for the es-
tablishment for them

p. with ⟨all nations except
the⟩ Soues, & Snake
indians

q. with the Shoe Tribe the
big bellies, Cheyennes

ravins & those to the S.
W. who visit them

r. on the Missouri 16000
[1600] mes up (*On both
sides of the Missouri, 1612
miles from its mouth*)

s. Their Villages are on
both Sides of the Mis-
souree 1605 miles up,
those Villages are the
remains of thirteen dif-
ferent Villages of this
nation and have been
reduced by the Small
Pox, and the wars which
the *Soues* have Caused
on them ⟨from⟩ to col-
lect & form their earli-
est tredition been
Compelled to unite in
two Villages and drove
back by the Sous, from
the Countrey below
white River to this
place, haveing made on
their retreat below, at
this place they have
resided 9 years in
2 Stockaded Towns
raise Corn Beans &c &
hunt a fiew miles
around   They trade
Horses with the Assin-
naboins for Sundrey ar-
ticles which is not
Sufficiently furnished
by their Traders from
the North

These are the most friendly, well disposed Indians inhabiting the Missouri. They are brave, humane and hospitable. About 25 years since they lived in six villages, about forty miles below their present villages, on both sides of the Missouri. Repeated visitations of the small pox, aided by frequent attacks of the Sioux, has reduced them to their present number. They claim no particular tract of country. They live in fortified villages, hunt immediately in their neighborhood, and cultivate corn, beans, squashes and tobacco, which form articles of traffic with their neighbors the Assinniboin: they also barter horses with the Assinniboins for arms, ammunition, axes, kettles, and other articles of European manufacture, which these last obtain from the British establishments on the Assinniboin river. The articles which they thus obtain from Assinniboins and the British traders who visit them, they again exchange for horses and leather tents with the Crow Indians, Chyennes, Wetepahatoes, Kiawas, Kanenavich, Stactan and Cataka, who visit them occasionally for the purpose of traffic. Their trade may be much increased. Their country is similar to that of the Ricaras. Population increasing.

13. a. Shoes Men
    (*Ahwâhhâway*)
   b. Mah-har-ha (*Ah-wâh-hâ-way*)
   c. Soulier
   d. *Minatarra* (big belly)
   e. 1
   f. [*blank*]
   g. 50
   h. ⟨300⟩ 200
   i. Hudsons Bay, N W. & X. Y, Companies from Assinniboin R. over Land N. 150 ms.
   j. at the Mandan Villages
   k. 300
   l. 1000
   m. The same [*as the Mandans*]
   n. The Same [*as the Mandans*]
   o. ⟨at Fort Mandan on the Missouri near their Village 16000 [1600] miles up in Lat. 47 N. Longtd. 101° 2′, West⟩ Those four nations [*Ricaras, Mandans, Shoes, and Big Bellies*] would move to the River Yellowstone at or about that place would be a proper place for the establishment for them
   p. with ⟨all nations except the⟩ Soues, & Snake indians
   q. with the ⟨Shoe tribe⟩

Big bellies Mandans,
Crows and those to the
S. W. who rove

r. in Sight of the mandans
(*On the S. W. side of the
Missouri, three miles about
the Mandans*)

s. This village is Situated
on the S W. Side of the
Missouries at the mouth
of Knife river in Sight
of the Mandans above,

those people Came
from the S W and are
of the Big Belley nation,
they raise Corn &c hunt
in their neigh-
bourhood   They trade
Horses with the Assina-
boins for Sundrey ar-
ticles which is not
Sufficiently furnished
by their Traders from
the North

They differ but very little, in any particular, from the Mandans, their neighbors, except in the unjust war which they, as well as the Minetares, prosecute against the defenceless Snake Indians, from which, I believe, it will be difficult to induce them to desist. They claim to have been once a part of the Crow Indians, whom they still acknowledge as relations. They have resided on the Missouri as long as their tradition will enable them to inform.

14. a. Big bellies (*Minetares*)
b. 1st Vilg. Me-ne-tar-re,
Me ta har ta 2 Vilg.
Me-ne-tar-re
c. Gross Ventre
d. Me ne tar re
e. 2
f. [*blank*]
g. 500 (*600*)
h. 2500
i. Hudsons Bay, N W. &
X. Y, Companies from
Assinniboin R. over
Land N. 150 ms.
j. at their Villages
k. 1,000
l. 3500 (*3,000*)
m. The Same [*as the Man-
dans*] except robes

n. The Same [*as the Man-
dans*] & White bear
o. The Same place [*as the
Mandans*] (or higher up)
p. with Souex, Snake Inds.
& partially with the
upper tribes of the As-
sinniboins, to the
N W
q. with the ⟨Shoe Tribe⟩
the Big bellies Man-
dans, Crows and those
to the S. W. who rove
r. in Sight of the Mandans
(*On both sides of the Knife
river, near the Missouri, 5
miles above the Mandans*)
s. Their Villages are on
the Knive river near its

mouth and about 2
Miles apart & 1 from
the Missouri   they
Came from the S E as
they Say   they raise
Corn Beans &c &c. and
hunt on both Sides of
the Missourie above

their Villages. They
trade Horses with the
Assinaboins for Sun-
drey articles which is
not Sufficiently fur-
nished by their traders
from the North

They claim no particular country, nor do they assign themselves any limits: their tradition relates that they have always resided at their present villages. In their customs, manners, and dispositions, they are similar to the Mandans and Ahwahhaways. The scarcity of fuel induces them to reside, during the cold season, in large bands, in camps, on different parts of the Missouri, as high up that river as the mouth of the river Yellow Stone, and west of their villages, about the Turtle mountain. I believe that these people, as well as the Mandans and Ahwahhaways, might be prevailed on to remove to the mouth of the Yellow Stone river, provided an establishment is made at that place. They have as yet furnished scarcely any beaver, although the country they hunt abounds with them; the lodges of these animals are to be seen within a mile of their villages. These people have also suffered considerably by the small-pox; but have successfully resisted the attacks of the Sioux. The N. W. company intend to form an establishment in the course of the next summer, and autumn, on the Missouri, near these people, which, if effected, will most probably prevent their removal to any point which our government may hereafter wish them to reside at.

15. a. Ayauwais
    b. Ah-e-o-war
    c. dis Iaways or ne persa
    d. Ottoes (*Missouri*)
    e. 1
    f. [*blank*]
    g. 250 (*200*)
    h. ⟨1600⟩ 800
    i. Mr Crawford (*and other merchants*) from Michilimacknac
    j. at the Villages (*and hunting camps*)
    k. 3800
    l. 6000
    m. Deer Beaver otter Mink Black Bear, ⟨fishes⟩ fox racoon Muskrat &c.
    n. Deer, Black Bear Beaver otter Mink Muskrats, Raccons Gray

foxes & Tallow & Bears Oile

o. on the Missourie at the mouth of Kanzus or at the [*blank*]

p. No Nation particularly, Sometimes join the Saukies

q. With the Saukees & re- nars, and all nations East of the Mississippi

r. 36 Lgs up Demoin (*40 leagues up the Demoin on the S. E. side*)

s. Their Village is 40 Leagus up the River

Dumoen, their Coun- trey join the Soues Lands and extend to the Missoure River they are a tribe of the Ottoes Nation and for- merley lived on the Mis- sourie (a fiew miles below the Antient Ot- toes Town) or their Town was at the 1st Bluff above R. platt on the N. Side   they culti- vate Corn Beans &c. &c.—

They are the descendants of the ancient Missouris, and claim the coun- try west of them to the Missouri; but as to its precise limits, or boundaries, between themselves and the Saukees and Foxes, I could never learn. They are a turbulent savage race, frequently abuse their traders, and commit depredations on those ascending and descending the Missouri. Their trade cannot be expected to increase much.

16. a. Saukees
b. O Sau-kee
c. la Sauk
d. *O Sau kee (like the Shaw o nee and Au- Chipaway[)]
e. 2
f. [*blank*]
g. 500
h. ⟨2800⟩ 2000
i. Merchants at the Prarie de Chain & St Louis & Illinois & Mick-a nak
j. at their Villages at prarie de Chien and on

the Mississippi (*and at Eel river on the Waubash*)
k. 4000
l. 6000
m. Deer skins principally
n. Deer, Black Bear Beaver otter mink Musk- rats, Racoons Gray foxes & Tallow & Bears Oile
o. At prarie de Chein
p. With the Osarge ⟨Kanzus, ottoes, Mis- souries⟩ & different ⟨bands⟩ tribes of the ⟨Panias &⟩ Chipaways

q. ⟨Soues⟩ and all the Nations on the East of the Mississippi ⟨Chipaways⟩ & ⟨partially⟩ with the Ayaways

r. on the West of the Mississippi above rock river (*140 leagues above St. Louis*)

s. They live in 3 Villages a fiew miles above the Mouth of Rock River on the West bank of the Mississippi, their Countrey is principally on the E. Side of the Missippi, they hunt on the waters of the Missourie low down, on the Demoin & the Mississippi on both Side from the oisconsin river down to the Ilinois river

Saukees and Renars, or Foxes. These nations are so perfectly consolidated that they may, in fact, be considered as one nation only. They speak the same language: they formerly resided on the east side of the Mississippi, and still claim the land on that side of the river, from the mouth of the Oisconsin to the Illinois river, and eastward towards lake Michigan; but to what particular boundary, I am not informed: they also claim, by conquest, the whole of the country belonging to the ancient Missouris, which forms one of the most valuable portions of Louisiana, but what proportion of this territory they are willing to assign to the Ayouways, who also claim a part of it, I do not know, as they are at war with the Sioux, who live N. and N. W. of them, except the Yankton ahnah. Their boundaries in that quarter are also undefined: their trade would become much more valuable if peace was established between them and the nations west of the Missouri, with whom they are at war: their population has remained nearly the same for many years: they raise an abundance of corn, beans and melons: they sometimes hunt in the country west of them, towards the Missouri, but their principal hunting is on both sides of the Mississippi, from the mouth of the Oisconsin to the mouth of the Illinois river. These people are extremely friendly to the whites, and seldom injure their traders; but they are the most implacable enemies to the Indian nations with whom they are at war. To them is justly attributable the almost entire destruction of the Missouris, the Illinois, Cahokias, Kaskaskias, and Piorias.

17. a. Renarz (*Foxes*)
    b. Ottar-car me
    c. la Renars
    d. *O Sau kee (like the Shaw o nee and Au-Chipaway[)]
    e. 1
    f. [*blank*]
    g. 300
    h. ⟨1600⟩ 1200
    i. Merchants at the Prarie de Chain & St Louis & Illinois & Mick-a nak
    j. at their Villages at prarie de Chien and on the Mississippi
    k. 2500
    l. 4000
    m. The Same [*as the Saukees*] (a greater perportion of other skins[)]
    n. Deer, Black Bear Beaver otter mink Muskrats, Racoons Gray foxes & Tallow & Bears Oile
    o. At prarie de Chein
    p. With the Osarge ⟨Kanzus, ottoes, Missouries⟩ & different tribes of the ⟨Panias &⟩ Chipaways
    q. ⟨Soues⟩ and all the Nations on the East of the Mississippi ⟨Chipaways⟩ & ⟨partially⟩ with the Ayaways
    r. on the West of the Mississippi above rock river (*Near the Saukees*)
    s. They live in 3 Villages a fiew miles above the mouth of Rock River on the west bank of the Mississippi, their Countrey is principally on the E. Side of the Missippi, they hunt on the waters of the Missourie low down, on the Demoin & the Mississippi on both Side from the oisconsin river down to the Ilinois river

18. a. Dar-co-tar's proper the Soos or Sioux
    b. Wah-pa-tone tribe
    c. Sioux
    d. *Dar-co-tar (or Sioux)
    e. (*One*)
    f. 80
    g. 200
    h. ⟨1000⟩ 700
    i. Mrs Campbell Dickson and other Merchants who trade to Michilimack
    j. (*On the Mississippi and*) on the R. St. Peters (*at sundry places not stationary*)
    k. 10000
    l. 18000
    m. Deer Beaver otter, fox mink Black bear, racoons fishers Muskrats and a greater perpotion of Deer
    n. Deer Bever otter red

fox Mink martains,
Muskrat fishers Black
bear, racoon and wolves

o. on the Mississippi R
(*west side*) about the Falls
of St Anthony on
mouth of St peters

p. with the Chipaways of
La fallowoine & leach
Lakes—(*and Sandy lakes;*
defensive with the Saukees,
Renars and Ayauwais)

q. The Saukie & Renards
and those who inhabit
East of the R Missis-
sippi, below the
Chipaways

r. rove on the Mississppi
(*On the north side of the*
river St. Peters, 18 leagues
from its mouth)

s. a Band of Sieux or Darcotas rove on both Sides
of the Mississippi about
the Mouth of the River
St. peters and Claim
jointly with the other
bands of the Sieux or

Darcotas all the Coun-
trey North of a ⟨West⟩
East line from the
Mouth of Little Sieux
River to the Mississippi
R on the west Side of
that river to the Oiscon-
sin, and up on both
Sides of the Mississippi,
and an Easterley &
westerley line passing
the otter tail portage &
between the head of St
Peter & river Rogue
and westerley ⟨to⟩ pass-
ing the heads of River
Jacque (or James) to the
head of *War re con ne*
River Down that to Mis-
sourie, and on both
Sides of that river (in-
cluding the *Ricareis*
Tribes) to the White
river, thence on the
West of the west Side of
the Missourie to the
little Soues R

Claim the country in which they rove on the N. W. side of the river St. Peters; from their village to the mouth of the Chippeway river, and thence north eastwardly towards the head of the Mississippi, including the Crow-wing river. Their lands are fertile, and generally well timbered. They are only stationary while the traders are with them, which is from the beginning of October to the last of March. Their trade is supposed to be at its greatest extent. They treat their traders with respect, and seldom attempt to rob them. This, as well as the other Sioux bands, act, in all respects, as independently of each other as if they were a distinct nation.

19.
a. Dar-co-tar's proper the Soos or Sioux
b. Min-da-war-car-ton tribe
c. Gens de Lake
d. *Dar-co-tar (or Sioux)
e. (*One*)
f. 120
g. 300
h. ⟨1500⟩ 1200
i. Mrs Campbell Dickson and other Merchants who trade to Michilimack
j. on the Mississippi & River St peters not Stationary
k. 8700
l. 16000
m. Deer Beaver otter, fox mink Black bear, racoons fishers Muskrats with a greater perpotion of Deer
n. Deer Bever otter red fox Mink Martains, Muskrat fishers Black bear, racoon and wolves

o. on the Mississippi (*west side*) about the Falls of St Anthony or mouth of S Peter
p. with the Chipaways of La fallovoine & leach Lakes—(*and Sandy lakes; with the Saukees, Renars and Ayauwais*) never go to war on the Missouri
q. The Saukie & Renards and those who inhabit East of the R Mississippi, below the Chipaways
r. rove on the Mississppi (*at the mouth of the river St. Peters*)
s. they rove above the mouth of the St Peters River, their Village is on the Mississippi they rove on both Sides of the river as far or high up as the Crow Wing river, they cultivate Corn Beans &c. &c.

'Tis the only band of Siouxs that cultivates corn, beans, &c. and these even cannot properly be termed a stationary people. They live in tents of dressed leather, which they transport by means of horses and dogs, and ramble from place to place during the greater part of the year. They are friendly to their own traders; but the inveterate enemies to such as supply their enemies, the Chippeways, with merchandise. They also claim the country in which they hunt, commencing at the entrance of the river St. Peters, and extending upwards, on both sides of the Mississippi river, to the mouth of the Crow-wing river. The land is fertile, and well watered;

lies level and sufficiently timbered. Their trade cannot be expected to increase much.

20.
a. Dar-co-tar's proper the Soos or Sioux
b. Wâh-pa-coo-tar tribe
c. people who Shoot at leaves
d. *Dar-co-tar (or Sioux)
e. [*blank*]
f. 60
g. 150
h. 700 (*400*)
i. Mrs Campbell Dickson and other Merchants who trade to Michilimack
j. on the Mississippi & River St peters not Stationary
k. 3800
l. 6000
m. the Same [*as the Wah-pa-tone*] (a greater perpn. of otter Skins)
n. the Same [*as the Wah-pa-tone*]
o. on the Mississippi R about the Falls of St Anthony or mouth of St peters

p. with the Chipaways of La fallowine & leach Lakes— but Sometimes go to war on the Missouri
q. The Saukie & Renards and those who inhabit East of the R Mississippi, below the Chipaways
r. St Peters (*south-west side, 30 leagues above its mouth, in Arrow Stone Prairies*)
s. they rove on St. peters river Claim the Countrey on the N W Side of the Mississippi to the Chipaway River and on both sides above, their Villag is 18 Lgs. up St Peters on the N. Side, do not Cultivate the land but live by hunting, and is only Stationary when Traders are with them

They rove in the country south west of the river St. Peters, from a place called the *Hardwood* to the mouth of the Yellow Medicine river: never stationary but when their traders are with them, and this does not happen at any regular or fixed point. At present they treat their traders tolerably well. Their trade cannot be expected to increase much. A great proportion of their country is open plains, lies level, and is tolerably fertile. They maintain a partial traffic with the Yanktons and Tetons to the west of them;

to these they barter the articles which they obtain from the traders on the river St. Peters, and receive in return horses, some robes and leather lodges.

21. a. Dar-co-tar's proper the Soos or Sioux
    b. Sis-sa-tone tribe
    c. [*blank*]
    d. *Dar-co-tar (or Sioux)
    e. [*blank*]
    f. 80
    g. 200
    h. ⟨1000⟩ 800
    i. Mr. Cammeron who trades to Mackilimack
    j. at the head of the St. peters river (*about 130 leagues from its mouth*)
    k. 17000
    l. 30000
    m. the Same [*as the Wah-pa-tone*] (a greater perpotion of Beaver otter & Bear[)]
    n. The Same [*as the Wah-pa-tone*]
    o. at the heads of St. Peters and red river (or R Rouch)
    p. with the Chipaways & Mandans Knistanoux & assinniboins
    q. The Saukie & Renards and those who inhabit East of the R Mississippi, below the Chipaways & Ricarras
    r. Head of St. peters (*and Red river of Lake Winnipie*)
    s. on the heads of St. Peters—not Seperate—Claim the Countrey on the N. W Side of the Mississippi—only Stationary when Traders are with them do not Cultivate the ground.

   They claim the country in which they rove, embracing the upper portions of the Red river, of lake Winnipie, and St. Peters: it is a level country, intersected with many small lakes; the land is fertile and free of stone; the majority of it open plains. This country abounds more in the valuable fur animals, the beaver, otter and marten, than any portion of Louisiana yet known. This circumstance furnishes the Sissatones with the means of purchasing more merchandise, in proportion to their number, than any nation in this quarter. A great proportion of this merchandise is reserved by them for their trade with the Tetons, whom they annually meet at some point previously agreed on, upon the waters of James river, in the month of May. This Indian fair is frequently attended by the Yanktons of the North and Ahnah. The Sissatones and Yanktons of the North here supply the others with considerable quantities of arms, ammunition, axes, knives, kettles, cloth, and a variety of other articles; and receive in return principally horses, which the others have stolen or purchased from the nations on the Missouri and west of it. They are devoted to the interests of their traders.

22. a. Dar-co-tar's proper the Soos or Sioux
    b. Yanktons of the N. tribe
    c. (*La Soo*)
    d. *Dar-co-tar (or Sioux)
    e. [*blank*]
    f. 200
    g. 500
    h. ⟨2500⟩ 1600
    i. a partial Trade [*Mr. Cammeron*] no trader of their own
    j. at the head of the St. peters river (*about 130 leagues from its mouth*)
    k. 1800
    l. 3000
    m. Buffalow robes & Wolves only
    n. The Same [*as the Wah-pa-tone*] (*and buffaloe robes, tallow, dried meat and grease in addition*)
    o. at the same place [*as the Sissatone*] or on the Mis-sourie (*near the mouth of the Chyenne river*)
    p. with the Chipaways & Mandans, Knistanoux & assinniboins
    q. The Saukie & Renards and those who inhabit East of the R Missis-sippi, below the Chipaways & Ricarras
    r. Hds of R Jacque E Side (*From the heads of the river St. Peters and Red river to the Missouri, about the great bend*)
    s. Soues or Darcota on the heads of Rivers Jacque & Big Sieux Claim the Countrey on the N W Side of the Mississippi, no traders, & but little acquainted with whites

This band, although they purchase a much smaller quantity of mer-chandise than the Sissatones, still appropriate a considerable proportion of what they do obtain in a similar manner with that mentioned of the Sissatones. This trade, as small as it may appear, has been sufficient to render the Tetones independent of the trade of the Missouri, in a great measure, and has furnished them with the means, not only of distressing and plundering the traders of the Missouri, but also, of plundering and massacreing the defenceless savages of the Missouri, from the mouth of the river Platte to the Minetares, and west to the Rocky mountains. The country these people inhabit is almost one entire plain, uncovered with timber; it is extremely level; the soil fertile, and generally well watered.

23. a. Dar-co-tar's proper the Soos or Sioux
    b. Yank-tons-Ah-nah tribe on River Demoin
    c. [*La Soo*]
    d. *Dar-co-tar (or Sioux)
    e. [*blank*]
    f. 80
    g. 200
    h. ⟨1000⟩ 700
    i. with Mr. Crawford on river Demoin
    j. on the river Demoin 30 Leagus up that R. (*and sometimes at the Ayauwais village Prairie de Chien*)
    k. 3000
    l. 5000
    m. Deer & racoon, Some Bear otter & Beaver
    n. Deer, rackoon, Bear otter ⟨Fox⟩ Beaver Buffalow roabs & Grees Elk, wolves
    o. ⟨with⟩ near the mouth of Chyanne or Dog River or at the Council Bluffs

    p. with the Nations on the West and lower part of the Missourie River (*except the Mahas and Poncars*) and with the Ricaras (*also with the Chippeways*)
    q. The Saukie & Renards and those who inhabit East of the R. Mississippi below the Chipaways & Ayauways
    r. River Demoin (*From the river All Jacque eastwardly, on the lower portion of the river Sioux and heads of Foids [Floyd's] river, Little, Sioux and Demoin rivers*)
    s. Soues or Darcota between the Missourie & River Desmoin, on the Little River Souix they rove live by hunting do not Cultivate the ground not good or verry bad

These are the best disposed Sioux who rove on the banks of the Missouri, and these even will not suffer any trader to ascend the river, if they can possibly avoid it: they have, heretofore, invariably arrested the progress of all those they have met with, and generally compelled them to trade at the prices, nearly, which they themselves think proper to fix on their merchandise: they seldom commit any further acts of violence on the whites. They sometimes visit the river Demoin, where a partial trade has been carried on with them, for a few years past, by a Mr. Crawford. Their trade, if well regulated, might be rendered extremely valuable. Their country is a very fertile one; it consists of a mixture of wood-lands and prairies. The land bordering on the Missouri is principally plains with but little timber.

24. a. Dar-co-tar's proper the Soos or Sioux
    b. Teton *Bous rouley* (burnt woods[)]
    c. Bous rouley
    d. *Dar-co-tar (or Sioux)
    e. [*blank*]
    f. 120
    g. 300
    h. ⟨1400⟩ 900
    i. with Louisell &c from St Louis
    j. at Cedar Island 1235 miles up the Missouri River
    k. 5000
    l. 7000
    m. Buffalow robes, Dressd Buffalow Skins Greece in bladders & meat
    n. Buffalow roabs, Dressed Buffalow Skins, Grees, Beaver, Deer, Cabbra, Skins, Small & large foxes ⟨Mink⟩ otter, wolves ⟨& Hair Pecon, Careajoe Skins⟩
    o. ⟨with⟩ near the mouth of Chyanne or Dog River Except the Council Bluffs
    p. with the nations on the West and lower part of the Missourie River except the Ricaras
    q. the Saukie & Renards and those East of the R Mississippi below the Chipeways & Ayauways
    r. 400 Lgs. up M[issouri] (*On the east side of the Missouri, from the mouth of White River to Teton river*)
    s. Soues or Darcota rove on both Sides of the Missourie about the Grand de tour (or big bend[)] & on Teton River above White River, they are but litle acquainted with the whites, uncivilised ⟨robbers⟩ rascals, they attempted to Stop the party for N W D[iscovery]

25. a. Dar-co-tar's proper the Soos or Sioux
    b. *Teton-O-kan-dan-das* tribe
    c. (*La Soo*)

d. *Dar-co-tar (or Sioux)
e. [*blank*]
f. 50
g. 120
h. 6oo [or] 360
i. with Louisell &c. from St Louis
j. above the mouth of Chien or *Shar ha* R (*and at the Rickaras*)
k. 1500
l. 2500
m. Buffalow robes, Dressd Buffalo Skins Greece in bladders & meat
n. Buffalow roabs, Dressed Buffalow Skins, Grees, Beaver, Deer, Cabbra, Skins, Small & large foxes ⟨Mink⟩ otter, wolves ⟨& Hair Pecon, Careajoe Skins⟩
o. ⟨with⟩ near the mouth of Chyanne or Dog River or at the Council Bluffs
p. with the Loup, Mahars Ponarer, Mandans & Big bellies
q. the Saukie & Renards and those East of the Mississippi Shar ha & Ricreras
r. on the Miss[ouri] (*On each side of the Missouri, from the mouth of Teton river to the mouth of Chyenne river*)
s. Soues or Darcota rove

on both Sides of the Missourie ⟨about⟩ below the Mouth of *Shar ha* (Chien or Dog) river on the Teton River above White River, they are but little acquainted with the whites

26. a. Dar-co-tar's proper the Soos or Sioux
b. *Teton*-Min-na-Kine-az-zo
c. (*La Soo*)
d. *Dar-co-tar (or Sioux)
e. [*blank*]
f. 100
g. 250
h. 1200 [or] 750
i. No trader (*Mr. Loisell and Co. of St. Louis*)
j. about the mouth of Chien and at Ceder Isd. (*and at the Rickaras*)
k. 2,000
l. 3,000
m. Buffalow robes, Dressd Buffalow Skins Greece in bladders & meat
n. Buffalow roabs, Dressed Buffalow Skins, Grees, Beaver, Deer, Cabbra, Skins, Small & large foxes ⟨Mink⟩ otter, wolves ⟨& Hair Pecon, Careajoe Skins⟩
o. ⟨with⟩ near the mouth of Chyenne or Dog River or at the Council Bluffs

p. with the Loup, Mahars,
Ponarer, Mandans &
Big bellies

q. the Saukie & Renards
and those East of the
Mississippi Shar ha &
Ricreras

r. on the Miss[ouri] up
(*From the mouth of the
Chyenne river on each side
of the Missouri as high as
the Rickaras*)

s. Soues or Darcota rove
on both Sides of the
Missourie above the
Sharha or Chien river
Visious but have be-
haved tolerably well to
the only trader Mr.
Haney but little ac-
quainted with the
whites, Some intercourse
with the Ricaras whome
they Sometimes treat
well but oftener bad (a
kind of an exchange
exists between them[)]

27. a. Dar-co-tar's proper the
Soos or Sioux

b. Teton-Sah-o-ne tribe

c. (*La Soo*)

d. *Dar-co-tar (or Sioux)

e. [*blank*]

f. 120

g. 300

h. 1400 [or] 900

i. no Trader (*Mr. Loisell
and Co. of St. Louis*)

j. about the mouth of
Chien and at Ceder Isd.
(*and at the Rickaras*)

k. 2,300

l. 3,500

m. Buffalow robes, Dressd
Buffalow Skins Greece
in bladders & meat

n. Buffalow roabs, Dressed
Buffalow Skins, Grees,
Beaver, Deer, Cabbra,
Skins, Small & large
foxes ⟨Mink⟩ otter,
wolves ⟨& Hair Pecon,
Careajoe Skins⟩

o. ⟨with⟩ near the mouth
of Chyanne or Dog
River or at the Council
Bluffs

p. with the Loup, Mahars,
Ponarer, Mandans &
Big bellies

q. the Saukie & Renards
and those East of the
Mississippi Shar ha &
Ricreras

r. on the Miss[ouri] above
(*On each side of the Missouri from the Ricaras to
the mouth of Warreconne
river*)

s. Soues or Darcota rove
on both Sides of the
Missourie above &
below the Ricaraas,
Visious but have be-
haved tolerably well to
the only trader Mr.
Haney but little ac-

quainted with the
whites   Some inter-
course with Ricaras
whome they Sometimes

treat well but oftener
bad (a kind of an ex-
change exists between
them[)]

Tetons Bois Brulé. Tetons Okandandas. Tetons Minnakineazzo. Tetons Sahone. These are the vilest miscreants of the savage race, and must ever remain the pirates of the Missouri, until such measures are pursued, by our government, as will make them feel a dependence on its will for their supply of merchandise. Unless these people are reduced to order, by coercive measures, I am ready to pronounce that the citizens of the United States can never enjoy but partially the advantages which the Missouri presents. Relying on a regular supply of merchandise, through the channel of the river St. Peters, they view with contempt the merchants of the Missouri, whom they never fail to plunder, when in their power. Persuasion or advice, with them, is viewed as supplication, and only tends to inspire them with contempt for those who offer either. The tameness with which the traders of the Missouri have heretofore submitted to their rapacity, has tended not a little to inspire them with contempt for the white persons who visit them, through that channel. A prevalent idea among them, and one which they make the rule of their conduct, is, that the more illy they treat the traders the greater quantity of merchandise they will bring them, and that they will thus obtain the articles they wish on better terms; they have endeavored to inspire the Ricaras with similar sentiments, but, happily, without any considerable effect. The country in which these four bands rove is one continued plain, with scarcely a tree to be seen, except on the water-courses, or the steep declivities of hills, which last are but rare: the land is fertile, and lies extremely well for cultivation; many parts of it are but badly watered. It is from this country that the Missouri derives most of its colouring matter; the earth is strongly impregnated with glauber salts, alum, copperas and sulphur, and when saturated with water, immense bodies of the hills precipitate themselves into the Missouri, and mingle with its waters. The waters of this river have a purgative effect on those unaccustomed to use it. I doubt whether these people can ever be induced to become stationary; their trade might be made valuable if they were reduced to order. They claim jointly with the other bands of the Sioux, all the country lying within the following limits, viz. beginning at the confluence of the river Demoin and Mississippi, thence up the west side of the Mississippi to the mouth of the St. Peters river, thence on both sides of the Mississippi to the mouth of Crow-wing river, and upwards with that stream, including the waters of the upper part of the same; thence to include the waters of the upper portion of Red river, of lake Winnipie, and down the same nearly to Pembenar river, thence a south westerly course to intersect the Missouri at or near the Mandans, and with that stream downwards to the entrance of the Warrecunne creek, thence passing the Missouri it goes to include the lower portion of the river Chyenne, all the waters of White river and river Teton, includes the lower portion of the river Quicurre, and returns to the Missouri, and with that stream downwards to the mouth of Waddipon river, and thence eastwardly to intersect the Mississippi at the beginning.

The subdivisions of the Darcotar or Sioux nation, with the names of the principal chiefs of each band and subdivision
[*found only in the printed document*]

Names of the Bands	Name of the Subdivisions	Names of the Chiefs	Remarks
Mindawarcarton	Mindawarcarton Kee-uke-sah Tin-tah-ton Mah-tah-ton	*Ne-co-hun-dah Tar-tong-gar-mah-nee Cha-tong-do-tah	Those marked with a star are the principal chiefs of their respective bands, as well as their own subdivisions.
Wahpatone	Wah-pa-tone O-ta-har-ton	*Tar-car-ray War-bo-sen-dat-ta	
Wahpacoota	War-pa-coo-ta Mi-ah-kee-jack-sah	*War-cah-to Chit-tah-wock-kun-de-pe	
Sissatone	Sissatone Caw-ree	*Wack-he-en-do-tar Tar-tung-gan-naz-a	
Yankton, (of the north)	Kee-uke-sah Sah-own Hone-ta-par-teen	*Mah-to-wy-ank-ka . . . . . Arsh-kane Pit-ta-sah	Said individually to be very friendly to the whites. He posseses

	Hah-har-tones	Mah-pe-on-do-tak	great influence in his
	Hone-ta-par-teen-waz	Tat-tung-gar-weet-e-co	band and nation.
	Za-ar-tar		
Yankton ahnah	Yank-ton,-sa-char-hoo	*Nap-pash-scan-na-mah-na	Accepted a medal and flag of the United States.
	Tar-co-im-bo-to	War-ha-zing ga	Do. a medal.
Teton, (Bois brûle)	E-sah-a-te-ake-tar-par	*Tar-tong-gar-sar-par . .	Do. do. & flag of U.S.
	War-chink-tar-he	Man-da-tong-gar	A great scoundrel; We
	Choke-tar-to-womb	Tar-tong-gar-war-har	gave him a medal before we were acquainted with his character.
	Oz-ash	Mah-zo-mar-nee	
	Me-ne-sharne	Wah-pah-zing-gar	
Teton,	She-o	*O-ase-se-char	
O-kan-dan-das	O-kan-dan-das	Wah-tar-pa	
Teton,	Min-na-kine-az-zo	*Wock-ke-a-chauk-in-dish-ka	
min-na-kine-az-zo	Wan-nee-wack-a-ta-o-ne-lar	Chan-te-wah-nee-jah	
	Tar-co-eh-parh		
Teton, sah-o-ne	Sah-o-ne	*Ar-kee-che-tar	
	Tack-chan-de-see-char	War-min-de-o-pe-in-doo-tar	
	Sah-o-ne-hont-a-par-par	Sharh-ka-has-car	

28. a. Chyennes
    b. Shar-ha
    c. Chien
    d. *Chyenne
    e. [*blank*]
    f. 110
    g. 300
    h. 1700 [or] 1200
    i. no Trader (*Mr. Loiselle, & Co. of St. Louis*)
    j. on the Chien River (*not stationary*) and at the Ri[c]aras
    k. (*1,500*)
    l. (*2,000*)
    m. Buffalow Robes (*of best quality*)
    n. Buffalow roabs, Dressed Buffalow Skins, Grees, Beaver, Deer, Cabbra,

Skins, Small & large foxes ⟨Mink⟩ otter, wolves ⟨& Hair Pecon, Careajoe Skins⟩ & Big horn anamal Skins

o. at the Mouth of *Shar ha* River or at the Mouth of Yellowstone R.

p. a Defensive War with Sioux (or Darcotas) and at war with no other that I know of

q. with the Ricaras, Mandans, Menataries, and all their neighbours in the plains to the S. W.

r. on Chien R. (*About the source of the river Chyenne, in the black hills*)

s. No Settled place   they rove to the S. W. of the

Ricaras, and on both Sides of the Cout noir or black hills, at the heads of the Chien River, do not Cultivate the Soil, they formerley lived in a Village and Cultivated Corn on the Cheyene River a fork of the red river of Lake winnipique, the Soues drove them from that quater across the Missourie, on the S W bank of which they made a Stand (a fort) a litte above the *ricares* a fiew years, and was Compelled to rove   well disposed Inds.

They are the remnant of a nation once respectable in point of number: formerly resided on a branch of the Red river of Lake Winnipie, which still bears their name. Being oppressed by the Sioux, they removed to the west side of the Missouri, about 15 miles below the mouth of the Warricunne creek, where they built and fortified a village, but being pursued by their ancient enemies the Sioux, they fled to the Black hills, about the head of the Chyenne river, where they wander in quest of the buffaloe, having no fixed residence. They do not cultivate. They are well disposed towards the whites, and might easily be induced to settle on the Missouri, if they could be assured of being protected from the Sioux. Their number annually diminishes. Their trade may be made valuable.

[*Ed: The printed versions of items 29 and 30 have two sets each: Wetepahatoes and Kiawas, and Kanenavish and Staetan. Where words from the printed source are used, we have two sets of parenthetical material.*]

29. a. We ta pa ha to Cay-au-wa nation

b. We ta pa ha to & ⟨Cas ta ha na⟩ Cay-au-wah

c. (*Wete-pahatoes*) (*Ki´âwâs*)

d. and e. [*blank*]

f. 70 (*including the Kiâwâs*)

g. 200 (*including the Kiâwâs*)

h. 1000 [or] 700 (*including the Kiâwâs*)

i. no Traders that visit them, what little trinkets they possess is acquired from their neighbouring Tribes or Nations

j. Sometimes visit the Ricaras

k., l., and m. [*blank*]

n. Buffalow roabs, Dressed Buffalow Skins, Grees, Beaver, Deer, Cabbra, Skins, Small & large foxes ⟨Mink⟩ otter, wolves ⟨& Hair Pecon, Careajoe Skins⟩ & Big horn Skins and Horses

o. at the Mouth of *Shar ha* River or at the Mouth of Yellowstone R.

p. a Defensive War with Sioux (or Darcotas) and at war with no other that I know of

q. with the Ricaras, Mandans, Menataries, and all their neighbours in the plains to the S. W.

r. Rivers platt & Loup (*On the Paduca fork of the river Platte*) (*and frequently with the Wetepahatoes*)

s. rove on the Paducar fork of the river platte on the Wolf or Loup river a N W branch of the Platt to the S W. of the Black hills or *Cout niree* a litte to the S. of West from the mouth of the *Chien or Sharha River* they are but little known they Sometimes Come to the ricaras and trade horses to them

They are a wandering nation, inhabit an open country, and raise a great number of horses, which they barter to the Ricaras, Mandans, &c. for articles of European manufactory. They are a well disposed people, and might be readily induced to visit the trading establishments on the Missouri. From the animals their country produces, their trade would, no doubt, become valuable. These people again barter a considerable proportion of the articles they obtain from the Menetares, Ahwahhaways, Mandans, and Ricaras, to the Dotames and Castapanas. [*The remainder comes from the second item.*] What has been said of the Wetephatoes is in all respects applicable to these people also. Neither these people, the Wetephatoes, nor the Chyennes have any idea of exclusive right to the soil.

30. a. Ca-ne-na-vich Sta-e-tan
       tribes
    b. Ca-ne-na-vich Sta-e-tan
    c. Kites
    d. and e. [*blank*]
    f. 190 (*150*) (*25*)
    g. 500 (*400*) (*75*)
    h. 3300 [or] 1900 (*1,500*)
       (*300*)
    i. no Traders that visit
       them, what little trin-
       kets they possess is ac-
       quired from their
       neighbouring Tribes or
       Nations
    j. Sometimes visit the
       Ricaras
    k., l., and m. [*blank*]
    n. Buffalow roabs, Dressed
       Buffalow Skins, Grees,
       Beaver, Deer, Cabbra,
       Skins, Small & large
       foxes ⟨Mink⟩ otter,
       wolves ⟨& Hair Pecon,
       Careajoe Skins⟩ & Big
       horn Skins and horses
    o. at the Mouth of *Shar ha*
       River or at the Mouth
       of Yellowstone R. or at
       the Mouth of the
       Cheyenne or the River
       Roche-joune yellow
       Rock
    p. a Defensive War with
       Sioux (or Darcotas) and
       at war with no other
       that I know of
    q. Mandans, Ricaras, and
       all their neighbours
    r. Heads of R Loup (*On*

*the heads of the Padoucas
fork of the river Platte,
and S. fork of Chyenne
river*) (*On the head of the
Chyenne, and frquently
with the Kanenavish*)
    s. no limits Can be dis-
       cribed for any of the
       Nations and tribes in
       this quarter as *War* with
       their neighbours fre-
       quently happen which
       force one party to re-
       move a Considerable
       distance from the
       others, untill peace is
       restored, at which pe-
       riod all lands are Gen-
       erally in Common—
       yet it is not common for
       two tribes to Camp to-
       gether for any long
       time or hunt in the
       Same place

31. a. Cataka Tribe
    b. Ca ta ka
    c., d., and e. [*blank*]
    f. 25
    g. 75
    h. 400 [or] 300
    i. no Traders that visit
       them, what little trin-
       kets they possess is ac-
       quired from their
       neighbouring Tribes or
       Nations
    j. Sometimes visit the
       Ricaras
    k., l., and m. [*blank*]

n. Buffalow roabs, Dressed Buffalow Skins, Grees, Beaver, Deer, Cabbra, Skins, Small & large foxes ⟨Mink⟩ otter, wolves ⟨& Hair Pecon, Careajoe Skins⟩ & Big horn anamal Skins and Horses

o. at the Mouth of *Shar ha* River or at the Mouth of Yellowstone R. or at the Mouth of the Cheyenne or the River Roche-joune yellow Rock

p. a Defensive war with the Soues & Assinni- boins & Ricaras at war with no other nation that I know of

q. Mandans Big bellies and their wandering neighbors

r. Heads of R Loup above (*Between the heads of the north and south forks of the river Chyenne*)

s. Those tribes [*Cataka, Nemousin, and Dotane*] rove on the heads of the *Wolf* or *Loup* River and on the head waters of the S E branches of the *river, Roche journe* or *yellow rock,* and between the Cout Noire and *rock* or Shineing moun- tains— one of those tribes is known to Speak

the Padoucan Lan- guage. Their Territories are in Common as above Stated— do not Cultivate the Soil but live by hunting in a countrey abounding in aniamals— inhabit a fine [country] for Beaver Otter &c.

32. a. Nemousin Tribe

b. Ni-mi-ou-Sin

c. (*Allebome*)

d. and e. [*blank*]

f. 15

g. 50

h. 300 [or] 200

i. no Traders that visit them, what little trin- kets they possess is ac- quired from their neighbouring Tribes or Nations

j. Sometimes visit the Ricaras

k., l., and m. [*blank*]

n. Buffalow roabs, Dressed Buffalow Skins, Grees, Beaver, Deer, Cabbra, Skins, Small & large foxes ⟨Mink⟩ otter, wolves ⟨& Hair Pecon, Careajoe Skins⟩ & Big Horn Skins and Horses

o. at the mouth of *Shar ha River* or at the mouth of Yellowstone R.

p. a Defensive war with the Soues (or Darcotas)

and at war with no
other nation that I
know of

q. Mandans, Ricaras, and
all their neighbours

r. Heads of R Loup above
(*On the head of the north
fork of the river Chyenne*)

s. Those tribes [*Cataka,
Nemousin, and Dotane*]
rove on the heads of the
Wolf or *Loup* River and
on the head waters of
the S E branches of the
*river, Roche journ*e or

yellow rock, and between
the Cout Noire and *rock*
or Shineing moun-
tains— one of those
tribes is known to Speak
the Padoucan Lan-
guage. Their Territories
are in Common as
above Stated— do not
Cultivate the Soil but
live by hunting in a
countrey abounding in
aniamals— inhabit a
fine [country] for
Beaver Otter &c.

These differ from the others (viz. Wetepahatoes, Kiawas, Kanenavich, Staetan and Cataka) in as much as they never visit the Ricaras; in all other respects they are the same.

33. a. Do-ta-ne tribe (*Dotome*)
    b. Do-ta-na
    c. (*Dotame*)
    d. Padouces
    e. [*blank*]
    f. 10
    g. 30
    h. 200 [or] 120
    i. no Traders that visit
       them, what little trin-
       kets they possess is ac-
       quired from their
       neighbouring Tribes or
       Nations
    j. Some times visit the
       Ricaras
    k., l., and m. [*blank*]
    n. Buffalow roabs, Dressed
       Buffalow Skins, Grees,
       Beaver, Deer, Cabbra,

Skins, Small & large
foxes ⟨Mink⟩ otter,
wolves ⟨& Hair Pecon,
Careajoe Skins⟩ & Big
Horn Skins and Horses

o. at the Mouth of *Shar ha*
   River or at the Mouth
   of Yellowstone R. or at
   the Mouth of the
   Cheyenne or the River
   Roche-joune yellow
   Rock

p. a Defensive War with
   Sioux (or Darcotas) and
   at war with no other
   that I know of

q. with the Ricaras, Man-
   dans, Menataries, and
   all their neighbours in
   the plains to the S. W.

425

r. Heads of the R. Loup
above (*On the heads of the
river Chyenne*)

s. Those tribes [*Cataka,
Nemousin, and Dotane*]
rove on the heads of the
Wolf or *Loup* River and
on the head waters of
the S E branches of the
river, Roche journe or
yellow rock, and be-
tween the Cout Noire
and *rock* or Shineing

mountains— one of
those tribes is known to
Speak the Padoucan
Language. Their Ter-
ritories are in Common
as above Stated— do
not Cultivate the Soil
but live by hunting in
a countrey abounding
in aniamals— inhabit
a fine [country] for
Beaver Otter &c.

The information I possess, with respect to this nation, is derived from Indian information: they are said to be a wandering nation, inhabiting an open country, and who raise a great number of horses and mules. They are a friendly, well disposed people, and might, from the position of their country, be easily induced to visit an establishment on the Missouri, about the mouth of Chyenne river. They have not, as yet, visited the Missouri.

34. a. Cas-ta-ha-na N
b. Cas-ta-ha-na *Nation*
c. Gens des Vache
d. Me na ta re (or big belly)
e. [*blank*]
f. 500
g. 1300
h. 7000 [or] 5000
i. what little trinkets they posses is acquired from their neigbouring Tribes or Nations (*No Trader*)
j. Some visit the Mandans & Wanataries
k., l., and m. [*blank*]
n. Buffalow roabs, Dressed

Buffalow Skins, Grees,
Beaver, Deer, Cabbra,
Skins, Small & large
foxes ⟨Mink⟩ otter,
wolves ⟨& Hair Pecon,
Careajoe Skins⟩ & Big
Horn Skins and Horses
(*and skins of the lynx or
louverin, and martens in
addition*)

o. at the mouth of Roche joune (or Yellow Stone R)
p. a Defensive War with the Sioux & Assinni- boins, at war with no other nation that I know of

q. Mandans Big bellies
   and their wandering
   neighbours
r. Yellowrock river &
   Loup (*Between the sources
   of the Padoucas fork, of the
   rivers Platte and Yellow
   Stone*)

s. rove on a S E. fork of
   the *Yellow Rock* River
   Called Big horn River,
   and the heads of the
   Loup. Their Territories
   are in common   do not
   cultivate the Soil but
   live by hunting

What has been said of the Dotames is applicable to these people, except that they trade principally with the Crow Indians, and that they would most probably prefer visiting an establishment on the Yellow Stone river, or at its mouth on the Missouri.

35. a. *Ravin* nation
    b. ⟨Arp-Sar-co-gah⟩
       Kee-hât-sâ
    c. Cor beaus
    d. Menetare (or big belly)
    e. [*blank*]
    f. 350
    g. 900
    h. 5000 [or] 3500
    i. what little trinkets they
       possess is acquired for
       their neigbouring
       Tribes or Nations (*No
       Trader*)
    j. Some visit the Mandans
       & Minataries
    k., l., and m. [*blank*]
    n. Buffalow roabs, Dressed
       Buffalow Skins, Grees,
       Beaver, Deer, Cabbra,
       Skins; Small & large
       foxes ⟨Mink⟩ otter
       wolves ⟨& Hair Pecon,
       Careajoe Skins⟩ & Big
       Horn Skins and Horses
       (*and skins of the lynx or*

*louverin, and martens in
addition*)
o. at the mouth of Roche
   joune (or Yellow Stone
   R)
p. a Defensive War with
   the Sioux & Assinni-
   boins, at war with no
   other nation that I
   know of & Ricaras
q. Mandans Big bellies
   and their wandering
   neighbours
r. on the Yellow Rock R.
   low down (*about the
   mouth of the Big-horn
   river*)
s. rove on both Sides of
   the River *Roche jone* (or
   Yellow Stone) a ⟨Short⟩
   Some distance above
   the mouth. Their Ter-
   ritories are in Com-
   mon   do not cultivate
   the Soil but live by
   hunting   Ther Coun-

trey is full of anamals or
Game of every Kind
perticularly Beaver, a

great perpotion Wood
Ld.

These people are divided into four bands, called by themselves A-hâh´-âr-ro´-pir-no-pah, Noo´-ta, Pa-rees-car, and E-hârt´-sâr. They annually visit the Mandans, Minetares, and Ahwahhaways, to whom they barter horses, mules, leather lodges, and many articles of Indian apparel, for which they receive, in return, guns, ammunition, axes, kettles, awls, and other European manufactures. When they return to their country, they are in turn visited by the Paunch and Snake Indians, to whom they barter most of the articles they have obtained from the nations on the Missouri, for horses and mules, of which those nations have a greater abundance than themselves. They also obtain from the Snake Indians, bridle-bits and blankets, and some other articles which those Indians purchase from the Spaniards. The bridle-bits and blankets I have seen in the possession of the Mandans and Minetares. Their country is fertile, and well watered, and in most parts well timbered.

36. a. Pau⟨nch tribe⟩ (*Paunch Indians*)

b. ⟨pa-Sha-pa-to-rah⟩ Kee-hât-sâ (*Al-la-ka-we-ah*)

c. Gens des panse

d. Menetarre (or big belly)

e. [*blank*]

f. 300

g. 800

h. 4000 [or] 2300

i. what little trinkets they possess is acquired from their neighbouring Tribes or Nations (*No Trader*)

j. Some visit the Mandans & Minataries

k., l., and m. [*blank*]

n. Buffalow roabs, Dressed Buffalow Skins, Grees, Beaver, Deer, Cabbra, Skins, Small & large foxes ⟨Mink⟩ otter, wolves ⟨& Hair Pecon, Careajoe Skins⟩ & Big Horn Skins no Horses (*and skins of the lynx or louverin, and martens in addition*)

o. at the mouth of Roche joune (or Yellow Stone R)

p. a Defensive War with the Sioux & Assinni-boins, at war with no other nation that I know of except Ricaras

q. Mandans Big bellies
and their wandering
neighbours

r. on the Yellow Rock R.
high up (*near the rocky
mountains, and heads of
the Big-horn river*)

s. rove on the River *Roche-*

jone high up   their
Countrey abounds in
animals of Different
kinds. Their Territories
are in Common   do
not cultivate the Soil
but live by hunting

These are said to be a peaceable, well disposed nation. Their country is a variegated one, consisting of mountains, vallies, plains, and woodlands, irregularly interspersed. They might be induced to visit the Missouri, at the mouth of the Yellow Stone river; and from the great abundance of valuable fured animals which their country, as well as that of the Crow Indians, produces, their trade must become extremely valuable. They are a roving people, and have no idea of of exclusive right to the soil.

37. a. As[sini]boins T[ribe]s as
cald. by the Chipaways
or Stone Sious

b. Ma-ne-to-par Tribe

c. or Band lar Gru Crain
or canoe

d. Soues (Dar co ta) with a
little Corruption

e. [*blank*]

f. 100

g. 200

h. 1200 [or] 750

i. Hudsons Bay N W. &
X. Y. Companies

j. The Establishments at
the mouth of Mous R.
on the assiniboin River
& at the Establishmts.
on R. Cappell abt. 150
mes. N. of Fort Mandan

k. 4500

l. 7000

m. Some Beaver a fiew
Roabs, Grees, meat
wolves & pemitigon
Some Brown Bear &c

n. Buffalow roabs, Dressed
Buffalow Skins, Grees,
Beaver, Deer, Cabbra,
Skins, Small & large
foxes ⟨Mink⟩ otter,
wolves ⟨& Hair Pecon,
Careajoe Skins⟩ & Big
Horn Skins and Horses
(*Buffaloe robes, tallow,
dried and pounded meat
and grease, skins of the
large and small fox, small
and large wolves, antelopes
(or cabri) and elk in great
abundance; also some
brown, white and grisly
bear, deer and lynx*)

o. at the mouth of Roche

joune (or Yellow Stone
R)

p. Sioux snake Indians
and partially with
Ricaras & Several na-
tions on the S. W. of
Missouri

q. the Knistanoes (or
Cristanoes & their own
tribes only)

r. on Mous river (*between
the Assinniboin and the
Missouri*) & R. Rogue

s. rove on the Mouse
River and the branches
of River *Ossinaboin*
North of the Mandans,
those people do not
cultivate the ground,
they are Vicious.   they
live by hunting pay but
little respect to their en-
gagements, great
Drunkards

38. a. As[sini]boins T[ribe]s as
cald. by the Chipaways
or Stone Sious

b. Na-co-ta O-ee-gah

c. Gens des fees or Girls
(*Gens des Tee*)

d. Soues (Dar co ta) with a
little corruption

e. [*blank*]

f. 100

g. 250

h. 1200 [or] 850

i. Hudsons Bay N W. &
X. Y. Companies

j. The Establishments at
the mouth of Mous R.
on the assiniboin River
& at the Establishmts.
on R. Cappell abt. 150
mes. N. of Fort Mandan

k. 6000

l. 6500

m. Some Beaver a fiew
Roabs, Grees, meat
wolves & pemitigon

n. Buffalow roabs, Dressed
Buffalow Skins, Grees,
Beaver, Deer, Cabbra,
Skins; Small & large
foxes ⟨Mink⟩ otter
wolves ⟨& Hair Pecon,
Careajoe Skins⟩, & Big
Horn Skins and Horses
(*Buffaloe robes, tallow,
dried and pounded meat
and grease, skins of the
large and small fox, small
and large wolves, antelopes
(or cabri) and elk in great
abundance; also some
brown, white and grisly
bear, deer and lynx*)

o. At the mouth of Roche-
joune (or Yellow Stone
R)

p. Sioux snake Indians
and partially with
Ricaras & Several na-
tions on the S. W. of
Missouri

q. the Knistanoes (or
Cristanoes & their own
tribes only)

r. between the R. Rouche
& Missouri (*about the
mouth of Little Missouri,
to the Assinniboin, at the
mouth of Capelle river*)

s. Rove on the heads of
the Mouse river & River
Capell (or that Calls)
and on a N West branch
of the Missourie Called
White earth River,
vicious & do not Culti-
vate the land live by
hunting   pay but little
respect to their engage-
ments, great Drunkards.

39. a. As[sini]boins T[ribe]s as
cald. by the Chipaways
or Stone Sious

b. Na-co-ta Mah-ta-pa-nar-to

c. Big Devils (*Gens des
grand Diable*)

d. Soues (Da co ta) with a
little corruption

e. [*blank*]

f. 200

g. 450

h. ⟨2000⟩ [or] 1600

i. Hudsons Bay N W. &
X. Y. Companies (*and
occasionally at the establishments on the river
Saskashawan*)

k. 8000

l. 8000

m. Some Beaver a fiew
Roabs, Grees, meat
wolves & pemitigon

n. Buffalow roabs, Dressed
Buffalow Skins, Grees,
Beaver, Deer, Cabbra,
Skins, Small & large
foxes ⟨Mink⟩ otter,
wolves ⟨& Hair Pecon,
Careajoe Skins⟩ & Big
horn Skins and Horses
(*Buffaloe robes, tallow,
dried and pounded meat
and grease, skins of the
large and small fox, small
and large wolves, antelopes
(or cabri) and elk in great
abundance; also some
brown, white and grisly
bear, deer and lynx, with
more bears and some mar-
ten, with more bears and
some marten*)

o. at the mouth of Roche-
joune (or Yellow stone R)

p. Sioux snake Indians
and partially with
Ricaras & Several na-
tions on the S. W. of
Missouri

q. the Knistanoes (or
Cristanoes & their own
tribes only)

r. between the R. Rouche
& Missouri & up White
earth R (*and on the head
of Assinniboin and Capelle
rivers*)

s. rove in the plains in
Different parties be-
tween the *Missouris* &
the *Saskashowan* rivers

above the Yallow Stone
River & heads of the
Ossiniboins River—

they are vicious do not
Cultivate the Soil live by
hunting.

Manetopa. Oseegah. Mahtopanato. Are the descendants of the Sioux,
and partake of their turbulent and faithless disposition: they frequently
plunder, and sometimes murder, their own traders. The name by which
this nation is generally known was borrowed from the Chippeways, who
call them *Assinniboan,* which, literally translated, is *Stone Sioux,* hence the
name of Stone Indians, by which they are sometimes called. The country
in which they rove is almost entirely uncovered with timber; lies extremely level, and is but badly watered in many parts; the land, however,
is tolerably fertile and unincumbered with stone. They might be induced
to trade at the river Yellow Stone; but I do not think that their trade
promises much. Their numbers continue about the same. These bands,
like the Sioux, act entirely independent of each other, although they
claim a national affinity and never make war on each other. The country
inhabited by the Mahtopanato possesses rather more timber than the
other parts of the country. They do not cultivate.

40. a. Knistanoes or
Cristanoes

b. Knis-ta-nau 2 *bands*

c. Crees

d. Corupted Chipaway

e. [*blank*]

f. 150

g. 300

h. 1000

i. Hudsons Bay N. W. &
X. Y. Companies

j. The Establishments at
the mouth of Mous R.
on the Assiniboin River
& at the Establishmts.
on R. cappell abt 150
mes. N. of Fort Mandan

k. 10000 (*15,000*)

l. 15000

m. Beaver, wolves, otter,
carkajeu (or wolverine
or Beaver robes)
Dressed Elk or Mose
little fox Loucirva
[picou?] or Lynx, Mink
Martin &c

n. Dressed Moos Skins &
Martins (*The skins of the
beaver, otter, lynx, wolf,
wolverine, marten, mink,
small fox, brown and
grizzly bear, dressed elk
and moose-deer skins, muskrat skins, & some buffaloe
robes, dried meat, tallow
and grease*)

o. at the mouth of Roche-
joune (or Yellow Stone R)

p. Sioux the fall Indians
Blood Indians, Crow,
&c.

q. Algonquins Chipaways
Assiniboins mandans
Grovantre &c. and the
Ah-nah-ha-ways or
Shoe Indians

r. Assiniboin River (*and*

*thence towards
Saskashawan*)

s. rove on Heads of Os-
siniboin & its waters
and to the Missouri in
the Countrey of the As-
siniboins, principally on
the head Assiniboin—
not Stationary.

They are a wandering nation; do not cultivate, nor claim any particular tract of country. They are well disposed towards the whites, and treat their traders with respect. The country in which they rove is generally open plains, but in some parts, particularly about the head of the Assinni-boin river, it is marshy and tolerably well furnished with timber, as are also the Fort Dauphin mountains, to which they sometimes resort. From the quantity of beaver in their country, they ought to furnish more of that article than they do at present. They are not esteemed good beaver hunters. They might, probably be induced to visit an establishment on the Missouri, at the Yellow Stone river. Their number has been reduced, by the small pox, since they were first known to the Canadians.

41. a. Fall Indians
b. (*A-lân-sâr*)
c. Fall Indians or Gen de rapid
d. Me ne tar re
e. [*blank*]
f. 260
g. 660
h. 2500
i. N W Company
j. ⟨about the great Falls of Missouri⟩ Eagle Moun-tain (*Upper establishment on the Saskashawan; but little trade*)
k. 1000
l. 4000

m. Beaver, wolves, otter, carkajeu (or wolverine or Beaver robes) Dressed Elk or Mose little fox Loucirva [picou?] or Lynx, Mink Martin &c

n. Dressed Moos Skins & Martins and Big horned animal Skins (*Skins of the beavers, brown, white and grizzly bear, large and small foxes, muskrat, mar-ten, mink, lynx, wolverine, wolves, white hares, deer, elk, moose-deer, antelopes of the Missouri, and some buffaloe*)

o. about the falls of
   Missouri
p. (*Defensive war with the*
   Christenoes)
q. [*blank*]
r. near Rock M (*On the*
   head of the south fork of
   the Saskashawan river,
   and same streams supposed

to be branches of the
Missouri)
s. rove between the Mis-
   souries and askaw or
   Bad river a fork of the
   Saskashawan, a tribe of
   Menetaries, but little
   known, they rove as far
   as the rock mountains

The country these people rove in is not much known: it is said to be a high, broken, woody country. They might be induced to visit an establishment at the falls of the Missouri: their trade may, no doubt, be made profitable.

42. a. Cat-tan a haws
    b. Cat an a haws
    c. none
    d. through h. [*blank*]
    i. (*No trader*)
    j., k., and l. [*blank*]
    m. Beaver, wolves, otter,
       carkajeu (or wolverine
       or Beaver robes)
       Dressed Elk or Mose
       little fox Loucirva
       [picou?] or Lynx, Mink
       Martin &c
    n. and Big horned animal
       Skins and all other
       northern animals inhab-
       iting a N. climate except
       racoons & fisher (*Skins*
       of the beavers, brown,
       white and grizzly bear,
       large and small foxes,

muskrat, marten, mink,
lynx, wolverine, wolves,
white hares, deer, elk,
moose-deer, antelopes of the
Missouri, and some
buffaloe)
o. about the falls of
   Missouri
p. and q. [*blank*]
r. near Rock M (*Between*
   the Saskashawan and the
   Missouri, on waters sup-
   posed to be of the Missouri)
s. on the heads of the
   South fork of the Sas-
   kas-ha-wan, and North
   branches of the Mis-
   souri ⟨near⟩ about the
   rock Mountain   but
   little known

What has been said of the Fall Indians is, in all respects, applicable to this nation. They are both wandering nations.

43. a. Blue Mud (*and Long Hair*) Indians
    b. [*blank*]
    c. (*Blue Mud and Long Hair Indians*)
    d. through h. [*blank*]
    i. (*No trader*)
    j., k., and l. [*blank*]
    m. Beaver, wolves, otter, carkajeu (or wolverine or Beaver robes) Dressed Elk or Mose little fox Loucirva [picou?] or Lynx, Mink Martin &c
    n. and Big horned animal Skins and all other northern animals inhabiting a N. climate except racoons & fisher (*Not*

known, but from the position of their country supposed to abound in animals similar to those mentioned in [42 o]
    o. about the falls of Missouri
    p. and q. [*blank*]
    r. near Rock M (*West of the Rocky mountains, and near the same on water courses supposed to be branches of the Columbia river*)
    s. In the Rock or Shineing mountains on the S. Side of a River Called *Great Lake* River, Supposed to run into the *Columbia* river, but little known

Still less is known of these people, or their country. The water courses on which they reside, are supposed to be branches of the Columbia river. They are wandering nations.

44. a. Alitan or Snake Ind.
    b. A-li-tan (*So-so-na, So-so-bâ, and i´-â-kâr*)
    c. Gen de Serpent
    d. *Ali tan
    e., f., and g. [*blank*]
    h. very noumerous
    i. Some of those Inds trade with the Spaniards ⟨North and S. of them⟩
    j. New Mexico
    k., l., and m. [*blank*]
    n. Carkajous wolverine or

Beaver eaters Loucirva Pichou or Lonkz (*The same with the Fall, Cattanahaws and Black Foot Indians, except buffaloes; but they have in addition immense quantities of horses, mules and asses*)
    o. Head of Platt or Arkansaws R (*At or near the Falls of Missouri*)
    p. act on the Defensive as far as I can lern   the most of the nearer na-

tions make war upon them

q. with those who wish to be friendly (*Mandans and Crow Indians, and all those who do not attack them*)

r. in and about Rockey Mounts. (*Among the rocky mountains, on the heads of the Missouri, Yellow Stone, and Platte rivers*)

s. rove on both Sides from the falls about 2500 miles up near the Rock mountain to the head and about those moun-

tains Southerley quite to the head of Arkansaw, verry moumerous all the nations on the Missouries below make war on them & Steal their horses   Those I have seen are mild and appear well disposed (I am told they are the best nation known) those to the South have some trade with the Spaniards of N. Mexico from whom those on the Missouries get some articles   they abound in horses

Aliatans, *Snake Indians.* These are a very numerous and well disposed people, inhabiting a woody and mountainous country; they are divided into three large tribes, who wander at a considerable distance from each other; and are called by themselves So-so-na, So-so bu-bar, and I-a-kar; these are again subdivided into smaller tho' independent bands, the names of which I have not yet learnt; they raise a number of horses and mules which they trade with the Crow Indians, or are stolen by the nations on the east of them. They maintain a partial trade with the Spaniards, from whom they obtain many articles of cloathing and ironmongery, but no warlike implements.

[*Ed: The printed version adds two other divisions to the Snake Indians, material not found on the manuscript. We repeat the item number.*]

44. a. (*Aliatans*)
b. (*A-lí-a-tân*)
c. (*Aliatâ*)
d. (*Aliatan*)
e. and f. [*blank*]
g. (*Very numerous*)

h. [*blank*]
i. (*With the Spaniards of New Mexico*)
j. (*The place at which this trade is carried on is not known*)
k., l., and m. [*blank*]

n. (*Immense quantities of horses, mules, asses, buffaloe, deer, elk, black bear, and large hares; and in the northern regions of their country, big horn and Missouri antelopes, with many animals of the fur kind*)

o. (*On the Arkansas, as high up as possible. It would be best that it should be west of the source of the Kansas, if it should be necessary even to supply it some distance by land*)

p. (*Defensive war with the Great and Little Osages, Paniapique, Kansas, Pania Proper, Pania Repeublican, Pania Loups, Ricaras, and Sioux*)

q. (*At peace with all who do not wage war against them*)

r. (*Among the rocky mountains and in the plains at the heads of the Platte and Arkansas rivers*)

Of the West. These people also inhabit a mountainous country, and sometimes venture in the plains east of the Rocky mountains, about the head of the Arkansas river. They have more intercourse with the Spaniards of New Mexico than the Snake Indians. They are said to be very numerous and warlike, but are badly armed. The Spaniards fear these people, and therefore take the precaution not to furnish them, with any warlike implements. In their present unarmed state, they frequently commit hostilities on the Spaniards. They raise a great many horses.

44. a. (*Alitan*)
   b. [*blank*]
   c. (*La Plays*)
   d. (*Aliatan*)
   e., and f. [*blank*]
   g. (*Very numerous*)
   h. [*blank*]
   i. (*With the Spaniards of New Mexico*)
   j. (*The place at which this trade is carried on is not known*)
   k., l., and m., [*blank*]
   n. (*Immense quantities of horses, mules, asses, buffaloe, deer, elk, black bear, and large hares; and in the northern regions of their country, big horn and Missouri antelopes, with many animals of the fur kind*)
   o. (*On the Arkansas, as high up as possible. It would be best that it should be west of the source of the Kansas, if it should be neces-*

sary even to supply it some distance by land)

p. (*Defensive war with the Great and Little Osages, Paniapique, Kansas, Pania Proper, Pania Repeublican, Pania Loups,*

Ricaras, and Sioux)

q. [*blank*]

r. (*The mountains on the borders of New Mexico, and the extensive plains at the heads of the Arkansas and Red rivers)*

La Playes. These principally inhabit the rich plains from the head of the Arkansas, embracing the heads of Red river, and extending with the mountains and high lands eastwardly as far as it is known towards the gulph of Mexico. They possess no fire arms, but are warlike and brave. They are, as well as the other Aliatans, a wandering people. Their country abounds in wild horses, besides great numbers which they raise themselves. These people, and the West Aliatans, might be induced to trade with us on the upper part of the Arkansas river. I do not believe that any of the Aliatans claim a country within any particular limits.

45. a. ⟨Padoucas⟩
 b. ⟨p⟩
 c. padoo
 d. *Padoucies
 e. Several V[illages]
 f. and g. [*blank*]
 h. verry noumerous
 i. Some of those Inds trade with the Spaniards ⟨North and S. of them⟩
 j. New Mexico
 k., l., and m. [*blank*]
 n. Carkajous wolverine or Beaver eaters Loucirva Pichon or Lonkz (except Moose Martin Picou & Carckjou Skins[)] (*they have in addition immense quantities of horses, mules and asses*)
 o. near the head of Platt, or Arkansaw Rivers
 p. act on the Defensive as far as I can lern   the most of the nearer nations make war upon them; q. with those who wish to be friendly
 r. Heads of Platt & Arkansaws R
 s. This nation live in Villages on the heads of River Platt & Arkansaws noumerous, well disposed, abound in horses, have Some [trade] with New Mexico, I can obtain no certain account of their Situation Numbers &c. &c.

This once powerful nation has, apparently, entirely disappeared; every inquiry I have made after them has proved ineffectual. In the year 1724, they resided in several villages on the heads of the Kansas river, and could, at that time, bring upwards of two thousand men into the field (see Monsr. Dupratz history of Louisiana, page 71, and the map attached to that work). The information that I have received is, that being oppressed by the nations residing on the Missouri, they removed to the upper part of the river Platte, where they afterwards had but little intercourse with the whites. They seem to have given name to the northern branch of that river, which is still called the Paducas fork. The most probable conjecture is, that being still further reduced, they have divided into small wandering bands, which assumed the names of the subdivisions of the Paducas nation, and are known to us at present under the appellation of Wetepahatoes, Kiawas, Kanenavish, Katteka, Dotame, &c. who still inhabit the country to which the Paducas are said to have removed. The majority of my information led me to believe that those people spoke different languages, but other and subsequent information has induced me to doubt the fact.

46. a. Chipaways
    b. Oo-chi-pa-wau
    c. Souteau
    d. *Oo he-pawau
    e. 1
    f. [*blank*]
    g. 400
    h. ⟨2000⟩ 1600
    i. British N W. Co.
    j. near their Village
    k. 12,000
    l. 16000
    m. Beaver Otter, racoon fox Min[k] Deer & B Bear Skins & Martens
    n. Beaver, otters, racoon, fox, Mink, Deer & B. Bear Skins & Martens
    o. head of Mississippi or at Red Lake (*Sandy Lake*)
    p. Sioux (or Darcotas) (*Saukees, Renars, and Ayouwais*)
    q. all the tribes of Chipaways and the nations about the Lakes & Down the Missippi
    r. in an Island in Leach Lake (*formed by the Mississippi river*)
    s. a village in a lake near the head of the Mississippi and an expansion of the Same Called Leach, they own all the Countrey West of L. Su-

439

peror & to the Sous
line— wild rice which
is in great abundance in

their [country] raise no
Corn &c.

Chippeways, *of Leach Lake*. Claim the country on both sides of the Mississippi, from the mouth of the Crow-wing river to its source, and extending west of the Mississippi to the lands claimed by the Sioux, with whom they still contend for dominion. They claim, also, east of the Mississippi, the country extending as far as lake Superior, including the waters of the river St. Louis. This country is thickly covered with timber generally; lies level, and generally fertile, though a considerable portion of it is intersected and broken up by small lakes, morasses and swamps, particularly about the heads of the Mississippi and river St. Louis. They do not cultivate, but live principally on the wild rice, which they procure in great abundance on the borders of Leach Lake and the banks of the Mississippi. Their number has been considerably reduced by wars and the small pox. Their trade is at its greatest extent.

47. a. Chipaways about L. Dubois (or wood) and the head of the Mississippi
    b. Algonquins 100 men & Chipaways 200
    c. Souteaus
    d. *Oochepawau
    e. [*blank*]
    f. ramble
    g. 300, 200, 100 (*200*)
    h. 500, 700, 350 (*700*)
    i. British N W. Co.
    j. at Dift. Camps (*At an establishment on Red Lake, and at their hunting camps*)
    k. 12000 (*8,000*)
    l. 16000 (*10,000*)
    m. Beaver Otter, racoon fox Min[k] Deer & B

Bear skins & Martens & some Berch Canoos
    n. Beaver, otters, racoon, fox, Mink Deer & B. Bear skins & Martens & Canoos
    o. head of the Mississippi or at Red Lake
    p. Sioux (or Darcotas)
    q. all the tribes of Chipaways and the nations about the Lakes & Down the Missippi & partially with the Assiniboin
    r. about the head of Mississippi & L. of Woods (*and around Red Lake*)
    s. in differant parts of the Countrey from the

heads of the Mississippi
Northerley to the N W.
part of Lake Dubois

do not cultivate the
land but live on Wild
rice hunting &c &c

[Chippeways] *Of Red lake*. Claim the country about Red lake and Red lake river, as far as the Red river of lake Winnipie, beyond which last river they contend with the Sioux for territory. This is a low level country, and generally thickly covered with timber, interrupted with many swamps and morasses. This, as well as the other bands of Chippeways, are esteemed the best hunters in the north west country; but from the long residence of this band in the country they now inhabit, game is becoming scarce; therefore, their trade is supposed to be at its greatest extent. The Chippeways are a well disposed people, but excessively fond of spirituous liquor.

48. a. Chipaways on River
       Rouge
    b. ⟨Kristanoe⟩
       Oo-che-pa-wau
    c. Souteu
    d. *Oochepawau
    e. [*blank*]
    f. ramble
    g. 100
    h. 800 (*350*)
    i. N W & X Y Co.
    j. at the mouth of
       Pembinar river
    k. 7000
    l. 10000
    m. Beaver Otter, racoon
       fox Min[k] Deer & B
       Bear Skins & Martens
    n. Beaver, otters, racoon,
       fox, Mink, Deer & B.
       Bear skins & Martens
       and Lynx, wolverine &
       wolves
    o. head of the Mississippi
       or at Red Lake (*On the*

    Red river of Lake Win-
    nipie, about the mouth of
    the Assiniboin river)
    p. Sioux (or Darcotas) (*and*
       partially with Assinniboins)
    q. all the tribes of
       Chipaways and the na-
       tions about the lakes &
       Down the Missippi &
       cristinoes
    r. on R. Ruge (*of Lake*
       Winnipie, and) about the
       Mouth of Pembina
    s. ramble near the Estab-
       lishment on the River
       ⟨Rogue⟩ Assiniboin &
       fork of red River run-
       ning into *Lake Wini-*
       picque This tribe of
       Chipaways formerley
       lived on the Mississippi
       at Sand Lake and en-
       couraged by the British
       traders to hunt on River
       Rogue

[Chippeways] *Of river Pembena.* These people formerly resided on the east side of the Mississippi, at Sand lake, but were induced by the north west company, to remove, about two years since, to the river Pembena. They do not claim the lands on which they hunt. The country is level and the soil good. The west side of the river is principally prairies or open plains; on the east side there is a greater proportion of timber. Their trade at present is a very valuable one, and will probably increase for some years. They do not cultivate, but live by hunting. They are well disposed towards the whites.

49. a. Algonquin
b. Oo Chipawau
c. Souters
d. *Oochepawau
e. [*blank*]
f. ramble
g. 200
h. ⟨1200⟩ 600
i. N. W. & X Y Co.
j. Portage de prarie (*Establishments on the Assiniboin at Fort de Prairie*)
k. 8000
l. 11000
m. Beaver Otter, racoon, fox Min[k] Deer & B Bear Skins & marten
n. Beaver, otters, racoon, fox, Mink, Deer & B. Bear Skins & Martens Lynx & Wolverines [*words crossed out, illegible*]
o. Mouth of Assinnoboin about the place the West line will cross from the L. of Wo[o]ds in Lat.

49° 37′ North or therabouts (*At the Red river establishment*)
p. Sioux (or Darcotas) (*and partially with the Assinniboins*)
q. all the tribes of Chipaways and the nations about the lakes & Down the Missippi & cristinoes
r. about the Mouth of the assiniboin (*on Red river*)
s. Those bands [*including No. 50*] rove on the river Rogue from the Pembaner down to the Lake Winipicque and about the *Lake Manitauber*, removed from the East encouraged by the British traders to hunt on River Rogue Those people do not Cultivate the earth but hunt beaver & valuable furs

[Algonquins] *Of Portage de Prairie.* These people inhabit a low, flat, marshy country, mostly covered with timber, and well stocked with game. They are emigrants from the lake of the Woods and the country east of it, who were introduced, some years since, by the N. W. traders, in order to hunt the country on the lower parts of the Red river, which then abounded in a variety of animals of the fur kind. They are an orderly, well disposed people, but like their relations on Rainy lake, extremely addicted to spirituous liquors. Their trade is at its greatest extent.

50. a. Algonquins [*word beginning with "K" crossed out, illegible*]
    b. Oo Chepa wau
    c. Souteau
    d. *Oochepawau
    e. [*blank*]
    f. ramble
    g. 100
    h. 500 (*300*)
    i. N W & X Y Co.
    j. Portage de prarie (*Establishments on the rivers Winnipie and Rainy Lake, and at their hunting camps*)
    k. ⟨4000⟩
    l. ⟨5000⟩ (*6,000*)
    m. Beaver Otter, racoon, fox Min[k], Deer & B Bear Skins & marten (*Principally birch bark canoes*)
    n. Beaver, otters, racoon, fox, min[k] Deer & B Bear Skins & martens Lynx & Wolverines & wolverines & wolves &
       Muskrats
    o. Mouth of Assinnoboin about the place the West line will cross from the L. of Wo[o]ds in Lat. 49° 37′ North or therabouts (*At the Red river establishment*)
    p. Sioux (or Darcotas) (*and partially with the Assinniboins*)
    q. all the tribes of Chipaways and the nations about the lakes & Down the Missippi & Algonquians
    r. low down the red R (*On the south side of Rainy Lake, Rainy Lake river, and Lake of the Wood*)
    s. Those bands [*including No. 49*] rove on the river Rogue from the Pembaner down to the Lake Winipicque and about the *Lake Manitauber*, removed from the East encouraged by

the British traders to	Cultivate the earth but
hunt on River Rogue	hunt beaver & valuable
Those people do not	furs

Algonquins, *of Rainy lake, &c.* With the precise limits of the country they claim, I am not informed. They live very much detached, in small parties. The country they inhabit is but an indifferent one; it has been much hunted, and the game, of course, nearly exhausted. They are well disposed towards the whites. Their number is said to decrease. They are extremely addicted to spirituous liquor, of which large quantities are annually furnished them by the N. W. traders, in return for their bark canoes. They live wretchedly poor.

51. a. Black foot Indians
    b. [*blank*]
    c. la peain noir
    d. through h. [*blank*]
    i. (*No trader*)
    j., k., and l. [*blank*]
    n. Beaver, otters, racoon, fox, Mink, Deer, B Bear Skins & martens Lynx & Wolverines & wolves & Muskrats and Elk & Big horn
    o. about the falls of Missouri
    p. and q. [*blank*]
    r. near the Rock M. (*Between the Saskashawan and the Missouri, on waters supposed to be of Missouri*)
    s. *Blackfot* rove near the Rock mountains on the East Side on the waters of the Missouries but little known   Those nations [*including*

Flatheads] being little known the information is from the Menerres

52. a. Flat head Inds.
    b. (*Tut-see-was*)
    c. Tate Platt
    d. through h. [*blank*]
    i. (*No trader*)
    j. through m. [*blank*]
    n. Beaver, otters, racoon, fox, Mink, Deer & B Bear Skins & Martens & Lynx & wolverines & wolves & Muskrats and Elk & Big horn
    o. [*blank*]
    p. (*Defensive war with Minetares*)
    q. [*blank*]
    r. on the W. of Rock M. (*On the west side of a large river, lying west of the Rocky mountains, and running north, supposed to be the south fork of the Columbia river*)

s. Flat heads live on a
    river running to the
    N W beyond the Mis-
    souri, Supposed to be a
    branch of the Colum-
    bia. Those nations
    [*including Blackfeet*]
    being little known the
    information is from the
    Menerres

The information I posses with respect to these people has been received from the Minetares, who have extended their war excursions as
far westerly as that nation, of whom they have made several prisoners,
and brought them with them to their villages on the Missouri: these prisoners have been seen by the Frenchmen residing in this neighborhood.
The Minatares state, that this nations resides in one village on the west
side of a large and rapid river, which runs from south to north, along the
foot of the Rocky mountains on their west side; and that this river passes
at a small distance from the three forks of the Missouri. That the country
between the mountains and the river is broken, but on the opposite side
of the river it is an extensive open plain, with a number of barren sandy
hills, irregularly distributed over its surface as far as the eye can reach.
They are a timid, inoffensive, and defenceless people. They are said to
possess an abundance of horses.

53. a. ⟨Chippaway tribe⟩ Pania
        Pickey
    b. ⟨O jib a no⟩
    c. ⟨Sou teaux⟩ Pania
        Pickey
    d. ⟨Chippaway⟩ * Pania
    e. 2
    f. [*blank*]
    g. 500
    h. 2000
    i. through n. [*blank*]
    o. 3 Forks of Arkansaw
    p. Little & Big Ossage
        Kanses & Panias
    q. [*blank*]
    r. on the head of Red
        River of Mississippi

These people have no intercourse with the inhabitants of the Illinois;
the information, therefore, which I have been enabled to obtain, with respect to them, is very imperfect. They were formerly known by the name
of the *White* Panias, and are of the same family with the Panias of the
river Platte. They are said to be a well disposed people, and inhabit a very
fertile country; certain it is that they enjoy a delightful climate.

[*Ed: Here end both the printed statistical view and Clark's manuscript table in its full coverage.*

Number 53 might also be added to this category. In the additional space at the foot of the table, Clark added the following information on the Southern tribes.]

54. a. Dellaways Kickapoos about the mouth of the Missouri
    c. Loups
    d. Dillaway &c.
    f. ramble
    g. 20
    h. 60
    r. above the Mouth of Missouri & up that river as high as Osarge Womans River

55. a. Deallaways Miamis &c. about De Moins & St Louis
    c. Loups
    d. Dellaway &c.
    f. ramble
    g. 25
    h. 80
    r. about St. Louis & [Dilliard? De Moins?] village.

56. a. Piories & Illinois
    f. camps
    g. 18
    h. 50
    r. near St. Genivieve

57. a. Shawonies
    d. Shawonies
    e. 3
    g. 150
    h. 600
    r. on apple River near Cape Gerardeau

58. a. Dillaways
    c. Loups
    d. Dillawais
    e. 2
    g. 200
    h. 800
    r. on a Small Creak near Cape Girardeau

59. a. Cherikees Creeks &c. delewais & Chickasaws
    f. ramble
    h. varies
    r. near New madrid

60. a. Chickasaws, Chocktaws & Cherikees
    f. ramble
    h. varies
    r. Between the Mississippi & Arkansaws Rivers

in Lower Louisiana

61. a. Arkansaws
    b. O-zar-jees
    d. Osage
    e. 2
    g. 260
    h. 1000
    r. Near the mouth of the Arkansaws R

62. a. Chacktaws
    f. ramble
    g. 300
    h. 1500
    r. from the Natchetouchs to the Mississippi

63. a. Biloxes ⟨Na⟩
    e. 2
    g. 40
    h. 150
    r. on red River below the Natchetouches

64. a. Chacktaws
    e. 1
    g. 25
    h. 100
    r. 26 Leagues up Red R. at the Rapids

65. a. Biloni N.
    e. 2
    g. 15
    h. 60
    r. on Red River near Avoyelles

66. a. Cadoquies
    e. ⟨1⟩
    f. ramble
    g. 400
    h. 1600
    r. on Red River 80 Leagues above Natchitoches

67. a. Conchates
    e. ⟨1⟩
    f. Dispersed
    g. 100
    h. 350
    r. Dispersed through the Opilousas countrey

68. a. Alibamas N
    e. 1 g. 30
    h. 100
    r. near Opiousas Chirch

69. a. Bilexis & Chacktaws
    e. 1
    g. 15
    h. 50
    r. Rochedile Beyou

70. a. Atacapas
    e. ⟨1⟩
    f. Dispersed
    g. 30
    h. 100
    r. Dispersed on vermillion Creek

71. a. Chitenachas
    d. Natachas
    e. 3
    g. 30
    h. 100
    r. 12 Leagues from the Sea on bayou Teeche

72. a. Tounicas
    e. 1
    g. 18
    h. 60
    r. Point Coupee E Side

IDENTIFICATIONS OF CLARK'S EASTERN INDIANS

Clark's Name	*Modern Name*
1. Grand Osarge	Grand Osages
2. Little Osarge	Little Osages

3.	Kanzas	Kansas
4.	Ottoes	Otos
5.	Missouries	Missouris
6.	Pania proper	Chawi Pawnees
7.	Pania Loup	Skiri Pawnees
8.	Pania Republicans	Kitkahahki Pawnees
9.	Mahar	Omahas
10.	Poncare	Poncas
11.	Ricaras	Arikaras
12.	Mandans	Mandans
13.	Shoes Men	Awaxawi
14.	Big Bellies	Hidatsas
15.	Ayauwais	Iowas
16.	Saukees	Sauks
17.	Renarz	Fox
18.	Sioux Wah-pa-tone	Wahpeton
19.	Sioux Min-da-war-car-ton	Mdewakanton
20.	Sioux Wah-pa-coo-tar	Wahpekute
21.	Sioux Sis-sa-tone	Sissetons
22.	Sioux Yanktons	Yanktons
23.	Sioux Yank-tons-Ah-nah	Yanktonais
24.	Sioux Teton Bous rouley	Brulé
25.	Sioux Teton O-kan-dan-das	Oglalas
26.	Sioux Teton Min-ne-kine-az-zo	Miniconjou
27.	Sioux Teton Sa-on-ne	Saone
28.	Chyennes	Cheyennes
29.	Wetapahato and Cay-au-wa	Kiowas
30.	Ca-ne-na-vich and Sta-e-tan	Arapahoes
31.	Cataka	Plains Apaches
32.	Nemousin	Comanches
33.	Do-ta-ne	Plains Apaches
34.	Cas-ta-ha-na	Arapahoes
35.	Ravin	Crows
36.	Paunch	Crows
37.	Assiniboin Ma-ne-to-par	Assiniboines
38.	Assiniboin Na-co-ta O-ee-gah	Assiniboines
39.	Assiniboin Na-co-ta Ma-ta-pa-nar-to	Assiniboines
40.	Knistanoes	Crees
41.	Fall Indians	Atsinas

42. Cat-tanahaws	Kutenais
43. Blue Mud Indians	Nez Perces
Long Hair	Crows?
44. Alitan or Snake Indians	Shoshones
Snake Indians	Shoshones
Of the West	Utes
La Playes	Comanches
45. Padoucas	Plains Apaches
Wetepahatoes	Kiowas
Kiawas	Kiowas
Kanevavish	Arapahoes
Katteka	Kiowa Apaches
Dotame	Plains Apaches
46. Chipaways of Leach Lake	Chippewas
47. Chipaways about Lake Dubois	Chippewas
48. Chipaways on River Rouge	Chippewas
49. Algonquins of Rainy Lake	Chippewas
50. Algonquins of Portage de Prairie	Chippewas
51. Black foot	Blackfeet
52. Flat head	Flathead (Salish)
53. Pania Pickey	Wichitas
54. Dellaways Kickapoos about the mouth of the Missouri	Delawares and Kickapoos
55. Dellaways Miamis about DeMoins and St. Louis	Delawares and Miamis
56. Piories and Illinois	Peorias and Illinois
57. Shawonies	Shawnees
58. Dillaways	Delawares
59. Cherikees Creeks &c. delewais and Chickasaws	Cherokees, Creeks, Delawares, and Chickasaws
60. Chickasaws, Chocktaws and Cherikees	Chickasaws, Choctaws, and Cherokees
61. Arkansaws	Osages
62. Chacktaws	Choctaws
63. Biloxes	Biloxis
64. Chacktaws	Choctaws
65. Biloni	Biloxis
66. Cadoquies	Caddoes
67. Conchates	Conchanty (Creek)

68. Alibamas		Alabamas
69. Bilexis and Chacktaws		Biloxis and Choctaws
70. Atacapas		Attacapas
71. Chitenachas		Natchez
72. Tounicas		Tunicas

Part 3: Botanical Collections

The following lists represent Lewis's botanical efforts during the first year of the expedition. The first document is Lewis's list of specimens from Codex R, pp. 4–49; it was probably prepared at Fort Mandan, perhaps from other notes now lost. The second document was prepared by John Vaughan of the American Philosophical Society as a receiving list of the specimens and was probably copied from identification labels accompanying the items or from a separate list. It is from the Donation Book at the American Philosophical Society (see Appendixes B and C, vol. 2). The "H" following some items in the Donation Book may represent an accession check and may stand for "have." The specimens are apparently the items in box 4 of the goods sent back from Fort Mandan in April 1805, and designated "Specimens of plants numbered from 1 to 60." See Jackson (LLC), 1:235, 239–40 n. 21; Clark's entry, April 3, 1805, and accompanying notes. The discrepancy in the number of items cannot be explained. Lewis has additional specimens numbered 100–108. Vaughan's numbers 61 and 62 may be his own convention for loose, unnumbered items, while his note on the "corolla of tobacco" may apply to items 106 or 108. These herberia (with some losses) are at the Academy of Natural Sciences, Philadelphia.

The discussion of this collection, here called the Fort Mandan collection, is necessarily brief in order not to duplicate a specialized volume which will appear as the final book in this edition. The natural history volume will be much like the *Atlas* with its introduction, calendar, and illustrations. The final volume will include a discussion of the party's botanical activities, an introduction to the Lewis and Clark herbarium at the Academy, and illustrations of those specimens. An excellent examination of this topic is available in Cutright (LCPN), 357–75.

We provide at this time a table of botanical identifications. A similar table, probably in the form of a calendar, will accompany the natural history volume and will include the whole of the Lewis and Clark herbarium. The present table gives the voucher number, approximate date and place of collection, and the current scientific and common name. Since Lewis's voucher numbers are not chronologically or systematically arranged from St. Louis to Fort Mandan, we have recorded the items in chronological fashion to provide easy comparison with the daily journals and their corresponding botanical annotation. The lack of chronology in the voucher numbers may be evidence that label numbers were not assigned at the time of collection, but later, possibly at Fort Mandan. The "1804 Dates" are those on labels at the Academy or from the lists of Lewis and Vaughan. The location was determined by comparing the specimen dates with journal entries, *Atlas* maps, and our annotation. In most instances Lewis's precise location for collecting the specimens is unclear, so we have given the closest geographic landmark for that day.

The most difficult task was to apply current scientific and common names to the herbaria. Since the first thirty items are missing from the Academy, we had to rely on Lewis's descriptions for identifications. The lack of existing specimens cannot be explained and accounts for several unidentified items. The remaining specimens at the Academy were examined by Dr. A. T. Harrison, formerly of the University of Nebraska, with the assistance of the Academy's curatorial staff. He also examined previous botanical work on the plants, current botanical literature, and employed his own familiarity with regional flora. Items number 37, 62, and 102 remain unidentified as they were not to be found in the collection. Numbers 62 and 102 may never have been accessioned, while number 37 remains a curious loss similar to the first thirty specimens.

[Lewis]   [*undated, winter 1804–5*]

A List of specimines of plants collected by me on the Mississippi and Missouri rivers— contain such observations on the vegitable kingdom spread to our view in this rich country as they have occurred to my mind.— or as the several subjects have presented themselves to my view.—

No. *1.* a species of Cress, taken at St. Louis May 10th 1804. it is common in the open growns on the Mississippi bottoms, appears in the uncultivated parts of the lots gardens and orchards, the seed come to maturity by the 10th of May in most instances.—

No. 2. was taken on the 22ed of May 1804 on the bank of the Missouri about 8 miles above St. Charles it is common in the botom lands— rises to the hight of two feet, and rarely puts forth more than two stalks from the same root and most commonly only one— it's root is spiral.

No. 3. Was taken on the 23rd of May 1804, near the mouth of the Osage Woman's creek, it is a srub and resembles much in growth the *blad-*

der scenna, it rises to hight of eight or ten feet and is an inhabitant of a moist rich soil.— usually the verge of the river bank.— it is a handsome Shrub

No. 4. Was taken at a small Village North side of the Missouri called Sharett, on the 25th of May 1804. this is the last settlement on the Missouri; and consists of ten or twelve families mostly hunters. this specimine is the seed of the Cottonwood which is so abundant in this country, it has now arrived at maturity and the wind when blowing strong drives it through the air to a great distance being supported by a parrishoot of this cottonlike substance which gives the name to the tree in some seasons it is so abundant as to be troublesome to the traveler— this tree arrives at great sise, grows extreemly quick the wood is of a white colour, soft spungey and light, perogues are most usually made of these trees, the wood is not durable nor do I know any othe valuable purpose which it can answer except that just mentioned—

this tree forms a great majority of the timber bordering the rivers Missouri and Mississippi; it extends itself throughout the extensive bottom lands of these streams and seases to appear when the land rises into hills— when these rivers form new lands on their borders or Islands in their steams, which they are pertually doing, the sweet willow is the first tree or shrub which usually makes it's appearance, this continues one two or three years and is then supplanted by the Cotton wood which invariably succeedes it.— this tree resembles much in it's air and appearance that beatifull and celibrated tree the Lombardy poplar; and more particularly so when in its young state; the young plants grow very close untill they have attained the age of four or five years, a proportion of them then begin to dye and the forrest opens and gives place to sundry other shrubs and plants which will be noticed in their proper places.—

No. 5. was taken on the 27th of May 1804 near the mouth of the Gasconade; it is a species of cress which grows very abundantly alonge the river beach in many places; my men make use of it and find it a very pleasant wholsome sallad.—

No. 6. Was taken on the 27th of may 1804 near the mouth of the Gasconade; it is a species of rape or kail, it grows on the beach of the river, when young my men used it a boiled green and found healthy and pleasent.—

No. 7. was found on the 27th of May 1804 near the water side about 10 miles below the mouth of the Gasconade, it rises to the hight of three feet and puts forth many large suculent branched stalks from the same root, this plant is a stranger to me.—

No. 8. Was taken the 29th of May 1804 below the mouth of the Osage Rivr. this plant is known in Kentuckey and many other parts of this western country by the name of the yellow root— it is a sovereighn remidy for a disorder common in this quarter called the Soar eyes— this complaint is common it is a violent inflamation of the eyes attended with high fevers and headach, and is extreemly distressing, and frequently attended with the loss of sight— this root affords a speady and efficasious remidy for this disorder prepared & used in the following manner— let the roots be geathered washed and carefully dryed in the shade; brake them in pieces of half an inch in length and put them in a bottle or viol, taking care to fill the vessel about two thirds full of the dryed root, then fill the vessell with could water, rain water is preferable; let it remain about six hours shaking it occasionally and it will be fit for use; the water must remain with the root and be applyed to the eyes frequently by wetting a piece of fine linin touching them gently with it.— this root is a fine aromatic bitter, and a strong asstringent; it is probable that it might be applyed in many cases as a medicene with good effect, but I have not learnt that any experiment has been made by an inward application— it makes an excellent mouth water, and a good outward applycation for wounds or inflamations of every kind.— native of rich bottom lands on the rivers—

No. 9. Was taken on the 30th of May 1804 below the mouth of the Osage river; it rises from 18 Inches to 2 feet in hight; is a beautifull green plant found most generally on the sides of rich hills in the forrest it's radix is fiberous—

No. 10. This plant was taken the 1st of June at the mouth of the Osage river; it is known in this country by the name of the *wild ginger,* it resembles that plant somewhat in both taste and effect; it is a strong stomatic stimelent, and frequently used in sperits with bitter herbs— it is common throughout the rich lands in the Western country.

No. 11. Was taken the 3rd of June above the mouth of the Osage river; it is the groath of high dry open praries; rises to the hight of 18 inches or two feet puts forth many stems from the same root; the radix is fiborous; the Indians frequently use the fruit of this plant to alay their thirst as they pass through these extensive dry praries common to many parts of the country bordering on the Missouri; it resembles much the Indigo in the appearance of it's growth. it bears it's fruit much like the indigo, a stem projects about three inches from the main stem at an angle of about 20 degrees, and bears from [two?] to four podds, which in their succulent and unripe state as at this season of the year are about the sise of a pullet's egg, somewhat flattened on two sides; the matrix is formed in two lobes and the seed are like pees and attached to the matrix in the same manner, single and adhering to the center the pulp is crisp & clear and tasts very much like the hull of a gardin pee.— when ripe the fruit is of a fine red coulour and sweet flavor.— it dose not ripen untill the middle of June.—

No. 12. 1st of August 1804. one of our hunters brought us a bough of the purple courant, which is frequently cultivated in the Atlantic states; the fruit was ripe; I presume it is a native of North America— here it grows generally in the praries but is not very abundant.— No. 12 is a specimine of it's leaves.—

No. 13. The *narrow leaf willow* taken on the 14th of June— this tree is male and female, the female bearing it seed in a small pod small ova form of three lobes, or devisions— these pods are attached to a stem which projects from the small boughs, and are from thirty to fifty in number, about this season they begin to ripen, when the pods burst and a great number of small seeds each furnished with a parrishoot of a cotton-like substance are discharged from those cels. they readily float in the air and are driven by the wind to a great distance, they are so abundant at some times as to be disagreeable to the traveller— the *male* plant has sucession of it's flowers, commencing to bloom about the 1st of June and continuing untill the 1st of August, they are a small tausel of a half, or ¾ of an inch in length, round, and tapering to the extremity, putting frort from it's sides an infinite number of small stamens of a brown colour. it's leaves are numerous narrow, slightly indented, of a yellowish ⟨deep⟩ green, on the uper side, and whiteish green underneath, pointed, being widest in the middle which rarely exceeds ⅛th of an inch, it is smoth, tho' not glossey

This tree is invariably the first which makes it's appearance on the newly made Lands on the borders of the Mississippi and Missouri, and seems to contribute much towards facilitating the operation of raisin this ground still higher; they grow remarkably close and in some instances so much so that they form a thicket almost impenetrable the points of land which are forming allways become eddies when overflown in high water these willows obstruct the force of the water and makes it more still which causes the mud and sand to be deposited in greater quantities; the willow is not attal imbarrassed or injured by this inundation, but ⟨the moment the water subsides⟩ puts forth an innumerable quantity of small fibrous roots from every part of its trunk near the surface of the water which further serve to collect the mud, if there happens not to be a sufficient quantity of mud depossited in the one season to cover the trunk of the willow as high as these capillery roots when the water subsides they fall down and rest on the trunk of the tree and conceal it for 18 or 20 Inches; these capillery roots now perish and the willow puts forth other roots at the surface of the ground which enter it and furnish the tree with it's wanted nutriment— this willow never rises to any considerable sise, it is seldom seen larger than a mans arm, and scarcely every rises higher than 25 feet. the wood is white light and tough, and is generally used by the watermen for *setting poles* in preference to anything else.— as the willow incrases in size and the land gets higher ⟨and more dry⟩ by the annul inundations of the river, the weeker plants decline dye and give place to the cotton-wood which is it's ordinary successor, and these last in their turn also thin themselves as they become larger in a similar manner and leave the ground open for the admission of other forest trees and under brush— these willow bars form a pleasant beacon to the navigator at that season when the banks of the river are tumbling in, as they seldom high and rearly falling in but on the contrary most usually increasing.—

No. 14. The *wide leaf willow* or that species which I believe to be common to most parts of the Atlantic States.   it grows in similar situations to that discribed with rispect to the narrow leaf willow, but is never found in such abundance, it arrives to greater size some times to forty feet in hight and eighteen inches in diameter, the leave is smoth ovate, pointed, finely indented, a pale green on the upper side and of a whiteis green or silver colour underneath—   like the narrow leaf willow the leaf is widest in the middle where it is from one inch to ¾ wide.—   it bears it's seed in the manner discribed of the other and the plants ar likewise male and female.

No. 15.   Was taken on the 20th of July, a pieniel plant, an inhabitant of the open praries or plains, high situations, where the grass is low.   the flower is a pale purple colour small form a kind of button of a long conic like form which terminate it's branches which are numerous—   it grows abot 2½ or three feet high—   it is a stranger to me.—   the leaves are small and narrow, and divided into three on a stem

No. 16.   this is much the same as No. 15 with this difference that the blume of the conic tausel are white in stead of purple and it's leaves single fewer and longer—

No. 17.   Taken on the 27th of July, the appearance of the bush is much like the privy and about the same hight   it grows about the borders of the open praries   it's leaf is a deep green, ovate 1½ to 1¼ inches long ½ inch wide finely indented—   pla[n]t piennial.   the buries or fruit a small round bury of a deep perple coulour nearly black, has three seed formed like the third part of a globe split by the meeting of two plains at it's axcis.—   I do not know whether birds eat them or not.   they look handsome but tast insipid.   this is a groath with which I am not acquainted.—

No. 18.   was taken 30th July grows in the praries in high situations, it's radix ⟨matrix⟩ is peennial, it grows about three ½ or 4 feet high   it has a long tap root it is but little branced, it's colateral brances are short and furnished with many leaf stems which are garnished by a great number of small leaves which are attatch by pairs on either side and resemble some of the sensative bryers, tho I could not discover that this plant partook of that quality.—   it's flower is of a gloubelar form composed of a number of fibers of a yellowish white, and produces as a fruit a bunch of little pees which are all bent edgeways into the form of a semicircle and so

456

closely connected and compressed as to form a globular figure of a curious appearance—

No. 19. Taken at the old village of the little Osages; the seed were now ripe; it grew in great abundance in the prarie from five to six feet high; it gave the plain much the appearance of an extensive timothy meadow ready for the sythe, the small birds feed on the seed which are very abundant resembling in size shape and colour those of the ⟨timothey⟩ flax; when ripe they fall very easily from the stem. the leaf of this grass does not decline or wither as many others do at the time the seed ripens but still continues succulant and green. it continues throughout the summer to put up a succession of young succors which in turn bear a larger quantity of seed: this succession of crops continues throughout the season without the declining or withering of the stalk or leaves of the mother plant. the horses were very fond of this grass and I am disposed to believe that it would make a valuable grass for culture.— this grass is common in the praries or bottom lands as high as the river Platte and perhaps further— it is a fine sweet grass and I am confident would make good hay.—

No. 20. A specemine of wild Rye taken on the 27th of July, this grass is common to all the low praries above the Cancez river it rises to the hight of six feet and upwards and resembles the rye extreemly in appearance the geese and ducks feed on it when young, as they do also on the grain when ripe in September and October it produces much grain tho of an inferior quality compared with cultivated rye.—

No 21. is another species of the wild rye it dose not grow as tall as No. 20 neither does it like that species confine itself so much to the open ground; it is sometimes found in the timbered land. the grain it produces is [n]either so large or so abundant as the former.—

No. 22. 23. 24 & 25. Are various species of grasses which appear in the praries, No. 23 is the most common of any other grass, it rises to the hight of from 4 to 8 feet and never bears any flower or seed that I ever observed and suppose therefore that it must propegate by means of the root: *common* to all praries in this country.

No. 26.— Taken on the 2ed of August in the parie at the Cuncil bluff.

it is a species of honeysuccle; the flower is small and the tube of the flour is very small and short   they smell precisely like the English Honeysuccle so much admired in our gardens; this is a shrub and does not run or vine. the vining honesuccle which bears a red flour is also common to the Illinois and is found as high up the Missoury as the mouth of the Kancez river above which I have not observed it.— this species of shrub Honesuccle has some of it's leaves much indented; the fruit nearly ripe when the plant is still in blume; it makes a pretty groath and is a pleasant looking pla[n]t rises to three or four feet high and limbs are much branchd.

No. 27.   taken 4th of August, and furst observed at the bald prarie— it is beatifull plant with a variagated leaf— these leaves incompass the flowers which are small and in the center of them; at a small distance they resemble somewhat a white rose   the leaf near the large stem is green and is edged with white; they grow smaller and more numerous as they approach the flower or the extremity of the limb.   the plant is much branched; the leaf is smoth on both sides and edge, of an ovate form and pale green colour, rises to five or six feet, is annual   at every point that it branches it has a pair of opposite leaves and from thee to four branches—

No. 28.— taken on the 17th July at the bald prarie— is a large convolvalist a fine white colour; the vines are very extensive and run in every direction intwining themselves about the larger weeds and bending them down is [in] such manner as to make the open grownds ⟨impassable⟩ or praries where they grow almost impassable; the root is about the size and shape of the vine and enters it so deep that I could not find it's brances tho' I dug as much as 2 feet in surch of it.— the leaf is of a tonge like form pale green even on the edges.   leaf thus [*see fig. 10*]—

No. 29.   Taken on the 18th of July.— an annuel plant puting up many branches from the root has a leaf like the pateridge bea[n], is jointed bears a number of yllow *pea-like* flowers which grow on the seed stems which project from the main branches and which are unattended with leaves; these flowers grow all arround this stem and give it the appearance of a tausell.   the [l]eaf stems ar long and have 24 par of leaves.

No. 30.   was taken at the bald praries and is common to both low and high praries   it usually grows in a single stem and appears to be an annual groath   the leaves are white and like the stem appear to be covered

10. Large "convolvalist" leaf (*Convolvulus sepium* L.,
hedge bindweed), July 17, 1804, Codex R, p. 37

with a white down— this is common to all the praries above the Kancez
river; from it's resemblence in taste smell &c to the *common Sage* I have
called it the wild Sage.—

No. 31. Taken on the 10th of August, a species of sand rush, joined
and so much branched as to form a perfect broom; it is common to every
part of this river at least as far as Latitude 42 N. it grows near the water's
edge in moist sand; the horses are remarkably fond of it.

No. ⟨32⟩ *40.*— Taken at our camp at the Maha vilage August 17th
1804. it is a handsome plant about 3 feet high much branched bears
a yellow circular flower carnished with meany small narrow ovate petals
of the same colour, the leaf about an inch and a quarter in length thick
smoth indent finely, incompassing the stalk about ⅔'s and of a tongue-
like form; ynnual plant is covered with a gumlike substance which ad-
heres to the fingers and yealds a pleasent smell.—

No. (100) Novr. 17th the seed of a plant given me by the recaray chief who accompanyed us to the mandanes he informed me that a tea of the seed was a strong diaerettic— and that the squaws chewed them and rubed their hair with them as a perfume.

No. (101.) the root wen pounded in either green or dryed state makes an excellent poltice for swellings or soar throat.— information of the same chief.

No. (102) by the information of the same chief— is an excellent purge— the root is dryed and pounded in that state as much as you can hold betwen the finger and thumb thrise is a doze— it is the growth of the open praries— has many small stalks 2 feet high. radix piennl

No. 103. is the growth of the open praries—it seldom grows higher it is said to be good for inflamed eyes the leaves are immerced in water and being bruised with the fingers a little the water is squeezed from it and occasionally droped when could upon the eyes.—

(104 No.) October the 16th a dwarf cedar of the open praries seldom ever rises more than six inches high— it is said to be a stimilating shrub— it is used as a tea by the Indians to produce sweat— they would make a handsome edging to the borders of a gardin if used as the small *box* sometimes is.—

N 105. seed of the Larger species of recarre tobacco pre[se]nted us by *Lepoy* an Indian chief of that nation commanding the *middle town.*

No. 106— is the corrollars of the same prepared for smoking. they are plucked and dryed in the shade—

No. 107. is the seed of the smaller species.—

The recarres cultivate two species of tobacco,[1] for the purpose of smoking in which way they use it altogether as they neither snuff nor chew—

The *Larger species* (see specimine plants No. 108) rises to the hight of three feet. it's round green and succulent much branched when suffered to grow singly. in that sittuation it branches near the ground and continues to branch and rebranch as it rises at the distance of an inch or 2 inches, thus forming an infinite number of boughs at the top which are terminated by the flowers which are tubelar; trunnicated scalluped on the edges and five pointed, white colour, order, *pentandria moniginia,*— the leaf is of a toung-like form. ⟨The indians⟩ the larger of which are attached to the lower part of the stalk. one inch wide in the broadest part, & 2½ inches long.— the demins as they are higher on the stalk, tho' they increas in number— The indians cultivate it in the following manner— they prepare hills at the distance of about 2½ feet from each other, and leavel the top nearly leaving it somewhat convex. in these hills they sew the seed as early in the spring as the climate will permit them to prepare the earth say latter end of April; they keep the hill clear of weeds and grass by plucking it from among the stalks of tobacco with their fingers— and sometimes allso thin the stalks of tobacco by plucking up the weaker stalks tho they leave many stalks to grow on each hill. when the tobacco begins to form it's seed poods it is then ready for the knife when a great portion from each hill is cut and hung on sticks untill it is nearly dry— when they form them into carrots of the thickness of a mans arm role them closely with willow bark and hang them in the smoke of their lodges to dry. in forming the carrot, they put the butts or lower parts of the stalks together. where the tobacco is cultivated with a view to make carrots the stalks are so thick that they do not attain a thickness at the largest part of the stem greater than that of a small quill— They esteem much more the carraller [corolla] dryed for the purpose of smoking—and for this purpose leave some plant more widely seperated from each other—in which situation they produce a greater abundance of flowers & seed. they begin to blume in the month of [*blank*] and continue untill the first frost;— during the full blume of the flower they pluck the carrallar together with the flower and discarding the latter suffer the former to dry in the shade when perfectly dryed it resembles at first view the green *tea* and in that state it is smoked by the indians and I found it very pleasent— it dose not affect the nerves in the same manner that the tobacco cultivated in the U' S. dose— The smaller species of this plant differs but little from this just discribed— it is cultivated in the same manner and bears a flower like the other only smaller— the only difference is the form of the leaf, which is larger (say) 4 times the size and *ovate*— they dry this on sticks and use it in that manner   it is reather stronger than the large kind and is seldom made into carrots by the Recares.—

☞ it is worthy of remark that the recares never use *sperituous liquors*. Mr. Tibeau informed me that on a certain occasion he offered one of their considerate men a dram of sperits, telling him it's virtues— the other replyed that he had been informed of it's effects and did not like to make himself a fool unless he was paid to do so— that if Mr. T. wished to laugh at him & would give him a knife or *breech-coloth* or something of that kind he would take a glass but not otherwise.—

[Vaughan]

Donations   November 16, 1805 from Meriwether Lewis   Dried Plants &c put into Dr. B. S Bartons hands for examination

No. 1 At St. Louis May 10th 1804

2 May 10th 1804

3 May 23, 1804

4 May 25th 1804   The Cottonwood found on every part of the Missouri as high as the mandans, generally grows in the river bottoms & near is borders.—   H

5. May 27, 1804

6 May 27, 1804

7 May 27, 1804

8 May 29, 1804   This plant is known in Kentucky & many other parts of the Western Country by the name of the yellow root—   It is said to be a Sovereign remedy in a disorder common to the Inhabitants of the Country where found, usually termed Sore eyes—   frequently attended with high fever & Sometimes terminates in the loss of sight, always gives great pain & continues for a length of time in most cases. The preparation & application of the root is as follows—   having procured a quantity of the roots, wash them clean & Suffer them to dry in the Shade, break them with the fingers as fine as you conveniently can, put them in a glass vessel, taking care to fill it about ⅔ with the Broken root, then add rain or river water until the Vessel is filled, shake it frequently & it will be fit for use in the course of 6 hours. The Water must not be decanted but remaining with the root is to be frequently applied by wetting a piece of the fine linnen and touching thee Eyes gently with it—   This root has a fine aromatic bitter taste, it is probable that it might be appplied internally in many cases with good effect, but I have not learnt that any experiments have yet been made with it in that way. It makes an excellent *mouth water*

& is an excellent outward application in cases of wounds or local application of any kind— It is the Growth of rich bottom lands. M. Lewis

  9—

  10 Usually called wild ginger   grows in rich bottom Land   June 1,
1804

  11. June 3d 1804

  12 The purple Currant.   1 Augt. 1804

  13 Narrow leaf willow common to the borders of the Missouri   June
14, 1804

  14 Broadleaf Willow found on the missouri   not So common as the
Narrow leaf willow but grows much larger sometimes rising to 30 feet
June 14, 1804

  15 found in the open plains—   20 July, 1804   H

  16 same as No 16   H

  17 found on the Edges of the Prairies, rises about 8 foot high   the leaf
is a deep green, the bush has a handsome appearance with its fruit—   27
July, 1804   H

  18. growth of the high plains taken the 30 July, 1804.   H

  20 S. ⟨gr:⟩

  20. # Growth of the rich Prairie bottoms found 27 July, 1804   S. ⟨gr.⟩

  21 Another Speecis of the wild Rye it does not grow as tall as No 20 S
27 July

  22, ⟨23, 24,⟩ S   No 22, 23, 24, 25 are various Species of grass which
grow in the prarie Bottom lands of the Missouri   No 23 is the most common   it rises to the height of 4 & 5 feet & never bears any Seed or flower,
it propagates itself by the root—   27 July

  23,

  24—   H

  25 H

  26 H

  26 #

  26 ∅ Species of Honey Suckle common to the prairies   this Specimen
was obtained at the Council Bluffs 2d Aug. 1804   H

  27 Growth of the Prairie Bottoms taken on the 4th Aug. 1804

  28   Do—   Do—   15 July 1804

29 Growth of the open praries 18 July 1804

30.   Do—   Do—   13 July

No 31. Growth of the Sand Bars near the Banks of the Rivers   10 Aug 1804

32 Specimens of the aromatic plants on which the Antelope feeds these wer obtained 21 Sep. 1804 at the upper part of the Big bend of the Missouri—   H

33 an evergreen plant which grows usually in the open plains, the natives smoke its leaves mixed with Tobacco called by the french engages *Sacacommé*   obtained at Fort Mandon

34 The leaf of Oak which is common to the Prairies.   5 Sep. 1804

35. Sept. 18 The Growth of the Prairies   H

36 Sept. 18 Growth of the high Prairies—

37 Sept. 22   Do—   Do—

38 Oct. 15, 1804—   Growth of the high Prairies or Plains—

A 39 Obtained at the mouth of the River Quicoarre from which place upwards, it is abundant in the Missouri bottoms, it is a pleasant Berry to eat, it has much the flavor of the Cranbury & continues on the bush thro' the Winter   This is an Evergreen shrub—

Some plants are sent down by the barge to the care of Capt Stoddart at St. Louis—   H

40. 17 Aug 1804   Growth of Prairies at our Camp near the old Maha Village ⟨the Gr⟩   H

41. 2d Sep. 1804   on the Bluffs   grows in open high Situations   H

42. 27th Augt.   At the Chalk Bluff   grows in the mineral earth at the base of the Hill   H

43. 25th Augt.   Growth of the open Prairies.—   H

44 Sepr 1st.   Do—   Do   H

45. Oct. 12.   Specimen of Tobacco the Indians cultivate called Ricaras Tobacco—   at the Ricares Town

46. Sep. 15, 1804   The growth of the Upper Prairis   H

47 Oct. 17   Species of Juniper common to the Bluffs   H

48. Oct. 17   a Decoction of this plant used by the Indians to wash their Wounds.—   103

49. Oct. 16 (104)   never more than 6 Inches high   Dwarf Cedar.

50— Oct. 18 The small rose of the Prairies it rises from 12 to 14 Inch high does not vine H

51. Oct. 3d 1804 Radix Perennial three to 8 Stalks as high as the specimen growth of the high sides of the Bluff (Camomile taste)

52. Sep. 15 1804 Growth of the plains. H

53 Oct. 3d Flavor like the Cammomile Radix Perennial— High Bluffs

53 (A) Sep. 2 The Indians use it as an application to fresh wounds they bruise the leaves add a little water & use it—

54. Oct. 2d grows from 18 Inches to 2½ feet many stalks from the same root, from which they issue near the ground The Radix perennial— The goat or antelope feed on it in the winter, it is the growth of the high bluffs S H

55 Oct. 2d 1804 Growth of the high Bluffs

56 Oct. 2d 1804. Growth of the open plains

57 Oct. 1, 1804 first discovered in the neighborhood of the Kancez River—now very common, the growth of the little Cops, which appear on the steep declivities of the Hills where they are sheltered from the ravages of the fire. H

58. 2d Oct. 1804 A species of Cedar found on the Bluffs the trees of which are large, some 6 feet in the Girth— H

58. 12 Sepr. growth of the high dry Prairie H

59— 19th Sepr. 1804 The growth of the high & bare Prairies which produce little Grass— Generally mineral earth H

59. Growth of moist & very wet prairies— 8 Sep. H

60. Oct 1, 1804— another variety of wild Sage growth of High & bottom Prairies— H

Seeds

61 Wild Prairie Timothy Seeds H

62 Seeds of a Species of Pine with a Pod H

The Fang of a Rattle Snake, they are abundant on the Missouri

Specimen of the fur of the Antelope, this animal affords but little, it is intermixed with the coarse hair & is not perceptible but by close examination—

Two Small quadrupeds.

a few Insects

The Corolla of the Indian Tobacco as prepared for the purpoe of Smoking by the Mandans, Ricaras, Minetares & Ahwahhaways, in this State it is mixed with a small quantity of Buffaloes Tallow, previous to charging the pipe— It is esteemed a great delicacy among these people, they dispose of it to their neighbors the Assinouboins & others who visit them for the purpose of Traffick from whom they obtain a high price—

BOTANICAL IDENTIFICATIONS

Voucher Number	1804 Dates	Approximate Location	Current Scientific and Common Names
1	May 10	St. Louis, MO	perhaps *Thlaspi arvense* L. (field pennycress naturalized from Europe)
2	May 22	above St. Charles, St. Charles County, MO	unknown
3	May 23	near mouth of Femme Osage River, St. Charles County, MO	*Amorpha fruiticosa* L. (false indigo)
4	May 25	near Marthasville, Warren County, MO	*Populus deltoides* Marsh. var. *deltoides* (cottonwood)
5	May 27	near mouth of Gasconade River, Gasconade County, MO	Possibly one of the following species of *Rorippa:* a. *R. palustris* (L.) Bess. (bog yellow cress) b. *R. sessiliflora* (Nutt.) Hitchc. (sessile-flowered cress) c. *R. sinuata* (Nutt.) Hitchc. (spreading yellow cress)
6	May 27	near mouth of Gasconade River	unknown, but no native species of rape or kale (*Brassica*)

7	May 27	about ten miles below mouth of Gasconade River	unknown
8	May 29	near Osage-Gasconade county line, MO	*Hydrastis canadensis* L. (golden seal, yellowroot)
9	May 30	near Osage-Gasconade country line	unknown
10	June 1	mouth of Osage River Osage-Cole county line, MO	*Asarum canadense* L. (wild ginger)
11	June 3	east of Jefferson City, Cole County, MO	*Astragalus crassicarpa* Nutt. var. *berlandieri* Barneb. (ground plum, buffalo bean)
13	June 14	near Miami, Saline County, MO	*Salix exigua* Nutt. ssp. *interior* (Rowlee) Cronq. (sandbar, or coyote, willow)
14	June 14	near Miami	*Salix amygdaloides* Anderss. (peach-leaved willow)
19	undated, June 16?	Carroll County, MO opposite Lafayette-Saline county line	*Phalaris arundinacea* L. (reed canarygrass)
61	undated, June 16?	Carroll County, opposite Lafayette-Saline county line	*Phalaris arundinacea* L. (reed canarygrass)
30	July 13	above Rulo, Richardson County, NE	*Artemisia ludoviciana* Nutt. var. *ludoviciana* (white sage)
28	July 15 or 17	near Iowa-Missouri state line	*Convolvulus sepium* L. (hedge bindweed)
29	July 18	near Nebraska City, Otoe County, NE	*Cassia fasciulata* Michx. (partridge pea)
15	July 20	near Cass-Otoe county line, NE	*Petalostemum purpureum* (Vent.) Rydb. (purple prairie clover)

16	undated, July 20?	near Cass-Otoe county line	*Petalostemum candidum* (Willd.) Michx. (white prairie clover)
17	July 27	near Bellevue, Sarpy County, NE	unknown
20	July 27	near Bellevue	*Elymus canadensis* L. (Canada wild rye)
21	July 27	near Bellevue	*Elymus virginicus* L. (Virginia wild rye) or *E. villosus* Muhl. (slender wild rye)
22	July 27	near Bellevue	unknown
23	July 27	near Bellevue	*Andropogon gerardi* Vitman (big bluestem)
24	July 27	near Bellevue	unknown
25	July 27	near Bellevue	unknown
18	July 30	near Fort Calhoun, Washington County, NE	*Desmanthus illinoensis* (Michx.) MacM. (bundleflower)
12	August 1	near Fort Calhoun	*Ribes americanum* Mill. (wild black currant)
26	August 2	near Fort Calhoun	*Symphoricarpos occidentalis* Hook. (western snowberry) or *S. orbiculatus* Moench (buckbrush)
27	August 4	near Blair, Washington County, NE	*Euphorbia marginata* Pursh (snow-on-the-mountain)
31	August 10	near Decatur, Burt County, NE	*Equisetum arvense* L. (field horsetail)
40	August 17	south of Dakota City, Dakota County, NE	*Grindelia squarrosa* (Pursh) Dun. var. *squarrosa* (curly-top gumweed)
43	August 25	near Vermillion, Clay County, SD	*Cleome serrulata* Pursh (Rocky Mountain bee plant)

42	August 27	near Yankton, Yankton County, SD	*Psoralea lanceolata* Pursh (lemon scurf pea)
44	September 1	west of Yankton-Bon Homme county line, SD	*Mirabilis nyctaginea* (Michx.) MacM. (wild four o'clock)
41	September 2	near Springfield, Bon Homme County, SD	*Artemisia frigida* Willd. (prairie sagewort)
53 A	September 2	near Springfield	*Petalostemum purpureum* (Vent.) Rydb. (purple prairie clover)
39 A	undated, September 4?	mouth of Nio-brara River, Knox County, NE	*Shepherdia argentea* (Pursh) Nutt. (buffaloberry)
34	September 5	near Verdel, Knox County, NE	*Quercus macrocarpa* Michx. (bur oak)
59 [a]	September 8	near Nebraska-South Dakota state line	*Zizania aquatic* L. (wild rice)
58 [a]	September 12	near Charles Mix-Brule county line, SD	*Liatris aspera* Michx. (rough gayfeather)
46	September 15	near mouth of White River	*Astragalus canadensis* L. var. *mortoni* (Nutt.) S. Wats. (Canada milkvetch)
52	September 15	near mouth of White River	*Artemisia dracunculus* L. (silky wormwood)
35	September 18	near Chamberlain, Brule County, SD	*Liatris pycnostachya* Michx. (tall blazing star gayfeather)
36	September 18	near Chamberlain	*Astragalus missouriensis* Nutt. (Missouri milkvetch)
59 [b]	September 19	lower part of Big Bend of Missouri; Buffalo County, SD	*Gutierrezia sarothrae* (Pursh) Britt. & Rusby (broom snakeweed)
32	September 21	upper part of Big Bend of Missouri; Hughes County, SD	*Gutierrezia sarothrae* (Pursh) Britt. & Rusby (broom snakeweed)

37	September 22	near Lyman-Stanley County line, SD	unknown
57	October 1	near mouth of Cheyenne River, Stanley County, SD	*Rhus aromatica* Ait. var. *trilobata* (Nutt.) Gray (aromatic sumac)
60	October 1	near mouth of Cheyenne River	*Artemisia cana* Pursh (silversage, hoary sagebrush)
54	October 2	near Sully-Potter county line	*Chrysothmnus nauseosus* (Pall.) Britt. ssp. *graveolens* (Nutt.) Piper (rabbit brush)
55	October 2	near Sully-Potter county line	*Artemisia cana* Pursh (silversage, hoary sagebrush)
56	October 2	near Sully-Potter county line	*Artemisia cana* Pursh (silversage, hoary sagebrush)
58 [b]	October 2	near Sully-Potter county line	*Juniperus scopulorum* Sarg. (Rocky Mountain red cedar)
51	October 3	near Sully-Potter county line	*Artemisia frigida* Willd. (prairie sagewort)
53	October 3	near Sully-Potter county line	*Artemisia longifolia* Nutt. (long leaf sage)
45	October 12	above Walworth-Campbell line, SD	*Nicotiana quadrivalvis* Pursh (Indian tobacco)
38	October 15	near Fort Yates, Sioux County, ND	*Poinsettia cyathophora* (Murr.) Klotzsch & Garcke (fire-on-the-mountain)
49 (same as 104)	October 16	near Little Beaver Creek, Emmons County, ND	*Juniperus horizontalis* Moench (creeping juniper)

47	October 17	below mouth of Cannon Ball River, Sioux County, ND	*Juniperas communis* L. (dwarf juniper)
48 (same as 103)	October 17	below mouth of Cannon Ball River	*Psoralea argophylla* Pursh (silver-leaf scurf pea)
50	October 18	near mouth of Cannon Ball River	probably *Rosa arkansana* Porter (prairie wild rose)
33	undated	at Fort Mandan	*Arctostaphylos uva-ursi* L. (bearberry)
100	November 17	at Fort Mandan	*Aquilegia canadensis* L. (columbine)
62	undated		unknown
101	undated		*Echinacea angustifolia* DC. (narrow leaf purple coneflower)
102	undated		unknown
103 (same as 48)	undated		*Psoralea argophylla* Pursh (silver-leaf scurf pea)
104 (same as 49)	undated		*Juniperus horizontalis* Moench (creeping juniper)
105	undated		*Nicotiana quadrivalvis* Pursh (Indian tobacco)
106	undated		*Nicotiana quadrivalvis* Pursh (Indian tobacco)
107	undated		possibly *Nicotiana rustica* L. var. *pumila* Schrank (small Arikara tobacco)
108	undated		*Nicotiana quadrivalvis* Pursh (Indian tobacco)

NOTES FOR PART 3

1. The mention of seeds of two varieties of tobacco cultivated by the Arikaras has not been entirely resolved. Voucher 105 is the seed of the larger tobacco variety and 107 is the seed of the smaller variety. The large variety, based on Lewis's excellent description, is clearly *Nicotiana quadrivalvis* Pursh. The voucher specimen 45 is the plant with flowers. The small variety, described by Lewis as being similar but with smaller flowers, and with larger, ovate leaves, is very different and fits the description of *Nicotiana rustica* L. var. *pumila* Schrank. Goodspeed, 356; Cronquist et al., 72. This is important primary evidence that two different species of tobacco were cultivated by the Arikaras. Cf. Gilmore (UPI), 61–62; Gilmore (SCAT), 480–81. Unfortunately, Lewis did not collect a specimen of this smaller species. The tobacco seeds were returned to Jefferson and apparently cultivated in the gardens of William Hamilton and Bernard McMahon. Jackson (LLC), 1:238–39 n. 17, 269, 356, 357 n. 1, 2:389, 392 n. 1, 529.

Part 4: Mineralogical Collections

The following list of mineralogical specimens is found in the Donation Book of the American Philosophical Society (see Appendices B and C, vol. 2). John Vaughan, librarian of the Society, may have copied these notes into the book from an original list by Lewis or he may have taken the notes directly from identifying tags which were once with the specimens. The specimens are apparently the items in box 4 of the goods sent back from Fort Mandan in April 1805, and designated "Specimens of earths, salts, and minerals, numbered 1. to 67." See Jackson (LLC), 1:235, 239–40 n. 21; Clark's entry, April 3, 1805, and accompanying notes. The discrepancy in the number of items (Lewis numbers 67, Vaughan 68) may be attributed to last minute hurrying by Lewis or to a clerical error in Philadelphia. Adam Seybert, a physician, scientist, and member of the Society, added some comments further identifying the specimens. Those additions are italicized and placed in brackets in this section. The "H" following some items may represent an accession check and may stand for "have."

Modern identifications of the specimens are nearly impossible because the descriptions here are so slight and because the specimens have been lost. When Thwaites prepared his edition he called on Edwin H. Barbour, curator of the geological museum, University of Nebraska, to identify the specimens, but the professor had little success. It is doubtful that Barbour saw the specimens so he was at the same disadvantage as we and we are unable to advance identifications much beyond him. Readers are referred to journal entries which correspond to specimen dates for possible geologic references and accompanying annotation.

The specimens may not have all arrived safely at Philadelphia considering that some items have the note "label only." Apparently at some unknown time the specimens were moved to the Academy of Natural Sciences, Philadelphia, where they were integrated with the Academy's general collections and not differentiated as Lewis and Clark pieces. Only one item (number nine) has been discovered; it had the original tag still attached, so it could easily be associated with the expedition. It is pictured in Jackson (LLC), 2: following 566.

———————

M. Lewis' Donation continued 16 Nov. 1805.

No. 1. Specimen of compact salt formed by concretion & found adhering to the rocks, thro' which a Salt fountain Issues, Situated on the South Side of the Southern Branch of the Arcansus River, called by the osage Indians Ne-chu-re-thin-gar. [*Muriat of Soda. This salt beyond all doubt is formed in a consequence of water, we held it in solution, having been evaporated in consequence of exposure to the Sun's rays & atmosphere. The crystals are small cubes heaped together and in every respect resemble those procured by art.*]

2. Found just above the entrance of the cannon Ball river, the butt[e] is principally composed of this sand & strongly impregnated with ⟨a Substance supposed to be blue vitriol⟩ [*Sulphat of Iron in consequence of the decomposition of Pyrites.*]

3. Flint found at the white Chalk Bluffs 1804

4— 23 Aug 1804, found exuding from a Strata of Sand rock on [one] of the Bluffs— [*Much resembles the "Atrausent Stein" of the Germans found near Goslar, and consists principally of Sulphat of Iron derived from decomposed Sulphuret of Iron, intermixed with Clay.*]

5. Specimen of the Sand of the Missouri. [*It is Siliceous sand with a mixture of particles of Mica.*]

6 Augt 21, 1804 In the interstices of a blue clay which forms the majority of the Bluffs, Strata of all earth or Stone make their appearance & Horizontal. [*Alum formed in consequence of a decomposition of aluminous Shistus—& Sulphat of Lime on the lower surface crystallized.*]

7 Petrefaction on the Missouri, May 30, 1804

8 Found among the loose earth of the Bluff 23 Aug. 1804 [*regular crystals of Gypsum or Sulphat of Lime. Trapezoid*]

9 a Petrified Jawbone of a fish or some other animal found in a cavern a few miles distance from the Missouri S side of the River. 6 Aug. 1804, found by Searjant Gass

10. A Specimen of Earth which forms a narrow Strata in the Bluffs above the Sand rock & beneath a large Strata of blue earth Augt 22, 1804— [*Tripoli, nearly colourless & shistose*]

11. Generally met with in the Surface of the earth in the level plains & is very common from the calumet Bluff to Fort mandan [*Clay with aluminous impregnation derived from decomposed Shistus.*]

12. Pebble found at the entrance of the River Quicourre. [*Agatised Flint.*]

13. 22d Aug. 1804.   found occupying the interstices of a blue clay which forms the middle Strata of the Bluff & is about 15 feet in Depth. [*same as No. 6.*]

14 Specimen of the granulated Spontaneous Salt, found at the licks on Salt River bran[ch] of the River Platte, obtained from the Oteoes— [*Muriat of Soda in form of an efflorescence.*]

15 Sept. 1, 1804.   found exuding from a Strata of firm blue earth which forms the majority of the River Bluffs— [*a yellowish clay, probably arising from decomposed Slate.*]

16 Presented to me by a Mr. Griffith near the entrance of the Missouri—   This mineral was presented me by a Mr Griffith who informed me that it had been procured from an earth, found in a cave of limestone rock on the Mississipi a few miles from the entrance of the Missouri, by the Same process observed in extracting Saltpetre from the earth of Caverns— [*a mixture of different kinds of Salts.*]

17

18 Aug. 22.   on the Upper part of the Bluff

19

20—   Aug 22, 1804. Is usually found incrusting or overlaying a black Rock which crowns the Summits of most of the river Hills in this quarter. [*Sulphat Lime?*]

21—   a specimen of a firm blue Earth which formed a large Strata of the Bluffs which we passed from 21 Augt. to 15 Sep 1804 [*Aluminous Shistus in a state of decomposition.*]

22. found at the Calumet Bluff. [*also resembling "Atramentstein" similar to No. 4.*]

23. Salt obtained the 17 Sept. 1804 overlaying a dark blue Clay on the Sides of the river hills, it is So abundant that it impregnates the little rivulets in Such a degree that the water is unfit to drink. [*Alum intermixed with Clay.*]

24 Carbonated wood found on the Std. side of Riv near fort Mandane 60 feet above high water mark in the Bank Strata 6 Inch thick.

25. Precipitate of one pint of Missouri water weight 80:65 grs [*pincipally common Clay.*]

26 Pebbles common to the Sand Bars of the Missouri— [*Agatised flint & small quartzose pebbles.*]

27 Specimen of lead ore of Bertons mine on the Marimeg River— [*Galena or sulphuret of Lead.*]

28. *Green Earth*, Presented by Mr Charbono, who informed me that the natives procure this earth in the neighberhood of the Rocky mountain, but cannot ⟨find⟩ point out the place.— The Indians mix this Earth with glue & paint their arrows with it, when thus boiled with Glue it gives a fine green color to wood, but easily yield to Water the Indians also paint their Skins with it. M. L: Feby. 13, 1804 [*Green Clay coloured by Iron.*]

29. Specimen of the lead ore of Bertons' mine on the Marrimic River Upper Louisiana [*Galena*]

30. Sep. 15, 1804 found in the interstices of a Brown rock which Sometimes makes its appearance in a Strata of 6 or 8 feet usually about half of the Elevation of the Bluffs— [*Similar to 4 & 22.*]

31. Specimen of ⟨quartz⟩ Carbonat of Lime found on many parts of the Missouri common to the Mississipi & Ohio. ⟨probably a mixture of Glauber, common & Epsom Salts with alumine.⟩ [*Rhomboidal carbonat of Lime.*]

32. Specimen of Globar Salts taken in Prairie of Std. Shore 22 Octr. 1804 many bushels could have been obtained.— [*a misture of various kinds of Salt with alumine.*]

33 Specimen of the Sand of the river Quicourre or Rapid River. [*quartz ore Sand of a greyish white colour.*]

34 Obtained at the Calumet Bluffs— [*principally fragments of argillaceous Iron ore.—*]

35 Found on the N. Side of the River quicourre just above its entrance [*Slate in a State of decomposition—with some Sulphat of Lime.*]

36. Found Sep. 6 on Larbord Shore encrusting a Rock— [*Alumine probably from decomposition of Shistus with Saline impregnation tho' very Slight.*]

37. Found at the upper part of the Big Bend

38. found at the base of the Bluffs intermixed with loose earth 22 Aug. 1804 [*Pyrites.*]

39. Petrefactions obtained on the River ohio in 1803

40 Specimen of the Sand rock which forms the base of the Limestone Clifts in the neighborhood of the osage Woman's river on the Missouri. [*fine grained Sand Stone.*]

41. Specimen of Earth which constitutes the majority of the Bluffs— 23d Aug 1804   when taken was in a firmer state than at present— [*Slate decomposed with Pyrites decomposed.*]

42. found at the upper Point of the Big Bend of the Missouri

43. found above the white chalk Bluff in the Interstices of the Chalk rock [*Shistus decomposing with Small crystals of Gypsum.*]

44— Aug 23, 1804 Specimen of a bituminous substance found on the face of a Sand rock, from which it appears to exude & forms by exposure to the air. This Strata of Sand rock is about 10 feet thick & forms a proportion of the lower part of the River Bluffs— [*Aluminous Shistus in a state of decomposition.*]

45. Specimen of the Earth which forms the base of the Banks of the Missouri   H. [*fine grey coloured Sand.*]

46. Found at the Burning Cliffs 23 Aug. 1804— [*Pyrites.*]

47 Specimen of the Earth of which the Hills of the Missouri are principally formed from the entrance of the river Sioux to fort mandan & if Indian information may be depended upon, for several hundred miles further up— It is in this tract of country that the Missouri acquires it coloring matter of which it abates but little to its junction to the Mississipi. This earth when saturated by the rains or melting snows becomes so Soft for many feet in depth, that being unable to support its own weight, it

Seperates into large masses from the hills, & Slipping down their Sides precipitates itself into the Missouri & mingles with its waters— great quantities of this earth are also thrown into the river by its Subsidiary Streams & rivulets which pass thro' or originate in this tract of open Country. M. L. [*Slate in a decomposed state.*]

48. Sep. 10th   found on the side of the Bluffs not very abundant [*same as 47—with Streaks of green clay.*]

49. Aug. 22, 1804   found overlaying & intermixed with the Earth which forms the bluffs of the River. [*crystallized Sulphat of Lime.*]

50 Aug. 24, 1804   Specimen of Pirites at the base of the Bluffs on the South side of the Missouri. [*Principally cubic Pyrites imbedded in argillaceous Shistus.*]

51. Specimen of Pirites found 22 Aug. 1804 at the base of the bluffs on the S. Side of the Mississipi— only the label

52 A Specimen of the Chalk found at the white ⟨Chalk⟩ Clay Bluffs on the S. Side of the Missouri. [*Argill?*]

53 Found at the White ⟨Chalk⟩ Clay Bluffs on S. Side Missouri (only the label) [*Pyrites in a state of efforescence*]

54 from 24 Aug. to 10 Sept. 1804   Pyrites found intermixed promiscuously with the earth which form the Bluffs of the Missouri in a great variety of places. [*same as 53.*]

55 Incrustations of large round masses of rock which appear in a Sand bluff just above the entrance of the Cannonball river. This river derives its name from the appearance of these Stones   many of them are as perfectly globular as art could form them. [*Carbonate of Lime be caustious that you do not confound this with the globular Pyrites.   see No. 58 below.*]

56 Found on the side of the River bluffs.   22d Aug. 1804   Irregularly intermixed with the Earth. [*Pyrites.*]

57. Pyrites found along the borders of the Missouri from 20 Augt to 10 Sepr, they are very common on the borders of all the little Rivulets in this open Country. [*Some of these Pyrites are in a state of efflorescence.*]

58 Found 23d Aug. 1804 at the base of the Bluff. [*Carbonat of Lime indeterminately crystallised & invested by ⟨indurated argill⟩ compact carbonat of Lime*]

59 A Specimen of calcareous rock, a thin Stratum of which is found

overlaying a soft Sand rock which makes its appearance in many parts of the bluffs from the entrance of the River Platte to Fort Mandon. [*Mass of shells*]

60. Found on the River Bank 1 Aug. 1804 (petrified [*Ed: blank*] Nest)

61

62 Specimen of the pummice Stone found amongst the piles of drift wood on the Missouri, Sometimes found as low down as the mouth of the osage river. I can hear of no burning mountain in the neighborhood of the Missouri or its Branches, but the bluffs of the River are now on fire at Several places, particularly that part named in our chart of the Missouri *The Burning Bluffs*. The plains in many places, throughout this great extent of open country, exhibit abundant proofs of having been once on fire— Witness the Specimens of Lava and Pummicestone found in the Hills near fort mandon— [*Pumice.*]

63 Specimen of a Substance extremely common & found intermix'd with the loose Earth of all the Cliffs & Hills from the Calumet Bluff to Fort Mandon. [*crystallized Gypsum. Sulphated Lim*]

64 Specimen of Carbonated wood with the loose Sand of the sand-Bars of the Missouri & Mississipi, it appears in considerable quantaties in many places— [*carbonated wood*]

65. Specimen of Stone commonly met with on the Surface of the Earth thro' a great proprotion of the plain open country above the River Platte— [*Carbonate of Lime.*]

66 Found in the Bluffs near Fort mandan. [*Petrefied wood.*]

67. A Specimen of Lava & pummice Stone found in great abundance on the Sides of the Hills in the Neighborhood of Fort Mandan 1609 miles above the mouth of the Missouri— exposed by the washing of the Hills from the rains & melting Snow.— These are merely the river Hills which are the banks only of a Valley formed by the Missouri, passing thro' a level plain— from the tops of these hills the country as far as the eve can reach is a level plain. The tract of Country which furnishes the Pummice Stone seen floating down the Misouri, is rather burning or burnt plains than burning mountains— [*Lavas*]

68 Brought us by one of our hunters, John Shields who found it at the Allum Bluff 22 Aug. 1804. [*Pyrites or Slate.*]

Part 5: Missouri River Miscellany

The following are a collection of miscellaneous documents by Clark that do not fit into other sections of this chapter. These documents were all apparently made at Fort Mandan, although the second (Clark's "A Slight View of the Missouri River") may have been a postexpeditionary piece intended for Nicholas Biddle and copied from a lost original. One other possible document for inclusion is not printed here because of its duplication of existing material. Apparently at Fort Mandan Clark made a list of his courses and distances up the Missouri River in 1804 drawn from his daily log of journal entries. A check of this document against Clark's journals shows no significant differences and only occassional errors in copying. The document ("The *courses* and *Computed Distance's* of each day assending the *Missouri River;* commencing at the mouth") is in the Voorhis Collection of the Missouri Historical Society.

[Clark]   [*undated, winter 1804–5*][1]

    The Number of Officers & Men for to protect the Indian trade and Keep the Savages in peace with the U. S. and each other   1805   if Soldiers act as Boatmen & Soldiers

Names of elegable Situations of Establishments	Agents	Colonel	Majors	Captains	Loutents.	Ensigns	Serjons Mates	Interpeters	Sergeants	Corporals	Musick	Privats	Total	Distance from each oth[er]
At St Louis—	1	1	1	1	1	1	1	1	3	1	4	60	68	
at the Osarge, or Arkansaw				1		1	1	1	1	1	1	45	48	
" the mouth of Kanzes—				1		1		1	2	1		25	28	366
" the Council Bluff—				1		1		2	2	2	2	30	36	316
" " *Chien* or *Shar ha* R—				1	1	1	1	3	4	4	4	75	88	640
" " Rochejone river—	1			1	1	1		4	3	3	3	45	54	500
" " Falls of Missourie—				1		1		2	2	1	1	30	38	700
" " Head of Kanzes or Arkansas				1	1	1	1	2	4	4	4	75	87	

	Agents	Colonel	Majors	Captains	Loutents.	Ensigns	Serjons Mates	Interpeters	Sergeants	Corporals	Musick	Privats	Total	Distance from each oth[er]
on the Mississippi Prarie de Chien	1			1	1	1	1	2	4	4	4	70	82	
St Peters or Falls of St Anthony					1		1	1	2	2	2	30	36	
do — do Sand Lake—				1	1	1	1	1	2	4	2	40	48	
on the St Peters River				1	1	1	1	1	4	4	4	75	82	
	3	1	1	8	9	8	12	22	32	32	32	600	700	

[Clark]   *[undated, winter 1804–5]*[2]

A Slight View of the Missouri River.

This River is a turbilant & muddey Stream Containing great number of Islands below the River *Platte* which falls in on its S. side   6 miles up above the Platte but fiew Islands, more Sand bars and the ⟨Stream⟩ Current less rapid—   The rapidity of the Missouri may be Setimated from the mouth to the Osages ⟨Kansas to⟩ from 6 miles pr. Hour to the Kansas 6½ to 7 miles from thence to the Platte 5½ to 6 miles pr. Hour, & from thence to the *Rochejone* about [*blank*] miles and I am told from thence to the falls less Rapid, The bottoms is very extensive perticularly on the N. Side as high as Floyds River & Bluff 880 miles up, there they become narrow from 3 to 5 miles wide as high as River Jacque 974 miles up   abov as high as this place the high open Countrey approach the River—   The fish Common in the Missouri is perincipally Cat.   Some white, its tributary Streams abound in a variety of fish, its bank Contain a variety of mineral

The Climate, Winds, & Diseases

The Climate thro which the Missouri passes is Certainly pleasing & desireable between the Latituds of 38° & 48° North—   The winter wind are

Changeable, the Summer Spring & fall wind are for maney days Stationary at the Same point   a S. E. wind is Common in Summer

The Diseases Commons to our party was Tumers in Summer & Ploure-
sis in Winter, Some few Rhumatics, and on one part of this River above
the Mahars the party much incomoded frequently with a Lax, (owing to
the minerals) &c

The Face of the Countrey, ⟨water⟩ Soil & productions

The Countrey bordering on the Missourie as high as the Kanzas is rich
and well watered, extinsive planes back which is also Rich—   to the Plate
less timbered land, Countrey Rich and fertile—   from the Plate to the
Fort Mandan the Countrey is Generally open Plains, intersperced with
Groves of Timber, which is to be found on the Rivers & Smaller Streams
Generally—   This Countrey abounds in a variety of wild froot, Such
as Plumbs, Cherris, Currents, Rasburies, Sarvis berry, High bush Cram
burry (or Pimbanah)[3] Grapes, a Red Biry Called by the french Greas au
Beff &. &.

Ores Minirals Salts & Salt Salines

I know of no Body of ore, it is said that the Sioux know of a Silver mine
on the R. De Moin,—and I am also told that Lead ore has been descovered
in Several places. I am told by Several that Several Small Lakes [& &c?] N E
of the Mandans is So much the quality of Glober Salts as to be unpleasing
to drink—   the runs in the hils above the Jacque is so much impregnated
with glover Salts as to have its effect   The Bluffs of the Missouri above
R. Jacque abounds in minerals of various Kinds, Such as Cobalt, Piritus,
Alum, Coparas, & a variety of other mineral   Salt is Collected in various
parts of the Missourie Country perticularly on a Creek 60 Lgs. up the
Republican fork of the Kanzas River   it is Collected by Sweeping it together with a Broom of feathers on a hard Surface, The Grand Saline
one fork of the Arkansas, also the red Satem pot Saline, & Cristict Salt on
the waters of that River—   Salt is made in 3 places on the River Rogue of
Lake Winnipic. Maney Small licks near the Missouri in different posts, no
doubt (from their appearance) equal to any.

The Different kinds of wild Animals &
where to be found White Bear &c.

The wild ammals Common below the River Platt is Such as are Common in the Indiana Territory   Those on the Missouri from the Plate to the Mandans are Elk Common Deer, fallow Deer, Mule Deer with Black tail, Antalope or Goats Buffalow Har[e]s Rabits large wolves, Small wolves (Red foxes & Small Grey foxes above the Chayenne River) Porcupins Braroes, a Small Dog or Squirel which lives in Burrowed Villages & Barks at the approach at any thing they do not understand weasel mice of Different kinds in great abundance Beaver & otter, the upper part a fiew Loucirvea and Grisley Bear which is said to be verry dangerous. The Countrey above the Mandans Contain great numbers of those anamils Common below and the White & Rid Bear[4] (The White Bear is larger and more dangerous than eithr the Grey or Rid bear and frequently Kill the Indians, Two of the *minetarees* has been Killed and eate up this winter ⟨near⟩ on thier hunting parties—[)]   The Black hills is Said abound in Bear of every kind, and in addition to all those animals Common on the Missouri an Animmal with verry large horns Curved about the Size of a Small Elk, and a Booted Turkey commonly white—   maney othr animals is Said to inhabit the Rockey mountains Such as Branded Goats Squirels of Different kinds & Sizes uncommon in the U. S. (I have seen the Skins of Several)

Birds Waterfowls uncommon in the U S.

about 1150 miles up the Missouri and from thenc up we have the Magpy, the Calumet eagle is Scerce, but to be found on the Missouri above the Kanzas—   this Bird is about the Size of a ⟨Grey⟩ Bald Eagle, a part of its tail & wings white, much prised by all the Indians, the owl is Smaller & high up the Missouri white,[5] a fiew white Brant is to be Seen as low as the Chyenne River (Rattle Snakes are ⟨not numerous⟩)

Indians [Nt. Ch.? *nation's character?*]

The Kanzas ottoes Missouris Poncars ⟨the Different bands of Sious⟩ are fierce pilfering Set and viewed as bandittes by the Traders who visit them. The Pancas, Loups, Republicans Mahars and majority of the *Ricaras* are mild Sincere and well disposed towards the whites   live in villages &—

The Different Bands of the Tetons a tribe of Sioux are fierce deceitfull unprencipaled robers, they rove on either side of the Missouri about Chyennes, River   The *Mandans Minetarras & Ma harhas* are certainly the most mild sincere Indians I ever Saw, the Mandans particularly

Indians Claims to Lands

No limits can be discribed for any of the Nations & tribes except the Sioux Osages as war with each other frequently happen which forces one party to remove, a considerable distance from the other, untill peace is restored, at which period all lands are Generally in common— yet it is not common for two tribes to Camp together for any long time or hunt in the Same neighbourhood.

The Osage Claim a great extent of Countrey on the Osage Kanzas & Arkansaw Rivers   The Sioux Claim on both Sides of the Missouri from the Mahars to near the Mandans & to the Mississippi from Crow Wing River Down to near the Demoin & to the Mouth of Little River Sioux, the Ayawwas & Saukes & Renards Claim the lower potion of the Missouri on the N E Side.

I have never herd of any Treaty haveing been entered into betwen Spain and the Indian for a boundery or Lands and I belive that Nation are userpers, on the Missouri & high up the Mississippi

The Geography may be Seen as well as is at this time Know by a refurence to my map of the Missouri and its waters &c.

The Different nations are written in red Ink on the Map, as they are Situated numbers &. &.

Their Trade, Cultivation & mode of Life.

The Osage, Kansas, Ottoes & Missouri, Pania, Republican & Loups, Ayauwais Saukies & Renars, *Ricaras* Mandans, Menatarres & Ma har,hars live in Vilages and raise Corn beeen, Semmins &c. artichoaks all except the three latter nations Trade with the merchants from St. Louis & mickellimaken Sackes Renars & Ayawais, with the latter, the Mandans Minatarra & Ma har ha Trade with the British Companies from the Assinniboin River—   The Sioux near the Mississippi Trade with Merchants from Michillenmackinac, the Yankton *ah nah* & one the bands of Tetons trade partially with the mrchants from St Louis, The Mahars & poncassars as also all the Nations west of the Missouri, have no Trader and what little trafick they have is with other nations for which they give horses Garment of the Skin of the Big horn animal &. &. The Assiniboins and those nations N and N E of them Trade with the British Traders Scattered on the waters of Lake *Winnipic*— The Snake Nation and those on the heads of the River Platte & *Rockjone* R have some little trafick with the Spaniards of New Mixico, all those nations on the main branch of the Missouri & near it the Indians have no trade or aney intercourse with the whites all those last mintioned Nations, rove in the Plains & Mount[ains] no Settled place of abode, and do not raise Corn Beans tho fond to trade for them

The articles which the nations apper
perticularly fond of

The Tetons & Yanktons are fond of Tobacco Guns Powder & Ball Horses Knives & alls & pertically Spirrits

The Ricaras appear fond of Paint Blue Beeds rings the Tale & feathers of the Calumet Eagle and partially of any other article of merchandize also horses. do not drink Spiritious Licquer— The Mandans Menetaries & Maharhas are fond of War axes in a perticular form [*here a drawing of war ax*][6] Blue beeds, pipes, paint, The tale & [top?] feathers of the Calumet Eagle, Knives, Guns, Powder & Ball, White Buffalow Skin, & Horses &. &. arrow points

The nations in every quarter I am told are fond of Blue Beeds, red Paint, Knives, axes, Guns & ammunition.

Their arms and method of takeing their game.

The arms of the nations on the Missouri is fusees & Bows & Arrows The fusies are Short and tight. The lower nations make use of fusies principally those higher up i e the Mahas, Poncaris, Sioux, Ricaras, Mandans, Minetarras, Ma har has Assinniboins and the wandering Bands make much more use of Bows & arrows than of fusees— they most of those nations have Guns but find it much Cheaper to kill their game with arrows than with Ball— Those nations pursue the Buffalow on horse Back and after fatiegueing them a little, ride Close by the Side of the

Fatest and Shoot her with arrows, their bows being Strong backed with Sinears [sinews] Some times force an arrow through a Cow— They are bad Deer hunters, and those they kill is Generally with the fusee, also the Elk and wilder game. the Antelope or Goat they Sometimes drive them into pens, they also get them in the rivers, parties on each Sides & the Boys Kill them with Sticks in the River— The wolves & foxes Catch in holes or traps of logs.

⟨The method⟩ What is their Form of Carrying on
War & making peace

The Different nations have peculiarities of their own— The *Me ne tarras* when a Chief intends to go to war he makes a feest & Some one man informs of his intentions in a harrang, & at the time they Set out it is not known by those that go how maney the party will Consist, the leave the village at Different times ⟨Chiefly⟩ Prompally at night and meet a Some given point— on their return they enter their village with great pomp if they are suckcessfull, if not they Steel in as they went out. all Boy Prisoners & men they addopt, the feamales they make Slaves of which is Custom of the nations generally— The pipe is the Semblem of peace with all, The different nations have their different fashions of Dilivering and receiving of it— The party delivering generally Confess their Errors & request a peace, the party receiving exult in their Suckcesses and receive the Sacred Stem &c—

orrigian

It is probable from the Similarity of maney of those nations that they were at Some period embodied in a more Civillised State, perhaps the decendants of Several Great nations— Some of those nations Say their forefathers imigrated from the S. & others from the East or up the river— Some from the *Ohio*

Their mode of Punishment for
Larger & Lesser Crimes

The Mandans punish Capatal Crimes with Death, Smaller Crimes by reason Contempt & Conventrey, The man So treated proves his deturmination to reform by penance, runing arrows through the flesh, Cutting themselves in Different places, going into the Plains necked & Starveing maney Days, and returns, this being a proofe of his determination to reform, they after much Serimony take him into favour, "a punishment for boys too fond of women" is to Dress and perform the Duties of Women dureing Life.[7] The Minitars Maharhas have Similar Customs—

Our reception and treatment Generally

all nations at all times with great attention and appearent friendship, The Tetons Treated us roughfly as before discribed— The other nations have at all times have appeared friendly and well disposed towards us (the Sioux & ottoes are great Beggers— The nations above the Sioux perticularly the mandans never beg altho, they may be in great want of the article[)]

our peculiar Situations as to provision &c. &c

we by the aide of our Black smiths precured Corn Sufficient for the party dureing the winter and about 70 or 90 bushels to Carry with us.   we Soon found that no Dependance Could be put in the Information of our Interpreter Jessomme's Information respecting the Supplies of meat we were to recive of the Indians, and Sent out hunters and frequently went ourselves to hunt the Buffalow Elk & Deer, and precured a Sufficency dureing the winter—, also Skins for our mens Shoes— The Indians being without meat half the winter—fearfull of going out at any great Distance to hunt for fear of the Sioux who are Continually harrassing the mandans &c. We had at one period of the Winter Buffalow in great numbers near us   the weather being excessively Cold we Could, we found it imprackable to precure at that tinme a Sufficiency of Meat without the riesque of friesing maney of our men, who frequently, were Slightly frosted.

The Mountains & their Situation—

The *Cote-Noir* or Black Mountains are Situated in Several ranges on the S W Side of the Missouri and run N. N. W. & S. S. E from the heads of the Kanzas and Arkansaws as far North as about Latd. 46° N. and back of 4 ranges of those mountains is the Rockey or Shineing Mountains, which run in nearly the Same Derection, a Small Mountain is Situated at the head of Knife River N W. of Fort Mandan about 30 Leagues Called Turtle Mountain— a long narrow mountain is Situated about N W. of fort Mandan about 30 or 40 Leages Called Moose Deer Mountain,[8] North of Fort Mandan & no Great Distance from the Establishments on the Assinniboin River is situated a high wooded Countrey on which there is several Small lakes, this high Countrey is Called Turtle Mountain, Several detached mountains are Situated above this in different Derections

The Traders & Their Conduct &c. &c.

The traders who frequented the nations below heretofore were such as purchased the privilage of tradeing with the different nations, and as their terms of trade was not certain for any length of time, did not interest themselves in diswadeing the Indians from any vicious act which they might have had in view, being at all times jellous of their temporary provilegeis— The Traders who visit the Seoux are from different quarters and in Course jealous of each, those jelousies in Trade leads those trades to Speak unfavourable of each other, which gives the Indians an unfavourable opinion of ⟨them⟩ all the whites &. The Trades who frequnt the Mandans & Minetarres are from two British Companie N W. & Hudsons Bay, Those British Companies have carried their jelousy to Such hite, as to give the Indians a bad oppinion of all whites from that quarter, they not only do every thing in their power to Injur each other, but oppose each other in the presence of the Indians, Several instancs of violance on the property & persons of each other & one Deaths not long Since—[9]

What is Genl. Shape, Sise, Colr and Dress & Amusements.

The Indians of the Missoury is will Shaped Generally The Sioux Ottoes & Missouri are Smaller than the Indians are Generally. The Sioux normeley Dark, with small legs The Osage, Kanzes, Panias Mahars Ricaras, & Mandans, are large men, women of all Generally Small The Minetarras Maharhas & Crow Indians are large portley men, Tall women well proportioned.— The Assininiboins & Christiones are much like the Sioux— The Chyennes, Castihania Can nar vesh and those Indians which I have seen that rove between the *Cote Noir* & rock mountains are large & fine looking fellows— The Snake Squars are remarkably Small, the men I am told are also Small— The Indians low down the Missouri dress in Skins & what clothes and trinkets they can precure from the whites— The Sioux dress in leather except a Breach Cloth, except on their first days then those who have them put on better Clothes— The Ricaras & Mandans men, Dress in Leather Leagens & mockasons a flap of Blanket Generally before & a Roabe of Buffalow Skin Dressed, the womin the Same and a Shift of the Antelope or big horn animal, fringed & decerated with Blue Beeds Elk tusks & pieces of red Cloth, the Minatares & other Squars in the nighbourhood the Same the Minatars men ware a shirt in winter Generally of Dressed Elkskin maney decrattions about the head feet & Legs of Skins Shells, Talents [talons] &c. &c. &c.

The amusements of the men of Mandans & nighbours are playing the Ball & Rackets, Suffustence Feists to bring the Buffalow (in which all the young & handsom women are giving to the old men & Strangers to embrace,[)] many others feists & Dances of a similar kind— The women have a kind of game which they play with a Soft Ball with their foot, they being viewed as property & in course Slaves to the men have not much leisure time to Spear— (maney men have 4. 5. 6 & 7 wives Generally Sisters in marying or Purches the eldest he Genly. Gets all)

The Superstitions & Mode of Deposeing the Dead

All the nations which I have Seen are Superstitious and have a faboulous tale of their Tredition, but none So much So as the nations high up the Missouri, The Ricaras *Mandans* & *Minetarras* have Stones Situated in the plain which they Consult every year for They Say that the See figers on the Stone's early in the morning Emblematical of what is to take place the Suckceeding year— The Ricaras and the nations below them Cover their Dead with earth the Mandans and the nations about them Scaffold their dead and pay great Devotion to them after Death, frequently Sacrifice to them, They have Certain Animals &c. which they worship, or view as enspired with asserting power to which they make great Sacrifices of their property, it is not uncommon to thro away to those medisons 10 horses, Robes &c &c— that they never attend to after. They Show their greif by Cutting off their hair and Small fingers and pierceing their flesh.

The nations ⟨high up⟩ on the Missouri are Generly helthy but few of them have remidies for Diseases, they make great use of the Coal bath & Swets— Sioux Cure the Bite of the Mad Dog & Snake with a root common in all open Countrey before discribed the Goitre is common, womin perticularly.

Their houses & Lod[g]es Mode of life
& how Convay burthen

The house & Lodges of the Indians on the Missouri are nearly resembling each other— Their Houses (also Cald. Lodges) are built in a Circular form of different Sises from 20 to 70 feet Diameter and from 8 to 14 feet high, Supported with 4 pillars Set in a Squar form near the Center near the hight of the hut. around the huts forks about 4 feet with Beems from one to the other, which form the Circle and Support the Top, around and on the top of those beems they place neet round poles, on the top of those poles Small willows & grass, & cover all (except a hole 4 or 5 feet Squars at top) with earth, laveing also a Dore Generally on the South Side from which they have a projection about 5 feet covered— Their Lodges are made of Dressed Buffalow Skinns, to Stretch on poles So as to form a Cone & Some of them will hold Conveniently 20 men— The Mandans & Minnetarras & live in 2. 3 & 4 families in a Cabin, their horses & Dogs in the Same hut, all provisions killed are in Common, not only in the different Lodges but frequently throughout the nation, they Seldom [dust?] the hut or Clean the horse appartment The Squars do all the Lavour & Carry the burthens with the assistance of their Dogs which the Homes in a Small Stay or two poles which with one of the ends of each on the Ground, and the Load across the poles &c.[10]

Their Laws & Government & Similarity
of Language &

The Sioux have regular police ⟨no Stationary⟩ no fixed Laws but what is brought on by Custom, and all the other nations have no other Laws the Good or bad government of the nations are owing and Depend in a great measure on the dispositions & Correctness of the Chiefs who are feared

489

11. Area about Fort Mandan and North to the
Assinboine River, undated (winter 1804–5),
Voorhis Collection, Missouri Historical Society

by the majority— all nations Harrang. Genl. the old men perform this Service by the derection of the Cheifs

In all the languages of the Different nations on the Missouri maney words are the Same, The Osage, Kanzas, Mahars & Poncars speak the Same language with different promouncation and Some words Different The Pania, Loups, Republican, Pania Pickey and Ricaras Speake the Same Language with much [Coruptn?]

The Sioux & Assinniboins the Same Language— The Mandans some fiew words of Several language (They lern with great facility) The *Mini-tarres Ma har ha* Crow & fall Indians Speake the Same language The Ottoes Missoures Ayuwuais, & [Poucons?][11] Speake the Same Language.

[Clark]   [*undated, winter 1804–5*][12]

The Course from the Fort Mandan to the Fort *Chaboillez's* on the Assinna Boin is North 150 Miles

	ms	
Mirey creek	12	& Big C. of wood 16 to the E to a lake
Mous river ⎫ 30 yd wide ⎭	50	to the river La Sou 4 L
and	20	Legues to a Small creek of the Mous R
&	3	do to the next—
&	1	League cross the Lasou or M.
&	20	L Cross the Ditto to the R Pass Turtle Hites [Hills?] a 6 L.
&	7	to Assinibon
	51	

NOTES FOR PART 5

1. This table from document 67 of the Field Notes was presumably written before the departure from Fort Mandan and before the captains had actually seen the "Rochejone" (Yellowstone) or the Falls of the Missouri. It outlines an ambitious scheme for control of the Louisiana Territory and its inhabitants and trade. It would be decades before the federal government summoned the will or the resources to implement it fully. In 1819 a military expedition set out up the Missouri to establish a post at the mouth of the Yellowstone, but it got no farther than the Council Bluffs in Nebraska, where it erected Fort Atkinson, abandoned in 1827. There would be no military post at the mouth of the Yellowstone, or anywhere near the Great Falls of the Missouri, until the 1860s. The army did not establish a lasting presence beyond the eastern edge of the Great Plains until 1848. Nonetheless, the captains' astuteness is indicated by the fact that military posts were eventually established at or near about two-thirds of the sites they selected. "Musick" refers to drummers, buglers, and other military musicians. Several columns of figures do not add up as given. Nichols & Halley, 61–100; Prucha (SR), 81–102, 139–67.

2. This brief summary by Clark of most aspects of the Missouri valley is part of the Biddle Family Deposit of "seven manuscript items" (see Appendix B, vol. 2) in the American Philosophical Society. It is a combined printing of items two and four which appear to be one continuous document that has become separated over time. From internal evidence it is clear that it was composed at Fort Mandan, but may have been copied later for the use of Nicholas Biddle after 1810.

3. The "sarvis berry" is *Amelanchier alnifolia* Nutt., juneberry or serviceberry. The high bush cranberry, or pembina, may be identified as *Viburnum opulus* L. var. *americanum* Ait., although its distribution is more northerly. It may be that Clark or his informants were actually seeing the nannyberry and applying the name pembina to it. Pembina is a corruption of the Chippewa word *nepin-minan*, "summer berry." Barkley, 137, 329–30; Gilmore (UPI), 63–64, 63 n. 1.

4. This "red bear" is perhaps the cinnamon color phase of the black bear, *Ursus americanus*, since Clark's Indian informants seem to have distinguished its behavior from that of the grizzly. Jones et al., 264.

5. Clark had perhaps either seen or been told of the snowy owl, *Nyctea scandiaca* [AOU, 376], during the winter at Fort Mandan; this arctic bird sometimes winters in the northern United States.

6. This drawing is a simplified sketch of the war hatchet shown and discussed on January 28 and February 5, 1805. See fig. 6.

7. Evidently a reference to the "berdashes" (see above, December 22, 1804), although being "too fond of women" hardly conveys what Clark apparently means.

8. One or more of various high buttes and low mountains in west-central North Dakota and east-central Montana.

9. Perhaps a reference to the death of Ménard. See above, October 25, 1804.

10. A description of the travois of the plains tribes.

11. Perhaps the Winnebagos who are linguistically related to the other named tribes. A synonymy of names lists terms similar to Clark's word, for example, Pouans. Hodge, 2:961.

12. Clark must have gathered this material and the accompanying map (fig. 11) at Fort Mandan; it concerns the route from there to the North West Company's principal post on the Assiniboine River in Manitoba, managed by Charles Chaboillez. The source would be the company agents—Larocque, McKenzie, and Heney—who visited the captains during the winter. Clark's "Mous" is the present Souris River (Clark's "La Sou"), also known as the Mouse. It enters the Assiniboine River southeast of Brandon, Manitoba, Canada. The document is in the Voorhis Collection of the Missouri Historical Society on a sheet which also has an undated Lewis document to be found in Chapter 3 of this edition.

Part 6: Baling Invoices

The following lists appear on pp. 256–74 of Codex C, reading backward; the hand is unknown. The first part is an invoice of presents to be given to Indian chiefs, the second lists "necessary stores" for the expedition. There seems to be no way of determining when the lists were written, but since they are found in a journal sent back from Fort Mandan they are printed here.

Baling Invoice of Sundries for Indian Presents

No. 30 a Bag Contg.
   2 Chief's Coats
   2 hats & plumes
   2 White Shirts
   2 Medals 2d Sise
   2 hair pipes   for first Chiefs of Ottos or Panis—
   2 wrist Bands
   2 Arm Bands
   2 Bundles Gartg.
   2 pr Leggins
   2 Britch Clouts

   3 Medals 3d Size
   3 Blue Blankets
   3 pr Scarlet Leggins   2d Chief
   3 Britch Clouts
   3 Bundles Gartg.

   3 medals 3d Sise
   3 Scarlet Leggins
   3 white Shirts   3d Chief
   3 Britch Clouts
   3 Bundles Gartg.

No 13 a Bag,
   1 medal 2d Sise
   1 Chiefs Coat
   1 white Shirt
   1 Hat & Plume
   1 Hairpipe   1st Chief of Ponkas or any other
   1 Wrist Band   that may be met this Side of
   1 Arm Band   Mahar—
   1 pr Scarlet Leggins
   1 Blue Britch Clout
   1 Flag of 2d sise

   2 pr Scarlet Leggins
   4 Blue Britch Clouts
   4 pr Leggins
 14 Silk Handkfs.

26 pocket Ditto

    4 Rolls Ribbon   this part intended for foreign

    4 Callico Shirts   nations—   Should any of the

    4 hairpipes   three above Nations be met; the

    4 Rolls Gartg. small Bundles   presents of Small articles may be

    5 looking Glasses   taken from the Bags no. 33, 15,

  14 Small Bundles Ribbon   42, 9, 36, 16, 45 or 26—

    1 large Roll Gartg.

    1 Blue Blanket

    1 d Cold thread

    1 d White do

  10 pieces nonsoprettys

No 33 a bag Contg.

    1 Chiefs Coat

    1 hat & Circle feather

    1 white Shirt

    1 pr Scarlet Leggins

    1 Britch Clout Scarlet

    1 Large Medal   for the Maha Chief

    1 Small Bundle Gartg.

    1 Silver Moon

    1 wrist Band

    1 Arm Band

  (1 Flag)

    1 Medal 2d Sise

    1 Blue Blanket

    1 pr Leggin & Britch Clout

    1 Callico Shirt   for 2d Do

    1 Wampum hairpipe

    1 Small Bundle tape

    1 Medal 3d Sise

    1 Britch Clout & Shirt   for 3d Do

    1 pr Leggins, 1 Bundle Gartg.

    1 Scarlet Blanket

    1 Roll Ribbon   for 1st Chief's wife

    1 Silk handkf

    1 Callico Shirt   Some Great man

    1 tomy hawk   Some Considered man

5 handkfs	1 to each young men
1 Ivory Comb	Some woman of consideration
2 Bunches of thread	1 Skaine to Sundry women
2 Bundles Gartg.	to Some young women
1 Doz. Knives 5 Lookg Glasses	1 to Sundry men
2 Bead Neck Laces	for young women
3 Burng. Glasses	to young men
1 Small Bundle Gartg. (say Ribbon)	to some Girl
3 pieces Dutch Tape	by ½ pce. to young women
10 maces White Rd. Beads	to Girls
2 maces Sky blue Rd do	"
3 do Yellow do	"
3 do Red Do	"
14 do Yellow Seed Do	"
5 do Mock Garnets	"
1 Dos Small Hawk Bells	young men
5 large do	"
6 tinsel hat Bands	"
1 needle Case	woman
3 pr Glass Ear Bobs	do
100 Broaches	by 10 to young warriors
6 Silver Rings	to women
9 pr Scissars	"
2 Collars of Guilt wire	men of Consequence
3 Rolls Snare do	young men by 1 fathom
1 Bunch Knitting pins	by 3, to men abt. 35 or 40
412 needles	by 10, to women
61 fish hooks	by 4 or 5 to men
½ doz. Iron Combs	to Women
14 thimbles (Steel)	by 1 to [⟨Sachem⟩?] women
1 [lb?] vermillion in 10 papers	to young warriors
50 Awls	1 at a time to men
½ doz. Jews harps	to young men
3 Rasors	to men
1 large flat file	to some elderly man
1 smaller do	"
1 Doz fire Steels	to young men
5 Skaines Silk	to women
1 Roll Gartering	by 1 fathom to women
3 pewter lookg. glasses	young girls

18 Curtain Rings	young women
1 piece nonsopretty	by 2 fathoms to women
1 paper Verdigrease	by 1 oz: to young men

No 15 The Same—(Chief dress for Rickaras) & one Flag

" 42 The Same—Ditto for Mandanes & a Flag of 2d size

" 45 The Same, except no Scarlet Britch Clouts blue ones in lieu, and no large medals for 1st Chiefs, But medals of 2d sise—& no Scarlet Blanket, but 1 Shirt in lieu & a Flag 2d Sise

" 36 The Same as "no 45" & a Flag of 2d Size

" 16 The Same Do & a Flag of 3d Sise

" 26 The Same Do (a flag of 3d sise) & No 9 (a Flag of 3d Sise)   these two Bales have artillery Coats

Two Carrots of Tobacco will be Added to every 1st Chief Dress, and 1 Carrot to the 2nds & 3ds—   and 6 Carrots to to be given to the Nation—

The followg. Bales intended for foreign Nations: that is those beyond the mandanes

No 18, a Bag Containing

1 Chiefs Coat	
1 Medal 2d Sise	
1 pr Leggins	
1 Britch Clout	
1 White Shirt	1st Chief
1 Small Bundle Gartg.	
1 lookg. Glass	
1 Burng. Glass	

1 Callico Shirt	
1 Medal 4th & 5th Sise	
1 Small bundle gartg.	
1 pr Leggins	2d Chief
1 Britch Clout	
1 Wampum hair pipe	

1 Medal 5 Size	
1 Britch Clout	
1 Shirt	3d Chief
1 Small Bundle Gartg.	

3 Rolls Ear Wire

3　Do　Snare Wire

1　″　Knitting pins

　½ [lb.?] Vermillion in 5 papers

18 Knives

1 Dos: fire Steels

3 pewter lookg. glasses

24 Curtain Rings

1 piece nonsopretty

1 Tomyhawk

2 pieces Dutch Tape

3 Bead Necklaces

2 Rolls Ribbon　　　　　　　　　by fathoms to Girls

4 Lookg. Glasses

4 Burng.　Do

10 Maces White Rd Beads

2　do　Blue　Do

2　do　Yellow　Do

3　do　Mock Garnets

1 Dos hawk Bells

5 large　do

1 Needle Case

6 Cotton handkfs

3 Silk　Do　　　　　　　　　to women of Consideration

　½ dos: Iron Combs

10 Skaines thread

3 Dos: Brass thimbles　　　　　(by 4 or 5 to children[])]

6 pr Scissars

1 fine necklace

2 Romall hkf

6 Silver Rings—　　　　　　　women of consideration

100 Needles

50 Broaches

2 pr Bracelets—　　　　　　　to Some Young Chiefs or

3 pr Glass Ear Bobs　　　　　Chiefs Sons

4 fathoms Red flannel in 2 pieces

1 Gro Awls

2 Wampun Shells

1 Extra Chiefs Coat
1 medal 3 Sise
1 white Shirt
1 Britch Clout   for a 1st Chief
1 lookg. Glass
1 Burng. Glass
1 piece fancy handkf
1 [lb?] Cold. thread

No 14 The Same

No 24

5 Callico Shirts
8 fathoms Red flannel in 4 pieces
2 Bunches Blue Beads
2   do— Red— do
10 Small bunches white Seed do
14 Rolls Wire difft Sises
7 Bunches White Rd Beads
17 maces mock Garnets
6 ½ doz: pewter lookg. Glasses
18 pr of Scissars difft. Sises
1 Extra Bunch of Beads
9 Dos thimbles
6 Medals Dom: Animals
20 do Sowing
5 [lb?] Vermillion in 10 papers Ea.
12 d Silver Rings
2 dos: Small hawk Bells & 2 Gro: do
5 Bunches large Do
10/12 Gro Rings
6 Dos: Jews harps
3 Rolls Binding
200 Needles
12 pr Glass Ear Bobs
2 pr Braslets
1 Card of Beads
20 Single Ps. Narrow Ribbon
1 needle Case
7 white metal Ear rings

1 [lb?] Nuns thread
1 [lb?] Col[ore]d thread
1 pce Bandano Hkf:
3 Britch Clouts
4 Bunches Yellow Beads
4 Silk Handkfs
50 Broaches
4 pce dutch tape
2 pce Nonsopretty
20 fancy handkfs
2 hair pipes
1 Silver Arm Band
1 Wrist Band
1 Tomyhawk
3 ¾ dos: paper lookg. Glasses
2 ⅓ Dos: Burng. Glasses

No 3 The Same, Except the followg. articles more— vt. [viz.] 1 Gorget, 1 medal, 1d vermillion, 1 Bunch Bells, 3 hair pipes, 1 Burng. glass, 1 necklace & 1 remnant of Scarlet—. and the followg. article, less— vt. [viz.] 1 Arm & Wrist Band, 1 Bunch Yellow Beads & 1 Callico Shirt

No 4 a Case
15 Dos: Butchers Knives
5 ^{10}/$_{12}$ ″ Bone handle do
3 ⅓ ″ Staghandle Do
6 half round files
12 tomyhawks
2 Dos: fire Steels
7 Dos: Iron Combs
1 Gro: Awls
8 Bundles Knitting Pins
48 Collar needles
2 ⅓ Dos: Small Scissars
1 ¾ Dos: large Do
8 [lb?] Red Lead
24 Squaw Axes
2 Bundles of Pieces of Brass & Iron
28 fish Spears
5 large Canoe Awls

499

In a Box of necessary Stores No. 8 are the follg. belongg. to Indian Department   27 fish Spears   5 large Canoe Awls

Recapitulation of the Above fourteen Bags & 1 Box of Indian Presents. Vizt [viz.]—

15 Chief Coats (of which 9 are Artillery Coats)
11 hats & 6 Circle feathers, & 5 Soldier's plumes
18 White Shirts

20 Scarlet Leggins
 1 Remnant Scarlet
 2 Britch Clouts Do
 3 Blankets   Do   equal to 1 pce Scarlet
 3 large medals
13 2d Size Do   Likenesses

71 Medals 3d & 4th Sise
 8 Silver moons
12 Wampum Do
24 hairpipes Do
12 Silver Arm Bands
12 Wrist   Do—   Do
72 Rings Silver
1500 Broaches do

12 Blue Blankets
20 prs Leggins   equal to 3 pces Strouds
45 Britch Clouts

44 Callico Shirts
12 Rolls Gartg.
 2 dos: Dutch tape
 2 dos: nonsoprettys
12 Rolls narrow Ribbon
24 Tomy hawks
 8 Ivory Combs
 7 pces fancy handkf:
 5 pce, Bandano Do
 ½ pce Romall handkf
10 [lb?] threads
35 Dos: Knives, of which 22 doz Butchers Knives
12 dos. Dutch paper lookg. glasses

2 Cards of Bead necklaces

3 fine   Ditto

7 ¾ doz. Burning Glasses

120 Small Maces white Rd Beads

7 Bunches Sky Blue Beads

17   Do   Yellow   Do

20   do   White Seed Do

4   do   Red   Do

1   Do   Green   Do

18   Do   Mock Garnets or 80 Maces

8 ⅓ Doz: large Sise hawk Bells

6 Gro: Small   Do

3 Dos: Tinsel hat Bands

48 pr Glass Ear Bobs

8 pr   Do   Braslets

12 ½ Dos: Scissars large & Small

30 Collars of Brass Wire, quill Sise

16   Do   Ear Wire

34 Bunches Snare Do

18 Bunches Knitting Pins

3900 Needles Assorted

12 Needle Cases

about 500 fish hooks

12 Dos: Iron Combs

9 ⅓ Dos: taylors Steel thimbles

19 [lb?] Vermillion

5 ¾ Gro: Awls

3 Dos: Rasors

22 files

12 Dos: fire Steels

40 Skaines Silk

18 Dos: Pewter lookg. Glasses

3 Gro: Curtain Rings

10 [lb?] Verdigrease or near abt.

24 fathoms of Red flannel in 12 pieces—   to a piece of flannel

48 Collar Needles

8 [lb?] Red Lead

24 Squaw Axes

2 Bundles of pieces of Brass & Iron

55 fish Spears

5 large Canoe Awls

130 Pigtail Tobacco wt 63 lb

176 Carrots tobacco abt 500 in 9 Bales.—

26 Silver Ear Rings

Bailing Invoice of Sundries, being necessary Stores Vizt. [viz.]

No 1. a Bale Contg.

4 Blankets

3 fine Cloth Jackets

6 flannel Shirts

3 pr Russia Over Alls

5 frocks

4 White Shirts

200 flints

2 Spike Gimblets

2 Small Do

12 pr Socks

2 tin Boxes; with 2 memm. Books in Ea.

½ [lb?] Col[ore]d. thread

1 Romall Handkf

1 Paper Ink Powder

1 pce Catgut

3 Setts Rifle Locks

1 Screw Driver

″ 2. The Same

″ 3 The Same

″ 4 The Same, except 1 p. trowsers less and 1 flannel Shirt in lieu

″ 5 a Bale

4 Blankets

1 Cloth Jacket

4 flannel Shirts

2 frocks

2 Watch Coats

50 flints

1 White Shirt

1 Spike Gimblet

6 pr Socks

½ [lb?] Nuns thread

1 pce Catgut

1 pce Silk Handkf

4 Quire Comn fool's Cap

9 half quires post paper

4 Sticks Sealing wax

1 Romall Handkf:

1 Vice

1 Sett of Gunlocks

1 nipper

" 6 The Same, except 1 watch Coat less & 3 Cloth overalls, 2 pr ox hide Shoes, ½ m fish hooks, & 1 Gro: awls more.—

" 7 a Bale

6 Blankets

1 Watch Coat

2 pr ox hide Shoes

4 papers of fish hooks

1 Gro Awls

1 Vice Smallest Sise

1 Screw Driver

1 quire paper fools Cap

5 Romall Handkfs

1 fancy   Do

1 Drawing Knife

3 pr Socks

3 pr Cloth over Alls

2 flannel Shirts

2 frocks

1 pr English Shoes

1 fine Cloth Jacket

11 Cartridge Box Belts

¼ [lb?] nuns thread

25 flints

" 8 a Box

27 fish Spears

the Glue

Sundry Iron Works for Guns

3 Screw Augurs

62 files difft Sizes

1 Dradle [treadle?]

1 Brace
5 Chisels
5 large Canoe Awls
2 Gimblets
  Primg. wires & Brushes
  Capt: Lewis Gunlock
1 Bundle Iron Wire
18 Axes
2 howels
1 Adse
  Iron Weights

    Recapitulation of Seven Bales & 1 Box of necessy Stores Vit. [viz.]

30 Blankets
15 fine Cloth Jackets
35 flannel Shirts
11 pr Russia Over Alls
6 pr Cloth   Ditto
26 frocks
18 White Shirts
925 flints
11 Spike Gimblets
8 Small   Do
63 pr Socks
8 tin Boxes with memm. Books
2 [lb?] Col[ore]d thread
¼ [lb?] Nuns thread
11 Romall Handkf
4 papers Ink powder
6 pces Catgut
14 Setts Gunlocks
5 Screw Drivers
2 pcs Silk Handkf
9 quires fools Cap paper
18 half quires post
8 Sticks sealing Wax
3 vices
2 nippers
4 Watch Coats

    4 pr. ox hide Shoes
    1 pr English Do
    2 Gro Awls
1000 fish hooks
    1 fancy handkf.
    1 Drawg. Knife
       the Glue
    3 screw Augurs
  62 files difft Sises
    5 Chisels
  18 Axes
    2 howels
    1 adse

Sources Cited

Abel (CJ) Abel, Annie Heloise. *Chardon's Journal at Fort Clark, 1834–1839*. . . . Pierre: State of South Dakota, 1932.

Abel (TD) ———. "Trudeau's Description of the Upper Missouri." *Mississippi Valley Historical Review* 8 (June–September 1921): 149–79.

Abel (TN) ———, ed. *Tabeau's Narrative of Loisel's Expedition to the Upper Missouri*. Norman: University of Oklahoma Press, 1939.

Allen Allen, John Logan. *Passage Through the Garden: Lewis and Clark and the Image of the American Northwest*. Urbana: University of Illinois Press, 1975.

Anderson (EDM) Anderson, Gary C. "Early Dakota Migration and Intertribal War: A Revision." *Western Historical Quarterly* 11 (January 1980): 17–36.

Anderson (CFP) Anderson, Irving W. "A Charbonneau Family Portrait." *American West* 17 (March–April 1980): 4–13, 58–64.

Anderson (SSS) ———. "Sacajawea, Sacagawea, Sakakawea?" *South Dakota History* 8 (Fall 1978): 303–11.

AOU American Ornithologists' Union. *Check-list of North American Birds*. 6th ed. Baltimore, Md.: American Ornithologists' Union, 1983. [AOU] in brackets with numbers refers to a species item-number in the book.

Appleman (LC) Appleman, Roy E. *Lewis and Clark: Historic Places Associated with Their Transcontinental Exploration (1804–06)*. Washington, D.C.: United States Department of the Interior, National Park Service, 1975.

Atlas	Moulton, Gary E., ed. *Atlas of the Lewis and Clark Expedition*. Lincoln: University of Nebraska Press, 1983.
Bakeless (LCPD)	Bakeless, John. *Lewis and Clark, Partners in Discovery*. New York: William Morrow, 1947.
Baraga	Baraga, R. R. Bishop. *A Dictionary of the Otchipwe Language, Explained in English*. 1878. Reprint. Minneapolis: Ross & Haines, 1966.
Barkley	Barkley, T. M., ed. *Atlas of the Flora of the Great Plains*. Ames: Iowa State University Press, 1977.
Beckwith	Beckwith, Martha W., ed. *Mandan and Hidatsa Myths and Ceremonies*. Memoirs of the American Folk-Lore Society, vol. 32. New York: J. J. Augustin, 1938.
Benson	Benson, Keith R. "Herpetology on the Lewis and Clark Expedition: 1804–1806." *Herpetological Review* 3 (1978): 87–91.
Berthrong	Berthrong, Donald J. *The Southern Cheyennes*. Norman: University of Oklahoma Press, 1963.
Betts (SY)	Betts, Robert B. *In Search of York: The Slave Who Went to the Pacific with Lewis and Clark*. Boulder: Colorado Associated University Press, 1985.
Bowers (HSCO)	Bowers, Alfred W. *Hidatsa Social and Ceremonial Organization*. Smithsonian Institution, Bureau of American Ethnology, Bulletin 194. Washington, D.C.: Government Printing Office, 1965.
Bowers (MSCO)	———. *Mandan Social and Ceremonial Organization*. Chicago: University of Chicago Press, 1950.
Brown	Brown, Robert Harold. *Wyoming: A Geography*. Boulder, Col.: Westview Press, 1980.
Burroughs	Burroughs, Raymond Darwin. *The Natural History of the Lewis and Clark Expedition*. East Lansing: Michigan State University Press, 1961.
Catlin (NAI)	Catlin, George. *Letters and Notes on the Manners, Customs, and Condition of the North American Indians. . . .* 2 vols. London: privately published, 1841.
Catlin (OKP)	———. *O-Kee-Pa: A Religious Ceremony, and Other Customs of the Mandans*. Edited by John C. Ewers.

	1967. Reprint. Lincoln: University of Nebraska Press, 1976.
Chittenden	Chittenden, Hiram M. *The American Fur Trade of the Far West.* 2 vols. New York: Harper, 1902.
Chuinard (CMML)	Chuinard, Eldon G. "The Court-Martial of Ensign Meriwether Lewis (Some Observations Related to the Court-Martial of the Expedition's Private Newman)." *We Proceeded On* 8 (November 1982): 12–15.
Chuinard (OOMD)	———. *Only One Man Died: The Medical Aspects of the Lewis and Clark Expedition.* Glendale, Calif.: Arthur H. Clark, 1979.
Clark	Clark, William P. *The Indian Sign Language.* 1885. Reprint. Lincoln: University of Nebraska Press, 1982.
Clarke (MLCE)	Clarke, Charles G. *The Men of the Lewis and Clark Expedition: A Biographical Roster of the Fifty-one Members and a Composite Diary of their Activities from all Known Sources.* Glendale, Calif.: Arthur H. Clark, 1970.
Coues (HLC)	Coues, Elliott, ed. *History of the Expedition under the Command of Lewis and Clark. . . .* 1893. Reprint. 3 vols. New York: Dover Publications, 1965.
Coues (NLEH)	———, ed. *New Light on the Early History of the Greater Northwest.* 3 vols. New York: Harper, 1897.
Criswell	Criswell, Elijah Harry. *Lewis and Clark: Linguistic Pioneers.* University of Missouri Studies, vol. 15, no. 2. Columbia: University of Missouri Press, 1940.
Cronquist et al.	Cronquist, Arthur, Arthur H. Holmgren, Noel H. Holmgren, James L. Reveal, and Patricia K. Holmgren. *Intermountain Flora: Vascular Plants of the Intermountain West, U.S.A.* Vol. 4, *Subclass Asteridae (except Asteraceae).* New York: New York Botanical Garden, 1984.
Cutright (HLCJ)	Cutright, Paul Russell. *A History of the Lewis and Clark Journals.* Norman: University of Oklahoma Press, 1976.

Cutright (LCPN)	———. *Lewis and Clark: Pioneering Naturalists.* Urbana: University of Illinois Press, 1969.
Cutright (OMPD)	———. "The Odyssey of the Magpie and the Prairie Dog." *Bulletin of the Missouri Historical Society* 23 (April 1967): 215–28.
Davidson	Davidson, Gordon Charles. *The North West Company.* Berkeley: University of California Press, 1918.
DeMallie	DeMallie, Raymond J., trans. and ed. "Nicollet's Notes on the Dakota." In *Joseph N. Nicollet on the Plains and Prairies: The Expeditions of 1838–39 with Journals, Letters, and Notes on the Dakota Indians,* translated and edited by Edmund C. Bray and Martha Coleman Bray, 250–81. St. Paul: Minnesota Historical Society, 1976.
Denig	Denig, Edwin Thompson. *Five Indian Tribes of the Upper Missouri.* Edited by John C. Ewers. Norman: University of Oklahoma Press, 1961.
Densmore	Densmore, Frances. "Uses of Plants by the Chippewa Indians." Bureau of American Ethnology, Annual Report 44, 275–397. Washington, D.C.: Government Printing office, 1928.
DeSmet	DeSmet, Pierre-Jean. *Life, Letters, and Travels of Father Pierre-Jean DeSmet, S. J., 1801–1873.* Edited by Hiram M. Chittenden and Alfred T. Richardson. 4 vols. New York: Harper, 1905.
Diller (MMR)	Diller, Aubrey. "Maps of the Missouri River Before Lewis and Clark." In *Studies and Essays in the History of Science and Learning . . . ,* edited by M. F. Ashley Montagu, 503–19. New York: Henry Shuman, 1946.
Diller (PH)	———. "Pawnee House: Ponca House." *Mississippi Valley Historical Review* 36 (September 1949): 301–4.
Ewers	Ewers, John C. *Indian Life on the Upper Missouri.* Norman: University of Oklahoma Press, 1968.
Fernald	Fernald, Merritt Lyndon. *Gray's Manual of Botany.* 8th ed. New York: D. Van Nostrand, 1970.
Fletcher & La Flesche	Fletcher, Alice C., and Francis La Flesche. *The*

	Omaha Tribe. 1911. Reprint. 2 vols. Lincoln: University of Nebraska Press, 1972.
Foley & Rice (RMC)	Foley, William E., and C. David Rice. "The Return of the Mandan Chief." *Montana, the Magazine of Western History* 29 (July 1979): 2–14.
Foster	Foster, Steven. *Echniacea Exhalted! The Botany, Culture, History, and Medicinal uses of the Purple Coneflower.* Drury, Mo.: New Life Farm, 1984.
Gilmore (SCAT)	Gilmore, Melvin R. "Some Comments on 'Aboriginal Tobaccos.'" *American Anthropologist*, n.s., 24 (October–December 1922): 480–81.
Gilmore (UPI)	———. *Uses of Plants by the Indians of the Missouri River Region.* 1919. Reprint. Lincoln: University of Nebraska Press, 1977.
Glover	Glover, Richard, ed. *David Thompson's Narrative, 1784–1812.* Toronto: Champlain Society, 1962.
Goodspeed	Goodspeed, Thomas H. *The Genus Nicotina: Origins, Relationships, and Evolution of its Species in Light of their Distribution, Morphology, and Cytogenetics.* Waltham, Mass.: Chronica Botanica, 1954.
Graveline	Graveline, Paul. "Joseph Gravelines and the Lewis and Clark Expedition." *We Proceeded On* 3 (October 1977): 5–6.
Grinnell	Grinnell, George Bird. *The Cheyenne Indians: Their History and Ways of Life.* 2 vols. 1923. Reprint. Lincoln: University of Nebraska Press, 1972.
Hafen (JBC)	Hafen, Ann W. "Jean-Baptiste Charbonneau." In Hafen (MMFT), 1:205–24.
Hafen (TC)	Hafen, LeRoy R. "Toussaint Charbonneau." In Hafen (MMFT), 9:53–62.
Hafen (MMFT)	———, ed. *The Mountain Men and the Fur Trade of the Far West.* 10 vols. Glendale, Calif.: Arthur H. Clark, 1965.
Hall	Hall, E. Raymond. *The Mammals of North America.* 2d ed. 2 vols. New York: John Wiley and Sons, 1981.
Hanson	Hanson, Charles E. *The Northwest Gun.* Lincoln: Nebraska State Historical Society, 1955.
Hassrick	Hassrick, Royal B. *The Sioux: Life and Customs of a*

	Warrior Society. Norman: University of Oklahoma Press, 1964.
Hebard	Hebard, Grace Raymond. *Sacajawea, a Guide and Interpreter of the Lewis and Clark Expedition.* . . . Glendale, Calif.: Arthur H. Clark, 1933.
Hodge	Hodge, Frederick Webb, ed. *Handbook of American Indians North of Mexico.* 1912. Reprint. 2 vols. St. Clair Shores, Mich.: Scholarly Press, 1968.
Holder	Holder, Preston. *The Hoe and the Horse on the Plains.* Lincoln: University of Nebraska Press, 1970.
Hollow & Parks	Hollow, Robert G., and Douglas R. Parks. "Studies in Plains Linguistics: A Review." In Wood & Liberty, 68–97.
Holmgren	Holmgren, Virginia C. "A Glossary of Bird Names Cited by Lewis and Clark." *We Proceeded On* 10 (May 1984): 28–34.
Howard (Sac)	Howard, Harold P. *Sacajawea.* Norman: University of Oklahoma Press, 1972.
Hyde (IHP)	Hyde, George E. *Indians of the High Plains: From the Prehistoric Period to the Coming of the Europeans.* Norman: University of Oklahoma Press, 1959.
Hyde (RCF)	———. *Red Cloud's Folk: A History of the Oglala Sioux Indians.* Norman: University of Oklahoma Press, 1937.
Irving (Astor)	Irving, Washington. *Astoria.* 1836. Reprint. Portland, Oreg.: Binfords and Mort, 1967.
Jackson (JP)	Jackson, Donald, ed. *The Journals of Zebulon Montgomery Pike with Letters and Related Documents.* 2 vols. Norman: University of Oklahoma Press, 1966.
Jackson (LLC)	———, ed. *Letters of the Lewis and Clark Expedition with Related Documents, 1783–1854.* 2d ed. 2 vols. Urbana: University of Illinois Press, 1978.
Jones et al.	Jones, J. Knox, Jr., David H. Armstrong, Robert S. Hoffmann, and Clyde Jones. *Mammals of the Northern Great Plains.* Lincoln: University of Nebraska Press, 1983.
Josephy	Josephy, Alvin M. *The Nez Perce Indians and the*

Opening of the Northwest. New Haven: Yale University Press, 1965.

Kehoe   Kehoe, Alice B. "The Function of Ceremonial Sexual Intercourse Among the Northern Plains Indians." *Plains Anthropologist* 15 (May 1970): 99–103.

Kennedy   Kennedy, Michael S., ed. *The Assiniboines: From the Accounts of the Old Ones Told to First Boy (James Larpenteur Long).* Norman: University of Oklahoma Press, 1961.

Krause   Krause, Richard A. *The Leavenworth Site: Archaeology of an Historic Arikara Community.* University of Kansas Publications in Anthropology, no. 3. Lawrence: University of Kansas Press, 1972.

Lee et al.   Lee, David S., Carter R. Gilbert, Charles H. Hocutt, Robert E. Jenkins, Don E. McAllister, and Jay R. Stauffer, Jr. *Atlas of North American Freshwater Fishes.* Raleigh: North Carolina State Museum of Natural History, 1980.

Lehmer   Lehmer, Donald J. *Middle Missouri Archaeology.* National Park Service Anthropological Papers No. 1. Washington, D.C.: Government Printing Office, 1971.

Lehmer, Meston, & Dill   Lehmer, Donald J., L. K. Meston, and C. L. Dill. "Structural Details of a Middle Missouri House." *Plains Anthropologist* 18 (May 1973): 160–66.

Lewis   Lewis, T. H. "Lewis and Clarke and the Antiquities of the Upper Missouri River." *American Antiquarian and Oriental Journal* 13 (January–November 1891): 288–93.

Liberty   Liberty, Margot. "The Sun Dance." In Wood & Liberty, 164–78.

Link   Link, John Thomas. "The Toponomy of Nebraska." Master's thesis, University of Nebraska, 1932.

Loos   Loos, John Louis. "A Biography of William Clark, 1770–1813." Ph.D. diss., Washington University, 1953.

Lowie (TA)   Lowie, Robert H. *The Assiniboine.* Anthropological

	Papers of the American Museum of Natural History, vol. 4, part 1. New York: American Museum of Natural History, 1909.
Lowie (TC)	———. *The Crow Indians.* 1935. Reprint. Lincoln: University of Nebraska Press, 1983.
Ludwickson, Blakeslee, & O'Shea	Ludwickson, John, Donald Blakeslee, and John O'Shea. "Missouri National Recreational River: Native American Cultural Resources." A report prepared for the Heritage Conservation and Recreation Service, Interagency Archeological Services, Denver, Colorado, 1981.
Luttig	Luttig, John D. *Journal of a Fur-Trading Expedition on the Upper Missouri, 1812–1813. . . .* Edited by Stella M. Drumm. St. Louis: Missouri Historical Society, 1920.
McDermott (GMVF)	McDermott, John Francis. *A Glossary of Mississippi Valley French, 1673–1850.* St. Louis: Washington University, 1941.
McDermott (WCS)	———. "William Clark's Struggle with Place Names in Upper Louisiana." *Bulletin of the Missouri Historical Society* 34 (April 1978): 140–50.
McMillan	McMillan, Bruce R. "Man and Mastodon: A Review of Koch's 1840 Pomme de Terre Expeditions." In *Prehistoric Man and his Environments: A Case Study in the Ozark Highlands,* edited by W. Raymond Wood and R. Bruce McMillan, 81–96. New York: Academic Press, 1976.
Marx	Marx, Walter H. "A Latin Matter in the Biddle 'Narrative' or 'History' of the Lewis and Clark Expedition." *We Proceeded On* 9 (November 1983): 21–22.
Masson	Masson, L. R., ed. *Les Bourgeois de la Compagnie du Nord-ouest. . . .* 1889–90. Reprint. 2 vols. New York: Antiquarian Press, 1960.
Mattes	Mattes, Merrill J. "Report on Historic Sites in the Fort Randall Reservoir Area, Missouri River, South Dakota." *South Dakota Historical Collections* 24 (1949): 470–577.
Matthews	Matthews, Washington. *Ethnography and Philology*

of the Hidatsa Indians. Washington: Government Printing Office, 1877.

Mattison (GP) Mattison, Ray H. "Report on Historic Sites Adjacent to the Missouri River, Between the Big Sioux River and Fort Randall Dam, Including Those in the Gavins Point Reservoir Area." *South Dakota Historical Collections* 28 (1956): 22–98.

Mattison (GR) ———. "Report on Historic Sites in the Garrison Reservoir Area, Missouri River." *North Dakota History* 22 (January–April 1955): 5–73.

Mattison (OR) ———. "Report on Historical Aspects of the Oahe Reservoir Area, Missouri River, South and North Dakota." *South Dakota Historical Collections* 27 (1943): 1–159.

Mattison (BB) ———. "Report on the Historic Sites in the Big Bend Reservoir Area, South Dakota." *South Dakota Historical Collections* 31 (1962): 243–86.

Mehl Mehl, M. G. *Missouri's Ice Age Mammals.* Educational Series, no. 1. Jefferson City, Mo.: Division of Geological Survey and Water Resources, 1962.

Meyer Meyer, Roy W. *The Village Indians of the Upper Missouri: The Mandans, Hidatsas, and Arikaras.* Lincoln: University of Nebraska Press, 1977.

Moore Moore, Conrad T. "Man and Fire in the Central North American Grassland, 1535–1890; A Documentary Historical Geography." Ph.D. diss., University of California, Los Angeles, 1972.

Moulton Moulton, Gary E. "A Note on the White Pirogue." *We Proceeded On* 12 (May 1986): 22.

MRC Missouri River Commission. *Map of the Missouri River From Its Mouth to Three Forks, Montana, in Eighty-four Sheets.* Washington, D.C.: Missouri River Commission, 1892–95.

MRR *Missouri River: Rulo, Nebraska to Yankton, South Dakota.* Omaha, Nebr.: Corps of Engineers, 1947–49.

MRY *Missouri River: Gavins Point Near Yankton, South*

	Dakota to Stanton, North Dakota. Omaha, Nebr.: Corps of Engineers, 1949.
Munnick (FR)	Munnick, Harriet D. "François Rivet." In Hafen (MMFT), 7:237–43.
Munnick (PD)	———. "Pierre Dorion." In Hafen (MMFT), 8:107–12.
Nasatir (JBT)	Nasatir, Abraham P. "Jean-Baptiste Truteau." In Hafen (MMFT), 4:318–97.
Nasatir (BLC)	———, ed. *Before Lewis and Clark: Documents Illustrating the History of the Missouri, 1785–1804.* 2 vols. St. Louis: St. Louis Historical Documents Foundation, 1952.
Neiburger, Edinger, & Bonner	Neiburger, Morris, James G. Edinger, and William D. Bonner. *Understanding Our Atmospheric Environment.* 2d ed. San Francisco: W. H. Freeman, 1982.
Nichols & Halley	Nichols, Roger L., and Patrick L. Halley. *Stephen Long and American Frontier Exploration.* Newark: University of Delaware Press, 1980.
Nicollet (MMR)	Nicollet, Joseph N. Maps of the Missouri River, Joseph N. Nicollet Papers, vol. 2, pt. 2, Manuscripts Division, Library of Congress, Washington, D.C.
North Dakota Guide	*North Dakota: A Guide to the Northern Prairie State.* Compiled by workers of the Federal Writers' Project of the Works Progress Administration for the State of North Dakota. American Guide Series. 1938. Reprint. New York: Oxford University Press, 1950.
Oglesby	Oglesby, Richard Edward. *Manuel Lisa and the Opening of the Missouri Fur Trade.* Norman: University of Oklahoma Press, 1963.
Osgood (FN)	Osgood, Ernest S., ed. *The Field Notes of Captain William Clark, 1803–1805.* New Haven: Yale University Press, 1964.
Parks (BVAP)	Parks, Douglas R. "Bands and Villages of the Arikara and Pawnee." *Nebraska History* 60 (Summer 1979): 214–39.
Parks (NCL)	———. "The Northern Caddoan Languages: Their

Subgroupings and Time Depth." *Nebraska History* 60 (Summer 1979): 197–213.

Prucha (IPM)   Prucha, Francis Paul. *Indian Peace Medals in American History*. Lincoln: University of Nebraska Press, 1971.

Prucha (SR)   ———. *The Sword of the Republic: The United States Army on the Frontier, 1783–1846*. New York: Macmillan, 1969.

Pyne   Pyne, Stephen J. "Indian Fires." *Natural History* 92 (February 1983): 6–11.

Quaife (ECMJ)   Quaife, Milo Milton, ed. "Extracts from Capt. McKay's Journal—and Others." *Wisconsin Historical Society Proceedings* 63 (1915): 186–210.

Quaife (MLJO)   ———, ed. *The Journals of Captain Meriwether Lewis and Sergeant John Ordway kept on the Expedition of Western Exploration, 1803–1806*. Madison: State Historical Society of Wisconsin, 1916.

Reid   Reid, Russell, ed. *Lewis and Clark in North Dakota*. Bismarck: State Historical Society of North Dakota, 1947–48.

Robinson   Robinson, Doane. "Lewis and Clark in South Dakota." *South Dakota Historical Collections* 9 (1918): 514–96.

Ronda (IC)   Ronda, James P. "'A Chart in His Way': Indian Cartography and the Lewis and Clark Expedition." *Great Plains Quarterly* 4 (Winter 1984): 43–53.

Ronda (LCAI)   ———. *Lewis and Clark among the Indians*. Lincoln: University of Nebraska Press, 1984.

Russell (FTT)   Russell, Carl P. *Firearms, Traps, and Tools of the Mountain Men*. New York: Alfred A. Knopf, 1967.

Russell (GEF)   ———. *Guns on the Early Frontiers: A History of Firearms from Colonial Times Through the Years of the Western Fur Trade*. Berkeley: University of California Press, 1962.

Saindon (WP)   Saindon, Bob. "The White Pirogue of the Lewis and Clark Expedition." *WPO Publication* No. 1 (August 1976): 15–22.

Secoy	Secoy, Frank Raymond. *Changing Military Patterns on the Great Plains (17th Century through Early 19th Century)*. Monographs of the American Ethnological Society, no. 21. Locust Valley, N.Y.: J. J. Augustin, 1953.
Smith (BBHS)	Smith, G. Hubert. *Big Bend Historic Sites*. River Basin Surveys Museum of Natural History, Smithsonian Institution. Publications in Salvage Archaeology, no. 9. Lincoln, Nebr.: [Smithsonian Institution], 1968.
Smith (LAFV)	———. *Like-a-Fishhook Village and Fort Berthold, Garrison Reservoir, North Dakota*. National Park Service, Anthropological Papers, no. 2. Washington, D.C.: Government Printing Office, 1972.
South Dakota Guide	*South Dakota: A Guide to the State*. Compiled by the Federal Writers' Project of the Works Progress Administration. American Guide Series. 2d ed. New York: Hastings House, 1952.
Speck	Speck, Gordon. *Breeds and Half-Breeds*. New York: Clarkson N. Potter, 1969.
Stearn & Stearn	Stearn, E. Wagner, and Allen E. Stearn. *The Effect of Smallpox on the Destiny of the Amerindian*. Boston: Bruce Humphries, 1945.
Stephenson	Stephenson, Robert L. "Blue Blanket Island (39WW9), An Historic Contact Site in the Oahe Reservoir near Mobridge, South Dakota." *Plains Anthropologist* 14 (February 1969): 1–31.
Stewart (APN)	Stewart, George R. *American Place-Names: A Concise and Selective Dictionary for the Continental United States of America*. New York: Oxford University Press, 1970.
Steyermark	Steyermark, Julian A. *Flora of Missouri*. Ames: Iowa State University Press, 1963.
Strong	Strong, William Duncan. *From History to Prehistory in the Northern Great Plains*. Smithsonian Miscellaneous Collections, vol. 100. Washington, D.C.: Government Printing Office, 1940.
Swanton	Swanton, John R. *The Indian Tribes of North America*. Bureau of American Ethnology, Bulletin

	145. Washington, D.C.: Government Printing Office, 1952.
Thompson	Thompson, Ralph Stanton. "Final Story of the Deapolis Indian Village Site." *North Dakota History* 28 (October 1961): 143–53.
Thwaites (EWT)	Thwaites, Reuben Gold, ed. *Early Western Travels.* 32 vols. Cleveland: Arthur H. Clark, 1905–19.
Thwaites (LC)	———, ed. *Original Journals of the Lewis and Clark Expedition, 1804–1806.* 8 vols. New York: Dodd, Mead, 1904–1905.
Tyrrell	Tyrrell, Joseph B., ed. *David Thompson's Narrative of His Explorations in Western America 1784–1812.* Toronto: Champlain Society, 1916.
Wallace	Wallace, W. Stewart, ed. *Documents Relating to the North West Company.* Toronto: Champlain Society, 1934.
Warren	Warren, Gouverneur K. "Original Sketches of a Reconnoissance of the Missouri River from the Northern Boundary of Kansas to a point sixty two miles above Fort Union made during the Summers of 1855 and 1856." Manuscript Map in 39 sheets, Record Group 77, National Archives, Washington, D.C.
Wedel (PV)	Wedel, Waldo R. "Observations on Some Nineteenth Century Pottery Vessels from the Upper Missouri." Bureau of American Ethnology, Anthropological Papers No. 51, Bulletin 164, 91–114. Washington, D.C.: Government Printing Office, 1957.
Wentworth	Wentworth, Edward N. "Dried Meat—Early Man's Travel Ration." *Agricultural History* 30 (January 1956): 2–10.
White (RD)	White, Richard. *The Roots of Dependency: Subsistence, Environment, and Social Change among the Choctaws, Pawnees, and Navajos.* Lincoln: University of Nebraska Press, 1983.
White (WW)	———. "The Winning of the West: The Expansion of the Western Sioux in the Eighteenth and Nineteenth Centuries." *Journal of American History* 65 (September 1978): 319–43.

Whitehead   Whitehead, Harriet. "The Bow and the Burden Strap: A New Look at Institutionalized Homosexuality in Native North America." In *Sexual Meanings: The Cultural Construction of Gender and Sexuality*, edited by Sherry B. Ortner and Harriet Whitehead, 80–115. Cambridge: Cambridge University Press, 1981.

Will   Will, George F. *Archaeology of the Missouri Valley*. Anthropological Papers, American Museum of Natural History, vol. 22, part 6. New York: American Museum of Natural History, 1924.

Will & Hecker   Will, George F., and Thad C. Hecker. "Upper Missouri River Valley Aboriginal Culture in North Dakota." *North Dakota Historical Quarterly* 11 (January–April 1944): 5–126.

Will & Spinden   Will, George F., and Herbert J. Spinden. *The Mandans: A Study of their Culture, Archaeology and Language*. Papers of the Peabody Museum of American Archaeology and Ethnology, Harvard University, vol. 3, no. 4. Cambridge, Mass.: Peabody Museum, 1906.

Williams   Williams, David. "John Evans' Strange Journey." *American Historical Review* 54 (January, April 1949): 508–29.

Wood (BS)   Wood, W. Raymond. *Biesterfeldt: A Post-Contact Coalescent Site on the Northeastern Plains*. Smithsonian Contributions to Anthropology, no. 15, Washington, D.C.: Smithsonian Institution Press, 1971.

Wood (JE)   ———. "The John Evans 1796–97 Map of the Missouri River." *Great Plains Quarterly* 1 (Winter 1981): 39–53.

Wood (NPF)   ———. *Nanza, the Ponca Fort*. Society for American Anthropology, Archives of Archaeology, no. 3. Madison, Wis.: Society for American Anthropology, 1960.

Wood (OHI)   ———. "The Origins of the Hidatsa Indians: A Review of Ethnohistorical and Traditional Data." A study conducted for the National Park Ser-

	vice, Midwest Archeological Center, Lincoln, Nebraska, 1980.
Wood (PT)	———. "Plains Trade in Prehistoric Intertribal Relations." In Wood & Liberty, 98–109.
Wood (TL)	———. "Theodore H. Lewis and his Northeastern Nebraska 'Forts.'" *Plains Anthropologist* 23 (February 1978): 77–79.
Wood & Moulton	Wood, W. Raymond, and Gary E. Moulton. "Prince Maximilian and New Maps of the Missouri and Yellowstone Rivers." *Western Historical Quarterly* 12 (October 1981): 373–86.
Wood & Liberty	Wood, W. Raymond, and Margot Liberty, eds. *Anthropology on the Great Plains*. Lincoln: University of Nebraska Press, 1980.
Wood & Thiessen	Wood, W. Raymond, and Thomas D. Thiessen, eds., *Early Fur Trade on the Northern Plains: Canadian Traders among the Mandan and Hidatsa Indians, 1738–1818*. Norman: University of Oklahoma Press, 1985.
Woodward	Woodward, Arthur. *The Denominators of the Fur Trade*. Pasadena: Socio-Technical Publications, 1970.
Wyoming Guide	*Wyoming: A Guide to Its History, Highways, and People*. Compiled by workers of the Writers' Program of the Work Projects Administration in the State of Wyoming. New York: Oxford University Press, 1941.

Index

Bellevue Public Library